Special Edition

USING

MICROSOFT®

SQL SERVER

6.5

Special Edition

Using
Microsoft®
SQL Server
6.5

Bob Branchek

Peter Hazlehurst

Stephen Wynkoop

Scott L. Warner

Special Edition Using Microsoft SQL Server 6.5

Credits

About the Authors

Bob Branchek is an independent lecturer, writer, and the president of Bob Branchek Associates, Inc., a New Jersey-based Microsoft Solution Provider specializing in the delivery of customized training and consulting for Microsoft Windows NT and SQL Server. Bob has 19 years of experience in the computer industry and contributed to Que's *Using Windows NT*. Bob also lectures at the Information Technologies Institute of New York University in New York City and currently is teaching a course on client/server computing. He's the writer and on-camera talent for several video training courses, and is a Microsoft Certified Professional. He possesses both B.S. and M.A. degrees. While employed for Digital Equipment Corporation's Educational Training Services, he was awarded its Instructor Excellence Award in 1982, 1983 and 1984. Bob can be reached on the Internet at 73227.1627@compuserve.com or on CompuServe at 73227,1627.

Peter Hazlehurst, born in Oxford, England, and educated in Australia, has spent the past five years in the client/server development industry specializing in real-world business solutions. Peter moved to the U.S. three years ago to join Phoenix International as its first employee and currently is Senior Systems Architect. Phoenix is the leading client/server vendor of Banking Software and its product is installed in 13 institutions in the U.S. and six internationally. The relational database Phoenix selected is Sybase System 10, written entirely in Gupta's SQLWindows. Phoenix currently is in the process of porting to Microsoft SQL Server to target smaller domestic banks with the concept of the "bank in a box." Phoenix has shown that client/server works for real businesses. Peter can be reached via e-mail on the Internet at phazlehurst@phoenixint.com or on CompuServe at 73114,3145.

Stephen Wynkoop is an author and lecturer working almost exclusively with Microsoft-based technologies. Stephen has been a regular speaker at Microsoft's TechEd conferences and has written two other books on Access and Office 95 development technologies. He contributed to Que's *Special Edition Using Windows NT Server* and is working on other Que books regarding exciting technologies on the horizon. Stephen can be reached on the Internet at swynk@primenet.com.

Scott L. Warner is a programmer/analyst for Service Graphics, Inc. in Indianapolis. He received his degree from Purdue University's computer technology department. In addition to Delphi, Scott also develops applications in PowerBuilder and Visual Basic. He can be reached on the Internet at swarner@iquest.net.

Acknowledgments

I'd like to thank my family for their patience and understanding in providing the quality time necessary to complete the book. I'd especially like to thank my wife Cathy, who read and offered suggestions on my first, second, and sometimes third drafts of chapters. I'd like apologize to my son Jeffrey for not working out some way to include his picture in this book (as I did in QUE's *Using Windows NT*).

I'd like to thank Dick Vigilante and Howard Decklebaum of the Information Technologies Institute of New York University for the opportunity to teach courses on related computer topics the past 15 years. I'd also like to thank the students of those classes who, although they were attending evening classes and were tired from long work days, still managed to ask questions that helped me to learn along with them.

Thanks to the people at the various training organizations at which I've delivered training including: Mike, Jim, and Andy of Online Consulting in Wilmington, Delaware; Karen, Kenan, and Carmen at Dow Jones Training Services in Princeton, New Jersey; Bruce at Teltech and Ronnie at Creative Data Movers in New York City; and Jim at Professional Training Services in Nashua, New Hampshire.

I'd also like to thank Jim Walker and Howard Nusbaum. Jim, a former colleague at Digital Equipment Corporation, has provided me with opinions, often different than mine, which led me to re-examine my ideas. Howard has provided the questions of a novice user which have kept me attuned to the need for understanding the a complete range of users rather than just those who are technically savvy.

—*Bob Branchek*

I would like to thank my family, especially my father, for inspiration and guidance. I also would like to thank all my friends at Phoenix who are great to work with and who provide an excellent place to play with new toys like Java and the Internet. Finally, I'd like to thank my adopted U.S. family (they know who they are) for all their help, support, and friendship in the time that I've been lucky enough to know them. And final, final thanks to all the folks at Que, especially Deborah Abshier, Jeff Riley and Al Valvano for "learning me to read" and for bringing me into the world of publishing.

—*Peter Hazlehurst*

First, thank you to the team at Que, specifically Al Valvano and Jeff Riley for their persistence in making this book become a reality and working through the changing landscape with SQL Server to make this book the best it can be. Many thanks to my family for putting up with the continuous push on schedules and "just one more section." Without their help and support, this would not have been possible. A special thank you to my wife for her adding a much-needed round of editing on materials—it was very much appreciated. Also, many thanks to Mike B. for all of the foresight, commitment, and pushing to the edge of technologies. Without his passion for technology, life would not be what it is today.

—*Stephen Wynkoop*

We'd Like To Hear From You!

As part of our continuing effort to produce books of the highest possible quality, Que would like to hear your comments. To stay competitive, we *really* want you, as a computer book reader and user, to let us know what you like or dislike most about *Special Edition Using Microsoft SQL Server 6.5* or other Que products.

You can mail comments, ideas, or suggestions to the address below, or send us a fax at (317) 581-4663. For the online inclined, Macmillan Computer Publishing has a forum on CompuServe (type `GO QUEBOOKS` at any prompt) through which our staff and authors are available for questions and comments. Our Internet site is at `http://www.mcp.com` (World Wide Web).

In addition to exploring our forum, please feel free to contact me personally on CompuServe at `74671,3710` to discuss your opinions of this book. You can also reach me on the Internet at `avalvano@que.mcp.com`.

Thanks in advance—your comments will help us to continue publishing the best books available on computer topics in today's market.

Al Valvano
Acquisitions Editor
Que Corporation
201 W. 103rd Street
Indianapolis, Indiana   46290
USA

Contents at a Glance

VI | Appendixes

Contents

III | Defining Retrieval Structures

Introduction

All data processing is involved with the operations of storing and retrieving data. A database, such as Microsoft SQL Server, is designed as the central repository for all the data of an organization. The crucial nature of data to any organization underlies the importance of the method used to store it and enable its subsequent retrieval for processing.

Microsoft SQL Server uses the features of other databases and some features that aren't required for other databases to store data. Most of these additional features are made possible by SQL Server's tight integration with the Windows NT operating system. SQL Server contains the data storage options and the capability to store and process the same volume of data as a mainframe or minicomputer.

Like most mainframe or minicomputer databases, SQL Server is a database that has seen an evolution from its introduction in the mid-1960s until today. Microsoft's SQL Server is founded in the mature and powerful relational model, currently the preferred model for data storage and retrieval.

Unlike mainframe and minicomputer databases, a server database is accessed by users—called clients—from other computer systems rather than from input/output devices, such as terminals. Mechanisms must be in place for SQL Server to solve problems that arise from the access of data from perhaps hundreds of computer systems, each of which can process portions of the database independently from the data on the server.

Within the framework of a client/server database, a server database also requires integration with communication components of the server in order to enable connections with client systems. Microsoft SQL Server's client/server connectivity uses the built-in network components of Windows NT.

Unlike a stand-alone PC database or a traditional mainframe or minicomputer database, a server database, such as Microsoft SQL Server, adds service-specific middleware components—such as *Open Database Connectivity* (ODBC)—on top of the network components. ODBC enables the interconnection of different client applications without requiring changes to the server database or other existing client applications.

SQL Server also contains many of the front-end tools of PC databases that traditionally haven't been available as part of either mainframe or minicomputer databases. In addition to using a dialect of *Structured Query Language* (SQL), GUI applications can be used for both the storage, retrieval, and administration of the database. ■

Who Should Use This Book

This book is written for all users of Microsoft SQL Server— from database users to database administrators. It can be used by new users to learn about any feature of Microsoft SQL Server. It can also serve as a reference for experienced users who need to learn the use of a feature of the product that they haven't yet employed.

The CD-ROM that accompanies this book provides example Transact-SQL statements and demonstration applications provided by many third-party vendors to give you a feeling for many of the products and services available in the market, as well as to give you ideas for using SQL Server in your organization.

In addition, you can use the electronic version of this book that is included on the CD, enabling you to reference the information in the book on your monitor alongside an actual SQL Server database.

How to Use This Book

This book is divided into six sections. The sections are intended to present the use of SQL Server as a logical series of steps in the order in which the reader would most likely use the product. Ideally, you will go through the sections and their chapters in sequence.

Part I: Understanding SQL Server Fundamentals and Background Information

In Part I, the basic features of Microsoft SQL Server are discussed, and an overview of it's capabilities is presented. In this section, you'll learn about necessary information that is related to Microsoft SQL Server. The background information about SQL Server is recommended for all new readers and current users of SQL Server who may be unfamiliar with it.

In Chapter 1, "Introducing Microsoft SQL Server," you'll learn the origin and evolution of SQL Server and its implementation as a relational database. You'll also learn about the components of SQL Server, including the installation and configuration of the database and its client components. In Chapter 2, "Data Modeling and Database Design," you'll learn how to design a database. Moreover, you'll become familiar with the terminology that's associated with a relational database, such as SQL server.

Chapter 3, "Understanding the Underlying Operating System, Windows NT," explains the features of the operating system that SQL Server takes advantage of to obtain optimal performance. The SQL Server database components are designed solely for implementation on the Windows NT system.

Part II: Defining and Manipulating Data and Data Storage Units

In Part II, you learn how to create the storage areas and other storage structures of the database. You'll also learn to manipulate the stored data, including combining data from multiple sources. If you are already familiar with SQL or the previous version of SQL Server, you'll still want to read the chapters in this section to learn how this version differs from the earlier version. You'll also want to learn about the additions that support the ANSI SQL standard.

Chapter 4, "Creating Devices, Databases, and Transaction Logs," explains how you create the storage areas on a disk where you create your database and backups of your database. Chapter 5, "Creating Database Tables and Using Datatypes," provides you with instructions on how to create database tables and choose the datatypes of the table columns. You can also read about the considerations involved in your choice of table and table column characteristics.

Chapter 6, "Retrieving Data with Transact-SQL," provides instruction in the use of the SELECT statement and the addition of clauses to the SELECT statement for controlling the retrieval of targeted data. Chapter 7, "Performing Operations on Tables," continues the instruction on retrieving data begun in Chapter 6. Included in the discussion is instruction on how to combine data from multiple tables. Chapter 8, "Using Functions," provides a comprehensive treatment of the functions that you can use in Transact-SQL. The examples presented in the chapter are simple and direct, which facilitate the understanding of the use of the functions.

Part III: Defining Retrieval Structures

In Part III, you learn how to define database objects that are used to control the retrieval of data. The retrieval objects are stored in a database and provide both convenient and rapid ways of retrieving data.

In Chapter 9, "Managing and Using Views," you learn the definition and use of stored SELECT statements that are subsequently used like an actual table. You'll also learn of the problem of disappearing rows, a phenomena that occurs with the storage of rows through a view.

In Chapter 10, "Managing and Using Indexes and Keys," you learn how to define the database objects that are used to insure fast retrieval of the rows of database tables. In addition, you'll learn to use the database object that is a basis for insuring referential integrity in a database.

Part IV: Defining and Using Advanced Data Definition and Retrieval Structures

The chapters of Part IV continue the discussion of database objects and structures that enable data to be retrieved faster and more precisely. Chapter 11, "Managing and Using Rules and

Defaults," contains information on how to restrict the values that may be inserted into database tables and other database structures.

Chapter 12, "Understanding Transactions and Locking," provides an understanding of the synchronization mechanism used by SQL Server to ensure the integrity of database tables and operations.

Chapter 13, "Managing Stored Procedures and Using Flow-Control Statements," and Chapter 14, "Creating and Managing Triggers," discuss the capability of creating a set of Transact-SQL statements that can be stored and subsequently executed as a group. You can use flow-control statements, including conditional statements, to effectively write a SQL program that manipulates your database. In addition, you'll learn to create a set of SQL statements that are automatically activated when SELECT, INSERT, UPDATE, or DELETE statements are executed on a database.

Chapter 15, "Creating and Using Cursors," provides you with instruction on the use of a feature of SQL Server that enables you to perform selection operations on individual rows of a database table. You can also randomly access an individual row and manipulate it without affecting other rows.

Part V: Performing Administrative Operations

Chapter 16, "Understanding Server, Database, and Query Options," provides you with the information necessary to configure your server and database for various uses and situations. In addition, you'll also learn to configure your queries against the database.

Chapter 17, "Optimizing Performance," explains how you can enhance a database and the retrieval of information from the database using important calculations based on different storage factors. Moreover, you'll learn to use the built-in monitoring tool of the Windows NT system to monitor the performance of SQL Server components and applications.

Chapter 18, "SQL Server Administration," provides you with information about how to keep data consistently available to the users of client systems. Availability of data from a database is ensured by a combination of fault-tolerant mechanisms and the duplication of data before it's lost.

Chapter 19, "SQL Server Security," continues the discussion of maintaining data availability by explaining the implementation of proper security for SQL Server and its databases. Chapter 20, "Setting Up and Managing Replication," discusses how you implement the automatic creation and maintenance of multiple copies of a database to enhance performance in the access of data.

The remaining chapters depart from the others in this section in that they discuss products that are used with SQL Server for communication and querying. Chapter 21, "Communicating with SQL Server," provides you with information about the client and server components used for the interconnection of systems. The network components and protocols are the basis on which SQL Server and client applications depend for communication.

Chapter 22, "Accessing SQL Server Databases Through Front-End Products," discusses the access of a SQL Server database through programming and non-programming applications. The chapter uses representative examples of the most prevalent client products.

Part VI: Appendixes

Appendix A, "Installation and Setup of the Client and Server Software," teaches you the different steps and considerations to keep in mind as you set up your server system and the clients who will access it.

Appendix B, "SQL Server and Web Pages," teaches you how to work with Web pages, specifically with the query utility tool MS Query. MS Query can provide access to to SQL Server and many other databases, making it a versatile tool for viewing stored data.

Appendix C, "Using SQL Trace," covers how to monitor and record database activity for SQL Server 6.5. It shows how to display server activity in real time and how to create filters for monitoring particular users, applications, and hosts.

Appendix D, "Redundant Arrays of Inexpensive Drives (RAID)," explains the six implementations used by RAID to provide a set of physical devices that will offer better data device integrity and performance.

Appendix E, "Case Study: New York Metropolitan Museum of Art," provides a real-world example of a system used by Jay Hoffman of Gallery Systems in New York.

Appendix F, "What's on the CD?" teaches you about the materials included on the CD-ROM that accompanies this book. It contains applications, tools, and demonstration products.

Conventions Used in This Book

Que has over a decade of experience writing and developing the most successful computer books available. With that experience, we've learned what special features help readers the most. Look for these special features throughout the book to enhance your learning experience.

The following font conventions are used in this book to help make reading it easier.

- *Italic type* is used to introduce new terms.
- Screen messages, code listings, and command samples appear in `monospace type`. For more details about syntax, see the following section, "Syntax Guidelines."
- Code that you are instructed to type appears in **`monospace bold type`**.
- Shortcut keys are denoted with strikethrough. For example, "choose File, Edit" means that you can press Alt+F, then press E to perform the same steps as clicking on the File menu and the clicking on Edit.

 Tips present short advice on a quick or often overlooked procedure. These include shortcuts.

N O T E Notes present interesting or useful information that isn't necessarily essential to the discussion. A note provides additional information that may help you avoid problems or offers advice that relates to the topic. ■

> **CAUTION**
>
> Cautions look like this and warn you about potential problems that a procedure may cause, unexpected results, or mistakes to avoid.

This icon indicates you can also find the related information on the enclosed CD-ROM.

Syntax Guidelines

It's important to have a clearly defined way of describing Transact-SQL commands. In this book, the following rules apply:

- Anything in *italics* means that you have to substitute the italicized text with your own text.
- Anything placed inside square brackets "[...]" means that it can be optionally left out of the command.
- Anything placed inside curly braces "{ ... }" means that one of the values must be chosen to complete the syntax.
- The available values are separated by the bar (or pipe) character "|" (meaning "OR"). Consider the following example:

  `{DISK ¦ TAPE ¦ DISKETTE}`

  It would be translated as "DISK or TAPE or DISKETTE."
- Finally, if you see "..." after any bracketed block in a Transact-SQL statement, it means that section can be repeated as many items as is appropriate.

Understanding SQL Server Fundamentals and Background Information

Introducing Microsoft SQL Server

A s the computer industry continues to move to more distributed environments and moves a significant portion of its data from mainframe to servers, you need to understand the concepts behind a client/server database environment.

In several respects, server databases such as Microsoft SQL Server are identical to mainframe databases. The overwhelming majority of databases used on computer systems are relational databases. Also, server databases, such as relational databases on mainframe or minicomputer systems, support the use of Structured Query Language (SQL) as well as proprietary tools to access data.

Where you start to see differences in a PC-based client server solution is in the architecture and physical implementation of the system. With a SQL Server solution, your users will be using intelligent client systems such as personal computers. In a mainframe or minicomputer environment, users likely use a terminal or a PC using terminal-emulation software. With more intelligent client systems, users can retrieve information from the server and manipulate it locally. This type of implementation optimizes the processing of the information, allowing each component to work on the information independently in the manner best suited for that component. The server focuses on the database processes, while the client focuses on the presentation of the information. ■

A brief history of SQL Server

SQL Server has been around nearly 10 years and has been developed by several companies for many different platforms.

What language SQL Server uses to implement and maintain the relational model

Transact-SQL is a subset standard SQL that SQL Server uses to implement, maintain, and access databases.

What software is used to access SQL Server

SQL Server comes with several utilities to access its services. These utilities may be used locally or remotely to manage a SQL Server system.

How to obtain help

With a system as complex as SQL Server, it's very difficult to know every last detail. Online help is available in an easily searchable book-type format.

Why the Move to SQL Server?

Two key features of a server database become important because of the client access to data. The first feature is providing a single point of access to the data in the database. The second feature is the division of processing and manipulation between the client and server systems.

Microsoft SQL Server permits client applications to control the information retrieved from the server using several specialized tools and techniques. These include options such as stored procedures, server-enforced rules, and triggers that permit processing to be done on the server automatically. You don't have to offload all processing to the server, of course. You still can do appropriate information processing as needed on the client workstation.

Since with mainframe or minicomputer systems all processing is done at the host side, it can be initially simpler to implement systems in this environment than with a true client/server implementation. This is because users work at terminals that are directly connected to the mainframe or minicomputer and manipulate only the original copy of the database using the processing power of the mainframe or minicomputer.

Although organizations routinely use Microsoft SQL Server to manipulate millions of records, SQL Server provides a number of tools that help manage the system and its databases and tables. The Windows-based tools that come with SQL Server are easy to use for all database operations. These tools can be used to

- Perform the administration of the databases
- Control access to data within the databases
- Control the manipulation of data within the databases

You can also use a command-line interface to perform all operations with Microsoft SQL Server. A dialect of SQL is used with SQL Server for interactive and application program access to data. (SQL is the *de facto* standard for database operations, and every vendor's database product should include a version of it.)

N O T E The *Microsoft Open Database Connectivity model* (ODBC) uses SQL to connect to databases even in those cases where the underlying database doesn't natively know SQL. In those cases, SQL is translated into a set of commands that will accomplish the requested call. After you master SQL, you can work with any ODBC data source that you need to access. ■

Although this book includes coverage of how to use the command-line tool for issuing interactive SQL commands, you should remember that you can perform most operations through the application tools that use the Windows Graphical User Interface. You can use either interface or both interfaces, depending on your interest. If you're already familiar with another SQL dialect, you may initially find that it's simpler to issue direct SQL commands for all operations.

Exploring the Origin and Evolution of SQL Server

Microsoft SQL Server evolved from the older Sybase SQL Server database, a product that was introduced in 1987. Sybase SQL Server, one of the earliest relational database systems for the PC marketplace, was developed by members of INGRES.

In 1988, SQL Server for OS/2 was co-developed by Sybase, Microsoft, and Ashton-Tate when it first came to the PC platform. After SQL Server was ported to NT, Microsoft became the lead partner in the project and Ashton-Tate left the picture. Both Microsoft and Sybase sold and supported the product through version 4.21, as they were by and large the same product. In 1993, partly due to the Windows NT operating system version developed by Microsoft, the co-development/licensing agreement ended. Since that time, Microsoft has focused on the NT Server versions of SQL Server, while Sybase has worked on and sold the minicomputer versions of the SQL Server. Version 6.5, released in April, is the latest version in the progressive tuning and enhancement of the database engine.

If you start Microsoft SQL Server using a command line, the information returned in a separate window (which also is written to a separate log file) includes a Sybase copyright notice—evidence of Microsoft SQL Server's origin. Three Sybase copyright notices can be seen in the following excerpt from the startup of an earlier version of SQL Server on Windows NT.

```
94/08/09 16:17:37.92 kernel   SQL Server for Windows NT 4.21 (Intel X86)
      Jan 27 1994 21:47:39
Copyright (c) 1988-1994 Microsoft Corporation;  Copyright Sybase, Inc 1987-1994
94/08/09 16:17:38.08 kernel   Copyright (C) 1988-1993 Microsoft Corporation.
94/08/09 16:17:38.08 kernel   Copyright Sybase, Inc. 1987, 1993
94/08/09 16:17:38.08 kernel   All rights reserved.
94/08/09 16:17:38.08 kernel   Use, duplication, or disclosure by the United
States Government is subject
94/08/09 16:17:38.10 kernel   to restrictions set forth in FAR
subparagraphs 52.227-19(a)-(d) for civilian
94/08/09 16:17:38.16 kernel   agency contracts and DFARS 252.227-7013(c)
(1)(ii) for Department of Defense
94/08/09 16:17:38.16 kernel   contracts. Sybase reserves all unpublished
 rights under the copyright laws of
94/08/09 16:17:38.16 kernel   the United States.
94/08/09 16:17:38.16 kernel   Sybase, Inc. 6475 Christie Avenue,
Emeryville, CA 94608, USA.
94/08/09 16:17:38.16 kernel   Logging SQL Server messages in file
'G:\SQL\LOG\ERRORLOG'
94/08/09 16
```

N O T E The copyright notice for Sybase no longer appears in the latest version of Microsoft SQL Server, version 6.5. ∎

Microsoft originally licensed the core components of SQL Server from Sybase to make the product available on PC platforms running OS/2 and, more recently, Windows NT.

You can see from the heritage of SQL Server that it's by no means a new product to the marketplace. Indeed, it's been through many different rounds of revisions, updates, and upgrades, and certainly represents a world-class database platform on which you can develop mission-critical applications. You don't need to worry about "breaking in" a new-to-the-marketplace platform in your organization.

Understanding Relational Features of SQL Server

A key characteristic of SQL Server is that it's a relational database. You must understand the features of a relational database to effectively understand and access data with SQL Server. You can't construct successful queries to return data from a relational database unless you understand the basic features of a relational database.

The model for relational databases was designed by Dr. E.F. Codd in 1970 to store, retrieve, and manipulate data in a way that was easier than the hierarchical and network databases. Hierarchical and network databases were difficult to design and sometimes difficult to write proper queries for access to data.

Hierarchical and network databases were difficult to work with for several reasons. The physical and logical definitions of data storage in hierarchical and network databases had to be done by using a cryptic definition language syntax. Another difficulty of working *with* data definitions came from the fact that different types of internal pointers, numeric references to data locations, and more had to be set up and stored through the database. The pointers were used for the subsequent direct retrieval of data.

In Codd's relational database model, the data is referenced as though it's stored in a two-dimensional table. The actual physical storage of the data—although significant for the time it takes to store, change, or retrieve data—is insignificant syntactically for reference. The two-dimensional table model permits data to be referenced as the rows and columns of the table.

In a relational database, data is referenced as the rows and columns of a table. You can easily visualize data stored as a table because you often encounter data stored in tables in everyday life. For example, you reference train or plane schedules in the form of a table and you also create typical worksheets in the form of a table.

FIG. 1.1
Example of common table.

Flights out of Tucson - Que Airways

Time	Dest.	Flt.	Gate
6:45a	Indianapolis	2332	3
8:30a	Phoenix	617	4
9:15a	Los Angeles	4325	3
12:00p	San Carlos	17	7
5:45p	Seattle	7548	4
7:30p	Las Vegas	777	7

The rows of a table are unordered in Codd's relational model. In the relational model implemented in Microsoft SQL Server, the rows of a database table are also unordered (they're in the order in which they were entered), unless a clustered index is created for the table. After you create a clustered index for a table, the rows are stored in ascending order by the one or more columns that you use to create the index. Later, this book covers more about clustered indexes.

▶ For more information about clustered indexes and the other types of indexes supported by SQL Server, see Chapter 10, "Managing and Using Indexes and Keys."

It's important, however, that the statements you use in the retrieval language to access table rows are independent of the order of the rows. If you require that the rows of a table are retrieved and displayed in an order, the statement that you issue to retrieve the rows must specify the row order. The rows are sorted as they're retrieved for your query.

The original relational model required each row to be uniquely defined by at least one column of a table, the unique key. The unique row requirement ensures that each row is accessed or changed independently and uniquely from other rows of the table. The query language used to access table rows can use only data stored within each row to separate one row from another.

SQL Server, however, doesn't require you to define unique table rows. You can create two or more rows of a table that can't be referenced separately from one another. Although you may not find a use for duplicate rows, some users feel such rows are desirable in some applications. In Chapter 2 you'll learn more about relational design concepts and techniques, but for now it's important to understand what's possible, if not practical. If you do want to prevent duplicates, you can add a constraint to tables to prevent duplicate rows.

CAUTION

As you'll see in Chapter 2, unless you're absolutely certain you must allow the storage of duplicate rows, you should ensure that table rows are unique. In the absence of enforced uniqueness, it's too easy to accidentally add one or more duplicates to the table. After you add the duplicate rows, it's difficult to remove or update them.

In the relational database model, data that's stored across tables in one or more databases is combined during the access of the rows during an inquiry. For example, if the Employees table contains columns such as Name, Department, and Badge, a second table named Pays can contain the columns Hours_Worked, PayRate, and Badge.

You can define the Badge column in both tables. This way, you can subsequently retrieve column values from both tables in a single query. You combine columns from multiple tables by using statements that call out the columns you need and specify the information common to both tables in the Where clause. You'll read more about the syntax of this operation, but for now, it's important to understand only that this pulling together of information based on common values is known as a *join*.

▶ For more information on Where clauses, see Chapter 6, "Retrieving Data with Transact-SQL."

The example in the Employees and Pays tables uses the relational capabilities of SQL Server to retrieve information from each table using the corresponding badge numbers. An example Select statement would be as follows:

```
Select * from Employees, Pays where Employees.Badge = Pays.Badge
```

Not surprisingly, if you modify or delete a badge number in the Employees table, the corresponding badge number in the Pays table must also be modified. This process of ensuring that corresponding values of related tables are maintained to keep table relationships intact is called *referential integrity*. This process can even include deleting related information in other tables if you remove a master record, as would be the case if the Employees record were deleted if it referred to records in the Pays table.

It's easiest to maintain referential integrity if table rows are unique. This ensures that there will be only a single row in a second table. Make sure you maintain the badge number if it is modified or deleted in the first table. In the relational-database model, the column, or set of columns, that uniquely defines the rows of a table is referred to as a *key*.

N O T E A key that uniquely defines the rows of a table is called a *primary key*. If you add the column(s) that is a primary key in one table to a second table, the column(s) added to the second table is called the *foreign key*. It's a foreign key because the new columns referencing the first table are used only to allow the matching of corresponding rows between the tables. For more information, see Chapter 10, "Managing and Using Indexes and Keys." ■

In earlier database systems, internal pointers were created and maintained within the database to link the corresponding rows stored in the tables. The pointer mechanism created a problem, however, because when the database was created, you had to define the data that was later combined during retrieval.

N O T E Older hierarchical and network databases don't use terms such as *table* or *row*. Hierarchical and network databases use their own terminology to describe data. For example, the equivalent of a row of a relational database is called a *record type*. The equivalent of a column of a relational database is called a *data item*. ■

If you neglected to identify data that must be combined later during retrieval, you couldn't do it once the database structure was created. You had to re-create the logical and physical structure of the database. The main problem involved with using hierarchical and network databases was that changes in data-retrieval combinations were impossible to make without redesigning the database.

In relational databases such as SQL Server, you can add a new column to a table at any time. This allows you to create relationships with other tables. Unlike typical hierarchical or network databases, the database doesn't need to be redefined; only a single table must be redefined. You don't need to unload the rows of the table and later reload the table to add a new column. You can use SQL's ALTER TABLE statement to make modifications to existing tables.

▶ For more information about the ALTER TABLE statement, please see Chapter 7, "Performing Operations on Tables."

Exploring Client/Server Features of SQL Server

Client/server computing is a type of distributed model for data storage, access, and processing. In a distributed processing system, multiple computers collectively perform a set of operations. A client/server system uses at least two computers, one of which is nearly always a personal computer.

N O T E Distributed processing was introduced by minicomputer systems to provide the capabilities of large mainframe computers. The data storage, access, and processing capabilities of several minicomputers could match the processing capabilities of a mainframe computer for some operations by working together. ■

Each system in a client/server model performs on _____, access, or processing operations. Client/server comp_____ uses terminals or PCs running terminal emula_____ rangement, the terminal or the PC that's _____ s and displays sets of characters.

When PCs and servers ar_____ n the server, mainframe, or mini_____ ver each process work within its _____ efficiency and speed of the ov_____

When PCs and servers are conn_____ server, mainframe, or minicompu_____ er each process work within its own _____ s to the efficiency and speed of the over_____

Client/server, as the name implies, al_____ in-equality results from the processing di_____ the larger and faster server computer transfers data fas_____ .ta, and typically performs more extensive processing than_____

Smaller PC systems are used as the client i_____ ver system because the PCs perform proportionally less of the overall work, relying primarily on the server for heavy-duty data manipulation. Also, the PC's keyboard and monitor allow it to work as an input device (generating commands and data) and as a output device (displaying data to the user).

N O T E A client and a server also are defined by the direction of the data flow and operational responsibilities. A large and powerful PC system can function as a server if it receives commands and data from one or more PC systems, processes the data, and returns information to other PC systems. The server is the computer system that receives requests for processing or information from other computer systems.

You can use large, powerful PCs as servers with less powerful PCs as clients and still qualify as using client/server technology. In this environment, the PC servers are usually more powerful than an average PC; this helps them perform processing requests from many clients. ■

[Handwritten note: Data from mf in one table — Data from user input? another table. sp - help]

Microsoft SQL Server is a perfect example of a client/server system. The SQL Server database must be installed on the Windows NT platform. The Windows NT operating system provides you with an extremely broad range of processor systems to use as your server. Windows NT is supported on I86 processor-based systems, PPC, MIPS, and Alpha AXP RISC-processor-based systems

Microsoft SQL Server is provided with the server software that's installed on the server system and some client software that's installed on the client PC systems. Windows GUI application tools allow the database and all objects to be created, maintained, and accessed from the client.

The network software components required for the interconnection of clients and the server computer are built into the Windows NT system. Windows NT also provides a choice of network protocols for communication between the client and server systems. A client can run Windows 95, which also contains built-in network software for connection with the Windows NT server system. The Windows 95 client and Windows NT server systems support a wide range of network cards.

In a client/server system where the server application is a database such as SQL Server, the server is responsible for the creation and maintenance of database objects such as the table and indexes. The server maintains referential integrity and security and ensures that operations can be recovered in the event of numerous types of failures.

The client performs all user interaction, including information display and allowing manipulation of the application with the graphical user interface. After rows of data are retrieved from the server, the application can create copies to be held locally and the data can be manipulated. You also can control the type of access to the information. Read-only access is often an excellent option, insulating the user from the master copies of the information that they work with on the server.

If you work with local copies of the information, you can work with the information locally without communicating with the server. After you complete your work, you can send changes back to the server or, if the information was for review only, simply discard the working databases. Of course, you also can manipulate the data directly in the SQL Server database from the client, if needed. You must be sure to update the server with all changes so that other users can access the most recent data in the database.

You can also access SQL Server directly from the server. Direct server access is convenient, especially for administrative operations, but it isn't a client/server approach because the operations occur locally rather than across the network. Microsoft SQL Server comes with 32-bit versions of the SQL Windows application tools for the Windows NT server that are normally used on the clients.

Although you can have client applications validate new or updated data, the validation should optimally be done at the server. For example, a column such as Badge can be checked to ensure that each new or updated badge number is unique and within a specified range. It's safer for the data to be validated at the server as a part of a SQL Server-defined mechanism. If the validation is defined at the server, it will always be in force whether or not the connected client performs a validation.

N O T E A big benefit of using server-side validation is that you'll protect the database from access from applications that may access the database in "non-standard" manners. This includes applications (such as Excel, Access, and Word) that can connect to the database using ODBC. In each case, rules and integrity checks that you implement on the server will still be enforced, even though the client application may be unknown. ■

If you rely on client applications to validate data before it's sent to the server, you must ensure that all the client applications do it consistently. You must also ensure that changes aren't made directly at the server, where no validation mechanism has been defined. It's simpler and more reliable to implement server validation.

T I P You also can perform validation in client applications in addition to validation on the server. Client validation can be specific to the client application that isn't enforced by server validation mechanisms. When the updates are sent to the server, it will still enforce its own validation.

Examining SQL Server Features and Components

The core component of Microsoft SQL Server is the relational database and its structure. As you no doubt agree, SQL Server is a powerful, comprehensive database environment. There are certain parameters to using SQL Server and they're pointed out here.

Microsoft SQL Server allows you to define up to 32,767 databases. If you realize that the definition of a database is a centralized repository for the storage of information, it is difficult to be overly constrained by the 32,767-database limit. It's unlikely you'll encounter any situation in which you need to define more than this very liberal limit. If you do, you'll certainly want to be looking at adding additional servers to your network to help balance the load. In a typical production installation, you'll often find that less than five—and often only one—application-oriented databases will be in service on any given server.

You can also define up to 2 billion tables within each of your 32,767 databases. It's not likely that you'll need anywhere near 2 billion tables in a database. With most typical systems, you'll have only several hundred tables in a database.

You can define up to 250 columns for each table. In Chapter 2, where you'll learn about database design, you'll see that when you normalize your database tables, you largely overcome this limitation. As you'll see, SQL Server allows columns from as many as 16 tables to be combined in a single query.

The number of rows in a table is effectively unlimited for Microsoft SQL Server. You're limited in practice by the capacity of the storage medium on which tables are stored, and databases and their tables can be stored across multiple physical disks. Microsoft SQL Server allows databases to expand to include up to 32 physical disks.

N O T E The 32-disk limit is imposed indirectly through subordinate logical structures. You store
SQL Server databases, transaction logs, indexes, and tables on logical structures called
segments. You can expand a database by adding segments that are created on devices. A database
can include up to 32 segments. See Chapter 4, "Creating Devices, Databases, and Transaction Logs,"
for information about creating databases and segments. ■

You can define up to 250 indexes for each table, only one of which can be defined as a clustered
index. An *index* is a structure that allows the table rows to be retrieved more quickly than they
could without using an index. In a *clustered index*, the table rows are sorted and maintained in
storage in a physically ordered state. That is, rows that are sorted before and after one another
are also stored in that sorted order. An index is often defined for the columns that are referenced in retrieval statements. 250 indexes should provide fast retrieval of table rows.

Indexes require additional storage space in the database for the index structure that must be
created and stored. One performance recommendation is to define as few indexes as you need
because of the space they take up. You still need to define enough indexes to allow the rapid
retrieval of rows. You should define the minimum number of indexes that you require; it would
be unusual for you to need more than 250 for a single table.

Devices and Databases

You store databases and all the objects within them in disk files. Microsoft SQL Server calls
your database files *devices*, but they're logical units rather than physical devices. You create a
database on the logical devices. Remember that you can create up to 32,767 databases.

Each database is created with a set of system tables in which SQL Server records data about
the database objects such as tables or indexes that you subsequently create. Like a relational-
database product, SQL Server keeps the control information about your database objects in a
relational database—the set of system tables.

Transact-SQL

Structured Query Language (SQL) is the query language developed by IBM in the 1970s that
has become the *de facto* standard database query language for relational databases. The dialect
of SQL that you use with SQL Server is Transact-SQL, which Microsoft implements as a core
component of SQL Server.

Transact-SQL adds additional keywords to those of the original SQL for the formation of data
retrieval, storage, and manipulation. When SQL Server's implementation of SQL was put into
place, like other database vendors, Microsoft added features and extensions to the language.

Compared to other vendors' SQL dialects, Transact-SQL has less unique syntax. Arguably, the
SQL dialect SQL-PLUS, used with the relational database Oracle, has the most additional
unique syntax. Although the large set of unique syntax in some SQL dialects is useful, the use
of dialect-specific syntax makes stored sets of SQL commands non-portable and can be the
cause of many headaches when moving your systems between servers.

N O T E Remember that some SQL dialect is used with all relational databases. If you work with more than one relational database, or if you must convert from one to another, it's easier to use the SQL syntax that's the most generic. Stored sets of SQL statements—if they use generic syntax—can be easily converted or used across relational databases. ■

Transact-SQL is best characterized as lean and mean. You have just enough enhancements to basic SQL to write functional queries. Transact-SQL contains statements to create logical storage units, the devices, as well as the databases that reside on the devices. You can also use Transact-SQL statements to create the objects, such as tables, that are stored within the databases.

Not surprisingly, you can also use Transact-SQL statements to add and manipulate data and other database objects. Four keywords are used to form statements that perform all basic data storage, retrieval, and manipulation. Use INSERT to add new rows to a database table. Use DELETE to delete rows from a table and use UPDATE to change rows of a table. Use SELECT to form various statements for the retrieval of data from one or multiple tables.

The INSERT, DELETE, UPDATE, and SELECT statements—as well as other statements—use a generic form of SQL for data manipulation. The extensions to Transact-SQL are principally for flow control to direct the execution order of statements. Use flow-control statements in organized sets of SQL statements that are stored as objects within your database.

Stored sets of Transact-SQL statements contained within the SQL Server database are called *stored procedures*, which are compiled so that they rapidly execute SQL statements. You can use stored procedures in addition to programs for database access and manipulation because they can use variables and parameters, return errors and status, and use flow control to control the execution order of SQL statements.

▶ For more information on Stored Procedure and how to implement them, see Chapter 13, "Managing Stored Procedures and Using Flow-Control Statements."

A *trigger* is a special type of stored procedure used to maintain referential integrity in a SQL Server database. You create insert, delete, and update triggers to control the addition, deletion, or updates to corresponding rows of related tables for which the trigger is defined. Triggers are an excellent way to maintain referential integrity because you have complete control over the operations that they perform, and they're server-based.

You also use several additional objects—rules, defaults, and constraints—to help control or apply values automatically to table columns. You use a *default* to supply a value to the column of a database table when the insertion of a new row doesn't specify a value for the column. A *rule* constrains the values that can be entered into the column of a table. A *constraint* is used to define a characteristic of a table column, such as requiring only unique values.

Two Windows NT processes are part of the SQL Server set of components. You issue Transact-SQL statements that are conveyed to and performed by the two server processes. You can use a tool such as the Performance Monitor to display the characteristics of the SQL Server processes. For example, in Figure 1.2, shows the working set for the two SQL Server processes SQLSERVR and SQLEXEC. The *working set* of a process is the percentage of processor time that's directly allocated to a process.

FIG. 1.2

The Performance Monitor
displays the characteristics of
the SQL Server processes.

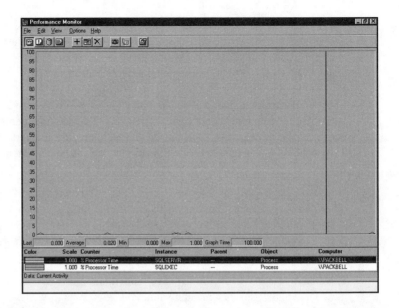

The SQLSERVR process is divided into multiple threads for execution. *Threads* are the separate
units of execution on a Windows NT system. The division of one of the two SQL Server processes into multiple threads allows multiple execution in a multiprocessor environment such as
Windows NT. If your server has more than one processor, different operations on the SQL
Server databases can be executed simultaneously.

 You can buy a wide range of computer systems with multiple processors and increased memory to
enhance the Windows NT version of Microsoft SQL Server and have your transactions performed as
rapidly as you need.

You can use Windows NT's Performance Monitor not only to monitor the performance of SQL
components, but to learn about the function of components. For example, you can perform
different Transact-SQL statements and use the Performance Monitor to determine which
component is activated to perform the operation.

Command-Line Applications

You can issue SQL statements through the Interactive Structured Query Language (ISQL)
utility. *ISQL/w* is the Windows tool that allows you to use Transact-SQL with SQL Server from
a graphical interface (see the section entitled "ISQL/w" later in this chapter). If you become
familiar enough with Transact-SQL syntax, or if you prefer working at the DOS command line,
you can perform all operations on your databases through ISQL command lines.

From a command-line session, you invoke ISQL with the command isql. You can use several
parameters on the ISQL command line. For example, you can enter the user name and password following ISQL to bring you directly into an ISQL command session.

The following example shows the initiation of a command session. The command prompt is successively numbered until the termination command GO is entered.

```
isql /Usa /P<password> /S<server>
1>
```

You can use the `-?` or `/?` switch to display a list of the syntax for the use of the ISQL command, as shown in the following example:

```
usage: isql [-U login id] [-e echo input]
     [-p print statistics] [-n remove numbering]
     [-c cmdend] [-h headers] [-w columnwidth] [-s colseparator]
     [-m errorlevel] [-t query timeout] [-l login timeout]
     [-L list servers] [-a packetsize]
     [-H hostname] [-P password]
     [-q "cmdline query"] [-Q "cmdline query" and exit]
     [-S server] [-d use database name]
     [-r msgs to stderr] [-E trusted connection]
     [-i inputfile] [-o outputfile]
     [-b On error batch abort]
     [-O use Old ISQL behavior disables the following]
          <EOF> batch processing
          Auto console width scaling
          Wide messages
          default errorlevel is -1 vs 1
     [-? show syntax summary (this screen)]
```

N O T E   ISQL command-line parameters are case-sensitive. Be sure to observe the upper- and lowercase indications provided by the help from ISQL.

Table 1.1 summarizes the function of each parameter. Each parameter (also called a *switch* in the Microsoft SQL Server documentation) is preceded with a forward slash (/) or a hyphen (-). The command isql /? displays the hyphens (-), although the hyphen or forward slash can be used. (The use of the hyphen in command-line ISQL is inherited from the Sybase version of SQL Server.) ■

Table 1.1   ISQL Command-Line Parameters

Parameter	Function
a *packet_size*	Packet size for data transfer 512 through 65535; NT default is 8192
b	On error batch abort
c *cmdend*	Specifies the command terminator; default is GO
d *dbname*	Issues a USE dbname command on entry into ISQL
E	Use trusted connection
e	Echo input
H *wksta_name*	Specifies the workstation name

continues

Table 1.1 Continued

Parameter	Function
h *headers*	Number of rows to print between column headings
i *inputfile*	Specifies an input batch file for execution
L	Lists the local and remote servers
l *timeout*	login timeout
m *errorlevel*	Sets error-level displays to this level or higher
n	Omit prompt line numbers
O	Use old behavior
o *outputfile*	Specifies file where statement output is directed
P *password*	Specifies password; prompted for if not specified
p	Display performance statistics
Q *"query"*	Executes a .SQL batch file and exits the ISQL session
q *"query"*	Executes a .SQL batch file
r [0¦1]	Controls redirection of error-level messages
S *servername*	Specifies the server name; default is local
s *colseparator*	Set column separator; default is blank
t *timeout*	Command timeout in seconds; default is no timeout
U *login_id*	Case-sensitive SQL Server user account name
w *columnwidth*	Set column width; default is 80
?	Shows syntax

Table 1.2 lists the set of commands used after you enter ISQL. These commands must be used at the beginning of a command line (a 1> prompt).

Table 1.2 ISQL Commands

Command	Purpose
GO	Default command terminator; executes a statement
RESET	Clears statements before execution
ED	Invokes the default system editor
!! *command*	Executes a NT command
QUIT or EXIT()	Exits ISQL

Command	Purpose
Ctrl+C	Terminates a query without exiting ISQL
SHUTDOWN	Stops the SQL Server and exits ISQL

 TIP You can use the command-line recall feature of Windows NT (the ⬆ key) to recall previous commands that you've entered within ISQL. Your ISQL commands are limited to a maximum of 1,000 characters per line.

Applications

Four GUI applications are available to access and manage SQL Server installations.

The first of the applications allows you to enter Transact-SQL statements. The second, the SQL Client Configuration Utility, allows you to define the set of database and network library routines for database operations performed from a client system. The third, SQL Server Books Online, provides you with a complete set of SQL Server manuals organized for retrieval through the Books Online Browser. The final major tool is the Enterprise Manager. It's likely that you'll spend a fair amount of time in this utility as it provides access to the core administrative functions for SQL Server.

ISQL/w A Windows version of ISQL called ISQL/w issues Transact-SQL statements. You enter Transact-SQL commands in a separate query window within the ISQL/w main window. You can cut, copy, paste, print, save, and edit previous queries more easily in ISQL/w than you can through an ISQL command line.

After you start the ISQL/w application, you sign in to SQL Server by indicating your user name, password if necessary and the server you want to use. SQL Server maintains its own list of users who may connect to a server from a client system by using a valid login ID and user name.

▶ For more information on implementing and managing SQL Server security, see Chapter 19, "SQL Server Security."

Figure 1.3 shows a SELECT statement used to retrieve all rows from the system table sysdatabases, which contains a list of all defined databases. The tabular list of columns of information kept for the databases is displayed on the Results screen.

Your query output is displayed in a separate Results screen, which you can reach by clicking the Results tab. In addition, when you submit a query, ISQL/w automatically switches the current view to the Results tab. The Results tab shows information such as the rows returned by a query and error messages. You can use the scroll bars to view the entire query output. For example, Figure 1.4 shows the tables that are automatically created when SQL Server is installed.

FIG. 1.3

SQL statements are entered in the Query page of ISQL/w.

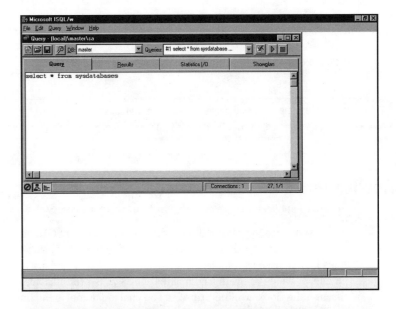

FIG. 1.4

You can use ISQL/w from both the client and server systems.

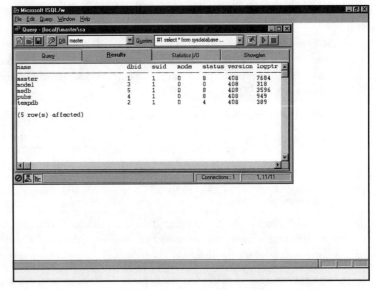

The SQL Client Configuration Utility The SQL Client Configuration Utility defines the Net-Library and DB-Library used for communication between the client and server. Figure 1.5 shows the SQL Client Configuration Utility dialog box. Click Locate to check for multiple copies of client libraries on your client or server system. You must consult the documentation of your client product to confirm that the correct version of the DB-Library is chosen.

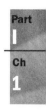

FIG. 1.5

Establish the client configuration by selecting the appropriate tab.

N O T E You should use the latest version of the network and database libraries on your system. If you have a mixed version environment, you'll have to consider either upgrading all servers to the most-recent server software, or attempting to use previous-versions drivers with the newer servers. While this will work in most cases, you might experience some problems using new features. ■

The Net-Library default is set to Named Pipes when you install the SQL Server client application tools on a client system. *Named Pipes* is the default communication mechanism used for communication between the client application and the SQL Server system. You can choose a different network library to use an alternate communication mechanism from named pipes. For example, as Figure 1.6 shows, you can choose alternate mechanisms for the TCP/IP, IPX/SPX, and Banyan VINES transport protocols.

FIG. 1.6

Several communication mechanisms are available.

N O T E The SQL Client Configuration Utility is helpful because a client may need to connect to more than one server. By installing all different protocols needed, the client workstation will have access to the routines located in network and database libraries. ■

Using SQL Server Books Online   The SQL Server Books Online help facility contains the contents of 13 books (see fig. 1.7) and a glossary on SQL Server. Like ISQL/w and the SQL Client Configuration Utility, the SQL Server Books Online application can be installed automatically on a client or server system. You'll find it extremely convenient to have quick access to such extensive documentation without leaving your computer system. These books include the entire text of the SQL Server documentation as provided by Microsoft.

FIG. 1.7

You can print or copy pages or complete sections of the Books Online information.

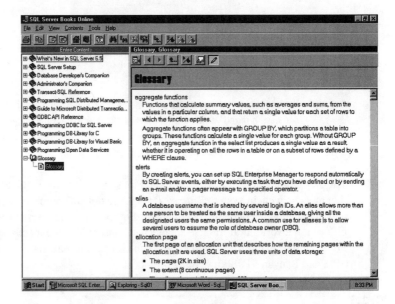

SQL Service Manager   The SQL Server Manager is one of the only utilities available when physically working on the server. The SQL Service Manager application starts, stops, or pauses the SQL Server processes. You must start SQL Server before you can perform any operations with the databases. The SQL Service Manager is the easiest way to start either a local or remote server. Figure 1.8 shows the SQL Service Manager dialog box after the MSSQLServer service is started.

> **N O T E**   A service on Windows NT such as the MSSQLServr and SQLExecutive of SQL Server are system processes that run in the background within NT. These background processes are used by SQL Server and client systems that require their functions. ■

The traffic light metaphor simplifies the starting, stopping, and pausing of SQL Server. Double-click Stop or the red light to stop SQL Server; double-click Pause or the yellow light symbol to temporarily pause SQL Server if the server has been started.

FIG. 1.8
If you pause the MSSQLServer
service, no additional client or
server connections are
permitted.

Status also shown here

 TIP You can minimize the SQL Service Manager and still observe the traffic lights to determine whether
server service is stopped (red light) or started (green light). The icon that represents the service
manager will still show the traffic light.

SQL Enterprise Manager SQL Enterprise Manager is the server application that you use to
perform nearly all administrative operations with local or remote servers. You can even use
SQL Enterprise Manager to start and stop both SQL Server services rather than use the SQL
Service Manager. SQL Enterprise Manager is also used to do the following:

- Manage user-account and server logins
- Back up and restore databases and transaction logs
- Start, stop, and configure servers
- Check database consistency
- Display server statistics
- Set up and manage database replication
- Create and manage database objects and tasks
- Create and control user accounts and groups
- Control the access control lists

You also may find that it's convenient to perform queries by using Transact-SQL commands
from within SQL Enterprise Manager. Click the SQL Query Tool toolbar button of SQL Enterprise Manager's main window (see fig. 1.9) to bring up a window through which you can issue

ISQL statements. Unlike ISQL/w, you won't have to connect and log in because you're already connected when you started SQL Enterprise Manager.

FIG. 1.9

In Enterprise Manager, you can issue SQL statements directly by using the Query Analyzer button.

Query Tool ―

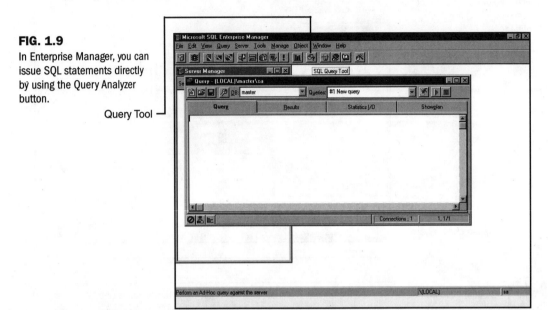

Although you also can perform all the administrative operations for SQL Server through ISQL, SQL Enterprise Manager allows you to perform the operations with pull-down menus and dialog boxes rather than a command line. In Figure 1.10, the grouping of server objects under folders have been expanded to display several different types of server entities.

FIG. 1.10

Server objects are displayed in a hierarchical fashion in the Server Manager window.

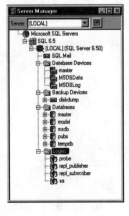

SQL Performance Monitor   The SQL Performance Monitor is a standard administrative application of the Windows NT operating system. SQL Server was written to allow SQL Server objects and counters to be displayed within the Performance Monitor with Windows NT object counters. For convenience, an additional icon is added that has a predefined set of objects and counters used for monitoring SQL Server.

Figure 1.11 shows a chart view of several important SQL counters that you can use to monitor the performance of SQL Server on your system. The integration of the SQL Server objects, counters—such as the cache hit ratio—and user connections enables you to select and display SQL Server statistics with NT objects and counters.

FIG. 1.11

The Performance Monitor is used to display statistics on the performance of both the system and SQL Server.

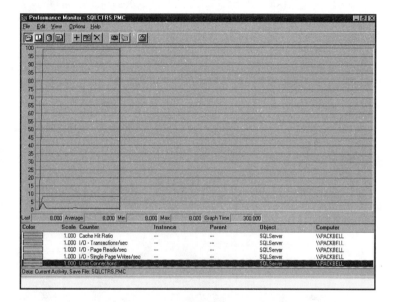

In addition to the chart display in Figure 1.11, you also can dynamically switch to display the counter information as a vertical bar graph rather than a chart. You can also record object counters in a log for later display, or you can display the information in the form of a tabular report.

The Performance Monitor also allows you to set threshold values for SQL Server counter values. When the threshold value is reached, an alert is displayed within an Alert view of the Performance Monitor. A message can also be sent to you about the alert even if you're working on a client workstation.

▶ For more information on performance monitoring techniques, see Chapter 17, "Optimizing Performance."

SQL Security Manager The SQL Security Manager administers SQL Server accounts. Choose one of the following three security types you want to implement on your system during the installation of SQL Server:

■ *Standard security.* Standard security requires you to log in to SQL Server using a user name and ID.

■ *Integrated security.* Integrated security requires you to log in only to Windows NT. You don't need to log in a second time when you access SQL Server. You'll still be prompted to sign in, but your user name in SQL Server will be taken from your network login ID.

■ *Mixed security.* Mixed security allows you to log in to SQL Server or use the integrated login of Windows NT. Integrated logins can be used only with connections to the server from clients using named pipes.

Figure 1.12 shows the main window of the SQL Security Manager. The Security Mode in the lower left corner is standard for the Windows NT domain PACKBELL. Login access through named pipes has been granted to users who are members of the SQL Server group Administrators.

FIG. 1.12
Integrated security provides the simplest account management in SQL Server.

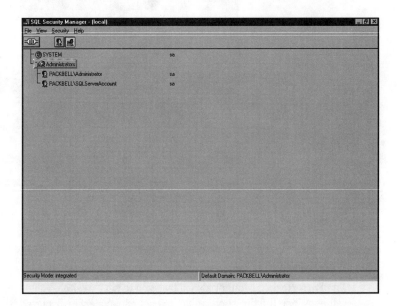

The SQL Security Manager graphically maps Windows NT groups and users to SQL Server accounts and passwords. You can also use the SQL Security Manager to find SQL Server access permissions for mapped accounts.

From Here...

Now that you've learned the basics of how SQL Server will be implemented in your organization, we'll begin working with the topics that will really make SQL Server get to work for you.

Be sure to also review Appendix A, "Installation and Setup of the Client and Server Software," so you understand what will be installed and where it will be located on your system.

For more information about selected topics, see the following Chapters:

- Chapter 10, "Managing and Using Indexes and Keys," shows you how to create and use keys and indexes.
- Chapter 11, "Managing and Using Rules and Defaults," shows how to create and use rules and defaults.
- Chapter 14, "Creating and Managing Triggers," shows how to create and use triggers to maintain referential integrity in the database.
- Chapter 15, "Creating and Using Cursors," shows you how to use cursors in a programming language to manipulate rows of a database table one at a time.

Data Modeling and Database Design

Chances are good that when you started learning about development in the programming world, you began with flowcharting. Flowcharts are a great tool for diagramming programmatic flow and for help in laying out the different components of your system. The purpose is to discover logic flaws and missing functionality before coding, rather than later during the cycle.

The reality is that flowcharts are rarely done. In fact, how many times have you been in a crunch to pull one together for a project, but waited until after the project was done to do the chart? This happens more often than any of us would like to admit. It's easy to pull it together after the fact because you already know what you've designed into the program, and you're not going to flowchart something you opted not to include in the application. It's a pretty safe way to approach things, provided you've reviewed the program along the way to ensure that the functionality meets the needs of your customer.

Database design isn't nearly as open to modification along the way. Because changing a database table after the fact alters the foundation for all other parts of the system, even in subtle ways, it often requires major overhaul work in the balance of the system. A simple change to a table can mean that entire portions of the application will stop functioning. ■

How you approach database design and architecture

There are many issues to designing and implementing a database. These issues can vary widely depending on the scope of a project.

What normalization is and how you accomplish it

Information is very powerful. Databases store large amounts of data. Unfortunately, data cannot always be used as information. Normalization is a way to guarantee that data will be available and flexible.

What client/server is, and what pieces of the SQL Server system can be used to help implement it to add value to your application

Client/server systems can share resources of many different systems within an organization and even beyond the boundaries of an organization.

How to make design easier and faster

There are many tools that can be used to aid in the design and even implementation of a database system.

Probably the most important thing you can do when you bring up a database-oriented system is to diagram and design the database structure that will support the application. If you don't do this, you'll end up making some subtle—and often not-so-subtle—changes to the structure later, probably at a time when the changes are far more expensive in the development cycle.

When you decide to develop a system based on Microsoft SQL Server, you've taken the first step toward implementing two separate architectures in your software. These are client/server and relational database tables. Both are powerful if used correctly and present a real-life advantage to your system if you take time to pay attention to the rules along the way.

This chapter introduces you to those rules. We'll show you the theory and practice that make up a client/server system, including how you can start to determine the best location (client or server) for a given piece of functionality to be implemented, guidelines for breaking apart procedural flow, and much more.

We'll also show you other parts of this book that can help you implement these concepts in your application. Since the decision to move to client/server depends heavily on the flow of the application and where things are physically being completed, SQL Server provides an ideal component to provide server-side functionality to bring client/server to your applications. It's important to understand what pieces of the database design will dovetail into your desires to move to the client/server world.

Understanding the Basics: Normalization

When you start working with relational databases, you inevitably end up hearing about data normalization and bringing things into third normal form. *Normalization* refers to how you implement the relationships and storage of data in your database tables. When you normalize a table, you try to limit the redundant data in the table. Many different levels, or types, of normalization exist, and we'll provide a brief overview here to help get you started.

Your overall goal is likely a 3NF, or *third normal form*, database. This will be the best compromise in most cases between extremes when it comes to normalization versus functionality and ease of implementation. There are levels beyond 3NF but, in practice, they can begin to cloud the database design with more design issues than functional issues.

When you delve into the world of normalized databases, you are, by definition, starting down the road of relational databases. Structures before normalized databases used a series of pointers to retain relationships between different tables and values. You may recall implementing linked lists, where each row in a database table contained a pointer to both the next and previous rows. To traverse the database, you simply walked up and down this list of links between records.

In the relational world, you define columns that relate to each other among tables. These columns are *keys* to other values. Keys are used to uniquely define a relationship to another instance or set of information. This chapter will get into more about keys as you work with the definitions of the different normalization levels.

What's In A Name?

A key difference between SQL Server-type database implementations and other more traditional PC-based databases is the terminology used to describe the databases and their information. Keep in mind that a device, or physical file on the disk drive of the server, contains one or more databases. Databases contain one or more tables, and tables contain one or more columns of information. For each table of columns, one or more rows may exist.

In more traditional terms, there was no concept of a database as in SQL Server. Instead, you had a file that contained records of fields. The following table shows a basic comparison of terms between a SQL Server implementation and a more traditional database such as Btrieve or dBASE.

New Term	Old Term
Device	N/A
Database	File
Table	N/A
Column	Field
Row	Record

You'll need to keep these terms in mind and, if you use the newer terms in describing the tables you're designing, you can avoid problems with ambiguity between developers and designers.

With relational databases, you don't use ordered, or sorted, rows. You use real-time statements—those that are evaluated when they are called or issued—to control the presentation of the information. You also use joins and views to control how information is retrieved, rather than try to store the information in the most advantageous format possible at the outset. This allows for more dynamic access to the information in the database tables. It also lets you simply store the information, and then retrieve it in any manner you like.

Take a look at the different types of normalization up to, and including, the third normal form.

First Normal Form

In first normal form (denoted 1NF), the foundation for the relational system is put into place. In 1NF, you don't have multiple values represented in any single column. In database terms, this means that each value in the database table is *atomic*, or represented only once.

In the past you may have implemented a database schema where, for example, you stored the item code for each item ordered—such as in a point of sale system, with the order record. Later, when your program queried the order, it retrieved and parsed this field and could determine what was ordered with that order record. Figure 2.1 shows an example of this. You had the opportunity to store one or more item numbers in with the order record.

FIG. 2.1

Without 1NF, you could store more than one logical item in a physical record. This isn't valid when you normalize your database.

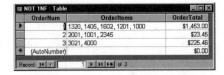

> **N O T E**   We've created these examples using Microsoft Access working with SQL Server because it's a good tool for creating tables quickly and easily. The tool you use is entirely up to you; even the SQL Enterprise Manager, although a bit less "visual," will still serve your purposes fine. You'll also want to take a look at the end of this chapter and consider one or more of the database tools that you can use to help the process of creating tables and relationships. ■

With 1NF, duplicates aren't allowed. You need to create a schema where only one item will be recorded for each order record on file. So to implement the point-of-sale solution mentioned earlier, you would have an order represented by one to *n* records containing the item code information that made up the order. This provides a slightly different challenge to retrieve the information for the record. You must have a means of retrieving each record associated with the order and making sure that you've retrieved each record, but no more or less. Of course, this will lead to order numbers, called out in each record. Later, this chapter gets more into the database design and entity relationship models. Figure 2.2 shows the results of this first pass at normalizing a database table.

FIG. 2.2

With a 1NF table, each row is a single, atomic record. It must be able to stand alone.

OrderNum	OrderItem	Description
1	1320	Milk
1	1405	Cookies
1	1602	Bread - French
1	1201	Bread - Italian
1	1000	Bread - American
2	2001	Cheese
2	1001	Bread - Swedish
2	2345	Bologna
3	3021	Paper Towels
3	4000	Eggs
	0	

For now, simply remember that with 1NF, you must have each row contain only one instance of the information, and all column values must be atomic.

Second Normal Form

The first requirement for second normal form (denoted as 2NF) is that it fulfill the requirements of 1NF. The second requirement—the major requirement to fulfill the 2NF rule—is that each instance or row in the database table must be uniquely identifiable. To do this, you must often add a unique ID to each row. In the case in the preceding section, where you broke apart the orders table, at first blush it looks as though the structure fits this rule. You have, after all, instituted an order ID, and if you combine the order ID and the item code, you'd have a unique handle on the row, right? Wrong. You could conceivably have a single order with more than one instance of an item. Consider the case when you go grocery shopping and buy your milk for the week. It's easy to see that you'd be buying multiple half-gallons of milk on the same order.

You'll need to add an OrderItemID column to the table to fulfill the requirements for 2NF (see fig. 2.3). You'll keep the OrderNum, but the OrderItemID will be the primary unique identifier for the item in a given row.

FIG. 2.3

After you add a unique row ID for each line item, this table now fits the 2NF model.

Part
I
Ch
2

OrderItemID	OrderNum	OrderItem	Description
1	1	1320	Milk
2	1	1405	Cookies
3	1	1602	Bread - French
4	1	1201	Bread - Italian
5	1	1000	Bread - American
11	1	1320	Milk
6	2	2001	Cheese
7	2	1001	Bread - Swedish
8	2	2345	Bologna
9	3	3021	Paper Towels
10	3	4000	Eggs
(AutoNumber)		0	

2NF : Table

Record: 1 of 11

N O T E Notice that although we've added a new item as item 11, it can still be related back to the order based on the order number. All we've done is provide a way to uniquely identify the row within the table.

Third Normal Form

Third normal form, or 3NF, is really a lifesaver for the developer. All the work to normalize your database tables really pays off when you move to the 3NF model. As with 2NF reliance on first being in 1NF, 3NF requires that you also be compliant with the 2NF model. In layperson's terms, when you have a table that's in 3NF, you won't have redundant non-key information in your table that relies on non-key information in another table.

That's a strange definition until you understand what's really happening here. The whole goal of normalizing your tables is to remove redundant, non-key information in your tables. Reviewing Figure 2.3 shown earlier, you'll quickly see that this model is broken quite nicely. Because you're storing descriptions in the table, and because these descriptions probably are used elsewhere in the database, storing them individually in the table is a problem.

Here's where you start to see the real advantages of moving to 3NF. Remember, the simple examples that we're using here relate to a grocery store. Imagine if you were storing your information as shown in Figure 2.3, and that you needed to change the description of "Milk" to "Milk 2%" because your vendor has maliciously introduced "Milk 1%" to the mix. You'd need to write a utility to update the sales database tables and any other table that ever referenced "Milk" to show the correct percentage. A real nightmare that will often lead to problems is inconsistent information in the database. It would take forgetting or not knowing about only one table that needed to be updated to completely invalidate your use of the item "Milk" for sales history.

Normalization is the key to taking care of this. In Figure 2.4, the problem is corrected quite simply by removing the description from the table altogether.

FIG. 2.4

To fit the 3NF model, the description column is removed from the order items table.

OrderItemID	OrderNum	OrderItem
1	1	1320
2	1	1405
3	1	1602
4	1	1201
5	1	1000
6	2	2001
7	2	1001
8	2	2345
9	3	3021
10	3	4000
11	1	1320
(AutoNumber)	0	0

Since an item code is already assigned to Milk, you have the information you need to set up the Inventory table, as shown in Figure 2.5.

FIG. 2.5

By creating an inventory table, you create a "home base" to refer to and use any time you reference inventory items.

ItemCode	Description	Cost	Retail	SalePrice	SaleStart	SaleEnd
1000	Bread - American	$0.54	$0.99	$0.00		
1001	Bread - Swedish	$0.54	$0.99	$0.00		
1201	Bread - Italian	$0.54	$0.99	$0.00		
1320	Milk 2%	$1.25	$1.89	$0.00		
1321	Milk 1%	$1.10	$1.79	$1.50	12/31/95	1/15/96
1405	Cookies	$2.43	$3.29	$0.00		
1602	Bread - French	$0.54	$0.99	$0.00		
2001	Cheese	$0.69	$1.19	$0.00		
2345	Bologna	$1.72	$2.19	$0.00		
3021	Paper Towels	$0.34	$0.59	$0.00		
4000	Eggs	$0.52	$0.69	$0.00		
0		$0.00	$0.00	$0.00		

Of course, once you've begun normalizing your table, it brings to mind the question of how to get a complete picture of the item sold. How can you find out all the information about the line item, what its description is, the sale price, and so forth? This is where relational databases and their use of Views come into play. In the example, you can create a quick query that returns the information you need quickly and easily. Figure 2.6 shows what a sample view would return to your application for the table examples.

FIG. 2.6

When you create a relational view of the database tables, you can retrieve and work with a complete picture of the information, although it may be dispersed across several tables.

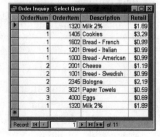

OrderNum	OrderItem	Description	Retail
1	1320	Milk 2%	$1.89
1	1405	Cookies	$3.29
1	1602	Bread - French	$0.99
1	1201	Bread - Italian	$0.99
1	1000	Bread - American	$0.99
2	2001	Cheese	$1.19
2	1001	Bread - Swedish	$0.99
2	2345	Bologna	$2.19
3	3021	Paper Towels	$0.59
3	4000	Eggs	$0.69
1	1320	Milk 2%	$1.89

▶ **See** Chapter 6, "Retrieving Data with Transact-SQL," for more information. **p. 141**

▶ **See** Chapter 9, "Managing and Using Views," for more information. **p. 245**

You can see that by using the combined information between the tables, you still have the same full data set to work with, but at the same time, you're limiting the sources of information. You'll find quite often that the way you end up working with the information may not change, only the methods used behind the scenes to retrieve that information. This is the case with the 3NF table in this example. You're still storing the same information base—you're just retrieving the information using a different means, which in this case is a logical view of the two related tables.

Next, you'll look into the logical pieces of the functional parts of your system. These pieces will play a key role in your database and overall system design decisions.

Part

I

Ch

2

Understanding the Client/Server Model

Before you start designing your database, you'll need to understand where the functional components of your system will reside. It's important to understand where data manipulation is done and what should be stored in the database vs. what should be calculated or determined on-the-fly.

With SQL Server, you can implement true client/server systems. By this we mean that these systems can adhere to the concepts of client/server, allowing you to divide functional components into cooperative operations that accomplish your application's goal. This sounds strange, but what it amounts to is dividing processing between the client and server in a way that makes sense to the application. With database-oriented systems, especially those where the database subsystem is open and accessible from many different points, it makes sense to implement an intelligent database layer that will manage the data. This layer is responsible only for storage and inquiries as they relate to the information. It has no responsibility for the presentation of information.

In the next couple of sections, you'll review what types of functions and operations reside in the client and server sides of the client/server model. Although these concepts aren't exhaustive, you need to understand them. For many people, *client/server* is just a fancy term for a PC database that resides in a common location and is accessed by many different workstations. After reading this chapter, you should understand that client/server is much more than a common storage location. You can't create a client/server system by using Microsoft Access database tables, for example, regardless of whether the tables are stored on a file server or a local system because no intelligent engine can process the database independently of your application. The logic controlling the data is still driven by your client-side application.

N O T E   You can create Access-based client/server systems by creating linked or attached tables to an Access system. These tables can be based in a server-based intelligent database system and will help you create a client/server system in Access. By saying that Access database tables aren't client/server, we're referring only to the native Access database tables, typically contained in physical files with an .MDB extension. ▪

Typical Roles: The Client Side

Client-side applications are responsible for displaying information to users, manipulating information in the database and on the user display, reports, and user-interruptible operations. This means that any operation you submit to the server component of your system should never require intervention by users in order to complete the operation.

The client application will typically be written in a host language—often Delphi, PowerBuilder, Visual Basic, C, or C++, for example. These applications allow users to perform add, change, and delete operations against the database, where applicable.

The client application should avoid, at nearly all costs, having to work with the entire database table's contents. When a set of information is worked with, you should always think of it as a *results set*, not the entire data set available to you. By results set, we mean that you should ask the server application to filter and limit the information that will be presented to you so that the operations you carry out are completed against as small a set of information as possible.

One of the best descriptions we've heard comparing older systems with client/server is that of a file cabinet versus a folder. In older systems, you'd typically be doing the equivalent of asking for a file cabinet full of information, so you can take the time to sift through the contents to find the file you want. In this scenario, your client-side application is the piece doing the sifting. All information from the database table is passed through the client, and the client does the filtering to find the information you want to work with.

In the client/server world, you simply request the file folder you want, and that's what's returned. You don't filter through the file cabinet—the server process does. This limits network traffic, as only the results set is passed back over the network. The other very significant benefit of this is that it also increases performance for your application. Typically, server systems are powerful, very strong computing platforms. Since this optimized server platform can work with all information locally, it can do so at top speed. It will be processing the information at the best rate possible.

In short, your client-side application should be optimized to work with results sets. This works hand in hand with database structure and design because you need to make sure that you create the database in such a way that it can support this requirement. You'll have to define the joins, queries, stored procedures, and table structures to support this optimized query into the contents of the database.

In summary, here are some guidelines for the client side of your application:

- It should gather all needed information before making a request of the server.
- The client is responsible for all data display to the user.
- The client should work with results sets rather than tables.
- The client should do all data-manipulation operations.
- The client provides for all formatting of data and information presentation in reports.

Typical Roles: The Server Side

The server side of the client/server equation is typically very task-oriented. This means that operations are broken into logical components. This is what you're starting to see now with Microsoft's BackOffice offerings. You now have server-side components that control mainframe connectivity with the SNA Server, database access with SQL Server, electronic mail with the Exchange Server, internet and intranet access with Internet Information Server, and more products on the horizon that will continue in this vein.

With SQL Server, your goal is to create the results sets required by the client-side applications. The database engine will be responsible for carrying out the information storage, update, and retrieval in the system. When you first start working with SQL Server, notice that it has no user interface (UI) at all. Yes, utilities are available to help you manage it, but SQL Server in and of itself has no UI. This is by design. SQL Server exists to fulfill requests made of it to the point of returning the results from those requests. Unlike Access, dBASE, FoxPro, and others like them, SQL Server has no involvement in showing users the results of these queries.

When you're designing your database structures, you need to keep a very close eye on how you implement informational control in your system. For example, it may be that different people will need different access levels to the information. Security may be—and often is—a major issue in the query of the database. If this is the case, your table structures and joins need to reflect this requirement. Chapter 19, "SQL Server Security," provides additional information about the security considerations for your system.

You'll also need to keep in mind how users are going to be accessing your information. Remember that in today's world of open systems, new challenges exist in presenting and controlling information. As you create your database tables and the rules that govern them, you need to assume absolutely nothing about the client side of the application. A good question to ask yourself is, "When I receive this information, what needs to happen with it?" You can answer it by saying, "It needs to be stored for later retrieval." But is that all?

If you're storing sales information, you should validate the item code being sold. Does it exist in the inventory database? Is sufficient stock on hand to sell this item? Do you force sufficient stock levels, or do you allow a "negative stock" situation to occur and simply log the discrepancy in a suspected transactions table?

Each issue requires work on the database side through rules and triggers. It's true that you could expect the client application to complete these tasks, but what if someone is accessing your database from Excel or Word? Can you really assume that they've had the presence of mind to make sure that these checks are taking place? These important issues should be carried out by the server to make sure that they happen, regardless of the point of entry.

For additional information about rules and triggers, see Chapter 14, "Creating and Managing Triggers," and see Chapter 11, "Managing and Using Rules and Defaults." In addition, see Chapter 22, "Accessing SQL Server Databases Through Front-End Products."

Part
I

Ch
2

Exceptions to the Rules and Roles

There are exceptions to any rule, and the client/server model is certainly subject to this fact. You'll find times where you want to do more processing at the respective ends of the client/server model. These may be times where you need to do more processing on the client, or cases on the server where you want to blindly store information received. You'll need to address these on a case-by-case basis, but keep in mind that the client/server model is there to help and guide your efforts. Always be very cautious when developing systems that fall outside the model because more often than not, you'll be asking for trouble.

It may seem like the right thing to do at the time you're implementing that really intricate trigger or rule, but a caution is in order: it can become a nightmare trying to move too much functionality into the wrong side of the client-server model. Think long and hard about other ways you can implement something if you find yourself putting into place an operation that breaks the client/server model. You'll be glad you did.

Establishing a Roadmap to Your Database

Earlier we mentioned that one way you can best go about designing your database is to diagram it and work out the relationships between tables on paper first. This helps point out any flaws in the different points of information that you may need to be able to extract from the system.

Database flowcharts consist of *entity relationship diagrams*, or ERDs. ERDs show exactly how a database is structured, what the relationships are between the tables, what rules and triggers are involved in maintaining referential integrity, and so forth. One big benefit of the ERD is that you can sit down with the client and take a logical walk through the database, making sure that the system serves the client's needs.

N O T E It's beyond the scope of this book to provide an all-encompassing view of the intricacies of entity relationship diagramming. The information and approach we'll be providing here are meant to fit 90 percent of the cases for what you'll be doing. In some cases, you'll need to implement slightly different or less frequently used facets of the ERD systems. In those cases, you'll be best served by consulting the capabilities of your design software and database back end, as well as the resources available on the Internet and in other sources of information regarding the world of ERD. ■

Entity Relationship Diagramming: The Flowcharts of the Database World

Entity relationships are shown by drawings that include several different objects. These objects include entities, attributes, and relationships. There are specific ways to depict each aspect of your system. In Figure 2.7, you can see what a basic diagram would look like for the point-of-sale system that you've been working with in the examples.

FIG. 2.7

This diagram shows a relational diagram for the grocery sales system.

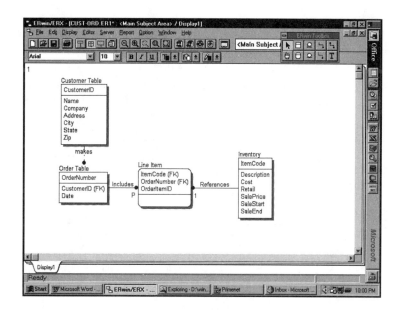

We've added the customer table to be able to track an order for a customer, but apart from this addition, the table structure reflects the earlier tables and relationships. Take a look at how these basic objects—the entities, attributes, and relationships—apply to the simple model.

Using and Referencing Entities   First, notice four boxes in Figure 2.8. Each box represents a table, or entity. These entities are what will become the tables in the database, and each box includes the columns that will be created for the table. Each entity's object has two sections, with a portion shown above the dividing line and a portion below it.

FIG. 2.8

The basic entity is represented by a box that typically contains two sections.

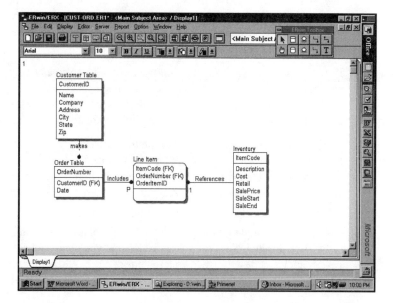

TIP When you name entities, you should always make the name singular. It will help reinforce the fact that they contain only one instance of the object they represent.

The portion above the dividing line represents the identifying portion of the row. Remember, to have a normalized database in 3NF, you need to be able to uniquely identify each row instance in the database table. By placing the identifying characteristics above the line, it's easy to read and determine how the record will be retrieved in most cases.

In Figure 2.8, you can see that, by the definition for the customer table, you'll most likely be retrieving records from it by using the CustomerID.

N O T E Although a record may usually be retrieved by this identifier, it's not an exclusive handle to the row. In most systems you'll need to provide other avenues to retrieve rows. On the customer table, for example, it's likely that you'll need to implement some name searches. These searches wouldn't include the Customer ID, but after you found the customer the user wanted to work with, you'd likely retrieve the Customer ID for the selection and then retrieve the entire customer record that was selected. ■

Using and Referencing Attributes   Attributes go hand in hand with the entity object. *Attributes* is the term for the different column elements that make up the entity object, the table in the database. Attributes for the Customer table include the CustomerID, Name, Company, and so forth. Attributes are described as *key* or *non-key*.

As the name implies, non-key attributes are those items that make up the entity that don't depend on any other entity. In other words, they don't make up, nor are they a part of, a key that's used in the entity.

Key attributes come in two different types: primary and (for lack of a better term) non-primary. Primary keys are always shown above the line, indicating that they're identifying attributes for this entity. If the attribute is a key to the entity but not a part of the identifying structure for the entity, it's placed below the line.

If an item refers to a key value in another table, it's known as a *foreign key*. Again, if you reference the basic model as in Figure 2.9, you can see that the Customer table doesn't have any foreign-key segments, but the Order table does, as indicated by the "(FK)". The foreign keys in the Order table are non-identifying, but help designate the customer that the order refers to.

Moving from the Order table to the Line Item table, you'll see that the OrderNumber *is* listed as an identifying component of the Line Item table. This means that to find a specific instance of an order line item, you need to know the OrderItemID, the ItemCode, and the OrderNumber. In this implementation, the Line Item table is an associative table between the Inventory table and the Order table.

Using and Referencing Relationships   If a "proof-is-in-the-pudding" segment to database design ever existed, it's in the relationships that you define between the different entities. It's easiest and most descriptive to look to your database ERDs to tell a story, in plain English, about what's happening in the database. Referring to Figure 2.9, you can see verbs between the entities. These verbs describe the relationships between the two entities and are also indicated by the relationship line between them.

FIG. 2.9

The basic ERD shows foreign keys as primary (identifying) and non-primary (non-identifying) columns in the sample tables.

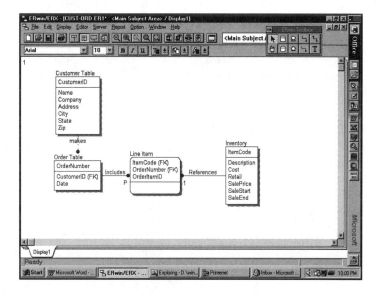

A customer makes orders in the Order table, and an order includes line items that reference inventory items. You can also read the diagram in the other direction. For example, you could also say that inventory items are referenced by line items. In any event, you should be able to show concise paths for information to follow when trying to reach an end result.

In the examples, we're using ERwin by Logic Works. This tool allows you to define the different objects, and then place the relationships between the objects appropriately. In the relationship between the Customer and Order tables, Figure 2.10 shows that the relationship is non-identifying and that the relationship is a zero, one or more relationship.

FIG. 2.10

ERwin allows you to easily define the relationship between the Customer and Order tables.

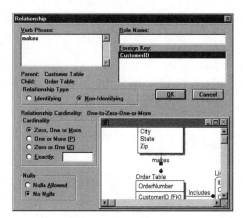

You can also see that the key in the Order table that will be used to retrieve the customer information is CustomerID. It's automatically added to the Order table, and it's added to the non-key portion of the record. If you define an identifying relationship, CustomerID will be moved to the top portion, or identifying key portion, of the Order table entity.

Each of the other relationships is defined in a similar manner. You can walk down the table structure and determine exactly how the different entities will interact. The next couple of sections look at a methodology that will guide you through the design process with the customer.

System Architecture Definition

There are several steps to creating a solid definition for a database structure. In many cases it's possible to point to flaws in the database design, only to realize that if the customer were involved more completely in the process, the problem could have been avoided.

While bringing a customer up to speed, terminology, methodology, and approach aren't the goal of client reviews. The goal of any system you'll endeavor to write is making sure that the database structure will support the functionality of the system. This is where the old maxim of "Determine the output first, the input will follow" comes to bear on a project. It's certainly true that the test of any system is the output. If you've created the best system ever devised to allow input of information, it's a sure bet that if you don't have a way to get meaningful information out of the system, your time has been all but wasted.

Review the User's Goals for the System

The first thing you need to do is to decide what it is you'll be providing for the customer. We think it's probably safe to say that reports and output are nearly always a developer's least favorite part of a system to develop and implement. Often, one of the first statements made to the customer is, "We'll give you reporting tools to create your own reports. All we need to do now is figure out what needs to happen in the program." This is a formula for problems!

If you didn't know that the users needed to have an aging report from their point-of-sale system's accounts receivable subsystem, would you automatically store the date that the original invoice went out?

N O T E It may seem that involving the user only prolongs the development process. Many studies have shown, as has personal experience, that it's not the case. Spending the time now pays off manyfold later in the project in terms of more accurate deadlines, correct designs, and more. ■

Truly the only way you can ensure that you're not coding in vain is to make sure that you can fulfill the output needs for the system.

Here's a general set of guidelines that not only will allow you to ensure that you've hit at least the high points of your target audience, but will also map nicely to the database design topics we've covered here:

- Meet with your users and get a good overview of what they need from the system. Get as specific as possible with your discussion. Get copies of current forms, reports, screen shots of what they may have on their current systems, and so on.

- Create a functional overview of the system. An overall system flowchart will be a good component of the overview, allowing the customers to review the system and make sure that you understand what's happening at different steps in the flow of work through the system.

- Present the functional overview to the users. Walk through the system carefully to make sure that it's correct.

- Create a set of tables using a good ERD tool. Don't worry initially about foreign keys and the like. It's more important at this point to simply make sure that you're gathering the right informational items for the users.

- Present the database tables to the users—not from the perspective that they should understand how and why you've laid out the tables the way you have, but more from the standpoint of "OK, ask me any question about where some bit of information will be stored. We want to make sure that we can show you all the information you need." Of course, the first thing you should do—even before meeting with the customers—is to review the reports and samples that you obtained early on and make sure that you're addressing them appropriately.

- Next, put into place the relationships between the tables as needed. Make sure that you can walk down all the logical paths that you expect the users will need, based on your needs analysis. There will be more information about resolving many-to-many joins later in this chapter.

- Present this new schema to the users with a challenge. Ask them to present you with a query for information from the system. Can you satisfy it with identifying and/or non-identifying relationships? Can you get there from here? This is the test of your database design. You should be able to address each and every one of the stated intentions for the system.

N O T E Systems get very complex very fast. We can't overemphasize the importance of reviewing with the users all the different requests that may be made of the system. In one such case, we prevented a substantial design rewrite by meeting with users. We found that, although the information was available to determine a specific-case customer, we hadn't correctly laid out the relationships. By preventing this oversight early on, you'll save many, many hours of development time in the long run. ■

Avoid Many-to-Many Joins

In some cases, you'll be faced with a join situation that won't resolve to a single instance on either side of the database table equation. When this is the case, you'll want to consider implementing an associative table that provides a link between the tables. You can see a simple example of this technique in the sample system, since you really could just add ItemCode to the Order table.

NOTE   A *join* is a way of creating a logical view of your data. You specify how the information is retrieved, if it's related to other tables, and what information you'd like to see. From there SQL Server will return the results set to your client application in the form of a view on the table as you've defined it. ▨

If you didn't have the associative table between the Order table and the Inventory table, you would end up with a many-to-many relationship between the two. This isn't a good way to accomplish this, as you wouldn't have a singular path for *identifying an instance* of an order record. Figure 2.11 shows the associative table.

FIG. 2.11
An associative table has been implemented to remove the many-to-many relationship problem imposed by the Order and Inventory tables.

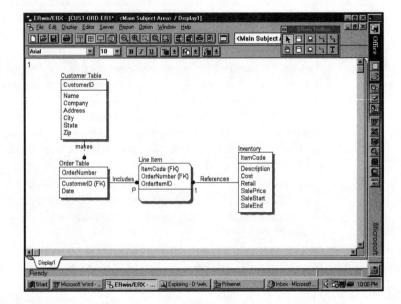

When to Break the Mold

Sometimes, having the database tables be fully normalized just won't work with the model you're putting into place. This is most likely to be encountered in terms of performance. You may end up with a join to return information that simply takes too long to complete.

For example, if you're working with static tables in your application, as may be the case with the inventory table in the example, you may want to load that table to a local Access table for access by your application. If you were to do this once a day, you'd be reasonably assured of having the correct and up-to-date information at the workstations.

It may be that you're loading down tables that, when taken alone, don't provide a complete picture. For example, if you have a customer table, an account balance table, and a sales representative table—all related based on customer number—you'll end up with a three-way join to return a complete picture of the information.

You may want to consider denormalizing this set of tables at the client. In this case, you could create a single table that would hold the information from all three tables as a single row of information. That way, when you request information for customer X, you'll receive all the information you need, and a further join won't be required.

N O T E Of course, in reality you wouldn't want to be manipulating something as potentially dynamic as the customer account balance in a remote mode. As a rule, you'll want to consider this method of denormalization only for static tables, or at least those that change only infrequently. ▨

Part

I

Ch

2

From Here...

In this chapter, you've reviewed a lot of information that can pay off in the long run for your applications. Be sure to normalize your database tables to the highest degree possible. If you find exceptions to the normalization goals, that's fine, but you should make sure that you're not overlooking some other method of getting the same task accomplished.

Review things carefully with your customers, whether the customer is internal or an external client, and this will provide substantial leverage in your projects and will help you toward coming in on time and on budget.

The following chapters provide additional information that you'll find useful in your database design efforts:

■ Chapter 6, "Retrieving Data with Transact-SQL," will show how you create the joins that this chapter talked about. It will also show how you can create the SQL statements that you'll need to retrieve the information in the format, order, and filtered results sets that you can most optimally work with.

■ Chapter 9, "Managing and Using Views," shows how you can create the logical data sets that you'll be working with in SQL Server's relational environment.

■ Chapter 11, "Managing and Using Rules and Defaults," shows how to implement business rules and data integrity in your database tables.

■ Chapter 14, "Creating and Managing Triggers," will help you add referential integrity to your applications by enabling server-side processes when certain data-driven events occur.

■ Chapter 19, "SQL Server Security," will help determine the best approach for securing your database and the objects contained within it.

CHAPTER 3

Understanding the Underlying Operating System, Windows NT

Understand the Windows NT features of multiprocessors and multithreading

Windows NT supports advanced operating systems features such as multithreading and multiprocessors.

Understand and use the built-in networking components

Windows NT provides support of the interconnection of client systems to the SQL Server database.

Use the reporting facilities of Windows NT

Windows NT contains built-in monitoring and reporting tools which are used to monitor SQL Server.

Windows NT, the operating system that Microsoft SQL Server runs on, has several mechanisms that you should understand to help you use SQL Server more effectively. *Operating system mechanisms* are sections of computer code that control how the computer's hardware and other software is used. For example, some NT mechanisms control how one or more central processors are used by applications. The MSSQLServer and MSQLExecutive processes of Microsoft SQL Server use Windows NT mechanisms to service client systems.

Windows NT is also responsible for managing the security of the network and its associated resources. You create system users for the server and can control their access to resources, including SQL Server, on that system. Although it's outside the scope of this book to review the entire Windows NT security model, domain administration, and how these components control your network, it's important that you have a comprehensive understanding of how your network is set up, what users are defined, and whether you plan to use this same security model in your SQL Server implementation. Consult Que's *Special Edition Using Windows NT* for additional information about the Windows NT system.

In addition to mechanisms of Windows NT that control the use of resources such as the CPUs, several system applications control aspects of the operating system that affect Microsoft SQL Server. You can monitor the use of Windows NT and SQL Server components through the Performance Monitor and change usage based on the statistics collected. You can display errors and other events returned as the results of SQL Server's activity through the Event Viewer and, by using the information returned, interpret and correct them.

It's also helpful to understand the different configurations of interconnections among the Windows NT Servers that Microsoft SQL Server is on. The interconnection of server and client is accomplished primarily through network software, which you must understand the basics of to communicate between client and server or server and server. ■

Understanding Multiprocessing, Multitasking, and Multithreading

Many times, working with and understanding the difference between the terms *multiprocessing*, *multitasking*, and *multithreading* can be confusing. But they're important in your use of SQL Server because they affect the performance and scalability of the system. This section will briefly review each of them.

Multitasking and multiprocessing are two mechanisms of an operating system (such as Windows NT) that are used to share one or more central processors (CPUs) of the computer system. Earlier operating systems permitted only one application at a time to use a computer's resources. It wasn't long before operating system designers realized that the core resources of a computer system, such as the CPU, could be shared by multiple application programs.

The terms *multiprocessing* and *multitasking* refer to the sharing of the CPU(s) of a computer system by more than one application program. The simplest form of multiprocessing is when an operating system switches use of a computer system's CPU among multiple applications. The operating system must keep track of where each program has left off so that the program can be started back up again when the program receives use of the central processor again. This is *round-robin scheduling*. Round-robin scheduling permits each process to use a CPU for a period of time rather than allowing a CPU to be used exclusively by a process.

Each application must receive use of a CPU long enough to get some reasonable amount of work done. Also, the switching of the CPU must be accomplished quickly. If an operating system provides each application with enough time to use a CPU, and the switch among applications is done quickly enough, a user interacting with one application might work as if a CPU were dedicated to their exclusive use. Of course, this performance can also be influenced by having too many applications waiting to use the CPU(s).

N O T E The interval of time at which Windows NT exchanges use of the central processor is several hundred milliseconds. Windows NT maintains an elaborate technique to determine what program receives the use of the central processor next. Programs are assigned a priority from 0 to 31. NT grants use of the central processor to the program that has the highest priority (has been waiting to use the central processor the longest) and works down the list of priorities in order. ■

Operating systems such as Windows NT perform a more sophisticated sharing of the use of a central processor than the simple round-robin approach mentioned earlier. A program on Windows NT can be written in several functional sections, and each section can receive use of a central processor independently. One definition of the term *multitasking* refers to the sharing of the use of a central processor by multiple sections of a program simultaneously.

A complete application program that can use the resources of a system is called a *process* in the Windows NT system. Each program section that can receive use of a Windows NT central processor is called a *thread*. A thread must have its own priority as well as other characteristics for Windows NT to schedule use of system resources separately for each thread. The term *multithreading* on Windows NT also refers to the use of the central processor of an NT system by multiple threads of the same or different processes.

N O T E There are two types of multiprocessing capabilities: *symmetric* and *asymmetric*. Windows NT uses symmetric multiprocessing, which is the most commonly implemented. Symmetric multiprocessing spreads the processes for both the operating system and applications among all available system CPUs. Asymmetric multiprocessing allows the operating system to be placed on a single CPU and applications spread among others. ■

Part
I

Ch
3

A feature such as multitasking with multiple threads is most advantageous when more than a single processor is available to be shared. An application that's written in several threads can have each thread execute simultaneously on Windows NT. The two major components of Microsoft SQL Server, the server and monitor process, are written as multiple threads to take advantage of the multithread form of multitasking available on Windows NT. This is referred to as a *multiprocessor environment*.

You can use a powerful single-processor system for SQL Server such as a Digital Alpha AXP, MIPS R4000, PowerPC, or Intel Pentium Pro system. Multiple CPU systems can be used by Windows NT because of its symmetric multiprocessing capability. *Symmetric multiprocessing* allows several threads to execute simultaneously, regardless of whether they're running application or operating-system code.

N O T E Multi-CPU systems are particularly advantageous for use as servers for a SQL Server database because I/O requests from client systems can be handled while other operations, such as account validation, are done in a second processor of the system. Multiple server requests can be done at a time that greatly increases the number of workstation clients that can be served by the server. ■

Understanding Multi-Architecture

An important characteristic of Windows NT is its multi-architecture feature. The term *architecture* refers to different types of hardware components that can be used on a computer system, especially different central processors. Windows NT runs on computer systems that use different microprocessors for their central processing units.

For example, Windows NT can run on a system that uses Intel 386, 486, or Pentium processors. NT can also run on x86 clones produced by such vendors as Cyrix and AMD. Windows NT will also run on Digital's Alpha AXP, MIPS R4000 series processors, and Motorola's PowerPC. The Windows NT distribution CD contains the separate versions of the installation software for all four systems, with more compatible systems planned.

As you can see, a key advantage to using Windows NT as the paltform for SQL Server is that you have so many choices of computer systems to use as a server for a SQL Server database. Windows NT and SQL Server are scalable from a desktop PC to a large Alpha AXP or MIPS system. It will even scale to systems with one or more processors that have enough power to replace a minicomputer or even a large mainframe system.

Understanding the Multiuser Environment of SQL Server on Windows NT

Traditional mainframe and minicomputer system databases were accessed by users sitting in front of input/output devices. Windows NT is unlike minicomputer or mainframe systems in that users don't use dumb terminals as the input or output devices. Instead, each user gains access to an NT system running SQL Server by using a computer system with its own operating system. As discussed in Chapter 1, "Introducing Microsoft SQL Server," this is referred to as the *client system*. The multiple users of a Windows NT server access an application such as SQL Server from their own client computer system.

N O T E *Dumb terminals* got their nickname because they simply transfer characters to and from the CPU, using the CPU to perform the work with the information. Dumb terminals, unlike PCs or other workstations, can't perform any processing. Dumb terminals replaced the card readers and printers that were used as input and output devices on early computer systems. A dumb terminal combines separate input and output devices in a simple device for input and output. ▣

Each user typically runs Windows for Workgroups, Windows 95, DOS, OS/2, or Windows NT Workstation on a client workstation system. Each operating system allows a user to run applications independently of a central server system. A user at a workstation uses connectivity software—usually, the network operating system—to establish a connection to a central server computer running Windows NT Server.

Understanding the Windows NT Network Components

Windows NT provides the capability to establish networks and to connect to other computer systems. The connectivity feature of Windows NT is used for several purposes. A network connection can be made for the purpose of sharing the resources of different systems. You might create the connection to access information on a remote disk of another Windows NT or a non-Windows NT system. You might also need to transfer data between two systems. When you access the SQL Server database on the server system from a client system, you're wholly dependent on the communication connections that are established by the NT system.

You can also perform administrative operations through network connections to Windows NT. You use commands to learn the connection status of systems, monitor the flow of control and user data between connections, and alter the characteristics that affect the connections. You can also change the size of network and disk buffers, the temporary storage space in RAM used to store the data coming from one system and received into a second system.

The connectivity components of Windows NT are also used to connect an application on a client workstation to the SQL Server database on the NT server. All the previously specified uses for client/server connectivity—such as remote administration, monitoring, and data transfer—are necessary in a system using Microsoft SQL Server.

▶ **See** Chapter 17, "Optimizing Performance," for a more detailed discussion of using NT performance monitoring. **p. 445**

▶ **See** Chapter 18, "SQL Server Administration," for more information on administration of SQL Server. **p. 459**

Part

I

Ch

3

Sharing Resources

Windows NT networks are set up as domains. Each domain can have a number of workgroups. A *domain* is a Windows NT network. Before a computer can be added to a domain, an account must be set up. Rights for this account are controlled by the administrator. *Workgroups* are users of a domain that are grouped together by department, task, or some other method. Users are placed into workgroups because they want to share each other's resources. By joining a workgroup(s) with only resources a user needs, it's easier to locate and use shared resources.

Both methods for sharing resources could work for sharing a SQL Server resource. But workgroups are geared towards users and therefore don't offer very sophisticated or versatile security measures. Windows NT offers excellent built-in security through its use of domains for implementation and administration. SQL Server can take full advantage of this security.

▶ **See** Chapter 21, "Communicating with SQL Server," for more information on how SQL Server uses the built-in security of Windows NT. **p. 535**

Installing Network Software

You add additional network protocols to allow access to and from different network types through the Network properties dialog box (see fig. 3.1). To access this dialog box, choose Settings, Control Panel from the Start menu and double-click the Network icon. Or you can right-click the Network Neighborhood icon on the desktop and choose Properties. Components can be added, removed, configured, or updated in this dialog box.

After entering new configuration information for a network component, you'll be prompted to either reboot the system or leave the system up and running (see fig. 3.2). You network components won't be available until you reboot.

FIG. 3.1
You can manipulate several
network software properties
together.

FIG. 3.2
After the installation is
complete, you'll need to
reboot the system for the
changes to take effect.

If you're adding the additional network software that comes with Windows NT, you need to confirm or change the path for the NT distribution. If you're installing optional network software, enter the path for its distribution.

Configuring Adapter Cards

If your NT workstation has a built-in network hardware interface or an installed network interface card (NIC), its associated network software is installed during the Windows NT Workstation or Server installation. You might add or change network interface cards on PC workstations that don't have network interfaces on their motherboards.

The manufacturers of network interface cards use software, referred to as *drivers* for their NIC. If you change from one NIC to another, you have to change the driver software. The need to change network adapters can arise for a number of reasons. For example, you might want to upgrade as faster cards become available, replace a faulty card, or add a new, special-function card to the system.

As mentioned, one of the reasons you might want to update your card is to improve network performance. You can change from a slower 8-bit NIC to a faster 16- or 32-bit NIC. The 16- or 32-bit NICs perform some network operations more quickly than 8-bit NICs. Other NIC characteristics can also affect performance, including items such as the buffer sizes and types of media supported.

You might need to change the NIC on the server system to get adequate performance for queries made against your SQL Server database. You might also change the NIC on selected client systems that require faster access to the server database.

Choose the Add button from the Adapters page in the Network properties dialog box to bring up the Select Network Adapter dialog box. Select the name of the network adapter card from the Network Adapter card list. The selected adapter card in Figure 3.3 is the 3Com Etherlink II Adapter.

FIG. 3.3

You'll need to add adapter card software if you add a second or different NIC to your system.

Part

I

Ch

3

Network adapter cards typically require that an IRQ level and an I/O base address be specified when the adapter software is added. The IRQ level and I/O base address should match the one specified by the manufacturer. Windows NT can automatically detect and configure a number of adapter cards.

Before buying an NIC, you should consult with a reputable dealer, who can tell you whether the card can be set up automatically by Windows NT. You can also check with Microsoft to learn of NICs that can be automatically configured. Some of the major manufacturers provide NICs that also allow the IRQ and addresses to be set through software rather than jumpers on the card. Cards that can be automatically set up can be advantageous to use, especially if you have a large number of other interface cards installed in your PC workstation.

The more cards you've installed in your system, the easier it is to have conflicts. Two cards that have identical IRQ and/or address settings by default will, if unchanged, cause one another to not work as expected. Some interface cards provide few changes to be made to their IRQ or address settings. If some of your interface cards can be set through software to a large number of values, you can more easily prevent card-setting conflicts.

Ideally, you should check the specification of all cards that you want to use in your PC workstation to determine whether all IRQ and address conflicts can be eliminated. If you don't do this, you might have to later change one or more cards to eliminate conflicts and allow all cards to work, including your network card.

You should also check that the interface cards, including the network interface cards that you buy for NT, are supported. Microsoft provides a list of the supported interface cards, including network NICs that can be used with Windows NT.

You should know the factory default settings for your network adapter card and the current settings, if you've changed them from the factory defaults. You should also run any diagnostic program, to learn quickly if the network adapter cards functions properly.

Select the adapter card from the Installed Adapter Card list and click OK to install the network adapter using the default NT driver (or click <u>H</u>ave Disk to use a manufacturer's driver). Involvement of the user in the installation of adapter cards depends on the abilities of the card and the sophistication of the driver software. All of the settings might be automatically determined or some might need to be supplied to properly install an adapter card.

> **N O T E** Many manufacturers repackage network adapter cards that are manufactured by other companies for PC workstations. If your network adapter card doesn't appear in the list, it might be shown under a different name. Check with the vendor from whom you bought the card, the documentation that came with the card, a diagnostic display of the card characteristics, or the labeling on the adapter board itself to find its designation. ■

> **T I P** Consider buying identical network adapter cards for PC workstations. Several adapter manufacturers provide you additional software to diagnose and monitor network interface card operation, but only if you have matching NICs among PCs.

Understanding Workgroups

The capability to form workgroups is a part of the built-in network features of Windows NT. Windows NT allows the interconnection of Windows NT systems into groups that can share each other's resources. A *workgroup* is a logical set of NT workstations that require the sharing of resources with one another. This is the basis for designating workstations as the members of the same workgroup.

The members of a workgroup can typically share the resources of one another equally. An example of a resource that can be shared among workgroup members equally is a disk drive, and the directories and files on it.

This capability to share between workstations without a requirement to have a designated server system is called *peer-to-peer networking*. Each system can share access to the other's resources after they become shared. In such an arrangement, the systems function as both clients and servers to one another. In this case, a *server* is a workstation that makes a resource such as a disk available to another workstation. A *client* is a workstation that accesses the resources of another workstation.

Workstations in a network that share each other's resources should be placed in a logical organization, which is the NT workgroup. You must designate which NT workstations become members of the same group. After you form workgroups, the resources for sharing can be set up. The underlying capability of peer-to-peer networking of workgroups permits workgroup client access to a Microsoft SQL Server database. The peer-to-peer features of a workgroup can also be used to share related information about SQL Server (such as the documentation, which could reside on any shared disk in a workgroup).

After the disk-sharing feature is enabled on each system, for example, you can access another workgroup member's disks. You can execute applications, read or write databases, create documents and spreadsheets, and delete or rename files on the shared disk of another workstation in the workgroup.

A disk drive that's part of the hardware components of a workstation is called a *local drive*. Local disk drives are directly connected to a workstation.

A remote drive is a disk drive that's accessible to a workstation that physically isn't one of its hardware components. The remote drive is the local drive of another workstation. The physical connection to a remote drive is through the LAN.

Workstations that are part of the same network can be made members of the same workgroup. Workstations that need to assess each other's resources should be made members of the same workgroup. This is the basic criteria for the formation of workgroups.

You can, however, define a workgroup based on your own criteria. The placement of two or more workstations into a workgroup is arbitrary, the meaning of which is that you, as an administrator, have full control over who's made a member of the workgroup. You can have groups of only two members each if you have a need for such a configuration. You can even place workstations into the same workgroup that share no resources (although this serves no purpose).

You'll find that there's a practical limit on the number of systems that can be members of the same workgroup. A constraint results from the speed of the workstation's hardware, including its disk drives, amount of memory, processor, and system bus. The individual hardware components of a workstation that's used as a server in a workgroup might not be fast enough to allow it to serve many workgroup members.

Members of a workgroup might access a SQL Server database in a different workgroup as well as their own. However, it's more likely that the SQL Server database will be installed on a Windows NT server system in a domain. However, members of one or more workgroups can still access the SQL Server database even though it's placed into a different type of logical organization of client and server systems.

In a client/server network system, as an alternative to the peer-to-peer model that Windows for Workgroups is based on, you can buy a large, powerful, and fast single system that's the only server in a group of workstations. If your server system is a Pentium, MIPS R4000, Alpha AXP processor, or multiple i486 processors, it can function as a server for a much larger number of workstations.

Traditional networking definitions have typically been that a network configuration is either a workstation/server network or a peer-to-peer network, not usually both. The fact is, with the introduction of Windows for Workgroups and continuing with Windows 95, systems are more

Part

I

Ch

3

typically a mixture of server-based and peer-to-peer based networks. The appeal of the peer-to-peer type of network often is cost. You don't have to implement a huge system to act as a server to other workstations on the network in this environment. The disadvantage is that you won't typically be running hard-core server applications, such as SQL Server, on the workstation of these environments.

Also, as you implement your workgroups, you'll find logical groupings of your users emerging, even beyond the groups you've established. You should consider Windows NT domains if you find it difficult to administer workgroup networks. Domains allow you to group users into logical cross-sections and then use these groupings to manage security, access to the network, user names, and more.

This latter type of centralized organization provides some of the features of a client/server network. If you require more of a client/server configuration for your workstations, including the capability to serve dozens or hundreds of clients, you'll want to use the additional features provided by the Windows NT Server.

A simple rule of thumb for peer-to-peer configured workgroups is to limit their members to no more than 20 or so. Microsoft suggests that you define fewer than 20, but it depends on how many members interact with one another simultaneously that determines the actual limit. You'll find that you can deviate from the suggested limit of 20 workstations, although you should certainly keep the recommended values in mind as you configure your workgroups.

You might want to limit the numbers of members of a workgroup to less than 20 to allow for the occasional load put on your system by connections to your resources from outside your workgroup. Unlike the domain model mentioned earlier, a workgroup isn't a security mechanism and doesn't serve to restrict access to the resources of member workstations. Other members of the network can access the resources of workstations outside their own workgroups after they know the share name and optional password.

It might help you to understand workgroups by thinking of them as a loosely organized confederation rather than as an integrated republic. The members of a workgroup log on to their workstations, establishing their user names for the network. Their user names and passwords are checked in an account database that resides on a local disk. You administer each workstation separately, including the definition of separate accounts for each workstation.

You designate a workstation as a member of a workgroup when you install Windows NT. You can later use the Network Control Panel to change your membership in a workgroup. You can designate a workstation as a member of only one workgroup at a time.

A new workgroup is created the first time you use its name. This occurs either during the installation of a Windows NT system or when you later change the name of your workgroup. Members of the same workgroup are displayed together when you examine the workstations of your network.

Members of a workgroup are together to simplify the sharing of resources. There's no restriction on the workstations that might become a member of a workgroup that's provided by Windows NT; you define the criteria for workstation membership.

You can use workstations with faster processors or multiple processors, and large fast disks in your workgroup to extend the 20-workstation limit of the workgroup network. Faster processors and faster disks help extend the limit by performing server tasks more quickly. This allows more workstations to interact as clients and servers with one another and still have acceptable performance.

You won't, however, be able to extend your network to a configuration in which your servers support 10,000 or more NT workstations. Although you can have several tens of thousands of interconnected NT systems, the maximum number is far less and is limited by the number of systems that can perform well while interconnected. For information about networks supporting users in these quantities, see the next section regarding the domain model available with NT Server.

In a workgroup, you create and administer user accounts on each workstation. You log on to each workstation, and your user name and password are validated at the local workstation. If you have the responsibility for the administration of more than one workstation, you must log on to each one to maintain its account database. This is particularly inconvenient if a user has accounts on several workstations and changes must be made to each one.

Part
I
Ch
3

Another possibility is to specify a domain for your computer rather than a workgroup. As mentioned previously, a domain is a more tightly administered group of workstations. You can read about domains in the next section "Understanding NT Domains."

TROUBLESHOOTING

I tried to establish a connection between my client system and the SQL Server database on the Windows NT Server system. No matter what I do, I can't even see the Windows NT system. You probably have not installed the proper network drivers. Try checking your network properties. If the network components are all configured correctly, check to see that the proper SQL Server network files are properly installed.

Understanding NT Domains

A different name and configuration can be given to the set of systems in the client/server configuration provided and controlled by a Windows NT Server. A *domain* is the group of NT workstations that are part of a Windows NT Server-based network. The domain is the rough equivalent of the workgroup discussed thus far in this chapter. When you set up an NT Server domain-based system, you run the main network management software on the NT Server. This server becomes the domain controller, adding new capabilities to the network configuration.

One feature that you gain with use of the NT Server is the capability to centralize the creation and maintenance of user accounts. User accounts are stored and validated from a single server workstation when you log on, rather than at each workstation.

The centralized account feature of a domain organization will permit you to install Microsoft SQL Server using integrated security. The integrated security feature of SQL Server uses the

Windows NT domain accounts rather than the internal login IDs of SQL Server. See Chapter 19, "SQL Server Security," for a discussion of integrated security.

The centralization of account information includes the user environment of Windows NT. The NT Workstation system allows characteristics—such as the desktop settings and program groups and items—to be modified for each workstation user. The Server allows this user environment information to be stored and maintained on a single workstation.

You create user accounts from the domain controller as one of the centralized administration features of NT Server. The user account is a domain account that allows you to log on to any workstation in the domain, unless you're restricted to log on from selected workstations for security reasons. Logins to the domain are checked against the entries kept in the account server database on the domain controller.

An additional type of group that can be referenced throughout the domain can be defined on an server network. You use these groups to selectively control access to resources. This type of group is called a *global group* because it can be referenced through the domain rather than locally at a single workstation. After a successful logon, global groups are used to provide access control to the resources of the workstations in the domain. The defining component of the domain is the centralized control of account information. When you log on to a workstation that's part of a domain, you're prompted to log on with your user name and the domain to which you belong. After you successfully log on to the domain, you have access to the resources of the domain that have been provided by the system administrator.

Another feature provided by Windows NT Server allows for the automatic duplication of directories and files from a server to one or more workstations. Files and directories are replicated across workstations and automatically updated. These copies are used to improve performance or provide backup copies. Although you can use the Windows NT Server replication feature to copy your SQL Server database, it's preferred that you use the built-in replication of SQL Server, which is discussed in Chapter 20, "Setting Up and Managing Replication."

You also gain additional fault tolerance features for the storage of information on disks. For example, a continuous copy of all the information on a disk can be made on a second disk of a server workstation. Data also can be stored across multiple disks, along with error-correction information, to allow the restoration of data, if it's corrupted.

The server also allows you to fully use features that are provided with the NT Workstation system. A feature that's fully utilized with the Windows NT Server is Remote Access. You're more likely to use the Remote Access features of Windows NT to log on to a server system to perform centralized account administration or other administrative operations for the entire network.

N O T E You can use the Remote Access service in NT Workstation, Windows for Workgroups, or Windows 95 (called *dial-up networking*) for remote access as well, but you're limited in the number of sessions that you can support simultaneously. ■

The first of the additional features provided with the server system is the capability to organize a network of workstations in a client/server—rather than peer-to-peer—configuration. You can do this without sacrificing the peer-to-peer capabilities of the workstation system configuration. The capability to implement features of both client/server and peer-to-peer models provides an opportunity to tailor the configuration of a Windows NT network to meet your work requirements.

Understanding the NT Performance Monitor

You must be able to monitor the use of system resources by applications such as the components of Microsoft SQL Server to properly control the system. An extensive performance monitoring capability is provided as part of the Windows NT system. The Performance Monitor administrative tool controls the monitoring and display of the use of system resources.

The Performance Monitor tool graphically displays the performance of one or more computers of a network. Resources or entities that can be monitored are called *objects* and can include processes, threads, processors, and memory. Counters are used with objects to record usage statistics. You can record and later review performance information graphically displayed in a representation called a *chart*.

Part

I

Ch

3

You can closely monitor the characteristics of the main resources of the computer system, the CPU(s), RAM, and disks in Windows NT by using the Performance Monitor. For example, you can collect and display the percentage of time both system code and user code use the CPU, such as the SQL Server and SQL Monitor processes. See Chapter 17, "Optimizing Performance," for a discussion on how to use the information returned by the Performance Monitor.

The Chart window, one of four displays called *views*, is brought up in an initialized state. Open the Performance Monitor from the Windows NT Administrative Tools group. Figure 3.4 shows the main window of the Performance Monitor.

FIG. 3.4

The statistics are automatically collected from the currently running system after you select them.

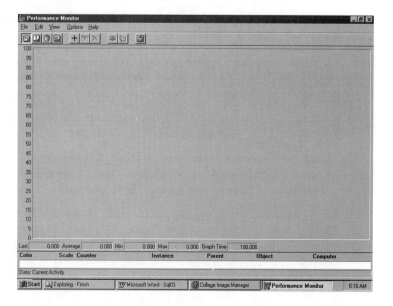

NOTE You need to manually start the logging process after you select the components you want to monitor. By default, when the monitor is loaded, the logging isn't yet active. ■

Logging isn't enabled when the Performance Monitor is started, so no information is displayed. The three additional views you can display are Alert, Log, and Report. To select objects to be monitored and displayed (or recorded in a log file), choose Add to Chart from the Edit menu. The Add to Chart dialog box appears, allowing you to select the objects for monitoring (see fig. 3.5).

FIG. 3.5
If you have a multiple processor server you can monitor each processor using the Instance field.

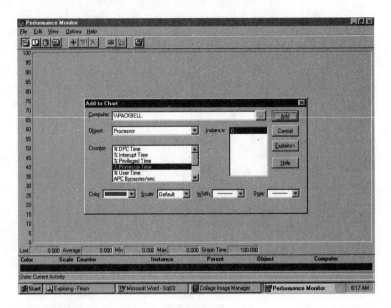

Selecting Objects and Counters in a Chart View

You select objects for monitoring in the Object drop-down list box. You select a counter for an object in the Counter list box. Each object has a different default counter. The default object is Processor with a default counter of % Processor Time.

In the example shown in Figure 3.5, the percentage of processor time for the CPU of the system PACKBELL is selected for monitoring and display.

You can use the Explain button to bring up an explanation of the selected counter. For example, the counter % Processor Time is explained at the bottom of the Add to Chart dialog box as the percentage of time a processor is executing an executable thread of code (refer to fig. 3.5).

After you select an object counter, use the Add button to add the counter line to the display. After you select all object counters, use the Done button to display the chart view. (The Cancel button changes to Done when you select a counter for display.) In the chart view shown in Figure 3.6, the percentage of time the processor was busy executing code is displayed graphically.

FIG. 3.6

The display of each counter is automatically assigned a different color.

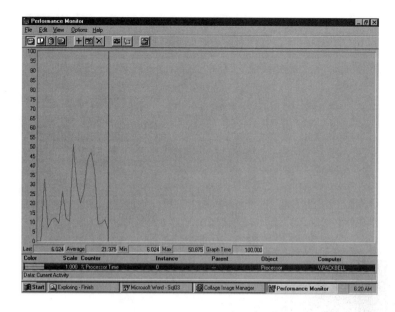

Displaying Information in a Report View

You can display the information collected by the Performance Monitor for object counters in the form of a report rather than in a graphical representation. A report view presents the information in a tabular format rather than graphical. You might find a report format preferable for viewing statistics because the numeric representation of all counters is displayed. You can create a report by choosing the Report view from the View menu.

A new report is blank because you haven't selected any object counter information. You select the object counters for a report by opening the Edit menu and choosing Add to Report. Only object counter values will be displayed in the report. In the Add to Report dialog box, the counter % Processor Time for the object Processor on the system PACKBELL is added to the report (see fig. 3.7).

After you select the object counters, click the Done button to bring up the report view. The report is organized by objects, with all counters for the same object group together under a column header. Instances of the same object are displayed across the page, rather than in a single column.

The report view shown in figure 3.8 shows the counters for each of the three objects specified to be included in the report. For the Processor and PhysicalDisk, the second column shows the instance. PhysicalDrive 0 denotes the first hard drive of the system. Instance 0 of the Processor denotes the first and only CPU of the computer system NT486.

FIG. 3.7

Multiple counters are available for monitoring most objects in the Performance Monitor.

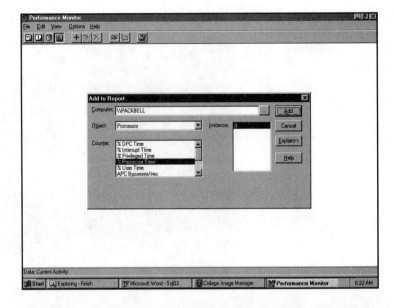

FIG. 3.8

You should obtain a baseline report of your system to use for later comparisons.

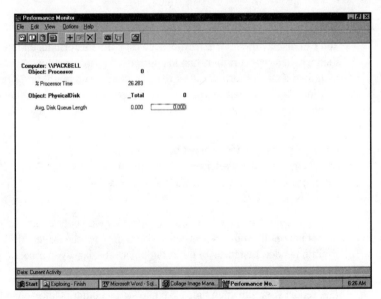

Selecting Objects and Counters in an Alert View

An *alert* is a line of information displayed in the alert view of the Performance Monitor, when the value of an object counter is above or below a value that you define. The entry in the log includes a date and time stamp, the actual object counter value, the criteria for returning it, the object value counter, and the system.

Choose Alert from the View menu to bring up an alert view. The alert view is initialized by default. Choose Add to Alert from the Edit menu to bring up the Add to Alert dialog box (see fig. 3.9).

FIG. 3.9

A program can be automatically started when the alert value is reached.

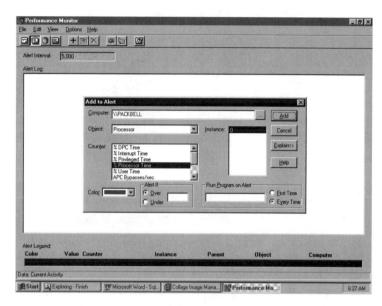

Part

I

Ch

3

You select the computer, object counter, color, and instance (if appropriate), similar to the way you did for chart views. Alerts are different in that they result in the display of information only if the object counter value is greater than or less than a value you define.

Selecting Objects in a Log View

The log view allows the selection of objects and their counters to be logged for subsequent display and analysis. You bring up the log view by choosing Log from the View menu. Like the other views, it's initialized by default; no object counters are defined for it.

Choose Add to Log from the Edit menu to open the Add To Log dialog box (see fig. 3.10). You can select objects from this dialog box. Click the Done button—Cancel changes to Done when an item is added—to bring up the log view with your selected objects.

The selected objects appear in the view with all counters collected for each object. Choosing Log from the Options menu brings up the Log Option dialog box, in which you can specify the name to be given to the log file, its location, and the interval at which counters will be written to the log file. You can pause the log with the Pause button or stop it with the Stop button. Counters for the objects included in the log file are available for subsequent viewing.

FIG. 3.10

You can log the performance statistics from another Windows NT system running SQL Server by entering its name in the Computer text box.

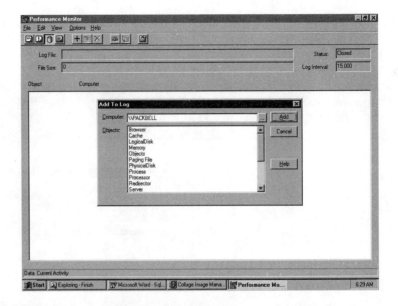

Displaying and Interpreting SQL Server Events

An integrated logging tool is used on Windows NT to log information about application, system, and security operations called *events*. The Event Viewer controls the logging and subsequent display of information about all events.

The Event Viewer records the date and time of occurrence, source, type, category, ID number, user name, and computer system for Windows NT and application-defined operations. You can then display these events by various categories, order, and amount of detail. Information about operations related to the use of Microsoft SQL Server is recorded primarily in the application log. It's also possible that information recorded in the system section is related to the use of SQL Server's system processes.

Events are occurences that you should know about that happen during the execution of user or system code. The events are logged in the event log file, which is enabled automatically at system startup. You can keep event logs and examine them later as printed reports. You can disable event logging through the Control Panel's Services item.

N O T E   You shouldn't disable event logging when using SQL Server. Otherwise, you'll lose the information recorded about database operations, which might help you correct problems later. ■

The first time you use the Event Viewer, its window displays events from the system log. In the example shown in Figure 3.11, the window is large enough to display one-line listings of 21 system events. The most recent event is listed first and is selected. If you've chosen Save Settings on Exit from the Options menu, the last log viewed will come up in the Event Viewer window when it's run again.

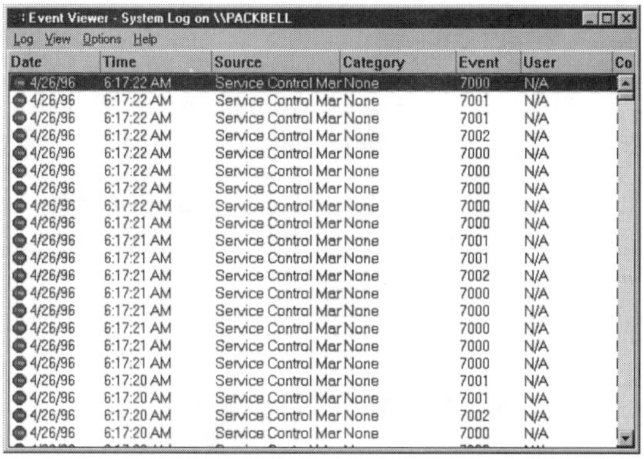

FIG. 3.11

The subsequent startup of the Event Viewer can optionally bring up information in the last log that you've examined.

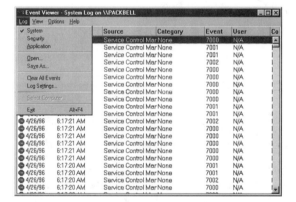

The Log menu allows you to choose from the System, Security, or Application logs to view events (see fig. 3.12).

FIG. 3.12

Information about SQL Server events is recorded in the application log.

Configuring the Application Event Log

You should configure the application log of the Event Viewer after you install SQL Server. Choose Log Settings from the Log menu to bring up the Event Log Settings dialog box. You can set the maximum size for the log file in kilobytes, the period of time events are kept, and whether to overwrite events if the log file is full. Separate settings are kept for each of the three logs—system, security, and application. In Figure 3.13, the system log file is set to a maximum size of 512K and events are set to be overwritten in a week.

FIG. 3.13

Select Overwrite Events as Needed to ensure that no new events are lost at the expense of losing the oldest recorded events.

Displaying Event Details

Detail about an event can be viewed by double-clicking a selected event or by choosing Detail from the View menu in the main windows of the Event Viewer. You must examine the detail of an event to learn the meaning of the event numbers.

The information at the top of the detail display is similar to an event line in the initial display of events. The description section of the Event Detail dialog box provides additional information about the event. Figure 3.14 shows the detail for an event from the application log recorded about a SQL Server event.

FIG. 3.14

If the Type field displays Information or Success, the event isn't an error but just the record of an event that occurred on the system.

For each logged event, several items of information are displayed. The items of information recorded for each event are the date, time, user, computer, event ID, source, type, and category.

You can use the information shown in Table 3.1 to help you interpret the information that's displayed in the Event Detail dialog box for events in all application logs.

Table 3.1   Item Descriptions for Logged Events

Item	Description
Event	Windows NT-assigned event number
Category	Event source; security source can be Login, Logoff, Shutdown, Use of User Rights, File, Print, Security Changes, or None
Computer	Name of computer on which error occurred
Date	Date of event
Event ID	Unique number for each source to identify event
Source	Program that was logged—for example, an application or a system component, including a driver

Item	Description
Time	Time of event
Type	Severity of error—for example, Error, Warning, Information, Success, Audit, or Failure Audit displayed as an icon
User	User name when error occurred; can be blank (N/A)

The Event Detail dialog box (refer to fig. 3.14) shows information about a normal stop of the SQL Server process, probably issued through the SQL Service Manager. You can use the Description list box's scroll bar to display additional information, if any, for an event. The SQL Service Manager is discussed in Chapter 1, "Introducing Microsoft SQL Server."

The last section of information in the Event Detail dialog box displays a byte dump in hexadecimal. Not all events display a dump—only those where the information is relevant. The information within the dump can be interpreted by someone with knowledge of the application code or the Windows NT system, which resulted in the event. You can select the Words radio button to display the dump in words rather than bytes.

Part

I

Ch

3

Use the Previous and Next buttons to display the detail for the previous and next events in the current log.

Using the View Menu

You can use the View menu to control other characteristics of the display of events in the main window of the Event Viewer (see fig. 3.15). For example, by default, the newest events are listed first in the window. Optionally, you can display events beginning with the oldest—rather than the most recent—listed first.

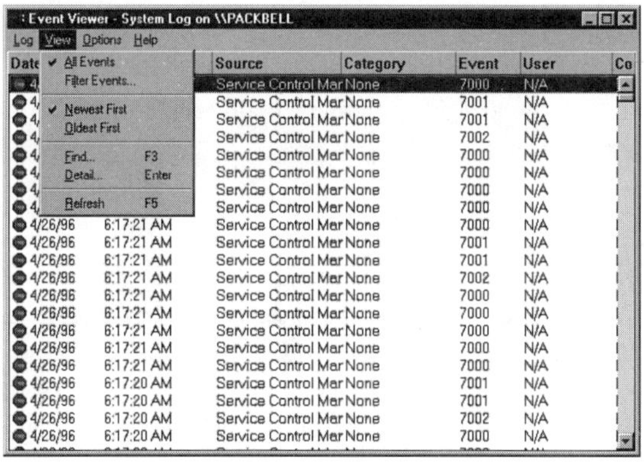

FIG. 3.15

Choose Oldest First to reverse the order of displayed events.

Choose Find from the View menu to bring up the Find dialog box (see fig. 3.16). Use Find to locate events by a criteria that you specify in the Find dialog box. You can enter various items for an event in the Find dialog box, including the source, category, event ID, computer, user, and any part of the description. If the event is found, the main Event Viewer window appears with the specified error selected. If the event isn't found, you see a `Search failed` error message.

In the Find dialog box, the events to be located are restricted to only a single SQL Server event generated that is related to the activity of the SQL Server process, one of the two components of SQL Server. You can use the Find Next button to display the next entry that matches the criteria that you've specified in the Find dialog box.

You can bring up the Filter dialog box to allow the selection of events using a criteria based on one or more items of an event. You can select the events based on the date and time of all events or the first and last events of a range of dates and times. Also, you can enter the source, category, user, computer, and event ID to filter the events displayed.

FIG. 3.16

Use the Direction radio buttons to define the direction of the search through the log.

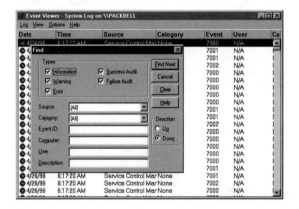

By default, Information, Warning, Error, Success Audit, and Failure Audit are selected but can be deselected to restrict the events returned. Success Audit and Failure Audit are valid only for the security log.

Clearing the Event Log

Choose Clear All Events from the Log menu to empty a log file of all recorded events. If you choose Clear All Events, a precautionary dialog box appears. You can select the Cancel button to cancel the emptying of the event log.

TROUBLESHOOTING

I've looked at the event log, and sometimes I see several transactions that are completed each time the MSSQLServer process is started. Is this a problem? SQL Server will automatically roll back uncommitted transactions each time the server starts up. This is most likely to occur if you stopped the system or server incorrectly—for example, by turning the power off. You should ensure that you stop the server and formally shut down the system each time to minimize the number of pending transactions that must be examined each time the server is started.

From Here...

In this chapter you've learned about the relevant characteristics of Windows NT on which you install Microsoft SQL Server. Windows NT's multithreaded design and support for multiple processors is ideally suited for a multithreaded application such as SQL Server. In addition, the built-in network support of the Windows NT system makes possible a simple and straightforward connection from clients to SQL Server. Lastly, you learned that information returned by SQL Server is returned to the built-in reporting facilities of Windows NT, the Performance Monitor and Event Viewer.

For information that discusses selected aspects of the topics mentioned in this chapter, you can review the following chapters:

- Chapter 17, "Optimizing Performance," teaches you how to optimize the performance of SQL Server including the use of SQL Server–specific information returned by the Performance Monitor.

- Chapter 22, "Accessing SQL Server Databases Through Front-End Products," teaches you how to use client-workstation-based applications to access the server database.

Part

I

Ch

3

Defining and Manipulating Data and Data Storage Units

CHAPTER 4

Creating Devices, Databases, and Transaction Logs

The storage of physical data in SQL Server is controlled through the creation of data devices. *Data devices* are areas of disks that are preallocated for the use of SQL Server. SQL Server can use devices for the storage of either data, logs, or dumps.

Databases are logical areas that SQL Server reserves for the storage of tables and indexes. One or many databases may be created on a data device provided the device is an appropriate size.

Transaction logs, covered in Chapter 12, "Understanding Transactions and Locking," are the work areas that SQL Server uses to manage the transactions performed by client processes. The transaction logs are used to store the information required by SQL Server to roll back a transaction if a client process issues a ROLLBACK TRANSACTION. ∎

Learn how to create and use devices

SQL Server places databases onto devices. Devices must be created on a computer sytstem's storage device, usually a hard drive.

Learn how to create and use databases and transaction logs

Databases store data. Transaction logs store transactions that were made against a database.

Become familiar with tempdb and its use

SQL Server uses a temporary table to work with data. There are several things that can be done to tempdb to enhance performance.

Learn how to create and use a removable media database

Many applications are sent to a remote site to be executed or are for temporary applications. Databases stored on removable media might be more efficient and cost-effective for such applications.

Defining Devices

Devices are the physical files that SQL Server creates on disk for storing databases and logs. Devices must be created before databases can be created. A device can be of two types: *database* (used for storing databases) and *dump* (used for storing transaction logs).

Devices can store more than one database or transaction log in them; however, you often can get better performance with a single database per device, because each device is managed by a single I/O thread from the operating system. A database can span multiple devices if it needs to grow, and this can be an optimizing method due to striped physical disk access over multiple drives.

Creating Database Devices

You can create a disk device in SQL Server in two ways: graphically or through Transact-SQL. The graphical method is performed by using SQL Enterprise Manager. The Transact-SQL method is performed using the DISK INIT command. Both methods are discussed in the following sections.

Using SQL Enterprise Manager   *SQL Enterprise Manager* is a versatile tool that permits DBAs to perform most of the administrative functions of SQL Server without knowledge of the often cryptic Transact-SQL commands required. However, SQL Enterprise Manager does not permit an automated installation or "scripted" installation procedure. For this you will need to use Transact-SQL.

To use SQL Enterprise Manager to create a device, follow these steps:

1. Start SQL Enterprise Manager from the Microsoft SQL Server 6.5 group. Figure 4.1 shows SQL Enterprise Manager just after it's been started.

FIG. 4.1

Note that no server is selected and that all the main toolbar buttons are disabled.

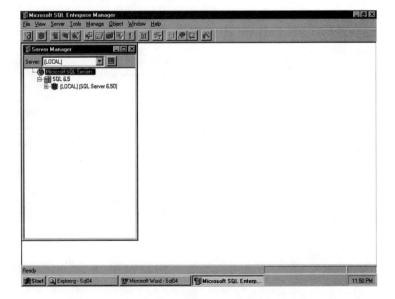

2. Select the server that's going to be managed. Then from the Manage menu, choose Devices. The Manage Database Devices window appears (see fig. 4.2).

FIG. 4.2

Each existing device is shown as a bar on the graph, with the dark area representing unused space in the device.

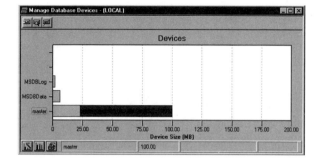

3. Click the New Device toolbar button to create a new device. The New Database Device dialog box appears (see fig. 4.3).

FIG. 4.3

SQL Enterprise Manager's New Database Device dialog box. Note that you can use the slider to specify how big the device should be by dragging the "thumb."

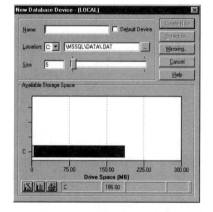

Part

II

Ch

4

4. Enter the details about the device being added, including the name, the location that the device should be placed, and the size of it (see fig. 4.4).

5. Click Create Now to begin creating the device. This process could take some time, depending on the size of the device being created and the speed of the physical drives being used. After the device is successfully created, you see the message box shown in Figure 4.5.

N O T E This device could have been scheduled to be created by using the Schedule button. This option allows the user to enter a time (single or recurring instance) for the operation to be performed. In addition, the Transact-SQL script that SQL Server will use to complete the operation may be edited. Additions or modifications could make the scheduled operation more powerful than simply creating a table. ▪

FIG. 4.4

SQL Enterprise Manager's New Database Device dialog box; the information entered will create a 5M device called NewDevice on the C drive using the physical file C:\MSSQL\DATA\ NewDevice.DAT.

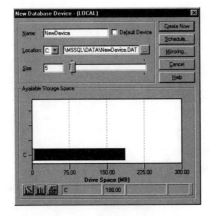

FIG. 4.5

SQL Enterprise Manager displays a message after all operations indicating success or failure. This message indicates that no errors occurred during the allocation of disk space for the database device's creation.

After successful creation of the device, SQL Enterprise Manager will add it to the graph of devices (see fig. 4.6).

FIG. 4.6

The NewDevice device has been added and is now empty (all dark).

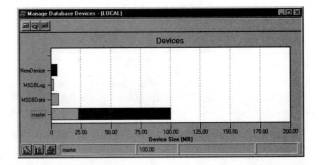

N O T E   SQL Server creates a physical file on the drive when the device is created. If you are using Windows NT's NT File System (NTFS), the operating system will return control to the application (SQL Enterprise Manager) immediately after executing the create command because of the way NTFS represents files to calling programs. Don't be concerned if you were used to seeing device creation take a long time on FAT or OS/2 HPFS and now it's suddenly very quick. This is one of the blessings of NT's new file system. ■

Using *DISK INIT*   DISK INIT is the SQL equivalent of creating a device through SQL Enterprise Manager. In fact, SQL Enterprise Manager's graphical front end is actually just creating the right DISK INIT command to be sent to the server. The syntax for the use of DISK INIT is as follows:

```
DISK INIT
    NAME = 'logical_name',
    PHYSNAME = 'physical_name',
    VDEVNO = virtual_device_number,
    SIZE = number_of_2K_blocks
    [, VSTART = virtual_address]
```

▶ **See** the "Syntax Guidelines" section of the Introduction for clarification of the syntax used in this book. **p. 6**

The options for the Transact-SQL command DISK INIT are as follows:

- ▪ *logical_name*—Any valid SQL Server identifier. A shorter name is probably preferable because it has to be used each time a database is created.

- ▪ *physical_name*—The full path and file name of the file to be used on the operating system to store the data.

- ▪ *virtual_device_number*—This is the unique system identifier for the device. It can range from 0 to 255, where 0 is reserved for the master database.

- ▪ *number_of_2K_blocks*—This is how a device is sized. The minimum value is 512 (meaning 1M).

- ▪ *virtual_address*—This parameter controls the virtual paging of the data device and how SQL Server accesses it. This parameter should be used only when you're told to by a Microsoft Service Provider.

The following SQL statement creates the same data device that was created earlier using the SQL Enterprise Manager:

```
DISK INIT
    Name = 'NewDevice',
    PhysName = 'C:\SQL60\DATA\NewDevice.DAT',
    VDevNo = 6,
    Size = 2500
```

Using Device Options   You should consider two important device options when creating devices in SQL Server: *mirroring* and *default devices*. Both options are important to mission-critical environments where downtime needs to be minimized.

Mirroring   *Mirroring* is used to provide an absolute copy of the database (usually) on a different physical device so that if a hardware failure occurs on the primary device, the database can be switched over to run on the mirror device. SQL Server performs mirroring by installing a mirror-handling "user" on the server. This user is listed as spid 1 in the system processes, which you can list by running the system procedure sp_who. Mirroring is a continuous operation and provides maximum redundancy in the event of a failure.

Mirroring can be performed at two levels with SQL Server: either by the underlying operating system (Windows NT Advanced Server) or by SQL Server. More information on mirroring the

Part
II

Ch
4

operating system can be found in the Microsoft documentation that accompanies NTAS 3.51. In most cases, the operating system's implementation of mirroring will provide better performance and options—such as various different implementations of Redundant Arrays of Inexpensive Drives (RAID)—than SQL Server. There are six levels of RAID (levels 0 to 5) that can be implemented, and they provide different methods of distributing physical data (and its copies) across multiple drives.

▶ **See** Appendix D, "Redundant Arrays of Inexpensive Drives (RAID)," for more information about levels of RAID. **p. 595**

Furthermore, with NTAS it's possible to mirror whole drives, thereby protecting all devices that reside on the drive.

SQL Server's mirroring works by creating an additional device on the specified disk and then using the mirror handler to copy every transaction that the device receives to the mirror device.

To enable mirroring on a device by using SQL Enterprise Manager, follow these steps:

1. Start SQL Enterprise Manager, select the server that's going to be managed, and then choose De_v_ices from the _M_anage menu. The Manage Database Devices window appears (refer to fig. 4.6).

2. Double-click the device to be mirrored in the graph. The Edit Database Device dialog box appears (see fig. 4.7).

FIG. 4.7

SQL Enterprise Manager's Edit Database Device dialog box allows you to change the size of a device by using the spinner controls on the _S_ize (MB) field.

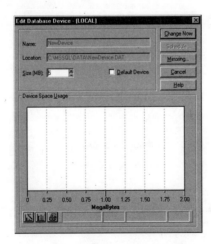

3. Click the _M_irroring button to display the Mirror Database Device dialog box (see fig. 4.8). SQL Enterprise Manager will automatically place an appropriately named mirror device in the Mirror Device Filename field.

CAUTION

If you're using long file names for your devices (such as *NewDevice*), be aware that there seems to be a bug in the way that SQL Enterprise Manager assigns the name of the mirror device. SQL Enterprise Manager defaults the name to be limited by the old FAT 8.3 limitations and will truncate *NewDevice* to *NewDevic*. This isn't a major problem, but it could result in duplicate files being attempted to be created due to the difference in the name not being considered until after the eighth byte of the file. For example, *NewDevice* and *NewDevice2* will have a default mirror name created that's identical and will cause an error condition in SQL Enterprise Manager.

FIG. 4.8

SQL Enterprise Manager's Mirror Database Device dialog box. The filename has been corrected to read c:\mssql\data\newdevice.mir to work around the bug in SQL Enterprise Manager.

4. Click the <u>M</u>irroring button to create the mirror device.

Mirroring can also be done by using Transact-SQL. The DISK MIRROR command's syntax is as follows:

```
DISK MIRROR
    NAME = 'logical_name',
    MIRROR = 'physical_name'
    [, WRITES = {SERIAL ¦ NOSERIAL }]
```

■ *logical_name*—This is the name of the device that will be mirrored.

■ *physical_name*—This is the full file name of the mirror device. Use an extension of .MIR for compatibility with SQL Enterprise Manager.

■ WRITES—This option isn't used on NT. It's provided only for backward compatibility with earlier versions of SQL Server that ran on OS/2.

The following example shows how to mirror the NewDevice created earlier:

```
DISK MIRROR
    Name = 'NewDevice',
    Mirror = 'C:\SQL60\DATA\NEWDEVICE.MIR'
```

Default Devices   Default devices are used by SQL Server when the CREATE DATABASE command isn't accompanied by a specific device that it should be placed on. Many devices can be specified as default. SQL Server will use them alphabetically until each device is filled.

To make a device a default device, select the Default Device check box on the Edit Database Devices dialog box in SQL Enterprise Manager. Alternately, use the `sp_diskdefault` system-stored procedure. The syntax for `sp_diskdefault` is as follows:

```
sp_diskdefault device_name, {defaulton ¦ defaultoff}
```

device_name is the logical device name that's being made default or not. If your device name has special characters, you may need to enclose the device name in single quotes so that SQL Server will recognize it.

In the following example, the device NewDevice is made a default device:

```
sp_diskdefault NewDevice, defaulton
```

Displaying Device Information   Here are two ways to find information about the devices that are now installed/active on a SQL Server: by using SQL Enterprise Manager or by using the system-stored procedure `sp_helpdevice`. Viewing device information by using SQL Enterprise Manager's Manage Database Devices window has been demonstrated several times earlier in this chapter; refer to those examples for help.

The syntax for `sp_helpdevice` is as follows:

```
sp_helpdevice [logical_name]
```

logical_name is the name of the device that's to be inspected. If no device is specified, `sp_helpdevice` will report information on all the devices on the SQL Server.

N O T E   The `sp_helpdevice` command must be entered through Transact-SQL. See the command-line applications section of Chapter 1, "Introducing Microsoft SQL Server," for help on starting a command-line ISQL session. There is also a graphical interface for ISQL/w. And Transact-SQL commands can be entered in SQL Enterprise Manager by choosing Tools, SQL Query Tool. ■

CAUTION

If you use the command-line ISQL application, remember to enter a go command to perform the commands entered to that point. The go command is the default commandend identifier. This identifier can be changed by using a switch when starting the ISQL session. Again, see the command-line applications section in Chapter 1.

The following example shows the output and use of `sp_helpdevice` to view all the devices on the server:

```
/*---------------------------
sp_helpdevice
---------------------------*/
device_name    physical_name            description
status cntrltype device_number low       high
-------------------------------------------------
diskdump        nul                      disk, dump device
16     2         0            0           20000
```

```
diskettedumpa  a:sqltable.dat              diskette, 1.2 MB, dump device
16     3          0            0            19
diskettedumpb  b:sqltable.dat              diskette, 1.2 MB, dump device
16     4          0            0            19
master         C:\SQL60\DATA\MASTER.DAT    special, default disk, physical
disk, 40 MB
3      0          0            0            20479
MSDBData       C:\SQL60\DATA\MSDB.DAT      special, physical disk, 2 MB
2      0          127          2130706432   2130707455
MSDBLog        C:\SQL60\DATA\MSDBLOG.DAT   special, physical disk, 2 MB
2      0          126          2113929216   2113930239

(1 row(s) affected)
```

Creating Dump Devices

Dump devices are special devices that SQL Server uses to perform backups and to *dump* (clear out) the transaction logs on databases. By default, SQL Server creates dump devices for the use of backups and log clearing. Several types of dump devices can be created, based on the medium that's being used to write the data to:

- *Disk.* A disk device can be a local disk device or a network disk device that's used for dumping data from the database—in the form of a backup. If the device is on the network, make sure that the NT server that's running SQL Server can access the network share where the device is placed.

- *Tape.* A tape dump device is used to back up a database directly to a tape device attached to the local computer. It isn't possible to dump to a tape attached to a remote computer.

- *Diskette.* A diskette dump device is provided for backward compatibility with earlier versions of SQL Server. Not recommended for use, it's supported only through the server console, because `sp_volchanged` commands must be used to tell the backup server that the diskettes have been changed.

- *Named pipe.* SQL Server has a named pipes interface to perform backups that allows third parties to hook in custom backup software and utilities. Named pipe devices aren't managed by SQL Enterprise Manager and must be explicitly referenced in a manual `DUMP` or `LOAD` command issued through ISQL.

- *NULL.* This is the special device that's used to dump the transaction logs of a database so that they're freed for more transactions to be posted against the server. Performing a dump to a NULL device will remove log entries from the database/log without adding data to the device itself. The NULL device is named DISKDUMP and is added to the system automatically when SQL Server is created. You can't manually add a NULL device to an existing SQL Server.

▶ **See** the Chapter 1 section entitled "Command-Line Applications." **p. 20**

There are two ways to add a dump device to the system: through SQL Enterprise Manager or by using the system-stored procedure `sp_addumpdevice`. The following two sections show you how to use both methods.

Part

II

Ch

4

Using SQL Enterprise Manager to Add a Dump Device   Using SQL Enterprise Manager to add a dump device removes the burden on the DBA to remember the syntax required for the system-stored procedures that must be executed to perform the task.

To add a dump device by using SQL Enterprise Manager, follow these steps:

1. Launch SQL Enterprise Manager from the Microsoft SQL Server 6.5 group. Select the server that's going to be managed. From the Tools menu, choose Database Backup/ Restore. The Database Backup/Restore dialog box appears (see fig. 4.9).

FIG. 4.9
The Backup tab is chosen by default when entering this dialog box.

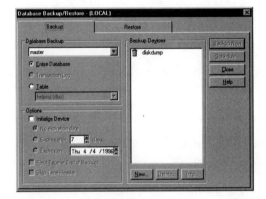

2. Click the New button to create a new dump device. The New Backup Device dialog box appears (see fig. 4.10).

FIG. 4.10
SQL Server places all disk-based dump devices in the BACKUP subdirectory by default.

3. Enter a Name and specify a Location for the device.

T I P   Click the ... button to find a particular directory on the server or network.

4. Specify whether the device is Tape or Disk, and then click the Create button. The device is added to SQL Server and to the list of available devices.

N O T E   SQL Server allocates resources for a dump device in the list and in the `sysdevices` system catalog table; however, it doesn't actually create a file/output item until a backup is actually performed to the device. If you click the dump device to inspect it before you perform a backup, you'll receive error #3201, and SQL Server will say that the device is offline. Don't worry about this error unless you're sure that a backup has been performed to the device. ■

Using *sp_addumpdevice*   SQL Server's system-stored procedure `sp_addumpdevice` is used to add dump devices to the system. `sp_addumpdevice` is the only way that you can add a diskette-based device for dumping to the SQL Server. The syntax for `sp_addumpdevice` is as follows:

```
sp_addumpdevice {'disk' ¦ 'diskette' ¦ 'tape'},
     'logical_name',
     'physical_name'
```

N O T E   Prior versions of SQL Server had some other parameters for `sp_addumpdevice` that were used to define the characteristics of the media being added. This is no longer necessary because SQL Server now inspects the device to determine its characteristics automatically. ■

The options for the system-stored procedure `sp_addumpdevice` are as follows:

- ■ *logical_name*—This is the logical name of the device that's going to be used for backups/dumps.

- ■ *physical_name*—This is the physical name of the device that's going to be used for the dump. For a `'disk'` or `'diskette'` dump device, specify the full path of the output file that should be created. For a `'tape'` device, reference the locally attached tape device by using Windows NT's Universal Naming Convention (UNC)—for example, `"\\.\tape0"`.

The following example adds a disk-based dump device to SQL Server:

```
sp_addumpdevice
     'DiskBackup',
     'C:\SQL60\Data\DISKBACKUP.DAT'
```

The following example adds a remote disk-based dump device on the network workstation/ server `MainFileServer`:

```
sp_addumpdevice
     'NetworkBackup',
     '\\MainFileServer\Data\NETBACKUP.DAT'
```

The following example adds a tape dump device to SQL Server:

```
sp_addumpdevice
     'TapeBackup',
     '\\.\Tape0'
```

Dropping Devices

Microsoft provides two ways to drop a device: by using SQL Enterprise Manager or by using the system-stored procedure `sp_dropdevice`. Dropping a device completely deallocates the disk space associated with the device and frees the space for other uses by the operating system or server.

If a device is not in use any more or is not correctly sized, it may be necessary to drop it so that it can be appropriately resized or the disk space given back to the operating system for other uses.

Part
II

Ch
4

Using SQL Enterprise Manager to Remove Devices   SQL Enterprise Manager provides a simple interface for the removal of database devices and is a convenient tool for managing large enterprises where lots of servers are involved. The DBA no longer has to know all the physical layouts of the server's devices because they are represented graphically by SQL Enterprise Manager.

> **CAUTION**
>
> For some reason, the drop device feature of SQL Enterprise Manager defaults to not removing the device file physically from the hard drive, nor does it give you an option to tell it to do so. Consequently, using SQL Enterprise Manager to remove a disk device won't actually make any disk space available for use on the server. You must go to a command prompt or to an Explorer Window and manually delete the file.
>
> If you're deleting a device so that the server frees up some allocated disk space, you're probably better off using sp_dropdevice and specifying DELFILE.

To use SQL Enterprise Manager to remove a database device, follow these steps:

1. In the SQL Enterprise Manager screen, select the server from which you want to remove the device. From the Manage menu, choose Devices. The Manage Database Devices window appears (see fig. 4.11).

FIG. 4.11
SQL Enterprise Manager's Manage Database Devices window lists all the devices that are available on the server that is being managed.

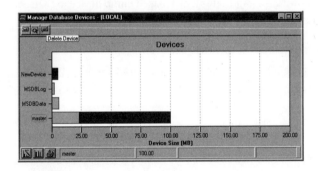

2. Click the device that you want to remove. From the Manage Database Devices window's toolbar, click the Delete Device button. A message box appears to confirm that you want to delete the device (see fig. 4.12).

FIG. 4.12
This is the last chance to abort a device deletion.

If the database device has one or many databases or logs on it, a second warning dialog box appears, asking permission to drop all the databases/logs that reside on it (see fig. 4.13).

FIG. 4.13
This dialog box lists databases that are using the device about to be deleted. You must drop these databases before the device can be deleted.

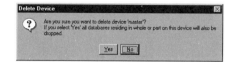

Using *sp_dropdevice* to Remove Devices   The system-stored procedure sp_dropdevice is provided for dropping devices from SQL Server. The syntax for sp_dropdevice is as follows:

sp_dropdevice *logical_name*[, DELFILE]

The options for the system-stored procedure sp_dropdevice are as follows:

■ *logical_name*—This is the name of the device to be removed.

■ *DELFILE*—If DELFILE is included, the physical file that was created on the server will also be removed.

An error will occur if this procedure is run against a device that has databases in it. The databases must be dropped before the device can be deleted.

Defining Databases and Transaction Logs

Databases are logical entities in which SQL Server places tables and indexes. A database exists on one or many database devices; correspondingly, a database device can have one or many databases on it.

Every database has a transaction log that belongs or is associated with it. The transaction log is a place that SQL Server writes all the database transactions to before writing them to the database. The transaction log is used to hold "open" transactions (transactions started with a BEGIN TRAN statement) until they're "closed" or COMMITted. By default, the transaction log is placed on the same database device as the database; however, better performance can be achieved by creating two devices—one for the log and one for the database itself.

SQL Server can logically maintain up to 32,767 databases on a single server. However, it's more likely that the server will run out of disk, memory, and CPU resources before this limit is ever reached. A database can be up to 1T (terabyte) in size and can have as many as 32 device *fragments* (that is, placements on database devices).

Given that a physical disk will unlikely be greater than 10G (gigabytes) in size, it would seem to be impossible to get a database much bigger than 320G by using SQL Server (which would suggest that Microsoft should increase the number of device fragments permitted). However, a database device actually can be mapped to multiple physical devices, provided some form of

Part

II

Ch

4

software- or hardware-based striping is in use. *Striping* is highly recommended because it provides substantial performance gains due to multiple physical disk drives being used for a single database device. When used with RAID, striping also provides an extra level of data integrity in case of a media failure.

▶ **See** Appendix D, "Redundant Arrays of Inexpensive Drives (RAID)," for more information. **p. 595**

Creating a Database and Transaction Log

The process of creating a database causes SQL Server to copy the *model* database to the new database name. This process copies all the items in the model database's catalog. If you want to have custom default tables and objects in every database created on a server, add them to the model just like you would add them to any database.

You can take two approaches to create a database and transaction log: you can use either SQL Enterprise Manager or the CREATE DATABASE command.

Using SQL Enterprise Manager to Create Database and Transaction Logs   To create a database using SQL Enterprise Manager, follow these steps:

1. Launch SQL Enterprise Manager from the Microsoft SQL Server 6.5 group. Select the server that's going to be managed. From the Manage menu, choose Databases. The Manage Databases window appears (see fig. 4.14).

FIG. 4.14
Each existing database is shown as a bar on the graph, with the dark area representing unused space in the database.

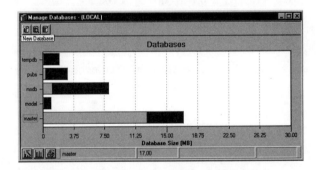

2. Click the New Database toolbar button to create a new database.
3. Enter the details about the database being added, including the name, the devices that the data and logs should be placed on, and how much disk space should be used for each (see fig. 4.15).

SQL Server 6.0 introduced a new database creation option that stops any users from accessing a database until a load operation is performed. This option is very useful for a database administrator who wants to create a database without having any users connect to it. Click the Create For Load check box in the New Database dialog box if you want to stop any users from accessing the database until the load operation has been completed.

FIG. 4.15

SQL Enterprise Manager's New Database dialog box. The required information is entered to add a 3M database called NewDatabase on the NewDevice for data and logs.

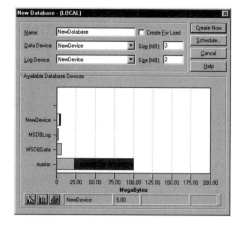

4. Click Create Now. After the database is successfully created, the Manage Databases window appears, showing the new database in the graph (see fig. 4.16).

FIG. 4.16

The NewDatabase database has been added and is mostly empty.

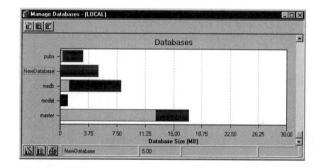

Using the *CREATE DATABASE* Command to Create Database and Transaction Logs The CREATE DATABASE command is the Transact-SQL method for creating a database. The syntax for CREATE DATABASE is as follows:

```
CREATE DATABASE database_name
     [ON {DEFAULT ¦ database_device} [= size]
     [, database_device [= size]]...]
     [LOG ON log_device [= size]
     [,log_device[= size]]...]
     [FOR LOAD]
```

The options for the Transact-SQL command CREATE DATABASE are as follows:

- *database_name*—This is the name of the database to be created. The database name must comply with the standard rules for naming objects.

- *database_device*—This is the device or list of devices that this database is to be created on and how much disk space, in megabytes, is to be reserved on each. If DEFAULT is specified, SQL Server will choose the next free default database device to use.

- *log_device*—The LOG ON parameter is where the log device is specified. Like the database device, it's possible to specify more than one device to be used for the logging of the database being created.

- FOR LOAD—This parameter disallows user access until a LOAD operation has been completed on the database.

The following example creates the same database that was created in the preceding section by using SQL Enterprise Manager:

```
CREATE DATABASE NewDatabase
    On NewDevice = 3
    Log On NewDevice = 2
```

Displaying Database Information

The Manage Databases window in SQL Enterprise Manager provides a graphical display of all the information about a database. To view this information in ISQL, use the system-stored procedure sp_helpdb. The syntax for sp_helpdb is

```
sp_helpdb database_name
```

If a *database_name* is supplied, sp_helpdb reports information about that database; otherwise, it reports information about all the databases on the server.

The following example shows the use of sp_helpdb for all the databases on the server. The information provided shows only the total size of the database and any options in effect:

```
/*-----------------------------
sp_helpdb
-----------------------------*/
name          db_size   owner dbid created     status
------------------------------------------------------------
master        17.00 MB  sa    1    Jun  7 1995 trunc. log on chkpt.
model          1.00 MB  sa    3    Jun  7 1995 no options set
msdb           4.00 MB  sa    5    Nov 23 1995 trunc. log on chkpt.
NewDatabase    5.00 MB  sa    6    Jan  7 1996 no options set
pubs           3.00 MB  sa    7    Jun  7 1995 select into/bulkcopy, trunc.
    log on chkpt., dbo use only
tempdb         7.00 MB  sa    2    Jan  7 1996 select into/bulkcopy, single
    user
```

In the following example, a database is supplied, and more detailed information, including device fragment information, is returned from SQL Server:

```
/*-----------------------------
sp_helpdb NewDatabase
-----------------------------*/
name          db_size   owner dbid created     status
------------------------------------------------------------
NewDatabase   5.00 MB   sa    6    Jan  7 1996 no options set

device_fragments                    size          usage
-------------------------------   -----------   -------------------
NewDevice                           2.00 MB log only
NewDevice                           3.00 MB data only
```

```
device                                segment
----------------------------          ----------------------------
master                                default
master                                logsegment
master                                system.
```

N O T E The `segment` information is displayed only if you're executing `sp_helpdb` from the database that you're inspecting. ∎

Increasing the Size of the Database and Transaction Log

SQL Server allows the size of a database to be resized in case its space is consumed by user data. In the same way, transaction logs can be increased in size if they get full too quickly and require excessive dumping.

Using SQL Enterprise Manager   To increase the size of a database or transaction log by using SQL Enterprise Manager, follow these steps:

1. Run SQL Enterprise Manager, select the required server, and from the Manage menu choose Databases. Double-click the database that needs to be adjusted; the Edit Database dialog box appears (see fig. 4.17).

Part

II

Ch

4

FIG. 4.17

SQL Enterprise Manager's Edit Database dialog box allows you to configure options that apply to the currently selected database.

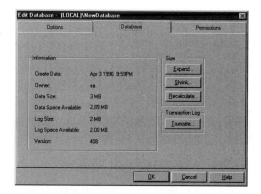

2. Click the Expand button to display the Expand Database dialog box (see fig. 4.18).

3. If you're expanding the database, select from the Data Device drop-down list box the device that you want to expand the database into. In the Size (MB) text box next to the drop-down box, enter the amount of megabytes that are required.

4. If you're expanding the log, select from the Log Device drop-down list box the device that you want to expand the log into. In the Size (MB) text box next to the drop-down box, enter the amount of megabytes that are required.

T I P To add a new device for the database or log to grow into, select <new> from either drop-down list box, and the New Database Device dialog box will appear.

FIG. 4.18

At the bottom of the dialog box is a graph showing all the devices on the server and the amount of free space in each.

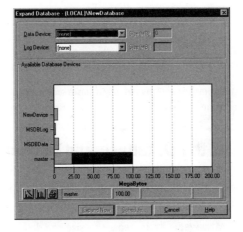

5. Click Expand Now to expand the database/log and return to the Edit Database dialog box. The Edit Database dialog box will be updated and will reflect adding the new log or database devices in the Log Space Available or Database Space Available fields.

N O T E SQL Enterprise Manager also provides an option to shrink a database. This is done by internally calling DBCC SHRINKDB. However, what SQL Enterprise Manager neglects to inform you is that the SQL Server must be started in single-user mode to perform these operations. If it's not started in single-user mode, there will be users (system handles such as the CHECKPOINT and MIRROR handlers) that can't be removed from the database. To start SQL Server in single-user mode, use the -m keyword and start SQL Server from the command-line. ■

Using the _ALTER DATABASE_ Command to Extend a Database   Transact-SQL provides the ALTER DATABASE command to allow a database to be extended. Transaction logs are also extended by using the ALTER DATABASE command; however, after the database is extended, the system-stored procedure sp_logdevice is used to specify that the extension to the database is actually for transaction log use.

The syntax for ALTER DATABASE is as follows:

```
ALTER DATABASE database_name
    [ON {DEFAULT ¦ database_device} [= size]
    [, database_device [= size]]...]
    [FOR LOAD]
```

The options for the Transact-SQL command ALTER DATABASE are as follows:

- _database_name_—This is the name of the database that's being extended.

- _database_device_—This is one or more database devices and the size (in megabytes) to be allocated to the database.

- ON DEFAULT—If DEFAULT is specified, SQL Server will allocate the requested space to the first free database device or devices that have enough space to meet the request.

- FOR LOAD—If FOR LOAD is specified, SQL Server will stop any user processes from connecting to the database until a LOAD has completed. FOR LOAD can be specified only if the database was initially created with the FOR LOAD option.

In this example, NewDatabase is extended by 5M on the NewDevice database device:

```
ALTER DATABASE NewDatabase
    On NewDevice = 5
```

In the following example, NewDatabase is extended by a further 5M, and the logs are placed on the extended portion:

```
ALTER DATABASE NewDatabase
    On NewDevice = 5
Go
sp_logdevice NewDatabase, NewDevice
```

Dropping Databases

Dropping a database frees up any space that it consumed on any database devices, and removes any objects that it contained. Dropping a database isn't reversible, so be careful; a restore will be required to recover the database.

N O T E Be sure to remember the difference between dropping a database and dumping one. Dropping a database drops all the tables and indexes and removes the logical area on the database device reserved for the database. Dumping a database creates a backup of the database's data onto a disk, diskette, or other type of media. ■

User accounts that had their default database as the database that's being dropped will have their default database changed to *master*. Only the System Administrator (SA) or the database owner (dbo) can drop a database. The master, model, and tempdb databases can't be dropped by any user account. Also, any databases that are participating in replication or have active users can't be dropped until the replication is suspended or until the users have disconnected from the database.

Using SQL Enterprise Manager to Drop a Database   To use SQL Enterprise Manager to drop a database, follow these steps:

1. Run SQL Enterprise Manager, select the server that the database resides on, and from the Manage menu choose Databases. The Manage Databases window appears (see fig. 4.19).
2. Click the database that you want to drop.
3. Click the Delete Database toolbar button. A message box appears, asking for confirmation to drop the database (see fig. 4.20).
4. Click Yes; the database is dropped.

Using the *DROP DATABASE* Command to Drop a Database   The syntax for the DROP DATABASE command in Transact-SQL is as follows:

Part
II

Ch
4

```
DROP DATABASE database_name, [database_name...]
```

database_name is the name of the database to be dropped.

Databases in all "states" (including Active, Damaged, Suspect, Offline, or Not recovered) can be dropped by using the DROP DATABASE command. A database that's still in Recovery status must be dropped by using the system-stored procedure sp_dbremove.

FIG. 4.19

SQL Enterprise Manager's Manage Databases window lists all the active databases on the currently managed server.

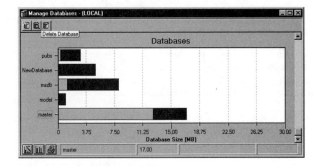

FIG. 4.20

This message box is the last chance that you have to abort a database being dropped before SQL Enterprise Manager performs the drop.

Defining Segments

Segments are logical groups of disk devices (or portions of devices) on which database objects are placed. Database segments are created in a database, which in turn can be placed on a particular database disk device. The advantage of segments is that individual objects, such as tables and indexes, can then be explicitly placed in a segment, allowing for greater performance.

Typically, two segments would be created for a database that spans two disk devices. These segments would then be used in such a way that all the tables with non-clustered indexes would be created on one segment and the non-clustered indexes for these tables would be created on the other segment. Non-clustered indexes are indexes that are binary search trees of the data. This has a tremendous performance advantage because the reading and writing of the data and index pages can execute concurrently on two physical devices rather than run serially.

▶ **See** Chapter 10, "Managing and Using Indexes and Keys," for more information about creating indexes. **p. 273**

N O T E SQL Enterprise Manager doesn't have any user interface to data segments, and so all the work has to be done with ISQL. ▄

Segments are also good for allowing the TEXT and IMAGE data associated with a database table to be stored on a separate physical device, and for splitting large tables across separate physical devices.

 TIP Better performance and far easier management is provided by splitting the database devices themselves across multiple disks at the operating system or hardware level by the use of RAID, rather than by using segments.

Using Default Segments

When a new database is created, three default segments are created for it. The SYSTEM segment houses all the system tables and their indexes. The LOGSEGMENT stores the transaction log for the database. The DEFAULT segment stores any user-created objects, unless they're explicitly moved or placed on a different segment.

Adding Segments

You add segments by using the system-stored procedure sp_addsegment. The syntax for sp_addsegment is as follows:

```
sp_addsegment segment_name, database_device
```

The options for the system-stored procedure sp_addsegment are as follows:

- *segment_name*—The name of the segment that's being added.
- *database_device*—The name of the database device that this segment should be placed on.

The following example creates a segment on the database device NewDevice:

```
sp_addsegment seg_newdevice1, NewDevice
```

Extending Segments

You can extend segments by using the system-stored procedure sp_extendsegment. When a segment is extended, it simply allocates more database disk devices to it for the use of any objects placed in the segment. The syntax for sp_extendsegment is as follows:

```
sp_extendsegment segment_name, database_device
```

The options for the system-stored procedure sp_addsegment are as follows:

- *segment_name*—The name of the segment to be extended.
- *database_device*—The name of the database device that this segment should be extended on.

The following example extends the segment seg_newdevice1 on to the database device NewDevice2:

```
sp_extendsegment seg_newdevice1, NewDevice2
```

T I P If you want to extend the DEFAULT segment, you must enclose default in quotation marks because default is a reserved word. For example,

```
sp_extendsegment 'default', NewDevice
```

Using Segments

After segments are created on a database, you can place an object on those segments in two ways. Both CREATE TABLE and CREATE INDEX have an ON SEGMENT option that allows a table or index to be created on a particular segment.

▶ **See** Chapter 5, "Creating Database Tables and Using Datatypes," for more information about creating tables on segments. **p. 105**

SQL Server also provides a system-stored procedure, sp_placeobject, that will direct the server to place any new data for a table onto a new segment. You would need to use this for tables that you want to partially load on one segment and then switch over to another segment. Executing sp_placeobject doesn't move any previously existing data allocations to the new segment; all it does is cause future allocations to occur on the requested new segment.

The syntax for sp_placeobject is as follows:

```
sp_placeobject segment_name, object_name
```

The options for the system-stored procedure sp_placeobject are as follows:

- *segment_name*—This is the name of the segment that the object should be placed on.
- *object_name*—This is the object that's to be moved. The object can be a fully qualified table column if the column's data type is IMAGE or TEXT. Because SQL Server doesn't store IMAGE or TEXT data in the same data pages as the rest of the table data, these column types can be placed on their own segment. This provides substantially better performance. IMAGE or TEXT data should be placed with sp_placeobject before table population to ensure that all rows' data is stored in the correct segments.

The following example makes all further data allocations for the table authors on the new segment seg_data2:

```
sp_placeobject seg_data2, authors
```

The following example moves the logo column from the pub_info table to a new segment for ImageData:

```
sp_placeobject seg_ImageData, 'pub_info.logo'
```

Dropping Segments

Dropping segments removes them from the database devices that they reside on. A segment can't be dropped if it contains any database objects; those objects need to be dropped first. For information about dropping tables see Chapter 5, "Creating Database Tables and Using Datatypes." For information about dropping indexes, see Chapter 10, "Managing and Using

Indexes and Keys." Segments are dropped by executing the system-stored procedure `sp_dropsegment`. The syntax for `sp_dropsegment` is as follows:

```
sp_dropsegment segment_name[, device_name]
```

- *segment_name*—This is the name of the segment that's to be dropped.
- *device_name*—This is the database device from which the segment should be removed. If no database device is specified, the segment is dropped from all the devices that it spans. If, however, a database device name *is* specified, the segment is removed only from that device.

Using the tempdb Database

Tempdb is a special database that's used by SQL Server to handle any "dynamic" SQL requests from users. Tempdb is a workspace for SQL Server to use when it needs a temporary place for calculations, aggregations, and sorting operations. The sorts of things that tempdb is used for include the following:

- Creating temporary tables for sorting data
- Holding temporary tables created by users and stored procedures
- Storing the data that matches any server cursors that are opened by a user process
- Holding values for temporary user-created global variables

One key advantage to using tempdb is that its activity isn't logged. This means that any data manipulation activity done on tempdb temporary tables are much faster than normal disk devices.

This is a double-edged sword, however, because if SQL Server is brought down at any time, all the information in tempdb is lost. Take care not to rely on tempdb without having application code that can restart itself in the event of a server shutdown.

Part
II

Ch
4

Adjusting tempdb's Size

The default size of tempdb when SQL Server is installed is 2M. For most production environments, this size will be insufficient for tempdb. If the environment is highly active with large queries or lots of requests for queries, it's recommended that tempdb be extended.

Tempdb is created in the master device by default and can be expanded in that device, or it can be moved so that it spans multiple database devices. To increase the size of tempdb, follow the same steps outlined earlier in the section entitled "Increasing the Size of the Database and Transaction Log" for resizing any other database.

Placing tempdb in RAM

Because tempdb is so critical to server performance (since SQL Server uses it for just about every query/operation that occurs), tempdb has a unique option of being able to be placed in RAM. Placing tempdb in RAM dramatically improves the amount of time required for sorting.

Before you consider placing tempdb in RAM, you must consider how tempdb uses memory now available in the server. All RAM that's allocated to SQL Server is paged based on a least recently used (LRU) algorithm. What this means is that quite often, data in tempdb will be in memory anyway as part of a regular page.

You shouldn't place tempdb in RAM unless sufficient RAM is available to the server to handle its normal operations. It's unlikely that you'll perceive any benefit from tempdb being in RAM unless the server has more than 64M of memory. With 128M or more of RAM, it's quite likely that you'll achieve performance gains by having tempdb in RAM.

There are no data-integrity considerations with tempdb in RAM, because none of the operations that occur on tempdb are logged. What this means is that tempdb is rebuilt every time the server is restarted, and any data that was in it—whether or not tempdb was in RAM or on a disk device—is lost.

To place tempdb in RAM, you must use the system-stored procedure `sp_configure` and restart the server. For more information on using `sp_configure` and other configurable options of SQL Server, refer to Chapter 16, "Understanding Server, Database, and Query Options."

Using Removable Media for Databases

A new feature—introduced in SQL Server 6.0 and continued with 6.5—enables databases to be placed on removable media such as CD-ROMs and magneto-optical (MO) drives. This feature permits the mass distribution of databases in a more friendly form than a backup tape, which the client must restore before using it. Also, a CD-ROM-based database is truly read-only and is a great way of securing data integrity.

N O T E   SQL Enterprise Manager doesn't have any user interface to allow the creation of removable media, so all the work has to be done with ISQL. It's possible to create a device and database on a removable drive attached to the Windows NT system; however, this won't be the same as a removable-media-capable database and shouldn't be done. ▪

Creating a Removable Database

A removable database has to be created in such a way that three devices are used: one for the system catalog, one for the user data, and one for the transaction log. Only the System Administrator (SA) can create removable databases.

SQL Server has a special system-stored procedure, `sp_create_removable`, that will create a database and devices that will be acceptable for use when creating a database for removable media purposes. It's important that you use this stored procedure because it will guarantee that the database created is usable on a removable device. The syntax for `sp_create_removable` is as follows:

```
sp_create_removable database_name, sysdevice_name_,
    'sysdevice_physical', sysdevice_size,
    logdevice_name, 'logdevice_physical', logdevice_size,
    datadevice1_name, 'datadevice1_physical',
    datadevice1_size [... , datadevice16_name,
    'datadevice16_physical', datadevice16_size]
```

The options for the system-stored procedure `sp_create_removable` are as follows:

- *database_name*—The name of the database to be created.

- *sysdevice_name*—The logical name to use for the device that will hold the system catalog tables.

- *sysdevice_physical*—The physical device path and file name that will be used to store the data for the system catalog device.

- *syssize*—The size in megabytes of the device.

- *logdevice_name*—The logical name to use for the device that will hold the transaction log.

- *logdevice_physical*—The physical device path and file name that will be used to store the data for the log device.

- *logsize*—The size in megabytes of the device.

- *datadeviceN_name*—The logical name to use for the device that will hold the user data. There can be up to 16 data devices.

- *datadeviceN_physical*—The physical device path and file name that will be used to store the data for *datadevice*.

- *datasize*—The size in megabytes of the device.

The following example creates a 1M data, log, and system catalog database and appropriate devices called `MyRemovable`:

```
/*----------------------------
sp_create_removable MyRemovable, MySys, 'C:\SQL60\DATA\REMOVABLE\MYSYS.DAT', 1,
    MyLog, 'C:\SQL60\DATA\REMOVABLE\MYLOG.DAT', 1,
    MyData, 'C:\SQL60\DATA\REMOVABLE\MYDATA.DAT', 1
----------------------------*/
CREATE DATABASE: allocating 512 pages on disk 'MySys'
Extending database by 512 pages on disk MyData
DBCC execution completed. If DBCC printed error messages, see your System
    Administrator.
Extending database by 512 pages on disk MyLog
DBCC execution completed. If DBCC printed error messages, see your System
    Administrator.
DBCC execution completed. If DBCC printed error messages, see your System
    Administrator.
```

Using the Removable Database

While the database is in development, the following rules should be observed to ensure that the database is usable on removable media:

- Keep the System Administrator (SA) as the Database Owner (DBO) of the database.
- Don't create any views, or any stored procedures that reference objects that can't be found in the database.
- Don't add any users to the database or change any of the user permissions on the database. You can, however, add groups, and permissions may be assigned to those groups.
- Don't alter any of the database devices created by `sp_create_removable`.

After database development is completed and you want to test that the database is acceptable for removable media, you should run the system-stored procedure `sp_certify_removable`. This procedure checks all the conditions required for a removable database and can automatically fix anything that it finds unacceptable. The syntax for `sp_certify_removable` is as follows:

```
sp_certify_removable database_name[, AUTO]
```

The options for the system-stored procedure `sp_certify_removable` are as follows:

- *database_name*—This is the name of the database to be certified.
- AUTO—If AUTO is specified, the stored procedure will correct any problems that it encounters. If you don't specify AUTO, you should correct any problems found using normal SQL Server tools.

> **CAUTION**
>
> If `sp_certify_removable` reports that it corrected anything when the AUTO flag was specified, it's highly recommended that you retest your application program to make sure that it's still compatible with the database. If no testing occurs, SQL Server could have rendered your application useless without you knowing about it.

As part of its execution, `sp_certify_removable` also takes offline all the devices that have been created for use in the removable database and makes them available for copying to the actual physical device. The output from `sp_certify_removable` is very important because it indicates the database characteristics to use when installing the removable database in a SQL Server.

The following example shows the MyRemovable database being certified and brought offline:

```
/*----------------------------
sp_certify_removable MyRemovable, AUTO
-----------------------*/
DBCC execution completed. If DBCC printed error messages, see your System
    Administrator.
DBCC execution completed. If DBCC printed error messages, see your System
    Administrator.
DBCC execution completed. If DBCC printed error messages, see your System
    Administrator.
File: 'C:\SQL60\DATA\REMOVABLE\MYLOG.DAT' closed.
Device dropped.
```

```
The following devices are ready for removal.  Please note this info. for
    use when installing on a remote system:

Device name  Device type  Sequence     Device frag. used by database
Physical file name
-----------------------------------------------------------------
--------------------
MySys        System + Log 1            1 MB
C:\SQL60\DATA\REMOVABLE\MYSYS.DAT
MyData       Data         2            1 MB
C:\SQL60\DATA\REMOVABLE\MYDATA.DAT

Database is now offline
Closing device 'MyData' and marking it 'deferred'.
Device option set.
Closing device 'MySys' and marking it 'deferred'.
Device option set.
```

Installing the Removable Database

After a distribution media/device is made, you must install it on the target SQL Server. Installation is achieved by using the information supplied in the output from sp_certify_removable. This information should be distributed with each CD-ROM or device that the removable media is placed on.

The system-stored procedure sp_dbinstall is used to install a database from removable media. The syntax for sp_dbinstall is as follows:

```
sp_dbinstall database_name, device_name, 'physical_device',
    size, 'device_type'[, 'location']
```

The options for the system-stored procedure sp_dbinstall are as follows:

- *database_name*—The name of the database to be installed. This can be any name that's valid for database and doesn't need to be the same as the original device.

- *device_name*—The name of the database device that's to be installed.

- *physical_device*—The full path information for the device on the removable media.

- *size*—The size of the device being created.

- *device_type*—The type of device being created on the target SQL Server. Valid types are 'SYSTEM' and 'DATA'. The 'SYSTEM' device must be created first. If more than one 'DATA' device exist, each should be installed by using sp_dbinstall.

- *location*—The location to use on the local drive for the device being installed. The system device must be installed locally; however, the data devices can be left on the removable media, if necessary or desired.

The following example installs the system device created earlier by the system-stored procedure sp_certify_removable in the section "Using the Removable Database" from a CD-ROM in drive E:

```
sp_dbinstall MyRemovable, MySys, 'e:\MySys.dat', 1,'SYSTEM',
➥'c:\sql60\data\invsys.dat'
```

After the system device is installed, the data device is installed but left on the CD-ROM:

```
sp_dbinstall MyRemovable, MyData, 'e:\MyData.dat', 1,'DATA'
```

After all the data devices are installed, you need to place the database online so that users can access it. This is achieved by using `sp_dboption`. The following example shows you how to bring `MyRemovable` online:

```
sp_dboption MyRemovable, OFFLINE, FALSE
```

▶ **See** the Chapter 16 section entitled "Displaying and Setting Database Options." **p. 433**

Uninstalling a Removable Media Database

If a removable media database is no longer required, you can remove it by using the system-stored procedure `sp_dbremove`. This procedure removes any entries from the system catalog relating to the database that was installed. The syntax for `sp_dbremove` is as follows:

```
sp_dbremove database_name[, dropdev]
```

The options for the system-stored procedure `sp_dbremove` are as follows:

- *database_name*—This is the name of the database to be removed/dropped.

- `dropdev`—If the keyword `dropdev` is supplied, `sp_dbremove` also removes any references in the system catalog to devices that were created as a result of the removable media database being created.

`sp_dbremove` doesn't remove the physical data files that were used to store the database devices. This needs to be done manually. See the *Caution* in the earlier section entitled "Using SQL Enterprise Manager to Remove Devices" for more information about removing device files manually.

From Here...

In this chapter, you learned all about devices, databases, and segments. This chapter provided you with information on how to create all the fundamentals for your server. From here you should consider looking at the following chapters to further develop your SQL Server and application programming knowledge:

- Chapter 5, "Creating Database Tables and Using Datatypes," shows how you can create tables in the databases and segments created in this chapter.

- Chapter 10, "Managing and Using Indexes and Keys," explains how to place the new indexes you create on the new index segments that you created in this chapter.

- Chapter 16, "Understanding Server, Database, and Query Options," explains how to further configure your SQL Server and databases for better performance.

- Chapter 18, "SQL Server Administration," tells you how to use the dump devices for backups and restores.

CHAPTER 5

Creating Database Tables and Using Datatypes

Data-processing systems involve the storage, processing, and retrieval of information. You must define where data will be stored before it can be processed and retrieved. All units of information, from characters to the logical definition of the entire database, can be defined through SQL Server components. ■

■ **Create database tables**

You'll learn how to create tables using a Transact-SQL statement or a Windows application.

■ **Define table columns by using different datatypes appropriate for the data to be stored in the columns**

Microsoft SQL Server has many datatypes for you to choose from for the storage of your data.

■ **Define and use user-defined datatypes**

SQL Server permits you to define your own datatypes facilitating the subsequent definition of table columns and other database structures.

■ **Add rows to a table using an insert statement**

The insert statement provides a simple way to store rows in a database table.

■ **Define and use table and column constraints**

Version 6 of SQL Server added the ability to define several characteristics of columns when the table is created rather than later using separate statements.

Creating Tables

Data in a relational database such as Microsoft SQL Server is stored in tables that are two-dimensional arrays. You'll recall from Chapter 1 that you've had experience working with tables from everyday life (such as train or bus schedules). The columns and rows of a table are already familiar to database users. Tables were chosen as the logical structure for storing data because of their familiarity to users and ease of use for retrieving, displaying, and manipulating data.

You can create Microsoft SQL Server database tables with the CREATE TABLE Transact-SQL statement. You can create up to 2 billion tables in each database. The major part of the creation of a table is the definition of the datatypes for columns. The syntax for CREATE TABLE is as follows:

```
CREATE TABLE [[database.]owner.]table_name
(column_name datatype [not null ¦ null] IDENTITY[(seed, increment)][constraint]
[, column_name datatype [not null ¦ null IDENTITY[(seed, increment)]]].
[constraint]…)
 [ON segment name]
```

> **N O T E**   For more information on identity columns, see the "*Identity* Property" section later in this
> chapter. ■

Enter the name of the table (*table_name*) following the keywords CREATE TABLE. You can use up to 30 characters to name a database object, such as a table. The column names are entered within parentheses. You define the name and type of the column by entering a column name up to 30 characters long, followed by a Transact-SQL datatype.

> **N O T E**   Everything stored in a database is stored as an object. A database object, such as a table,
> has information kept about it in system tables. For example, a table created by you has the
> name of the table, the type of data that is stored in its columns, and other characteristics stored in
> the system table sysobjects. ■

Optionally, you can enter the database in which the table is created, as well as an owner of the table. You'll find it more convenient to define the current database in which you're working first with a USE *database-name* command. After you define your current database with the USE command, all subsequent commands are performed within the database specified with the USE command.

> **N O T E**   Your SQL Server account is defined with a current database. The default database that
> you're directed to should be the one in which you work exclusively or more often. ■

If you don't enter the name of the owner of an object (such as a table) when you create a table, you'll be its owner. Often, tables are created from the system administrator's (sa) account, to restrict subsequent access to the tables.

The owner of the database in which the table is defined is automatically granted the CREATE TABLE permission, which allows the creation of tables. The database owner or the sa can grant CREATE TABLE permission to other users so that they can create tables in the database. You don't have to grant permission to create temporary tables in a database.

You can use ON *segment_name* to specify the segment on which the table is created. The segment must have already been created and assigned to a logical device. If you later create a non-clustered index for your table and don't specify a segment, the table and the non-clustered segment are placed in the default segment.

One use you might find for defining specific segments for a table is the separation of the table information and the clustered indexes that support it. You can optimize the system by placing the table on a specific segment that's different from its non-clustered indexes. If you specify the creation of a table and its non-clustered index on different segments, SQL Server can perform queries that use the index faster.

Queries that use a table's non-clustered index can be performed faster if both are located on different segments, and if the segments are on different logical devices located on different physical disks. Sets of information (such as an index and its associated table) that are stored on different physical disks can be accessed faster than a set stored on a single disk.

Data can be referenced faster because the underlying operating system and disk subsystems can perform a large part of the data transfer from two physical disks simultaneously. Sets of data located on a single physical disk must be accessed separately just due to physical layout of the disk drive.

 T I P You can obtain good performance with SQL Server databases without specifying multiple storage segments by using disk arrays that automatically spread data across multiple disks. For more information on this, investigate setting up striped disk sets at the operating system level. This capability is transparent to, and independent from, SQL Server.

Understanding Datatypes

The major part of defining a table is specifying the datatypes for the columns of the tables. Transact-SQL allows you to define several datatypes, including those for the storage of characters, numbers, and bit patterns. You can also define your own datatypes for use in stored procedures, tables, and other work that you'll be doing with the database tables.

You must define at least one column for a table, and you can define up to 250 columns. You're also limited to a maximum row length of 1,962 bytes.

T I P You can use image or text datatypes to get around the 1,962-byte limit for rows. Columns that are defined by using the image and text datatypes are stored outside the table and can store more than 2 billion bytes of data.

You should be careful to follow the rules for relational database design whenever feasible, however, to ensure the optimum response time and use of your SQL Server engine. For more information on database design, refer to Chapter 2, "Data Modeling and Database Design."

Tables are created by using a unit of measure called an *extent*. When you create a new table, the allocation of space for the table is initially set at one extent, which is eight pages, each of which is 2K in size. When the table fills the space in the already allocated extents, additional extents are automatically implemented up to the space allocated to the overall database size.

 T I P Use the system procedure `sp_spaceused` to obtain a report on the space allocated to a table or the graphical display in SQL Enterprise Manager. See Chapter 4, "Creating Devices, Databases, and Transaction Logs," for infomation on displaying allocated space.

Creating Temporary Tables

Creating a temporary table is a useful technique that you should take advantage of. You can create two types of temporary tables in SQL Server: local and global. A *local* temporary table is created if the first character of the table name is a pound sign (#). A local temporary table can be accessed only by the session in which it was created. A local temporary table is automatically dropped when the session in which it was created ends. You can't use more than 20 characters, including the pound sign, to name a local temporary table.

You create a temporary table that can be accessed by any session (each session can be created by a different user on a different client system) by defining a table with two pound signs (##) as the first two characters of the table name. A temporary table that's accessible from multiple sessions is called a *global temporary table* and is automatically dropped when the last session that's using it ends.

 T I P Constraints can be defined for temporary tables but foreign key constraints are not enforced.

You can use temporary tables to store sets of data that need to be operated on before permanently storing. For example, you can combine *the results of the data from multiple data sets* into a temporary table, and then access the combined data in the temporary table throughout your session. Data that has already been combined in a temporary table can be accessed faster than data that must be dynamically accessed from multiple tables. A temporary table that combines the results of two tables is faster to access because SQL Server doesn't need to reference the database tables to retrieve the information.

▶ **See** the section entitled "Performing Relational Joins" in Chapter 7. **p. 198**

N O T E Sessions are established differently depending on how you'll be accessing the server. A session is associated with a live connection to the database. For example, if you query a table and use a Dynaset type of dataset—that is, one that's active and updatable—the session will remain active. If you then connect to the database for another dataset inquiry, a separate and distinct session will be opened. Information in the temporary tables from the first session won't be available to the second session. ■

You might also find it convenient to use a temporary table to make a set of data available to a stored procedure that's invoked from another procedure. You'll find it easier to make data available to another procedure within a temporary table rather than pass data as a set of parameters.

▶ **See** Chapter 13, "Managing Stored Procedures and Using Flow-Control Statements."
p. 339

Selecting Datatypes

The *datatype* is the first characteristic you define for the column of a table. The datatype of a column controls the type of information that can be stored within the column. Define the datatype by following the column name with a keyword that may also require some parameters. After you define the datatype of a table column, it's stored as a permanent characteristic and can't be changed.

You can also use datatypes to define other data-storage structures, such as parameters and local variables. Parameters and local variables are storage structures defined in RAM rather than on disk. You're limited to a subset of the datatypes for the definitions of parameters and variables.

▶ **See** the Chapter 13 sections entitled "Using Parameters with Procedures," **p. 341**, and "Defining and Using Variables." **p. 358**

The next sections review each of the different system-defined datatypes that you can use in the definition of your SQL Server tables and stored procedures.

Part
II

Ch
5

Numeric *integer* Datatypes

Numeric integers are the first of several datatypes that you can use to define storage objects. Integer datatypes allow you to store whole numbers. You can directly perform arithmetic operations on integers without using functions. Numbers stored in integer datatypes always occupy the same amount of storage space, regardless of the number of digits within the allowable ranges for each of the integer datatype.

N O T E The name of a datatype, such as integer, is case-insensitive. ■

int or integer int (or integer) is the first of three integer datatypes. You can store negative and positive whole numbers within the range of –(2**31) to 2**31—approximately 4.3 billion numbers. The range is –2,147,483,648 to 2,147,483,647. Each value that's stored in an int datatype is stored in 4 bytes, using 31 bits for the size or magnitude and 1 bit for the sign.

> **N O T E** A set of two asterisks are used to denote exponentiation. The range of numbers for numeric digits are frequently referenced using a base number raised to a power because it allows the range to be specified precisely and compactly. ■

smallint smallint is the second integer datatype. You can store whole numbers within the range –32768 to +32767. Each value that's stored in a smallint datatype occupies 2 bytes and is stored as 15 bits for the magnitude and 1 bit for the sign.

tinyint You can store only whole positive numbers in a storage structure defined as tinyint within the range 0 to 255. Each value stored as a tinyint occupies one 1 byte.

The following example shows the creation of a table with three columns. The columns are defined as the int, smallint, and tinyint datatypes. A single row is inserted into the number_example table with values within the acceptable range for storage of each datatype. select is subsequently used to retrieve the row.

> **CAUTION**
>
> Database languages and programming languages have keywords. Keywords are the words that force an action to occur in an environment. To avoid confusion and error avoid using keywords when naming tables, columns, and so on.

```
create table number_example
(int1 int,int2 smallint,int3 tinyint)
insert into number_example
values (400000000,32767,255)
(1 row(s) affected)

select * from number_example
int1        int2    int3
---------- ------- ----
400000000   32767   255
(1 row(s) affected)
```

Enforcing Value Ranges Microsoft SQL Server automatically enforces the insertion of values within the range of each datatype. In the following two examples, values are inserted into columns that are defined as smallint and tinyint, although the values are outside the range of acceptable values.

The column values are specified in the values clause of the insert statement in the same order in which the columns were defined in the table. SQL Server returns an error message that describes the reason for the failed row insertion—the attempted insertion of a value is outside the allowable range for the datatype.

```
insert into number_example
values (1,32768,1)
Msg 220, Level 16, State 1
 Arithmetic overflow error for type smallint, value =  32768.
insert into number_example
values (1,1,256)
Msg 220, Level 16, State 2
 Arithmetic overflow error for type tinyint, value =  256.
```

T I P Use a `tinyint` or `smallint` to store integer values in one-quarter or one-half the storage space used for storing integer values in an `int` datatype. These are especially useful for use as flags, status indicators, and so forth.

Numeric *floating-point* Datatypes

Floating-point datatypes are the second group of several numeric datatypes you can use to define storage structures such as table columns. Unlike the `integer` datatypes, `floating-point` datatypes can store decimal numbers.

Unfortunately, the `floating-point` datatypes are subject to the rounding error. The storage of a value in a `numeric` datatype that's subject to the rounding error is accurate only to the number of digits of precision that's specified. For example, if the number of digits of precision is 15, a number that's larger than 15 digits can be stored, but the digits beyond 15 may inaccurately represent the initial number inserted into the storage. Also, the number may inaccurately return results of computations that involve `floating-point` datatypes. The rounding error affects a number's least-significant digits—the ones at the far right. You can accurately store numbers within the number of digits of precision available in `floating-point` datatype.

N O T E Microsoft calls datatypes such as the `floating-point` datatypes *approximate numeric datatypes* because values stored in them can be represented only within the limitations of the storage mechanism. You should avoid performing comparisons (such as in a WHERE clause) of data that's stored in approximate datatypes because a loaded value that's larger than the number of digits of precision is altered by the rounding effect during storage. ■

The *real* Datatype The first of the floating-point datatypes is `real`, which is stored in 4 bytes. You can store positive or negative decimal numbers in the `real` datatype, with up to seven digits of precision. You can store numbers in a column defined as `real` within the range of 3.4E–38 to 3.4E+38.

The range of values and representation is actually platform-dependent. Remember that Microsoft SQL Server evolved from the original Sybase SQL Server implementation. The REAL datatype stored on each of the several computer systems that a Sybase version was written for varied in the range of allowable characters and the actual representation of characters. For example, the range of decimal numbers stored by OpenVMS on Digital's VAX computers is 0.29E to 38 to 1.7E+38.

Part
II

Ch
5

The underlying operating system that Microsoft SQL Server runs on is supported on Intel, MIPS, PowerPC, and Alpha AXP systems. You should consider the previously stated value—the range of 3.4E–38 to 3.4E+38—as approximate and check the range of allowable numbers for the floating-point datatype that's stored in 4 bytes on your Windows NT system.

You should also realize that data stored in floating-point datatypes, which is moved between different NT platforms with different processor architectures, may require conversion to compensate for different representations and range of values.

float[(n)] Datatypes   The second of the floating-point datatypes is float, which is stored in 8 bytes if a value for *n* is omitted. You can store positive or negative decimal numbers in the float datatype with as many as 15 digits of precision. You can store numbers in a column defined as float within the range of 1.7E–308 to 1.7E+308.

If you specify a value for *n* within the range of 1 to 7, you're actually defining a real datatype. If you specify a value within the range of 8 to 15, the datatype has the identical characteristics as if *n* were omitted.

In the following example, a table is created with two columns defined as real and float. A single row is added with identical numbers that are subsequently added to each column of the table. The retrieval of the row from the table shows that the number stored in the real column was stored accurately to only 7 digits, the maximum number of digits of precision for a real datatype. The same 11-digit number was stored correctly in the column defined with the datatype float because float allows up to 15 digits to be stored accurately.

```
create table precision_example
(num1 real,num2 float)
insert into precision_example
values (4000000.1234,4000000.1234)
select * from precision_example
num1                   num2
------------------     ------------------
4000000.0              4000000.1234
(1 row(s) affected)
```

decimal[(p[, s])] and numeric[(p[, s])] Datatypes   You can use either the name decimal or numeric to select a datatype that, unlike float or real, allows the exact storage of decimal numbers. The scale and digits of precision is specified in the arguments *p* and *s*. You can store values within the range $10{**}38-1$ through $-10{**}38$ using 2 to 17 bytes for storage.

Use *p* to define the number of digits that can be stored to the left and right of the decimal point. Use *s* to define the number of digits to the right of the decimal point that must be equal to or less than the value of *p*. If you omit a value for *p*, it defaults to 18; the default of *s* is 0. Table 5.1 shows the number of bytes that are allocated for the specified precision (value of *p*).

Table 5.1   Number of Bytes Allocated for Decimal/Numeric Datatypes

Bytes Allocated	Precision
2	1–2
3	3–4

Bytes Allocated	Precision
4	5–7
5	8–9
6	10–12
7	13–14
8	15–16
9	17–19
10	20–21
11	22–24
12	25–26
13	27–28
14	29–31
15	32–33
16	34–36
17	37–38

The following example shows the storage and subsequent retrieval of a single row stored with the columns of a table defined as numeric/decimal datatypes. This example shows the default precision and scale and an explicit precision and scale being displayed.

```
create table definition_example
(num1 decimal,num2 numeric(7,6))
insert into definition_example
values (123456789123456789,1.123456)
select * from definition_example
num1                     num2
--------------------- ----------
123456789123456789      1.123456
(1 row(s) affected)
```

Part
II

Ch
5

N O T E The maximum precision permitted in the numeric/decimal datatypes is 28 unless you start SQL Server from the command line and change the precision. Use the command sqlservr with the option /p, which has the following syntax:

sqlservr [/dmaster_device_path][/pprecision_level]

For example, the following command starts SQL Server with a maximum precision of 38:

sqlservr /dg:\sql60\data\master.dat /p38.

If no value is specified after the precision qualifier /p, the precision for the numeric/decimal datatype is set to the maximum of 38. ■

Character Datatypes

You'll frequently use *character datatypes* to define table columns or other storage structures. Character datatypes allow the storage of a wider variety of symbols than numeric datatypes. Character datatypes enable you to store letters, numeric symbols, and special characters such as ? and >. You enter character data in either single or double quotation marks (' or ") when loading it into a storage area such as the column of a table.

char **Datatype**   char is the first type of character datatypes. When you store data in a char datatype, each symbol or character stored uses 1 byte. The number in parentheses specifies the size of storage for all sets of characters. For example, if you define a table column as the datatype char(15), each value of the column is 15 bytes in size and can store 15 characters. If you enter less than 15 characters, SQL Server adds blanks after the last specified character.

You can define a char(*n*) datatype to contain up to a maximum of 255 characters. Remember, the column value always contains the specified number of characters. SQL Server automatically adds spaces to the end of a char value to fill the defined length of space.

> **N O T E**   If a column is defined char and allowed to be null it will be treated as a varchar column. ■

> **N O T E**   Although the default installation of Windows NT uses the ASCII code to store character datatypes, you can install Windows NT so that UNICODE is used instead of ASCII. UNICODE stores character symbols in 16 bits (2 bytes) rather than ASCII's 1 byte. If Windows NT is defined to use UNICODE instead of ASCII, you must confirm the size of each character for character datatypes in applications such as Microsoft SQL Server. ■

varchar **Datatype**   You can use the varchar datatype to store a variable-length string of up to 255 characters. Unlike the char datatype, the storage space used varies according to the number of characters stored in each column value of rows of the table.

For example, if you define the table column as varchar(15), a maximum of 15 characters can be stored in the corresponding column of each table row. However, spaces aren't added to the end of the column value until the size of each column is 15 bytes. You can use a varchar to save space if the values stored in a column are variable in size. You can also specify a varchar datatype using the keyword char varying.

Using Character Datatypes   In the following examples, a table is created with two columns defined as char and varchar datatypes. The inserted row stores only two characters in each column of the row. The first column is padded with three spaces so that it occupies 5 bytes of storage. The second column of the row isn't padded and occupies only 2 bytes of storage to store the two characters. The retrieval of the row in the example displays each column value identically, masking the underlying storage difference.

```
create table string_example
(char1 char(5),char2 varchar(5))
insert into string_example
```

```
values ('AB','CD')
select * from string_example
char1 char2
---- ----
AB   CD
(1 row(s) affected)
```

In the following example, a row is inserted into the table that contains column values that are longer by one character than the maximum length of the datatypes of the table columns. The select statement in the example shows that the column values of the inserted row were truncated, or cut off, and contain only the first five characters of the column values. You don't receive a message that the truncation occurs when a row is inserted.

```
insert into string_example
values ('abcdef','abcdef')
select * from string_example
char1 char2
---- ----
AB    CD
abcde abcde
(2 row(s) affected)
```

 TIP Use the text datatype, which will allow the storage of more than 4 billion characters to store sets of characters that are longer than 255 characters.

TROUBLESHOOTING

Every time that I enter the name of a long department into the department column of a table, the department name is cut off at the end. Why? When a table column is defined using the char or varchar datatype, the maximum length is specified for all values that are later inserted into the column. SQL Server will automatically truncate (cut off) all characters that are longer than the maximum length that was defined. SQL Server doesn't notify you that's the truncation is being performed.

I've created several reports that I produce with code in my application. On some columns the values line up fine, but on others, they aren't lined up. What's causing the problem? When you use char datatypes, the fields are padded with extra spaces to fill the entire defined space for the column. These columns should appear fine on your report, depending on how you've read the values from SQL Server. If the extra spaces in the field are the problem, either use a trim statement in your query or store the data as a varchar.

Part
II

Ch
5

datetime and *smalldatetime* Datatypes

The datetime and smalldatetime datatypes store a combination of the date and time. You'll find it more convenient to store dates and times in one of the date and time datatypes rather than a datatype such a char or varchar. If you store data in one of these datatypes, you can easily display them because SQL Server automatically formats them in a familiar form. You can also use specialized date and time functions to manipulate values stored in this manner.

If you store date and time in char or varchar (or if you store time in numeric datatypes), date and time values aren't automatically formatted in conventional ways when they're displayed.

***datetime* Datatype**   datetime is the first type of date and time datatypes that you can use to define storage structures such as table columns. In the datetime datatype, you can store dates and times from 1/1/1753 AD to 12/31/9999 AD.

The total storage of a datetime datatype value is 8 bytes. SQL Server uses the first 4 bytes to store the number of days after or before the base date of January 1, 1900. Values that are stored as negative numbers represent dates before the base date; positive numbers represent dates since the base date. Time is stored in the second 4 bytes as the number of milliseconds after midnight.

N O T E   datetime values are stored to an accuracy of 1/300th of a second (3.33 milliseconds) with values rounded downward. For example, values of 1, 2, and 3 milliseconds are stored as zero milliseconds; the values of 4 through 6 milliseconds are stored as 3 milliseconds. ■

When you retrieve values stored in datetime, the default format for display is MMM DD YYYY hh:mmAM/PM—for example, Sep 23 1949 11:14PM. You must enclose datetime values in single quotation marks when they're used in an insert or other statement. You can enter either the date or time portion first, because SQL Server can recognize each portion and store the value correctly.

You can use upper- or lowercase characters for the date and one or more spaces between the month, day, and year when you enter datetime values. If you enter time without a date, the default date is January 1, 1900. If you enter the date without the time, the default time is 12:00AM. If you omit the date and the time, the default value entered is January 1, 1900 12:00 AM.

You can enter the date in several ways. Each is recognized and stored correctly by SQL Server. You can enter the date in an alphabetic format, using either an abbreviation for the month or the full name of the month. You can use or omit a comma between the day and year.

If you omit the century part of the year, decades that are less than 50 are represented as 20 and those that are 50 or more are entered as 19. For example, if you insert the year 49, the complete year stored is 2049. If you enter the year as 94, the complete year stored is 1994. You must explicitly enter the century if you want a century different from the default. You must supply the century if the day is omitted from the date value. When you enter a date without a day, the default entry is the first day of the month.

The set option dateformat isn't used if you specify the month of the year in alphabetic format. If you installed Microsoft SQL Server with the US_English Language option, the default order for the display of datetime values is month, day, and year. You can change the default order for the display of the date portion of a datetime value using the set dateformat command.

▶ **See** the section entitled "Understanding Query Options" in Chapter 16. **p. 436**

You can enter dates several ways, including the following examples:

- Sep 23 1949
- SEP 23 1949
- September 23 1949
- sep 1949 23
- 1949 sep 23
- 1949 23 sep
- 23 sep 1949

The numeric format for datetime values permits the use of slashes (/), hyphens (-), and periods (.) as separators between the different time units. When you use the numeric format with a datetime value, you must specify the month, day, and year of the date portion of the value.

In the numeric format, enter a separator between the month, day, and year entered in the order defined for dateformat. If you enter the values for a datetime datatype that's in the incorrect order, the month, day, or year will be misinterpreted and stored incorrectly. If you enter the information in the incorrect order, you may also receive an error message that tells you the date is out of range.

The following is an example of several entries for the numeric form of the date portion of a datetime datatype value with set dateformat defined as month, day, and year and the language as US_English:

- 6/24/71
- 06/24/71
- 6-24-1971
- 6.24.1971
- 06.24.71

The last of the possible formats for the date portion of a datetime datatype value is unseparated four-, six-, or eight-digit values or a time value without a date value portion. The dateformat controlled through set dateformat doesn't affect datetime datatype values referenced as the unseparated digit format.

If you enter a six- or eight-digit unseparated value, it's always interpreted in the order of year, month, and day. The month and day are always interpreted as two digits each. Four unseparated digit values are interpreted as the year, with the century and the month and day default to the first month and the first day of that month. Table 5.2 lists the possible interpretations of unseparated digit datetime datatype values:

Table 5.2   Interpretation of Unseparated Digit Dates for *datetime* Datatypes

Digits	Equivalent Representation in Alphabetic Format
710624	June 24, 1971
19710624	June 24, 1971
1971	January 1, 1971
71	Not valid
""	January 1, 1900 12:00AM

TROUBLESHOOTING

I omitted the entry of a value for a table column that was defined as the `datetime` datatype when I added a new row. When I subsequently displayed the new row, the entry for the column defined as `datetime` was January 1, 1900, and 12 midnight. When you inserted the new row, you must have used "" as a value for the `datetime` column, mistakenly thinking that it would result in a `null` entry. When two single quotation marks are used with no characters inserted between them as the value for either of the date and time datatypes, the entry January 1, 1900, and 12 midnight is always inserted by SQL Server.

You must enter the time with the time units in the following order: hours, minutes, seconds, and milliseconds. You must have a colon as a separator between multiple time units to allow a set of digits to be recognized as a time rather than a date value. You can use AM or PM, specified in upper- or lowercase, to specify before or after midnight.

You can precede milliseconds with a period or a colon, which affects the interpretation of the millisecond unit. A period followed by a single digit specifies tenths of a second; two digits are interpreted as hundredths of a second; three digits are interpreted as thousandths of a second. A colon specifies that the following digits will be interpreted as thousandths of a second. Table 5.3 shows several possible interpretations of the time portion of a `datetime` datatype value.

Table 5.3   *datetime* Datatype Values

Time	Interpretation
11:21	11 hours and 21 minutes after midnight
11:21:15:871	11 hours, 21 minutes, 15 seconds, and 871 thousandths of a second AM
11:21:15.8	11 hours, 21 minutes, 15 seconds, and eight tenths of a second AM
6am	Six AM
7 PM	Seven PM
05:21:15:500 AM	Five hours, 21 minutes, 15 seconds, and 500 milliseconds after midnight

smalldatetime smalldatetime is the second of the date and time datatypes you can use to define storage structures (such as table columns). In the smalldatetime datatype, you can store dates and times from 1/1/1900 AD to 6/6/2079 AD.

The total storage of a smalldatetime datatype value is 4 bytes. SQL Server uses 2 bytes to store the number of days after the base date of January 1, 1900. Time is stored in the other 2 bytes as the number of minutes after midnight. The accuracy of the smalldatetime datatype is 1 minute. You can use smalldatetime to store values that are within its more-limited range and lesser precision when compared to datetime.

TIP Use the smalldatetime datatype instead of the datetime datatype to store values in half the storage space.

In the following example, one column is defined by using the datetime datatype, and the second column is defined using the smalldatetime datatype. After the table is created, a minimum value is inserted into each column of a single row for the respective datatypes.

```
create table date_table
(date1 datetime,date2 smalldatetime)
insert into date_table
values ('Jan 1 1753','Jan 1 1900')
select * from date_table
date1                        date2
-------------------------- -------------------------
Jan 1 1753 12:00AM          Jan 1 1900 12:00AM
(1 row(s) affected)
```

In the following example, successive insert statements insert a date that's beyond both the range of the columns defined by using the smalldatetime and the range of datetime datatypes. An error is returned as a result of both insert statements.

```
insert into date_table
values ('May 19 1994', 'Jun 7 2079')
Msg 296, Level 16, State 3
```

In the preceding example, the conversion of char to smalldatetime resulted in a smalldatetime value out of range:

```
insert into date_table
values ('Jan 1 10000','May 19 1994')
Msg 241, Level 16, State 3
```

The example shows a syntax error converting datetime from a character string.

Specialized Datatypes

Transact-SQL contains a set of specialized datatypes for data storage. Most of the time you'll store data in more conventional datatypes such as integer, floating-point, and character. You can store dates and times in the datetime or smalldatetime datatypes.

Although you'll probably find that you can use the integer, floating-point, character, and date/time datatype formats for storing 90 percent of your data, in some cases you'll probably need a more custom solution.

Part
II

Ch
5

In these cases, you can use one or more of the specialized datatypes. For example, you may need to store only data that can be represented as true or false, yes or no. Since this is a binary condition, you may decide to create a custom datatype. As another example, you may need to store sets of data in a column that's larger than the 255-character limitation of the conventional character datatypes. Several additional datatypes are available to allow you to choose the best datatype for storing your information.

bit   You can use the `bit` datatype to store information that can be represented in only two states. A `bit` datatype is stored in a single bit; as a result, only two possible patterns can be stored—0 or 1. If you enter any other value than 0 or 1 in a data-storage structure such as a table column, 1 is stored. You can't define the `bit` datatype to allow `null` entries.

T I P   While it is not explicitly stated in the SQL Server documentation, the `bit` datatype corresponds to the boolean datatype in other DBMSes and programming languages.

You can also use a single byte to define up to eight different bit columns of a table by using the `bit` datatype. The amount of space allocated for one or more bits is a single byte, and the bit columns don't have to be contiguous. If you define nine columns of a table by using the `bit` datatype, 2 bytes are used for the total of nine `bit` datatypes.

N O T E   SQL Server stores information about columns defined using `bit` datatypes in the syscolumns system table by storing an offset to the bit column in the status column. You can't define an index that uses a column defined as a `bit` datatype. ■

timestamp   If you define a column of a table using the `timestamp` datatype, a counter value is automatically added to the `timestamp` column whenever you insert a new row or update an existing row. You can't explicitly enter a value into the column defined as a `timestamp`. A uniformly increasing counter value can be implicitly inserted only into a `timestamp` column by SQL Server.

The counter value inserted by SQL Server into a `timestamp` column specifies the sequence of operations that SQL Server has performed. Values entered into a `timestamp` column are stored in a `varbinary(8)` format, not a `datetime` or `smalldatetime` format. `Null` values are permitted in a `timestamp` column by default. A `timestamp` value isn't a date and time, but it's always unique within the table and database. You can define only a single column of a table as a `timestamp`.

N O T E   Timestamps are often used to ensure that a row can be uniquely identified. If you're updating columns in a row, it's a common practice to specify the timestamp field in the `where` clause of your `update` statement. This will make sure that you update only one row of the table. You can be assured of the uniqueness of the value because the server will maintain and update it any time you insert or update a row.

Timestamps are also used—again, as part of the `where` clause—to prevent two people from updating the same row. Because the timestamp is updated automatically whenever an update is made to the row, you can be sure that you're not going to overwrite someone else's information. If someone else updates a row that you're now working on, when they save their update, the row's timestamp will be *updated*, no longer matching your copy. When you issue the `update` command to save your changes, the `where` clause will fail because it can't find the specific row that you retrieved. Timestamps are excellent, server-maintained ways to make sure that you have a unique row identifier. ■

If you define a column with the column name timestamp and don't specify a datatype, the column is defined using the `timestamp` datatype. You can display the current `timestamp` value that's applied to the next timestamp column of a row that's updated or to a new row added using the global system variable `@@dbts`.

N O T E You can use a `select` statement to reference the global variable `@@dbts` by using the syntax:

`select @@dbts`

For example, the execution of this statement during the preparation of this chapter returned the following current `timestamp` value:

`0x01000000a3d2ae08` ■

binary(n) You can use the `binary` datatype to store bit patterns that consist of up to 255 bytes. Use the integer specified in parentheses to define the length of all bit patterns from 1 to 255 bytes. You must specify the size of a binary column to be at least 1 byte, but you can store a bit pattern of all zeros.

You must enter the first binary value preceded with `0x`. You can enter binary data using the characters 0 through 9 and A through F. For example, enter the value **A0** by preceding it with **0x**, in the form **0xA0**. If you enter values greater than the length that you defined, the values are truncated. Values are also padded with zeros after the least significant digit.

Here's another example. A column defined as `binary(1)` can store up to the maximum value of `ff`. In the following example, a table is defined with two columns with the datatypes `binary(1)` and `binary(2)`. Three `insert` statements are used to enter successive pairs of values of `0`, `1`, `ff`, and `fff` in both columns.

Part
II

Ch
5

```
create table binarytable
(x binary(1),y binary(2))
insert into binarytable
values (0x0,0x0)
insert into binarytable
values (0x1,0x1)
insert into binarytable
values (0xff,0xff)
insert into binarytable
values (0xfff,0xfff)
select * from binarytable
...
x     y
----  -------
0x00  0x0000
0x01  0x0100
```

```
0xff 0xff00
0x0f 0x0fff
(4 row(s) affected)
```

varbinary(n)   You can use the `varbinary` datatype to store bit patterns that consist of *up to 255 bytes*. You use the integer specified in parentheses to define the maximum length of all bit patterns from 1 to 255 bytes. You must specify the size of a binary column to be at least one byte, but you can store a bit pattern of all zeros.

Unlike the `binary` datatype, `varbinary` datatype storage is limited to just enough space for the length of the actual value. Like the `binary` datatype, you must enter the first binary value preceded with `0x`. You can enter binary data using the characters 0 through 9 and A through F. If you enter values that are greater than the maximum length you defined, the values are truncated.

In the following example, a table is defined with two columns with the `varbinary(1)` and `varbinary(2)` datatypes. Three `insert` statements are used to enter successive pairs of values of 0, 1, ff, and fff in both columns.

```
create table varbinarytable
(x varbinary(1),y varbinary(2))
insert into varbinarytable
values (0x0,0x0)
insert into varbinarytable
values (0x1,0x1)
insert into varbinarytable
values (0xff,0xff)
insert into varbinarytable
values (0xfff,0xfff)
select * from varbinarytable
...
x    y
---- ------
0x00 0x00
0x01 0x01
0xff 0xff
0x0f 0x0fff
```

Unlike the values entered into a table in which the columns are defined as binary(1) and binary(2), the values are stored in only the amount of space that's required. Values are truncated if they're greater than the maximum space defined when the table is created.

text and *image* Datatypes

Use `text` and `image` datatypes to store large amounts of character or binary data. You can store more than 2 billion data bytes in either a `text` or `image` datatype. It's wasteful to preallocate space for text or image datatypes to any significant extent, so only a portion of the space is preallocated. The remaining space is dynamically allocated.

N O T E   image datatypes are sometimes used for embedded OLE objects that are part of a row. ∎

text　Use a `text` datatype for storing large amounts of text. The characters stored in a text field are typically characters that can be output directly to a display device such as a monitor window or a printer. You can store from 1 to 2,147,483,647 bytes of data in a `text` datatype.

N O T E　You can store an entire resumé in a single column value of a table row. ∎

Your data is stored in fixed-length strings of characters in an initially allocated 2K (2,048 bytes) unit. Additional 2K units are dynamically added and are linked together. The 2K data pages are logically—but not necessarily physically—contiguous. If you use an `insert` statement to insert data into a column defined as `text`, you must enclose the data within single quotation marks.

T I P　If you define a column using the `text` datatype and permit `nulls`, using an insert statement to place a `null` value in the column doesn't allocate even a single 2K page, which saves space. However, any `update` statement will allocate at least one 2K page for the text column regardless of any value that may or may not be supplied for that column.

image　You can use the `image` datatype to store large bit patterns from 1 to 2,147,483,647 bytes in length. For example, you can store employee photos, pictures for a catalog, or drawings in a single column value of a table row. Typically, the data stored in an image column isn't directly entered with an `insert` statement.

Your data is stored in fixed-length byte strings in an initially allocated 2K (2,048 bytes) units. Additional 2K units are dynamically added and are linked together like the pages for a text column. The 2K data pages are logically—but not necessarily physically—contiguous.

Using *text* and *image* Datatypes　Values that are stored as either `text` or *image* datatypes are displayed just as other columns are when you use a `select` statement. The number of bytes displayed is limited by the global value `@@Textsize`, which has a default value of 4K. You can specify the `null` characteristic for `text` or `image` columns. A `null` for a `text` or `image` column of a table doesn't allocate any 2K pages of storage, unless an `update` is performed on a row containing the `null` value.

In the following example, two table columns are defined using `image` and `text`. Values are inserted into each column of a single row using an `insert` statement. The row is then retrieved from the table with a `select` statement.

```
create table imagetext_table
(image1 image,text1 text)
insert into imagetext_table
values ('123456789aczx+=\','12345678aczx+=')
select * from imagetext_table
image1                              text1
-------------------------------------------------------
0x313233343536373839961637a782b3d5c   12345678aczx+=

 (1 row(s) affected)
```

Part
II

Ch
5

Data in a column defined as an image datatype isn't translated from its ASCII representation automatically when it's displayed with a select statement. Data stored in a column defined as the text datatype is automatically translated to ASCII characters when the data is output with a select statement. An image column isn't meant to be direct output. It can be passed on to another program, perhaps running on a client system that processes the data before it's displayed.

Restrictions on *text* and *image* Columns   You'll encounter several restrictions on the use of data stored in text and image datatypes. You can define only table columns using the text or image datatypes. You can't define other storage structures (such as local variables or parameters) as text or image datatypes.

The amount of data that can be stored in a text or image table column makes each datatype unsuitable for use or manipulation in many Transact-SQL statements. This is simply because the amount of data that would have to be manipulated is too great. You can't specify a table column in an ORDER BY, GROUP BY, or compute clause that's a text or image datatype. SQL Server won't try to sort or group a table's rows using a column that can contain more than 4 billion bytes of data because too much data would have to be moved around and too large a space would have to be allocated in which to order the rows.

You also can't use a text or image column in a union unless it's a union all. You can't use a subquery that returns data values from a text or image datatype. You also can't use a text or image column in a where or having clause, unless the comparison operator like is used. You can't specify distinct followed by a table column that's defined as a text or image datatype.

Finally, you can't create an index or a primary or foreign key that's defined using a table column that you've defined as an image or text datatype.

money Datatype

The money datatype stores monetary values. Data values stored in the money datatype are stored as an integer portion and a decimal-fraction portion in two 4-byte integers. The range of values that you can store in the money datatype is from –922,337,203,685,477.5808 to 922,337,203,685,477.5807. The accuracy of a value stored in the money datatype is to the ten-thousandth of a monetary unit. Some front-end tools display values stored in the money datatype rounded to the nearest cent.

smallmoney Datatype

The smallmoney datatype stores a range of monetary values that's more limited than the money datatype. The values you can store in the smallmoney datatype ranges from –214,748.3648 to 214,748.3647. Data values stored in the smallmoney datatype are stored as an integer portion and a decimal-fraction portion in 4 bytes. Like values stored in a table column defined by using the money datatype, some front-end tools display values stored in the smallmoney datatype rounded to the nearest cent.

T I P You can store your monetary values in half the storage space if you choose the smallmoney rather than the money datatype.

When you add values to a table column defined as money or smallmoney, you must precede the most-significant digit with a dollar sign ($) or a sign of the defined monetary unit.

In the following example, a table is created with two columns that are defined using the money and smallmoney datatypes. In the first insert statements, values are incorrectly added because they aren't preceded with a dollar sign. A select statement shows that the values displayed are identical to those that were stored.

```
create table monetary_table
(money1 money,money2 smallmoney)
insert into monetary_table
values (16051.3455,16051.3455)
select * from monetary_table
money1                    money2
------------------------- -------------------------
16,051.35                 16,051.35
(1 row(s) affected)
```

In a continuation of the same example, a three-digit monetary value is added to both table columns, followed by a value that's outside the storage bounds for the datatype on the computer architecture.

```
insert into monetary_table
values ($123,$123)
insert into monetary_table
values (922337203685477,214748.3647)
Msg 168, Level 15, State 1
```

The integer value 922337203685477 is out of the range of machine representation, which is 4 bytes.

A large monetary value, which is defined as a money datatype, is added to the first column. It's incorrectly entered because it isn't preceded by a dollar sign ($). The select statements show that the number is stored incorrectly. If you enter a value into a table column that's defined as money or smallmoney, it's stored as a floating-point datatype, which makes it subject to the rounding error.

```
insert into monetary_table
values (922337203685476.,0)
money1                    money2
------------------------- --------
16,051.35                 16,051.35
123.00                    123.00
922,337,203,685,475.98    0.00
```

In the following example, the same large number that was previously entered without a dollar sign has been correctly entered with the dollar sign. A subsequent select statement shows that the large monetary value was correctly stored.

```
insert into monetary_table
values ($922337203685476.,0)
select * from monetary_table
money1                          money2
-------------------------- --------
16,051.35                       16,051.35
123.00                          123.00
922,337,203,685,475.98          0.00
922,337,203,685,476.00          0.00
```

Added to the table are values that contain four digits to the right of the decimal place. When the values are subsequently displayed with a select statement, the values are displayed to two decimal places, the nearest cent.

```
insert into monetary_table
values ($922337203685477.5807,$214748.3647)
select * from monetary_table
money1                          money2
-------------------------- --------
16,051.35                       16,051.35
123.00                          123.00
922,337,203,685,475.98          0.00
922,337,203,685,476.00          0.00
922,337,203,685,477.58          214,748.36
```

sysname Datatype

The sysname datatype is a user-defined datatype that's defined as varchar(30) and doesn't allow nulls. sysname is used for defining columns in system tables. You shouldn't use sysname to define the datatype of columns in your tables. You can use varchar(30), or you can define your own user-defined datatypes. See the section entitled "Creating User-defined Datatypes" later in this chapter.

Understanding *null* and *not null*

Now that you've learned about the additional datatypes that can be defined for Transact-SQL storage structures such as columns, parameters, and local variables, you should understand a second characteristic that you can define. In addition to specifying the datatype of a table column, you can specify an additional characteristic for each datatype: null or not null.

The null characteristic for a table column allows you to omit the entry of a column value in the column. If you define the characteristic for a column as not null, Microsoft SQL Server won't allow you to omit a value for the column when you insert a row. The null characteristic provides a type of validation.

The default characteristic for a column is not null, which doesn't allow an undefined column value. A null that's defined for a column is stored differently than a space, a zero, or a null ASCII character (which is all zeros). The interpretation of a null entry is undefined or unavailable because no explicit or implicit value is assigned to the column when a row is inserted.

If you reference a row that contains a `null`, the entry `(null)` is displayed in place of a column value to indicate that there's no entry in the row for that column.

There are two ways to designate that a column or storage structure contains a `null`:

- If no data is entered in the row for that column and there's no default value for the column or datatype, a `null` is entered automatically. You can define a default value that's inserted automatically into the table column when a column value is omitted. A default value can be added in place of a `null`.

- You can enter a `null` explicitly by using `null` or `null` without quotation marks when a row is inserted into the table. If you enter `null` within quotation marks, it's stored as a literal string rather than a `null`.

In the following example, a table is created that permits a `null` entry for numeric `integer` datatypes and character datatypes. A `null` is explicitly inserted into both columns of a single row in the table. In the following example, a `select` statement displays `(null)` for both column values of the row.

```
create table nulltable
(x int null, y char(10) null)
insert into nulltable
values (null,null)
select * from nulltable
x           y            1
---------- ----------
(null)      (null)
(1 row(s) affected)
```

> **N O T E** You can specify the keyword `null` in lower- or uppercase when you specify a `null` entry for the column of a row. The default display of a column that "contains" a `null` entry is "`(null)`." ■

To continue the example, `null` is entered in the second column (y) because only the x column precedes the `values` clause. A `null` value is added to the second column y implicitly because no value is specified in the list port (values within parentheses separated by a comma) of the `values` clause.

```
insert into nulltable
(x)
values (5)
select * from nulltable
x            y
------------------------
5            (null)
(2 row(s) affected)
```

ANSI Support for *null*s

You can change the behavior of SQL Server to automatically permit `null`s on table columns (or user-defined datatypes) if no reference to the `null` characteristic is specified when a column

Part

II

Ch

5

(or user-defined datatype) is defined. You can use a `set` command to change the `null` characteristic for columns or user-defined datatypes defined during a client session. You can also change the `null` characteristic for an entire database using the system procedure `sp_dboption`.

Use the following `set` command to cause `nulls` to be permitted automatically in table columns or user-defined datatypes:

```
SET ANSI_null_DFLT_ON
```

Use the following `sp_dboption` command to cause `nulls` to be permitted automatically in table columns or user-defined datatypes:

```
sp_dboption database-name, 'ANSI null default', true
```

ANSI nullability permits SQL Server not only to conform to a standard form of SQL but to be tailored to match the SQL dialect of other SQL used with other server databases. You can more easily use Microsoft SQL Server if you can modify the syntax and behavior of Transact-SQL to match a dialect of SQL that you've used previously. For example, if you change the default nullability of Microsoft SQL Server by defining the `sp_dboption` option as true, it automatically permits `nulls` in column definitions, like in Gupta's SQLBase database.

N O T E If you've changed the `null` characteristic during a session or for a database, you can set it back to the default by using the commands

```
SET ANSI_null_DFLT_OFF
```

or

```
sp_dboption database-name, 'ANSI null default', false ■
```

null **Manipulation**

When you compare a `null` value to any non-`null` value of a column or other data-storage structure, the result is never logically true. If you compare a `null` value to another `null` value, the result is also never a logical true. `null` values don't match each other because unknown or undefined values aren't assumed to be identical.

However, rows that contain multiple `null` values in a column referenced in an ORDER BY, GROUP BY, or DISTINCT clause of a `select` statement are treated as identical values. All three clauses group together rows with identical values. ORDER BY is used to sort rows, and, in the case of `nulls`, all entries in the same column are sorted together. Columns containing `nulls` appear at the beginning of a sequence of rows that are sorted in ascending order.

GROUP BY forms groups using identical values, and all `nulls` of a column are placed in a single group. The `distinct` keyword used in a `select` clause removes all duplicates from one or more column values and removes multiple `null` values as well. Columns that contain `nulls` are considered to be equal when you define an index that uses a `null` column.

▶ **See** the sections in Chapter 6 entitled "Using an *ORDER BY* Clause," **p. 168** "Using a *GROUP BY* Clause," **p. 176** and "Using *DISTINCT* to Retrieve Unique Column Values." **p. 171**

If you perform computations with columns or other data structures that contain `null`s, the computations evaluate to `null`. In the following example, the evaluation of the expression `x=x+1` evaluates to `null` because the x column contains only a single row with a `null` defined for the x column:

```
select * from nulltable
where x=x+1
x          y
---------- ----------
(0 row(s) affected)
```

The following example returns an error because a column defined as `not null` is compared with a `null` expression:

```
select * from employees
where badge=null
Msg 221, Level 16, State 1
```

A column of the datatype `integer` doesn't allow `null`s. It may not be compared with `null`.

Using *ISNULL()*

`ISNULL()` is a system function that returns a string of characters or numbers in place of `(null)` when a `null` is encountered in a data-storage structure such as a table column. The syntax of the function is as follows:

```
ISNULL(expression,value)
```

The expression is usually a column name that contains a `null` value. The value specifies a string or number to be displayed when a `null` is found. In the following example, `ISNULL()` is used to return a number when a `null` is encountered in the value of a row, or return the character string `'NO ENTRY'` when a `null` is encountered.

```
select x,ISNULL(x,531),y, ISNULL(y, 'NO ENTRY')
from nulltable
x                          y
---------- ---------- ---------- ----------
(null)        531      (null)      NO ENTRY
(1 row(s) affected)
```

N O T E You may decide that it's easier to avoid using `null` rather than deal with the intricacies of working with `null`s. You can decide to use a specific pattern that's entered for a datatype that has the meaning of no entry or undefined, rather than `null`. ■

Part

II

Ch

5

identity Property

In addition to defining the datatype of a column to allow or disallow `null`s, you can define a column with the property of `identity`. When you define a column with the property `identity`, you can specify both an initial value (seed) that's automatically added in the column for the first row, and a value (increment) that's added to that last value entered for the column. When you add rows to the table, you omit entering a value for the column defined with the `identity` property. The value for the identity column is automatically entered by adding the increment value to the column value of the last row.

In the following example, the second column is defined with the property `identity`. After two rows are added to the table, a subsequent retrieval of the table rows shows that the identity column values were generated by the `identity` mechanism.

```
create table identity_table
(name char(15),row_number integer identity(1,1))
insert into identity_table
(name)
values ('Bob Smith')
insert into identity_table
(name)
values ('Mary Jones')
select * from identity_table
name            row_number
-------------- ----------
Bob Smith       1
Mary Jones      2

(2 row(s) affected)
```

You can assign the `identity` property only to a column that's defined with the datatypes `int`, `smallint`, `tinyint`, `decimal(p,0)`, and `numeric(p,0)`—but not if the column permits `nulls`. If you omit a seed and increment value when specifying the `identity` property on a table column, they default to 1. Also, only a single column of a table can be defined with the property `identity`. The `identity` property doesn't guarantee that rows were be unique. You must establish a unique index on the identity column to guarantee unique table rows.

 TIP You can use the keyword `identitycol`, as well as the name of the column, to reference the column of a table that's defined with the property identity.

Creating and Using Constraints

Constraints are defined to provide data integrity on a table and individual columns. The `create table` statement allows you to create primary and foreign keys, define unique column and rows, and specify check and default constraints.

PRIMARY KEY Constraints

You use PRIMARY KEY constraints for column integrity as well as referential integrity. The definition of a PRIMARY KEY constraint for a table has several effects. The PRIMARY KEY constraint ensures that all rows of a table are unique by ensuring that one or more columns don't permit duplicate values to be entered. A PRIMARY KEY constraint also disallows `null` for the column(s) that the constraint is defined on. A PRIMARY KEY constraint also creates a unique index on the column(s) defined in the constraint. A secondary effect is that the index can be used for faster retrieval of rows of the table than if no index were defined on the table.

The definition of a PRIMARY KEY constraint on a single table doesn't by itself permit referential integrity. You must also define corresponding foreign keys in the tables whose rows will be combined with the table in which you define the PRIMARY KEY constraint. ■

The syntax of the PRIMARY KEY constraint is as follows:

```
CONSTRAINT constraint_name PRIMARY KEY CLUSTERED (column_name_1 column_name_n)
```

In the following example, the employees table has a PRIMARY KEY constraint defined on the badge column.

```
Create table employees4
(name char(20),department varchar(20),badge integer,
constraint badge_pays2 foreign key (badge) references employees4 (badge))
```

FOREIGN KEY constraint

A FOREIGN KEY constraint is used along with a previously defined PRIMARY KEY constraint on an associated table. A FOREIGN KEY constraint associates one or more columns of a table with an identical set of columns that have been defined as a PRIMARY KEY constraint in another table. When the column values are updated in the table in which the PRIMARY KEY constraint is defined, the columns defined in another table as a FOREIGN KEY constraint are automatically updated.

The PRIMARY KEY and FOREIGN KEY constraints ensure that corresponding rows of associated tables continue to match so that they can be used in subsequent relational joins. The automatic updating of the corresponding columns of different tables after they're defined as PRIMARY KEY and FOREIGN KEY constraints is called *declarative referential integrity*, a feature added to SQL Server in version 6.0.

The syntax of the FOREIGN KEY constraint clause is as follows:

```
CONSTRAINT constraint_name FOREIGN KEY (column_name_1 column_name_n) REFERENCES
_table_name (column_name_1 column_name_n)
```

The table named after the keyword REFERENCES is the table in which the corresponding column(s) are defined as a PRIMARY KEY constraint. In the following example, the badge column in the pays2 table is defined as a FOREIGN KEY constraint that is associated (references) with the badge column in the employees4 table.

```
Create table pays
(hours_worked integer, pay_rate integer,badge integer,
constraint badge_pays2 foreign key (badge) references employees4 (badge))
```

The corresponding columns that are defined as PRIMARY KEY and FOREIGN KEY constraints don't have to have the same names. However, it's simpler to understand the columns in different tables that are defined as associated PRIMARY KEY and FOREIGN KEY constraints if their names are identical. ■

Part
II

Ch
5

unique Constraint

You apply the unique constraint to any table column to prevent duplicate values from being entered into the column. A restriction is that the column can't be defined as the primary key or part of the primary key of the table. The unique constraint is enforced through the automatic creation of a unique index for the table that's based on the column. In the following example, a unique constraint is applied to the badge column of the employees2 table.

```
Create table employees2
(name char(20), department varchar(20),badge integer,
constraint badge_nodupes unique nonclustered (badge))
```

check Constraint

A check constraint limits the values that can be entered into one or more columns of a database table. You can use a check constraint, for example, to limit the range of values that can be stored in a column defined as a numeric datatypes that's smaller than the range permitted by the datatype.

The process of associating a check with a table column is called *binding*. You can define and associate multiple checks with a single column. A check can be defined for a column, even though a rule is already defined on the column. In the following example, a check constraint is defined on the column department to restrict subsequent entries to valid departments.

```
Create table employees5
(name char(20), department varchar(20),badge integer
check valid_department (department in
➡ ('Sales','Field Service','Software','Logistics')))
```

> **N O T E**   check and other constraints can seem as though they duplicate the function of other mechanisms that exist in SQL Server. If you've had this perception, it's accurate. In version 6.0 of SQL Server, Microsoft changed its version of SQL, Transact-SQL, to conform to a standardized form of SQL, ANSI SQL. Although Transact-SQL already had existing ways of performing some operations, such as rules and defaults, the addition of ANSI SQL syntax to Transact-SQL added alternate ways of performing the same operation.
>
> You can often choose to implement a feature such as a restriction on the values that can be entered into a column in the way that you feel is the easiest to set up. For example, you can choose to restrict the values entered into the columns of a table by using a check constraint rather than by defining a rule and binding it to the column.
>
> However, you should investigate each alternate mechanism, because one may be more appropriate for your use. Although a check constraint is quicker and simpler to set up to restrict the column values than a rule, a rule is more flexible in one way. After you define a rule, it can be bound to a column in multiple tables. A rule may prove more useful to you if you're going to use it to restrict column values on columns that are in multiple tables. ■

default Constraint

You use a `default` constraint to have a value that's automatically added to a table column when no value is entered during an insert. You can define a `default` constraint to the most frequent value that occurs within a table column, thus relieving a user of entering the defined `default` constraint value when a new row is added to the table. The syntax of the `default` constraint clause is as follows:

```
DEFAULT default_name value FOR column_name
```

In the following example, a default value is specified for the department column for the `employees6` table:

```
Create table employees6
(name char(20),department varchar(20),badge integer,
DEFAULT department_default 'Sales' for department)
```

You can also use a `default`, which you must define and then bind to a table column, to have a value automatically added to a table column. Although Microsoft recommends that you use a `default` constraint to add a value automatically to a table column, after a default is defined, it can be bound to columns in different tables, rather than in a single table.

▶ **See** Chapter 11, "Managing and Using Rules and Defaults." **p. 301**

Microsoft recommends that you use a `default` constraint rather than a `default` when you've defining a default value for a column in a single table because a `default` constraint is stored with the table, rather than as a separate database object. If you drop a table, the constraint is automatically dropped. When a table is deleted, a default bound to a column of the table isn't deleted.

N O T E   With a default constraint, you can use a set of functions called *niladic functions*. A niladic function inserts a value that's generated by SQL Server.

Niladic functions allow a system-supplied value that's information about the current user or a `timestamp` to be inserted when no value is specified. The ANSI niladic functions that can be used with a `default` constraint are `current_user()`, `session_user()`, `system_user()`, `user()`, and `current_timestamp()`. `current_user()`, `session_user()`, and `user()` return the user name stored in the database of the user issuing an insert or update. The `system_user()` function returns the SQL Server logon ID of the user, and the `current_timestamp()` function returns the date in the same form that's returned by the `getdate()` function. ■

Part

II

Ch

5

Creating User-Defined Datatypes

You can define your own datatype, which can then be used as a datatype for a storage structure such as a table column. You always define a user-defined datatype as one of the existing system datatypes. A user-defined datatype allows you to define a datatype that can contain a length specification, if necessary, and a `null` characteristic.

You can use a descriptive name for the user-defined datatype that describes the type of data that it contains.

Creating User-Defined Datatypes with *sp_addtype*   You can define a user-defined datatype with the system procedure sp_addtype, which uses the following syntax:

```
sp_addtype user_defined_datatype_name, system_datatype, null ¦ null
```

After you define a user-defined datatype, you can use it to specify the datatype of a storage structure such as a table column. You can use the system procedure sp_help to display a user-defined datatype. You can create and then bind defaults and rules to user-defined datatypes. You bind rules and defaults to user-defined datatypes with the same procedures used for system datatypes sp_bindefault and sp_bindrule.

An error message is generated if you specify not null for a column and don't create a default, or specify a value at insertion. You can also change the null or not null characteristic for a user-defined datatype when you define a column in a table.

In the following example, a user-defined datatype is created by using sp_addtype. The characteristics are displayed with sp_help. A new table is created in which the column is defined using the user-defined datatype.

```
sp_addtype names, 'char(15)', null
Type added.
sp_help names
Type_name       Storage_type     Length Nulls Default_name    Rule_name
-----------     --------------   ------ ---- -------------- --------

names           char             15     1    (null)         (null)
create table usertype_table
(charstring names)
```

In the following example, a value is inserted into the table and subsequently retrieved. The insertion of the string resulted in a truncation of the inserted string to 15 characters. The example also displays the table in which a column is defined by using a user-defined datatype.

```
insert into usertype_table
values ('this is a string')
select * from usertype_table
charstring
--------------
this is a strin
(1 row(s) affected)
sp_help usertype_table
Name                                Owner                             Type
--------------------------------    ----------------------------- -----------

usertype_table                      dbo                               user table
Data_located_on_segment             When_created
--------------------------------    -----------------------------

default                             May 19 1994 12:46PM
Column_name     Type             Length Nulls Default_name    Rule_name
--------------  -------------   ------ ---- -------------- -----------

charstring      names            15     1    (null)         (null)
Object does not have any indexes.
No defined keys for this object.
```

Creating User-Defined Datatypes with the Enterprise Manager   To define a user-defined datatype by using the Enterprise Manager, follow these steps:

1. Expand the databases by clicking on the plus (+) box next to the Databases folder. Click a database to select it. Your user-defined datatype will be created in the selected database.

2. Choose User Defined Datatypes from the Manage menu.

3. Enter a name in the New Name field of the Manage User-Defined Datatypes dialog box.

4. Enter a system datatype in the Datatype field. Enter a length for the datatype in the Length field if you choose a datatype such as char or varchar. You can also decide to allow nulls, apply a previously defined rule or default value to the user-defined datatype, or specifiy an owner.

5. Click OK to complete the creation process.

FIG. 5.1

You can list the user-defined datatypes from the Manage User-Defined Datatypes dialog box.

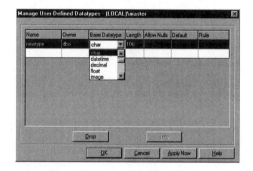

Dropping User-Defined Datatypes   You can use the system procedure sp_droptype to remove a user-defined datatype. The procedure uses the following syntax:

```
sp_droptype typename
```

You can't drop a user-defined datatype if one or more tables have a column that's defined using it. You can drop the user-defined datatype only if it isn't in use by any tables. In the following example, a user-defined datatype can't be dropped until you first drop the sole table in which a column is defined using the user-defined datatype.

```
sp_droptype names
Type is being used. You cannot drop it.
object                   type owner            column               datatype
--------------------     ---- ---------------  -------------------  --------
usertype_table           U    dbo              charstring           names
(1 row(s) affected)
drop table usertype_table
```

This command didn't return any data or rows:

```
sp_droptype names
Type has been dropped.
```

Part

II

Ch

5

You can also drop a user-defined datatype through the Enterprise Manager. To do so, follow these steps:

1. Expand the databases by clicking on the plus (+) box next to the Databases folder. Click a database to select it. Your user-defined datatype will be created in the selected database.

2. Choose User Defined Datatypes from the Manage menu.

3. Select the user-defined datatype.

4. Click Drop.

Working with Datatypes

You can't name objects with names of commands or other reserved works because datatypes are objects in the database. Datatypes are stored in the Systypes system table along with their coded values. You can use the following `select` statement to display the datatypes and their code value in the type column:

```
select name,type
from systypes
order by type
name                    type
----------------------- ----
image                   34
text                    35
timestamp               37
varbinary               37
intn                    38
sysname                 39
varchar                 39
binary                  45
char                    47
badge_type              47
tinyint                 48
bit                     50
smallint                52
int                     56
badge_type2             56
smalldatetime           58
real                    59
money                   60
datetime                61
float                   62
floatn                  109
moneyn                  110
datetimn                111
smallmoney              122
(24 row(s) affected)
```

You can use `sp_helpsql` to display information about the characteristics of system datatypes, as shown in the following example:

```
sp_helpsql 'datatype'
helptext
----------------------------------------------------------------
Datatype
Datatype                   Definition

Binary(n)                  Fixed-length binary data. Maximum
                           length=255 bytes.
Bit                        A column that holds either 0 or 1.
Char(n)                    Character data. Maximum length=255
                           bytes.
Datetime                   Dates and times with accuracy to milliseconds.
Float                      Floating-point numbers.
Image                      Large amounts of binary data (up to
                           2,147,483,647 characters.)
Int                        Integers between 2,147,483,647 and
                           -2,147,483,648.
Money                      Dollar and cent values.
Real                       Floating point numbers with 7-digit precision.
Smalldatetime              Dates and times with accuracy to the minute.
Smallint                   Integers between 32,767 and -32,768.
Smallmoney                 Monetary values between 214,748.3647 and
                           -214,748.3648.
Text                       Large amounts of character data (up to
                           2,147,483,647 characters.)
Timestamp                  Automatically updated when you
                           insert or update a row that has a timestamp
                           column, or use BROWSE mode in a
                           DB-LIBRARY application.
Tinyint                    Whole integers between 0 and 255.
Varbinary(n)               Variable-length binary data. Max
                           length=255 bytes.
Varchar(n)                 Variable-length character data. Max
                           length=255 bytes.
```

Creating Tables and Defining Columns Through the Enterprise Manager

In addition to creating a table with the create table statement, you can create a table through the Enterprise Manager. To do so, follow these steps:

▶ **See** the Chapter 1 section entitled "SQL Enterprise Manager." **p. 27**

1. Expand the databases by clicking on the plus (+) box next to the Databases folder. Click a database to select it. Your table will be created in the selected database.

2. Choose Tables from the Manage menu.

3. Enter a column name in the Column Name field.

4. Use the mouse or Tab key to move to the Datatype field. Select a datatype from the list that appears.

Part
II

Ch
5

5. If the datatype that you've chosen requires the specification of a length, enter it into the Length field.

6. To allow `null` values, leave the Nulls field selected.

7. If you've previously defined default values, you can choose one in the Default field.

8. Repeat steps 3 through 7 to continue specifying up to 250 columns and their characteristics. Figure 5.2 shows the Manage Tables window after information for three columns is entered.

FIG. 5.2

The `null` property is automatically enabled for each column that you enter, though you can uncheck it.

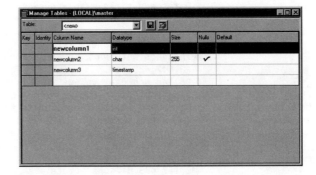

9. Click the Save Table button on the Manage Tables toolbar to bring up the Specify Table Name dialog box.

10. Enter a name for the new table in the Specify Table Name dialog box (see fig. 5.3).

FIG. 5.3

Name the table to complete the operation.

11. Click OK. The new table appears as the selected table in the Manage Tables window.

You also can define properties on columns such as an `identity`, `primary key`, or `constraint` by clicking the Advanced Features tool on the toolbar of the Manage Tables window while you're defining the table. For example, in Figure 5.4, a column has been defined as an identity column in the Identity Column combo box of the Manage Tables window after the Advanced Features tool is clicked.

FIG. 5.4

You can specify an initial value (seed) and increment for your identity column.

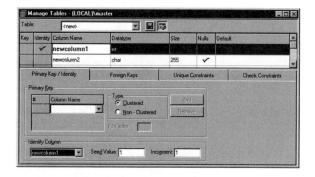

Adding Data to a Table with *insert*

After you create a table, you can add data by using an `insert` statement. Several forms of the `insert` statement can be used to add new rows to a table. Each `insert` statement can add only a single row to a table. The complete form of the `insert` statement uses the following syntax:

```
insert INTO table_name
(column_name_1,...,column_name_n)
VALUES ('string_1',...'lstring_')
```

List the table columns to receive values separately, enclosed by parentheses and separated by commas, after the `insert` clause. Enter the values that will be added to the table columns in parentheses in the same order as the column names in the previous line. The list of column values is preceded by the VALUES keyword.

You don't have to list the columns and their values in the same order as they were defined in the table. You must, however, enter the values in the VALUES clause in the correct order as the column names listed in the previous line; otherwise, data values may be inserted into the wrong columns.

In the following example, the columns are listed in the order in which they were defined in the table—but they don't have to follow the same order. The values are entered in the VALUES clause in an order that corresponds to the order of the columns named in the previous line.

```
insert into employees
(name, department, badge)
values ('Bob Smith', 'SALES', 1834)
```

If you omit one or more column names, a `null` or default value is entered into the table row. In the following example, the name and badge columns are listed in the `insert` statement. The `values` clause omits a value for the department.

```
insert into employees
(name, badge)
values ('Bob Mariah', 1999)
```

Part

II

Ch

5

Table 5.4 shows the resulting entry for a table if an explicit value isn't listed in the values list of an insert statement.

Table 5.4   Effect of *null* and Default Values on Table Column Entries

Column Characteristic(s)	User Entry	Resulting Entry
null defined	No default value defined	null
not null defined	No default value defined	Error, no row inserted
null defined	Default value defined	Default value
not null defined	Default value entered	Default value

N O T E Use (null) within the values list to insert a null into a column that has been defined to permit the null. ■

From Here...

In this chapter you've learned to create database tables. The process of creating a table involves the selection of the appropriate datatypes for your table columns. In addition, you've learned to add the additional characteristics that can be defined for a table column including the null characteristic and the various constraints. You learned to create, drop, and list the characteritics of a table using Transact-SQL syntax and the Enterprise Manager.

For further discussion about topics mentioned in this chapter, see the following chapters:

■ Chapter 6, "Retrieving Data with Transact-SQL," teaches you how to use Transact-SQL syntax to retrieve the data that you've stored in table columns.

■ Chapter 10, "Managing and Using Indexes and Keys," teaches you how to create and use keys and indexes and how to constrain rows and columns to unique values.

■ Chapter 11, "Managing and Using Rules and Defaults," teaches you how to create and bind rules and defaults to user-defined datatypes and table columns.

■ Chapter 13, "Managing Stored Procedures and Using Flow-Control Statements," teaches you how to define storage structures such as parameters and local variables by using system variables. You also learn how to reference global variables.

■ Chapter 16, "Understanding Server, Database, and Query Options," shows you how to use query options to control the display of data through set command options.

Retrieving Data with Transact-SQL

You usually don't want to access and display all the data stored in a database in each query or report. You may want some—but not all—of the rows and columns of data. Although you can access all the information, you probably don't need to display all rows and columns simply because it's too much information to examine at one time.

In Chapter 1, "Introducing Microsoft SQL Server," and Chapter 2, "Data Modeling and Database Design," you learned that the information stored in a relational database is always accessed in the form of a table. If you reference a printed table of information, you usually don't read all the rows and columns. You probably look at only part of the table to obtain the information you need. The table exists in a printed form only because it's a primitive way of storing information.

If you can reconsider your requests for information from the database, you can start to eliminate the queries that produce unwanted or unneeded results. In these cases, you can produce output that presents exactly what's needed and nothing more. ■

Retrieve data from a table by using a SELECT statement

The SELECT statement is used to display data from database tables.

Use comparison, Boolean, and range operators in SELECT statements to specify table rows

You can wirte queries that specify selected table rows.

Return rows of a table in sorted order by one or more columns and eliminate duplicate rows

You can manipulate the rows of a table, including changing their presentation order.

Use embedded queries to return rows used as the input values to outer queries

Use the ANY and ALL keywords to constrain the rows retrieved in a SELECT statement

Understanding Relevant Storage Characteristics for Retrieval

The data stored on your database—the disk of your computer system—is analogous to a set of printed tables. You don't need to retrieve an entire table when you issue queries to display information from the database. You construct a query using a Transact-SQL statement that returns only the relevant portion of the column or rows of your database tables.

Table 6.1 shows an example table structure and its data, which will be used for several examples in this chapter. For information on creating tables, see Chapter 4, "Creating Devices, Databases, and Transaction Logs" and Chapter 5, "Creating Database Tables and Using Datatypes."

Table 6.1   A Table Containing 12 Rows

Name	Department	badge
Bob Smith	Sales	1834
Fred Sanders	Sales	1051
Stan Humphries	Field Service	3211
Fred Stanhope	Field Service	6732
Sue Sommers	Logistics	4411
Lance Finepoint	Library	5522
Mark McGuire	Field Service	1997
Sally Springer	Sales	9998
Ludmilla Valencia	Software	7773
Barbara Lint	Field Service	8883
Jeffrey Vickers	Mailroom	8005
Jim Walker	Unit Manager	7779

The table is limited to 12 rows to make it easier to work with the examples. The typical size of a table for a production database might have more columns of information and will nearly always have more rows of information. The size of the table won't make any difference in showing the operation of Transact-SQL statements. The statements work identically regardless of the size of the tables operated on. The examples in this chapter are easier to understand if a small number of rows and columns are present in the table used to show SQL operations.

Retrieving Data from a Table with *SELECT*

Unless you retrieve all the columns and rows from all tables, your queries of a database are a selection process that narrows the information retrieved from the database. Your goal as you work with tables should always be to return only the information needed to fulfill the user's request. Any more information, and the user will be required to wait for a longer period of time than needed. Any less information than is needed will result in additional queries against the database. This modeling of sets of data is always a balancing act that requires continued refinement.

The Transact-SQL SELECT statement is used for the selection process. Various parts of a SELECT statement target some—but not all—of the data in the database tables. The complete syntax of the SELECT statement is as follows:

```
SELECT [ALL ¦ DISTINCT] select_list
       [INTO [new_table_name]]
[FROM {table_name ¦ view_name}[(optimizer_hints)]
      [[, {table_name2 ¦ view_name2}[(optimizer_hints)]
      [..., {table_name16 ¦ view_name16}[(optimizer_hints)]]]]
[WHERE clause]
[GROUP BY clause]
[HAVING clause]
[ORDER BY clause]
[COMPUTE clause]
[FOR BROWSE]
```

A SELECT statement is like a triangle superimposed on a database table. Using SQL keywords, the database is narrowed to target the columns and rows that are to be retrieved in a query. In the triangle comparison shown in Figure 6.1, the widest part of the triangle selects all the rows and columns of a database for retrieval. The point of the triangle opposite its wide base selects the least amount of data that can be retrieved from a table (a single row consisting of one column).

Most SQL queries retrieve rows and columns that are narrower than the entire table, represented by the base of the triangle in the figure, but wider than the single row and column as shown in the point of the triangle opposite the triangle's base. You'll typically need to retrieve more than a single row and column but less than all the rows and columns of the database.

Part

II

Ch

6

FIG. 6.1

SELECT queries are used to target specific columns and rows of a database. You can also use the SELECT statement to extract a single column or row, or all columns and all rows from the database.

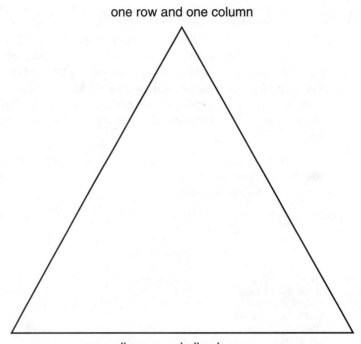

one row and one column

all rows and all columns

Specifying the Table with *FROM*

Different parts of the SELECT statement are used to specify the data to be returned from the database. The first part of the selection process occurs when fewer than all the database tables are referenced. You can retrieve data stored in the database separately by referencing some tables, but not others, in a SELECT statement.

A SELECT statement uses the FROM clause to target the tables from which rows and columns are included in a query. The syntax of the FROM clause is

```
[FROM {table_name | view_name}[(optimizer_hints)]
    [[, {table_name2 | view_name2}[(optimizer_hints)]
    [..., {table_name16 | view_name16}[(optimizer_hints)]]]]
```

In the following complete SELECT statement, the FROM clause specifies that the returned data should include only data from the Employee table:

```
SELECT *
FROM employee
```

N O T E In the examples shown in this chapter, the Transact-SQL keywords used to form clauses are written in uppercase. You can, however, use lowercase keywords. However, if you installed Microsoft SQL Server with the default binary sort order, the names of your database objects—including the names of tables and columns—must match in case. ■

You can also specify multiple tables in the FROM clause, as in the following example:

```
FROM table_name_1,…,table_name_n
```

Each table is separated from the names of other tables with a comma, a separator used with lists of information in FROM and other Transact-SQL clauses. The list in a FROM clause often specifies multiple tables rather than a single table.

In the following example of a SELECT statement, the FROM clause references the data from two tables:

```
SELECT *
FROM employee,pay
```

The Employee and Pay tables are targeted, from which all rows and columns are retrieved.

> **N O T E** As you'll see later in the section "Using a Wild Card in the *SELECT* Clause," using SELECT *
> returns all columns from the requested table or tables. This can cause queries that take
> quite some time to complete. You should avoid using Select * if possible. ■

> **N O T E** In a relational database, you must provide instructions within the SELECT statement to
> match the rows from two or more tables together. To learn how to match, or join rows from
> multiple tables, see Chapter 7, "Performing Operations on Tables." ■

Transact-SQL allows you to choose tables from different databases. You can specify the name of the database in which the table is located by inserting the database name to the left of the table name. Next, place a period, the database owner name, and another period, followed by the table you need to work with:

```
database_name.owner.table_name
```

In the following example, the Employee table in the company database and the owner dbo is specified:

```
SELECT *
FROM company.dbo.employee
```

> **N O T E** The DBO keyword specifies the database owner. You can refer to the dbo at any time. SQL
> will know that you're referring to the owner of the specific database. ■

In the previous example, the table was created by using the system administrator's account, so the owner is dbo. If you omit the name of the database and owner when you reference a table, SQL Server looks for the table or tables that you specified in the FROM clause in the current database. You must enter the name of the database in which a table was created, along with its owner, to include the rows and columns from tables in different databases.

Part

II

Ch

6

Specifying Columns with *SELECT*

The columns of values returned from database tables are specified as part of the SELECT clause immediately following the SELECT keyword. One or more of the columns are entered as a list. Each column, like the tables in a FROM clause, is separated by a comma:

```
SELECT column_name_1,...column_name_n
FROM table_name_1,...table_name_n
```

In the following code example, the Name and Badge columns are selected for retrieval. The results are shown in Figure 6.2. This example uses the SQL Windows application utility ISQL/w to perform the retrieval of rows.

```
Select name, badge
from employee
```

FIG. 6.2

SELECT statements are used to retrieve data from the database.

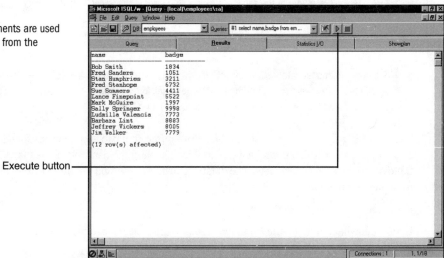

Execute button

N O T E The contents of the listings will be what should be entered into the query page of an ISQL/w session. Figures will then display what the results should look like when the Execute button (refer to fig. 6.2) is pressed. ■

Follow these steps to begin an ISQL/w session:

1. Click the ISQL/w icon in the SQL Server for Windows NT program group.

    The main window of ISQL/w appears, along with the Connect Server dialog box. You can connect to one or more SQL Server systems if you have a valid Login Id and Password. Use the List Servers button to see a list of the available servers. Figure 6.3 shows the connection to begin an ISQL/w session with a local Microsoft SQL Server system.

FIG. 6.3

You can also connect to a local Microsoft SQL Server through ISQL/w.

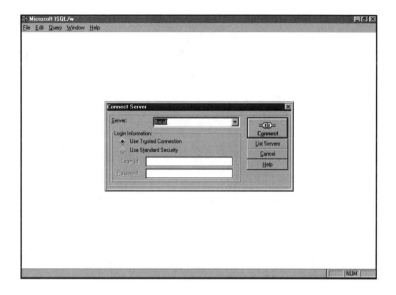

2. Enter a Server, Login Id, and Password.

N O T E If you've implemented Integrated Security, you don't have to specify a Login Id and Password. Your network name and password will be used to validate you on the server. ■

3. Click Connect.

If your server is available and your Login Id and Password are valid, a query window appears. Unless you've set the default database to the one in which you want to access tables and other objects, you must explicitly set ISQL/w to the correct database.

4. Enter the command **Use *name_of_your_database*** in the query window, or select the name of the database from the DB drop-down list box (above the Results tab).

5. Click the Execute button on the toolbar.

The example in Figure 6.4 shows the result of the execution of the USE command to set the database to employees. Use the Erase button on the toolbar to delete the previous command before you enter and execute a new command.

In Chapter 1, "Introducing Microsoft SQL Server," and Chapter 2, "Data Modeling and Database Design," you learned that one of the basic tenets of a relational database is that operations on database tables always return another table. The rows and columns of database tables that are targeted for retrieval are always assembled into a temporary table. In most cases, this table is maintained only until the data is provided to the requesting client.

The new temporary table shown in Figure 6.2 was constructed from the three-column employee table. According to the SELECT statement, "the temporary table targets all rows of the permanent table's *three columns* and eliminates the second column, Department." The temporary table is deleted after the rows are provided to the requesting client.

Part

II

Ch

6

FIG. 6.4

You can also define the database to which a user is automatically positioned when he starts a SQL Server session during the creation of the user logon.

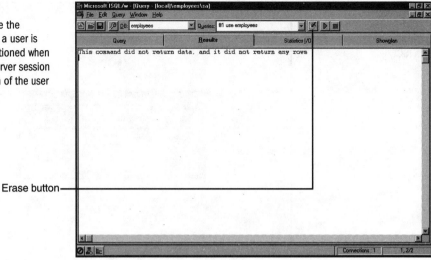

Erase button

Figure 6.5 shows the query with the Employee table performed with the command-line form of ISQL. As you can see, you must enter the default command-line terminator go at the end of each statement.

FIG. 6.5

Transact-SQL will produce the same results from a command-line prompt that it will in the GUI environment.

Use the ED command to edit a long statement to be entered at the command line. This will invoke the system editor with the previous command entered. Upon exiting the system editor, it will place the edited statement as the next statement.

You can display table columns in a different order than you originally defined. To change the default order for the display of table columns, simply list the names of the columns in the order in which you want the columns displayed. In the following example—the results are shown in

Figure 6.6—the order of display for the columns of the Employee table are reversed from the order in which they were defined.

```
select badge, department, name
from employee
```

FIG. 6.6

The SELECT clause determines the order in which columns are listed.

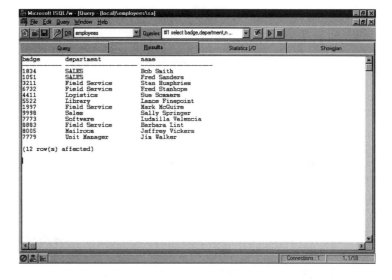

Changing the order of the displayed columns of a database table is consistent with the characteristics of a relational database. You learned in Chapter 2, "Data Modeling and Database Design," that the access of data from a relational database doesn't depend on the manner in which the data is physically stored. You simply specify the names of the columns in the order in which you want them returned in the SELECT clause of the SELECT statement.

 TIP You can display the same column of a table in multiple places if you need to improve the readability of the table, as in a train schedule.

Using a Wildcard in the *SELECT* Clause

You can use an asterisk (*) in the SELECT clause to specify all columns for inclusion in the retrieval. The following code shows a query that uses an asterisk to reference all columns of the Employee table with the results shown in Figure 6.7. The Name, Department, and Badge columns are displayed in the query results.

```
Select *
from employee
```

Part

II

Ch

6

FIG. 6.7

You can use the asterisk wild-card character in the SELECT clause of a SELECT statement.

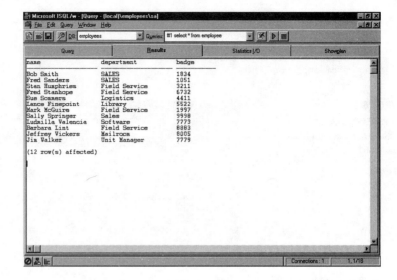

N O T E Although numerous examples throughout this book show SELECT statements with the asterisk (*) in the SELECT clause, you should always use caution in using the asterisk with production databases. The asterisk is used in the examples because it's convenient to use to reference all the columns. In many of the sample queries in which the asterisk is used, it has little effect on the amount of time it takes to perform the query.

You shouldn't use an asterisk with a production database because you probably need to access only some of the table columns in a query rather than all of them. Eliminating some table columns can dramatically reduce the time it takes to retrieve the rows when several rows are retrieved.

You can specify the column names even if all the columns should be retrieved so that the query is more descriptive. If the query is saved and later in need of revision, the columns and rows that the query retrieves will be easy to determine by reviewing the query. ■

Specifying the Rows of a Table

In the previous examples, all the table rows of a database are retrieved. Your goal often will be to retrieve only certain rows rather than all rows. For example, if you have tables that contain millions of rows, you'll probably never execute a query to retrieve all rows from the tables. Every query that you execute specifies a specific results set because it's impractical to retrieve or manipulate all rows in a single query.

The WHERE keyword is used to form a clause that you add to a SELECT statement to specify the rows of a table to be retrieved. A WHERE clause uses the following syntax:

```
SELECT column_name_n,...column_name_n
FROM table_name_1,...table_name_n
WHERE column_name comparison_operator value
```

A WHERE clause forms a row-selection expression that specifies, as narrowly as possible, the rows that should be included in the query. A SELECT statement that includes a WHERE clause may return a single row or even no rows if none of the rows matches the criteria specified in the SELECT statement.

In the example from the following code—the result is shown in Figure 6.8—a WHERE clause specifies that only the rows with the Sales department are retrieved. All rows that contain the Sales department, without regard for the case, are displayed.

```
select *
from employee
where department = "sales"
```

FIG. 6.8

The sort order that you defined during the installation of Microsoft SQL Server determines case-sensitivity.

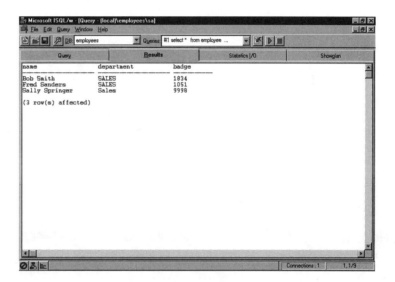

N O T E The default sort order is defined as case-insensitive during installation. If you change this after installation, you'll need to reinstall SQL Server. ■

The following code—the result is shown in Figure 6.9—shows the SELECT statement returns a single row because only one row contains the Mailroom department.

```
select *
from employee
where department = "mailroom"
```

The query result for a row that contains the personnel department retrieves no rows, as shown in the following code and in Figure 6.10. The count line, which displays the number of rows retrieved, is at the bottom of the output window. A retrieval in which no rows match the criteria of the SELECT statement doesn't return an error; instead, the message (0 row(s) affected) appears.

FIG. 6.9
The count message shows "row(s)" but only a single row is selected.

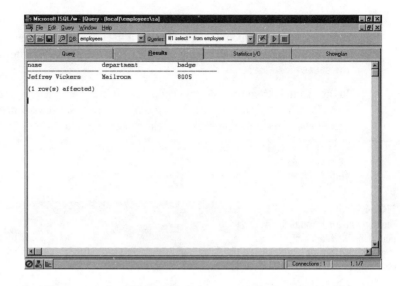

N O T E If you work with query products other than Transact-SQL, you may receive an error when no rows are retrieved. A query that returns no rows is considered valid by Transact-SQL—as well as other SQL dialects. ■

```
select *
from employee
where department = "personnel"
```

FIG. 6.10
You can enclose the value in the WHERE clause in single or double quotation marks. (Double quotes are used here.)

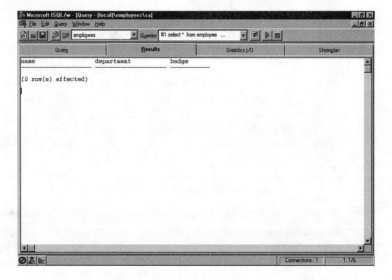

You can refer to the @@ERROR system symbol, which is called a *global variable*, to learn whether the previous operation was successful. Microsoft SQL Server returns a zero (0) to @@ERROR if the previous operation was successful. After you execute a SELECT query that retrieves zero rows, @@ERROR contains a zero (0), indicating that no error occurred (see fig. 6.11).

```
select @@error
```

FIG. 6.11
Conditional statements can be used to check @@ERROR and perform additional statements, if needed.

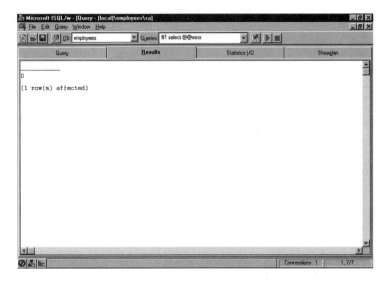

A SELECT statement is used in Figure 6.11 to display the contents of @@ERROR, so the results are returned in the form of rows retrieved from a table. The dashes (–) are displayed underneath the location of where a column header would appear if a column—rather than @@ERROR—was specified. A count message is also displayed for the one value (0) retrieved from the global variable. Error conditions and global variables are discussed in Chapter 13, "Managing Stored Procedures and Using Flow-Control Statements."

Using Comparison Operators in a *WHERE* Clause   The syntax for the WHERE clause allows the use of a comparison operator following the name of a table column and before a column value. In the earlier examples, only the comparison operator = (equal) was used. Additional comparison operators may be used to retrieve different rows. Table 6.2 lists the comparison operators that you can use in the WHERE clause.

Table 6.2   Comparison Operators

Symbol	Meaning
=	Equal
!=	Not equal
<>	Not equal

continues

Table 6.2 Continued	
Symbol	**Meaning**
<	Less than
>	Greater than
<=	Less than or equal to
>=	Greater than or equal to
LIKE	Equal to value fragment

N O T E   Table 6.2 lists the LIKE keyword as one of the comparison operators. Although LIKE isn't listed as one of the comparison operator symbols in the Microsoft documentation, LIKE is used exactly as a comparison operator. For more information on this operator, see the later section "Using the Comparison Operator *LIKE*." ■

The syntax for a WHERE clause that uses a comparison operator is as follows:

```
SELECT column_name_1,...column_name_n
FROM table_name_1,...table_name_n
WHERE column_name comparison_operator value
```

N O T E   You can optionally use spaces around the comparison operations if you wish. You query will execute correctly with or without spaces around the comparison operators. ■

In addition to the = (equal) comparison operator that was used in the preceding section (refer to figs. 6.8 through 6.11), you can use the <> (not equal) operator. You can use the not-equal operator to retrieve all rows except those that contain the value to the right of the <> operator. The following code—the result is shown in Figure 6.12—shows a SELECT statement that contains a WHERE clause for all rows from the Employee table except those that contain the Sales department.

```
select *
from employee
where department <> "sales"
```

The < (less than) comparison operator can be used to retrieve rows that are less than the value specified for the column in the WHERE clause. In the following code—the result is shown in Figure 6.13—the rows that contain a Badge number less than 5000 are retrieved from the Employee table.

```
select *
from employee
where badge < 5000
```

FIG. 6.12

You can use the comparison operators <> or ! = for 'not equal'.

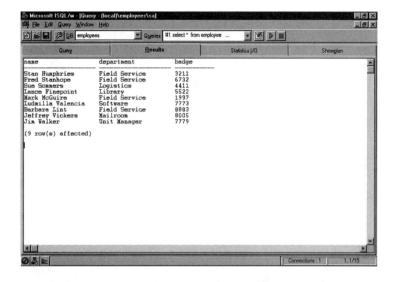

FIG. 6.13

The results include rows with Badge numbers less than 5000.

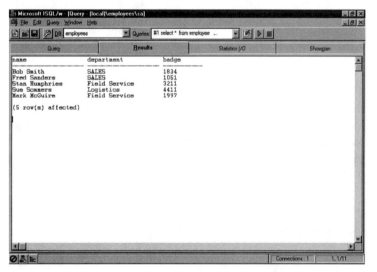

The > (greater than) comparison operator retrieves rows that contain a value greater than the value used in the WHERE clause. In the following code, rows with Badge numbers greater than 8000 are retrieved from the Employee table (see fig. 6.14).

```
select *
from employee
where badge > 8000
```

Part
II

Ch
6

FIG. 6.14

The results include rows with Badge numbers greater than 8000.

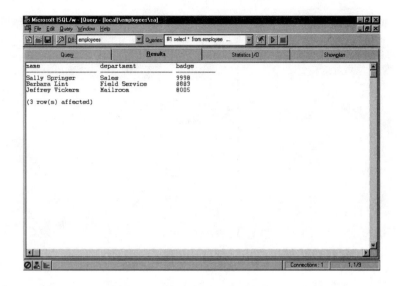

The <= (less than or equal to) comparison operator returns rows that have a value equal to or greater than the value in the WHERE statement. The following code returns rows that contain the value less than or equal to Badge number 3211 (see fig. 6.15).

```
select *
from employee
where badge <= 3211
```

FIG. 6.15

The results include rows with Badge numbers less than or equal to 3211.

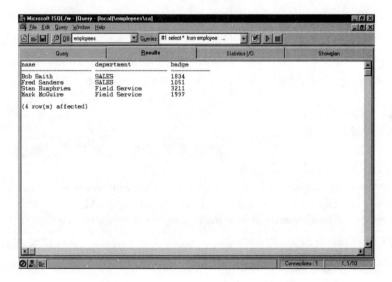

The >= (greater than or equal to) comparison operator returns rows that are greater than or equal to the value in the WHERE clause. Comparison operators can be used with columns that contain alphabetic values as well as numeric values. The following code uses >= in the WHERE clause to retrieve rows that are alphabetically greater than or equal to software for the Department column (see fig. 6.16).

```
select *
from employee
where department >= "software"
```

FIG. 6.16
The results include rows that contain the software department.

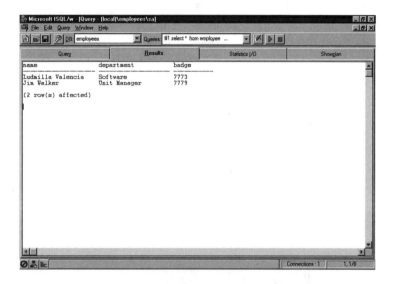

N O T E When you use comparison operations with columns that are defined as datatypes such as CHAR or VARCHAR, SQL Server uses the binary representation of all characters including alphabetic characters. For example, an uppercase letter A is stored with a lower binary value than an uppercase B. A character value of B is considered greater than the value of an uppercase A using its binary representation.

For values that are more than a single character, each character is successively compared using the binary representation. ■

Using the Comparison Operator *LIKE* The last of the comparison operators is a keyword—rather than one or two special symbols. The LIKE keyword is followed by a value fragment rather than a complete column value. The example query in the following code retrieves all rows that contain a department name beginning with the alphabetic character S (see fig. 6.17). A wildcard character such as the percent sign (%) can follow the letter S. This wildcard is used to match any number of characters up to the size of the column, minus the number of characters that precede the percent sign.

Part
II

Ch
6

> **TIP** You can also use the % before a value fragment in the WHERE clause of a SELECT statement, such as '%s'. You can also use wildcards multiple times.

```
select *
from employee
where department like "s%"
```

FIG. 6.17
The query retrieves only the rows that contain a department that starts with the letter s.

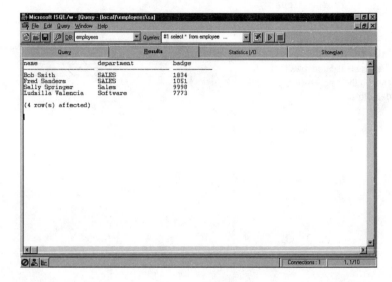

An underscore (_) is another wildcard that you can use to specify a value fragment. Each underscore used in the specification of a value fragment can match any one character. The example shown in the following code uses four underscores following the S to match any rows that contain a column value that begins with an s followed by any four characters (see fig. 6.18). Unlike the example shown in Figure 6.17, the query retrieves only the rows that contain Sales or SALES; it doesn't retrieve the rows that include Software.

```
select *
from employee
where department like "s____"
```

You can use square brackets ([ ]) as wildcards in a WHERE clause that uses the LIKE comparison operator. The square brackets specify a range of values. In the following code, the brackets are used to specify a range of any upper- or lowercase characters as the first character of the Department column (see fig. 6.19).

```
select *
from employee
where department like "[a-zA-Z]%"
```

FIG. 6.18

You can use the underscore (_) wildcard along with the percent sign *(%)* in a WHERE clause.

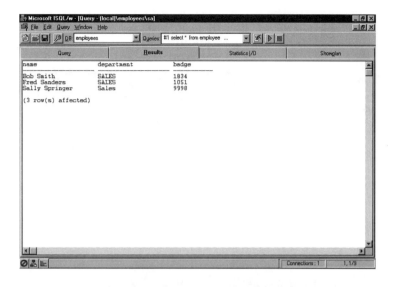

FIG. 6.19

You can use any wildcard combination in the value fragment.

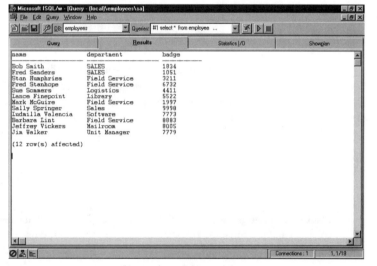

In Figure 6.19, % and [ ] are combined to specify that the rows for retrieval have any upper- or lowercase letter as their first character, as well as any additional characters up to the width of the column. The Department column was created wide enough to store 20 characters. The figure shows that you can combine wildcards to specify a value fragment.

You can also use a caret (^) after the left bracket to specify a range of values to be excluded from the rows retrieved in a SELECT statement. For example, the SELECT statement shown in the following code retrieves all rows from the Employee table except those with first characters that fall within the range F through M (see fig. 6.20).

```
select *
from employee
where department like "[^F-M]%"
```

FIG. 6.20

A SELECT statement that excludes a range of values from F through M.

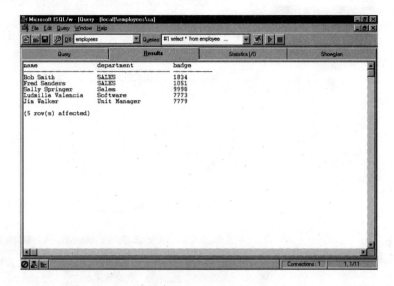

You can use wildcards only in a WHERE clause that uses the LIKE keyword. If you use the asterisk (*), underscore (_), brackets ([ ]), or caret (^) with any of the other comparison-operator symbols, they're treated as literal column values. For example, the following code contains the same query issued in Figure 6.20, but an equal sign (=) has been substituted for the LIKE query (see fig. 6.21). The identical query with an equal comparison operator rather than LIKE doesn't retrieve any rows.

```
select *
from employee
where department = "[^F-M]%"
```

Selecting Columns and Rows with the *WHERE* Clause   You can retrieve a subset of a table's columns and rows in a SELECT statement by combining the use of specific, called-out columns and the use of a constricting WHERE clause. In the following code, only two columns, Name and Department, are selected, and only for the rows that contain the Field Service value in the Department column (see fig. 6.22).

```
select name, department
from employee
where department = "field service"
```

FIG. 6.21

When you use wildcards with comparison operators other than LIKE, they're treated as literal column values.

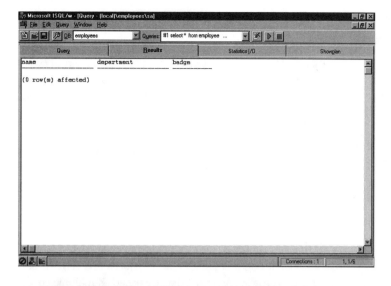

FIG. 6.22

A SELECT statement can limit both the rows and columns retrieved.

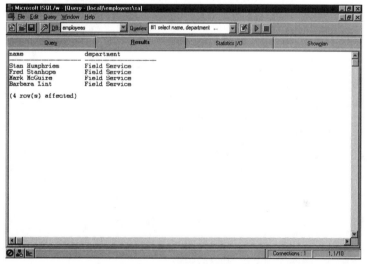

In Chapter 1, "Introducing Microsoft SQL Server," you learned that you can create more than 250 columns in a table and an unlimited number of rows. It's almost always impractical—except for small, simple tables—to try to retrieve all columns and rows of a table. If you correctly construct your query, you can also reference columns from multiple tables in a single query.

The SELECT clause is descriptive because it invokes a selection operation on a table's rows and columns. Keep in mind the analogy of the data-retrieval triangle introduced earlier in this chapter (refer to fig. 6.1). The SELECT statement effectively superimposes a triangle over a table to retrieve some (but not all) columns and some (but not all) rows.

Part
II

Ch
6

TROUBLESHOOTING

I executed a SELECT statement that resulted in no rows returned from a table, and I was surprised that SQL Server didn't return an error. SQL Server doesn't return an error for a query that results in no returned rows. Although this is not true of other software products—for example, some programming languages expect an error when no records are retrieved from a file—Microsoft SQL Server and Transact-SQL consider a query that returns no rows a valid query.

I executed a SELECT statement that resulted in no rows returned, but I'm certain information is in the database. How can I debug what went wrong? Try modifying your WHERE clause so only one condition is applied. Run the query with only the first condition. If no rows are returned, you can examine the WHERE clause to determine the problem. If information is returned, add the next portion or portions of the original WHERE clause, running the query after each. You should be able to quickly narrow down which portion of the constricting clause is going awry.

Using Boolean Operators and Other Keywords in a *WHERE* Clause   You can use Boolean operators to retrieve table rows that are based on multiple conditions specified in the WHERE clause. Booleans are used the way conjunctions are used in the English language. Boolean operators are used to form multiple row-retrieval criteria. Use Boolean operators to closely control the rows that are retrieved.

The syntax for the use of a Boolean is as follows:

```
SELECT column_name_1,...column_name_n
FROM table_name_1,...table_name_n
WHERE column_name comparison_operator value
Boolean_operator column_name comparison operator
```

Using the OR Operator   The first of the Boolean operators is OR, which you can use to select multiple values for the same column. In the following code, OR is used to form a WHERE clause to retrieve rows containing two column values (see fig. 6.23). Continue to add ORs to the WHERE clause to select additional values for the same column.

```
select *
from employee
where department = "field service"
or department = "logistics"
```

The following query retrieves the rows of the Employee table that contain three column values (see fig. 6.24).

```
select *
from employee
where department = "field service"
or department = "logistics"
or department = "software"
```

FIG. 6.23

You can use any number of ORs with different comparison operators in each comparison.

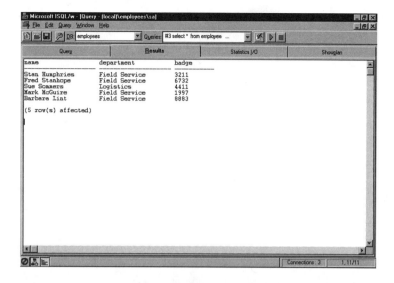

FIG. 6.24

You can use additional ORs to select more than two values of the same column.

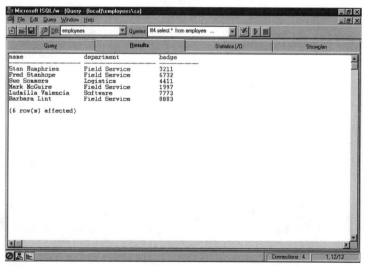

You can specify different columns in the WHERE clause of a SELECT statement that uses an OR. The query in following code retrieves rows that either are members of the Field Service department (with any Badge number) or have a Badge number that's less than 6000 (but are members of any department). See Figure 6.25.

```
select *
from employee
where department = "field service"
or badge < 6000
```

FIG. 6.25

You can use multiple Boolean
operators to specify a criteria
for the rows to be returned by
a SELECT statement.

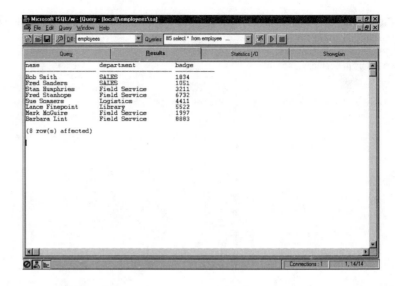

Using the AND Operator   Use the AND Boolean operator if you want the rows returned by the
query to meet both comparisons specified in the WHERE clause.

In the following code, a query is used to retrieve a row that contains a specific name and badge
combination (see fig. 6.26). If two rows in the table contained Bob Smith, the Boolean AND is
used to specify a criteria that requires the row to also contain the Badge value 1834. Multiple
rows would be returned only if more than one row contained the values Bob Smith and 1834.

```
select *
from employee
where name = "bob smith"
and badge = 1834
```

FIG. 6.26

You can also use AND (as
shown here) and OR together
in a WHERE clause.

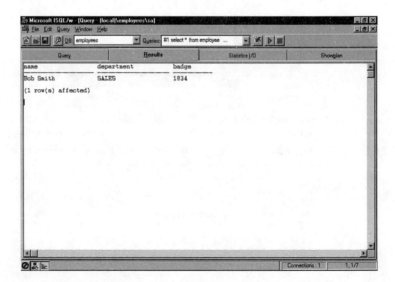

Populating one column of the table with unique values allows individual rows to be retrieved. A unique row is returned if one of the specified columns is the column that contains unique values.

TIP Defining a column with a unique row or a combination of rows allows individual rows to be retrieved or manipulated. In Chapter 1, "Introducing Microsoft SQL Server," you learned that Microsoft SQL Server allows you to store rows that have duplicate values across all table columns. If you allow rows to be individually selected, you establish the capability to reference one table row at a time, if necessary. Chapter 5, "Creating Database Tables and Using Datatypes," reviews the datatypes that are available. You may recall that the TIMESTAMP datatype is a perfect way to manage uniqueness for tables.

▶ **See** the section in Chapter 5 entitled "Specialized Datatypes." **p. 119**

Using the NOT Operator   NOT is an additional Boolean operator that you can use as part of a WHERE clause. Use NOT to specify negation. Use NOT before the column name and a comparison operator, such as = (equal), after the column name and before the value.

For example, the following query retrieves all rows of the Employee table that contain any department except Field Service (see fig. 6.27).

TIP You can use NOT instead of the not-equal comparison operators ! = and <>. A WHERE clause that uses NOT for negation is visually easier to understand than one that uses ! = (not equal).

```
select *
from employee
where not department = "field service"
```

FIG. 6.27
You can use NOT for negation the same way the not-equal comparison operators (! = and <>) are used.

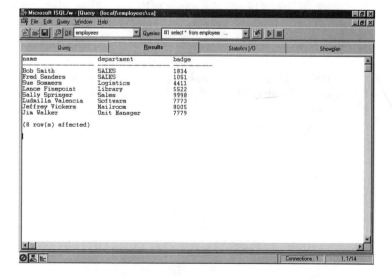

You can also use NOT in a WHERE clause in combination with AND and OR. In the following code, NOT is used to retrieve all rows of the Employee table that are members of the Field Service department, except for Mark McGuire (see fig. 6.28).

```
select *
from employee
where department = "field service"
and not name = "mark mcguire"
```

FIG. 6.28

You can use OR as well as AND with the NOT Boolean operator.

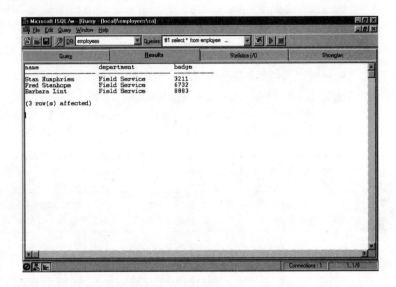

Using *BETWEEN* to Select a Range of Values   Although you can use a number of ORs in a WHERE clause to specify the selection of multiple rows, another construction is available in Transact-SQL. You can use the BETWEEN keyword with AND to specify a range of column values to be retrieved.

In the following code, a WHERE clause that includes BETWEEN is used to specify a range of Badge values to be retrieved from the Employee table (see fig. 6.29). Use BETWEEN after the name of the column, followed by one end of the range of values, the AND keyword, and the other end of the range of values.

```
select *
from employee
where badge between 2000 and 7000
```

FIG. 6.29

The table doesn't have to contain rows that are identical to the column values used to specify the range of values referenced by BETWEEN.

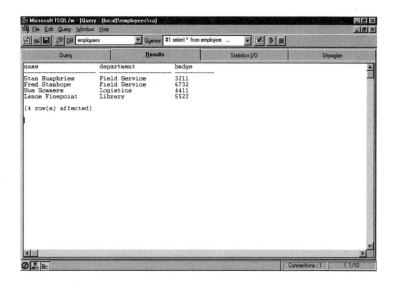

The two numbers that form the range of values for retrieval don't actually need to be stored in the table. For example, in Figure 6.29, Badge numbers 2000 and 7000 don't have to be stored in the table. Those numbers simply specify a range. Also, a successful query (one that returns an error code of 0) can return zero rows within the range specified by the WHERE clause that contains a BETWEEN. No rows need to be stored in the table for the query to execute correctly.

Using *IN* to Specify a List of Values You can't always use a WHERE clause with BETWEEN to specify the rows that you want to retrieve from a table in place of a WHERE clause that contains multiple ORs. The rows that contain the column values specified within the range of values will include rows that you don't want. However, you can use the IN keyword in a WHERE clause to specify multiple rows more easily than if you use multiple ORs with a WHERE clause.

A statement that uses IN uses the following syntax:

```
SELECT column_name_1,...column_name_n
FROM table_name_1,...table_name_n
WHERE column_name IN (value_1, ...value_n)
```

In the following code, IN is followed by a list of values to specify the rows to be retrieved (see fig. 6.30).

```
select *
from employee
where badge in (3211,6732,4411,5522)
```

Part
II

Ch
6

FIG. 6.30

A WHERE clause that contains IN is simpler to write than a WHERE clause that contains multiple ORs and is more specific than using the BETWEEN operator.

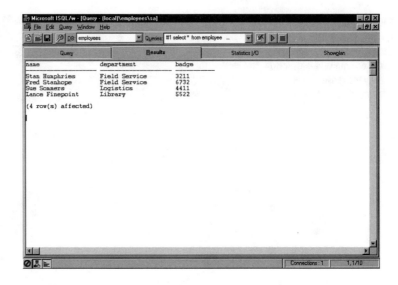

Using an *ORDER BY* Clause

In Chapter 1, "Introducing Microsoft SQL Server," you learned that the rows of a relational database are unordered. As part of your SELECT statement, you can specify the order in which you want the rows retrieved and displayed: Add an ORDER BY clause to sort the table rows that are retrieved by a SELECT statement.

N O T E   The rows of a SQL Server database usually will be retrieved in the order in which you inserted the rows into the table. If you create a clustered index for a table, the order of the rows returned by a query is the order of the clustered index. But you can't rely on the stored order of rows for two reasons:

■ You can create an index for a table that didn't have a clustered index. After the clustered index is created for the table, the rows will be retrieved in a different order than before the index is created.

■ The clustered index for a table can be deleted at any time, which affects the order in which rows are subsequently retrieved.

If you want to return the table rows in a specific order, you must add an ORDER BY clause to a SELECT statement. ■

The syntax of a SELECT statement that contains an ORDER BY clause is as follows:

```
SELECT column_name_1,...column_name_n
FROM table_name_1,...table_name_n
ORDER BY column_name_1,...column_name_n
```

The following code shows a SELECT statement in which the rows are ordered by Department (see fig. 6.31). The rows of the Employee table are retrieved in ascending order by default.

```
select *
from employee
order by department
```

FIG. 6.31

You can use multiple columns to determine the order of rows retrieved.

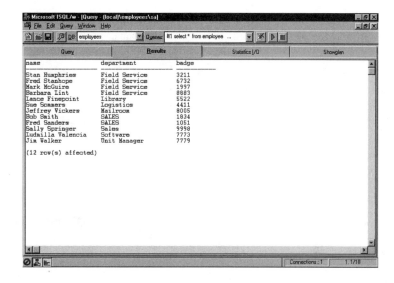

If you include the name of a second column after the name of the first column, the second column orders the rows that are duplicates of the first column. In the following code, ORDER BY is used to order the rows of the Employee table first by the Department and then by the Badge column (see fig. 6.32).

```
select *
from employee
order by department, badge desc
```

FIG. 6.32

You can reference a third column if you have the need.

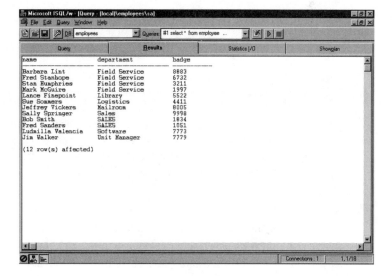

Part

II

Ch

6

Notice that the DESC keyword is added after the second named column to order the Badge numbers in descending orderbadge. You can also use the keyword ASC to specify explicitly that a column's order in the ORDER BY clause be ascending. However, it's unnecessary because the order of a column is ascending by default.

When you use ORDER BY in a SELECT statement, you can specify the columns in the ORDER BY clause by their order number in the SELECT clause. In the following code, the Department and Badge columns from the Employee table are referenced in the ORDER BY clause by their order of occurrence from left to right in the SELECT clause (see fig. 6.33).

```
select department, badge
from employee
order by 1, 2
```

FIG. 6.33

A SELECT statement that references the columns using column numbers rather than names.

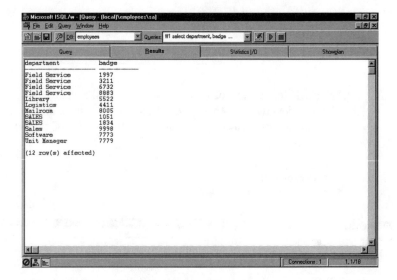

You must understand why SQL Server doesn't use the order of the column defined in a table such as Employee in the ORDER BY clause. In a relational database, the syntax of a query language that references database data should be independent of the manner in which the data is stored.

If Transact-SQL used the order of columns as they are defined in the table, the column number would be based as a physical characteristic of the stored data. It's more appropriate to reference the columns using the relative order of the columns in the SELECT clause.

Another problem exists in trying to reference table columns by the order in which the columns are defined in a table. You can specify columns from different tables in the SELECT clause. You can't, for example, reference two columns that are both defined as the third column in two tables, because the column numbers are identical.

You have complete control over specifying columns in the SELECT clause of a SELECT statement. You can reference the same column more than once in a SELECT clause, and the column values will be displayed multiple times. In the following code, the Badge column is referenced twice in the SELECT clause (see fig. 6.34).

```
select badge, name, department, badge
from employee
```

FIG. 6.34

Multiple copies of the same column can be used to improve readability.

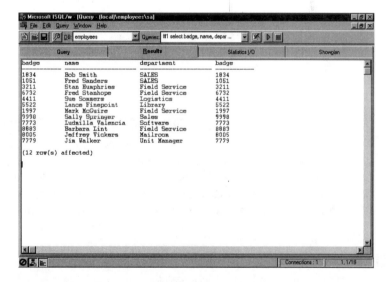

You may not immediately see a reason for displaying the values of a column more than once. If a listing is wide enough, it can be convenient to display a column—often the unique identifier for each row—as the first and last columns of a display, as Figure 6.34 shows. A train schedule is an example of a wide output in which the stations often are displayed in the first, last, and center columns to make the output display easier to read.

Using *DISTINCT* to Retrieve Unique Column Values

You can construct your database table so that you never allow duplicate rows to be stored or to allow duplicate rows. Unless you define a constraint on your table, such as a unique key, you can store duplicate rows in the table. Although you can disallow duplicate rows in the table, you

Part
II

Ch
6

may allow duplicates for some columns. You may want to find the unique entries that exist in a table column. The DISTINCT keyword is used to return the unique values of a column.

The following code shows the different departments of the Employee table (see fig. 6.35).

```
select distinct department
from employee
```

FIG. 6.35

You can use DISTINCT with multiple columns to return the unique values of a column.

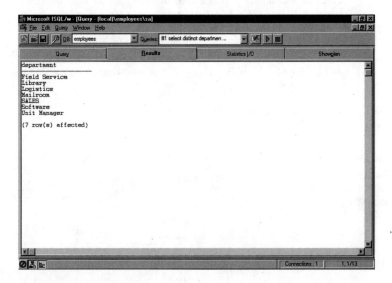

If you use DISTINCT with multiple columns, the rows retrieved are unique by the combination of the columns specified after the DISTINCT keyword. The combination of the values from the Department and Badge columns must return all rows. Whenever you combine a column that contains non-duplicate values (such as Badge) with a column that contains duplicate values (such as Department), the combination of the two is non-duplicate.

Using Arithmetic Operators

You can use arithmetic operators to form expressions in Transact-SQL. Expressions are evaluated within the statements in which they appear. You need arithmetic operators to manipulate the data retrieved from tables. You can use the arithmetic operators in the SELECT clause to add, subtract, multiply, and divide data from columns that store numeric data.

Table 6.3 shows the arithmetic operators you can use in Transact-SQL.

Table 6.3   Transact-SQL Arithmetic Operators

Symbol	Operation
+	Addition
–	Subtraction

Symbol	Operation
*	Multiplication
/	Division
%	Modulo (remainder)

You can form expressions by using arithmetic operators on columns defined with the datatypes TINYINT, SMALLINT, INT, FLOAT, REAL, SMALLMONEY, and MONEY. You can't use the modulo operator (%) on columns defined with the MONEY, SMALLMONEY, FLOAT, or REAL datatypes.

N O T E The modulo operator (%) is used to return an integer remainder that results from the division of two integer values. As a result, it can't be used with datatypes that can contain non-integer values. You'll receive an error message if you try to use the operator on columns defined as other than integer datatypes, even if the column values are whole numbers. ■

You can use arithmetic operators to form expressions in the SELECT clause of a SELECT statement with both numeric constants and columns. In the following code, an expression is used to increment the Badge numbers by 5 (see fig. 6.36).

```
select badge, badge + 5
from employee
```

FIG. 6.36
You can use multiple arithmetic operators to operate on column names, constants, or a combination of column names and constants.

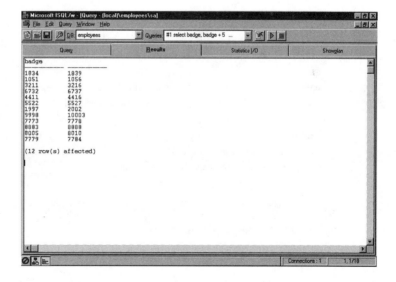

When you use an expression in a SELECT clause, the display for the evaluation of the expression doesn't have a column header. You can specify a column header for the expression by preceding the expression with a text string followed by an equal sign (=). For example, the following code shows the expression preceded by the specified column header in the SELECT clause of the SELECT statement (see fig. 6.37). You can enclose the text string in single or double quotation marks to retain embedded spaces.

N O T E If you perform an arithmetic operation on a column that contains a NULL, the result is an unknown value. ■

```
select badge, "badge + 5" = badge + 5
from employee
```

FIG. 6.37
You can also specify an alternate column header for any column without using the column name in an expression.

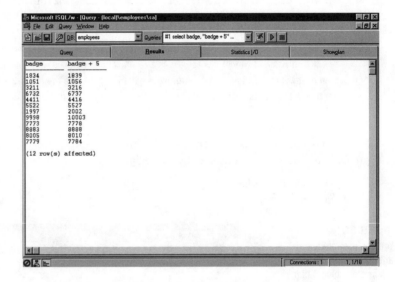

Computed columns are not stored in the database. They may exist in a temporary table that is created during the execution of the SELECT statement. Since the data is not in the database, there is no way to directly verify the results of a computed column. One easy way to compute a value incorrectly is to ignore operator precedence. Arithmetic operators are performed in predetermined order unless parentheses are used to force otherwise. Table 6.4 shows the order in which arithmetic operators are executed.

Table 6.4 Precedence Order of Arithmetic Operators

Operator	Order of Precedence
*	1st
/	1st
%	1st
+	2nd
–	2nd

If you use multiple arithmetic operators with the same order of precedence, the expressions are evaluated from left to right. You can use parentheses to control the order of execution. Expressions in parentheses are evaluated before any other expressions. Use parentheses to evaluate expressions that contain addition and subtraction before the expressions that contain multiplication, division, and modulo operators.

The following code shows the use of parentheses in the SELECT clause. The constant 5 is added to each value of the Badge column. After the constant is added to Badge, the sum is multiplied by 2. See Figure 6.38.

```
select "badge + 5 * 2" = (badge + 5) * 2
from employee
```

FIG. 6.38

You can use parentheses to make the evaluation order more descriptive, even if the parentheses are unnecessary.

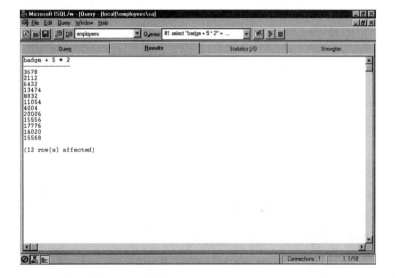

You can perform arithmetic operations on different numeric datatypes in the same expression—a procedure called *mixed mode arithmetic*. The datatype of the result is determined by the rank of the datatype code stored in a column of a system table.

You can use a SELECT statement to retrieve the datatype names and their code numbers from the systypes system table. Table 6.5 shows the codes for the numeric datatypes.

Part
II

Ch
6

Table 6.5   Type Codes for the Numeric Datatypes

Datatype	Code
TINYINT	48
SMALLINT	52
INT[EGER]	56

continues

Table 6.5	Continued
Datatype	**Code**
REAL	59
MONEY	60
FLOAT	62
SMALLMONEY	122

When you write expressions using different datatypes, the results are returned in the datatype of the highest ranked datatype. For example, the values of a column that's defined as either a TINYINT or a SMALLINT datatype is converted to INT if they're evaluated in a expression that contains an INT datatype.

One exception to the datatype code rule applies to expressions that include columns with the FLOAT and MONEY datatypes. The evaluation of an expression that contains FLOAT and Money is returned as the MONEY datatype, even though the code number for MONEY (60) is lower than FLOAT (62). You can retrieve the code numbers for all the Transact-SQL datatypes by using the query in following code.

```
select name, type
from systypes
order by type desc
```

This statement retrieves the names and codes for all Transact-SQL datatypes in order by the highest code numbers.

Using a *GROUP BY* Clause

The GROUP BY clause divides a table into groups of rows. The rows in each group have the same value for a specified column. Duplicate values for each different value are placed in the same group. Grouping allows you to perform the same functions on groups of rows.

You can group by any number of columns in a statement. Columns in the select list must be in the GROUP BY clause or have a function used on it. The syntax of a SELECT statement that contains a GROUP BY clause is as follows:

```
SELECT column 1,....column n
FROM tablename
GROUP BY columnname 1, columnname n
```

GROUP BY targets only unique column values after sorting by ascending column value (default). GROUP BY is unlike the ORDER BY clause, which though it also sorts records in ascending order, it doesn't remove duplicate column values.

The example query shown in the following code groups the rows by the Department column (see fig. 6.39). The departments are first sorted to group them together. The duplicate departments aren't displayed because the purpose of the GROUP BY clause in a SELECT statement is to form groups of rows for subsequent action by other clauses.

```
select department, "headcount" = count(*)
from employee
group by department
```

FIG. 6.39

A SELECT statement
containing a GROUP BY clause
that sorts rows by the column
referenced in the GROUP BY
clause.

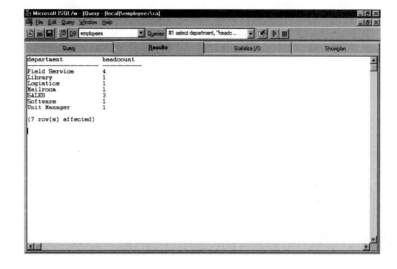

▶ **See** the Chapter 8 section entitled "Using *COUNT.*" **p. 217**

For example, you can select specific groups with a HAVING clause, which compares some property of the group with a constant value. If a group satisfies the logical expression in the HAVING clause, it's included in the query result. The syntax of a SELECT statement with a HAVING clause is

```
SELECT column 1,...column n
FROM tablename
GROUP BY columnname
HAVING expression
```

The HAVING clause is used to determine the groups to be displayed in the output of the SELECT statement. The following code shows the use of a HAVING clause (see fig. 6.40).

```
select department, "headcount" = count(*)
from employee
group by department
having count(*) = 1
```

Part

II

Ch

6

FIG. 6.40

A SELECT statement containing a HAVING clause that limits the returned rows.

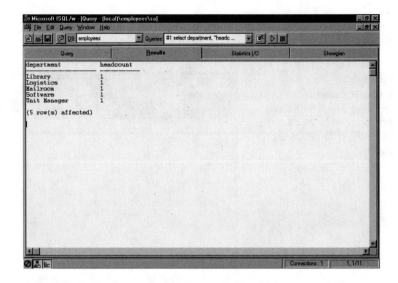

Using a *COMPUTE* Clause in a *SELECT* Statement

You can use a COMPUTE clause in a SELECT statement with functions such as SUM(), AVG(), MIN(), MAX(), and COUNT(). The COMPUTE clause generates summary values that are displayed as additional rows. The COMPUTE clause works like a so-called control break, a mechanism used in applications called *report writers*. You can use the COMPUTE clause to produce summary values for groups as well as calculate values using more than one function for the same group.

N O T E A report writer is an application that permits you to retrieve data from a database without using SQL statements. Nowadays, a report writer is designed with a graphical user interface which permits you to point and click on buttons and menu commands to retrieve database data. You might find it useful to purchase a report writer to retrieve data from your database as well as for using SQL statements. ■

The general syntax of the COMPUTE clause is as follows:

```
COMPUTE row_aggregate(column name)
[,row_aggregate(column name,...]
[BY column name [,column name...]
```

▶ **See** Chapter 8, "Using Functions," for more information. **p. 215**

Several restrictions apply to the use of a COMPUTE clause in a SELECT statement. The following list summarizes the COMPUTE clause restrictions:

■ You can't include text or image datatypes in a COMPUTE or COMPUTE BY clause.

■ DISTINCT isn't allowed with row aggregate functions.

■ Columns in a COMPUTE clause must appear in the statement's SELECT clause.

■ You can't use SELECT INTO in the same statement as a COMPUTE clause.

- If you use COMPUTE BY, you must also use an ORDER BY clause.

- Columns listed after COMPUTE BY must be identical to or a subset of those in the ORDER BY clause. They must also be in the same order, left to right, start with the same expression, and not skip any expressions.

- You must use a column name or an expression in the ORDER BY clause, not a column heading.

Using *COMPUTE* Without *BY*

You can use a clause that contains the keyword COMPUTE without BY to display grand totals or counts. You can also use both a COMPUTE and a COMPUTE BY clause in a SELECT statement.

Using Subqueries

You can nest a complete SELECT statement within another SELECT statement. A SELECT statement that's nested within another SELECT statement is called a *subquery*. The nested or inner SELECT statement is evaluated and the result is available to the outer SELECT statement. To use a subquery, enclose a SELECT statement within parentheses to specify that it should be evaluated before the outer query.

The row or rows returned by the SELECT statement in parentheses are used by the outer SE-LECT statement. The rows returned by the inner SELECT statement are used in the position of the value in the WHERE clause of the outer SELECT statement. For example, in the following code, all rows are retrieved for the Employee table, where the department is equal to the same Department to which Bob Smith is a member (see fig. 6.41).

```
select *
from employee
where department = (
select department
from employee
where name = "bob smith")
```

Some restrictions apply to the use of subqueries. The SELECT list of a subquery must return either a single value or one or more rows (if an EXISTS is used) unless IN is used in the outer query. This would result in the following error if a comparison operator such as = (equal to) was used in the WHERE clause of the outer query:

```
Msg 512, Level 16, State 1
Subquery returned more than 1 value. This is illegal when the subquery
follows =, !=, <, <= , >, >=, or when the subquery is used as an expression.
Command has been aborted.
```

N O T E Use NOT IN to eliminate rows that match the results of a subquery. ■

Part

II

Ch

6

FIG. 6.41
You can nest a subquery
within the subquery by using
an additional set of parentheses around an enclosed
SELECT statement.

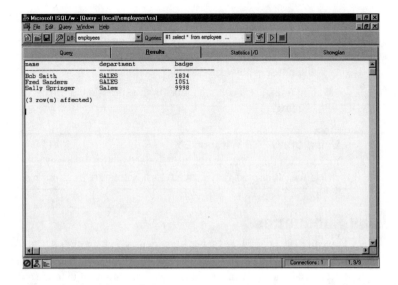

You're restricted in the choice of datatypes within subqueries. You can't use either the IMAGE
or TEXT datatypes in the SELECT clause of the subquery. Also, the datatype of the value(s) returned by the subquery must match the datatype used in the WHERE clause of the outer query.

TROUBLESHOOTING

**I tried to use the rows returned by a SELECT statement within another SELECT statement.
Although I enclosed the inner SELECT statement in parentheses, I received an error when the
statement executed.** Your nested SELECT statement probably returned more than one row value to
the WHERE clause of your outer SELECT statement. Unless you're sure that the inner SELECT
statement will return only a single row value, you should use an IN in the WHERE clause of the outer
SELECT statement.

Using *ANY* and *ALL*   You can use ANY and ALL to modify the comparison operators that precede a subquery. In Transact-SQL, ANY and ALL don't have the same meaning that they do in
the English language. For example, when > (greater than) is followed by ALL, it's interpreted as
greater than all values—including the maximum value returned by a subquery. When >
(greater than) is followed by ANY, it's interpreted as greater than at least one—the minimum.

T I P   If you have difficulty understanding the results of queries that contain one or more nested queries, you
can separately execute each subquery. If you record the result of the execution of an inner query, you
can use the values to help you interpret the results of the outer queries.

N O T E   The = ANY keyword is evaluated identically to IN. It would be clearer to use an IN instead
of = ANY. ∎

Specifying Optimizer Hints The optimizer hints clause is somewhat misleading. You use the optimizer clause of the SELECT statement to override the data-retrieval methods that are automatically chosen by the query optimizer. When a query is executed, a portion of SQL Server, called the *query optimizer*, determines how the retrieval of the data from the database is performed.

For example, although an index may exist on a table that's referenced in a query, the query optimizer may determine that it would be faster to retrieve the rows from the table without using the index. The query optimizer may not use an index because the number of rows requested by the query are few in number, and it would be faster to directly access the data rows rather than both the index rows and then data rows.

If multiple indexes exist on a table, the query optimizer will choose to return the rows of the table using the index that would result in the fastest retrieval of information.

You may, however, want to override the way in which the retrieval of rows will be done. For example, if two indexes—one clustered and one non-clustered—exist on a table, the query optimizer may choose to use the non-clustered index for the retrieval of the table rows. You can use the optimizer hints clause in a SELECT statement to force a retrieval using the clustered index. You want the rows to be retrieved by the clustered index because they will automatically be returned in ascending sorted order by the column or columns on which the clustered index was created.

For example, you can use the following optimizer hints clause in a SELECT clause to specify that the rows of a table will be retrieved by the clustered index:

```
select * from employee (index=0)
```

This statement specifies the index name or ID to use for that table. 0 forces the use of a clustered index (if one exists). If you use a optimizer hint of 1, a non-clustered index is used for retrieval of rows targeted in the SELECT statement.

N O T E You can confirm the method that's used to retrieve your rows by using the query option SHOWPLAN. This option returns information about how SQL Server performed your query. For example, if the rows of the query were retrieved without using an index, the method table scan appears in the information returned by SHOWPLAN. SHOWPLAN also clearly specifies if a clustered or non-clustered index *is used for retrieval in a query*. Click the Query Options button on the toolbar to bring up the Query Options dialog box, then select the Show Query Plan check box to return SHOWPLAN information. ■

Part

II

Ch

6

T I P You can also use the syntax *index=index_column_name* as an optimizer hint in a SELECT statement in place of the index number.

You can use a second set of optimizer hints to control the synchronization, or locking of the tables in your SELECT statement. You can use the locking optimizer hints to override the way in which SQL Server normally controls access to data from multiple clients.

Using NOLOCK   You use the NOLOCK optimizer hint to permit you to read rows that SQL Server would normally not permit you to access. For example, if you use NOLOCK in a SELECT statement, you can read uncommitted rows.

Using HOLDLOCK   You use HOLDLOCK to prevent other clients from changing rows that are part of your SELECT clause until your transaction is complete. Normally, other clients can modify the rows as soon as they're displayed. One restriction of HOLDLOCK is that you can't use it in a SELECT clause that also contains a FOR BROWSE clause.

Using UPDLOCK   You use an UPDLOCK like HOLDLOCK to prevent other clients from changing rows that are part of your SELECT clause. UPDLOCK releases the rows of your table and the end of the command or next transaction, rather than at the end of the transaction only.

Using TABLOCK   You use TABLOCK like HOLDLOCK to prevent other clients from changing rows. TABLOCK, unlike HOLDLOCK, acts on the entire table, rather than just on the rows of your table. You can use TABLOCK along with HOLDLOCK to prevent other clients from changing rows of your entire table until your transaction completes.

Using PAGLOCK   You use PAGLOCK like HOLDLOCK to prevent other clients from changing rows. PAGLOCK prevents other clients from changing rows a table page at a time, rather than the entire table.

Using TABLOCKx   You use TABLOCKx to prevent other clients from displaying as well as changing an entire table referenced in your SELECT clause until your command or transaction is complete.

Using FASTFIRSTROW   You use FASTFIRSTROW to retrieve the rows of a table using a non-clustered index. Unlike the index=1 optimizer hint, the first row of the query is returned more quickly through use of optimized read techniques. The total time that it takes to perform the query may be longer than if the non-clustered index *were used with the* FASTFIRSTROW *option.* You use FASTFIRSTROW to get better response time by returning the initial results of your query faster.

> **N O T E**   The *response time* for a database such as Microsoft SQL Server is usually defined as time that it takes to display on a client system monitor the first row of a query. *Throughput* is the amount of time that it takes to complete an operation, whether or not part of the operation involves the display of information as feedback to a client. Often enough in computer systems, better response time can be achieved though the throughput may be slower. ■

Using the *FOR BROWSE* Option

You can use the FOR BROWSE clause in a SELECT statement to read a table that another client is now adding, deleting, or updating rows within. Normally, SQL Server won't permit you to read a table while pending updates, deletes, or inserts are uncommitted. There are restrictions on what other clauses your SELECT statement can contain to use the FOR BROWSE clause.

To use the FOR BROWSE clause in a SELECT statement, the SELECT statement must contain a table with a timestamp column and a unique index. To use the FOR BROWSE clause in a SELECT statement, the SELECT statement can't contain a UNION clause. FOR BROWSE should be the last clause of a SELECT statement.

Unique indexes and timestamp columns are required attributes of tables to be used with the FOR BROWSE clause. If a table doesn't meet these requirements, a retrieval statement executes as if the FOR BROWSE clause weren't present in the SELECT statement. A SELECT statement that tries to read the rows from a table that's being modified waits up to the default query timeout interval of 5 minutes.

If the modification is completed within that time, the rows are displayed by the waiting query. If the pending modification doesn't complete within the timeout interval, the query fails. The FOR BROWSE clause in a SELECT statement permits you to read rows of a table while they're being changed.

> **CAUTION**
>
> If you use the FOR BROWSE clause in a SELECT statement, remember that you're looking at table rows whose values may not be kept by the user who's modifying the table. You must be willing to take a chance that a change you see in a table using a SELECT statement containing the FOR BROWSE clause may not be kept.

▶ **See** the section in Chapter 12 entitled "Defining Transactions." **p. 322**

From Here...

Part
II

Ch
6

In this chapter you've learned to write queries for the retrieval of data from a database which contains only the required rows or columns. In addition, you've learned to manipulate the returned data, performing arithmetic operations and sorting the rows. Finally, you've learned to use optimization techniques to override the default actions of SQL Server to retrieve data faster or in different ways.

For more information about the topics mentioned in this chapter, see the following chapters:

- Chapter 1, "Introducing Microsoft SQL Server," shows the syntax used for the command-line form of interactive SQL (ISQL).

■ Chapter 5, "Creating Database Tables and Using Datatypes," discusses the treatment of NULLs as column values as well as column datatypes.

■ Chapter 7, "Performing Operations on Tables," teaches you how to combine rows from multiple tables in the same query.

■ Chapter 10, "Managing and Using Indexes and Keys," teaches you how to create and use keys and indexes and how to constrain rows and columns to unique values.

■ Chapter 13, "Managing Stored Procedures and Using Flow-Control Statements," teaches you how to use conditional statements and check status in global variables such as @@ERROR.

Performing Operations on Tables

Information that's stored in multiple tables is often combined in a single query. To combine rows logically across tables, the tables must be created with related columns of data. You must be able to issue queries that not only combine but also eliminate rows from multiple tables, so that only the requisite rows appear in the resultant display.

You'll need to use an UPDATE statement to change one (or more) row's column values for a table. You may need to change a row simply to correct information that was incorrectly entered. You'll want to be able to remove rows that are no longer needed in a table. You use a DELETE statement to remove one or more rows from a table.

In addition to changing table rows, you'll find that you may need to add additional columns of information to a database table. You use the ALTER TABLE statement primarily to add one more columns to an already existing table, as well as change other characteristics of the table.

In this chapter, you'll learn to write queries that retrieve rows of related information from multiple tables. You'll also learn to update and delete the rows of a database table. Also, you'll learn to change the characteristics of database tables including how to add columns to a table. ■

How to change data and characteristics of your database tables

SQL Server permits you to change the column values of tables and add new columns to a table.

Operations made on multiple tables

You'll lean to combine data from multiple tables using relational joins and the UNION statement.

Remove one or more unwanted rows from a table

SQL Server permits you to remove selected rows from a table with the DELETE statement.

Updating Rows

Changing column values of rows is one of the operations that you must be able to perform to maintain a database. You use an UPDATE statement to modify the column values of table rows. The simplified syntax of an UPDATE statement is as follows:

```
UPDATE table_name
SET column_name_1 = value,......column_name_n = value
WHERE column_name comparison operator value
```

You use the WHERE clause to identify the rows to be changed. The WHERE clause, used as part of a SELECT statement, narrows the scope of your selection of rows that will be returned or affected by the query. In an UPDATE statement, the WHERE clause is used to identify the rows that are changed, rather than the rows to be displayed.

TIP   You can use the UPDATE statement to change erroneous entries or misspellings for the column values of existing rows of a table.

In the following example, the values for the Department and Badge columns of the Employees table are changed for the employee Bob Smith. If more than one row has an employee named Bob Smith, the department and badge number of each row is changed.

```
update employees
set department = 'SALES', badge = 1232
where name = 'Bob Smith'
```

N O T E   You can also update views as well as tables with the UPDATE statement. You simply use the name of the View in place of the table name in the UPDATE clause of the UPDATE statement. In many different operations, views are treated the same as tables. ▪

You can use UPDATE to change multiple rows that match the criteria specified by the WHERE clause. In the following example, all rows that contain the department SALES are changed to MARKETING.

```
update employees
set department = 'MARKETING'
where department = 'SALES'
```

> **CAUTION**
>
> You must be careful that you specify only the rows you want changed. If you omit a WHERE clause from an UPDATE statement, the change specified in the SET clause is made to every row of the table. The following example shows a change that's made to all rows of a table:
>
> ```
> update employees
> set wageclass = 'W0'
> ```
>
> There are usually two reasons why an UPDATE statement wouldn't contain a WHERE clause: because the WHERE was inadvertently omitted, or because you purposely want to change a column for all rows of a table.

For example, when you add a new column to a table with the ALTER TABLE command, you may have assigned a null values for the new column for all existing rows of the table. You can use an UPDATE statement without a WHERE clause to add a non-null value to the new column for all rows.

 TIP You can use a SELECT count(*) statement with the same criteria—specifically, your WHERE clause—that you plan to use in your UPDATE statement to learn the number of rows that will be subsequently changed by your UPDATE statement. By first determining the number of rows that will be affected by your UPDATE, you're more likely to notice any mistakes in your criteria.

▶ **See** the section in Chapter 8 entitled *"Using COUNT()."* **p. 217**

SET Clause Options

You can also use an expression or the keywords DEFAULT and NULL in the SET clause of an UP-DATE statement. If you use an expression in a SET clause rather than a constant value, the expression is first evaluated, and its result is assigned to the rows that are specified in the UPDATE statement.

In the following example, a raise in the hourly rate is given to all employees by updating the Rate column of the Pays table.

```
update pays
set rate=rate+2
```

You can use the keyword NULL to change the column value of the specified rows of a table to nulls. The table column that's to be assigned a null value must have been created with the NULL characteristic originally. In the following example, an employee who has been moved out of his current department but not yet assigned to another department has his department changed to a null.

```
update employees
set department=null
where name='Bob Smith'
```

You can also use the UPDATE statement to assign a DEFAULT value if a default value has been associated with the table column. In the following example, the department for an employee is changed to the default value which was previously established and associated with the Department column.

```
update employees
set department=default
where name ='Sally Springer'
```

▶ **See** the Chapter 11 sections entitled *"Creating Defaults"* **p. 314** and *"Binding Defaults."* **p. 315**

N O T E If a default doesn't exist for the column and the column permits nulls, the column value is changed to a null. ▧

Part
II

Ch
7

Overview of the Update Process

An update can be performed in SQL Server in two ways. Under certain conditions, changes can be made directly to the rows of database tables. When a direct update of the table row can be made, the operation is done quickly with little overhead to perform the operation. An update directly to the rows of a table is referred to as an *update in place*.

A second way in which you can change the rows of a table is an *indirect* or *deferred* update. In such an update, the change is made by deleting the row to be modified and then inserting the row as a new row with the new values in place. A deferred update is slower because two operations are required to change the row of a table.

The conditions under which a direct update can be performed are primarily determined by restrictions set on the database table. The following conditions must be met for a direct update to be performed on a table:

■ The updated column can't be part of a clustered index.
■ A update trigger can't be defined on the table.
■ The table can't be set up for replication.

Also, a number of conditions must be met for an update in place to be performed on updates that change a single row:

■ For a table column that's defined using a datatype of variable length (such as VARCHAR), the updated row must fit in the same database page. In general, this means that the information you're inserting can't be larger than the information you're replacing.
■ If a non-clustered index that allows duplicates is defined for the column, the updated column must be a fixed-size datatype or composed of multiple fixed datatypes.
■ If a unique, non-clustered index is defined on the column and the WHERE clause of the UPDATE statement uses an exact match for a unique index, the updated column must be a fixed-size datatype or composed of multiple fixed datatypes. The column in the WHERE clause can be the same column as the updated column.
■ The byte size of the updated row value can't be more than 50 percent different from the original row, and the total number of new bytes must be equal to or less than 24.

The following set of conditions must be met for updates that change multiple rows to be performed in place:

■ The updated column must be defined as a fixed-length datatype.
■ The updated column can't be part of a unique, non-clustered index.
■ If a non-unique, non-clustered index is defined on the column and the WHERE clause of the UPDATE statement isn't the same column as the updated column, an updated column must be a fixed-size datatype or composed of multiple fixed datatypes.
■ The table can't include a timestamp column.

▶ **See** the Chapter 12 section entitled "Understanding Locks." **p. 332**

▶ **See** the Chapter 10 section entitled "Defining Indexes." **p. 274**

▶ **See** the Chapter 14 section entitled "Using *INSERT* and *UPDATE* Triggers." **p. 378**

If needed—perhaps because you'll be making many subsequent updates on your database tables—you can plan the table design so that all updates are direct. You can consider all the restrictions for direct updates to ensure that your updates are performed as quickly as possible.

 You can use the query option SHOWPLAN to determine whether an update was direct or deferred.

Deleting Rows

Removing rows from a database table is another operation that you must be able to perform to maintain a database. Use a DELETE FROM statement to remove table rows. The syntax of a DELETE [FROM] statement is as follows:

```
DELETE [FROM] table_name
WHERE column_name = 'value'
```

You don't need to use the keyword FROM; it's optional in the DELETE statement. You can delete rows from tables, as well as update tables, through views.

In the following example, the operation of the DELETE statement removes all rows that match the criteria specified in the WHERE clause of the DELETE statement. In this case, we're removing all rows that contain the department 'SALES'.

```
delete from employees
where department = 'SALES'
```

 You can first use a COUNT function in a SELECT statement that has an identical WHERE clause to your DELETE statement to determine the number of rows that will be subsequently removed.

TROUBLESHOOTING

I executed a DELETE statement and, even though I uppercased all letters to reference the column values in the WHERE clause of my DELETE statement, it deleted rows that contain the same value in lowercase letters. Why did this happen? You must be aware of the default sort order that was selected when SQL Server was installed. Microsoft SQL Server installs with a case-insensitive sort order and this is why the DELETE statement didn't distinguish between upper- and lowercase. If you want all your subsequent DELETE statements—as well as UPDATE statements—to be case-sensitive, you might want to update SQL Server using SQL Setup from the SQL Server program group to effectively reinstall SQL Server with a case-sensitive sort order specified.

Part

II

Ch

7

▶ **See** the Appendix A section entitled "Installation and Setup of the Client and Server Software."
p. 569

You can use a DELETE FROM statement to remove multiple rows as well as individual rows. However, use the DELETE FROM statement carefully. If you don't use a WHERE clause in a DELETE FROM statement, all table rows are removed—leaving you with an empty table. You'll receive no warning before the DELETE FROM statement is executed. In the following example, all rows of the specified table are deleted:

```
delete from employees
```

N O T E You should define a transaction when you use statements such as DELETE FROM and UPDATE so that you can later change your mind and undo the removal or change of rows. See Chapter 12, "Understanding Transactions and Locking," to learn how to define and undo a transaction. It's often desirable to keep your transactions to as few statements as necessary, so that other users can access the latest information about a table. ■

TROUBLESHOOTING

I began entering a DELETE FROM statement and got as far as the name of the table when I accidentally executed the query. When I try to read the table, all the rows are gone. Other products ask me to confirm an unrecoverable action such as the deletion of all table rows. I'm surprised that SQL Server doesn't do this. How can I prevent this from happening again? Because SQL Server won't ask you to confirm the deletion or update of one or all table rows, you must be sure that you want the action to be performed before you allow it to execute.

N O T E The execution of a DELETE statement without a WHERE clause that removes all rows of a table is most often an accident. If you want to delete all rows of a table, but still keep the table intact, you should use the TRUNCATE statement. The syntax of TRUNCATE table is:

```
Truncate table_name
```

The advantage of using a TRUNCATE TABLE statement is that the removal of rows is completed faster than an equivalent DELETE statement. The truncate statement is faster because it removes pages of information that contain multiple tables rows at a time rather than the delete statement, which removes individual rows at a time. However, you can't recover table rows with the TRUNCATE TABLE statement. Unlike the DELETE statement, the TRUNCATE statement does not maintain a copy of the deleted rows even if it's part of a defined transaction.

TRUNCATE TABLE and DELETE TABLE retain the database table. If you want to permanently remove a table, as well as all rows that it contains, you can use the DROP TABLE statement (which uses the following syntax):

```
DROP TABLE table_name
```

After you drop a table, you can't recover the rows that it contained except from a previously made backup copy of the table. ■

T I P Another advantage of the truncate statement is that it won't log the removal of the information in the transaction log. If you have a situation where your transaction log has become full, you can still use the TRUNCATE statement to remove rows and free up space in the database.

Adding Columns with *ALTER TABLE*

You primarily use the ALTER TABLE command to add more columns to an existing table. You're limited in the operations you can perform on existing columns. For example, you can't delete a column or change the size or datatype of an existing column.

N O T E Other implementations of SQL do allow changes even to the datatype of existing columns to be performed through the ALTER TABLE statement. The ALTER TABLE statement in SQL Server and Transact-SQL, however, doesn't permit datatype changes to existing rows. In Microsoft SQL Server, you must create a new table, read the rows out of the old table and into the new table to effect such a change. ■

For more information, see the sections entitled "Changing the Width of a Table Column" and "Removing a Column from a Table" later in this chapter.

The syntax of the ALTER TABLE statement is as follows:

```
ALTER TABLE [[<database.>]<owner.>]<table_name>
ADD <column_name> <datatype> NULL [constraint],
<column_name> <datatype> NULL...] [constraint]
[WITH NOCHECK]
[DROP [CONSTRAINT]
        constraint_name [..., constraint_name_n]]
```

When ALTER TABLE is executed, it doesn't expand existing rows. It changes only the internal description of the added columns in the system tables. Each time an existing row is read from the disk, SQL Server adds the additional null entry for the new column or columns before it's available to a user.

When a new row is written to the disk, SQL Server creates the new row with the additional column and its value. SQL Server writes the row with the additional column unless no value is specified for the new row and its value remains a null. In the following example, sp_help is used to display the existing characteristics of a table in which three columns are defined:

```
sp_help employees3
Name                                Owner                          Type
------------------------------      ---------------------------    -------
employees3                          dbo                            user table
Data_located_on_segment             When_created
------------------------------      ---------------------------
default                             Jul 5 1994 10:08PM
Column_name     Type                 Length Nulls
Default_name    Rule_name
------------    ---------------      ------ ----  --------------  -------
```

Part

II

Ch

7

name	char	30	0	(null)	(null)
department	char	30	0	(null)	(null)
badge	int	4	0	(null)	(null)

```
Object does not have any indexes.
No defined keys for this object.
```

ALTER TABLE is used to add a new column to the table. You use the sp_help procedure to verify that the new columns have been added to the table. In the following example, SELECT displays all rows of the new table, including nulls in the new column for all rows:

```
alter table employees3
add wageclass char(2) null
sp_help employees3
```

Name		Owner		Type
employees3		dbo		user table
Data_located_on_segment		When_created		
default		Jul 5 1994 10:08PM		
Column_name	Type	Length Nulls		
Default_name	Rule_name			

name	char	30	0	(null)	(null)
department	char	30	0	(null)	(null)
badge	int	4	0	(null)	(null)
wageclass	char	2	1	(null)	(null)

```
Object does not have any indexes.
No defined keys for this object.
select * from employees3
```

name	department	badge	wageclass
Stan Humphries	Field Service	3211	(null)
Fred Stanhope	Field Service	6732	(null)
Sue Sommers	Logistics	4411	(null)
Lance Finepoint	Library	5522	(null)
Mark McGuire	Field Service	1997	(null)
Sally Springer	Sales	9998	(null)
Ludmilla Valencia	Software	7773	(null)
Barbara Lint	Field Service	8883	(null)
Jeffrey Vickers	Mailroom	8005	(null)
Jim Walker	Unit Manager	7779	(null)
Bob Smith	SALES	1234	(null)

```
(11 row(s) affected)
```

You can use an UPDATE statement to define values for new columns that are added to a table with ALTER TABLE.

The null values are inserted when a new column is added to the table with the ALTER TABLE statement. In the following example, all table rows have a new value added to the column that was added with an earlier UPDATE TABLE statement. A subsequent SELECT statement is used to display all rows of the table, which includes the new column values.

```
update employees3
set wageclass='w4'
(11 row(s) affected)
```

```
select * from employees3
name                      department              badge       wageclass
--------------------      --------------------    ----------   --------
Stan Humphries            Field Service           3211        w4
Fred Stanhope             Field Service           6732        w4
Sue Sommers               Logistics               4411        w4
Lance Finepoint           Library                 5522        w4
Mark McGuire              Field Service           1997        w4
Sally Springer            Sales                   9998        w4
Ludmilla Valencia         Software                7773        w4
Barbara Lint              Field Service           8883        w4
Jeffrey Vickers           Mailroom                8005        w4
Jim Walker                Unit Manager            7779        w4
Bob Smith                 SALES                   1234        w4
(11 row(s) affected)
```

You can also define a new column that you've added to a table with the identity characteristic. In Chapter 5, "Creating Database Tables and Using Datatypes," you learned that the identity characteristic permits you to define an initial value for the first row of the table (the seed) and a value that's added to each successive column to automatically generate a new column value (the increment).

N O T E You can't assign the identity characteristic to an existing column. Only new columns that are added to a table with the ALTER TABLE command can be defined with the identity characteristic. Also, if the value automatically generated for a new column by the identity mechanism exceeds the allowable values for the column's datatype, the ALTER TABLE statement fails and an error is displayed. ■

▶ **See** the Chapter 5 section entitled *"identity* Property." **p. 129**

In the following example, an additional column is added to table pays, which is defined with the identity characteristic and can be subsequently used as a row number.

```
Alter table pays
add row_number identity(1,1)
```

You can also add one or more columns to a table using the SQL Enterprise Manager. To add a column to an existing table through the SQL Enterprise Manager, follow these steps:

1. Right-click a selected table to which you want to add a column.

2. Choose Edit from the menu.

3. Enter one or more columns in the Manage Tables dialog box. You enter a column name, choose a datatype and a size for the datatype.

4. Click the Save Table tool on the toolbar to keep the additional columns that you've added to a table. In Figure 7.1, an additional column (wageclass) is added to the Employees table.

Part

II

Ch

7

FIG. 7.1

You can't deselect the null property on a column added to an existing table.

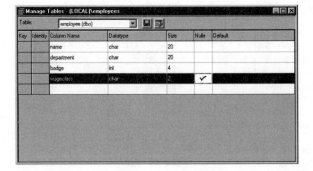

T I P You can also double-click a table to open it and edit its structure. This might be the case where you want to add a new column to the table.

Changing the Width of a Table Column

Recall that you can't use ALTER TABLE to change the size of an existing table column or its datatype. You can use ALTER TABLE only to add a new column. You also can't change the size of the column of a table through the SQL Enterprise Manager. You can, however, drop a column or narrow its datatype by creating a new table with smaller but compatible datatypes and fewer columns.

In the following example, a new table is created in which the name and datatype of the first column is identical to the first column in an existing table, but the first column in the new table is smaller in size. In the new table, the second column is defined as VARCHAR instead of CHAR, as it's defined in the second column of the existing table. The new table's third column is defined as SMALLINT instead of INT, as it's defined in the corresponding Badge column in the existing table. The SMALLINT datatype uses half the storage space of INT.

After the new table is created, all rows of the older table are loaded into the new table with an INSERT statement. A SELECT statement is then used to display the rows of the new table.

```
create table employees4
(name char(15), department varchar(20),badge smallint)
insert into employees4
select name,department,badge from employees
(11 row(s) affected)
select * from employees4
name            department           badge
-------------- -------------------- ------
Stan Humphries Field Service        3211
Fred Stanhope  Field Service        6732
Sue Sommers    Logistics            4411
Lance Finepoint Library             5522
Mark McGuire   Field Service        1997
Sally Springer Sales                9998
L. Valencia    Software             7773
```

```
Barbara Lint      Field Service     8883
Jeffrey Vickers Mailroom            8005
Jim Walker        Unit Manager      7779
Bob Smith         SALES             1234
(11 row(s) affected)
```

The sp_help procedure shows the difference between datatypes in the corresponding columns of the two tables used in the example. The example shows only the relevant parts of the display returned by sp_help.

```
sp_help employees
Name                            Owner                         Type
- - - - - - - - - - - - - - -  - - - - - - - - - - - - - - - - - - - - - - - -  - - - - -
employees                       dbo                           user table
...
name           char             20    0     (null)          (null)
department     char             20    0     deptdefault     (null)
badge          int              4     0     (null)          (null)
...
sp_help employees4
Name                            Owner                         Type
- - - - - - - - - - - - - - -  - - - - - - - - - - - - - - - - - - - - - - - -  - - - - -
employees4                      dbo                           user table
- - - - - - - - - - -  - - - - - - - - - - -  - - - - - -  - - - -  - - - - - - - - - - - - - -  - - - - - - - -
...
name           char             15    0     (null)          (null)
department     varchar          20    0     (null)          (null)
badge          smallint         2     0     (null)          (null)
...
```

The INSERT table statement successfully completes because the data from the earlier table is compatible with the columns defined for the new table. If the data isn't compatible between the tables, you'll receive an error. In the following example, a new table is created that defines a column as a character datatype. The attempted insertion of the corresponding column from one table results in an error because the datatypes can't be implicitly converted.

```
create table onecolumn
(badge char(4))
insert into onecolumn
select badge from employees
Msg 257, Level 16, State 1
Implicit conversion from datatype 'int' to 'char' is not allowed.
Use the CONVERT function to run this query.
```

N O T E If you're transferring a large number of rows between tables, you can first set a database option called select into/bulkcopy. If the select into/bulkcopy option is set, your rows are copied into a new table faster because SQL Server keeps less information in its transaction logs about your operation. The lack of complete log information about your operation, which prevents an undo or rollback operation to be done later, is probably not important because you still have the rows in the original table should the need arise to undo any operations.

Part

II

Ch

7

From an ISQL/W command line, the `select into/bulk copy` option can be set on or off by issuing the following command:

```
sp_dboption database_name, 'select into/bulkcopy', TRUE¦FALSE
```

For example, the following command turns on `select into/bulkcopy` for the database employees:

```
sp_dboption database_employees, 'select into/bulkcopy', true ■
```

TIP You can also change a database option using the graphical interface of the SQL Enterprise Manager rather than a command line.

Removing a Column from a Table

Although you can't remove a column from a table with the ALTER TABLE command, you can remove a column from a table through a series of operations. You also can't remove a column from a table with the SQL Enterprise Manager. First, create a new table that you define with all but one of the columns in an existing table. Then use an INSERT statement to copy rows from the original table to the new table, minus the column that you didn't define in the new table.

In the following example, a new table is defined that contains only two of the three columns defined in an existing table. INSERT is used with a SELECT statement that references only two of the three columns of the original table in the SELECT clause.

```
create table employees5
(name char(20), badge int))
insert into employees5
select name,badge from employees
```

Adding Constraints with *ALTER TABLE*

You can also use the ALTER TABLE command to add, drop, apply, or bypass constraints or checks on an existing table. Constraints are defined to provide data integrity on added columns. The ALTER TABLE statement, like the CREATE TABLE statement, allows you to add a column to a table with primary and foreign key, unique, and check and default constraints. You can add or drop constraints to or from a table without adding a new column. The syntax for constraints is identical to the syntax used for defining constraints in the CREATE TABLE statement.

▶ **See** the Chapter 5 section entitled "Creating and Using Constraints." **p. 130**

In the following example, a unique CONSTRAINT is added to the Badge column for the table employees2.

```
ALTER TABLE employees2
ADD
CONSTRAINT badgeunc UNIQUE NONCLUSTERED (badge)
```

N O T E Microsoft added a number of additional options to the ALTER TABLE statement in version 6 of SQL Server. All the additions were characteristics that were made to a table in other ways before version 6. You can continue to use the older and more direct ways of changing table characteristics. For example, an index, default, or rule can be defined and subsequently associated with a table using CREATE INDEX, CREATE RULE, or CREATE DEFAULT commands.

The changes that were made to the ALTER TABLE statement, as well as many other statements, allow Transact-SQL to meet the specifications of a standardized specification of SQL, ANSI SQL. The additions for ANSI compatibility result in multiple ways of performing the same operations, sometimes using different keywords or syntax. ■

You can easily drop a constraint from a table using the drop constraint clause of the alter table statement. You simply specify the name of the constraint to be removed from a table after the keywords drop constraint. For example, to remove a default constraint on the Department column for the Employees table, enter the following statement:

```
alter table employees
drop constraint department_default
```

Using the *WITH NOCHECK* Clause

You can add a NOCHECK clause to an ALTER TABLE statement to specify that a CHECK or FOREIGN KEY constraint shouldn't be applied on the existing rows of a table. The constraints added with the ALTER TABLE statement that contains the WITH NOCHECK clause are in effect only for rows that are subsequently changed or inserted. You can use a NOCHECK clause in an ALTER TABLE statement when you're certain that the existing data doesn't violate the constraints to speed up the execution of the ALTER TABLE statement.

You can't use WITH NOCHECK to override the initial checking of PRIMARY KEY and UNIQUE constraints. By default, SQL Server applies the constraints to existing rows in the table as well as new rows that are added or changed later. You'll receive an error message and the ALTER TABLE statement will fail if existing data violates your constraint.

You can also specify that a CHECK constraint that's added to a table through the ALTER TABLE statement isn't applied to the existing rows of a table through the NOT FOR REPLICATION clause. NOT FOR REPLICATION operates as though the WITH NOCHECK clause was added to the ALTER TABLE statement. The NOT FOR REPLICATION clause is added to an ALTER TABLE statement for a different purpose than the WITH NOCHECK clause.

If you set up the automatic copying of a table and table rows from one server system to another, the actual work of ensuring the server system that receives a copy of the data is done by an intermediate server. The NOT FOR REPLICATION clause is added to an ALTER TABLE statement to prevent the table copy on the intermediate server from being checked, an unnecessary operation.

Part
II

Ch
7

▶ **See** Chapter 20 "Setting Up and Managing Replication," for more information. **p. 505**

Adding Constraints Through the SQL Enterprise Manager

You can add table and column constraints through the SQL Enterprise Manager. To add a constraint to a table or column through the Enterprise Manager, follow these steps:

1. Right-click a selected table to which you want to add a constraint in the main window of the Server Manager.

2. Choose <u>E</u>dit from the menu. You can also double-click the table.

   Click the Advanced Features tool on the toolbar. You can click the Primary Key/Identity, Foreign Keys, Unique Constraints, or Check Constraints tabs to create each type of constraint.

3. Enter the requisite information in the <u>C</u>onstraint box that appears after you click a tab. For example, in Figure 7.2, a Chec<u>k</u> Constraint is entered on the Departments column for the Employees table to prevent any department from being entered and stored that isn't one of three department values.

FIG. 7.2
The <u>N</u>ot for Replication check box can also be checked when the Chec<u>k</u> Constraint option is defined.

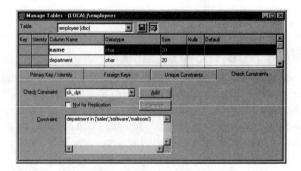

4. Click the Save Table toolbar button to apply the constraint to the table.

Performing Relational Joins

The rows of different tables can be combined to display and operate on the data using the same statements used in single tables. The rows of multiple tables can be combined in various ways. The first way is called an *equi-join* or *natural join*.

You perform a natural join or equi-join by matching equal values for rows in shared columns between multiple tables. You must define one of the two tables so that a column from one of the tables is duplicated in the second table. The column from the original table can be its primary key if it also is a column with values that make the rows of the table unique. The duplicate column that's added to a second table is referred to as a *foreign key*.

You define a foreign key to permit rows from different tables to be related. In a sense, the matching columns are used to form virtual rows that span a database table. Although each table is limited to 250 columns, matching columns to combine rows from multiple tables can result in almost an unlimited number of columns that can be combined across tables.

You use a standard SELECT statement with a WHERE clause to retrieve data from two or more tables. The syntax of a SELECT statement that's used to join two tables is as follows:

```
SELECT column_name_1,...column_name_n
FROM table_name_1, table_name_2
WHERE primary_key_column=
foreign_key_column
```

The following create table and insert statements are used to create a new table in the same database to be used for subsequent relational join examples. Each row that's added to the Pays table matches one row of the Employees table.

```
create table pays
(hours_worked int, rate int,badge int)
go
insert into pays
values (40,10,3211);
go
insert into pays
values (40,9,6732);
go
insert into pays
values (52,10,4411);
go
insert into pays
values (39,11,5522);
go
insert into pays
values (51,10,1997);
go
insert into pays
values (40,8,9998);
go
insert into pays
values (55,10,7773);
insert into pays
values (40,9,8883);
go
insert into pays
values (60,7,8005);
go
insert into pays
values (37,11,7779);
go
```

In the following example, three columns from two tables are displayed after the Badge column is used to combine the rows that have matching Badge numbers.

```
select name, department,hours_worked
from employees,pays
where employees.badge=pays.badge
name                department
hours_worked
-------------------  ------------------- --
Stan Humphries       Field Service          40
Fred Stanhope        Field Service          40
```

Part
II

Ch

7

```
Sue Sommers          Logistics        52
Lance Finepoint      Library          39
Mark McGuire         Field Service    51
Sally Springer       Sales            40
Ludmilla Valencia    Software         55
Barbara Lint         Field Service    40
Jeffrey Vickers      Mailroom         60
Jim Walker           Unit Manager     37
(10 row(s) affected)
```

An equi-join doesn't eliminate any of the table columns from the temporary tables that are formed by the join of tables. You must use a WHERE clause to match the corresponding rows of the tables. You also shouldn't use the asterisk wild-card character to reference all columns of the combined tables. If you use an asterisk, the columns with matching values are displayed twice.

In the following example, the rows of two tables are accessed without using a WHERE clause. SQL Server forms a cross-product of the rows in both tables. If you don't try to combine the rows using matching columns, each row of the second table in the FROM clause is added to every row of the first table. The Badge column is displayed from both tables because the asterisk wildcard is used in the SELECT clause.

```
select *
from employees,pays
name                 department       badge   hours_worked rate   badge
-----------------    -------------    -----   ------------ ----   ----
Stan Humphries       Field Service    3211    40           9      6732
Stan Humphries       Field Service    3211    40           10     3211
Stan Humphries       Field Service    3211    52           10     4411
Stan Humphries       Field Service    3211    39           11     5522
Stan Humphries       Field Service    3211    51           10     1997
Stan Humphries       Field Service    3211    40           8      9998
Stan Humphries       Field Service    3211    55           10     7773
Stan Humphries       Field Service    3211    40           9      8883
Stan Humphries       Field Service    3211    60           7      8005
Stan Humphries       Field Service    3211    37           11     7779
Fred Stanhope        Field Service    6732    40           9      6732
...
(100 row(s) affected)
```

The combination of all rows of the second table with the first table results in a *cross-product*, also called a *Cartesian Product*, of the two tables. In the example, the Employees table and the Pays table each contains 10 rows, so the resultant cross-product creates 100 rows in the temporary table. However, only 10 of the 100 rows belong together. The badge numbers match in one out of every 10 rows between the two tables.

TROUBLESHOOTING

I joined together two tables that didn't have matching columns with a SELECT statement that didn't contain a WHERE clause. I was surprised that SQL Server returned a huge table. The SELECT statement operates on multiple tables whether or not they were designed to be combined with a relational join. It's important to always use a WHERE clause, which eliminates rows that don't have matching column values. If you don't use a WHERE clause, you'll receive a temporary table that contains the cross-product of the number of rows in the first table multiplied by the number of rows in the second table. For example, two tables that each contains only 100 rows joined without a WHERE clause will return 10,000 rows.

If you reference one of the columns used to match the rows across both tables, you must indicate the table in which the column is defined. Any time you reference a column that has the same name in multiple tables, you must somehow specify which column from which table to prevent ambiguity. The following example displays an error because SQL Server doesn't know from which table to display the Badge column.

```
select badge
from employees,pays
where employees.badge=pays.badge
Msg 209, Level 16, State 1
Ambiguous column name badge
```

To avoid ambiguity, the table columns used for matching rows are preceded by the table in which they're defined and separated by a period (.). In the following example, the Badge column is displayed from the first table by preceding the name of the Badge column with its table name.

```
select employees.badge
from employees,pays
where employees.badge=pays.badge
badge
----------
3211
6732
4411
5522
1997
9998
7773
8883
8005
7779
(10 row(s) affected)
```

Using Range Variables

In the previous example, the name of the table is used to prevent ambiguity when referencing table columns in a SELECT statement when multiple tables are referenced. In fact, what appears in the examples to be the name of the table preceding the column name actually is a *range variable*.

N O T E   Other dialects of SQL refer to a range variable as an alias. ■

Part

II

Ch

7

Range variables are symbolic references for tables that are specified in the FROM clause of a SELECT statement. You can use a range variable in a preceding clause, such as the SELECT clause, or in a clause that comes after the FROM clause, such as a WHERE clause. Define a range variable by specifying a character constant following the name of a table in the FROM clause of a SELECT statement, as in the following syntax:

```
...
From table_name_1 range_name_1, ...,table_name_n range_name_n
...
```

You can define a range variable for each table that's specified in the FROM clause. You can use as many as 30 characters—the limit for any permanent or temporary object in Transact-SQL—to define the range variable. A range variable can be defined to provide a shorter reference to a table in a SELECT statement. In the following example, a range variable is defined for each table. The range variables are used in both the SELECT and WHERE clauses.

```
select e.badge,p.id
from employees e,pays p
where e.badge=p.id
badge       id
---------- ----
3211       3211
3211       3211
3211       3211
3211       3211
6732       6732
4411       4411
5522       5522
1997       1997
9998       9998
7773       7773
8883       8883
8005       8005
7779       7779
3211       3211
3211       3211
3211       3211
3211       3211
(17 row(s) affected)
```

Range variables are called range variables because after they're defined, the symbolic reference applies to, or ranges through, the table. As in the previous example, you can define a range variable to be a single character and use it as a short nickname for a table.

Range variables can be quite handy because several tables with long names can be specified in a SELECT statement. You can combine rows from as many as 16 tables in SQL Server using Transact-SQL. If you don't explicitly define range variables in the FROM clause, they're implicitly created using the complete name of each table.

In the following example, the rows from three tables are combined using the Badge columns that are defined in all the tables. The range variables are implicitly defined to the table names and are used in both the SELECT and WHERE clauses. The WHERE clause first combines the first and second tables; then the first and third tables use the AND Boolean operator.

```
select pays.badge, name,department, payrate
from employees,pays, salaries
where employees.badge = pays.badge
and employees.badge=salaries.badge
```

N O T E Transact-SQL automatically establishes range variables for use in queries. If you don't specify a range variable for the name of a table in the `FROM` clause, a range variable is created with the same name as the table, as in the following example:

```
select name
from employees
```

is internally rewritten as:

```
select employees.name
from employees employees
```

Although it seems unnecessary to create range variables when only a single table is named in the query, they are mandatory when you reference tables that contain columns with the same names in the same query. ▓

Using Many-to-One and One-to-Many Joins

You may not have tables that have only one corresponding row in each table. In previous examples, only a single row in the employees table matches the value of a single row in the pays table. It's possible that you'll have to create or work with existing tables in which more than one entry is a match for the entries in another table.

In the ensuing examples, rows have been added with identical badge numbers in the employees table. Three employees have been added, each with a last name of Smith and each with the same badge number. In the tables referenced in the following examples, Badge isn't defined as a primary key, so duplicate badge numbers can be present. Three employees with last names of Humphries have also been added, each with the same badge number as the original employee, Stan Humphries. The following example shows the rows of the Employees table after the additional seven rows are added.

N O T E Although you usually define a primary and foreign key using the corresponding columns of tables that you subsequently want to combine rows from for display, you aren't required to define the columns as keys. SQL Server will permit you to perform joins on tables that don't have primary or foreign key definitions. You should realize that the assignment of primary and foreign keys to a table isn't required, though it's often desirable, if you combine data from different tables. ▓

```
select * from employees
order by badge
name                    department              badge
------------------- ------------------- ----
Bob Smith               SALES                   1234
Henry Smith             Logistics               1234
Susan Smith             Executive               1234
Mark McGuire            Field Service           1997
```

Part

II

Ch

7

```
Gertie Humphries     Sales           3211
Stan Humphries       Field Service   3211
Stan Humphries Jr    Sales           3211
Winkie Humphries     Mailroom        3211
Sue Sommers          Logistics       4411
Lance Finepoint      Library         5522
Fred Stanhope        Field Service   6732
Ludmilla Valencia    Software        7773
Jim Walker           Unit Manager    7779
Jeffrey Vickers      Mailroom        8005
Barbara Lint         Field Service   8883
Sally Springer       Sales           9998
(16 row(s) affected)
```

The Pays table is unaltered and contains only the original 10 rows, as shown in the following example:

```
select * from pays
order by badge
hours_worked rate       badge
------------ ---------- ----
51           10         1997
40           10         3211
52           10         4411
39           11         5522
40            9         6732
55           10         7773
37           11         7779
60            7         8005
40            9         8883
40            8         9998
(10 row(s) affected)
```

You can combine tables that have an unequal number of matching rows. The following example joins the Employees table, in which two sets of entries match a single entry for the Badge column in the Pays table. The join of the Employees table with the Pays table is called *many-to-one*.

```
select name,pays.badge,hours_worked,rate
from employees,pays
where employees.badge=pays.badge
name                 badge    hours_worked    rate
----                 ----     ------------    ----
Fred Stanhope        6732     40              9
Stan Humphries       3211     40              10
Gertie Humphries     3211     40              10
Stan Humphries Jr    3211     40              10
Winkie Humphries     3211     40              10
Sue Sommers          4411     52              10
Lance Finepoint      5522     39              11
Mark McGuire         1997     51              10
Sally Springer       9998     40              8
Ludmilla Valencia    7773     55              10
Barbara Lint         8883     40              9
Jeffrey Vickers      8005     60              7
Jim Walker           7779     37              11
(13 row(s) affected)
```

If you switch the order of the joined tables, it becomes a *one-to-many join*. The following example returns the same rows that were returned in the previous example:

```
select name,pays.badge,hours_worked,rate
from pays,employees
where pays.badge=employees.badge
name                 badge        hours_worked    rate
----                 ----         ------------    ----
Fred Stanhope        6732         40              9
Stan Humphries       3211         40              10
Gertie Humphries     3211         40              10
Stan Humphries Jr    3211         40              10
Winkie Humphries     3211         40              10
Sue Sommers          4411         52              10
Lance Finepoint      5522         39              11
Mark McGuire         1997         51              10
Sally Springer       9998         40              8
Ludmilla Valencia    7773         55              10
Barbara Lint         8883         40              9
Jeffrey Vickers      8005         60              7
Jim Walker           7779         37              11
(13 row(s) affected)
```

Using Many-to-Many Joins

You may also want to join tables where more than one row matches more than one row in a second table, which is referred to as a *many-to-many join*. In the following example, two tables are combined after one row is added to Pays with a 3211 badge number, 73 hours_worked, and rate of 31.

```
select name,pays.badge,hours_worked,rate
from employees,pays
where employees.badge=pays.badge
name                 badge        hours_worked    rate
----                 ----         ------------    ----
Fred Stanhope        6732         40              9
Stan Humphries       3211         40              10
Gertie Humphries     3211         40              10
Stan Humphries Jr    3211         40              10
Winkie Humphries     3211         40              10
Sue Sommers          4411         52              10
Lance Finepoint      5522         39              11
Mark McGuire         1997         51              10
Sally Springer       9998         40              8
Ludmilla Valencia    7773         55              10
Barbara Lint         8883         40              9
Jeffrey Vickers      8005         60              7
Jim Walker           7779         37              11
Stan Humphries       3211         73              31
Gertie Humphries     3211         73              31
Stan Humphries Jr    3211         73              31
Winkie Humphries     3211         73              31
(17 row(s) affected)
```

Part

II

Ch

7

The additional row is added to the temporary table that's displayed. If the row value is restricted to only the badge number 3211, eight rows are returned.

Many-to-many queries are often not desirable and can produce results that are difficult to follow. In most cases, it's best to implement either a one-to-many or a many-to-one relationship, even if it entails adding an intermediary table.

▶ **See** Chapter 2, "Data Modeling and Database Design," for more information on database design approaches. **p. 33**

```
select name,pays.badge,hours_worked,rate
from employees,pays
where employees.badge=pays.badge
and pays.badge=3211
name                    badge        hours_worked   rate
----                    ----         ------------   ----
Stan Humphries          3211         40             10
Gertie Humphries        3211         40             10
Stan Humphries Jr       3211         40             10
Winkie Humphries        3211         40             10
Stan Humphries          3211         73             31
Gertie Humphries        3211         73             31
Stan Humphries Jr       3211         73             31
Winkie Humphries        3211         73             31
(8 row(s) affected)
```

Using Outer Joins

In the previous join examples, we excluded the rows in either of the two tables that didn't have corresponding or matching rows.

Previous examples, in which the rows of two tables were joined with a WHERE statement, included all rows of both tables. However, a query that includes all rows from both tables is probably never useful, except to understand the way in which SQL Server combines the rows. You can combine any two or more tables with a WHERE clause and receive a set of rows that were never meant to be combined and thus receive a meaningless result.

In practice, you'll combine only the rows from tables that have been created to be matched together. Tables that are designed to be combined have common columns of information so that a WHERE clause can be included in a query to eliminate the rows that don't belong together (those that have identical values).

N O T E   You must ensure that the information used to combine tables—the corresponding values in common columns—remains valid. If the value in one table is changed, the corresponding identical value (or values, if a one-to-many relationship exists) must also be updated in other tables.

Referential integrity involves ensuring that you have valid information in common columns across tables used to join tables. You'll read more about referential integrity in subsequent chapters. Chapter 14, "Creating and Managing Triggers," discusses the mechanism for maintaining referential integrity and Chapter 10, "Managing and Using Indexes and Keys," discusses the common table columns on which joins are based. ■

Use outer joins to return table rows that have both matching and non-matching values. You may need to return the rows that don't contain matching values in the common table columns for either one table or the other tables specified in the SELECT statement.

If, for example, you join the employees table with the pays table used in the previous examples, you can specify the return of rows with matching values along with rows without matching values. The specification of the outer join is positional, which means that you use a special symbol that precedes or follows the comparison operator in the WHERE clause of a SELECT statement.

An outer join references one of the two tables joined using the table's position in the WHERE clause. A *left-outer join* specifies the table to the left of a comparison operator and a *right-outer join* specifies the table to the right of a comparison operator. The following table shows the symbol combination used for outer joins.

Symbol Combination	Join
*=	Left-outer join
=*	Right-outer join

A left-outer join (*=) retains non-matching rows for the table on the left of the symbol combination in a WHERE statement. A right-outer join (=*) retains non-matching rows for the table on the right of the symbol combination.

In the following example, a SELECT statement specifies a join in the WHERE clause to return only rows that contain matching values in a common column for the two tables:

```
select *
from employees,pays
where employees.badge=pays.badge
name              department     badge    hours_worked rate    badge

Stan Humphries     Field Service  3211        40         10      3211
Gertie Humphries   Sales          3211        40         10      3211
Stan Humphries Jr. Sales          3211        40         10      3211
Winkie Humphries   Mailroom       3211        40         10      3211
Fred Stanhope      Field Service  6732        40          9      6732
Sue Sommers        Logistics      4411        52         10      4411
Lance Finepoint    Library        5522        39         11      5522
Mark McGuire       Field Service  1997        51         10      1997
Sally Springer     Sales          9998        40          8      9998
Ludmilla Valencia  Software       7773        55         10      7773
Barbara Lint       Field Service  8883        40          9      8883
Jeffrey Vickers    Mailroom       8005        60          7      8005
Jim Walker         Unit Manager   7779        37         11      7779
Stan Humphries     Field Service  3211        73         31      3211
Gertie Humphries   Sales          3211        73         31      3211
Stan Humphries Jr. Sales          3211        73         31      3211
Winkie Humphries   Mailroom       3211        73         31      3211
(17 row(s) affected)
```

Part
II

Ch

7

In the next example, a left-outer join is used in the WHERE clause of a SELECT statement to specify that both rows containing matching values for a common column and the rows from the left table (employees) are included in the rows returned. This might be the case where you needed to find out what employees don't have a pay rate associated with them.

Before the following query was executed, additional rows were added to the Employees table that don't have corresponding values in a common column in the Pays table:

```
select *
from employees,pays
where employees.badge*=pays.badge
name                     department      badge    hours_worked rate     badge
----------------         ------------    -------  ------------ -------- ----
Stan Humphries           Field Service   3211     40           10       3211
Stan Humphries           Field Servic    3211     73           31       3211
Fred Stanhope            Field Service   6732     40           9        6732
Sue Sommers              Logistics       4411     52           10       4411
Lance Finepoint          Library         5522     39           11       5522
Mark McGuire             Field Service   1997     51           10       1997
Sally Springer           Sales           9998     40           8        9998
Ludmilla Valencia        Software        7773     55           10       7773
Barbara Lint             Field Service   8883     40           9        8883
Jeffrey Vickers          Mailroom        8005     60           7        8005
Jim Walker               Unit Manager    7779     37           11       7779
Bob Smith                SALES           1234     (null)       (null)   (null)
Bob Jones                Sales           2223     (null)       (null)   (null)
Gertie Humphries         Sales           3211     40           10       3211
Gertie Humphries         Sales           3211     73           31       3211
Stan Humphries Jr.       Sales           3211     40           10       3211
Stan Humphries Jr.       Sales           3211     73           31       3211
Winkie Humphries         Mailroom        3211     40           10       3211
Winkie Humphries         Mailroom        3211     73           31       3211
Susan Smith              Executive       1234     (null)       (null)   (null)
Henry Smith              Logistics       1234     (null)       (null)   (null)
(21 row(s) affected)
```

N O T E Recall that null values don't match, so rows that contain nulls in the primary and foreign key columns are displaying only with outer joins and won't be seen with equi-joins. ■

In the next example, a right-outer join is used in the WHERE clause of a SELECT statement to specify that both rows that contain matching values for a common column and the rows from the right table (Pays) are included in the rows returned. Two additional rows are first added to the Pays table that don't have corresponding values in a common column in the Employees table.

```
insert into pays
values (40,10,5555)
insert into pays
values (40,10,5555)
select *
from employees,pays
where employees.badge=*pays.id
```

```
name                 department     badge    hours_worked rate    id
----------------     ----------     ------   ------------ -----   ----
Stan Humphries       Field Service  3211       40           10    3211
Gertie Humphries     Sales          3211       40           10    3211
Stan Humphries Jr.   Sales          3211       40           10    3211
Winkie Humphries     Mailroom       3211       40           10    3211
Fred Stanhope        Field Service  6732       40            9    6732
Sue Sommers          Logistics      4411       52           10    4411
Lance Finepoint      Library        5522       39           11    5522
Mark McGuire         Field Service  1997       51           10    1997
Sally Springer       Sales          9998       40            8    9998
Ludmilla Valencia    Software       7773       55           10    7773
Barbara Lint         Field Service  8883       40            9    8883
Jeffrey Vickers      Mailroom       8005       60            7    8005
Jim Walker           Unit Manager   7779       37           11    7779
Stan Humphries       Field Service  3211       73           31    3211
Gertie Humphries     Sales          3211       73           31    3211
Stan Humphries Jr.   Sales          3211       73           31    3211
Winkie Humphries     Mailroom       3211       73           31    3211
(null)               (null)         (null)     40           10    5555
(null)               (null)         (null)     40           10    5555
(19 row(s) affected)
```

TIP Left- and right-outer joins can be used to show rows that contain nulls which wouldn't have corresponding entries across tables, and would be displayed *only* with other non-matching entries.

Combining Query Results with *UNION*

Use a *UNION* to combine the results of two or more queries. A UNION merges the results of the first query with the results of a second query. UNION implicitly removes duplicate rows between the queries. A UNION returns a single results set that consists of all the rows that belong to the first table, the second table, or both tables.

You should define the queries that contain a UNION clause so that they're compatible. The queries should have the same number of columns and a common column defined for each table. You also can't use a UNION within the definition of a view.

The syntax for queries that include a UNION clause is as follows:

```
SELECT column_name_1, ..., column_name_n
FROM table_name_1, ... , table_name_n
WHERE column_name comparison_operator value
[GROUP BY...]
[HAVING ...
UNION
SELECT column_name_1, ..., column_name_n
FROM table_name_1, ... , table_name_n
WHERE column_name comparison_operator value
[GROUP BY...]
[HAVING...]
[ORDER BY...]
[COMPUTE...
```

Part
II

Ch
7

In the following example, the badge numbers that are common to both tables are displayed using two select statements that are bound with a UNION clause. The ORDER BY clause is used after the last query to order the final results. The ORDER BY clause appears only after the last SELECT statement. Recall that UNION implicitly removes duplicate rows, as defined by the query.

```
select badge from employees
union
select badge from pays
order by badge
badge
----------
1234
1997
3211
4411
5522
6732
7773
7779
8005
8883
9998
(11 row(s) affected)
```

In the following example, the same set of queries is used except the ALL keyword is added to the UNION clause. This retains query-defined duplicates (only the Badge column) in the resultant rows. The duplicate rows from both tables are retained.

```
select badge from employees
union all
select badge from pays
order by badge
badge
------
1234
1234
1234
1997
1997
3211
3211
3211
3211
3211
3211
4411
4411
5522
5522
6732
6732
7773
7773
7779
7779
```

```
8005
8005
8883
8883
9998
9998
(27 row(s) affected)
```

In the following example, the datatypes referenced in the query for one of the two columns aren't compatible. The execution of the example returns an error because of this.

```
select name,badge from employees
union
select hours_worked,badge from pay
Msg 257, Level 16, State 1
Implicit conversion from datatype 'char' to 'int' is not allowed.
 Use the CONVERT function to run this query.
```

You can use a UNION clause with queries to combine the rows from two compatible tables and merge the rows into a new third table. To illustrate this merge, in which the results are kept in a permanent table, a new table is created that has the same datatypes as the existing Employees table. Several rows are first inserted into the new table.

```
create table employees2
(name char(20),department char(20),badge int)
go
insert into employees2
values ('Rod Gilbert','Sales',3339)
go
insert into employees2
values ('Jean Ratele','Sales',5551)
go
insert into employees2
values ('Eddie Giacomin','Sales',8888)
```

Each table now has rows that contain employees records. If you use a UNION clause to combine the SELECT statements along with INSERT INTO, the resultant rows can be retained in a new table.

The SELECT statement that references the Employees table uses WHERE to restrict the rows returned to only those with the Sales department. All three rows of the employees2 table are in the Sales department, so no WHERE clause is necessary.

```
create table employees3
(name char(20),department char(20),badge int))
go
insert into employees3
select * from employees
where department='Sales'
union
select * from employees2
(6 row(s) affected)
select * from employees3
name                 department            badge
----                 ----------            ----
Eddie Giacomin       Sales                 8888
```

```
Gertie Humphries     Sales                    3211
Jean Ratele          Sales                    5551
Rod Gilbert          Sales                    3339
Sally Springer       Sales                    9998
Stan Humphries Jr    Sales                    3211
(6 row(s) affected)
```

As in the previous example, you can use UNION to combine multiple tables, or combinations of selected columns and rows from tables, into an existing or new table. You can have tables with identical columns at different office locations in which rows are added throughout the day.

At the end of the work day, you can use a set of SELECT statements with a UNION clause to add the separate collection tables to a master table at a central location. After the rows are copied to the master table, the rows of the collection tables can be removed using a DELETE FROM statement without a WHERE clause, or a TRUNCATE statement as mentioned earlier in this chapter.

You can combine up to 16 SELECT statements by adding additional UNION clauses between each set of SELECT statements. You can use parentheses to control the order of the UNIONs. The SELECT statements within parentheses are performed before those that are outside parentheses. You don't need to use parentheses if all the UNIONs are UNION ALL. You also don't need parentheses if none of the UNIONs is UNION ALL.

In the following example, three tables are combined using a UNION clause. IN is used with the first table to specify multiple forms of one department. The second table doesn't use WHERE and all rows are selected. The third table specifies only a single case-sensitive department name, assuming the sort order is case-sensitive.

You don't need parentheses to control the order of the merges because no UNIONs use ALL. The resultant rows are ordered by Badge and Name using an ORDER BY clause that can appear only after the last SELECT statement.

```
select name,badge
from employees
where department in ('SALES','Sales','sales')
union
select name,badge
from employees2
union
select name,badge
from employees3
where department='Sales'
order by badge,name
name                 badge
----                 ----
Bob Smith            1234
Gertie Humphries     3211
Stan Humphries Jr    3211
Rod Gilbert          3339
Jean Ratele          5551
Eddie Giacomin       8888
Sally Springer       9998
(7 row(s) affected)
```

From Here...

In this chapter you learned to add rows and delete rows from a database tables as well as change the characteristics of a table. You also learned how to perform operations on multiple tables using relational joins and UNION statements. Additional related information can be found in the following chapters:

- Chapter 2, "Data Modeling and Database Design," teaches you how you can create tables that logically lend themselves to the types of joins we've covered here.

- Chapter 10, "Managing and Using Indexes and Keys," teaches you how to define the common columns in tables that are used to perform joins.

- Chapter 12, "Understanding Transactions and Locking," teaches you how to set up a query so that you can undo it.

- Chapter 14, "Creating and Managing Triggers," teaches you how to maintain referential integrity, which ensures that correct rows are joined between tables.

Using Functions

Functions execute a section of code that performs an operation that returns a desired value. For the function to perform its operation, you must usually supply the required data as a list in which each element is called a parameter. You can use functions with columns of data and other storage structures of Transact-SQL. You can also use functions in the Select or Where clause of Select statements, in expressions, and, for selected functions such as system and niladic functions, in constraint defined in tables or views. ■

How to use functions to operate on the data in the database tables

Transact-SQL contains numerous functions to manipulate table data.

How to use system functions

You can use system functions to return information about your computer system and Microsoft SQL Server.

How to combine functions

You'll learn to use the information that is returned from one function within a second function in order to return needed information.

Basic SQL Functions

A small subset of Transact-SQL functions illustrate how functions are typically used in Transact-SQL statements. Also, the subset of SQL functions are generic and are typically available in any dialect of SQL.

> **N O T E**   If you've worked with another dialect of SQL, then you're probably familiar with the handful of basic functions. Unfortunately, the set of functions that are used across different vendors' dialects of SQL is extremely small. The remaining functions may be comparable across server database SQL dialects, though they aren't identical. ■

Some of the basic Transact-SQL functions are shown in Table 8.1.

Table 8.1   Basic Transact-SQL Functions

Function	Operation
AVG	Average
SUM	Sum
MIN	Minimum value
MAX	Maximum value
COUNT	Count

These, and other functions in a SELECT clause, are used as if they are column identifiers. The objects or arguments of a function must be enclosed in parentheses. If the function requires more than a single argument, the arguments are separated by a comma (,).

The syntax for the use of functions in the SELECT clause of a SELECT statement is as follows:

```
SELECT function (column_1 or *),...function (column_n)
FROM table
```

Note that NULL values aren't used for computation of AVERAGE, SUM, MIN, MAX. If all elements of a set are NULL, the function return is NULL. COUNT, when used with an asterisk (*), determines the number of rows in a column, even if it contains NULL values.

Using *AVG*

The AVG function returns the arithmetic average of the column values referenced. In the following example, AVG is used to return the average of the Pay Rate column for all rows of the Pays table.

```
select avg(pay_rate)
from pays
```

Using *COUNT*

The COUNT function returns the numbers of columns that match the selection expression. The asterisk wild card (*) is used as an argument for the COUNT function. If * is used in place of the column name in a SELECT clause, the asterisk specifies all rows that meet the criteria of the SELECT statement. The COUNT function counts all table rows that meet the criteria. The following syntax is used with the COUNT function:

```
SELECT COUNT(column_name)
FROM table_name
```

For example, the following SELECT statement returns the number of rows in the Employees table.

```
select count(*)
from employees
```

If a WHERE clause is used in your SELECT statement, the COUNT function applies to only the rows that match the criteria specified in the WHERE clause. For example, the following COUNT statement returns the number of employees in the Sales department.

```
select count(*)
from employees
where department='Sales'
```

 T I P You can improve the performance of the COUNT function by specifying a column name to count, and making sure that the column you specify is both indexed and not NULL. By doing so, SQL Server can use its optimization techniques to return the count of the rows more quickly.

Using *MAX*

MAX returns the largest value in a column. The syntax of MAX is as follows:

```
SELECT MAX(column_name)
FROM table_name
```

In the following example, MAX is used to return the maximum, or greatest number of hours_worked for all rows of the Pays table.

```
select max(hours_worked)
from pays
```

Using *MIN*

MIN returns the smallest value in a column. In the following example, MIN is used to return the minimum number of hours_worked for all rows of the Pays table.

```
select min(hours_worked)
from pays
```

In the next example, MIN is used to return the lowest rate of pay for employees in the Field Service department. Both the Pays and Employees tables must be referenced in the SELECT statement because the Department column is in the Employees table while the Rate column is in the Pays table. The corresponding badge numbers in each table are used to combine the appropriate rows.

```
select min(rate)
from employees,pays
where employees.badge=pays.badge
and department='Field Service'
```

Using *SUM*

SUM returns the summation of such entities as column values. The SUM function returns the total of the non-NULL values in the numeric expression, which is often just a column name, that follows the SUM keyword. The syntax for SUM is as follows:

```
SUM([DISTINCT] <expression>)
```

In the following example, the result would be the sum of the hours_worked for all rows of the Pays table.

```
select sum (hours_worked)
from pays
```

TIP Rows that contain a NULL value in the column referenced by the SUM function are automatically skipped in the calculation.

You can use multiple functions within a single statement. The following example returns the average, minimum, and maximum of the hours_worked column in the Pays table:

```
select avg(hours_worked), min(hours_worked), max(hours_worked)
from pays
```

In a more-complicated example that follows, a SELECT statement is used to return the maximum and average rate, minimum hours_worked, and the count of all rows of the Employees table.

```
select max(rate),min(hours_worked),avg(rate),count(*)
from employees,pays
where employees.badge=pays.badge
```

Using *DISTINCT* with *COUNT*

If the COUNT function is used to reference a column name, it returns the number of values. The COUNT function includes duplicates in its count, but it doesn't include NULL values. If you add the keyword DISTINCT, the COUNT function returns the number of each unique value. The following syntax for the COUNT function is used with the keyword DISTINCT in a SELECT statement:

```
SELECT COUNT(DISTINCT column_name)
FROM table_name
```

In the following example, the keyword DISTINCT is used with the COUNT function in a SELECT statement to display the number of different departments in the Employees table:

```
select count(distinct department)
from employees
```

Using *CUBE* and *ROLLUP*

The CUBE and ROLLUP operators were added to SQL Server 6.5 to make it easier to access large amounts of data in a summary fashion. When a select statement is cubed, aggregate functions are transformed into super-aggregate functions that return only the rows necessary to report a summary of the information requested. The ROLLUP operator differs from CUBE only because it is sensitive to the order of columns in the GROUP BY clause.

> **N O T E** There are several things to be aware of when using the CUBE and ROLLUP operators. First, a GROUP BY column list can be no more than 900 bytes. Second, there is a maximum of 10 columns. Next, columns or expressions must be specified in the GROUP BY clause; GROUP BY ALL can't be used. Finally, these operators are disabled when trace flag 204 is on. ■

Book sales are a perfect example. A query that returns a book title and the number of books ordered for each invoice in a database would return a row for each invoice. If the CUBE operator was applied to this query, it would only return a row for each title and the total quantity ordered for that title.

Using String Functions

Functions are used to perform various operations on binary data, character strings, or expressions (including string concatenation). String functions are used to return values commonly needed for operations on character data. The following list shows the set of string functions:

ASCII	PATINDEX	SPACE
CHAR	REPLICATE	STR
CHARINDEX	REVERSE	STUFF
DIFFERENCE	RIGHT	SUBSTRING
LOWER	RTRIM	UPPER
LTRIM	RTRIM	+

String functions are usually used on CHAR, VARCHAR, BINARY, and VARBINARY datatypes, as well as on datatypes that implicitly convert to CHAR or VARCHAR. For example, you can use the PATINDEX function on CHAR, VARCHAR, and TEXT datatypes.

You can nest string functions so that the results returned by an inner function are available for the operation performed by the outer function. If you use constants with string functions, you should enclose them in quotation marks. String functions are usually used in SELECT or WHERE clauses.

Part
II

Ch
8

> **CAUTION**
>
> You should ensure that the result returned by a nested function is compatible as input to the function in which it's embedded. In other words, if your function is expecting a string variable, be sure that the nested function returns a string, not a numeric value. Check your functions and datatypes carefully to determine if they're compatible. Otherwise, a the set of functions can't function correctly.

Using *ASCII*

ASCII returns the ASCII code value of the leftmost character of a character expression. The syntax of the ASCII function is as follows:

```
ASCII(<char_expr>)
```

> **N O T E** Remember that ASCII only returns the code associated with the leftmost character. If you need to have the ASCII value associated with the remaining portion of the string, you'll need to write a function that can walk down the string and return each value in succession. ■

Using *CHAR*

CHAR converts an ASCII code into a character. If you don't enter the ASCII code within the range of values between zero and 255, a NULL is returned. The syntax of the CHAR function is as follows:

```
CHAR(<integer_expr>)
```

In the following example, the ASCII and CHAR functions are used to convert a character to the decimal ASCII value, and the decimal ASCII value to a character:

```
select ascii('Able'),char(65)
----------- -
65          A
```

Using *SOUNDEX*

SOUNDEX returns a four-digit (SOUNDEX) code that is used in comparing two strings with the DIFFERENCE function. SOUNDEX could be used to search for duplicates with similar spellings in a mailing list. SOUNDEX can also be used in a word processor to return words that are similar to one that is misspelled.

The syntax for use of the SOUNDEX function is as follows:

```
SOUNDEX(<char_expr>)
```

SOUNDEX ignores all vowels unless they're the first letter of a string. In the following example, SOUNDEX is used to return evaluation values for a series of strings.

```
select soundex ('a'),soundex ('aaa'),soundex ('b'),soundex ('red'),
 soundex ('read')
```

```
---- ---- ---- ---- ----
A000  A000  B000  R300  R300
select soundex ('right'),soundex ('write')
---- ----
R230  W630
```

Using *DIFFERENCE*

DIFFERENCE returns the difference between the values of two character expressions returned by SOUNDEX. The difference is rated as a value from zero to four, with a value of four as the best match. Define the threshold within the range zero to four and perform subsequent operations defined by your criteria. The syntax of the DIFFERENCE function is as follows:

```
DIFFERENCE(<char_-expr1>, <char_-expr2>)
```

In the following example, the difference between "the" and "teh" is four, a value that is considered a good match. If you were using DIFFERENCE along with SOUNDEX in a program such as a spell checker, "teh" can be treated as a misspelling of "the."

```
select difference(soundex('the'),soundex('teh'))
----------
4
```

> **N O T E** The value that is returned by the DIFFERENCE function is fixed according to the design of the DIFFERENCE function. You must decide how you use the value returned. In the example, a value of 4 means that the two character strings, the and teh, are as alike as they can be using the soundex scale of values.
>
> If you're looking for a misspelling for the name of a department stored in the Department column of a table such as Employees, a value of 3 or less may be a different department or a misspelling of a department. ■

Using *LOWER*

LOWER, which converts uppercase strings to lowercase strings, uses the following syntax:

```
LOWER(<char_expr>)
```

Using *UPPER*

UPPER, which converts lowercase strings to uppercase strings, uses the following syntax:

```
UPPER(<char_expr>)
```

In the following example, UPPER and LOWER are used to convert a mixed-case string to all-uppercase and all-lowercase:

```
select upper('Bob Smith1234*&^'),lower('Bob Smith1234*&^')
---------------- ----------------
BOB SMITH1234*&^ bob smith1234*&^
```

Using *LTRIM*

LTRIM removes leading spaces from a string. To save space, you can remove leading spaces from a string before it's stored in the column of a table. The leading spaces can also be removed before you perform additional processing on the string. LTRIM uses the following syntax:

```
LTRIM(<char_expr>)
```

In the following example, LTRIM is used to remove leading spaces from a string:

```
select ltrim('    middle    ')
--------------
middle
```

> **N O T E** In this example, the return value of ('   middle   ') still contains trailing spaces. You need to use the next function, RTRIM, to remove trailing spaces. ■

Using *RTRIM*

RTRIM removes trailing spaces from a string. As with LTRIM, trailing spaces can be removed before you store the string in the column of a table. Like LTRIM, RTRIM can be used to remove trailing spaces before you perform further processing on the string. RTRIM uses the following syntax:

```
RTRIM(<char_expr>)
```

> **N O T E** In many cases, you'll want to work with the string without any leading or trailing spaces. Remember that you can nest these functions, so you can use the syntax as indicated in the following example:

```
select RTRIM(LTRIM('    middle    ')
```

This example returns only the word "middle" with no spaces surrounding it. ■

Using *CHARINDEX*

CHARINDEX returns the starting position of the specified character expression within a specified string. The first parameter is the character expression and the second parameter is an expression, usually a column name, in which SQL Server searches for the character expression. CHARINDEX cannot be used with Text and Image datatypes. The syntax of the CHARINDEX function is as follows:

```
CHARINDEX(<'char_expr'>, <expression>)
```

In the following example, CHARINDEX returns the starting character position of the word "Service" in a row of the Department column of the table Employees. An uppercase S—the first letter in Service—is the seventh character in the Field Service department.

```
select charindex('Service',department)
from employees
where name='Stan Humphries'
----------
7
```

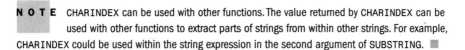

N O T E   CHARINDEX can be used with other functions. The value returned by CHARINDEX can be used with other functions to extract parts of strings from within other strings. For example, CHARINDEX could be used within the string expression in the second argument of SUBSTRING. ▦

Using *PATINDEX*

PATINDEX returns the starting position of the first occurrence of substring in a string such as the value of a table column. If the substring isn't found, a zero is returned. You can use the PATINDEX function with data stored as CHAR, VARCHAR, and TEXT datatypes.

Wild-card characters can be used in the substring as long as the percent sign (%) precedes and follows the substring. The syntax PATINDEX is as follows:

```
PATINDEX('%substring%', <column_name>)
```

In the following example, PATINDEX returns the character position for the first character of the substring within the string of characters stored in the department for the employee Stan Humphries. Stan Humphries is a member of the Field Service department.

```
select patindex('%erv%',department)
from employees
where name='Stan Humphries'
----------
8
```

Using *REPLICATE*

REPLICATE returns multiple sets of characters specified in the first argument of the function. The second argument specifies the number of sets to be returned. If the second argument, an integer expression, is a negative number, the function returns a NULL string. The syntax of REPLICATE is as follows:

```
REPLICATE(character_expression, integer_expression)
```

In the following example, REPLICATE returns a string of identical characters and also returns two iterations of the same sequence of two characters:

```
select replicate ('a',5),replicate('12',2)
----- ----
aaaaa 1212
```

Using *REVERSE*

REVERSE returns the reverse order of a string of characters. The character string argument can be a constant, a variable, or a value of a column. The syntax REVERSE is as follows:

```
REVERSE(character_string)
```

In the following example, the example would return the two constant strings that are enclosed in quotation marks, but their contents would be reversed:

```
select reverse('12345678910'),reverse('John Smith')
---------- ----------
01987654321 htimS nhoJ
```

In the following example, the result is a table column displayed without REVERSE, the same column is displayed in a different order using REVERSE, and the same string that is the name of the column of the Employees table is processed as a constant because it's enclosed in parentheses:

```
select name,reverse(name),reverse('name')
from employees
where name='Bob Smith'
name
------------------- -------------------- ----
Bob Smith           htimS boB            eman
```

Using *RIGHT*

RIGHT returns part of a character string, starting at the number of characters from the right as specified in the function argument. If the number of characters in the integer expression argument is negative, perhaps as the result of a nested function, RIGHT returns a NULL string. The syntax of the RIGHT function is:

```
RIGHT (character_expression, integer_expression)
```

The following example shows two identical strings, one that is displayed with a RIGHT function and also without a function. The second parameter of the RIGHT function 4 specifies to return from four characters from the end of the string to the rightmost character of the string.

```
select '12345678', right ('12345678',4)
-------- ----
12345678 5678
(1 row(s) affected)
```

> **CAUTION**
>
> You can't use a function such as the RIGHT function on TEXT or IMAGE datatypes. You must use the specialized set of string handling functions with TEXT and IMAGE datatypes. These special functions are discussed later in this chapter in the section entitled "Using TEXT and IMAGE Functions."

Using *SPACE*

SPACE returns a string of spaces for the length specified by the argument to the function. If the argument integer value is negative, SPACE returns a NULL string. The SPACE syntax is as follows:

```
SPACE(<integer_expr>)
```

In the following example, SPACE returns multiple spaces between two string constants:

```
select 'begin',space(15),'end'
-----  --------------- ---
begin                  end
```

Using *STR*

STR converts numeric data to character data. The STR syntax is as follows:

```
STR(<float_expr>[, <length>[, <decimal>]])
```

You should ensure that both the length and decimal arguments are non-negative values. If you don't specify a length, the default length is 10. The value returned is rounded to an integer by default. The specified length should be at least equal to or greater than the part of the number before the decimal point plus the number's sign. If *<float_expr>* exceeds the specified length, the string returns ** for the specified length.

In the following example, a series of constant numbers is converted to strings. The first number is completely converted because the second argument (the length) specifies the correct size of the resultant string, five numeric digits, the minus sign (–), and the decimal place (.). When the same constant value is converted using a length of six, the least-significant digit is truncated.

The third constant is correctly displayed using a length of six because it's a positive number. The same constant can't be displayed with a length of two, so two asterisks (**) are displayed instead.

```
select str(-165.87,7,2)
go
select str(-165.87,6,2)
go
select str(165.87,6,2)
go
select str(165.87,2,2)
go
-------
-165.87

------
-165.9
------
165.87

--
**
```

Using *STUFF*

STUFF inserts a string into a second string. The length argument specifies the number of characters to delete from the first string, beginning at the starting position. You can't use STUFF with TEXT or IMAGE datatypes. The STUFF syntax is as follows:

```
STUFF(character_string_1,starting_position,length,character_string_2)
```

In the following example, the string abcdef is inserted into the first string beginning at the second character position. The string 'abcdef' is inserted after the number of characters specified by the length argument are deleted from the first string:

```
select stuff('123456',2,4,'abcdef')
---------
1abcdef56
```

If the starting position or length is negative, or if the starting position is larger than the first character string, STUFF displays a NULL string. In the following example, a NULL is the result of the code shown because the starting position is a negative value:

```
select stuff('wxyz',-2,3,'abcdef')
(null)
```

If the length to delete is longer than the length of the first character string, the first character string is deleted to only the first character. In the following example, only the first character of the first character string remains after the second character string is inserted:

```
select stuff('123',2,3,'abc')
----
1abc
```

Using *SUBSTRING*

You can use SUBSTRING to return a part of a string from a target string. The first argument can be a character or binary string, a column name, or an expression that includes a column name. The second argument specifies the position at which the substring starts. The third argument specifies the number of characters in the substring.

Like several other string functions, you can't use SUBSTRING with Text or Image datatypes. The SUBSTRING syntax is as follows:

```
SUBSTRING(character_string, starting_position,length)
```

In the following example, multiple SUBSTRINGs are used along with the SPACE function to separate the first name from the last name, each of which is stored in a single column of the Employees table.

```
select substring(name,1,3),space(4),substring(name,5,5)
from employees
where badge=1234
--- ---- -----
Bob      Smith
```

Unlike earlier examples, the following example uses a function in several SQL statements. Multiple functions are often used in stored procedures or other batch objects. See Chapter 13, "Managing Stored Procedures and Using Flow-Control Statements," for more information about the use of local variables and the SELECT statement in the following example. Like the previous example, the first name is separated from the last name with multiple spaces added between the names, all of which is done by using multiple functions.

```
declare @x int
select @x=charindex(' ',(select name from employees where name='Bob Smith'))
```

```
select @x=@x-1
    select substring(name,1,@x), right(name,@x+2)
from employees
where badge=1234
-------------------
Bob              Smith
(d)+ (Concatenation)
```

The concatenation operator symbol (+) concatenates two or more character or binary strings, column names, or a combination of strings and columns. Concatenation is used to add one string to the end of another string. You should enclose character strings within single quotation marks. The syntax of the concatenation operator is as follows:

```
<expression> + <expression>
```

Conversion functions are used to concatenate datatypes that could not be concatenated without a change in datatype. CONVERT is one of the functions that you can use for datatype conversion. In the following example, a string constant is concatenated with the current date returned using the GETDATE date function. GETDATE is nested within CONVERT to convert it to a datatype, in this case VARCHAR, that is compatible with the string constant.

```
select 'The converted date is ' + convert(varchar(12), getdate())
---------------------------------
The converted date is Jul 11 1994
(1 row(s) affected)
```

Using Arithmetic Functions

Arithmetic functions operate on numeric datatypes such as INTEGER, FLOAT, REAL, MONEY, and SMALLMONEY. The values returned by the arithmetic functions are six decimal places. If you encounter an error while using an arithmetic function, a NULL value is returned and a warning message appears.

Two query processing options can be used to control the execution of statements that include arithmetic functions. The keyword for each of the two arithmetic operations is preceded by the SET keyword. You can use the ARITHABORT option to terminate a query when a function finds an error. ARITHIGNORE returns NULL when a function finds an error. If you set both ARITHABORT and ARITHIGNORE, no warning messages are returned.

There are numerous mathematical functions available in Transact-SQL (see Table 8.2).

Table 8.2   Transact-SQL Mathematical Functions

Function	Parameters	Return
ACOS	(float_expression)	Angle in radians whose cosine is a FLOAT value.
ASIN	(float_expression)	Angle in radians whose sine is a FLOAT value.

continues

Table 8.2 Continued

Function	Parameters	Return
ATAN	(*float_expression*)	Angle in radians whose tangent is a FLOAT value.
ATAN2	(*float_expr1*,*float_expr2*)	Angle in radians whose tangent is *float_expr1*/*floatexpr2*.
COS	(*float_expression*)	Trigonometric cosine of angle in radians.
COT	(*float_expression*)	Trigonometric cotangent of angle in radians.
SIN	(*float_expression*)	Trigonometric sine of angle in radians.
TAN	(*float_expression*)	Trigonometric tangent of expression in radians.
DEGREES	(*numeric_expression*)	Degrees converted from radians returned as the same datatype as expression. Datatypes can be INTEGER, MONEY, REAL, and FLOAT.
RADIANS	(*numeric_expression*)	Radians converted from degrees returned as the same datatype as expression. Datatypes can be INTEGER, MONEY, REAL, and FLOAT.
CEILING	(*numeric_expression*)	Smallest INTEGER >= expr returned as the same datatype as expression. Datatypes can be INTEGER, MONEY, REAL, and FLOAT.
FLOOR	(*numeric_expression*)	Largest INTEGER <= expr returned as the same datatype as expression. Datatypes can be INTEGER, MONEY, REAL, and FLOAT.
EXP	(*float_expression*)	Exponential value of expression.
LOG	(*float_expression*)	Natural log of expression.
LOG10	(*float_expression*)	Base 10 log of expression.
PI()		Value is 3.1415926535897936.
POWER	(*numeric_expression*,*y*)	Value of expression to power of *y* returned as the same datatype as expression. Datatypes can be INTEGER, MONEY, REAL, and FLOAT.
ABS	(*numeric_expression*)	Absolute value of expression returned as the same datatype as expression. Datatypes can be INTEGER, MONEY, REAL, and FLOAT.
RAND	([*integer_expression*])	Random flat number between zero and one using optional int as seed.
ROUND	(*numeric_expr*,*integer_expr*)	Rounded value to precision of *integer_expr* returned as the same datatype as expression.

Function	Parameters	Return
		Datatypes can be INTEGER, MONEY, REAL, and FLOAT.
SIGN	(*numeric_expression*)	One, zero, or –1 returned as the same datatype as expression. Datatypes can be INTEGER, MONEY, REAL, and FLOAT.
SQRT	(*float_expression*)	Square root of expression.

The following example shows the use of ABSOLUTE, RANDOM, SIGN, PI, and ROUND within an expression:

```
Select abs(5*-15),rand(),sign(-51.23),pi(),round((10*rand()),0)
----  ------------------- ---------- --------------------- ----
75    0.3434553056428724  -1.0       3.141592653589793     8.0
(1 row(s) affected)
```

In another example of the use of mathematical functions, FLOOR and CEILING are used to return the largest and smallest integer values that are less than or equal to, or greater than or equal to, the specified value.

```
select floor(81),ceiling(81),floor(81.45),
ceiling(81.45),floor($81.45),ceiling(-81.45)
--------- -------- ------------  ------------  ----------- ------
81        81       81.0          82.0          81.00       -81.0
(1 row(s) affected)
```

ROUND always returns a value, even if the length is invalid. If you specify that the length is positive and longer than the digits after the decimal point in ROUND, a zero is added after the least-significant digit in the returned value. If you specify that the length is negative and greater than or equal to the digits before the decimal point, 0.00 is returned by ROUND.

The following example shows the effects of using ROUND functions on various values. In the first example, the decimal number is rounded to two decimal places. The second number is displayed as 0.00 because the length is negative.

```
select round(81.4545,2), round(81.45,-2)
----------------------- --------------
81.45                   0.0
(1 row(s) affected)
```

In the following example, the first number is rounded down to three decimal places while the second number is rounded up to a whole number because it's more than half the value of the least-significant digit.

```
select round(81.9994,3),round(81.9996,3)
----------------------- -----------------------
81.999                  82.0
(1 row(s) affected)
```

Using *TEXT* and *IMAGE* Functions

In addition to PATINDEX, you can use several functions for operations on TEXT and IMAGE datatypes. You can also use relevant SET options and global variables with TEXT and IMAGE datatypes.

Using *SET TEXTSIZE*

SET TEXTSIZE specifies the number of bytes that are displayed for data stored as TEXT or IMAGE datatypes with SELECT statements. The SET TEXTSIZE syntax is as follows:

SET TEXTSIZE *n*

Use *n* to specify the number of bytes to be displayed. You must specify the value of *n* in the function SET TEXTSIZE as an INTEGER. If you specify *n* as zero (0), the default length in bytes (up to 4KB) is displayed. The current setting for TEXTSIZE is stored in the global variable @@TEXTSIZE.

In the following example, the TEXTSIZE default is first used to display a table column defined as the datatype TEXT. SET TEXTSIZE is defined to two (2), and as a result only two bytes of the table-column test are displayed. Finally, TEXTSIZE is reset to the default of 4KB using a value of zero (0).

```
select * from imagetext_table
image1              ...                                          text1
------------------------   ...   ------------------------------------
0x31323334353637383961637a782b3d5c   ... 12345678aczx+=
(1 row(s) affected)
set textsize 2
go
select text1 from imagetext_table
go
set textsize 0
go
select * from imagetext_table
go
text1
------------ ... ----------------------------------------
12
(1 row(s) affected)

image1              ...                                          text1
------------------------   ...   ------------------------------------
0x31323334353637383961637a782b3d5c   ... 12345678aczx+=
(1 row(s) affected)
```

Using *TEXTPTR*

TEXTPTR returns a value in VARBINARY format as a 16-character binary string that's a pointer to the first database page of stored text. The text pointer is used by the SQL Server system rather than by you, although the value is accessible by using TEXTPTR. SQL Server automatically checks if the pointer is valid when the function is used. The system checks that the return value points to the first page of text. The TEXTPTR syntax is as follows:

```
TEXTPTR(column_name)
```

Using *READTEXT*

READTEXT is a statement rather than a function; however, it is used along with the TEXT and IMAGE functions. READTEXT extracts a substring from data stored as a TEXT or IMAGE datatypes. You specify the number of bytes to include in the substring that follow an offset. The READTEXT syntax is as follows:

```
READTEXT [[<database.>]<owner.>]<table_name.><column_name>
 <text_pointer> <offset> <size>
```

In the following example, TEXTPTR retrieves the point to the first page of text for the one-and-only row of the table. The pointer is stored in a local variable @v. READTEXT is then used to extract a substring starting at the third byte—using an offset to skip past the first two bytes and retrieve the specified four bytes.

```
declare @v varbinary(16)
select @v=textptr(text1) from imagetext_table
readtext imagetext_table.text1 @v 2 4
(1 row(s) affected)
text1
--------------------------------------------...--------------------------------
3456
```

Using *TEXTVALID*

TEXTVALID returns either zero (0) or one (1), depending on whether a specified text pointer is invalid or valid. You must include the name of the table as part of your reference to the column defined as the datatype TEXT. The TEXTVALID syntax is as follows:

```
TEXTVALID('table_name.column_name', text_pointer)
```

In the following example, TEXTVALID determines the validity of a pointer to a data column stored as the datatype text. Recall that the output of one function can be used as the input to another function, as is the following example:

```
select textvalid('imagetext_table.text1',(select textptr(text1)
from imagetext_table))
go
----------
1
(1 row(s) affected)
```

In the next example, a SELECT statement that contains a WHERE clause returns a table row. As a result, TEXTVALID returns a zero—an invalid value because no row column was located.

```
select textvalid('imagetext_table.text1',(select textptr(text1)
from imagetext_table where text1 like '5'))
----------
0
(1 row(s) affected)
```

Using Conversion Functions

You often don't have to explicitly perform conversions because SQL Server automatically performs them. For example, you can directly compare a character datatype or expression with a DATETIME datatype or expression. SQL Server also converts an INTEGER datatype or expression to a SMALLINT) datatype or expression when an INTEGER, SMALLINT, or TINYINT is used in an expression.

▶ See the Chapter 5 section entitled "Numeric *integer* Datatypes." **p. 109**

Use a conversion function if you're unsure whether SQL Server will perform implicit conversions for you or if you're using other datatypes that aren't implicitly converted.

Using *CONVERT*

As mentioned earlier, CONVERT performs the explicit conversion of datatypes. CONVERT translates expressions of one datatype to another datatype as well as to a variety of special date formats. If CONVERT can't perform the conversion, you'll receive an error message. For example, if you attempt to convert characters contained in a column defined as a CHAR datatype to an INTEGER datatype, an error appears.

The CONVERT syntax is as follows:

```
CONVERT(<datatype> [(<length>)], <expression> [, <style>])
```

You can use CONVERT in SELECT and WHERE clauses or anywhere an expression can be used in a Transact-SQL statement. If you omit a length specification, it defaults to value of 30. Any unrecognized values that appear in DATATIME-to-SMALLDATETIME conversions aren't used. Not surprisingly, any conversions of BIT datatypes convert non-zero values to one (1) in keeping with the usual storage of BIT datatypes.

Integer values that you convert to MONEY or SMALLMONEY datatypes are processed as monetary units for the defined country (such as dollars for the United States). If you convert CHAR or VARCHAR datatypes to INTEGER datatypes such as INT or SMALLINT, the values must be numeric digits or a plus (+) or minus (–) sign.

Conversions that you attempt to make to a datatype of a different size can truncate the converted value and display a + after the value to denote that truncation has occurred. Conversions that you attempt to a datatype with a different number of decimal places can also result in truncation. Conversions that you specify as TEXT datatypes to CHAR and VARCHAR datatypes can be up to only 255 characters, the maximum length for CHAR and VARCHAR datatypes. The default of 30 characters is used if an explicit length is supplied.

The conversion of data stored as IMAGE datatypes to BINARY and VARBINARY datatypes can also be up to only 255 characters with a default of 30 characters. In the following example, a numeric constant is converted to a CHAR datatype, a decimal constant is converted to an INT datatype, and a decimal constant is converted to a BIT datatype:

```
select convert(char(4),1234),convert(int,12.345),convert(bit,87453.34)
---- ---------- --
```

```
1234 12          1
(1 row(s) affected)
```

In the next example of using CONVERT, several table columns are converted from an INT datatype to a CHAR datatype. The attempted conversion of the same table column to a VARCHAR datatype of an inadequate length results in truncation of each column value.

```
select badge,convert(char(4),badge),convert(varchar(2),badge)
from employees
badge
---------- ---- --
3211       3211 *
6732       6732 *
4411       4411 *
...
```

You can use the style argument of the CONVERT function to display the date and time in different formats. You can also use the style argument as part of a CONVERT function when you convert dates and times to CHAR or VARCHAR datatypes. Table 8.3 shows the different style numbers that can be used with CONVERT.

Table 8.3   Style Numbers for the *CONVERT* Function

Without Century (yy)	With Century (yyyy)	Standard	Display
-	0 or 100	default	mon dd yyyy hh:miAM(orPM)
1	101	USA	mm/dd/yy
2	102	ANSI	yy.mm.dd
3	103	English/French	dd/mm/yy
4	104	German	dd.mm.yy
5	105	Italian	dd-mm-yy
6	106		dd mon yy
7	107		mon dd, yy
8	108		hh:mi:ss
9	109		mon dd yyyy hh:mi:sssAM (or PM)
10	110	USA	mm-dd-yy
11	111	Japan	yy/mm/dd
12	112	ISO	yymmdd
13	113	Europe	dd mon yyyy hh:mi:ss:mmm (24h)
14	114	-	hh:mi:ss::mmm (24h)

In the following example, the current date and time are implicitly displayed using GETDATE, and GETDATE appears within CONVERT using different style numbers.

```
select getdate(),convert(char(12),getdate(),3),convert(char(24),
getdate(),109)
------------------------  ------------  ------------------------
Jul 12 1994  1:34PM        12/07/94      Jul 12 1994  1:34:49:440
(1 row(s) affected)
select convert(char(24),getdate(),114),convert(char(24),getdate(),112)
------------------------  ------------------------
13:36:45:223              19940712
(1 row(s) affected)
```

Using Date Functions

You can use several functions to perform operations with DATE datatypes. Use date functions to perform arithmetic operations on DATETIME and SMALLDATETIME values. Like other functions, date functions can be used in the SELECT or WHERE clauses, or wherever expressions can be used in Transact-SQL statements.

Using *DATENAME*

DATENAME returns a specified part of a date as a character string. DATENAME uses the following syntax:

```
DATENAME(<date part>, <date>)
```

Using *DATEPART*

DATEPART returns the specified part of a date as an integer value. DATEPART uses the following syntax:

```
DATEPART(<date_part>, <date>)
```

Using *GETDATE*

GETDATE returns the current date and time in SQL Server's default format for datetime values. Use a NULL argument with GETDATE. GETDATE uses the following syntax:

```
GETDATE()
```

Using *DATEADD*

DATEADD returns the value of the date with an additional date interval added to it. The return value is a DATETIME value that is equal to the date plus the number of the date parts that you specify. DATEADD takes the date part, number, and date arguments in the following syntax:

```
DATEADD (<date part>, <number>, <date>)
```

Using *DATEDIFF*

DATEDIFF returns the difference between parts of two specified dates. DATEDIFF takes three arguments: the part of the date and the two dates. DATEDIFF returns a signed integer value equal to the second date part, minus the first date part, using the following syntax:

```
DATEDIFF(<date part>, <date1>, <date2>)
```

Table 8.4 shows the values used as arguments for the date parts with the date functions.

Table 8.4   Date Parts Used in Date Functions

Date Part	Abbreviation	Values
Year	yy	1753-9999
Quarter	qq	1-4
Month	mm	1-12
Day of Year	dy	1-366
Day	dd	1-31
Week	wk	1-54
Weekday	dw	1-7 (Sun-Sat)
Hour	hh	0-23
Minute	mi	0-59
Second	ss	0-59
Millisecond	ms	0-999

The following examples show the use of several of the date functions. In the first example, the columns of a table that are defined as DATETIME and SMALLDATETIME datatypes are displayed without any functions.

```
select * from date_table
date1                      date2
-------------------------  -------------------------
Jan 1 1753 12:00AM         Jan 1 1900 12:00AM
(1 row(s) affected)
```

In the following example, the keyword year is used with DATENAME to return the year with the century from a DATETIME value:

```
select datename(year,date1) from date_table

1753
(1 row(s) affected)
```

In the following example, hour is used with DATENAME to return the hour from a DATETIME datatype value:

```
select datename(hour,date1) from date_table
----------------------------
0
(1 row(s) affected)
```

In the following example, month is used with DATENAME to return the number of the month from a DATETIME datatype value:

```
select datepart(month,date1) from date_table
-----------
1
(1 row(s) affected)
```

In the following example, GETDATE function is used in a SELECT statement to display the current date and time:

```
select now=getdate()
now
--------------------------
May 19 1994  2:00PM
(1 row(s) affected)
```

In the following example, GETDATE is nested within DATEPART to display only the current day as part of a SELECT statement:

```
select datepart(day,getdate())
-----------
19
(1 row(s) affected)
```

In the following example, GETDATE is nested within DATENAME to display only the name of the current month as part of a SELECT statement:

```
select datename(month,getdate())
----------------------------
May
(1 row(s) affected)
```

In the following example, the current date and the date stored in a DATETIME column are first displayed for reference. DATEDIFF is then used to display the number of days between the two datetime values.

```
select getdate()
--------------------------
May 19 1994  2:12PM
(1 row(s) affected)
select date1 from date_table
date1
--------------------------
Jan 1 1753 12:00AM
(1 row(s) affected)
select new=datediff(day,date1,getdate())
from date_table
new
```

```
----------
88161
(1 row(s) affected)
```

Using System Functions

You can use systems functions to obtain information about your computer system, user, database, and database objects. The system functions permit you to obtain information such as the characteristics of database objects within stored procedures and, using conditional statements, perform different operations based on the information returned.

You can use a system function, like other functions, in the SELECT and WHERE clauses of a SELECT statement as well as in expressions. If you omit the optional parameter with some system functions (see Table 8.5), information about your computer system and the current user database is returned.

Table 8.5 System Functions

Function	Parameter(s)	Information Returned
HOST_NAME()		The name of the server computer
HOST_ID()		The ID number of the server computer
SUSER_ID	(['login-name'])	The login number of the user
SUSER_NAME	([server_user_id])	The login name of the user
USER_ID	(['user_name'])	The database ID number of the user
USER_NAME	([user_id])	The database username of the user
DB_NAME	(['database_id'])	The name of the database
DB_ID	(['database_name'])	The ID number of the database
GETANSINULL	(['database_name'])	Returns 1 for ANSI nullability, 0 if ANSI nullability not defined
OBJECT_ID	('object_name')	The number of a database object
OBJECT_NAME	(object_id)	The name of a database object
INDEX_COL	('table_name', index_id, key_id)	The name of the index column
COL_LENGTH	('table_name', 'column_name')	The defined length of a column
COL_NAME	(table_id, column_id)	The name of the column
DATALENGTH	('expression')	The actual length of an expression of a datatype

continues

Table 8.5 Continued

Function	Parameter(s)	Information Returned
IDENT_INCR	('*table_or_view*')	The increment (returned as numeric(@@MAXPRECISION,0)) for a column with the identity property
IDENT_SEED	('*table_or_view*')	The seed value (returned as numeric(@@MAXPRECISION,0)) for a column with the identity property
STATS_DATE	(*table_id*, *index_id*)	The date that the statistics for the index (*index_id*) were last updated
COALESCE	(*expression1*, *expression2*, ... *expressionN*)	Returns the first non-NULL expression
ISNULL	(*expression*, *value*)	Substitutes value for each NULL entry
NULLIF	(*expression1*, *expression2*)	Returns a NULL when *expression1* is NULL when *expression1* is equivalent to *expression2*

In the following example, system function the HOST_ID is used to return the name of the Windows NT server system to which a user is connected.

```
select host_name ()
-----------------------------
NT1

(1 row(s) affected)
```

In the following example, multiple system functions are used to return information about the Windows NT server system, the current database and the current user.

```
select host_name (),host_id (),db_name (), db_id (), suser_name ()
---------- -------- --------- -------------------------
NT1       0000005e employees            6      sa

(1 row(s) affected)
```

N O T E You may not have reason to use any of the system functions. You may only need to use the system functions if you're performing some administrative operation with the database. Several of the system functions require that you have access to the system tables in order to return useful information. Access to these will depend on the security of your login ID.

You would not usually use the system functions in the SELECT clause of a SELECT statement that displays the information on your monitor. Rather, system functions, like other functions, can be used within other functions, and the information returned is recorded in local variables or a temporary or permanent table. System functions provide information that is usually used for advanced programming or administrative operations. Administrative operations can be performed within stored procedures as well as in an interactive session.

For example, the system function STATS_DATE returns the date the last time that statistics were updated for an index on a table. The database administrator must periodically update the statistics for a table so that the query optimizer has valid information to use to decide whether or not to use an index for the retrieval of rows from a table. Microsoft SQL Server does not automatically update the table statistics used by the query optimizer.

For example the following SELECT statement returns the statistics update date for two indexes on the table company.

```
select 'Index' = i.name,
       'Statistics Update Date' = stats_date(i.id, i.indid)
            from sysobjects o, sysindexes i
                where o.name = 'company' and o.id = i.id
Index                          Statistics Update Date
-----------------------------  --------------------------
badge_index                    Sep 18 1995   3:24PM
department_index               Sep 18 1995   3:27PM

(2 row(s) affected)
```

You can use a system function such as STATS_DATE, as shown in the previous example, to determine if it's time to update the statistics for the indexes of a table so the query optimizer will work properly.

You can also combine the system function STATS_DATE with the GETDATE and DATEDIFF functions to return the update statistics date, the current date, and the difference between the two dates. Using these three functions and a conditional statement in a procedure, you can run the procedure periodically to determine if the statistics for a table index have been updated within some period of time, for example a week.

If the difference between the STATS_DATE and the GETDATE is more than seven days, an UPDATE STATISTICS command should be issued (perhaps within the procedure as well). Other system functions can also be used to determine if a needed system operation on the database or its objects need to be performed. ■

▶ **See** the section entitled "Using Date Functions" (earlier in this chapter) for more information. **p. 234**

▶ **See** Chapter 13, "Managing Stored Procedures and Using Flow-Control Statements," for more information. **p. 339**

Using *ISNULL* and *NULLIF*

ISNULL is a system function that returns a string of characters or numbers in place of (NULL) when a NULL is encountered in a data-storage structure such as a table column. The syntax of the function is:

ISNULL(*expression,value*)

The expression is usually a column name that may contain a NULL value. The value specifies a string or number to be displayed when a NULL is found. In the following example, the ISNULL function is used to return the character string `'No entry'` when a NULL is encountered.

```
select ISNULL(y, 'No entry') from nulltable
y
----------
    No entry
(1 row(s) affected)
```

The NULLIF function returns a NULL if the two expressions are identical, otherwise the second expression is returned. The NULLIF function is usually used with the CASE statement. In the following example, a NULL is returned for identical strings while the first parameter is returned when the strings don't match.

```
select nullif ('same','same'),space (2),nullif ('same','different')
---- -- ----
        (null)    same
         (1 row(s) affected)
```

NOTE The space function is used in the example of the NULLIF function to provide a visual separation between the values returned by the use of the function twice in the SELECT statement. ■

Using *COALESCE*

The form of the COALESCE function that uses the syntax COALESCE (*expression1,expression2*) is similar to the NULLIF statement. Unlike the NULLIF statement, the COALESCE statement with two parameters returns *expression2* when a NULL is returned and returns *expression1* if NOT NULL is encountered.

You can also use COALESCE with more than two parameters. COALESCE returns the first non-NULL expression in the list of parameters when no NULL is used. If no non-NULL values are present, when COALESCE is used with more than two parameters, the function returns a NULL.

NOTE The COALESCE function is designed for use in a CASE statement, which is discussed in the chapter on stored procedures. Please consult the chapter on stored procedures for additional information on the COALESCE function. ■

▶ **See** the Chapter 13 section entitled "Using *CASE* Expressions." **p. 368**

Using Niladic Functions

Niladic functions return a user or timestamp value that is automatically placed in the row of a table when the value is omitted from an INSERT or UPDATE statement. Niladic functions are defined as part of a DEFAULT constraint in a CREATE or ALTER TABLE statement. You can use any of the following niladic functions:

USER

CURRENT_USER

```
SESSION_USER
SYSTEM_USER
CURRENT_TIMESTAMP
APP_NAME
```

The niladic functions USER, CURRENT_USER, and SESSION_USER all return the database username of the user executing an INSERT or UPDATE statement. The function SYSTEM_USER returns the user's login ID. CURRENT_TIMESTAMP returns the current date and time in the same form as the GETDATE function. APP_NAME returns the program name for the current session if one has been set.

Niladic functions can be used outside of the DEFAULT CONSTRAINT of a CREATE or ALTER TABLE statement. For example, you cannot use the niladic functions in the SELECT clause of a SELECT statement.

▶ **See** Chapter 11 "Managing and Using Rules and Defaults," for more information. **p. 301**

From Here...

In this chapter you've learned the use of various functions that return information about your system and characteristics of SQL Server. In addition, you learned how to use functions to perform operations on table data. Functions can be used both in an interactive session and in stored procedures.

For information about selected aspects of the topics mentioned in this chapter, review the following chapters:

- Chapter 5, "Creating Database Tables and Using Datatypes," discusses the values that can be stored in various Transact-SQL datatypes.

- Chapter 13, "Managing Stored Procedures and Using Flow-Control Statements," discusses the variables used for the temporary storage of values returned by functions as well as the global variables used to store information relevant to the use of functions.

- Chapter 16, "Understanding Server, Database, and Query Options," shows you how to use SET options to control the display of data through the use of functions used in SELECT statements.

Defining Retrieval Structures

Managing and Using Views

Views are static definitions for the creation of dynamic tables constructed from one or more sets of rows according to a predefined selection criteria. Views can be used to define numerous combinations of rows and columns from one or more tables. A defined view of the desired combination of rows and columns uses a simple SELECT statement to specify the rows and columns included in the view. ■

How to create a virtual table

In this chapter you'll learn to create stored SELECT statements that you subsequently use like database tables.

How to create views that are defined on multiple tables

You'll learn to create views that perform relational joins in order to combine information from multiple tables.

How manipulate data in views

You'll learn to add, update and delete rows through views and their underlying tables.

How to create a view of a view

You'll also learn to create a view that is based on views rather than tables.

How to manage views

You'll also learn to edit, list, and delete views through Transact-SQL statements and the Enterprise Manager.

Understanding Views

A *view* is a stored definition of a SELECT statement that specifies the rows and columns to be retrieved when the view is later referenced. You can define up to 250 columns of one or more tables in a view. The number of rows that you can define is limited only by the number of rows in the tables referenced.

Views are aptly named because they function as the set of rows and columns that you can see through their definition. Once the view is defined, you reference the view as if it is a table. Although a view appears as a permanent set of rows and columns stored on a disk in a database, it's not. A view doesn't create a permanent copy of the selected rows and columns of a database.

A view performs the SELECT statement contained within its definition when the view is later referenced like a table. The temporary table that is created and returned to the monitor is unavailable once the display of its rows is complete. A view enables you to execute a SELECT statement when you reference the view as a table.

> **CAUTION**
>
> It's easy to be misled and believe that a view is a table. Once the view is defined, you always access data through it as if it's a table. Try to remember that the data referenced through a view is always coming from its underlying table. Also, if you add columns to the underlying table that the view is defined on, the new columns don't appear in the view unless the view is first deleted and redefined.

A view can be used to access all of a table, part of a table, or a combination of tables. Because the portion of a table you access is defined within the view, you don't have to repeat the selection statements. You can use views to simplify access to the database. If you create even complicated views that use multiple clauses, you can perform the SELECT statement in the view just as easily as a view that contains a simple SELECT statement.

You can also use views to provide security in the database. You can grant permissions on a view that can be different than the permissions granted on the tables the view is based upon. You can provide access to only the rows and columns referenced through a view, but not provide access to all rows and columns directly through the table.

▶ **See** the Chapter 19 section entitled "SQL Server Security," **p. 487**

Creating a View

You can create a view either through a command-line isql session, an ISQL/w session, or through the SQL Enterprise Manager. A view is stored as a separate object in your database through which you have an alternate way of viewing and, with limitations, modifying a table. You should remember that you can only create a view in the current database. The syntax to create a view in an isql or ISQL/w session is as follows:

```
CREATE VIEW view_name [WITH ENCRYPTION] AS
SELECT statement...
FROM table_name ¦ view_name

[WHERE clause] [WITH CHECK OPTION]
```

You can also create a new view through the SQL Enterprise Manager by performing the following steps:

1. Within the current database select the Views folder.
2. From the View Folder menu click <u>N</u>ew View. Figure 9.1 shows the Manage Views dialog box for the current database.

Part
III
Ch
9

FIG. 9.1

Replace <VIEW NAME> with a name for your view.

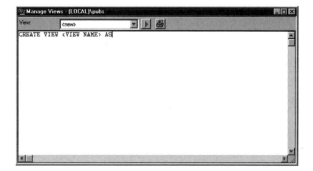

3. Enter the view definition within the Manage Views dialog box. (You can also select an existing view and edit it.) Figure 9.2 shows a previously designed view.

Execute button

FIG. 9.2

You can use the View list box to select other views for display or subsequent editing.

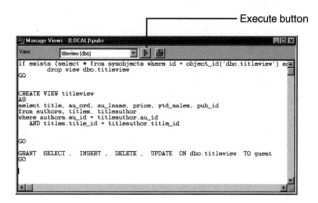

4. Click the Execute button (refer to fig. 9.2) to save the new view definition. You'll receive an error message if your view can't be created. The creation of your view will fail if a view already exists with the same name.

Selective Columns

You can define a view that is made up of some, but not all, of the columns of a table. In the following example, a view is defined as a pseudo-table that has two of the three columns of the Employees table:

```
create view twocolumns as
select name, badge
from employees
```

Once you've defined the view, you can use a SELECT statement to access it just like a table. For example, the twocolumns view created in the previous example can be referenced in the following manner to display the name and badge for all rows:

```
select *
from twocolumns
```

Selective Rows

You can also define a view that references some, but not all, of the rows of a table. In the following example, the sales1 view is defined to contain only the rows in which the department is equal to SALES from the Employees table:

```
create view sales1 as
select name, department, badge
from employees
where department='SALES'
```

You can also use one or more Boolean operators in the WHERE clause of a SELECT statement to specify the rows contained through the view. In the following example, a view is defined that contains all columns from the table that are members of the Sales department and that have a badge number greater than 1,000.

```
create view sales2 as
select name, department, badge
from employees
where department='Sales'
and badge>1000
```

 TIP You can use a WHERE clause in the SELECT statement that references a view even though the SELECT statement view within the view definition can include a WHERE clause. The view is treated just like an actual table.

See the section entitled "Creating a View" earlier in this chapter.

Selective Columns and Rows

You can also define a view that comprises a combination of only some columns and rows of a table. In the following example, the twocolumnsales view is defined and provides access to only two of the three columns, but only for the rows that contain the Sales department:

```
create view twocolumnsales as
select name,badge
from employees
where department='SALES'
```

You can continue to use a simple SELECT statement to reference the view like a table to retrieve the set of columns and rows defined in the view. For example, to show all rows and columns that are defined in the three previous views, you can use the following three SELECT statements:

```
select *
from twocolumns
select *
from sales1
select *
from twocolumnsales
```

TIP You can specify only some of the columns defined in the view within a SELECT clause of a SELECT statement. You don't need to use an asterisk (*) to reference all columns defined in the view.

You can't distinguish a view from a table in the way you use a view. You have to see the view definition to distinguish a view from a table. You can create views for all the combinations of rows and columns that you access together from database tables.

N O T E You can establish a naming convention for views and tables so that the name of each is self-descriptive as a table or view. For example, the table employees could be instead named employees_table, and the view sales could be named sales_view. Remember that you can use up to 30 characters for the name of an object, such as a view or table. You can also use a single character within the name of a view or table, such as a *v* for a view and a *t* for a table, if you run short of characters.

CAUTION

If you define views and tables so that each is obviously a table or view—for example, employees_table or sales_view—you may defeat the purpose of a view. A feature of the view is that it is nearly indistinguishable from a table. You work with a view in the same way that you work with a table. It can be an advantage to permit views and tables to be indistinguishable from one another to database users that needn't perform complicated queries. A complicated query can be defined within the view and the user told to use a simple SELECT statement to access the new "table," which is actually the view.

You can encounter some restrictions when you define a view. You can't define a view on a temporary table. Temporary tables are transitory database structures and exist only until data retrieved from a permanent table is displayed to an output device, such as a monitor.

If you were allowed to define a view that is based on a temporary table, the data may not be available when you reference it through the view. The temporary table on which the view was defined was automatically deleted.

▶ **See** the Chapter 5 section entitled "Creating Temporary Tables." **p. 108**

You also can't define a trigger (see following Note) on a view; a trigger can only be defined on a permanent table. It makes sense to only define a trigger on a table because a table is the permanent underlying source of the data for all views. If you were permitted to define a trigger on a view, SQL Server would still have to reference the underlying table to locate the data specified by the trigger. It's simpler to establish triggers that are based directly on tables.

N O T E   A *trigger* is a database object that is automatically executed when a table row is inserted, updated, or deleted. It's primarily designed to maintain referential integrity. See Chapter 14, "Creating and Managing Triggers," for more information. ■

In addition, you can't include ORDER BY in the definition of a view. The rows of a view are unordered like the rows of a database table. If you were permitted to use a SELECT statement that includes an ORDER BY clause in a view, the rows would be ordered and a view would have different characteristics than a database table. If a view is designed to be used like a permanent table, it must have similar or identical characteristics. You can use an ORDER BY clause when you retrieve rows from a view just like you would if you retrieve rows from a table.

▶ **See** the Chapter 6 section entitled "Using an *ORDER BY* Clause." **p. 168**

You also can't use COMPUTE in a view. COMPUTE creates a virtual column for the actual columns of a table or view.

▶ **See** the Chapter 6 section entitled "Using a *COMPUTE* Clause in a *SELECT* Statement." **p. 178**

You can't use DISTINCT in the SELECT clause in a view. You can however, use DISTINCT in a SELECT clause of the SELECT statement that references a view to return non-duplicate rows. You could also always ensure the rows retrieved through a view are unique by defining a unique key or index on the underlying table that the view references.

▶ **See** the Chapter 6 section entitled "Using *DISTINCT* to Retrieve Unique Column Values." **p. 171**

In the following example, a view that contains DISTINCT in its SELECT clause can't be successfully defined.

```
create view departments as
select distinct departments
from employees

Msg 154, Level 15, State 2
A DISTINCT clause is not allowed in a view.
```

You can't use INTO as part of a SELECT statement within a view. INTO redirects rows into another table rather than to a monitor. In the following example, a view can't be successfully created because it contains an INTO clause in its SELECT statement.

```
sp_help two
Name            Owner           Type
```

```
-------------------------------------------------
two                dbo              user table
Data_located_on_segment           When_created
---------------------------- --------------------------
default                            Oct 2 1994  1:33PM
Column_name   Type    Length Nulls Default_name   Rule_name
------------- ------------- ------ ---- -------------
name          char       25   0    (null)        (null)
badge         int         4   0    (null)        (null)
Object does not have any indexes.
No defined keys for this object.
create view selectinto as
select name,badge
into two
from employees
Msg 154, Level 15, State 3
An INTO clause is not allowed in a view.
```

Simple and Complex Views

In understanding views, you may find it helpful to further categorize them. Recall that you can define views that access multiple tables as well as individual tables. *Simple views* are those you define that access any combination of rows and columns from which single tables are called. *Complex views* are those that provide access to the rows and columns of multiple tables.

The syntax for a complex view uses the same syntax in the SELECT statement that is directly used for the retrieval of rows and columns. Use the following syntax to specify the rows and columns from multiple tables of a database:

```
CREATE VIEW view_name AS
SELECT column_1,…column_n
FROM table_1,…table_n
WHERE table_key_1=table_key_2
,…AND table_key_1=table_key_n
```

In the following example, the Name and Department columns are referenced from the Employees table and the Hours_Worked column is selected from the Pays table in the definition of the view. The WHERE clause is used to match the rows from the Employees table with the corresponding rows in the Pays table.

The Badge column is used in each table to match the rows in the same way in which a corresponding column can be used to match rows from a SELECT statement that is used outside a view.

```
create view combo as
select name,department,hours_worked
from employees,pays
where employees.badge=pays.badge
```

You access the rows and columns through a complex view the same way that you access rows and columns in a simple view. For example, you can reference the rows and columns defined in the combo view with the following SELECT statement:

```
select *
from combo
```

TIP Rather than require a user to perform a complicated SELECT statement, you can place the complex query within the view and have the user reference the view.

Displaying Views

When you create a view, the definition of a view is stored in the syscomments system table. One way that you can display the stored definition of a view from the syscomments table is by using the sp_helptext stored system procedure.

 TIP You can also use sp_helptext to display the text of a stored procedure, trigger, default, or rule as well as a view. Use sp_help to list the characteristics of a view or other objects.

In the following example, a simple view is defined that selects all rows of the Sales department. The rows of the Employees table are retrieved through the sales view. The sp_helptext sales procedure is used to display the definition of the view.

```
sp_helptext sales1
text
------------------
create view sale1s as
select * from employees
where department='Sales'
(1 row(s) affected)
```

The view definition that is stored in the syscomments table is retrieved by sp_helptext and displays the view definition as the row of a table. The column header is text, the view definition is the row, and the count message specifies the count of the one row retrieved.

TROUBLESHOOTING

I used sp_helptext to list the definition of a view that I defined the last time I used Microsoft SQL Server. Now when I use the procedure, SQL Server can't seem to find my view. Why? You're probably pointing to the wrong database. Microsoft SQL Server maintains separate system table syscomments for each database (along with 12 other system tables). You should first enter the USE command followed by the name of your database in which you created the view. If you have selected the correct database, the view should be shown when you use sp_helptext again.

You can also display the definition of a view through the SQL Enterprise Manager by performing the following steps:

1. Select the Views folder under the Objects folder in the database in which the view was created. Notice that an icon of a pair of eyeglasses appears to the left of each view to distinguish views from other objects. Figure 9.3 shows the expanded list of views that are currently defined for the pubs database.

FIG. 9.3
You can also double-click the selected view to display it.

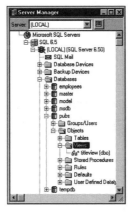

2. Click the right mouse button to bring up the Manage Views menu; open the Manage Views menu and choose Edit or open the Manage menu and choose Views. Figure 9.4 shows the definition of the view titleview displayed through the Enterprise Manager.

FIG. 9.4
You can edit the view displayed in the Manage Views dialog box of the SQL Enterprise Manager.

Editing Views

You must use the SQL Enterprise Manager to edit an existing view. You cannot edit a view from a command-line isql or ISQL/w session. You'd edit a view in order to change the columns or rows that are referenced by the view. For example, you'll need to add the name of a column that you inadvertently omitted when you originally defined the view.

To edit a view through the SQL Enterprise Manager, perform the following steps.

1. Select the Views folder under the Objects folder in the database in which the view was created.

2. Click the right mouse button to bring up the Manage Views menu and choose Edit from the Manage Views menu or Choose Views from the Manage menu or double-click the left mouse button on the selected view.

3. Make your changes after the keywords CREATE VIEW <view name> AS.

4. Click the Execute button (refer to fig. 9.2) in the Manage Views dialog box.

Figure 9.5 shows the view titleview after it has been changed. The view now shows only titles with a price greater than fifty.

FIG. 9.5
You can change the name of the view in the Manage Views dialog box to create a new view.

If you examine the SQL statements within the Manage Views dialog box within which your view is displayed, you'll note a conditional statement that precedes the definition of your view. The conditional statement, which begins with the keyword IF, checks to see if your view is already defined and deletes the view in order to redefine it as if it is a new view.

The deletion of your view is done to satisfy the requirements of Microsoft SQL Server, which does not permit the direct editing of an existing view. The Manager Views dialog box automatically generates the code to delete the view and recreate it with whatever changes you've made.

You could effectively edit an existing view from isql or ISQL/w only by deleting the existing view and creating a new one using the same name as the view that you deleted. You'll find it much easier to change views through the SQL Enterprise Manager.

Adding the *WITH ENCRYPTION* Clause

N O T E A GO command is used after the conditional statement and the CREATE VIEW statement. GO is a terminator that tells SQL Server to execute the previous statement. ▪

You may not want users to be able to display the definition of a view from the syscomments table. If you add the WITH ENCRYPTION in the CREATE VIEW statement, you can't subsequently list the definition of the view. In the following example, a view is created whose definition can't be subsequently displayed with the procedure sp_helptext.

```
create view test_view_encryption with encryption as
select * from company
go
sp_helptext test_view_encryption
go
The object's comments have been encrypted.
```

You also can't view the definition of an encrypted view from the SQL Enterprise Manager. Figure 9.6 shows the information returned when an encrypted view is displayed.

FIG. 9.6
The owner of an encrypted view can still drop it and create a new view with the name of the dropped view.

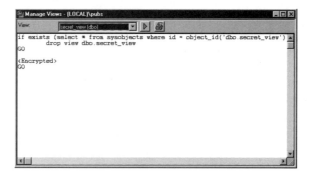

CAUTION
A disadvantage of encrypting view definitions is that views can't be re-created when you upgrade your database or SQL Server. During an upgrade, the definitions of a view are used to recreate the view—which can't be done if the view definition is encrypted. You would also be unable to upgrade a database if you delete the view definition stored as a row in the syscomments table.

N O T E You can also encrypt procedures and triggers. The reason for encryption is security. You can prevent users from displaying the objects (such as tables or views) that an object (such as a view) references to prevent them directly accessing the objects. You can use encryption along with object permissions to control access to objects and object definitions. ■

Displaying View Associations

One way that you can display the tables or views upon which a view is defined is to use the system procedure sp_depends. You may need to display the tables or views that a view references in order to discover and correct problems that you may encounter when you use the view.

In the following example, sp_depends shows that the sales view is defined from the Employees table user.

```
sp_depends sales
Things the object references in the current database.
object                  type            updated selected
---------------------------------------- ----------------
dbo.employees      user table          no          no
(1 row(s) affected)
```

N O T E   You can also use `sp_depends` to display information about tables and views that are
dependent upon procedures. `Sp_depends` references the sysdepends system table to
locate dependencies. `Sp_depends` shows only references to objects within the current database. ■

You can also display dependencies through the SQL Enterprise Manager. To display the dependencies of a view, click the right mouse button and choose Dependencies from the menu. For example, in Figure 9.7, the dependencies of the view titleview are displayed in the Object Dependencies dialog box. The Object Dependencies dialog box shows that the view is defined based on the four tables.

FIG. 9.7

The same icons used for tables and views in the Server Manager window of the SQL Enterprise Manager are used in the type column of the Object Dependencies dialog box.

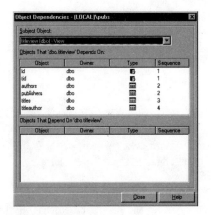

Creating Views of Views

You can define a view that references a view rather than a table. You can also create a view that references several views or a combination of views and tables. In the following example, the first view that is created is based on a table. A second view is created that references the first view. However many views are defined, they must all eventually reference a table because it is the permanent source of data.

```
create view salesonly as
select name,department,badge
from employees
where department='Sales'
go
This command did not return data, and it did not return any rows
create view salespersons as
select name
from salesonly
This command did not return data, and it did not return any rows
```

In a continuation of the previous example, the following example retrieves rows from the permanent table through a view that was defined on a previously created view. Sp_depends is used to confirm that the second view was defined based on the first view.

```
select * from salespersons
name
-------------------
Bob Smith
Mary Jones
John Garr
(3 row(s) affected)
sp_depends salespersons
go
Things the object references in the current database.
object                 type              updated selected
-------------------------- ---------------- --
dbo.salesonly          view               no     no
(1 row(s) affected)
```

Sp_depends doesn't iteratively translate views that are defined using other views. If a view references another view rather than a table, sp_depends shows the view rather than the original table. The sp_depends procedure shows only the view or table that the view directly references in the view definition.

CAUTION

Although sp_help shows you the columns included in the rows, it doesn't show you the rows included. Clauses, such as WHERE, aren't displayed by sp_help. You must examine the view definition with sp_helptext.

If you want to see the columns of rows that are included in a view that is defined on one or more views, you'll have to use sp_helptext to display all the view definitions. If a view is defined on only tables, the definition of the view displayed by sp_helptext specifies the rows and columns that are included. It's better to directly define views on tables rather than on other views.

You should use the Object Dependencies in the SQL Enterprise Manager to display object dependencies. Unlike sp_depends, the listing of object dependencies in the Object Dependencies shows the multiple level of views and tables that a view is based upon. For example, in Figure 9.8, the Object Dependencies dialog box shows that the view lowtitleview is defined directly based on the view (the eyeglasses icon in the type column) titleview (sequence number five) and indirectly to four tables (the table icon in the type column, sequence number four). The sequence numbers are used to illustrate level or depth of objects that the view is defined on.

FIG. 9.8
Object dependencies have
levels indicated by the
sequence number.

Renaming Columns in Views

You can also rename the columns of the base tables in the view. Define the list of alternate
column names following the name of the view and preceding the keyword (as in the view definition). Use the following syntax to assign alternate names for the columns referenced in a
view:

```
CREATE VIEW view_name [ (view_column_1,…view_column_n) ] AS
SELECT statement…
FROM table_name or view_name
[WHERE clause]
```

In the following example, alternate names for the columns of the Employees table are specified
as part of the view definition. A single letter is used for the alternate column name in the view.
Once the list of column names for the view is defined, the alternate column names appear as
new column headers as well as in other clauses, such as a WHERE clause.

```
create view view8 (a,b,c)
as
select name,department,badge from employees
(1 row(s) affected)
select * from view8
a                     b                     c
------------------    ------------------    ----------
Mary Jones            Sales                 5514
Dan Duryea            Shipping              3321
John Garr             Sales                 2221
Mark Lenard           Sales                 3331
Bob Smith             Sales                 1
Minty Moore           Sales                 7444
(6 row(s) affected)
```

N O T E You don't have to create a view to rename the column of a table during retrieval. Instead,
you can rename a column with a SELECT clause outside of a view using the following
syntax:

```
SELECT column_name=renamed_name
…
```

A new name that contains embedded spaces can be enclosed within single quotation marks. The new name isn't permanent—it only applies within the SELECT statement. ■

Renaming Views

You can use sp_rename to rename a view. The system procedure uses the following syntax:

```
sp_rename old_name, new_name
```

Use a comma (,) between the old_name and the new_name to separate the parameters from the procedure name. In the following example, the sales view is renamed sales2. Once the view is renamed, sp_depends shows that the renamed procedure is still based upon the permanent Employees table.

```
sp_rename sales, sales2
Object name has been changed.
sp_depends sales2
Things the object references in the current database.
object            type             updated selected
----------------  ----------------  ------ --------
dbo.employees     user table           no     no
(1 row(s) affected)
```

You can also rename a view using the SQL Enterprise Manager. To rename a view through the Enterprise Manager, perform the following steps:

1. Left-click the view to select it.
2. Click the right mouse button. Choose Rename.
3. Enter a new name for the view in the Rename Objects dialog box.
4. Click OK.

Figure 9.9 shows the Rename Object dialog box. When the Rename Object dialog box is first brought up, the current name of the view is displayed. Edit the existing name, or delete the old name and enter a new name to rename the view.

TIP You can use sp_rename to rename other database objects, including tables, columns, stored procedures, triggers, indexes, defaults, rules, and user-defined datatypes.

FIG. 9.9
The same Rename Object dialog box is used to rename other database objects.

CAUTION

Although you can rename views with the `sp_rename` procedure, SQL Server does not change the name of a table or view in the stored definition of a view in the table syscoments. It warns you of this when you rename a view or similar objects. In the following example, a warning is displayed when the table employees is renamed with the procedure `sp_rename`. The procedure `sp_helptext` shows that the old name of the table, employees, is retained in the definition of the view based on the renamed table.

```
sp_rename employees,newname
Warning - Procedures, views or triggers reference this object
and will become invalid.
Object name has been changed.
sp_helptext salesonly
go
text
- - - - - - - - - - - - - - - - - - - - - - - - - - - - - - - - - - - - - - - - - - - -
create view salesonly as
select name,department,badge
from employees
where department='Sales'
select * from salesonly
go
name                    department              badge
- - - - - - - - - - - -  - - - - - - - - - - -  - - - - - - - - -

Fred Sanders            SALES                   1051
Bob Smith               SALES                   1834
Sally Springer          Sales                   9998

(3 row(s) affected)
```

However, both the `sp_depends` procedure and the Object Dependencies dialog box will display the updated name of renamed tables and views. For example, Figure 9.10 shows the Object Dependencies for the view salespersons, which references the view salesonly while the view salesonly references the table newname, formerly named employees.

You should try not to rename objects unless it's absolutely necessary.

FIG. 9.10

You can display the dependencies for another view or table by selecting its name in the Subject Object list box.

Dropping Views

You can use the DROP VIEW command to remove a view from a database. Dropping a view has no effect on the permanent table that the dropped view is based upon. The definition of the view is simply removed from the database. The DROP VIEW syntax is as follows:

```
DROP VIEW view_name_1, … view_name_n
```

You can drop multiple views in a single DROP VIEW by using a list of views separated by commas after the DROP VIEW keywords. The following example drops the sales2 view:

```
drop view sales2
This command did not return data, and it did not return any rows.
```

You can also use the SQL Enterprise Manager to drop views by performing the following steps:

1. Left-click the view to select it.

2. Click the right mouse button. Choose Drop.

3. Click the Drop All button.

Figure 9.11 shows the Drop Objects dialog box. The view that was selected in the Server Manager dialog box is automatically selected in the Drop Objects dialog box.

FIG. 9.11

You can use the Show Dependencies button to display the object dependencies before you drop the view.

> **CAUTION**
>
> If you drop a view in which another view is defined, the second view returns the following error when you reference it (for example, in a SELECT statement).
>
> ```
> Msg 208, Level 16, State 1
> Invalid object name 'name_of_dropped_view'.
> Msg 4413, Level 16, State 1
> ```
>
> View resolution was unsuccessful because the previously mentioned objects, upon which the view directly or indirectly relies, don't currently exist. These objects need to be re-created in order to use the view.
>
> You should consider defining views directly on tables rather than other views. Tables are less likely to be dropped than views because tables are the objects in which rows are actually stored unlike views, which are simply a different way of looking at the data in a table.

Inserting Rows Through Views

In addition to retrieving rows of data through a view, you can also use the view to add rows to the underlying table on which the view is defined. To easily add a row, reference all table columns in the view. In the following example, a new row is added to the permanent Employees table through an INSERT statement that specifies the sales view.

Once you've created the view, you reference the view in an INSERT statement to add rows just as if you've referenced a table in the INSERT statement. The rows inserted through the view are added to the underlying table that the view was defined on.

In the following example, the view definition is first displayed to demonstrate that the view references the underlying table, employees, and is restricted only to rows that contain the department, Sales.

Once a new row is inserted through the view, the row is subsequently retrieved from both the view and the table.

```
sp_helptext sales
go
text
-----------------
create view sales as
select * from employees
where department='Sales'
go
insert into sales
values ('Mark Lenard','Sales',3331)
select * from sales
where badge=3331
go
name                    department            badge
------------------ -------------------- ----
Mark Lenard             Sales                 3331
(1 row(s) affected)
go
select * from employees
where badge=3331
name                    department            badge
------------------ -------------------- ----
Mark Lenard             Sales                 3331
(1 row(s) affected)
```

In the previous example, the row that was inserted through the view matched the criteria specified in the WHERE clause of the view; the inserted row contained the department, Sales. Although you may find it odd, SQL Server will permit you to insert a row through a view even though it doesn't match the criteria of WHERE clauses defined within the view.

Once a row is inserted through a view that does not match the criteria specified in the WHERE clause of the view, you can't retrieve the row through the view. The criteria for rows defined in the WHERE prevents you from retrieving the new row that you've just inserted. For example, in the following INSERT statement, a row is inserted through a view into the employees table on which the view sales is defined. As you'll recall from the definition of the sales view in the previous example, rows can have only the Sales department.

A subsequent SELECT statement is unable to retrieve the newly inserted row through the view. However, the row was added to the underlying table employees. A SELECT statement that references the table retrieves the new row that was added through the view. Both examples are shown here:

```
insert into sales
values ('Fannie Farmer','Logistics',6689)
go
select * from sales
where badge=6689
name                    department              badge
------------------ -------------------- ----------
(0 row(s) affected)
go
select * from employees
where badge=6689
go
name                    department              badge
------------------ -------------------- ----------
Fannie Farmer      Logistics            6689
(1 row(s) affected)
```

You can become confused when you add a row to the underlying table through a view in which the row doesn't match the criteria for inclusion in the view. The row can be inserted through the view (refer to previous example), but it cannot be retrieved and subsequently displayed through the same view. The row effectively disappears when retrieved through the view, but it still can be accessed through the table on which the view is based.

Fortunately, you can add the WITH CHECK OPTION clause to your view definition to prevent an operation, such as the insertion of a row through a view, that can't be subsequently displayed through the view.

The WITH CHECK OPTION, which is applied to the SELECT statement that is defined within the view, restricts all changes to the data to conform to the row selection criteria defined within the SELECT statement. For example, if a view is defined based on the table, employees, that contains a WHERE clause that specifies only the department, Sales, only rows that contain the department, Sales, can be inserted in the table, employees, through the view. WITH CHECK OPTION is illustrated in the following example:

```
create view check_with_check as
select * from company
where department='Sales' with check option
go
This command did not return data, and it did not return any rows
insert into check_with_check
values ('Bob Matilda','Field Service',3325,2)
go
Msg 550, Level 16, State 2
The attempted insert or update failed because the target view
```

Part III

Ch 9

```
either specifies WITH CHECK OPTION or spans a view which specifies
WITH CHECK OPTION and one or more rows resulting from the operation
did not qualify under the CHECK OPTION constraint.
Command has been aborted.
update check_with_check
set department='Hardware Repair' where department='Field Service'
go
(0 row(s) affected)
delete from check_with_check
where department='Field Service'
go
(0 row(s) affected)
```

TROUBLESHOOTING

I added a row to a view, but I can't seem to retrieve it when I reference the row in a subsequent SELECT statement. Why can't I retrieve the row through the view? You may have originally added a row that can't be retrieved because of the criteria specified in the view definition. (This is the aforementioned problem involved with disappearing rows.) Or the view may have been subsequently edited so that the row no longer meets the criteria for inclusion in the view.

Or the row may have been deleted through the view, another view, or directly from the underlying table. You can disable the disappearing row feature through the use of the WITH CHECK OPTION in the definition of the view.

In the previous example, a view was created that included all columns of the underlying table on which it was defined. If one or more columns of the underlying tables aren't present in the view, the missing columns must be defined to allow a NULL or have a default value bound to the missing columns. Otherwise, you can't add the row to the table through the view.

In the following example, a view is created that includes two columns of the employees table. The insertion of a row through the view is unsuccessful because the Department column was defined with NOT NULL.

```
create view namebadge as
select name,badge
from employees
go
insert into namebadge
(name,badge)
values ('Russell Stover',8000)
Msg 233, Level 16, State 2
The column department in table employees may not be null.
```

Once a default is defined for the Department column and bound to the column in the Employees table, a new row can be inserted through the namebadge view. The addition of the default for the Department column in the Employees table permits a value to be applied by default when a new row is inserted through the namebadge view. An example is shown in the following example:

```
create default deptdefault
as 'Sales'
go
sp_bindefault deptdefault, 'employees.department'
Default bound to column.
go
insert into namebadge
(name,badge)
values ('Russell Stover',8000)
(1 row(s) affected)
```

N O T E A default can be bound to a user-defined datatype or column of a table. A default can't be bound to the column of a view. However, the defaults bound to table columns that are referenced in a view are applied to the columns if a new row is inserted through the view. ■

The following example shows that once the row is inserted into the underlying employees table through the namebadge view, successive SELECT statements are used to retrieve the new row through the view and the table:

```
select * from namebadge
where name='Russell Stover'
go
name                    badge
-------------------- ----------
Russell Stover          8000
(1 row(s) affected)
select * from employees
where name='Russell Stover'
go
name                    department               badge
-------------------- -------------------- ----------
Russell Stover          Sales                    8000
(1 row(s) affected)
```

▶ **See** the Chapter 11 section entitled "Defining Defaults" for more information. **p. 313**

▶ **See** the Chapter 5 section entitled "Creating User-Defined Datatypes" for more information. **p. 133**

Using Views to Delete Rows

You can delete rows through views even though all columns are not referenced in the view. In the following example, a row that was previously added to the Employees table through the namebadge view is deleted by using the namebadge view. A subsequent SELECT statement demonstrates that the row is deleted.

```
delete from namebadge
where name='Russell Stover'
go
(1 row(s) affected)
select * from namebadge
where name='Russell Stover'
```

```
go
name                  badge
-------------------- ----------
(0 row(s) affected)
```

You can't delete a row if the criteria specified in the SELECT clause doesn't include the row specified for deletion. It isn't necessary to add the WITH CHECK OPTION to the definition of the view to prevent the deletion of rows that don't match the criteria specified by the WHERE clause of the view. In the following example, one or more rows of the Shipping department is specified for deletion through the sales view. Even if multiple rows were stored in the underlying permanent Employees table upon which sales is based, the rows can't be deleted through the sales view.

```
delete from sales
where department='Shipping'
go
(0 row(s) affected)
```

You also can't delete a row from the underlying table of a view if the column that you specify in the WHERE clause of a DELETE statement specifies a column that isn't specified in the view. The following example returns an error because the column specified in the WHERE clause isn't present in the namebadge view used in the DELETE statement:

```
delete from namebadge
where department='Shipping'
go
Msg 207, Level 16, State 2
Invalid column name 'department'.
```

You can, however, delete the row through a view that was defined with a WHERE clause that specifies a criteria that includes the row or rows specified in the DELETE statement. You can also delete one or more rows directly through the table in which the view was defined. In the following example, a row is deleted by using a DELETE statement that references the table containing the row:

```
delete from employees
where department='Shipping'
go
(1 row(s) affected)
```

Using Views to Update Rows

You can use an UPDATE statement to change one or more columns or rows that are referenced through a view. You can change one or more columns of the view. Any changes that you specify through the view are made to the underlying table in which the view is defined. In the following example, a single row is updated through the sales view:

```
select * from sales
go
name                  department              badge
-------------------- ----------------------- ----------
Bob Smith             Sales                   1234
```

```
Mary Jones              Sales                  5514
John Garr               Sales                  2221
Mark Lenard             Sales                  3331
(4 row(s) affected)
update sales
set badge=0001
where name='Bob Smith'
go
(1 row(s) affected)
select * from sales
where name='Bob Smith'
name                    department             badge
------------------      ------------------     ----------
Bob Smith               Sales                  1
(1 row(s) affected)
```

You can change one or more columns or rows so that they no longer meet the criteria for inclusion in the view. In the following example, a row is updated through a view and a column value is changed so that the row no longer matches the criteria defined in the view:

```
update sales
set department='Field Service'
where name='Bob Smith'
go
(1 row(s) affected)
select * from sales
where name='Bob Smith'
go
name                    department             badge
------------------      ------------------     ----------
 (0 row(s) affected)
```

You can also update the underlying table by updating through a view that is defined on a view. In the following example, the update to the Employees table is performed through a view that is defined using the sales view.

```
select * from onlyname
name
go
----------------------
Bob Smith
Fred Sanders
(2 row(s) affected)
update onlyname
set name='Bob Orieda'
where name='Bob Smith'
go
(1 row(s) affected)
select * from onlyname
go
name
----------------------
Fred Sanders
Bob Orieda
(2 row(s) affected)
```

```
select * from employees
where name like 'Bob%'
go
name                          department           badge
----------------------        ------------------   ------
Bob Orieda                    SALES                1834
(1 row(s) affected)
```

The updated row that was changed through the name onlyname view, which was based on the underlying employees table through the sales view, is displayed through both the nameonly view and the Employees table. The updated row is also displayed through the sales view. Here are the results:

```
select * from sales
where name like 'Bob%'
go
name                          department           badge
----------------------        ------------------   ------
Bob Orieda                    SALES                1834
(1 row(s) affected)
```

Any changes to the data that you make by updates through views are always reflected in the underlying tables. Views permit you to establish virtual tables with data rows organized like tables—though they are dynamically created as the view is referenced. It's convenient to use views as the only access to data; don't allow tables to be directly referenced.

N O T E   Users of older databases, such as hierarchical or network databases, may remember that their databases could only be manipulated through entities equivalent to views. Network databases had to be indirectly accessed through an entity called a *subschema*. A subschema functioned like a view.

The usual definition of a subschema is that it serves as the entity through which a programmer or user views the database. You always had to use a subschema to access a network database. Usually, a default subschema was created for a network database that permitted access to the entire database if necessary. ■

You can update underlying tables through multi-table views if the updated columns are part of the same table. The following example shows a row is successfully updated through the multi-table combo view.

```
create view combo (a,b,c) as
select name,employees.badge,pays.badge
from employees,pays
where employees.badge=pays.badge
go
This command did not return data, and it did not return any rows
update combo
set a='Jim Walker II'
where b=3211
go
(1 row(s) affected)
```

```
select * from combo
where b=3211
go
a                              b           c
-----------------------        ----------  ----------
Jim Walker II                  3211        3211
(1 row(s) affected)
```

You can't, however, update the view columns that are used to match rows between the tables because they're part of separate tables. In the next example, the column b and column c views are based on the Badge columns in the Employees and Pays tables. An error is returned that cites an unsuccessful update because the columns are from two tables.

```
update combo
set c=1111, b=1111
where b=8005
go
Msg 4405, Level 16, State 2
View 'combo' is not updatable because the FROM clause names multiple tables.
```

You can update a value in a single column directly through the view, and you can use a trigger to update the corresponding value in a related table. In the following example, a trigger has been defined to automatically update the Badge column in the Pays table if the Badge column in the Pays table is changed. When the badge is changed through the b column in the combo view, the trigger automatically activates to change the corresponding value in the Pays table.

```
update combo
set b=9999
where c=4411
go
(1 row(s) affected)
select * from combo
where b=9999
go
a                              b           c
-----------------------        ----------  ----------
Sue Sommers                    9999        9999
(1 row(s) affected)
```

Exploring Other View Characteristics

A view remains defined in the database if you drop the table upon which it's based. However, an error is returned when the view is referenced if its underlying table is undefined. If you create a new table with the same name as the one referenced by the view that was dropped, you can again retrieve data from the underlying new table through the view.

The following example drops a table upon which a view is based. As shown in the following example, sp_help confirms that the view remains defined even though you have deleted the table upon which it's based. When the view is used in a SELECT statement, an error is returned because the table doesn't exist. Once the table is re-created and rows are loaded from an existing table, the view is used to reference rows for the underlying new table.

```
drop table employees3
go
This command did not return data, and it did not return any rows
sp_help namebadge3
go
Name                    Owner              Type
---------------------------- ----------------
namebadge3          dbo                view
Data_located_on_segment When_created
---------------------- --------------------------
not applicable          Oct 2 1994 11:45AM
Column_name Type Length Nulls Default_name Rule_name
-------------- ------------- ---- -------------- -
name        char     25     0     (null)     (null)
badge       int      4      0     (null)     (null)
No defined keys for this object.
select * from namebadge3
go
Msg 208, Level 16, State 1
Invalid object name 'employees3'.
Msg 4413, Level 16, State 1
View resolution could not succeed because the previously mentioned
objects, upon which the view directly or indirectly relies, do not
currently exist.  These objects need to be re-created for the view
 to be usable.
create table employees3
(name char(25),department char(20),badge int)
go
This command did not return data, and it did not return any rows
insert into employees3
select * from employees
go
(12 row(s) affected)
select * from namebadge3
where name='Sally Springer'
go
name                    badge
---------------------- ----------
Sally Springer          9998
(1 row(s) affected)
```

If you use a SELECT clause in a view with an asterisk (*) to specify columns, the new columns added to the table with an ALTER TABLE statement won't be available in the old view. The new table columns are made available only if the view is dropped and re-created.

In the following example, a view is defined that uses an asterisk (*) in the SELECT clause of a SELECT statement to reference all columns of the Employees table. After an additional column is added to the table with an ALTER TABLE statement, the view doesn't display the NULL entries in the new column that was added to the table. The new Wageclass column is available through the view only after the view is dropped and re-created.

```
sp_helptext sales3
go
text
------------------
create view sales3
as
select * from employees3
where department='SALES'
go
(1 row(s) affected)
select * from sales3
go
name                    department         badge
----------------------------------- ----------
Fred Sanders            SALES              1051
Bob Orieda              SALES              1834
(2 row(s) affected)
alter table employees3
add wageclass int null
go
This command did not return data, and it did not return any rows
select * from sales3
go
name                    department         badge
----------------------------------- ----------
Fred Sanders            SALES              1051
Bob Orieda              SALES              1834
(2 row(s) affected)
select * from employees3
where department='SALES'
go

---------------------- --------------- ----------
Fred Sanders            SALES              1051      (null)
Bob Orieda              SALES              1834      (null)
(2 row(s) affected)
drop view sales3
go
This command did not return data, and it did not return any rows
create view sales3 as
select * from employees3
where department='SALES'
go
This command did not return data, and it did not return any rows
select * from sales3
go
name                    department      badge  wageclass
---------------------- ---------- ----------
Fred Sanders            SALES              1051      (null)
Bob Orieda              SALES              1834      (null)
(2 row(s) affected)
```

From Here...

In this chapter you've learned to create virtual tables that use a stored SELECT statement to create a subset of the rows, columns or a combination of the rows and columns of one or more database tables. You've also learned to change previously defined views using the Enterprise Manager and display and remove views when they're no longer needed. Finally, you learned to add, update, and delete rows through views applying the changes to the underlying tables from which the views are defined.

For information about selected aspects of the topics mentioned in this chapter, see the following chapters:

- Chapter 5, "Creating Database Tables and Using Datatypes," discusses the treatment of NULLs as column values, as well as the column datatypes.

- Chapter 7, "Performing Operations on Tables," teaches you how to combine rows from multiple tables in the same query, including the use of COMPUTE and COMPUTE BY.

- Chapter 10, "Managing and Using Indexes and Keys," teaches you how to create and use keys and indexes and how to constrain rows and columns to unique values.

- Chapter 14, "Creating and Managing Triggers," teaches you how to create and use triggers to maintain referential integrity in the database.

Managing and Using Indexes and Keys

One of the most important responsibilities of a database designer is to correctly define a database table for optimal performance. SQL Server's basic design of a table doesn't in any way define how data is to be accessed or stored physically, beyond the data-type constraints and any referential constraint placed on a column or columns designated as PRIMARY KEY. Instead, SQL Server provides a mechanism of indexes or keys to a table that help SQL Server optimize responses to queries.

Without an index, SQL Server must *table scan*, or read every row in a table, before it can know the answer to any given query. In large tables this is obviously an expensive option for the server to take. Indexes provide a way for SQL Server to organize pointers to the data required. An index in a database works the same way as an index in a reference book. Like an index in a book, an index in a database is a list of "important" values that contain references to pages in the database table that contain the information that matches the index value. This allows the database to read from a (usually) smaller list of index pages that will in turn point to the data that will answer any given request. ■

What indexes are for and how to create them

Indexes are used to make it easier and faster to retrieve data. They can be created at the same time a table is created or they can be added to the table at a later time.

The different kinds of indexes that can be created

There are several types of indexes. Each index tracks data and stores that tracking information in different ways. Some indexes also affect the way the data is physically stored in the database.

What keys are for and how to create them

Rows of data contain unique values that can be used to identify each individual row. The columns that contain these unique values are called key columns. For key columns to be guaranteed unique, they must be declared when creating a table. Key column definitions can also be added or modified after a table is created.

Defining Indexes

Indexes are SQL Server's internal method of organizing the data in a table in such a way that it can be retrieved in an optimal fashion. *Optimal*, in this case, refers to the quickest way. Indexes are collections of unique values in a given table and their corresponding list of pointers to the pages of data where those values are physically represented in a table.

At a high level, indexes are a shorthand way of the database recording information that it's storing in tables. Indexes are just another kind of object in the database and have storage needs like tables. Just as tables require pages of data to store their rows in, indexes require pages to store their summary data in. The advantage of an index is that, generally, it reduces the number of I/Os required to reach any given piece of data in a table.

When you create an index in SQL Server, you tell the database to scan the table, gather the discrete values in the particular column or column(s) being indexed, and then write a list of data pages (and row identifiers) to the index page that match the value being indexed. This allows the server to scan a list of index pages, before choosing to scan the whole table, looking for matching data.

Creating Indexes

SQL Server has two methods of creating indexes: a graphical method provided in SQL Enterprise Manager, and a Transact-SQL interface using the CREATE INDEX statement. Only the table's owner can create an index on a table.

N O T E SQL Enterprise Manager has a limitation when you create indexes through it in which you can't specify a data segment for the index to be created on. Moving indexes on to different data segments can significantly improve performance on non-clustered indexes because multiple I/O threads can be used to read the data from the index and data pages concurrently. Use the CREATE INDEX statement in ISQL/w to create an index if you need to specify a segment for the index data. ■

Creating an Index with SQL Enterprise Manager   To create an index using SQL Enterprise Manager, follow these steps:

1. Run SQL Enterprise Manager from the Microsoft SQL Server 6.5 group. Figure 10.1 shows the main screen shortly after the startup of SQL Enterprise Manager.
2. Select the server, database, and table that you want to work on (see fig. 10.2).
3. From the Manage menu choose Indexes. The Manage Indexes dialog box appears (see fig. 10.3).

FIG. 10.1

SQL Enterprise Manager's Explorer view after having just being started. Note that no server is selected.

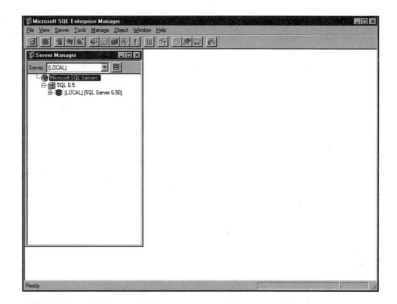

FIG. 10.2

The Explorer view of SQL Enterprise Manager, with the authors table selected from the pubs database.

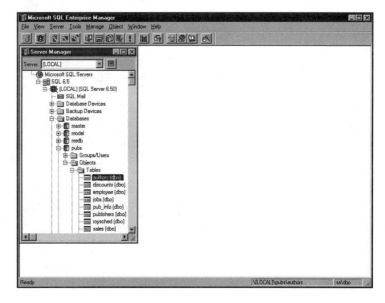

FIG. 10.3

The authors table is selected in the top-left combo box, and the aunmind index is selected in the top-right combo box.

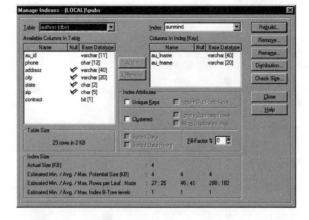

4. Select the value (New Index) from the Index combo box. This clears the Index combo box, enabling you to enter the new index name; the Columns In Index list also is cleared.

5. Enter `fk_au_id` as the index name, highlight the au_id column, and click the Add button. Select the check boxes Unique Keys and Ignore Duplicate Keys (see fig. 10.4).

FIG. 10.4

The Manage Indexes dialog box is ready to build a new index.

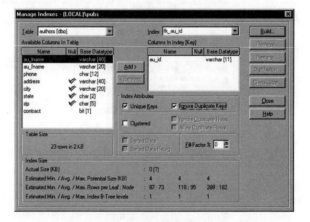

TIP Prefixing index names with *pk* for primary key or *fk* for foreign key makes it easier to identify the index type without having to inspect its properties.

6. Click the Build button to build the index. A message box appears, asking whether the index should be built now or scheduled as a task to run later (see fig. 10.5). Choose the option that's appropriate for your environment.

FIG. 10.5

The Index Build message box seeks confirmation of whether the index should be built immediately or scheduled as a task.

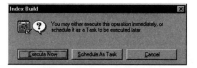

Creating an Index with *CREATE INDEX*

The Transact-SQL command CREATE INDEX is used by SQL Enterprise Manager to perform the index creation when the Build button is clicked in the Manage Indexes dialog box. The syntax for CREATE INDEX is as follows:

```
CREATE [UNIQUE] [CLUSTERED ¦ NONCLUSTERED] INDEX index_name
    ON [[database.]owner.]table_name (column_name [, column_name]...)
[WITH
    [FILLFACTOR = x]
    [[,] IGNORE_DUP_KEY]
    [[,] {SORTED_DATA ¦ SORTED_DATA_REORG}]
    [[,] {IGNORE_DUP_ROW ¦ ALLOW_DUP_ROW}]]
[ON segment_name]
```

The options for the Transact-SQL command CREATE INDEX follow.

UNIQUE   If an index is created as UNIQUE, SQL Server disallows duplicate values in the index and therefore stops a client from inserting a record into the base table. This is the most common use of an index to enforce integrity on a table. Unique indexes can't be created on tables that have duplicate values in the columns being indexed—the duplicate data must be removed first. If enabled, the IGNORE_DUP_KEY option (described later) allows UPDATE or INSERT statements, affecting several rows, that modify index keys to complete, even if the new index key values become duplicates. The duplicate values will be rolled back and the transaction will continue—no error will be generated.

CLUSTERED   A *clustered index* is a special index that forces SQL Server to store the table data in the exact order of the index. Using a clustered index to physically store the data in the table in a particular way can greatly improve access performance to the table. Data requested from tables that are scanned repeatedly by the index key value for an individual record or set of records in a range can be found very quickly, because SQL Server knows that the data for the index page is right next to it. Any further values are guaranteed to be in the following data pages.

If CLUSTERED isn't specified in the CREATE INDEX statement, the index is assumed to be NONCLUSTERED.

There can be only one clustered index per table because the data can be in only one physical order.

Part

III

Ch

10

> **CAUTION**
>
> Specifying a segment for a clustered index to be placed on will actually move the table data too. Be careful using the ON *segment_name* keyword when creating a clustered index. You must have approximately 1.2 times the space required for the entire table available on the target segment for the clustered index and data; otherwise, the segment free space will be filled and a new segment will need to be created. SQL Server won't warn you before index creation that the segment space is inadequate because it has no way of knowing or accurately estimating the size required for the index.

NONCLUSTERED   This is the default index type and means that SQL Server will create an index whose pages of index data contain pointers to the actual pages of table data in the database. You can create up to 249 non-clustered indexes in a table.

index_name   An index name must be unique by table—that is, the same index name can be given to two indexes, provided that they're indexing different base tables in the database. Index names must follow standard SQL Server naming conventions for objects.

table_name   *table_name* is the table that's going to be indexed.

column_name   The column that's being indexed. If more than one column is placed here, a composite or compound index is created. Multiple columns should be separated by spaces. You can specify up to 16 columns to create a composite key; however, the maximum width of the data types being combined can't exceed 256 bytes.

FILLFACTOR = x   Specifying a FILLFACTOR on a index tells SQL Server how to "pack" the index data into the index data pages. FILLFACTOR tells SQL Server to preserve space on the index data page for other similar rows that are expected for the same index keys or similar index key values.

> **CAUTION**
>
> The FILLFACTOR should rarely be used. It is included solely for fine-tuning purposes. Even for fine-tuning, it should only be used if future changes in the data can be made with accuracy.

Specifying a FILLFACTOR for frequently inserted database tables can improve performance because SQL Server won't have to split data onto separate data pages when the index information is too different to fit on a single page. Page splitting is a costly operation (in terms of I/O) and should be avoided, if possible.

The number of the FILLFACTOR refers to the percentage of free space that should be preserved on each index page.

A small FILLFACTOR is useful for creating indexes for tables that haven't got their complete dataset yet. For example, if you know that a table is going to have many more values than it does now and you want SQL Server to preallocate space in the index pages for those values so that it won't need to *page split*, specify a low FILLFACTOR of about 10. A page split occurs when the index fills up such that no further values will fit in the current 2K data page. Consequently

SQL Server *splits* the page in two and puts references to the newly created page in the original page.

A high FILLFACTOR will force more frequent page splits because SQL Server will have no room on the index page to add any additional values that may be necessary if a record is inserted into the table. A FILLFACTOR of 100 will force SQL Server to completely fill the index pages. This option is good for highly concurrent, read-only tables. It's extremely bad, however, for tables that are inserted or updated frequently; every insert will cause a page split, and many of the updates (if key values are updated) will also cause page splits.

If no FILLFACTOR is specified, the server default (usually 0) is used. To change the server default, use the system-stored procedure sp_configure.

▶ **See** the section entitled "Displaying and Setting Server Options" in Chapter 16. **p. 408**

Part
III

Ch
10

Be careful when specifying a FILLFACTOR for a clustered index—it will directly affect the amount of space required for the storage of the table data. Because a clustered index is bound to a table, (the physical order of the table data is mapped to the order of the clustered index), a FILLFACTOR on the index will space each data page of the table apart from the others according to the value requested. This can consume substantial amounts of disk space if the FILLFACTOR is sparse.

N O T E Specifying a FILLFACTOR when creating an index on a table without data has no effect because SQL Server has no way of placing the data in the index correctly. For tables that have dynamic data sets that need to be indexed with an index specifying a FILLFACTOR, you should rebuild indexes periodically to make sure that SQL Server is actually populating the index pages correctly. ▪

IGNORE_DUP_KEY   When SQL is executed, this option controls SQL Server's behavior that causes duplicate records to exist in a table with a unique index defined on it. By default, SQL Server will always reject a duplicate record and return an error. This option allows you to get SQL Server to continue processing as though this isn't an error condition.

This configuration option can be useful in highly accessed tables where the general trend of the data is more important than the actual specifics. It shouldn't be used for tables where each individual record is important, however, unless application code is providing appropriate referential constraints to the data. If multiple records are affected by an update or insert statement, and the statement causes some records to create duplicates, the statement will be allowed to continue. Those records that created duplicates will be rolled back with no error returned.

CAUTION

When enabling IGNORE_DUP_KEY, be careful that you don't lose required data due to unwanted updates occurring. If IGNORE_DUP_KEY is enabled for a unique index and an update is done to data that causes duplicate records to exist, not only will the duplicates be rejected by the update, but the original records will also be removed. This is because of the way SQL Server performs updates—by deleting the record and then reinserting it. The reinsertion will fail (due to the duplicity of the record), so neither the original record nor the updated record will exist.

SORTED_DATA   SQL Server uses the SORTED_DATA keyword to speed up index creation for clustered indexes. By specifying SORTED_DATA, you're saying that the data to be indexed is already physically sorted in the order of the index. SQL Server will verify that the order is indeed correct during index creation by checking that each indexed item is greater than the previous item. If any item isn't found to be sorted, SQL Server will report an error and abort index creation. If this option isn't specified, SQL Server will sort the data for you as it would do normally.

Using the SORTED_DATA keyword greatly reduces the amount of time and space required to create a clustered index. The time is reduced because SQL Server doesn't spend any time ordering the data; the required space is reduced because SQL Server no longer needs to create a temporary workspace to place the sorted values before creating the index.

SORTED_DATA_REORG   SORTED_DATA_REORG is similar to SORTED_DATA in that it helps SQL Server's overall performance by making the data physically reside in the database table in the order of the index. The SORTED_DATA_REORG keyword tells SQL Server to physically reorder the data in the order of the index. This can be especially useful on non-clustered indexed tables that you want to reduce the amount of page splits on due to data no longer being in adjacent data pages. This will help the data be physically adjacent in the database and will reduce the number of non-sequential physical I/Os required to fetch data, which in turn improves performance.

IGNORE_DUP_ROW   This option is for creating a non-unique clustered index. If enabled at index creation time on a table with duplicate data in it, SQL Server will

- Create the index
- Delete the duplicate values
- Return an error message to the calling process indicating the failure. At this point the calling process should initiate a ROLLBACK to restore the data.

If data is inserted into or updated in the table after the index is created, SQL Server will

- Accept any non-duplicate values
- Delete the duplicate values (and possibly the original record, if a duplicate occurs during an update)
- Return an error message to the calling process indicating the failure. At this point the calling process should initiate a ROLLBACK to restore the data.

> ▶ **See** the section entitled *"ROLLBACK TRAN,"* in Chapter 12. **p. 327**

N O T E   This option has no effect on non-clustered indexes. SQL Server internally assigns identifiers to the records being indexed and doesn't have to manage the physical order of the data according to the clustering. ■

ALLOW_DUP_ROW   This option can't be set on an index that's allowed to IGNORE_DUP_ROW. It controls behavior for inserting or updating records in a non-unique clustered index. If ALLOW_DUP_ROW is enabled, no errors are returned and no data is affected if multiple duplicate records are created in a clustered index.

ON segment_name   Specifying a segment for the index to reside on allows the placement of an index on a different segment of the data. This will improve performance of non-clustered indexes because multiple I/O handlers can be used to read and write from the index and data segments concurrently.

Clustered indexes that have a segment name specified will move the data that's being indexed, as well as the index to the indicated segment.

Understanding Statistics

The value of an index for helping SQL Server resolve a query largely depends on how accurately the index's data reflects the actual data in the database. SQL Server maintains heuristical or trend statistics on the data that the index contains to help it choose the appropriate index that will yield the least number of I/Os to get to the actual table data. Clustered indexes (when available) will almost always be chosen as a valid key over non-clustered indexes. Clustered indexes are favored because there is no physical I/O after the data is found in the index because it's on the same page.

SQL Server's statistics-gathering engine is based on an as-needed basis, in that the statistics are maintained only when an index is built or the statistics on those indexes are forced to be updated by the UPDATE STATISTICS statement. SQL Server doesn't maintain statistics on the fly purely for performance reasons. The additional overhead of maintaining the statistics dynamically generally isn't considered advantageous to fetching the data because it will consume (on average) more resources than would have been saved by the additional data. SQL Server's statistics indicate trends in the data and don't necessarily represent every key data element. These trends are what SQL Server uses to determine the best index to use.

The exception of where dynamic index statistic management would be beneficial is when an index is created on a table with no data in it. SQL Server has no way of knowing what the trends in the data are and, as a result, makes very basic assumptions of normal distribution. These assumptions are often very wrong after a number of records are added to the table; thus, SQL Server will table scan even though there's an appropriate index. In this situation, perform an UPDATE STATISTICS on the table, and the index's distribution information will be updated.

To determine the last time statistics information was updated on a given index, the DBCC command SHOW_STATISTICS can be used. An example of its use follows:

```
/*---------------------------
dbcc show_statistics( authors, fk_au_id )
---------------------------*/
Updated              Rows      Steps       Density
```

```
----------------------  ----------  ----------  --------
Dec 10 1995  2:20PM  23             22          0.0434783

(1 row(s) affected)

All density             Columns
----------------------  ------
0.0434783               au_id

(1 row(s) affected)

Steps
----------
172-32-1176
213-46-8915
238-95-7766
267-41-2394
274-80-9391
341-22-1782
409-56-7008
427-17-2319
472-27-2349
486-29-1786
527-72-3246
648-92-1872
672-71-3249
712-45-1867
722-51-5454
724-08-9931
724-80-9391
756-30-7391
807-91-6654
846-92-7186
893-72-1158
899-46-2035

(22 row(s) affected)

DBCC execution completed. If DBCC printed error messages, see your
System Administrator.
```

In the output from the DBCC SHOW STATISTICS command, you can see that the statistics have been kept up-to-date as of December 10th. In the second example, shown in Listing 10.1, the authors2 table is re-created with the same structures as authors and the data are copied to it.

On the CD

Listing 10.1   10_01.SQL—Creating the Table authors2 and Its Indexes

```
CREATE TABLE authors2
    (
        au_id id NOT NULL ,
        au_lname varchar (40) NOT NULL ,
        au_fname varchar (20) NOT NULL ,
        phone char (12) NOT NULL ,
        address varchar (40) NULL ,
```

```
        city varchar (20) NULL ,
        state char (2) NULL ,
        zip char (5) NULL ,
        contract bit NOT NULL
)
GO

 CREATE  INDEX aunmind ON dbo.authors2(au_lname, au_fname)
 WITH  FILLFACTOR = 5
GO

 CREATE  UNIQUE  INDEX barny ON dbo.authors2(au_id) WITH  IGNORE_DUP_KEY
GO

 CREATE  UNIQUE  INDEX fk_au_id ON dbo.authors2(au_id) WITH  IGNORE_DUP_KEY
GO

insert into authors2 select * from authors
GO
```

The previous listing was generated by doing a SQL script generation using SQL Enterprise Manager and then changing the table name from *authors* to *authors2*. Here's the same DBCC command reporting very different results, because the STATISTICS are out of date:

```
/*---------------------------
dbcc show_statistics( authors2, fk_au_id )
---------------------------*/
Updated              Rows       Steps      Density
-------------------- ---------- ---------- ------
                NULL 23          0          0.0

(1 row(s) affected)

All density            Columns
---------------------- ------
0.0                    au_id

(1 row(s) affected)

Steps
----------

(0 row(s) affected)

DBCC execution completed. If DBCC printed error messages, see your
System Administrator.
```

Performing an UPDATE STATISTICS on the authors2 table and then doing the DBCC command yields the identical results to the initial DBCC on the authors table:

```
/*---------------------------
update statistics authors2
go
dbcc show_statistics( authors2, fk_au_id )
```

Part III

Ch 10

```
------------------------------*/
Updated              Rows        Steps       Density
-------------------- ----------- ----------- --------
Dec 11 1995 12:08PM  23          22          0.0434783

(1 row(s) affected)

All density             Columns
----------------------- ------
0.0434783               au_id

(1 row(s) affected)

Steps
----------
172-32-1176
213-46-8915
238-95-7766
267-41-2394
274-80-9391
341-22-1782
409-56-7008
427-17-2319
472-27-2349
486-29-1786
527-72-3246
648-92-1872
672-71-3249
712-45-1867
722-51-5454
724-08-9931
724-80-9391
756-30-7391
807-91-6654
846-92-7186
893-72-1158
899-46-2035

(22 row(s) affected)

DBCC execution completed. If DBCC printed error messages, see your
System Administrator.
```

Updating Statistics   SQL Server has two ways of updating the statistics that relate to a table. The graphical way can be performed using SQL Enterprise Manager. The Transact-SQL command is UPDATE STATISTICS.

Using SQL Enterprise Manager to Update Statistics   To use SQL Enterprise Manager to update statistics on a table, follow these steps:

1. Launch SQL Enterprise Manager from the Microsoft SQL Server 6.5 group.

2. Select the server, database, and table that you want to work on.

3. From the Manage menu choose Indexes. The Manage Indexes dialog box appears (see fig. 10.6).

FIG. 10.6

The authors table is selected in the Table combo box, and the aunmind index is selected in the Index combo box.

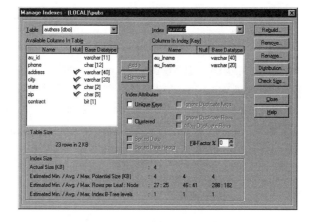

4. Click the Distribution button to view the Index Distribution Statistics dialog box (see fig. 10.7).

FIG. 10.7

This dialog box uses the output of DBCC SHOW_STATISTICS to display the information.

5. Click the Update button to update the statistics. A message box appears, asking whether the statistics should be updated now or scheduled as a task to run later (see fig. 10.8). Choose the option that's appropriate for your environment.

FIG. 10.8

The Update Distribution Statistics message box confirms whether the index statistics should be updated immediately or scheduled as a task.

By default, only the index highlighted in the Manage Indexes dialog box will have its statistics updated. If you want to update all of the indexes on the table selected, check the option Apply to ALL Indexes Of check box before either scheduling the task or executing it.

Using UPDATE STATISTICS   The UPDATE STATISTICS statement is used to update the index statistics on a table or index. The syntax for UPDATE STATISTICS is as follows:

```
UPDATE STATISTICS [[database.]owner.]table_name [index_name]
```

The options for the Transact-SQL command UPDATE STATISTICS are as follows:

- *table_name*—The name of the table that the index resides on. If no index is specified, all the indexes on the table are updated at the same time.

- *index_name*—The name of the index that's to have its statistics updated.

N O T E   Performing an UPDATE STATISTICS on a database table can affect the plan that a stored procedure has generated for accessing data. Because stored procedures are compiled and stored in the procedure cache when they're first executed, they can store invalid access paths to data based on the index statistics at the time the procedure was first run. To force a stored procedure to refresh its access path, use the system-stored procedure sp_recompile and pass the table that was updated as a parameter. For example, sp_recompile authors will force all the procedures that use the authors table to be recompiled the next time they're executed. ■

Forcing the Use of a Particular Index   If SQL Server fails to pick an index that you know should provide better performance than the index it chose, you can force the use of an index by specifying it in the FROM clause. To force an index, use the *optimizer hints* or (INDEX = ...) section of the SELECT statement's syntax. In simplified syntax, here's a SELECT statement:

```
SELECT ...
FROM table_name (INDEX = n) /* optimizer hints are placed after the table */
...
```

▶ **See** Chapter 6, "Retrieving Data with Transact-SQL," for more information on the syntax of SELECT statements. **p. 141**

The INDEX keyword tells SQL Server to use the index specified by the numeric *n*. If *n* equals 0, SQL Server will table scan. If *n* equals 1, SQL Server will use the clustered index if one is in the table. The other values of *n* are determined by the number of indexes on the table.

 T I P   An index name can also be used in the optimizer hint instead of an identifying id number.

Listing 10.2 shows SQL Server using the optimizer hints when selecting from the authors table.

Listing 10.2   10_02.SQL—Same *SELECT* Statement Performed Four Times to Demonstrate Use of Forced Index

```
/* Turn on statistics IO, so that the results can be seen */
set statistics io on
go
```

```
/* Basic Select with no hints to show the optimizer
   choosing the clustered index */
Select      AU_ID, AU_FNAME
From  AUTHORS
Where AU_ID between '172-32-1176' and '238-95-7766'
Order By AU_ID
go

/* Force a table scan */
Select      AU_ID, AU_FNAME
From  AUTHORS (INDEX = 0)
Where AU_ID between '172-32-1176' and '238-95-7766'
Order By AU_ID
go

/* Force the clustered index */
Select      AU_ID, AU_FNAME
From  AUTHORS (INDEX = 1)
Where AU_ID between '172-32-1176' and '238-95-7766'
Order By AU_ID
go

/* Force the first alternate index */
Select      AU_ID, AU_FNAME
From  AUTHORS (INDEX = 2)
Where AU_ID between '172-32-1176' and '238-95-7766'
Order By AU_ID
  go
```

The output is as follows:

```
AU_ID       AU_FNAME
---------- --------------------
172-32-1176 Johnson
213-46-8915 Marjorie
238-95-7766 Cheryl

(3 row(s) affected)

Table: authors  scan count 1,  logical reads: 1,  physical reads: 0
AU_ID       AU_FNAME
---------- --------------------
172-32-1176 Johnson
213-46-8915 Marjorie
238-95-7766 Cheryl

(3 row(s) affected)

Table: authors  scan count 1,  logical reads: 1,  physical reads: 0
Table: Worktable  scan count 0,  logical reads: 4,  physical reads: 0
AU_ID       AU_FNAME
---------- --------------------
172-32-1176 Johnson
213-46-8915 Marjorie
238-95-7766 Cheryl
```

```
(3 row(s) affected)

Table: authors  scan count 1,  logical reads: 2,  physical reads: 0
AU_ID       AU_FNAME
---------- --------------------
172-32-1176 Johnson
213-46-8915 Marjorie
238-95-7766 Cheryl

(3 row(s) affected)

Table: authors  scan count 1,  logical reads: 29,  physical reads: 0
Table: Worktable  scan count 0,  logical reads: 4,  physical reads: 0
```

> **CAUTION**
>
> The effects of forcing an index are clearly shown in these examples. The last example shows an extremely expensive option being forced on the server. You can cause major performance problems by forcing index use, and so it's generally not recommended that you update the indexes.
>
> Forcing index selection in a query is also dangerous if the application code is left unchanged and the indexes are changed or rebuilt. Changing the indexes may cause severe performance degradation due to the forcing of indexes that no longer provide optimal performance.
>
> If you must resort to index forcing and believe that the optimizer should have chosen a different index, it's recommended that you call Microsoft or your local support provider and log a bug with the query optimizer.

Displaying Index Information

SQL Server has two ways to show information about indexes. The graphical method is via SQL Enterprise Manager's Index Manager; the command-line method is via the system-stored procedure `sp_helpindex` and the ODBC stored procedure `sp_statistics`.

SQL Enterprise Manager's Index Manager has been discussed in detail in previous sections in this chapter. Please refer to the section "Using SQL Enterprise Manager to Update Statistics" for instructions on how to view the statistics associated with an index.

sp_helpindex   The system-stored procedure `sp_helpindex` has been provided to get information about indexes. The syntax for the procedure's use is

```
sp_helpindex table_name
```

table_name should be replaced with an unqualified table name. If the table you want to inquire on isn't in the current database, you must change to the required database before executing this procedure.

`sp_helpindex` will return the first 8 indexes that are found on a database table. In the following example, `sp_helpindex` shows all the indexes on the authors table:

```
/*--------------------------
sp_helpindex authors
```

```
---------------------------*/
index_name            index_description
index_keys
-------------------------------------
UPKCL_auidind         clustered, unique, primary key located on default
au_id
aunmind               nonclustered located on default
au_lname, au_fname
barny                 nonclustered, ignore duplicate key, unique located on
default au_id
fk_au_id              nonclustered, ignore duplicate key, unique located on
default au_id

(1 row(s) affected)
```

sp_statistics   sp_statistics is a special stored procedure that has been created to help
Microsoft "publish" information for the ODBC interface to the database. Microsoft created this
stored procedure so that an ODBC driver could retrieve all the relevant information about an
index from a single call to the database. The information returned can be gathered in a number
of other ways; however, it's often convenient to use sp_statistics to summarize all the relevant information on a table. The syntax for sp_statistics is as follows:

```
sp_statistics table_name [, table_owner] [, table_qualifier]
    [, index_name] [, is_unique]
```

The options for the system-stored procedure sp_statistics are as follows:

- *table_name*—This is the name of the table that you require the index information on.
- *table_owner*—This is the owner of the table.
- *table_qualifier*—This is the name of the database in which the table resides.
- *index_name*—This is the specific index that's being requested.
- *is_unique*—If this parameter is set to 'Y', SQL Server will return only unique indexes
  on the table.

> **TIP**   Many stored procedures have many of parameters. To save time, rather than specify all the parameters,
> you can indicate a particular one by placing an @ sign in front of the parameter name—for example,
> sp_statistics authors, @is_unique = 'Y'

Dropping Indexes

SQL Server has two ways of dropping indexes on a table. The graphical way can be performed
by using SQL Enterprise Manager. The command-line way is by using the SQL statement DROP
INDEX.

Using SQL Enterprise Manager to Drop an Index   To use SQL Enterprise Manager to drop
an index, follow these steps:

1. Launch SQL Enterprise Manager from the Microsoft SQL Server 6.5 group.
2. Select the server, database, and table that you want to work on.

3. From the Manage menu choose Indexes. The Manage Indexes dialog box appears.

4. Click the Remove button to drop the index required. A message box appears, asking whether the index should be removed now or scheduled as a task to run later (see fig. 10.9). Choose the option that's appropriate for your environment.

FIG. 10.9

The Index Removal message box confirms whether you want the index removed immediately or scheduled as a task.

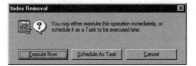

Using the *DROP INDEX* Command   To remove an index using Transact-SQL, use the DROP INDEX statement. The syntax for DROP INDEX is as follows:

```
DROP INDEX [owner.]table_name.index_name
[, [owner.]table_name.index_name...]
```

The options for the Transact-SQL command DROP INDEX are as follows:

■ *table_name*—The name of the table that the index resides on. If the user running DROP INDEX is the DBO or SA and the table isn't owned by that user, *table_name* can be prefixed by the *owner* of the table.

■ *index_name*—The name of the index to be removed. You can remove multiple indexes by indicating them in the same statement, separated by commas.

The following example drops the barny index on the authors table:

```
Drop Index authors.barny
```

No output is generated after executing this command.

Defining Keys

Keys and indexes are often synonymous in databases; however, in SQL Server a slight difference exists between them. In SQL Server, keys can be defined on tables and then can be used as referential integrity constraints in the same fashion as the ANSI standard for SQL.

A *primary key* is a unique column or set of columns that defines the rows in the database table. In this sense, a primary key performs the same integrity role as a unique index on a table, except that notionally SQL Server allows only one primary key to be defined for a table; on the other hand, there can be many unique indexes. Primary keys enforce uniqueness by creating a unique index on the table on which they're placed.

Foreign keys are columns in a table that correspond to primary keys in other tables. The relationship of a primary key to a foreign key defines the domain of values permissible in the foreign key. The domain of values is equivalent to a distinct list of values in the corresponding primary key. This foreign key domain integrity is a useful way of enforcing referential integrity between associated sets of columns. Foreign keys don't create indexes on the table when the key is created.

Starting in version 6.0, primary and foreign keys in SQL Server offer much of the functionality that previously had to be coded with triggers in prior versions of SQL Server. In prior versions of SQL Server, primary and foreign keys weren't much more than documentation and were useful to third-party programs that needed to know key information about a table. Keys provide needed functionality and should be used as a referential integrity enforcer.

Adding Primary and Foreign Keys

In SQL Server you can add primary and foreign keys in two ways. The graphical method is performed by using SQL Enterprise Manager. The command-line method is done by using Transact-SQL commands ALTER TABLE...ADD CONSTRAINT, or by specifying PRIMARY/FOREIGN KEY in the CREATE TABLE statement.

Using SQL Enterprise Manager to Add Primary and Foreign Keys   To use SQL Enterprise Manager to add a primary key, follow these steps:

1. Launch SQL Enterprise Manager from the Microsoft SQL Server 6.5 group.
2. Select the server, database, and table that you want to work on.
3. From the Manage menu choose Tables. The Manage Tables screen appears (see fig. 10.10).

FIG. 10.10
The authors table is selected in the top combo box, and a key icon is in the Key column of the au_id row.

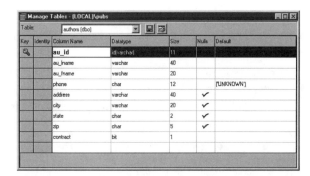

4. Click the Advanced Features toolbar button (with a green plus sign on it) to show the advanced options at the bottom of the window (see fig. 10.11).

FIG. 10.11
This figure shows SQL Enterprise Manager's Manage Tables window with the Advanced Features visible and the Primary Key/Identity page active.

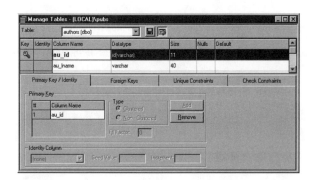

Part
III

Ch
10

5. Remove the existing primary key by clicking the <u>R</u>emove button and then re-enter the information (see fig. 10.12).

FIG. 10.12
The Primary Key has been reentered and the <u>A</u>dd button is now enabled to allow you to create the Primary Key on the table.

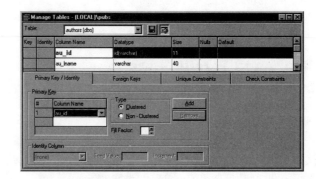

6. Click the <u>A</u>dd button to add the primary key. No message will be shown, but the key icon will return to the table.

7. Click the Save button to save the changes to the table. For the purposes of this exercise, you'll get an error because a foreign key was defined referencing this table. Ignore the error and close the window without saving changes.

Using _CREATE TABLE...PRIMARY KEY_   The CREATE TABLE syntax has a place for adding a PRIMARY KEY or a FOREIGN KEY in the CONSTRAINT section. A simplified syntax of the CREATE TABLE is shown as follows:

```
CREATE TABLE table_name
( column_name data_type CONSTRAINT ...,...)
```

In Listing 10.3, you'll see tables created in different styles with different types of CONSTRAINTs.

On the CD

Listing 10.3   10_03.SQL—Creating Tables with Different _CONSTRAINTs_

```
/* create a table where the primary key name is not
    specified, and the database will assign it */

Create TABLE TABLE_A
( COLUMN_A smallint PRIMARY KEY)
go

/* Now create a primary key specifying the name */
Create TABLE TABLE_B
( COLUMN_B smallint CONSTRAINT PK_COLUMN_B PRIMARY KEY)
go

/* Now create a foreign key referencing TABLE_A */
Create TABLE TABLE_C
( COLUMN_C smallint FOREIGN KEY (COLUMN_C) REFERENCES TABLE_A(COLUMN_A))
go

/* Now Create a multi-column primary key */
```

```
Create TABLE TABLE_D
( COLUMN_D1 smallint CONSTRAINT PK_D_COLUMNS PRIMARY KEY
(COLUMN_D1, COLUMN_D2), COLUMN_D2 smallint)

go

/* now create a foreign key referencing the multi-column
   primary key */
Create TABLE TABLE_E
( COLUMN_E1 smallint FOREIGN KEY (COLUMN_E1, COLUMN_E2)
                REFERENCES TABLE_D( COLUMN_D1, COLUMN_D2),
  COLUMN_E2 smallint)
go
```

N O T E   When you add a PRIMARY KEY to a table with the ALTER TABLE...ADD CONSTRAINT
syntax or in the CREATE TABLE statement, if you don't indicate any parameters for the key,
a clustered, unique index is created on the table. To specify a non-clustered index, add
NONCLUSTERED immediately after PRIMARY KEY to the statement. ■

Using *ALTER TABLE...ADD CONSTRAINT*   The ALTER TABLE...ADD CONSTRAINT syntax is very
similar to the CREATE TABLE logic. In Listing 10.4, the same tables are created, but the ALTER
TABLE syntax is used to add the keys.

On the CD

Listing 10.4   10_04.SQL—Altering Tables to Add Primary and Foreign Keys

```
/* create the table */
Create TABLE TABLE_A
( COLUMN_A smallint)
go

/* add the basic primary key without specifying the name */
Alter Table TABLE_A ADD PRIMARY KEY (COLUMN_A)
go

/* create the table */
Create TABLE TABLE_B
( COLUMN_B smallint)
go

/* add the primary key specifying the name */
Alter Table TABLE_B ADD CONSTRAINT PK_COLUMN_B PRIMARY KEY (COLUMN_B)
go

/* create the table */
Create TABLE TABLE_C
( COLUMN_C smallint)
go

/* Now create a foreign key referencing TABLE_A */
Alter Table TABLE_C ADD FOREIGN KEY (COLUMN_C) REFERENCES TABLE_A(COLUMN_A)
go
```

Part
III

Ch
10

continues

Listing 10.4 Continued

```
/* create the table */
Create TABLE TABLE_D
( COLUMN_D1 smallint,
  COLUMN_D2 smallint)
go

/* Now add the multi-column primary key */
Alter Table TABLE_D ADD CONSTRAINT PK_D_COLUMNS PRIMARY KEY
(COLUMN_D1, COLUMN_D2)
go

/* create the table */
Create TABLE TABLE_E
( COLUMN_E1 smallint,
 COLUMN_E2 smallint)
go

/* now add the foreign key referencing the multi-column
   primary key */
Alter Table TABLE_E ADD CONSTRAINT FK_E_COLUMNS FOREIGN KEY
(COLUMN_E1, COLUMN_E2)
REFERENCES TABLE_D( COLUMN_D1, COLUMN_D2)
go
```

N O T E SQL Server 6.5 adds two new options to the ALTER TABLE...ADD CONSTRAINT syntax: WITH CHECK ¦ NOCHECK, and NOT FOR REPLICATION. The WITH NOCHECK option is provided so that a constraint can be added without checking the existing data for referential integrity constraints. Microsoft added the NOT FOR REPLICATION option to allow replication to occur without requiring constraints to be dropped and re-added after the replication took place. ■

▶ **See** the section entitled "Creating and Using Constraints," in Chapter 5. **p. 130**

Displaying Key Information

SQL Server has two ways to show information about keys. The graphical method is via SQL Enterprise Manager's Table Manager. The command-line method is via the system-stored procedures sp_help and sp_helpconstraints, and the ODBC stored procedures sp_pkeys and sp_fkeys.

SQL Enterprise Manager's Table Manager has been discussed in detail in previous sections in this chapter. Please refer to the section entitled "Using SQL Enterprise Manager to Add Primary And Foreign Keys" for information on how to view the constraints on a table.

sp_helpconstraint SQL Server's primary way of displaying information about keys is through the system-stored procedure sp_helpconstraint. Its syntax is as follows:

```
sp_helpconstraint table_name
```

sp_help `sp_help` is a generic system-stored procedure that returns information about database tables. Part of the output from `sp_help` is information on keys on a table. The syntax for `sp_help` is

```
sp_help table_name
```

sp_pkeys and sp_fkeys SQL Server provides two system-stored procedures, `sp_pkeys` and `sp_fkeys`, that can be used to view key information stored in the database. `sp_pkeys` and `sp_fkeys` are procedures that have been created to help ODBC implementers access SQL Server's system catalog tables easily.

The syntax for the two procedures is identical and is as follows:

```
sp_pkeys ¦ sp_fkeys table_name
```

table_name is the table for which the keys need to be found.

Examples of Using System-Stored Procedures to View Primary and Foreign Keys Here are some examples of the output from `sp_pkeys`, `sp_fkeys`, and `sp_help`:

```
/*---------------------------
sp_helpconstraint TABLE_D
-----------------------*/
Object Name
-----------------------
TABLE_D

constraint_type            constraint_name      constraint_keys
---------------------      ---------------      -------------------
PRIMARY KEY (clustered)  PK_D_COLUMNS         COLUMN_D1, COLUMN_D2

Table is referenced by
---------------------------------------------------------------------
pubs.dbo.TABLE_E: FK_COLUMNS
/*---------------------------
sp_help table_d
---------------------------*/
Name         Owner         Type         When_created
------------------------------------------------------
TABLE_D      dbo           user table Dec 11 1995  7:42PM

Data_located_on_segment
-----------------------------
default

Column_name  Type                           Length Prec  Scale Nullable
------------------------------------------------------------------------
COLUMN_D1    smallint                       2      5     0     no
COLUMN_D2    smallint                       2      5     0     no

Identity     Seed     Increment
-----------------------------
No identity column defined.   (null)  (null)

index_name   index_description      index_keys
```

Part
III

Ch
10

```
-----------------------------------------------
PK_D_COLUMNS clustered, unique, primary key located on default
      COLUMN_D1, COLUMN_D2

constraint_type      constraint_name      constraint_keys
-------------------------------------------------------
PRIMARY KEY (clustered)   PK_D_COLUMNS   COLUMN_D1, COLUMN_D2

Table is referenced by
----------------------
pubs.dbo.TABLE_E: FK_COLUMNS
/*--------------------------
sp_pkeys table_d
--------------------------*/
table_qualifier   table_owner   table_name   column_name   key_seq
pk_name
---------------------------------------------------------------------
pubs              dbo           TABLE_D      COLUMN_D1     1
PK_D_COLUMNS
pubs              dbo           TABLE_D      COLUMN_D2     2
PK_D_COLUMNS

(2 row(s) affected)
/*--------------------------
sp_fkeys table_d
--------------------------*/
pktable_qualifier      pktable_owner      pktable_name       pkcolumn_name
fktable_qualifier      fktable_owner      fktable_name       fkcolumn_name

key_seq update_rule delete_rule fk_name              pk_name
---------------------------- ------------------------- --------------
pubs                    dbo                TABLE_D            COLUMN_D1
pubs                    dbo                TABLE_E            COLUMN_E1
1       1           1           FK_COLUMNS           PK_D_COLUMNS
pubs                    dbo                TABLE_D            COLUMN_D2
pubs                    dbo                TABLE_E            COLUMN_E2
2       1           1           FK_COLUMNS           PK_D_COLUMNS
```

Dropping Keys

SQL Server has two methods for dropping primary and foreign keys. The graphical method is performed by using SQL Enterprise Manager. The command-line method is done by using the Transact-SQL command ALTER TABLE...DROP CONSTRAINT.

Using SQL Enterprise Manager   To use SQL Enterprise Manager to drop a key, follow these steps:

1. Launch SQL Enterprise Manager from the Microsoft SQL Server 6.5 group.

2. Select the server, database, and table that you want to work on.

3. From the Manage menu choose Tables. The Manage Tables dialog box appears.

4. Click the Advanced Features toolbar button (with a green plus sign on it) to show the advanced options at the bottom of the window. Refer to Figure 10.11 for a picture of the Manage Tables dialog box.

5. Remove the existing primary key by clicking the Remove button; or click the Foreign Keys tab and remove the required foreign key.

6. Click the Save button (looks like a diskette) to save the changes to the table. If you get any referential constraint errors, you'll need to go to those tables and remove the primary/foreign keys that are causing the problem.

Using *ALTER TABLE...DROP CONSTRAINT*   To drop a foreign key using SQL, use the ALTER TABLE...DROP CONSTRAINT statement. The syntax for this SQL statement is as follows:

```
ALTER TABLE table_name DROP CONSTRAINT constraint_name
```

The *table_name* is the name of the table that the constraint applies to. The *constraint_name* is the name of the constraint.

N O T E   You can't drop a primary key if other tables reference it as a foreign key. You must drop those foreign keys first. ▨

Part
III

Ch
10

From Here...

In this chapter you learned how to create, view, and manage indexes on your data tables. This information is very important to help you create an optimized database that won't be bogged down by user queries that force table scans.

From here you should look at the following chapters for more information:

■ Chapter 6, "Retrieving Data with Transact-SQL," shows how you can examine your queries to make sure that they're hitting the indexes defined on the tables.

■ Chapter 16, "Understanding Server, Database, and Query Options," explains how to make changes to your global server, database, and query configurations to further optimize your queries.

Defining and Using Advanced Data Definition and Retrieval Structures

Mananging and Using Rules and Defaults

Rules constrain the values that can be stored within table columns and within user-defined datatypes. *Rules* use expressions that are applied to columns or user-defined datatypes to restrict the allowable values that can be entered. A *default* supplies a value for an inserted row when a user doesn't supply one. ■

How to use rules and defaults

Rules are used to enforce value restrictions on columns. Defaults encourage column values or provide a value when a column is inserted into a view that does not include that column.

What associates rules and defaults with columns

Rules and defaults can be defined and stored in the database but are still not enforced on any columns. They must be bound to a column to enforce the rule or default.

How to display information about rules and defaults

Rules and defaults can be bound to multiple columns. It might be necessary to periodically review the use of rules and defaults.

N O T E You can also restrict the values that are entered in columns of a table using constraints. Constraints are defined on a table column when the column is defined in a CREATE TABLE statement. The type of constraint that is comparable to a rule is a CHECK constraint.

Microsoft considers constraints preferable to rules as a mechanism for restricting the allowable values that can be entered into a table column because you can define multiple constrains on a column while you can only define a single rule for a column.

However, a rule is stored as a separate database object and can be applied to both columns of a table as well as user-defined datatypes. When a table is dropped, its CHECK constraints are no longer available. A rule, as a separate object, is still available even though the column of a table that it's defined on is dropped.

You should consider the advantages of using both constraints and rules. You might even use both constraints and rules. For example, a table column can have both a rule (only one, remember) and several CHECK constraints defined on it. A table column is restricted by the combination of a rule and one or more CHECK constraints that apply to the column. ▪

▶ **See** the Chapter 5 section entitled "Creating and Using Constraints." **p. 130**

Defining Rules

A rule provides a defined restriction on the values for a table column or a user-defined datatype. Any data that you attempt to enter into either a column or a user-defined datatype must meet the criteria defined for the user-defined datatype or column. You should use rules to implement business-related restrictions or limits.

For example, you can use a rule that is defined on a column to limit the values added into a column that records the departments of the company to only the allowable departments. If there are only four departments of which an employee can be a member, you can define a rule to limit the values entered into the Department column to only the four department names. Use a rule to specify the range of allowable values for a column of user-defined datatype.

N O T E You should recall that SQL Server provides an automatic validation for datatypes. You'll receive an error if you enter a value that is outside the range of allowable values for the datatype and if you enter a value that is incompatible with the datatype. For example, you can't enter alphabetic or special characters—such as an asterisk (*) and question mark (?)—in an int integer datatype.

You should keep this in mind when you define a column or user-defined datatype. If you choose a correct datatype for a column or user-defined datatype, it may make the definition of the rule simpler or even unnecessary. ▪

Remember, you can use a user-defined datatype to define a new datatype based on one of the system datatypes (such as char and int) or specialized datatypes. You'll find that user-defined datatypes for table columns must be identically defined across tables. In addition, you can't define a rule for a system datatype—only for a user-defined datatype.

For example, instead of redefining a column, such as Badge Number that is defined in multiple tables to be used for relational joins, you can define a user-defined datatype and use it as the datatype of badge in each table that it's defined. If the range of values can be identical for the Badge Number columns, you can define a rule for a user-defined datatype called badge and use it as the datatype for all Badge columns across tables.

Creating Rules

You create a rule with a CREATE RULE statement. The syntax of the CREATE RULE statement is as follows:

```
CREATE RULE rule_name
AS condition_expression
```

Create a rule in the current database, and it applies to only columns or user-defined datatypes within the database in which it is defined. You can use any expression in a rule that is valid in a WHERE clause, and your rule can include comparison or arithmetic operators. The conditional expression you use in a rule must be prefixed by the symbol @ (at). Use @ to specify a parameter that refers to the value later entered into a table column with either an UPDATE or INSERT statement.

In the following example, CREATE RULE is used to create a list of values using an IN keyword to form a condition expression. Although the parameter used in the condition expression is descriptively identical to the column name in the table to which it's later bound, the parameter can be defined using any set of alphanumeric characters.

```
create rule department_values
as @department in ('Sales','Field Service','Logistics','Software')
```

Part

IV

Ch

11

> **N O T E** If you add a rule (and other database objects) to the database model, the rule will be automatically available in any database that is created subsequently. When you create a new database, it's created using the model database as an template. Any objects that are in the model database are automatically duplicated in new database.
>
> If you create a set of rules that can and should be used throughout all your databases, create the rules first in the model database using the database administrator's account (sa) for access before you create your databases. ▪

The rule must restrict values to those that are compatible with the column datatype. You can't use constants within a condition expression that aren't compatible with the column or user-defined datatype to which the rule is subsequently applied. You can define the name of the rule so that it includes the name of the column or user-defined datatype to which it will be bound to make it descriptive.

You can also create a rule through the SQL Enterprise Manager by performing the following steps:

1. After your start the SQL Enterprise Manager, select the server and the database in which the rule is to be defined.

2. Expand the Objects folder and select Rules.

3. Click the right mouse button and select New Rule to bring up the Manage Rules dialog box. Alternatively, you can choose Rules from the Manage menu to bring up the Manage Rules dialog box.

4. Enter the description of the rule in the Description field and a name for the rule in the Rule field.

5. Click Add to create the new rule.

6. Click Close to close the Manage Rules dialog box.

Figure 11.1 shows the Manage Rules dialog box for the creation of the rule, department_values, through the SQL Enterprise Manager.

FIG. 11.1

The Rules page of this dialog box creates the rule but does not bind it to a column or user-defined datatype.

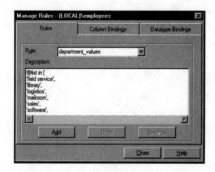

Binding Rules

The definition of a rule doesn't include the specification that applies the rule to either a table column or user-defined datatype. If you only define a rule, it's never in effect. Once you define a rule, you must bind it to a column or user-defined datatypes. A rule bound to a column or user-defined datatype specifies that the rule is in effect for the column or user-defined datatype. All values that you enter into a column or user-defined datatype must satisfy the criteria defined by the rule.

You can use sp_bindrule to bind a rule to a column or user-defined datatype, which uses the following syntax:

```
sp_bindrule rulename, table_name.column_name, [futureonly]
```

After you bind a rule to a column or user-defined datatype, information about the rule is entered into system tables. A unique rule ID number is stored in the syscolumns and systypes system tables. A rule has a row in syscolumns if it is bound to a column and in systypes if it is bound to a user defined datatype.

The first parameter of sp_bindrule specifies the name of the rule. You can use as many as 30 characters for the name of the rule, so you may be able to include the name of the table column or user-defined datatype within the name of the rule.

Enter the name of either the table column or the user-defined datatype to which the rule will be applied. You must enter the name of the table column preceded by the name of the table in which it's defined, enclosed in single quotation marks. If you enter only the name of an object, it's interpreted by SQL Server as the name of a user-defined datatype. When you enter a column name, use a period (.) to separate the table name from the column name to which the rule is to be bound. A rule that is bound to a datatype restricts the values that can be added to the table column that is defined using the user-defined datatype.

The third parameter, futureonly, is used only for the definition of user-defined datatypes. Futureonly prevents the rule from being applied to table columns that are already defined using the user-defined datatype. Use futureonly to specify that the rule only applies to columns that are subsequently created using the user-defined datatype to which the rule is bound.

You can also bind a rule to a table column or user-defined datatype using the SQL Enterprise Manager by performing the following steps:

1. After you start the SQL Enterprise Manager, select the server and the database in which the rule is defined.
2. Expand the Objects folder and select Rules.
3. Select the rule to be bound. Click the right mouse button and select Edit. Alternatively, you can choose Rules from the Manage menu to bring up the Manage Rules dialog box.
4. Click the Column Bindings or Datatype Bindings tab.
5. For a column binding, select the name of the table in the Table field, the column in the Column field, and the rule in the Bindings field. For a datatype binding, select the user-defined datatype in the User-Defined Datatype field and the rule in the Binding column.
6. Click Bind.
7. Click Close to close the Manage Rules dialog box.

Part
IV

Ch
11

Figure 11.2 shows the Manage Rules dialog box for the binding of the department_values rule to the Department column in the Employee table.

FIG. 11.2
You can bind a rule to the columns of multiple tables.

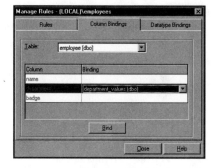

TIP You can double-click the left mouse button on a selected rule to bring up the Manage Rules dialog box.

Figure 11.3 shows the Manage Rules dialog box for the binding of rules to a user-defined datatype.

FIG. 11.3
You can bind a rule to a user-defined datatype when you create the datatype through the SQL Enterprise Manager.

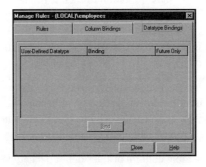

You may have already realized that conflicts can occur with rules and some precedence conventions that are used to resolve the conflicts. You might encounter a situation in which you have a table column that is defined using a user-defined datatype, and both the datatype and column have rules that are bound to them. The following list includes three precedence rules that apply to rule binding:

- Rules that you've bound to columns take precedence over rules bound to datatypes. If rules are bound to both a table column and the user-defined datatype with which the column is defined, the rule that is bound to the table columns is used. If you bind a new rule to a table column, it also overrides a rule bound to the user-defined datatype to which the column is defined.

- If you bind a new rule to a column or datatype, the new rule replaces the old one. You can have only a single rule bound to a column or user-defined datatype.

- If you bind a rule to a user-defined datatype, it doesn't replace a rule bound to a column of that datatype (which isn't surprising). Table 11.1 summarizes rule precedence.

Table 11.1   Rule Precedence

New Rule Bound to...	Old Rule Bound to User Datatype	Old Rule Bound to Column
User datatype	Replaces old rule	No change
Column	Replaces old rule	Replaces old rule

Rules don't apply to the data that has already been entered in the table. Values that are currently in tables don't have to meet the criteria specified by rules. If you want a rule to constrain the values entered in the table, define a rule directly or indirectly (through a user-defined datatype) before you allow data to be entered into a table.

In the following example, the procedure sp_bindrule is used to bind the rule department_values to the Department column in the Employees table. A subsequent INSERT statement fails its attempt to enter a value in the table column that doesn't meet the criteria defined by the rule. SQL Server returns a descriptive error message that specifies the attempted INSERT violates the rule bound on the table column.

```
sp_bindrule department_values, 'employees.department'
go
Rule bound to table column.
insert into employees
values ('Dan Duryea','Shipping',3321)
go
Msg 513, Level 16, State 1
A column insert or update conflicts with a rule imposed by a previous
CREATE RULE command. The command was aborted. The conflict occurred in
database 'master', table 'employees', column 'department'
Command has been aborted.
```

The following example defines a new user-defined datatype and rule that is later bound to the datatype:

```
sp_addtype badge_type2, int, 'not null'
go
Type added.
create rule badgerule2
as @badge_type2 >000 and @badge_type2 <9999
go
This command did not return data, and it did not return any rows
sp_bindrule badgerule2, badge_type2
Rule bound to datatype.
```

TIP You can restrict the range of allowable values by using the appropriate system datatype, for example, smallint instead of integer.

N O T E Microsoft says that there are three types of rules that you can define: rules with a range, a list, or a pattern. The two previous examples use a range (...@badge_type2 >000 and @badge_type2 <9999) and a list (...@department in ('Sales','Field Service','Logistics')) to restrict values for the rule. The following example shows the third type of rule: a rule that uses a pattern to restrict values. The example restricts values to any number of characters that end with S through U.

```
Create rule pattern_rule
@p like '%[SU]'
```

You may find it easier to define and use rules if you understand the types of rules that you can create. ▆

Displaying Rule Bindings

You can use the system procedure sp_help to display information about the user-defined datatypes or table columns that have rules bound to them. In the following example, information displayed about the user-defined datatype created in an earlier example includes the rule that is bound to the datatype:

```
sp_help badge_type2
Type_name  Storage_type  Length Nulls Default_name Rule_name
-------------  -------------- ------ ---- -------------
badge_type2 int         4     0     (null)      badgerule2
```

You can also display rule binding information by clicking <u>B</u>indings in the Manage Rules dialog box. In Figure 11.4, the Manage Rule Info dialog box shows a rule bound to a table column.

FIG. 11.4

You can also unbind a rule from the Manage Rule Info dialog box.

Displaying Rules

Sp_help displays information about a database object (such as a user-defined datatype or column), including the name of a rule that is bound to the datatype or column. Sp_help doesn't show the rule itself when information about the object to which it's bound is shown.

You can use sp_help to display information about a rule. However, it doesn't return much information about a rule. In the following example, sp_help returns information about the rule, badgerule2, and shows only its owner, the type of object, a defined segment on which it's located, and the date and time it was created:

```
sp_help badgerule2
Name                    Owner                 Type
----------------------------- --------------
badgerule2         dbo                    rule
Data_located_on_segment     When_created
--------------------- --------------------
not applicable           Oct 24 1994 10:40AM
```

You're probably more interested in displaying the rule itself rather than the characteristics of the rule as an object. To display the definition of a rule itself, use sp_helptext. The definition of a rule is saved as the row of a system table, so the definition of a rule is returned as the row of a table. The following example shows the rule that is used to constrain the range of allowable badge numbers defined in previous examples:

```
sp_helptext badgerule2
text
- - - - - - - - - - - - - - - - - - - - - - - - - -
create rule badgerule2
as @badge_type2 >000 and @badge_type2 <9999
(1 row(s) affected)
```

You can also use the SQL Enterprise Manager to display rules. A rule definition is shown in the Description field of the Manage Rules dialog box. Double-click a selected rule or right click and select Edit to bring up the description of a rule in the Manage Rules dialog box. Figure 11.1 presented the Manage Rules dialog box with the description of the rule within the description field.

TROUBLESHOOTING

I created a rule and bound it to a table column. When I tried to bind the rule to a column in a table in another database, I couldn't reference the rule. Rules are defined within a set of system tables that is local to each database. The rules defined within one database aren't available within another database. You can select the rule definition within an ISQL/w session, store it as a file, and then open the file to recover the rule. You can define the rule once you use a USE command to position yourself to the database in which the rule will be used.

Part
IV

Ch
11

Unbinding Rules

At some point, you may no longer want the values that are entered into a column or user-defined datatype to be constrained by a rule. You can unbind a rule using sp_unbindrule, which removes the constraint from a bound column or user-defined datatype. Unbinding a rule makes it non-applicable to a column or user-defined datatype. The sp_unbindrule syntax is as follows:

sp_unbindrule *table_name.column* or *user_datatype* [, futureonly]

Like sp_bindrule, if the first parameter of sp_unbindrule is a column, it must be preceded by the name of the table in which it's defined and entered in single quotation marks. Otherwise, the first parameter is interpreted as the name of a user-defined datatype.

Use futureonly—the optional third parameter—only with rules that are bound to user-defined datatypes. Table columns that are already defined using the user-defined datatype have the rule applied to the columns unless the futureonly optional parameter is present. The futureonly option prevents existing columns from inheriting the rule; only new columns that are defined using the user-defined datatype are affected by the rule.

You can also use the SQL Enterprise Manager to unbind a rule from a table column or user-defined datatype by clicking Unbind after selecting the rule in the Manage Rules Info dialog box (see fig. 11.5).

FIG. 11.5

The name of the rule is removed from the Bound Columns field of the Manage Rules Info dialog box.

In the following example, sp_help displays the Employees table, which has a rule that is defined on the Department column. Sp_unbindrule unbinds the rule from the Department column of the Employees table. A subsequent display of the Employees table shows that the rule has been unbound from the Table column.

```
sp_help employees
go
Name            Owner                    Type
------------------------------ ------------
employees       dbo                      user table
Data_located_on_segment        When_created
------------------------------ ------------
default                    May 12 1994 10:15AM
Column_name Type Length Nulls Default_name  Rule_name
------------- --------------- ------ ---- ------
name       char   20     0     (null)        (null)
department char   20     0     (null) department_values
badge      int    4      0     (null)        (null)
Object does not have any indexes.
No defined keys for this object.
sp_unbindrule 'employees.department'
go
Rule unbound from table column.
sp_help employees
go
Name            Owner                    Type
------------------------------ ------------
employees          dbo                   user table
Data_located_on_segment        When_created
------------------------------ ------------
default                    May 12 1994 10:15AM
Column_name  Type Length Nulls Default_name Rule_name
------------- --------------- ------ ---- --------
name         char   20     0     (null)      (null)
department   char   20     0     (null)      (null)
badge        int    4      0     (null)      (null)
Object does not have any indexes.
No defined keys for this object.
```

You can also unbind a rule by replacing the current rule with a new one. Sp_bindrule binds a new rule to that column or datatype. The old rule is automatically unbound from the user-defined datatype or table column.

In the following example, the attempted redefinition of the existing department_values rule is unsuccessful because a rule can't be replaced by one with the same name. A new rule is created and it's bound to the same column to which the department_values rule is bound; the new rule replaces the old department_values rule.

```
create rule department_values
as @department in ('Sales','Field Service','Logistics','Shipping')
go
Msg 2714, Level 16, State 1
There is already an object named 'department_values' in the database.
create rule depart2
as @department in ('Sales','Field Service','Logistics','Shipping')
go
This command did not return data, and it did not return any rows
sp_bindrule depart2, 'employees.department'
go
Rule bound to table column.
```

In the following example (a continuation of the previous example), an INSERT into the Employees table demonstrates that the new rule has been bound to the Department column. The old rule for Department would have disallowed the addition of a row that contains the Shipping department. A SELECT statement shows that the new row was added to the table. Finally, sp_help shows that the new depart2 rule is bound to the Department column of the Employees table and replaces the old department_values rule.

```
insert into employees
values ('Dan Duryea','Shipping',3321)
go
(1 row(s) affected)
select * from employees
go
name                department              badge
------------------  --------------------    ----------
Bob Smith           Sales                   1234
Mary Jones          Sales                   5514
Dan Duryea          Shipping                3321
(3 row(s) affected)
sp_help employees
go
Name                             Owner                              Type
----------------------------     -----------------------------      ------------
employees                        dbo                                user table
Data_located_on_segment          When_created
----------------------------     -----------------------------      ------------
default                          May 12 1994 10:15AM
Column_name     Type             Length Nulls Default_name      Rule_name
------------    -------------    ------ ----- --------------    --------------
name            char             20     0     (null)            (null)
department      char             20     0     (null)            depart2
```

```
badge             int          4     0      (null)            (null)
Object does not have any indexes.
No defined keys for this object.
```

Renaming Rules

You can rename rules, like other objects, using `sp_rename`. You can also use `sp_rename` to rename other user objects (such as tables, views, columns, stored procedures, triggers, and defaults). The `sp_rename` syntax is as follows:

`sp_rename` *object_name, new_name*

In the following example, an existing rule is renamed. Once the rule is renamed, a display of the Employees table shows that the new name of the rule is in effect for the Department column.

```
sp_rename depart2, depart3
go
Object name has been changed.
sp_help employees
go
Name                                Owner                        Type
------------------------------      ---------------------------  ----------------
employees                           dbo                          user table
Data_located_on_segment             When_created
------------------------------      ---------------------------
default                             May 12 1994 10:15AM
Column_name    Type                 Length Nulls Default_name    Rule_name
-------------  --------             ------ ----- -------------   -------------
name           char                 20     0     (null)          (null)
department     char                 20     0     (null)          depart3
badge          int                  4      0     (null)          (null)
Object does not have any indexes.
No defined keys for this object.
```

You can also rename a rule using the SQL Enterprise Manager with the Rename Object dialog box by clicking the right mouse button on a selected rule and selecting <u>R</u>ename. In the Rename Object dialog box, enter a new name in the <u>N</u>ew Name field. Click OK. Figure 11.6 shows the Rename Object dialog box.

FIG. 11.6

The new rule name immediately replaces the old name in the Server Manager dialog box of the SQL Enterprise Manager.

Dropping Rules

You can use the DROP RULE statement to permanently remove a rule from a database. The rule is immediately removed if it's not bound to any columns or user-defined datatypes. If the rule is bound to a column or a datatype, you must first unbind the rule from all columns and user datatypes to be able to drop the rule. You can drop multiple rules with a single DROP RULE statement. The DROP RULE syntax is as follows:

```
DROP RULE rule_name_1[,…rule_name_n]
```

In the following example, an initial attempt to remove a rule is unsuccessful because the rule is bound to a table column. Once the rule is unbound from the table column, it's successfully removed. Sp_helptext demonstrates that the object is gone.

```
drop rule depart3
go
Msg 3716, Level 16, State 1
The rule 'depart3' cannot be dropped because it is bound to one or more column.
sp_unbindrule 'employees.department'
go
Rule unbound from table column.
drop rule depart3
go
This command did not return data, and it did not return any rows
sp_helptext depart3
go
No such object in the current database.
```

You can also drop rules through the SQL Enterprise Manager. Select the name of the rule in the Rule field of the Manage Rules dialog box. Click Drop to remove the rule (refer to fig. 11.1). Click Close to close the Manage Rules dialog box.

TROUBLESHOOTING

I defined a rule and bound it to a user-defined datatype. I was surprised that a rule that I had previously bound to the same datatype isn't in effect any longer. You can only have a single rule bound to either a user-defined datatype or a table column. In addition, if you bind a rule to a user-defined datatype without using futureonly, it effectively replaces the rule for all table columns defined from the user-defined datatype.

Defining Defaults

You can use defaults to define a value that is automatically added to a column if no value is explicitly entered. You bind a default to a column or user-defined datatype using sp_binddefault. You must define a default value that is compatible with the column datatype. A default also can't violate a rule that is associated with a table column.

Default definitions are stored in the syscomments table like rule definitions. Also like rules, if you bind a new default to a column, it automatically overrides an old rule. A default bound to the column takes precedence over a default bound to the user-defined datatype.

Creating Defaults

You can define a default using the CREATE DEFAULT statement. The name used in the second parameter of the sp_bindefault is interpreted as a user-defined datatype unless it's preceded with the table name. It must be preceded by the name of a table to be interpreted as a column of a table. The CREATE DEFAULT syntax is as follows:

```
CREATE DEFAULT default_name AS constant value
```

> **CAUTION**
>
> If you define a default with a value that's longer than the table column to which it's subsequently bound, the default value entered into the column is truncated.

You can also create a default using the SQL Enterprise Manager by performing the following steps:

1. After your start the SQL Enterprise Manager, select the server and the database in which the default is to be created.

2. Expand the Objects folder and select Defaults.

3. Click the right mouse button and select New Default to bring up the Manage Defaults dialog box. Alternatively, you can choose Defaults from the Manage menu to bring up the Manage Defaults dialog box.

4. Enter a value for the default in the Description field and a name for the default in the Defaults field.

5. Click Add to create the new default.

6. Click Close to close the Manage Defaults dialog box.

Figure 11.7 shows the Manage Defaults dialog box for the creation of the default department through the SQL Enterprise Manager.

FIG. 11.7

You can also manage existing defaults using the Manage Defaults dialog box.

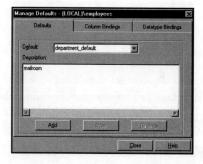

Binding Defaults

You can use the system procedure, `sp_bindefault`, to bind a default to a user-defined datatype or table column. The second parameter can be the name of a table column or a user-defined datatype. Use the third parameter to specify that the default value should only be applied to new columns of tables that are defined—not to existing columns of tables. The `sp_bindefault` syntax is as follows:

```
sp_bindefault default_name, table_name.column_name, [futureonly]
```

In the following example, a default is defined and bound to the Department column of the Employees table. A row is inserted into the table that omits a value for the Department column in the list of values. A subsequent SELECT statement demonstrates that the default value was added to the Department column for the newly inserted row.

```
create default Department_default as 'Sales'
go
sp_bindefault Department_default, 'employees.department'
go
Default bound to column.
insert into employees
(name, badge)
values ('John Garr',2221)
go
(1 row(s) affected)
select * from employees
where badge=2221
go
name                    department              badge
------------------      --------------------    ----------
John Garr               Sales                   2221
(1 row(s) affected)
```

In the following example, a default is defined and bound to a user-defined datatype. The second parameter of `sp_bindefault` is interpreted as a user-defined datatype because no table name precedes the object name. The third parameter isn't specified, so the default value is applied to any table columns that are defined using the user-defined datatype.

```
create default badge_default
as 9999
sp_bindefault badge_default, badge_type2
Default bound to datatype.
```

> **N O T E** When you define a table column that permits NULL values, a NULL is added to a row when the column isn't referenced when a row is inserted into the table. A NULL entry is automatically inserted, just as a default value is automatically inserted. The definition of a NULL remains the same; however, its meaning is still undefined, which is different from the automatic insertion of an actual value. ■

▶ **See** the Chapter 5 section entitled "Understanding *null* and *not null*." **p. 126**

Part
IV

Ch
11

You can also bind a default to a table column or user-defined datatype using the SQL Enterprise Manager by performing the following steps:

1. After your start the SQL Enterprise Manager, select the server and the database in which the default is defined.

2. Expand the Objects folder and select Defaults.

3. Select the default to be bound. Click the right mouse button and select Edit. Alternatively, you can choose Defaults from the Manage menu to bring up the Manage Rules dialog box.

4. Click the Column Bindings or Datatype Bindings tab.

5. For a column binding, select the name of the table in the Table field, the column in the Column field, and the default in the Bindings field. For a datatype binding, select the user-defined datatype in the User-Defined Datatype field and the default in the Binding column.

6. Click Bind.

7. Click Close to close the Manage Defaults dialog box.

Figure 11.8 shows the Manage Defaults dialog box for the binding of the department_default default to the Department column in the Employee table.

FIG. 11.8
You can bind a default to the columns of multiple tables.

Displaying Bindings

You can use sp_help to display the defaults bound to either table columns or user-defined datatypes. In the following example, sp_help displays the default that's bound to the Badge column:

```
sp_help employees
go
Name                              Owner                    Type
-------------------------------   ----------------------   ----------
employees                         dbo                      user table
Data_located_on_segment           When_created
-------------------------------   ----------------------
default                           Oct 18 1994 12:52PM
Column_name      Type             Length Nulls Default_name    Rule_name
--------------   --------------   ------ ----- --------------  --------
```

```
name            char          20      0    (null)         (null)
department      char          20      0    (null)         (null)
badge           int            4      0    badge_default  (null)
Object does not have any indexes.
No defined keys for this object.
```

You can also display default bindings using the SQL Enterprise Manager. One way in which you can display default bindings through the SQL Enterprise Manager is from the Manage Default dialog box. Click Bindings to display default bindings in the Manage Default Info dialog box (see fig. 11.9).

FIG. 11.9

You can bind a default to both a user-defined datatype and a table column.

T I P A default bound to a table column is also displayed in the Default file of the Manage Table dialog box in the SQL Enterprise Manager.

Displaying Defaults

You can use the procedure sp_helptext to display the value that's defined for the default. The definition of defaults are stored as rows in the syscomments system table. The display of a default definition is shown as the row of a table. In the following example, the default for a table column is shown using sp_helptext:

```
sp_helptext Department_default
go
text----------------------------------------
create default Department_default as 'Sales'
(1 row(s) affected)
```

You can also use the SQL Enterprise Manager to display a default. A default definition is shown in the Description field of the Manage Defaults dialog box. Double-click a selected rule or right-click and select Edit to bring up the description of a default in the Manage Defaults dialog box. Figure 11.7 presented the Manage Defaults dialog box with the default value.

Unbinding Defaults

When you no longer want the default value automatically entered into a column or user-defined datatype, you must unbind the default by using sp_unbindefault, which removes the default

Part

IV

Ch

11

from a bound column or user-defined datatype. Unbinding a default makes it non-applicable to a column or user-defined datatype. The sp_unbindefault syntax is as follows:

```
sp_unbindefault table_name.column_name [,futureonly]
```

Use the third parameter, which is optional, to specify that only new columns defined using the user-defined datatype aren't bound using the default. You only use the third parameter for user-defined datatypes; you don't use it for table columns. In the following example, a default is unbound from a table column. Sp_help is first used to verify that the default is bound to the table column. Thereafter, sp_help is used after the default is unbound to verify that the default was unbound from the table column.

```
sp_help employees
go
Name                             Owner                             Type
-----------------------------    -----------------------------     ---------------
employees                        dbo                               user table
Data_located_on_segment          When_created
-----------------------------    -----------------------------
default                          Oct 18 1994 12:52PM
Column_name     Type             Length Nulls Default_name      Rule_name
-------------   -------------    ------- ---- --------------    --------
name            char                20    0    (null)           (null)
department      char                20    0    (null)           (null)
badge           int                  4    0    badge_default    (null)
Object does not have any indexes.
No defined keys for this object.
sp_unbindefault 'employees.badge'
go
Default unbound from table column.
sp_help employees
go
Name                             Owner                             Type
-----------------------------    -----------------------------     ----------
employees                        dbo                               user table
Data_located_on_segment          When_created
-----------------------------    -----------------------------
default                          Oct 18 1994 12:52PM
Column_name     Type             Length Nulls Default_name      Rule_name
-------------   -------------    ------- ---- --------------    ----------
name            char                20    0    (null)           (null)
department      char                20    0    (null)           (null)
badge           int                  4    0    (null)           (null)
Object does not have any indexes.
No defined keys for this object.
```

You can also use the SQL Enterprise Manager to unbind a default from a table column or user-defined datatype by clicking Unbind after selecting the default in the Manage Defaults Info dialog box. Figure 11.10 shows the Manage Default Info box after the department_default default has been unbound from the user-defined datatype department.

FIG. 11.10
The name of the default is immediately removed from the Bound Columns or Bound Datatypes field of the Manage Default Info dialog box.

Renaming Defaults

You can use system procedure, sp_rename, to rename a default. In the following example, a default is renamed using sp_rename. After the default is renamed, the table in which the default is bound to a column is displayed using sp_help to confirm that the default was renamed.

```
sp_rename Department_default, dept_default
go
Object name has been changed.
sp_help employees
go
Name                              Owner                             Type
-------------------------------   -----------------------------     ----------
employees                         dbo                               user table
Data_located_on_segment           When_created
-------------------------------   -------------------------
default                           May 12 1994 10:15AM
Column_name     Type            Length Nulls Default_name      Rule_name
-------------   ------------    ------ ----- --------------    --------
name            char              20     0    (null)            (null)
department      char              20     0    dept_default      (null)
badge           int                4     0    (null)            (null)
Object does not have any indexes.
No defined keys for this object.
```

You can also rename a default using the SQL Enterprise Manager with the Rename Object dialog box by clicking the right mouse button on a selected default and selecting Rename. In the Rename Object dialog box, enter a new name in the New Name field (refer to fig. 11.6). Click OK.

N O T E All database objects can be renamed using the sp_rename system procedure of the Rename Object dialog box in the SQL Enterprise Manager. ■

Dropping Defaults

You can permanently remove a default with the DROP DEFAULT statement. The default is immediately removed if it's not bound to any columns or user-defined datatypes. If the default is bound to a column or a datatype, you must first unbind the default from all columns and user datatypes to be able to drop the default. You can drop multiple defaults with a single DROP DEFAULT statement. The DROP DEFAULT syntax is as follows:

```
DROP DEFAULT default_name_1 [,...default_name_n]
```

In the following example, an attempt to drop a default is unsuccessful because the default is bound to a table column. Once the column is unbound from a table column, the default is successfully dropped.

```
drop default dept_default
go
Msg 3716, Level 16, State 1
The default 'dept_default' cannot be dropped because it is bound to one or
more columns.
sp_unbindefault 'employees.department'
go
Default unbound from table column.
drop default dept_default
go
This command did not return data, and it did not return any rows
sp_helptext dept_default
No such object in the current database.
```

You can also drop defaults through the SQL Enterprise Manager. Select the name of the default in the Default field of the Manage Defaults dialog box. Click Drop to remove the default (refer to fig. 11.7). Click Close to close the Manage Defaults dialog box.

From Here...

Rules are very powerful tools used to enforce limitations on column and user-defined datatype values. Once a rule is created it must then be bound to columns and/or datatypes. Rules and datatypes can be bound to multiple table columns or user-defined datatypes. Defaults provide a way to provide an initial value to columns. Initial values can be used as suggestions or as a way to allow users with a limited view of a table to insert rows that will contain data in columns to which they do not have access.

For information about the type of restrictions that are provided by constraints, see the following chapter:

- Chapter 5, "Creating Database Tables and Using Datatypes," teaches you how to define data columns and user-defined datatypes. You'll also learn the allowable range of values for each system datatype.

Understanding Transactions and Locking

Learn what transactions are and how to use them

SQL Server deals in transactions. Unless specifically stated, transactions are not actually written to the database until SQL Server deems it necessary.

Learn the different types of isolation levels at your disposal

Depending on the isolation level being used, a SELECT statement may not return completely valid data.

Learn how to interpret and avoid locks

Locks can be placed on pages, tables, and now even rows. The type of lock used can avoid or cause deadlock between users.

A good understanding of transactions and locking is essential for anybody who is going to write database applications for more than one user. Even single-user applications require some understanding of locking, though the impact of locking yourself is not nearly as drastic as that of locking an enterprise network of hundreds of users.

SQL Server has a number of different styles of locking available to the programmer. This chapter will provide you with the information required to make an accurate assessment of what is needed for your application in terms of transaction control and locking.

You can never be too cautious in a multiuser application. As a programmer you should always concentrate on attempting to minimize the amount of locking that can occur so that there is less chance of users interfering with each other. ■

Defining Transactions

A *transaction* is a logical unit of work that you want the SQL Server to perform for you. That unit of work may include one or many SQL statements, provided the unit of work is delineated appropriately to the server.

Single-statement transactions can be executed in ISQL just by entering their text and typing **go**. Single-statement transactions are ideal where the results required are simple and self-contained. For example, the following statement will return a list of tables from the database currently being used. (The text for this statement can be found in 12_01.SQL on the CD-ROM.)

```
Select        *
From   SYSOBJECTS
Where TYPE = 'U'   /* user defined tables */
Order By NAME
```

But what do you do when you need to do more than one thing in a transaction and conditionally undo it if something goes wrong? That is where multi-statement transactions come into play. Multi-statement transactions enable you to put two or more SQL statements together and send them to the server for processing; then, on some basis that you decide, you may choose to undo the work submitted. An example of a multi-statement transactions is as follows. (The text for this statement can be found in 12_02.SQL on the CD-ROM.)

```
Create Table TABLE_A(
       X     smallint null,
       Y     smallint null)
Go
Create Table TABLE_B(
       Z     smallint null)
Go

Begin Tran
       Update       TABLE_A
       Set    X = X + 1
       Where        Y = 100

       Update TABLE_B
       Set    Z = Z + 1

       If @@rowcount = 0 or @@error !=0 /* no rows where hit by our update */
       Begin
              Rollback Tran
              Print 'Error Occurred, no rows were updated'
              Return
       End
Commit Tran
```

> **TIP** To make your scripts and stored procedures easier to read, format them with indented sections inside transaction blocks.

Optimistic vs. Pessimistic Locking

When you write multiuser database applications, you can take one of two approaches to transaction control: optimistic or pessimistic locking. *Optimistic locking* assumes that you are going to do nothing in your application code to explicitly enforce locks on records while you work on them. Instead, you will rely on the database to manage this on its own while you concentrate on application logic. Pessimistic locking assumes that the application code will attempt to enforce some type of locking mechanism.

To implement optimistic locking in your application without having it grind to a halt under excessive locks on the server, you must take care to observe some simple rules, as follows:

- Minimize the amount of time that a transaction is held open by limiting the amount of SQL that occurs inside a BEGIN TRAN...COMMIT TRAN section.
- Rely on application code to guarantee that updates are hitting the right record rather than holding locks while a user browses data.
- Ensure that all application codes update and select from tables in the same order. This will stop any deadlocks from occurring.

Most marketing literature has attempted to tell us, as application developers, that SQL Server is going to manage locking and that there is nothing to worry about. This is a *very* optimistic locking approach. Unfortunately, it is not very pragmatic because it assumes that there is nothing a programmer or user can do to explicitly cause locking. In fact, there are many situations that will cause a large amount of locking to occur on a server, potentially disabling it for the enterprise that it is supporting.

Background Information on Locking

We think it will be useful as background to first discuss some of the basics of locking as they pertain to (and are implemented by) SQL Server, so that some of the more detailed items discussed in the sections below are not without a base of understanding. Specifically, we want to focus on the following two key areas of locking:

- Page Sizes and Granularity of Data
- Types of Locks

Page Sizes and Granularity of Data   SQL Server's internal basic unit of work is a 2K data page. What this means is that any activity that is executed on the server must do work on at least 2K of data. To further explain, a table has a number of pages of data associated with it (depending on the number and size of rows that it contains); SQL Server can only reference data in that table a page at a time. So, if an update hits a single record in a table and a lock is held for some period of time, it is more than likely that more than one row is in fact being locked.

How does this affect a database application? One of the most important considerations when writing a multiuser application is that there must be a way for multiple users to work independently of one another. For example, two users must be able to update customer records at the same time while answering phone calls from customers. The greater the capability to manipulate data in the same table without affecting other users by locks, the greater the concurrency of an application and the greater the chance of being able to support a lot of users.

A highly accessed table (such as a table of unique values for the rest of the system) should be made as concurrent as possible by forcing as few as possible rows of data onto the same data page—thereby limiting the number of coincidental rows locked as the result of a user action. Additionally, users' transactions should be kept to a minimum duration when hitting these tables.

Two other types of locks can occur that lock data more greatly than a singe data page: table and extent. *Table* locks occur because a user issued a query to update a table without including a WHERE clause (thereby implicitly saying that "I want to update every row"), and when the number of data pages locked exceeds the Lock Escalation Threshold defined for the particular table or database. *Extent* locks occur when SQL Server needs to create a new database extent (eight pages of data) to respond to a user query. Unfortunately, there are no controls at our disposal to handle or deal with extent locks, so you simply should know that they occur and what they mean. For more information, see the section entitled "LE Thresholds" later in this chapter.

Types of Locks   SQL Server can place several types of locks on database pages and tables. The page locks that are possible are SHARED, EXCLUSIVE, and UPDATE. SHARED locks and EXCLUSIVE locks are reasonably self explanatory in that they either allow another process to acquire a lock on the same page or they don't.

Multiple processes may have SHARED locks on the same data page, and they are usually acquired when data is being read. Importantly though, no other process may take an EXCLUSIVE lock (to perform DML) until all SHARED locks have been released.

EXCLUSIVE locks of table pages are given to a process that is updating a record on a page, inserting a new record at the end of a page, or when a process deletes a record from a page. EXCLUSIVE locks disallow any other process from accessing the page.

The UPDATE lock type is a middling lock. It sits in between SHARED and EXCLUSIVE in that it will allow a process to acquire a SHARE on the page until an actual update has occurred on it. UPDATE locks are acquired when a CURSOR is being built in the server. UPDATE locks are automatically promoted to EXCLUSIVE when an update occurs on one of the pages associated with the cursor.

At the table level, SQL Server has SHARED and EXCLUSIVE locks that work in the same fashion as the page level. SQL Server also has INTENT locks. INTENT locks indicate that a table has a number of pages on it that SQL Server is *intending* to lock at the page level in response to a user process.

SQL Server 6.5 has added *insert row-level locking*. This new lock allows multiple users to insert records into the same page. It was added because of a large amount of contention with inserts at the end of tables.

▶ **See** Chapter 15, "Creating and Using Cursors," for additional information. **p. 389**

Defining Isolation Levels

There are a number of ways in SQL Server that you can cause locks to be held or released while querying the database. One of those ways is by setting a transaction's isolation level. As its name implies, an *isolation level* specifies to the database how "isolated" to keep the data that is currently being worked on by the other users and requesters of data on the server. SQL Server has three different types of isolation levels and they are documented in the following three sections.

N O T E Transaction isolation levels are set for the entire time that a session is connected to the database. If you change isolation levels for a specific part of your application, do not forget to change back to the default so that other parts of the application are not adversely affected.

To achieve the same effects as isolation levels for a single SELECT statement, refer to the section below, "Holding a Lock Explicitly," for more information. ▩

Read Committed Read Committed is the default method of operation for SQL Server. It does not allow you to have data returned from the database that is "dirty" or *uncommitted*. Read Committed acquires SHARE locks on all the pages it passes over inside a transaction. It is possible that, due to another user performing a delete or insert that is committed or rolled back during the life of your query, you may receive some data pages that are not re-readable or that may contain values that only temporarily exist in the database.

If it is important that the query's results be completely unaffected by other users during the life of a particular transaction, so make sure that you use the Repeatable Read isolation level.

To set your isolation level to Read Committed, perform the following SQL:

```
Set Transaction Isolation Level Read Committed
Go
```

Read Uncommitted Read Uncommitted is the same as the NOLOCK keyword on an individual SELECT statement. No SHARED locks are placed on any data that you pass over in the query; additionally, no locks held by other users are observed. For example, if another user has deleted a whole table that you are about to select from, but has yet to COMMIT a transaction, you will still be able to read the data from it and not receive any error conditions.

Part
IV

Ch
12

> **CAUTION**
>
> The Read Uncommitted transaction isolation level is not recommended for any applications that require data integrity because you cannot be guaranteed that the data you are working with is still as it was or, indeed, in the database at all. Use Read Uncommitted sparingly in your applications and possibly only for such procedures as reporting applications on tables that are statistically unaffected by the average transactions that post against your server.

To set your isolation level to Read Uncommitted, perform the following SQL transaction:

```
Set Transaction Isolation Level Read Uncommitted
Go
```

Repeatable Read (a.k.a. Serializable)   Repeatable Read is the most *exclusive* type of locking that you can force SQL Server to maintain. Repeatable Read guarantees that the data you are reading will be unaffected by other transactions issued from other users during the life of a given transaction that you are working on. Because of Repeatable Read's explicit locking of data from other users, Repeatable Read reduces the concurrency of the database. It reduces the number of different users that can access data at the same time without affecting each other. Take care that you do not use Repeatable Read unwisely in your application; there are not that many places where it is actually required.

To set your isolation level to Repeatable Read, perform the following SQL transaction:

```
Set Transaction Isolation Level Repeatable Read
Go
```

Creating and Working with Transactions

In the opening section of this chapter, you saw how to delineate a transaction using BEGIN, COMMIT, and ROLLBACK. SQL Server's keywords or Transact-SQL statements that are required for transaction control are described below for clear definition.

> **CAUTION**
>
> It is very important to remember that every BEGIN TRAN must be followed at some point in the code by a matching COMMIT TRAN or ROLLBACK TRAN. Transactions *must* begin and end in pairs, otherwise the server will continue holding locks until the client is disconnected.

BEGIN TRAN   When you issue a BEGIN TRAN to the database, SQL Server marks a point in the database's transaction logs identifying a point to be returned to in the event of a ROLLBACK TRAN. BEGIN TRAN explicitly tells SQL Server that all the work following, until a COMMIT or ROLL-BACK is encountered, should be treated as one logical unit—despite the fact that it may contain many operations.

It is possible to issue operations without a BEGIN TRAN statement, and they will affect a database. However, you will not be able to conditionally undo the work that you sent to the server if it is not preceded by a BEGIN TRAN so that SQL Server knows to what state the database must be returned.

N O T E SQL Server's transaction logs monitor those transactions that are contained inside of BEGIN and COMMIT statements. In the event of a media failure on a database before data is physically changed on the database, SQL Server will recover or ensure that those changes are applied by "rolling forward" those unapplied transactions to the database when the server is next brought back online. ■

COMMIT TRAN Issuing a COMMIT TRAN to the database signals SQL Server that you are happy with the work done so far and no longer want to group any additional work inside the transaction. COMMIT TRAN is not reversible.

ROLLBACK TRAN ROLLBACK TRAN is SQL Server's equivalent of the Edit, Undo menu option in your favorite word processor. Sending a ROLLBACK to the database server will cause it to undo all the work to the most recent BEGIN TRAN statement. Typically, a ROLLBACK TRAN would be issued during a long transaction if any particular part of it encountered a SQL error of some kind.

CAUTION

SQL Server will enable you to call *remote* stored procedures inside a transaction; however, because of the nature of the *Remote Procedure Call* (RPC) interface with the other server upon which the RPC executed, SQL Server will not be able to ROLLBACK any such calls. Take care when writing applications that require RPCs that there are additional RPCs to programmatically undo the work you did previously.

Part
IV

Ch
12

DDL and Database Statements

DDL (Data Definition Language) and database modification statements are now allowed inside a transaction. The following statements can appear in transactions:

ALTER TABLE	CREATE DEFAULT	CREATE INDEX
CREATE PROCEDURE	CREATE RULE	CREATE TABLE
CREATE TRIGGER	CREATE VIEW	DROP DEFAULT
DROP INDEX	DROP PROCEDURE	DROP RULE
DROP TABLE	DROP TRIGGER	DROP VIEW
GRANT & REVOKE	SELECT INTO	TRUNCATE TABLE

 T I P SQL Server does not allow a table column to be dropped, but there is a way to work around it. Create a new table with the required schema (minus the column) and use the SELECT INTO Transact-SQL command to copy the data.

Using Named Transactions and SavePoints

One thing that becomes obvious during the writing of large stored procedures and applications with large bodies of SQL code is that no matter how it is looked at, the code is pretty unreadable. It is text based and there is a great reliance on programmers all working with the same style of format and layout. When transactional programming is involved, it becomes even more important for people to use good indenting to clearly mark blocks of code.

N O T E A new type of transaction has been added that allows transactions to be distributed. Such transactions are controlled by *the Distributed Transaction Coordinator*. This type of transaction is very useful for transactions that occur at remote locations but affect centralized inventory levels. ■

However, even the most careful programmer will find that it becomes a bit of a nightmare to remember how many indents to ROLLBACK out of in the event of an error condition or some programmatic constraint. Named Transactions and SavePoints are used for just this purpose: they provide a way of rolling back work to a given *named* or *saved* portion of the code that has been executing (even if it is at a higher nesting level).

Named Transactions Named transactions provide a convenient way of attaching an identifier to a whole body of work. Use named transactions to make it easier to undo large portions of code. To create a named transaction, add the name of the transaction to the BEGIN TRAN statement, as follows. (The text for this statement can be found in 12_05.SQL on the CD-ROM.)

On the CD

```
/* Open outer transaction */
Begin Tran UPDATE_AUTHORS
        Update AUTHORS
        Set     CONTRACT = 1
        Where   AU_ID = '341-22-1782'

        /* Open inner transaction */
        Begin Tran UPDATE_TITLEAUTHOR
                Update TITLEAUTHOR
                Set     ROYALTYPER = ROYALTYPER + 25
                Where AU_ID = '341-22-1782'
                If @@error != 0
                Begin
                        Rollback Tran UPDATE_TITLEAUTHOR
                        Print 'Failed to update Royalties'
                        Return
                End
        Commit Tran UPDATE_TITLEAUTHOR
Commit Tran UPDATE_AUTHORS
```

NOTE If you omit the transaction's identifier or name when committing or rolling back a transaction, SQL Server will simply undo the work to the most recent BEGIN TRAN regardless of its name. Take care when using named transactions that all work is coded in a consistent manner—either using names or not. Otherwise, programmers may end up stepping on each others' transactions inadvertently. ■

Using SavePoints SavePoints are really just another way of doing a named transaction. They provide a method of marking a place in the code to which a ROLLBACK may be used to undo work. To create a SavePoint, issue the SQL command

```
SAVE TRANSACTION <TRAN_NAME>
```

Then just use the identifier, <TRAN_NAME>, when performing your ROLLBACK.

The text for this statement can be found in 12_06.SQL on the CD-ROM.

On the CD

```
Begin Tran
      Update AUTHORS
      Set     CONTRACT = 1
      Where   AU_ID = '341-22-1782'

      /* save our work to this point */
      Save Transaction AuthorDone

      Update TITLEAUTHOR
            Set     ROYALTYPER = ROYALTYPER + 25
            Where   AU_ID = '341-22-1782'
      If @@error != 0 Or @@RowCount > 1
      Begin
            /* rollback and exit */
            Rollback Tran AcctDataDone
            Print 'Error occurred when updating TitleAuthor'
            Return
      End
Commit Tran
Print 'Transaction Committed'
```

Part
IV

Ch
12

CAUTION

Despite the fact that the transaction above rolled back the UPDATE on TITLEAUTHOR, SQL Server will hold locks on the TITLEAUTHOR table until the entire transaction is completed by either COMMIT or ROLLBACK. This is a side-affect of using a SavePoint and is something that may cause unexpected locking in an application.

TROUBLESHOOTING

I have an application that seems to continuously hold locks after the first transaction executes.
I'm sure that I'm committing properly. What's going on? The most likely scenario is that you have
issued more `BEGIN` `TRAN`s than you have corresponding `COMMIT` `TRAN`s or `ROLLBACK` `TRAN`s.
Remember that transactions must be enclosed in pairs of `BEGIN` and `COMMIT`/`ROLLBACK`. If you fail
to do so, SQL Server will think that you want to keep the transaction open for a longer period.

To help identify your code problems, do a walk through of your application, and monitor error
conditions carefully. Chances are that an error condition is occurring and some code is returning
control before closing an open transaction. Also, check the value of the system variable `@@trancount`
to tell you how deeply nested in transactions you really are.

Serialized Columns Without *IDENTITY*

SQL Server 6.0 introduced a new *serial* datatype, called the `IDENTITY`, in which SQL Server will
automatically assign the next sequential value to a column in a table. `IDENTITY`s are very valuable in applications that have high transaction volume and want to identify each record
uniquely.

For some applications that must support multiple database back ends and for those applications that require SQL Server 4.x compatibility, it is possible to implement the same kind of
feature as an `IDENTITY` column by performing the following steps:

1. Create a table with columns in it to store a table name and the current value. (The text
   for all the following statements can be found in 12_07.SQL on the CD-ROM.)

On the CD

```
/* create the table */
Create Table Record_IDs(
      Table_Name  varchar(30),
      Current_ID  int)
Go

/* add a primary clustered index */
Create     Unique Clustered Index PK_Record_IDs
      on Record_IDs( Table_Name ) with FILLFACTOR = 1
Go
```

2. Insert records into the table that correspond to tables in the target database:

```
Insert Record_IDs
      Select   Name,      1
      From   Sysobjects
      Where  Type = 'U'    /* user defined tables */
```

3. Create a stored procedure that will have a consistent access interface to the table and will lock the table so that no other users can modify the data while a given process is accessing it:

```
Create Procedure up_GetID                        /* up = user procedure */
        @psTableName         varchar(30),             /* p = parameter */
        @rnNewID    int OUTPUT          /* r = receive or output parameter */
As
Declare
        @nSQLError    int,
        @nRowCount    int

Begin Tran
        /* Update the record to acquire the exclusive lock on the page */
        Update Record_IDs
        Set     Current_ID = Current_ID + 1
        Where   Table_Name = @psTableName

        /* Check for errors */
        Select      @nSQLError = @@error,
            @nRowCount = @@rowcount
        If @nSQLError != 0 OR @nRowCount != 1
        Begin
            Rollback Tran
            Return -999 /* failed to update record correctly */
        End

        /* Select back the value from the table that we've already locked */
        Select      @rnNewID = Current_ID
        From    Record_IDs
        Where   Table_Name = @psTableName

        /* Check for errors */
        Select      @nSQLError = @@error,
            @nRowCount = @@rowcount
        If @nSQLError != 0 OR @nRowCount != 1
        Begin
            Rollback Tran
            Return -998 /* failed to select record correctly */
        End
    Commit Tran
    Return 0
    Go
```

4. Test the new procedure:

```
Declare
        @nRecordID    int,
        @nRC          int,
        @sMsg         varchar(255)

/* Fetch a record ID for use in inserting new record */
Exec @nRC = up_GetID 'table_A', @nRecordID OUTPUT

If @nRC != 0
        Print 'An error occurred fetching new Record ID'
```

Part
IV

Ch
12

```
      Else
      Begin
           Select @sMsg = 'New Record value is ' + Convert( varchar(4),
     ➥@nRecordID )
           Print @sMsg
      End
      Go
```

TIP Always use the new IDENTITY column to create identifying columns instead of the TIMESTAMP datatype. The IDENTITY column is far easier to reference and use in application code and can impose less data overhead if you use a small datatype for it (such as TINYINT or SMALLINT).

Understanding Locks

In addition to the background information provided previously in the section entitled "Types of Locks," it is important to know how to handle locking when it occurs in your database.

Displaying Lock Information

There are two ways to review information about locks held in the database: using the SQL Enterprise Manager or through the execution of the system stored procedure, sp_lock. SQL Enterprise Manager, under the covers, is calling sp_lock to get the information to display.

Using SQL Enterprise Manager   To view information that is being locked using the SQL Enterprise Manager, perform the following steps:

1. Run SQL Enterprise Manager from the Microsoft SQL Server 6.5 group (see fig. 12.1).

FIG. 12.1

After just being started, SQL Enterprise Manager shows that no server is selected.

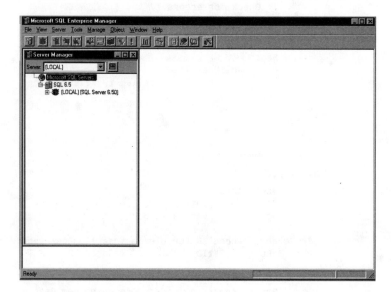

2. Select the server on which you want to work (see fig. 12.2).

FIG. 12.2

Clicking the plus next to the server expands its tree of devices, databases, and logins.

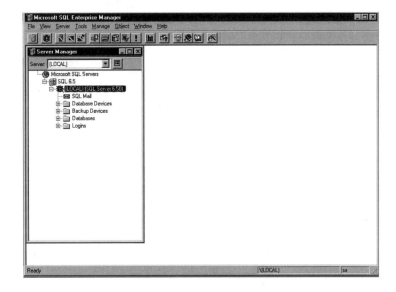

3. From the Server menu, select Current Activity and click the Object Locks page (see fig. 12.3).

FIG. 12.3

The Object Locks page of the Current Activity window shows the objects that are currently being locked.

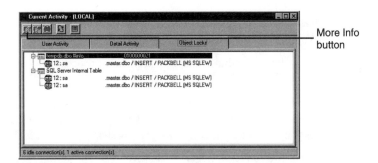

More Info button

To get more information about the individual statement that is causing locking (see fig. 12.4), you can either double-click the process that is in the Object Locks page or click the More Info toolbar button (see reference in fig. 12.3).

FIG. 12.4

The Process Details dialog box shows additional information about the SQL statement that is causing locks.

Using *sp_lock* The sp_lock system stored procedure will return a list of processes and the types of locks that they are holding on the system. To get the locks held by a particular process, add the process ID to the command (sp_lock *spid*). Here is some example code to show you the output of sp_lock:

```
Begin Tran
     Update authors
     set au_id = au_id
go
sp_lock
go
rollback tran
go
```

The output of the sp_lock follows:

spid	locktype	table_id	page	dbname
10	Sh_intent	640005311	0	master
10	Ex_table	16003088	0	pubs
10	Sh_table	288004057	0	pubs
10	Ex_extent	0	320	tempdb

TIP Many system procedures return an OBJECT_ID column to identify a database object. To quickly get the name of that object, use the system function OBJECT_NAME( ). For example, select OBJECT_NAME(1232324).

Killing a Locking Process

Before killing a process that is holding locks on the database, verify with the sp_who and sp_lock system procedures that the spid (server process id) that you are targeting to kill is in fact the user holding the locks.

When reviewing the output from sp_who, look at the blk spid column to identify a user that is blocked. Trace the tree of the blocks back the parent spid, and kill that user. To kill a user process you can either use SQL Enterprise Manager, or execute the Kill command.

Using SQL Enterprise Manager Using SQL Enterprise Manager to kill a process involves first finding the process that is causing locking, and the steps to do this are outlined previously in the section entitled "Using *sp_lock*."

Having found a process that needs to be killed, you can press the Kill Process button on the toolbar of the Current Activity window (see reference in fig. 12.5).

FIG. 12.5
The Kill Process toolbar button enables you to halt an activity.

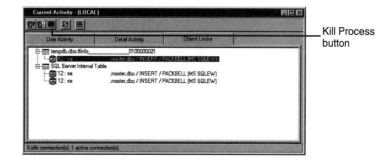

Kill Process button

A warning dialog box appears so you can change your mind and undo your action (see fig. 12.6).

FIG. 12.6
The warning dialog box enables you to confirm whether or not you really want to kill a process.

Using *KILL*   Having identified the user process (spid) that you want to kill, execute the following SQL to kill it:

```
KILL spid
```

This will kill most processes that are existing on the server. Under some circumstances, it is possible to have processes that can't be killed. Usually this occurs when it is in an Extent or Resource lock awaiting the underlying operating system to complete a task. Monitor the process with sp_who until it leaves this condition and then execute the KILL command.

Holding a Lock Explicitly

If you have application code that really needs to explicitly hold locks on particular sets of data, SQL Server provides you with extensions to the basic SELECT statement that perform this functionality. SQL Server enables you to add *optimizer hints* or keywords to your SELECT statements that tell it how to process the data that matches your results. There are several kinds of hints that you can place on a set of data affected by a SELECT statement: NOLOCK, HOLDLOCK, UPDLOCK, TABLOCK, PAGLOCK, and TABLOCKX. Some of these options are discussed below.

NOLOCK   NOLOCK is an option that enables the query to read from dirty data. *Dirty* data is data that may or may not have been affected by other users' updates and deletes. Selecting records from a table with the NOLOCK keyword ignores any other user's EXCLUSIVE locks (indicating that they had updated a record) and does not place any locks on the data itself.

Part

IV

Ch

12

NOLOCK is a very useful option for those people writing applications in which the data is statistically unaffected by a small sample of records having fluctuating values (i.e., you are more interested in trends of data than in the actual values themselves). Care should be taken, and it is important to clearly differentiate between data fetched with the NOLOCK keyword and data that is legitimately accurate according to the known condition of the database as a whole.

> **CAUTION**
>
> When selecting data with the NOLOCK keyword, it is possible that another user has affected your data in such a way as to make it invalid during the time you are reading from the data page in which it resides. For example, another user could have deleted a record that you are reading, and while you are reading it, their COMMIT is processed and the record is removed.
>
> If you are reading data and it is no longer available, you will receive error messages 605, 606, 624, or 625. It is recommended that you process these errors in the same way that you process a deadlock condition. That is, inform the users that an error has occurred and ask them to retry their operations—advanced applications may want to auto retry the first time to avoid confusing the users unnecessarily.

HOLDLOCK   Normal SELECTs on tables acquire a SHARED lock on a page while the SELECT is passing through the data. A SHARED lock does not prohibit another user from updating a record or attempting to gain an EXCLUSIVE lock on the data page that is currently being processed by the SELECT. In addition, the SHARED lock expires on a data page as the next page is being read. If you want to maintain data integrity for the life of the SELECT (because you may need to scroll backwards and forwards through the result set), use the HOLDLOCK command to force SQL Server to hold the SHARED lock until the transaction is complete.

TABLOCK and TABLOCKX   As its name implies, TABLOCK forces a SELECT statement to lock the entire table or tables affected by the SELECT for the duration of the statement. TABLOCKX forces an exclusive table lock for the life of the transaction, denying any other user access to the table until the transaction has been completed.

 Do not place a table lock (TABLOCK) on a table unless you have a good programmatic reason. TABLOCKs often create unnecessary overhead and undue locking in the server. Instead, rely on Lock Escalation (LE) thresholds to manage TABLOCKs for you.

Lock Escalation Options

SQL Server locks data on the page level. Any query that you execute on the server will hold locks on at least one full page. If you start updating or locking multiple pages on a table, SQL Server starts consuming resources to manage your requests. At a certain point (based on a percentage of pages locked per table), it becomes more efficient for the database to lock the entire table (a table lock) than to keep managing the individual pages being locked by a given transaction.

Fortunately, SQL Server enables you to configure the way in which it chooses to *escalate* locks from page level to table level. These are options that are set at the server level with the server stored procedure, `sp_configure`.

LE Thresholds   Using `sp_configure`, it is possible to set three different types of *Lock Escalation (LE) thresholds*: LE threshold maximum, LE threshold minimum, and LE threshold percent.

The threshold maximum is used by the server to determine when to escalate a set of page locks to a table lock. The default for the server is 200 pages. To change this value, follow these steps. (The text for this statement can be found in 12_08.SQL on the CD-ROM.)

```
Use Master
Go
sp_configure 'LE threshold Maximum', NNN   /* where NNN is the new number
                                              of pages */
Go
Reconfigure
Go
```

The threshold minimum is used in conjunction with the threshold percent to stop a table lock escalation occurring on a table with few rows. Suppose you set the LE threshold percent to 50 percent, meaning that if more than half the data pages where being locked you wanted the whole table locked. This is not an unreasonable proposition until you have a small table with only a few pages. The threshold minimum that defaults to 20 pages stops the threshold percentage from escalating page locks to table locks unless its minimum number of pages has been locked.

The threshold percentage is used to enable you to generically set a level at which you want to escalate a set of page locks to a single table lock relative to the number of rows in the table. The default value of this configuration option is zero (0), meaning that the LE threshold maximum should be used to determine escalation.

> **TIP**
> As we saw above, despite the LE thresholds it is possible to force locking on pages and tables by using the HOLDLOCK and TABLOCK keywords when issuing a SELECT statement to the server.

From Here...

In this chapter you learned about the fundamentals of locking and transactions and how they will affect your application. In addition, you learned about the internals of SQL Server and how it manages many users hitting the same table.

Take a look at the following chapters to further develop your SQL Server and application programming knowledge:

- Chapter 5, "Creating Database Tables and Using Datatypes," tells you how you can redefine some of your tables to enable better concurrency.

Part
IV

Ch
12

- Chapter 10, "Managing and Using Indexes and Keys," shows you how you can optimize table access through the creation of a clustered index with a sparse FILL FACTOR.
- Chapter 16, "Understanding Server, Database, and Query Options," provides an understanding of how the options you set up for the server affect database applications and transaction locks.

Managing Stored Procedures and Using Flow-Control Statements

What flow-control statements are available and how to use them

Programming languages were built around flow control but databases were built around data. Flow-control statements were added to databases to facilitate the writing of stored procedures.

How to work with a host language, returning information about the success or failure of your routine

Return codes or visual output to the user can increase the effectiveness of a stored procedure.

How to work with variables within your procedures

Variables must be assigned a data type and a scope.

As your systems become more complex, you'll need to spend more time carefully integrating SQL code with your host application code. In this chapter, you'll be reviewing the logic and flow control statements that you have available to you in your SQL code. ■

N O T E It's important to keep in mind the client/server model when you're building your systems. Remember that data management belongs on the server, and data presentation and display manipulation for reports and inquiries should reside on the client in the ideal model. As you build systems, be on the lookout for those items that can be moved to the two different ends of the model to optimize the user's experience with your application. ■

Although SQL is defined as a non-procedural language, Microsoft SQL Server permits the use of flow-control keywords. You use the flow-control keywords to create a procedure that you can store for subsequent execution. You can use these stored procedures instead of writing programs using conventional programming language, such as C or Visual Basic, to perform operations with a SQL Server database and its tables.

Some of the advantages that Stored Procedures offer over dynamic SQL Statements are

- Stored procedures are compiled the first time that they're run and are stored in a system table of the current database. When they are compiled, they are optimized to select the best path to access information in the tables. This optimization takes into account the actual data patterns in the table, indexes that are available, table loading, and more. These compiled stored procedures can greatly enhance the performance of your system.

- Another benefit is that you can execute a stored procedure on either a local or remote SQL Server. This enables you to run processes on other machines and work with information across servers, not just *local* databases.

- An application program written in a language, such as C or Visual Basic, can also execute stored procedures, providing an optimum "working together" solution between the client side software and SQL Server.

Defining Stored Procedures

You use the CREATE PROCEDURE statement to create a stored procedure. Permission to execute the procedure that you create is set by default to the owner of the database. An owner of the database can change the permissions to allow other users to execute the procedure. The syntax that you use to define a new procedure is as follows:

```
CREATE PROCEDURE [owner,] procedure_name [;number]
[@parameter_name datatype [=default] [OUTput]
…
[@parameter_name datatype [=default] [OUTput]
[FOR REPLICATION] ¦ [WITH RECOMPILE] , ENCRYPTION
AS sql_statements
```

> **CAUTION**
>
> Be sure you reload your stored procedures again after information has been saved in the database tables that represents, both in volume and content, the information that your application can expect to see. Since stored procedures are compiled and optimized based on the tables, indexes, and data loading, your query can show significant improvement just by reloading it after "real" information has been placed in the system.

In the following example, a simple procedure is created that contains a SELECT statement to display all rows of a table. Once the procedure is created, its name is simply entered on a line to execute the procedure. If you precede the name of a stored procedure with other statements, you use the EXECUTE procedure-name statement to execute the procedure.

```
create procedure all_employees
as select * from employees

all_employees

name                    department            badge
------------------- -------------------- ----------
Bob Smith               Sales                 1234
Mary Jones              Sales                 5514
( 2 row(s) affected)
```

N O T E As mentioned earlier, naming conventions for SQL objects are an important part of your implementation plan. In a production system, you will often have hundreds of stored procedures, many tables, and many more supporting objects. You should consider coming up with a naming convention for your stored procedures that will make it easy to identify them as procedures and will make it easier to document them. In many installations, a common prefix for the stored procedure name is sp_. ■

You can create a new procedure in the current database only. If you're working in ISQL or ISQL/w, you can execute the USE statement followed by the name of the database to set the current database to the database in which the procedure should be created. You can use any Transact-SQL statement in a stored procedure with the exception of CREATE statements.

N O T E Stored procedures are treated like all other objects in the database. Therefore, they are subject to all of the same naming conventions and other limitations. ■

Using Parameters with Procedures

You can define one or more parameters in a procedure. You use parameters as named storage locations just like you would use the parameters as variables in conventional programming languages, such as C and VB. You precede the name of a parameter with an *at* symbol (@) to designate it as a parameter. Parameter names are local to the procedure in which they're defined.

You can use parameters to pass information into a procedure from the line that executes the parameter. You place the parameters after the name of the procedure on a command line, with commas to separate the list of parameters if there is more than one. You use system datatypes to define the type of information to be expected as a parameter.

In the following example, the procedure is defined with three input parameters. The defined input parameters appear within the procedure in the position of values in the VALUE clause of an INSERT statement. When the procedure is executed, three literal values are passed into the

INSERT statement within the procedure as a parameter list. A SELECT statement is executed after the stored procedure is executed to verify that a new row was added through the procedure.

N O T E   When a procedure executed as the first statement in a series of statements, the procedure does not have to be preceded by the keyword EXECUTE. The name of the procedure to be executed is simply placed as the first keyword on the line. ■

T I P   Be sure to check the documentation for the host language you are using with SQL Server to determine the correct calling sequence for the host language. Actual calling syntax varies by language.

```
create procedure proc4 (@p1 char(15), @p2 char(20), @p3 int) as
insert into Workers
values (@p1, @p2, @p3)

proc4 'Bob Lint',Sales,3333

select * from Workers
where Badge=3333
```

Name	Department	Badge
Bob Lint	Sales	3333

```
(1 row(s) affected)
```

The semicolon and integer after the name of a procedure enables you to create multiple versions of a procedure with the same name. In the following example, two procedures with the same name are created as version one and two. When the procedure is executed, the version number can be specified to control the version of the procedure that is executed. If no version number is specified, the first version of the procedure is executed. This option is not shown in the example above, but is available if needed by your application.

In the following example, two procedures are created with the same name, but as version one and two and are then subsequently executed once both are defined. Both procedures use a PRINT statement to return a message that identifies the procedure version. When the procedure is executed without the version number specified, the first version of the procedure is executed.

```
create procedure proc3;1 as
print 'version 1'

create procedure proc3;2 as
print 'version 2'

proc3;1

version 1

proc3;2
```

```
version 2

proc3

version 1
```

In the previous example, proc3 is executed without preceding it with the keyword EXECUTE because it is executed interactively as the first statement on a line.

 TIP You can use the SET NOEXEC ON command the first time that you execute a procedure to check it for errors, rather than executing it when errors may cause it to fail.

You can create a new stored procedure through the SQL Enterprise Manager as well as in ISQL or ISQL/w. Perform the following steps to create a new stored procedure through the SQL Enterprise Manager:

1. Select Stored Procedures under the Objects of the selected database in the Server Manager window.

2. Right-click Stored Procedures and select New Stored Procedures from the menu. You can also select Stored Procedures from the Manage menu to bring up the Manage Stored Procedures dialog box. You can enter Transact-SQL statements in the dialog box. The Manage Stored Procedures dialog box is brought up with the keys that are used to define a stored procedure. Figure 13.1 shows the Manage Stored Procedures dialog box before any statements are typed into the dialog box.

FIG. 13.1

You can also edit an existing stored procedure in the Manage Stored Procedures dialog box.

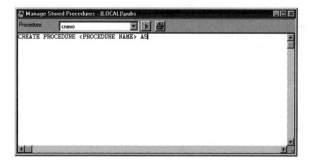

3. You must overwrite <PROCEDURE NAME> in the Manage Stored Procedures dialog box with the name of your new procedure.

4. Click the Execute button to create and store your procedure. Figure 13.2 shows a simple Transact-SQL statement and a new procedure name entered in the Manage Stored Procedures dialog box.

Part
IV

Ch
13

FIG. 13.2

Click the Procedures list box to display a list of the procedures in the selected database.

Displaying and Editing Procedures

You use the system procedure sp_helptext to list the definition of a procedure, and sp_help to display control information about a procedure. The system procedures sp_helptext and sp_help are used to list information about other database objects, such as tables, rules, and defaults, as well as stored procedures.

Procedures with the same name and version number are displayed together and dropped together. In the following example, the definition of procedures proc3, version one and two, are both displayed when the procedure is specified with the sp_helptext system procedure.

```
sp_helptext proc3

text
-------------------------------------------------
create procedure proc3;1 as
print 'version 1'
create procedure proc3;2 as
print 'version 2'

(1 row(s) affected)
```

In the next examples, the system procedure sp_help is used to display information about the procedure proc3. If the version number is used with the sp_help system procedure, an error is returned.

```
sp_help proc3

Name                            Owner                           Type
----------------------------    ----------------------------    ----------------
proc3                           dbo                             stored procedure
Data_located_on_segment When_created
----------------------          -------------------------
not applicable                  Dec 7 1994  1:50PM
```

You can use an additional system procedure just to return information about stored procedures. The system procedure sp_stored_procedures is used to list information about stored procedures. In the following example, the procedure sp_stored_procedures is used to display information about a previously stored procedure.

```
sp_stored_procedures procall

procedure_qualifier  procedure_owner  procedure_name  num_input_params
num_output_params num_result_sets remarks
-------------------------------------------------------------------------------
----------
master  dbo  procall;1  -1  -1 -1  (null)

(1 row(s) affected)
```

 T I P You can use the command SET SHOWPLAN ON before you execute a procedure to see the way in which SQL Server will perform the necessary reads and writes to the database tables when the statements in your procedure are executed. You can use this information to help determine whether additional indexes or different data layout would be beneficial to the query.

You use the SQL Enterprise Manager to list and edit existing procedures. Double-click the procedure to be edited in the list of stored procedures in the main window of the server Manager. The selected procedure is displayed and can be changed in the Manage Stored Procedures dialog box that is brought up.

You actually can't directly edit stored procedures. You'll notice that the Manage Stored Procedures dialog box (refer to figures 13.1 and 13.2) that is brought up for an existing procedure has additional Transact-SQL statements added previous to the procedure definition. The conditional IF statement is used to check if the procedure is already defined (which it will be if you were able to select it) and delete the procedure. The old procedure definition must be removed and a new procedure, with the name you specify, will be substituted for the old procedure.

Dropping Procedures

You use the DROP PROCEDURE statement to drop a stored procedure that you've created. Multiple procedures can be dropped with a single DROP PROCEDURE statement by listing multiple procedures separated by commas after the keywords DROP PROCEDURE in the syntax:

```
DROP PROCEDURE procedure_name_1, …,procedure_name_n
```

Multiple versions of a procedure can't be selectively dropped. All versions of a procedure with the same name must be dropped by using the DROP PROCEDURE statement that specifies the procedure without a version number. All versions of a procedure with the same name must be dropped together.

In the following example, the two versions of the procedures proc3 are dropped.

```
drop procedure proc3
This command did not return data, and it did not return any rows
```

You can also drop a selected procedure in the SQL Enterprise Manager. Click the right mouse button for the selected procedure and choose Drop from the menu that is brought up.

Part
IV

Ch

13

TROUBLESHOOTING

I created a procedure in a previous session, but I was unable to find the procedure again in a subsequent session. Procedures are defined within a database. In your subsequent session, you probably found yourself in a different database than the database in which the procedure was originally defined. You can ask the database administrator to define the database that your procedure was defined in to your default database and you'll always be positioned to it each time you begin a session. You can also enter the USE command followed by the name of the database in which your procedure was defined to position yourself to it so that you can locate the procedure.

Understanding Procedure Resolution and Compilation

The benefit of using a stored procedure for the execution of a set of Transact-SQL statements is that it is compiled the first time that it's run. During compilation, the Transact-SQL statements in the procedure are converted from their original character representation into an executable form. During compilation, any objects that are referenced in procedures are also converted to alternate representations. For example, table names are converted to their object IDs and column names to their column IDs.

An execution plan is also created just as it would be for the execution of even a single Transact-SQL statement. The execution plan contains, for example, the indexes to be used to retrieve rows from tables that are referenced by the procedure. The execution plan is kept in a cache and is used to perform the queries of the procedure each time it's subsequently executed.

TIP You can define the size of the procedure cache so that it is large enough to contain most or all the available procedures for execution and save the time that it would take to regenerate the execution plan for procedures.

Automatic Recompilation

Normally, the procedure's execution plan is run from the memory cache of procedures that permits it to execute rapidly. A procedure, however, is automatically recompiled under the following circumstances:

- A procedure is always recompiled when SQL Server is stated (usually after a reboot of the underlying operating system), and the procedures are first executed.

    N O T E It's often the case that SQL Server remains up and running on the server system continuously. As a database server, it must be available whenever users on client PC workstations must access the SQL Server databases. The server computer and SQL Server may never be stopped and restarted unless a major error occurs, a hardware malfunction, or an update to a new version of SQL Server or Windows NT. The recompilation of stored procedures would not be done frequently on systems that run non-stop. ■

- A procedure's execution plan is also automatically recompiled whenever an index on a table referenced in the procedure is dropped. A new execution plan must be compiled because the current one references an object, the index, for the retrieval of the rows of a table that doesn't exist. The execution plan must be redone to permit the queries of the procedure to be performed.

- Compilation of the execution plan is also re-initialized if the execution plan in the cache is currently in use by another user. A second copy of the execution plan is created for the second user. If the first copy of the execution plan weren't in use, it could have been used rather than a new execution plan being created. When a user finishes executing a procedure, the execution plan is available in the cache for reuse by another user with appropriate permissions..

- A procedure is also automatically recompiled if the procedure is dropped and re-created. All copies of the execution plan in the cache are removed because the new procedure may be substantially different from the older version and a new execution plan is necessary.

Note that because SQL Server attempts to optimize stored procedures by caching the most recently used routines, it is still possible that an older execution plan, one previously loaded in cache, may be used in place of the new execution plan. To prevent this problem, you must either drop and re-create the procedure or stop and restart SQL Server to flush the procedure cache and ensure that the new procedure is the only one that will be used when the procedure is executed.

You can also create the procedure using a WITH RECOMPILE option so that the procedure is automatically recompiled each time that its executed. You should do this if the tables accessed by the queries in a procedure are very dynamic. Tables that are very dynamic have rows added, deleted, and updated frequently, which results in frequent changes to the indexes that are defined for the tables.

In other cases, you may want to force a recompilation of a procedure when it would not be done automatically. For example, if the statistics used to determine whether an index should be used for a query are updated or an entire index is created for a table, recompilation is not re-done automatically. You can use the WITH RECOMPILE clause on the EXECUTE statement when you execute the procedure to do a recompilation. The syntax of the EXECUTE statement with a recompile clause is:

```
EXECUTE procedure_name AS
.Transact-SQL statement(s)
...
WITH RECOMPILE
```

If the procedure you're working with uses parameters and these parameters control the functionality of the routine, you may want to use the RECOMPILE option. This is due to the fact that if

Part
IV

Ch
13

the routine's parameters may determine the best execution path, it may be beneficial to have the execution plan determined at runtime, rather than determining it once and then using this plan for all accesses to the stored procedure.

N O T E   It may be difficult to determine whether a procedure should be created with the WITH RECOMPILE option. If in doubt, you'll probably be better served by not creating the procedure with the RECOMPILE option. Because—if you create a procedure with the RECOMPILE option—the procedure is recompiled each time the procedure is executed, you may waste valuable CPU time to perform these compiles. You can still add the WITH RECOMPILE clause to force a recompilation when you execute the procedure. ■

You can't use the WITH RECOMPILE option in a CREATE PROCEDURE statement that contains the FOR REPLICATION option. You use the FOR REPLICATION option to create a procedure that's executed during replication.

▶ **See** Chapter 20, "Setting Up and Managing Replication." **p. 505**

You can add the ENCRYPTION option to a CREATE PROCEDURE statement to encrypt the definition of the stored procedure that is added to the system table syscomments. You use the ENCRYPTION option to prevent other users from displaying the definition of your procedure and learning what objects it references and what Transact-SQL statements it contains.

CAUTION

Unless you absolutely must encrypt procedures for security reasons, you should leave procedures unencrypted. When you upgrade your database for a version change or to rebuild it, your procedures can only be recreated if the entries in syscomments are not encrypted.

Defining Procedure Auto Execution

You can use the system stored procedure, sp_makestartup, to define a procedure to execute automatically when SQL Server is started up. You can mark any number of procedures to execute automatically at start up. The syntax sp_makestartup is as follows:

```
sp_makestartup procedure_name
```

The procedures that are defined to execute automatically at start up execute after the last database has been automatically started and recovered at start up of SQL Server. You can use the system procedure sp_helpstartup to list the procedures that are defined to execute at start up. You use the system procedure, sp_unmakestartup, to prevent a procedure from executing automatically.

In the following example, a new procedure is created that is marked for the automatic execution when SQL Server is started. In addition, the list startup procedures are also listed before and after the procedure is removed from automatic execution at start up.

```
create procedure test_startup as
print 'test procedure executed at startup'
go
sp_makestartup test_startup
go
Procedure has been marked as 'startup'.
sp_helpstartup
go
Startup stored procedures:
-----------------------------
test_startup

(1 row(s) affected)
sp_unmakestartup test_startup
go
Procedure is no longer marked as 'startup'.
sp_helpstartup

Startup stored procedures:
```

Understanding Procedure and Batch Restrictions

Sets of Transact-SQL statements are referred to as batches, which includes stored procedures. The rules or syntax for the use of Transact-SQL statements in batch apply to the following list of objects:

- Procedures
- Rules
- Defaults
- Triggers
- Views

The syntax is primarily a set of restrictions that limit the types of statements that can be used in batch. Most of the restrictions are the statements that create objects or change the database or query environment don't take effect within the current batch.

For example, although rules and defaults can be defined and bound to a column or user-defined datatype within a batch, the defaults and rules are in effect until after the completion of the batch. You also can't drop an object and reference or re-create it in the same batch.

Some additional Set options that are defined with a batch don't apply to queries contained in the batch. For example, the Set option SET NOCOUNT ON will affect all queries that follow it with a stored procedure and suppress the count line for the execution of SELECT statements. The SET SHOWPLAN ON option does not affect the queries used within a stored procedure, and a query plan isn't displayed for the queries in the procedure.

Part
IV

Ch
13

Understanding the End-of-Batch Signal *GO*

As you've seen throughout this book, if you use the command-line ISQL for the execution of a set of Transact-SQL statements, the GO command is used to specify the end of the set of statements. GO is used on a line by itself. The GO command is required if you interactively use a set of statements or read in statements from an input file to ISQL.

The GO command is not required to execute a set of Transact-SQL statements that are used in the Windows GUI application form of ISQL, ISQL/w. GO is also not required in a series of Transact-SQL statements that are executed within batch objects, such as stored procedures, rules, defaults, triggers, or views. In the following example of an interactive ISQL session, the GO command is used first to cause the execution of the USE command and then to signal the end of the second batch, two SELECT statements.

```
C:>isql/U sa
Password:
1>use employees
2>go
1>select * from Workers
2>select count(*) from Workers
3>go
```

```
Name                            Department       Badge
------------------------------  ---------------  ----------
Bob Smith                       Sales            1234
Sue Simmons                     Sales            3241
Mary Watkins                    Field Service    6532
Linda Lovely                    Library          7888

(4 row(s) affected)
----------


----------
4

(1 row(s) affected)
```

In the following example, the GO command is used with the file query1.sql, which contains the following commands:

```
use employees
go
select * from Workers
select max(Rownum) from Rownumber
go
```

The Transact-SQL statements within the file are executed with the invocation of ISQL, which returns the following display:

```
isql /U /i query1.sql /n /P ''
Name                            Department               Badge
------------------------------  -----------------------  ------------
Bob Smith                       Sales                    1234
Sue Simmons                     Sales                    3241
```

```
Mary Watkins              Field Service        6532
Linda Lovely              Library              7888

(4 rows affected)

- - - - - - - - - - -
           19

(1 row affected)
```

 TIP You can also use a /o file-spec to direct the output of the execution of ISQL to a file rather than to your monitor and *capture* the output of any statements executed during the ISQL session.

Using Flow-Control Statements

Transact-SQL contains several statements that are used to change the order of execution of statements within a set of statements such as a stored procedure. The use of such flow-control statements permit you to organize statements in stored procedures to provide the capabilities of a conventional programming language, such a C or COBOL. You may find that some of the retrieval, update, deletion, addition, and manipulation of the rows of database tables can more easily be performed through the use of flow-control statements in objects, such as stored procedures.

Using *IF...ELSE*

You can use the keywords IF and ELSE to control conditional execution within a batch, such as a stored procedure. The IF and ELSE keywords permit you to test a condition and execute either the statements that are part of the IF branch or the statements that are part of the ELSE branch. You define the condition for testing as an expression following the keyword IF. The syntax of an IF…ELSE statement is as follows:

```
IF expression
     statement
[ELSE]
     [IF expression]
     statement]
```

NOTE It's impossible to show examples of the use of conditional statements that can be formed with the keywords IF and ELSE without using other keywords. The examples shown next use the keywords PRINT and EXISTS. In the subsequent examples, the keyword PRINT is used to display a string of characters. ■

The keyword EXISTS is usually followed by a statement within parentheses when used in an IF statement. The EXISTS statement is evaluated to either True or False, depending upon whether the statement within the parentheses returns one or more rows, or no rows, respectively.

You needn't use an ELSE clause as part of an IF statement. The simplest form of an IF statement is constructed without an ELSE clause. In the following example, a PRINT statement is used to display a confirmation message that a row exists in a database table. If the row doesn't exist in the table, the message No entry is displayed. Unfortunately, the message is also displayed after the verification message is displayed because you're not using the ELSE option.

```
if exists (select * from Workers
where Badge=1234)
     print 'entry available'
print 'No entry'
```

```
entry available
No entry
```

In the following example, the row isn't found in the table, so only the PRINT statement that follows the IF statement is executed.

```
if exists (select * from Workers
where Badge=1235)
     print 'entry available'
print 'No entry'
```

```
No entry
```

The previous two examples shows the problem of using an IF statement that doesn't contain an ELSE clause. In the examples, it's impossible to prevent the message, No entry, from appearing. You would add an ELSE clause to the IF statement to print the message, No entry, if a row isn't found and the condition after the IF isn't True.

In the following example, our previous examples are rewritten to use an IF and ELSE clause. If a row that is tested for in the IF clause is in the table, only the message employee present is displayed. If the row isn't found in the table, only the message employee not found is displayed.

```
if exists (select * from employees
where name='Bob Smith')
     print 'employee present'
else print 'employee not found'
```

> **CAUTION**
>
> Unlike some programming languages you may have used, when used alone, the Transact-SQL IF statement can have only one statement associated with it. As a result, there is no need for a keyword, such as END-IF, to define the end of the IF statement. See "Using BEGIN...END" in the next section for information on grouping statements and associating them with an IF...ELSE condition.

Using *BEGIN...END*

You use the keywords BEGIN and END to designate a set of Transact-SQL statements to be executed as a unit. You use the keyword BEGIN to define the start of a block of Transact-SQL statements. You use the keyword END after the last Transact-SQL statement that is part of the same block of statements. BEGIN...END uses the following syntax:

```
BEGIN
     statements
END
```

You often use BEGIN and END with a conditional statement such as an IF statement. BEGIN and END are used in an IF or ELSE clause to permit multiple Transact-SQL statements to be executed if the expression following the IF or ELSE clause is True. As mentioned earlier, without a BEGIN and END block enclosing multiple statements, only a single Transact-SQL statement can be executed if the expression in the IF or ELSE clause is True.

In the following example, BEGIN and END are used with an IF statement to define the execution of multiple statements if the condition tested is True. The IF statement contains only a IF clause, no ELSE clause is part of the statement.

```
if exists (select * from employees
where badge=1234)
     begin
           print 'entry available'
           select name,department from employees
           where badge=1234
     end
```

```
entry available
name                    department
--------------------    --------------------
Bob Smith               Sales
```

```
(1 row(s) affected)
```

In the second example, an ELSE clause is added to the IF statement to display a message if the row isn't found.

```
if exists (select * from employees
where department='Sales')
     begin
           print 'row(s) found'
           select name, department from employees
           where department='Sales'
     end
else print 'No entry'
```

```
row(s) found
name                    department
--------------------    --------------------
Bob Smith               Sales
Mary Jones              Sales
```

```
(2 row(s) affected)
```

The third example returns the message that follows the ELSE clause because no row is found.

```
if exists (select * from employees
```

Part

IV

Ch

13

```
where department='Nonexistent')
      begin
            print 'row(s) found'
            select name, department from employees
            where department='Nonexistent'
      end
else print 'No entry'

No entry
```

Using *WHILE*

You use the keyword WHILE to define a condition that executes one or more Transact-SQL statements when the condition tested evaluates to True. The statement that follows the expression of the WHILE statement continues to execute as long as the condition tested is True. The syntax of the WHILE statement is as follows:

```
WHILE
      <boolean_expression>
      <sql_statement>
```

N O T E   As with the IF...ELSE statements, you can only execute a single SQL statement with the WHILE clause. If you need to include more than one statement in the routine, you'll need to use the BEGIN...END construct as described earlier. ■

In the following example, a WHILE statement is used to execute a SELECT statement that displays a numeric value until the value reaches a limit of five. The example uses a variable that is like a parameter in that a variable is a named storage location. You define the datatype of a variable using a DECLARE statement to control the way information is represented in the variable. A variable is always referenced preceded by an *at* sign (@) like a parameter.

In the example, the value stored in the variable is initialized to one and subsequently incremented. The statements associated with the WHILE execute until the variable x reaches a value of five.

```
declare @x int
select @x=1
while @x<5
begin
print 'x still less than 5'
select @x=@x+1
end
go
(1 row(s) affected)
x still less than 5
(1 row(s) affected)
x still less than 5
(1 row(s) affected)
x still less than 5
(1 row(s) affected)
x still less than 5
(1 row(s) affected)
```

A more meaningful example of the use of a WHILE statement can be shown after two additional Transact-SQL keywords are introduced and explained. An example using WHILE along with the keywords BREAK and CONTINUE will be shown a little later in this section.

Using *BREAK*

You use the keyword BREAK within a block of Transact-SQL statements that is within a conditional WHILE statement to end the execution of the statements. The execution of a BREAK results in the first statement following the end of block to begin executing. The syntax of a BREAK clause is as follows:

```
WHILE
  <boolean_expression>
  <sql_statement>
BREAK
  <sql_statement>
```

In the following example, the BREAK within the WHILE statement causes the statement within the WHILE to terminate. The PRINT statement executes once because the PRINT statement is located before the BREAK. Once the BREAK is encountered, the statements in the WHILE clause aren't executed again.

```
declare @x int
select @x=1
while @x<5
begin
      print 'x still less than 5'
      select @x=@x+1
      break
end

(1 row(s) affected)
x still less than 5
(1 row(s) affected)
```

Using *CONTINUE*

You use a CONTINUE keyword to form a clause within a conditional statement, such as a WHILE statement, to explicitly continue the set of statements that are contained within the conditional statement. The syntax of the CONTINUE clause is as follows:

```
WHILE
  <boolean_expression>
  <statement>
BREAK
  <statement>
CONTINUE
```

In the following example, a CONTINUE is used within a WHILE statement to explicitly define that execution of the statements within the WHILE statement should continue as long as the condition specified in the expression that follows WHILE is True. The use of CONTINUE in the following example skips the final PRINT statement.

Part
IV

Ch

13

```
declare @x int
select @x=1
while @x<5
begin
      print 'x still less than 5'
      select @x=@x+1
      continue
      print 'this statement will not execute'
end

(1 row(s) affected)
x still less than 5
(1 row(s) affected)
x still less than 5
(1 row(s) affected)
x still less than 5
(1 row(s) affected)
x still less than 5
(1 row(s) affected)
```

Examples of Using *WHILE*, *BREAK*, and *CONTINUE*

Although the two previous examples use BREAK and CONTINUE alone, you don't typically use either CONTINUE or BREAK within a WHILE statement alone. Both BREAK and CONTINUE are often used following an IF or ELSE that is defined within a WHILE statement, so an additional condition can be used to break out of the WHILE loop. If two or more loops are nested, BREAK exits to the next outermost loop.

In the following example, a BREAK is used with an IF statement, both of which are within a WHILE statement. The BREAK is used to terminate the statements associated with the WHILE if the condition specified by the IF statement is True. The IF condition is True if the value of the local variable, @y, is True.

```
declare @x int
declare @y tinyint
select @x=1, @y=1
while @x<5
begin
      print 'x still less than 5'
      select @x=@x+1
      select @y=@y+1
      if @y=2
      begin
            print 'y is 2 so break out of loop'
            break
      end
      end
print 'out of while loop'

(1 row(s) affected)
x still less than 5
(1 row(s) affected)
(1 row(s) affected)
y is 2 so break out of loop
out of while loop
```

In the following example, a WHILE statement is used to permit only the rows of a table that match the criteria defined within the expression of the WHILE statement to have their values changed.

```
begin tran
while (select avg(price)from titles) < $30
begin
      select title_id, price
      from titles
      where price >$20
      update titles set price=price * 2
end
```

```
(0 row(s) affected)

title_id price
-------- -------------------------
PC1035   22.95
PS1372   21.59
TC3218   20.95

(3 row(s) affected)
(18 row(s) affected)
(0 row(s) affected)

title_id price
-------- -------------------------
BU1032   39.98
BU1111   23.90
BU7832   39.98
MC2222   39.98
PC1035   45.90
PC8888   40.00
PS1372   43.18
PS2091   21.90
PS3333   39.98
TC3218   41.90
TC4203   23.90
TC7777   29.98

(12 row(s) affected)
(18 row(s) affected)
(0 row(s) affected)
```

You must be careful in defining the WHILE statement and its associated statements. As shown in the following example, if the condition specified with the WHILE expression continues to be True, the WHILE loop will execute indefinitely.

```
while exists (select hours_worked from pays)
print 'hours worked is less than 55'

(0 row(s) affected)
hours worked is less than 55
(0 row(s) affected)
...
```

Part
IV

Ch

13

If the evaluation of the expression following the WHILE returns multiple values, you should use an EXISTS rather than any comparison operators. In the following example, the error message that is returned is descriptive of the problem.

```
while (select hours_worked from pays) > 55
print 'hours worked is less than 55'

Msg 512, Level 16, State 1
Subquery returned more than 1 value.  This is illegal when the subquery follows
=, !=, <, <= , >, >=, or when the subquery is used as an expression.
Command has been aborted.
```

Defining and Using Variables

You may recall that earlier in this chapter variables were described as similar to parameters in that they are named storage locations. Variables in Transact-SQL can be either local or global. You define local variables by using a DECLARE statement and assigning the variable a datatype. You assign an initial value to local variables with a SELECT statement.

You must declare, assign a value, and use a local variable within the same batch or stored procedure. The variable is only available for use within the same batch or procedure, hence the name local variable.

You can use local variables in batch or stored procedures for such things as counters and temporary holding locations for other variables. Recall that local variables are always referenced with an @ preceding their names. You can define the datatype of a local variable as a user-defined datatype as well as a system datatype. One restriction that applies to local variables is that you can't define a local variable as a text or image datatype.

The syntax of a local variable is as follows:

```
DECLARE @variable_name datatype [,variable_name datatype…]
```

The SELECT statement is used to assign values to local variables, as shown in the following syntax:

```
SELECT @variable_name = expression ¦select statement
[,@variable_name = expression select statement]
[FROM list of tables] [WHERE expression]
[GROUP BY…
[HAVING …]
[ORDER BY…]
```

If the SELECT statement returns more than a single value, the variable is assigned to the last value returned. In the following example, two local variables are defined and used to return the number of rows in the table. The CONVERT function must be used to convert the numeric format of the number of rows to a text datatype for the PRINT statement. The message that is displayed by the PRINT statement is first built and assigned to a local variable because the concatenation can't be done within the PRINT statement.

```
declare @mynum int
```

```
select @mynum = count(*)from Workers
declare @mychar char(2)
select @mychar = convert(char(2),@mynum)
declare @mess char(40)
select @mess ='There are ' + @mychar + 'rows in the table Workers'
print @mess

(1 row(s) affected)

(4 row(s) affected)

(1 row(s) affected)

There are 4 rows in the table Workers
```

Each SELECT statement returns a count message in the previous example. If you want the count message suppressed, you must first execute the SET NOCOUNT statement. In the following example, the same statements that were executed in the previous example are re-executed with the count turned off.

```
declare @mynum int
select @mynum = count(*)from Workers
declare @mychar char(2)
select @mychar = convert(char(2),@mynum)
declare @mess char(40)
select @mess ='There are ' + @mychar + 'rows in the table Workers'
print @mess

There are 4 rows in the table Workers
```

Using *PRINT* with Variables

You'll recall that in examples shown earlier in this chapter, PRINT was used to display a message to the assigned output device. You use the keyword PRINT to display ASCII text or variables up to 255 characters in length. You can't use PRINT to output other than CHAR or VARCHAR datatypes or the global variable @@VERSION.

Recall that you can't concatenate string data in a PRINT statement directly. You must concatenate text or variables into a single variable and output the results with the PRINT statement. The syntax of the PRINT statement is as follows:

```
PRINT 'text' |@local_variable | @@global_variable
```

Using Global Variables

A global variable is a variable that is defined by SQL Server. You can't define a global variable with your routines; you can only use the pre-declared and defined global variables. You always reference a global variable by preceding with two *at* signs (@@). You reference a global variable to access server information or information about your operations. You can only declare local variables. You shouldn't define local variables that have the same name as system variables because you may receive unexpected results in your application.

Part
IV

Ch

13

Table 13.1 lists the names of all Microsoft SQL Server global variables and a brief description of the information that's contained within them.

Table 13.1   Global Variables for Microsoft SQL Server

Global Variable	Description
@@CONNECTIONS	Total logins or attempted logins
@@CPU_BUSY	Cumulative CPU Server time in ticks
@@DBTS	Value of unique timestamp for database
@@ERROR	Last system error number : 0 if successful
@@FETCH_STATUS	Status of the last FETCH statement
@@IDENTITY	The last inserted identity value
@@IDLE	Cumulative CPU Server idle time
@@IO_BUSY	Cumulative Server I/O time
@@LANGID	Current language ID
@@LANGUAGE	Current language name
@@MAX_CONNECTIONS	Max simultaneous connections
@@MAX_PRECISION	Precision level for decimal and numeric datatypes
@@MICROSOFTVERSION	Internal version number of SQL Server
@@NESTLEVEL	Current nested level of calling routines from 0 to 16
@@PACK_RECEIVED	Number of input packets read
@@PACKET_SENT	Number of output packets written
@@PACKET_ERRORS	Number of read and write packet errors
@@PROCID	Current stored procedure ID
@@ROWCOUNT	Number of rows affected by last query
@@SERVERNAME	Name of local server
@@SERVICENAME	Name of the running service
@@SPID	Current process server ID
@@TEXTSIZE	Current max of text or image data with default of 4K
@@TIMETICKS	Number of microseconds per tick-machine independent; tick is 31.25 milliseconds or 1/32 second.
@@TOTAL_ERRORS	Number of errors during reads or writes

Global Variable	Description
@@TOTAL_READ	Number of disk reads (not cache)
@@TOTAL_WRITE	Number of disk writes
@@TRANCOUNT	Current total active user transactions
@@VERSION	Date and version of SQL Server

In the following example, a global variable is used to retrieve the version of SQL Server, which is concatenated with a string literal and the contents of a second global variable.

```
PRINT @@VERSION
declare @mess1 char(21)
select @mess1 = 'Server name is ' + @@servername
PRINT @mess1

SQL Server for Windows NT 4.20 (Intel X86)
      Aug 24 1993 00:00:00

(1 row(s) affected)

Server name is BOB486
```

Using Additional Procedure and Batch Keywords

Several additional keywords can be used within stored procedures or batches of Transact-SQL commands. These additional keywords don't fall into a single descriptive category of similar function. Some of these keywords are GOTO, RETURN, RAISERROR, WAITFOR, and CASE.

Using *GOTO*

You use a GOTO to perform a transfer from a statement to another statement that contains a user-defined label. A GOTO statement used alone is unconditional. The statement that contains the destination label name follows rules for identifiers and is followed by a colon (:).

You only use the label name without the colon on the GOTO line. The syntax of the GOTO statement is

```
label:
```

```
GOTO label
```

The following example shows the use of the GOTO statement that is used to transfer control to a statement that displays the word yes until the value of a variable reaches a specified value. The COUNT was turned off prior to execution of the statements in the example.

```
declare @count smallint
select @count =1
restart:
```

Part

IV

Ch

13

```
print 'yes'
select @count =@count + 1
while @count <= 4
goto restart

yes
yes
yes
yes
```

Using *RETURN*

You use the RETURN statement to formally exit from a query or procedure and optionally provide a value to the calling routine. A RETURN is often used when one procedure is executed from
within another. The RETURN statement, when used alone, is unconditional, though you can use
the RETURN within a conditional IF or WHILE statement. The syntax of the RETURN statement is:

```
RETURN [integer]
```

You can use a RETURN statement at any point in a batch or procedure. Any statements that follow the RETURN are not executed. A RETURN is similar to a BREAK with one difference. A RETURN,
unlike a BREAK, can be used to return an integer value to the procedure that invoked the procedure that contains the RETURN. Execution of statements continue at the statement following the
statement that executed the procedure originally.

To understand the use of the RETURN statement, you must first understand the action performed by SQL Server when a procedure completes execution. SQL Server always makes an
integer value available when a procedure ends. A value of zero indicates that the procedure
executed successfully. Negative values from –1 to –99 indicate reasons for the failure of statements within the procedure. These integer values are always returned at the termination of a
procedure even if a RETURN statement isn't present in a procedure.

You can optionally use an integer value that follows the RETURN statement to replace the SQL
Server value with your own user-defined value. You should use non-zero integer values so that
your return status values don't conflict with the SQL Server status values. If no user-defined
return value is provided, the SQL Server value is used. If more than one error occurs, the
status with the highest absolute value is returned. You can't return a NULL value with a RETURN
statement. Table 13.2 shows several of the return status values that are reserved by SQL
Server.

Table 13.2 Selected Microsoft SQL Server Status Values

ReturnValue	Meaning
0	Successful execution
–1	Missing object
–2	Datatype error
–3	Process was chosen as a deadlock victim

ReturnValue	Meaning
–4	Permission error
–5	Syntax error
–6	Miscellaneous user error
–7	Resource error, such as out of space
–8	Nonfatal internal problem
–9	System limit was reached
–10	Fatal internal inconsistency
–11	Fatal internal inconsistency
–12	Table or index is corrupt
–13	Database is corrupt
–14	Hardware error

You must provide a local variable that receives the returned status in the EXECUTE statement that invokes the procedure that returns status. The syntax to specify a local variable for the returned status value is the following:

```
EXEC[ute] @return_status=procedure_name
```

The following example shows a return value from a called procedure that executes successfully and returns zero (0). The example shows the definition of the called procedure proc1. This stored procedure is executed from a set of Transact-SQL statements entered interactively.

N O T E When a set of Transact-SQL statements execute together, whether the statements are part of a procedure or not, the rules for batch operations apply. This is true even if the set of statements are typed in interactively. ▪

N O T E A procedure that is invoked within another procedure with an EXECUTE statement is most often referred to as a *called procedure*. Call refers to an equivalent operation used in some programming languages. The keyword used in these languages to invoke the equivalent of a section of code from a program is CALL. This is the same as running a subroutine or function in these other languages. ▪

Part
IV

Ch
13

Although the called procedure doesn't contain a RETURN statement, SQL Server returns an integer status value to the procedure that called proc1.

```
create procedure proc1 as
select * from employees

declare @status int
execute @status = proc1
```

```
select status = @status

name                    department              badge
-------------------     --------------------    ----------
Bob Smith               Sales                   1234
Mary Jones              Sales                   5514

(2 row(s) affected)

status
----------
0

(1 row(s) affected)
```

In the following example, proc2 is identical to the procedure proc1 that was used in the previous example except that proc2 contains a RETURN statement with a user-defined positive integer value. A SELECT statement is to display the returned status value from proc2 to confirm that the specified value on the RETURN statement in proc2 is returned to the next statement after the statement that executed proc2.

```
create procedure proc2 as
select * from employees
return 5

declare @status int
execute @status = proc2
select status = @status

name                    department              badge
-------------------     --------------------    ----------
Bob Smith               Sales                   1234
Mary Jones              Sales                   5514

(1 row(s) affected)

status
----------
5

(1 row(s) affected)
```

In the following example, the returned value is checked as part of a conditional statement and a message displayed if the procedure executed successfully. This third example of Transact-SQL return statements is more typical of the usage of return status in a production environment.

```
declare @status int
execute @status = proc1
if (@status = 0)
begin
      print ''
      print 'proc1 executed successfully'
end
```

```
name                  department            badge
-------------------   -------------------   ----------
Bob Smith             Sales                 1234
Mary Jones            Sales                 5514

proc2 executed successfully
```

 TIP You can nest procedures within other procedures up to 16 levels in Transact-SQL.

Using *RAISERROR*

You use the RAISERROR statement to return a user-specified message in the same form that SQL Server returns errors. The RAISERROR also sets a system flag to record that an error has occurred. The syntax of the RAISERROR statement is

```
RAISERROR (<integer_expression>¦<'text of message'>, [severity] [, state[,
argument1] [, argument2] )
[WITH LOG]
```

The integer_expression is a user-specified error or message number and must be in the range 50,000 to 2,147,483,647. The integer_expression is placed in the global variable, @@ERROR, which stores the last error number returned. An error message can be specified as a string literal or through a local variable. The text of the message can be up to 255 characters and is used to specify a user-specified error message. A local variable that contains an error message can be used in place of the text of the message. RAISERROR always sets a default severity level of 16 for the returned error message.

In the following example, a local variable is defined as a character datatype that is large enough to receive the error number specified in the RAISERROR statement after the error number is converted from the global variable, @@ERROR. The RAISERROR statement first displays the message level, state number, and the error message, Guru meditation error. The error number 99999 is then displayed separately using a PRINT statement.

```
declare @err char(5)
raiserror 99999 'Guru meditation error'
select @err=convert(char(5),@@ERROR)
print @err
go
Msg 99999, Level 16, State 1
Guru meditation error

(1 row(s) affected)

99999
```

You can also add your message text and an associated message number to the system table sysmessages. You use the system stored procedure, sp_addmessage, to add a message with a message identification number within the range 50,001 and 2,147,483,647. The syntax of the sp_addmessage system procedure is as follows:

```
sp_addmessage message_id, severity, message text' [, language [, {true ¦ false}
[, REPLACE]]]
```

> **CAUTION**
>
> If you enter a user-specified error number that has not been added to the sysmessages table and do not explicitly specify the message text, you'll receive an error that the message can't be located in the system table as shown in the following example:
>
> ```
> raiserror (99999,7,2)
> go
> Msg 2758, Level 16, State 1
> RAISERROR could not locate entry for error 99999 in Sysmessages.
> ```

User-defined error messages that are generated with a RAISERROR statement without a number in the sysmessages table return a message identification number of 50,000.

The severity level is used to indicate the degree or extent of the error condition encountered. Although severity levels can be assigned in the range of one through 25, you should usually assign your system message a severity level value from 11–16.

Severity levels of 11–16 are designed to be assigned through the sp_addmessages statement and you can't assign a severity level of from 19–25 unless you're logged in as the administrator. Severity levels 17–19 are more severe software or hardware errors, which may not permit your subsequent statements to execute correctly.

Severity levels of 20–25 are severe errors and won't permit subsequent Transact-SQL statements to execute. System messages that have severity levels over 19 can be such problems as connection problems between a client system and the database server system or corrupted data in the database.

N O T E Microsoft suggests that severe errors—those that have a severity level of 19 or higher—should also notify the database administrator. The database administrator needs to know of these problems because such problems are likely to impact many different users and should be attended to as soon as possible. ■

When specifying messages, you enter an error message within single quotes of up to 255 characters. The remaining parameters of the sp_addmessage procedure are optional. The language parameter specifies one of the languages SQL Server was installed with. U.S. English is the default language if the parameter is omitted.

The next parameter, either True or False, controls whether the system message is automatically written to the Windows NT application event log. Use True to have the system message written to the event log. In addition, True results in the message being written to the SQL Server error log file.

The last parameter, REPLACE, is used to specify that you want to replace an existing user-defined message in the sysmessages table with a new entry.

The following example shows the use of the sp_addmessage system stored procedure that adds a system message with an associated identification number and severity. A subsequent SELECT statement retrieves the message from the system table sysmessages. Finally, the RAISERROR statement is used to return the user-defined system message.

```
sp_addmessage 99999,13,'Guru meditation error'
go
select * from sysmessages where error=99999
go
raiserror (99999, 13,-1)
go
New message added.
error        severity dlevel description              languid
..........   ........ ...... .................... ......
99999        13       0       Guru meditation error    0

(1 row(s) affected)

Msg 99999, Level 13, State 1
Guru meditation error
```

You can use the system stored procedure, sp_dropmessage, to remove a user-defined message from the system table sysmessages when it is no longer needed. The syntax of the sp_dropmessage is as follows:

```
sp_dropmessage [message_id [, language ¦ 'all']]
```

You're only required to enter the message number to drop the message. The two additional optional parameters permit you to specify the language from which the message should be dropped. You can use the keyword all to drop the user-defined message from all languages.

In the following example, a user-defined message in the default language of U.S. English is removed from the system table, sysmessages.

```
sp_dropmessage 99999
go
Message dropped.
```

Using *WAITFOR*

You use a WAITFOR statement to specify a time, a time interval, or an event for executing a statement, statement block, stored procedure, or transaction. The syntax of the WAITFOR statement is as follows:

```
WAITFOR {DELAY <'time'> ¦ TIME <'time'> ¦ ERROREXIT ¦ PROCESSEXIT ¦ MIRROREXIT}
```

The meaning of each of the keywords that follow the WAITFOR keyword is shown in the following list:

- DELAY—Specifies an interval or time to elapse
- TIME—A specified time (no date portion) of up to 24 hours
- ERROREXIT—Until a process terminates abnormally
- PROCESSEXIT—Until a process terminates normally or abnormally
- MIRROREXIT—Until a mirrored device fails

In the following example of a WAITFOR statement, a DELAY is used to specify that a pause of forty seconds is taken before the subsequent SELECT statement is executed.

```
waitfor delay '00:00:40'
select * from employees
```

In the second WAITFOR example, a TIME is used to wait until 3:10:51 PM of the current day until the subsequent SELECT statement is executed.

```
waitfor time '15:10:51'
select * from employees
```

Using *CASE* Expressions

You can use a CASE expression to make a execution decision based on multiple options. Using the CASE construct, you can create a table that will be used to lookup the results you are testing and apply them to determine what course of action should be taken. The syntax of the CASE expression is as follows:

```
CASE [expression]
WHEN simple expression1¦Boolean expression1 THEN expression1
[[WHEN simple expression2¦Boolean expression2 THEN expression2] […]]
      [ELSE expressionN]
END
```

If you use a comparison operator in an expression directly after the CASE keyword, the CASE expression is called a *searched expression* rather than a *simple* CASE expression. You can also use a Boolean operator in a searched CASE expression.

In a simple CASE expression, the expression directly after the CASE keyword always exactly matches a value after the WHEN keyword. In the following example, a CASE expression is used to substitute alternate values for the Department column in the Company table. In the following example, a CASE expression is used to return a corresponding set of alternate values for three department values of the table company.

```
select name,division=
case department
      when "Sales" then "Sales & Marketing"
      when "Field Service" then "Support Group"
      when "Logistics" then "Parts"
      else "Other department"
end,
badge
from company
go
name                    division            badge
------------------      ----------------    ----------
Fred Sanders            Sales & Marketing   1051
Bob Smith               Sales & Marketing   1834
Mark McGuire            Support Group       1997
Stan Humphries          Support Group       3211
Sue Sommers             Parts               4411
Lance Finepoint         Other department    5522
Fred Stanhope           Support Group       6732
```

```
Ludmilla Valencia    Other department  7773
Jim Walker           Other department  7779
Jeffrey Vickers      Other department  8005
Barbara Lint         Support Group     8883
Sally Springer       Sales & Marketing 9998

(12 row(s) affected)
```

If you don't use an ELSE as part of the CASE expression, a NULL is returned for each non-matching entry, as shown in the following example.

```
select name,division=
case department
when "Sales" then "Sales & Marketing"
when "Field Service" then "Support Group"
when "Logistics" then "Parts"
end,
badge
from company
go
name                division          badge
------------------- ----------------- ----------
Fred Sanders        Sales & Marketing 1051
Bob Smith           Sales & Marketing 1834
Mark McGuire        Support Group     1997
Stan Humphries      Support Group     3211
Sue Sommers         Parts             4411
Lance Finepoint     (null)            5522
Fred Stanhope       Support Group     6732
Ludmilla Valencia   (null)            7773
Jim Walker          (null)            7779
Jeffrey Vickers     (null)            8005
Barbara Lint        Support Group     8883
Sally Springer      Sales & Marketing 9998

(12 row(s) affected)
```

You'll recall that a searched CASE expression can include comparison operators and the use of AND as well as OR between each Boolean expression to permit an alternate value to be returned for multiple values of the column of a table. Unlike a simple CASE expression, each WHEN clause is not restricted to exact matches of the values contained in the table column.

In the following example, comparison values are used in each WHEN clause to specify a range of values that are substituted by a single alternative value.

```
select "Hours Worked" =
case
when hours_worked < 40 then "Worked Insufficient Hours"
when hours_worked = 40 then "Worked Sufficient Hours"
when hours_worked > 60 then "Overworked"
else "Outside Range of Permissible Work"
end
from pays
go
```

```
Hours Worked
---------------------------------
Worked Sufficient Hours
Worked Sufficient Hours
Overworked
Worked Insufficient Hours
Overworked
Worked Sufficient Hours
Overworked
Worked Sufficient Hours
Outside Range of Permissible Work
Worked Insufficient Hours
Worked Sufficient Hours
Worked Sufficient Hours

(12 row(s) affected)
```

N O T E   When a CASE construct it executed, only the first matching solution is executed. ■

CAUTION

You must use compatible datatypes for the replacement expression of the THEN clause. If the replacement expression of a THEN clause is a datatype that is incompatible with the original expression, an error is returned.

For example, a combination of original and replacement datatypes is compatible if the one is a variable length character datatype (varchar) with a maximum length equal to the length of a fixed length character datatype (char). In addition, if the two datatypes in the WHEN and THEN clauses are integer and decimal, the resultant datatype returned will be decimal in order to accommodate the whole and fractional portion of the numeric value.

You can also use both the COALESCE and NULLIF functions in a CASE expression. You use the COALESCE function to return a replacement value for any NULL or NOT NULL values that are present in, for example, the column of a database table. The syntax of one form of the COALESCE function is

COALESCE (expression1, expression2)

In the following example, the COALESCE function is used to display either the product of hours_worked times rate or a zero if the columns hours_worked and rate are NULL.

```
select badge, "Weekly Pay in Dollars"=coalesce(hours_worked*rate,0)
from pays2
go
badge       Weekly Pay in Dollars
----------  ----------------------
3211        400
6732        360
4411        520
5522        429
1997        510
```

```
9998        320
7773        550
8883        360
8005        420
7779        407
1834        400
1051        360
3467          0
3555          0
7774          0

(15 row(s) affected)
```

N O T E A COALESCE function is equivalent to a searched CASE expression where a NOT NULL expression1 returns expression1 and a NULL expression1 returns expression2. An equivalent CASE expression to a COALESCE function is as follows:

```
CASE
     WHEN expression1 IS NOT NULL THEN expression1
     ELSE expression2
END
```

You can use a COALESCE function as part of a SELECT statement simply as an alternative way of returning an identical display or because you find the COALESCE function simpler to use. ■

You can also use a NULLIF function with or in place of a CASE expression. The NULLIF function uses the following syntax:

```
NULLIF (expression1, expression2)
```

In the following example, a simple SELECT statement is first used to display the table without using a NULLIF function to show all column values for all rows. A second SELECT statement is used to operate on the columns, badge and old_badge.

```
select * from company2
go
name                 department           badge       old_badge
-------------------- -------------------- ----------- ----------
Mark McGuire         Field Service        1997        (null)
Stan Humphries       Field Service        3211        (null)
Sue Sommers          Logistics            4411        (null)
Fred Stanhope        Field Service        6732        (null)
Ludmilla Valencia    Software             7773        (null)
Jim Walker           Unit Manager         7779        (null)
Jeffrey Vickers      Mailroom             8005        (null)
Fred Sanders         SALES                1051        1051
Bob Smith            SALES                1834        1834
Sally Springer       Sales                9998        9998
Barbara Lint         Field Service        8883        12
Lance Finepoint      Library              5522        13

(12 row(s) affected)

select name,nullif(old_badge,badge)
from company2
```

Part
IV

Ch

13

```
go
name
------------------- ----------
Mark McGuire          (null)
Stan Humphries        (null)
Sue Sommers           (null)
Fred Stanhope         (null)
Ludmilla Valencia     (null)
Jim Walker            (null)
Jeffrey Vickers       (null)
Fred Sanders          (null)
Bob Smith             (null)
Sally Springer        (null)
Barbara Lint          12
Lance Finepoint       13

(12 row(s) affected)
```

The example only returns non-null values for rows that contain old_badge values that are different than new column values. In addition, a NULL is returned if no old column values were present. You can combine the use of the NULLIF and COALESCE functions to display the returned information in a more organized way.

The following example combines a COALESCE and NULLIF function to return an old badge number only if it was different than the current badge number or if it was defined. Otherwise, a new badge number is displayed.

```
select name,badge=coalesce(nullif(old_badge,badge),badge)
from company2
go
name                  badge
------------------- ----------
Mark McGuire          1997
Stan Humphries        3211
Sue Sommers           4411
Fred Stanhope         6732
Ludmilla Valencia     7773
Jim Walker            7779
Jeffrey Vickers       8005
Fred Sanders          1051
Bob Smith             1834
Sally Springer        9998
Barbara Lint          12
Lance Finepoint       13

(12 row(s) affected)
```

From Here...

In this chapter, you've seen how you can use Transact-SQL to control the flow of your SQL Server–based application. Remembering to use these techniques to manipulate information on the server can significantly improve performance for your application.

Here are some other areas of interest that relate to the materials you've been working with here:

- Chapter 4, "Creating Devices, Databases, and Transaction Logs," teach you how to create and use user-defined datatypes.
- Chapter 11, "Managing and Using Rules and Defaults," teaches you how to create and use rules and defaults.
- Chapter 14, "Creating and Managing Triggers," teaches you how to use triggers to maintain referential integrity in the database.
- Chapter 17, "Optimizing Performance," teaches you ways to optimize the operation of Microsoft SQL Server, including the correct sizing of the procedure cache.

Part
IV

Ch
13

Creating and Managing Triggers

Triggers are methods that SQL Server provides to the application programmer and database analyst to ensure data integrity. Triggers are very useful for those databases that are going to be accessed from a multitude of different applications because they enable business rules to be enforced by the database instead of relying on the application software. ■

How to use triggers to enforce data integrity

SQL Server's triggers allow you to enforce very customized referential integrity.

How to find out information about triggers

SQL Server provides a number of system-stored procedures that can be used to view information on triggers.

Trigger examples and tips on how to write your own triggers

In this chapter you will see practical examples of how to write triggers that, for example, send e-mail.

Understanding SQL Server Triggers

A *trigger* is a special type of stored procedure that is executed by the SQL Server automatically when a particular table modification is applied by SQL Server (or hits) a given table. The most common use of a trigger is to enforce business rules in the database. Triggers are used when the standard constraints or table-based *Declarative Referential Integrities* (DRI) are not adequate. If a DRI constraint is enforced by SQL Server, then the trigger will not be executed because it was not needed.

Triggers have a very low impact on performance to the server and are often used to enhance applications that have to do a lot of cascading operations on other tables and rows.

▶ **See** Chapter 10, "Managing and Using Indexes and Keys," **p. 273** and Chapter 11, "Managing and Using Rules and Defaults," for more information about DRI. **p. 301**

In SQL Server 6, Microsoft added ANSI compliant DRI statements that can be used in the CREATE TABLE statement. The sorts of rules that can be enforced by them are relatively complex; however, it makes the understanding of the table creation quite difficult.

Besides the inability to perform complex business rule analysis based on values that are supplied when a trigger is executed, DRI has one important limitation: the current implementation does not permit referencing values in other databases. Although this may seem a relatively insignificant problem, it has a substantial impact on those people trying to write distributed applications that may need to check data constraints/values on other databases and servers.

Creating Triggers

Creating a trigger is much like declaring a stored procedure, and it has a similar syntax, as follows:

```
CREATE TRIGGER [owner.]trigger_name
ON [owner.]table_name
FOR {INSERT, UPDATE, DELETE}
[WITH ENCRYPTION]
AS sql_statements
```

The options for the Transact-SQL command CREATE TRIGGER are as follows:

- trigger_name—The name of the trigger must conform to standard SQL Server naming conventions.

- INSERT, UPDATE, DELETE—With these keywords, the trigger's scope is defined. This determines which actions will initiate the trigger.

- WITH ENCRYPTION—This option is provided for developers to prevent users in their environment from being able to read the text of the trigger after it has been loaded onto the server. This is very convenient for third-party application developers who embed SQL Server into their products and do not want their customers to be able to disassemble the code and modify it.

SQL Server stores the text of a trigger in the system catalog table syscomments. Use the WITH ENCRYPTION option with care because if the original trigger text is lost, it will not be possible to restore the encrypted text from syscomments.

> **CAUTION**
>
> SQL Server uses the unencrypted text of a trigger stored in syscomments when a database is upgraded to a newer version. If the text is encrypted, it will not be possible for the trigger to be updated and restored into the new database. Make sure that the original text is available to upgrade the database when necessary.

N O T E To provide a good level of recovery for your applications, you should always maintain an offline copy of your stored procedures, triggers, table definitions and overall structure of the server-side of your SQL Server application. This information can be used to reload the server in case of any problems. ▪

- sql_statements—A trigger may contain any number of SQL statements in Transact-SQL, provided they are enclosed in valid BEGIN and END delimiters. Limitations on the SQL permitted in a trigger are described in the next section.

N O T E When a trigger is executed, a special table is created by SQL Server into which the data that caused the trigger to execute is placed. The table is either inserted for INSERT and UPDATE operations or deleted for DELETE and UPDATE operations. Because triggers execute after an operation, the rows in the inserted table are always a duplicate of one or more records in the trigger's base table. Make sure that a correct join identifies all the characteristics of the record being affected in the trigger table so that data is not accidentally modified by the trigger itself. (See the following examples to get an idea of how to construct a trigger.) ▪

Examining Limitations of Triggers

SQL Server has some limitations on the types of SQL statements that can be executed while performing the actions of a trigger. The majority of these limitations are because the SQL cannot be rolled back (or inside a transaction), which may need to occur if the UPDATE, INSERT, or DELETE that caused the trigger to execute in the first place is also rolled back.

The following is a list of Transact-SQL statements that are not permitted to be in the body text of a trigger. SQL Server will reject the compilation and storing of a trigger with these statements:

- All database and object creation statements: CREATE DATABASE, TABLE, INDEX, PROCEDURE, DEFAULT, RULE, TRIGGER, and VIEW
- All DROP statements
- Database object modification statements: ALTER TABLE and ALTER DATABASE
- TRUNCATE TABLE

Part IV
Ch 14

N O T E   DELETE triggers will not be executed when a TRUNCATE operation is initiated on a table. Because the TRUNCATE operation is not logged, there is no chance for the trigger to be run. However, permission to perform a TRUNCATE is limited to the table owner and to *sa*—and it cannot be transferred. ■

- Object permissions: GRANT and REVOKE
- UPDATE STATISTICS
- RECONFIGURE
- Database load operations: LOAD DATABASE and LOAD TRANSACTION
- All physical disk modification statements: DISK...
- Temporary table creation: either implicit through CREATE TABLE or explicit through SELECT INTO

Additionally, the following are limitations that should be clearly understood:

- A trigger may not be created on a view, but only on the base table or tables that the view was created on.
- Any SET operations that change the environment, while valid, are only in effect for the life of the trigger. All values return to their previous states once the trigger has finished execution.
- Manipulating binary large object (BLOB) columns of datatype TEXT or IMAGE, whether logged or not by the database, will not cause a trigger to be executed.
- SELECT operations that return result sets from a trigger are not advised because of the very special handling of result sets that would be required by the client application code (whether in a stored procedure or not). Take care to make sure that all SELECT operations read their values into locally defined variables available in the trigger.

Using Triggers

In this section you will see several types of triggers being created for use. These examples aren't very sophisticated but should give you ideas on how you might implement triggers in your own environment.

Triggers are *fired* or *executed* whenever a particular event occurs. In the following sections you will see the different events that can cause a trigger to be executed and some idea of what you may want to do on those events.

Using *INSERT* and *UPDATE* Triggers

INSERT and UPDATE triggers are particularly useful because they can enforce referential integrity constraints and make sure that your data is valid before it enters the table. Typically INSERT and UPDATE triggers are used to verify that the data on the columns being monitored by the trigger meets the criteria required or to update timestamp columns. Triggers are used when the criteria for verification is more complex than what can be represented in a declarative referential integrity constraint.

In Listing 14.1, the trigger is executed whenever a record is inserted into the Sales table or when it is modified. If the order date is not during the first 15 days of the month, the record is rejected.

On the CD

Listing 14.1   14_01.SQL—*SALES* Trigger Disallowing Specified Records

```
Create Trigger Tri_Ins_Sales
On      SALES
For     INSERT, UPDATE
As

/* declare local variables needed */
Declare      @nDayOfMonth        tinyint

/* Find the information about the record inserted */
Select      @nDayOfMonth = DatePart( Day, I.ORD_DATE )
From   SALES S, INSERTED I
Where  S.STOR_ID = I.STOR_ID
And    S.ORD_NUM = I.ORD_NUM
And    S.TITLE_ID = I.TITLE_ID

/* Now test rejection criteria and return an error if necessary */
If @nDayOfMonth > 15
Begin
      /* Note: always Rollback first, you can never be sure what
      kind of error processing a client may do that may force locks
      to be held for unnecessary amounts of time */
      ROLLBACK TRAN
      RAISERROR ( 'Orders must be placed before the 15th of
                  the month', 16, 10 )
End
Go
```

N O T E   Notice the way the inserted table is referred to in the previous join. This *logical* table is created specially by SQL Server to allow you to reference information in the record being modified. Using an alias I (as shown) makes it easy to reference the table in the join criteria specified in the Where clause. ■

Using *DELETE* Triggers

DELETE triggers are typically used for two reasons. The first reason is to prevent deleting records that will have data integrity problems if they indeed are deleted (for example, they are used as foreign keys to other tables). The second reason for a DELETE trigger (which is really an extension of the first reason) is to perform a cascading delete operation that deletes children records of a master record such as deleting all the order items from a master sales record.

Part
IV

Ch
14

In Listing 14.2, the trigger is executed whenever a user attempts to delete a record from the Stores table. If there are sales at that store, then the request is denied.

On the CD

Listing 14.2   14_02.SQL—*STORES* Trigger Disallowing Removal of More Than One Store

```
Create Trigger Tri_Del_Stores
On    STORES
For   DELETE
As

/* First check the number of rows modified and disallow
anybody from deleting more than one store at a time */
If @@RowCount > 1
Begin
     ROLLBACK TRAN
     RAISERROR ( 'You can only delete one store at a time.', 16, 10 )
End

/* declare a temp var to store the store
that is being delete */
Declare    @sStorID char(4)

/* now get the value of the author being nuked */
Select     @sStorID = D.STOR_ID
From   STORES S, DELETED D
Where S.STOR_ID = D.STOR_ID

If exists (Select *
           From    SALES
           Where   STOR_ID = @sStorID )
Begin
     ROLLBACK TRAN
     RAISERROR ( 'This store cannot be deleted because there are
                 still sales valid in the SALES table.', 16, 10 )
End
Go
```

TIP   Use RAISERROR as an easy way to send the calling process or user detailed and specific information about the error to the calling process or user. RAISERROR allows you to specify error text, severity levels and state information—all of which combined make for more descriptive errors for the user (it also makes it easy to write generic error-handlers in your client applications).

Using Triggers That Send E-Mail

One of the better features of SQL Server is its ability to invoke behavior directly from the operating system. The sort of behavior must be predefined through SQL Server's Extended procedures, but they allow you to create incredibly powerful trigger operations. SQL Server is relatively unique in its ability to support operating system-specific features. This is achieved because it only runs on Windows NT, which has a very standardized programming interface across all of its supported hardware platforms (Intel, MIPS, Alpha, and PowerPC).

Triggers can call any of the extended procedures (xp_*) available to the server and any external procedures that you add to the server with the sp_addextendedproc command. In Listing 14.3, the trigger demonstrates sending e-mail when a record is deleted from the underlying Authors table.

On the CD

Listing 14.3   14_03.SQL—Trigger Sending E-Mail to *ChiefPublisher* Indicating Author Deleted from System

```
Create Trigger Tri_Del_Authors_Mail
On      AUTHORS
For     DELETE
As

/* declare some variables to store the author's name */
Declare     @sLName varchar(40),
      @sFName varchar(20),
      @sAuthor varchar(60)

/* now get the value of the author being removed */
Select      @sLName = D.AU_LNAME,
      @sFName = D.AU_FNAME
From  AUTHORS A, DELETED D
Where A.AU_ID = D.AU_ID

/* Send mail message */
Select @sAuthor = @sLName + ', ' + @sFName
exec master.dbo.xp_sendmail @recipient = 'ChiefPublisher',
@message = 'deleted ' + @sAuthor
Go
```

Using Nested Triggers

Triggers can be nested up to 16 layers deep. However, if it is not desirable to have nested trigger operations, SQL Server can be configured to disallow them. Use the nested triggers option of sp_configure to toggle this option.

▶ **See** the Chapter 16 section entitled "Displaying and Setting Server Options," for more information on sp_configure and other options. **p. 408**

Triggers become nested when, during execution of one trigger, it modifies another table on which there is another trigger—which is therefore executed.

Part
IV

Ch
14

T I P

You can check your nesting level at any time by inspecting the value in @@NestLevel. The value will be between 0 and 16.

SQL Server cannot detect nesting that causes an infinite loop during the creation of a trigger until the situation occurs at execution time. An infinite loop could be caused by having a trigger, TRIGGER_A on TABLE_A, that executes on an update of TABLE_A, causing an update on TABLE_B. TABLE_B has a similar trigger, TRIGGER_B, that is executed on an update and causes an update of TABLE_A. Thus, if a user updates either table, then the two triggers would keep executing each other indefinitely. If SQL Server detects such an occurrence, it shuts down or cancels the trigger.

N O T E If a trigger causes an additional modification of the table from which it was executed, it does not cause itself to be executed recursively. SQL Server has no support for *re-entrant* or *recursive* stored procedures or triggers in the current version. ∎

For example, suppose we have two triggers: one on the Sales table and one on the STORES table. The two triggers are defined in Listing 14.4.

On the CD

Listing 14.4   14_04.SQL—Two Triggers Nested if Delete Occurs on Sales Table

```
/* First trigger deletes stores if the sales are deleted */
Create   Trigger Tri_Del_Sales
On       SALES
For      DELETE
As


/* Announce the trigger being executed */
Print "Delete trigger on the sales table is executing..."

/* declare a temp var to store the store
that is being deleted */
Declare @sStorID char(4),
        @sMsg    varchar(40)

/* now get the value of the store being deleted */
Select  @sStorID = STOR_ID
From    DELETED          /* DELETED is a fake table created
                           by SQLServer to hold the values of
                           records deleted */
Group By STOR_ID

/* Now delete the store record */
Select @sMsg = "Deleting store " + @sStorID

Print @sMsg

Delete      STORES
Where       STOR_ID = @sStorID
Go


/* Second trigger deletes discounts if a store is deleted */
Create   Trigger Tri_Del_Stores
On       STORES
```

```
For     DELETE
As

/* Announce the trigger being executed */
Print "Delete trigger on the Stores table is executing..."

/* declare a temp var to store the store
that is being deleted */
Declare @sStorID char(4),
        @sMsg    varchar(40)

/* now get the value of the store being deleted */
Select  @sStorID = sTOR_ID
From    DELETED            /* DELETED is a fake table created
                             by SQLServer to hold the values of
                             records deleted */
Group By STOR_ID

If @@rowcount = 0
Begin
        Print "No Rows affected on the stores table"
        Return
End

/* Now delete the store record */
Select @sMsg = "Deleting discounts for store " + @sStorID

Print @sMsg

Delete  DISCOUNTS
Where   STOR_ID = @sStorID
Go
```

If a DELETE is executed on the Sales table (as shown in Listing 14.5), the trigger is executed on the Sales table, which in turns causes a trigger to execute on the Stores table.

Listing 14.5 Results of Executing Delete on Sales Table

```
/*---------------------------
Delete from sales where stor_id = '8042'
---------------------------*/
Delete trigger on the sales table is executing...
Deleting store 8042
Delete trigger on the Stores table is executing...
Deleting discounts for store 8042
```

TIP Triggers and DRI don't typically work together very well. For example, in Listing 14.5, you must first drop the Foreign Key constraint on the Discounts table for it to actually complete the delete. It is recommended that wherever possible you implement either triggers or DRI for integrity constraints.

Displaying Trigger Information

If you need to view the behavior that is being enforced on a table due to a trigger, you must display the information that describes the triggers (if any) that a table owns. There are a number of ways of obtaining information about a trigger that is on any given table. In this section, the two most common, using SQL Enterprise Manager (SQL EM) and the system procedures sp_help and sp_depends, will be demonstrated.

Using SQL Enterprise Manager

To view information about a trigger using the SQL Enterprise Manager, perform the following steps:

1. Run SQL Enterprise Manager from the Microsoft SQL Server 6.5 group.

2. Select the server that you want to work on.

3. Select the table that you want to work on (see fig. 14.1).

FIG. 14.1

Once a table is highlighted you can click on the right mouse button and use quick menu to perform common operations that are also available on the Manage menu.

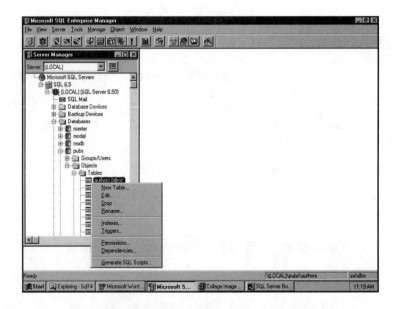

4. From the Manage menu, select Triggers (see fig. 14.2).

FIG. 14.2

In the Manage Triggers window of SQL Enterprise Manager, the second combo box on the toolbar lists the triggers that are active on the table in the first combo box.

Using *sp_help*, *sp_depends*, and *sp_helptext*

The system procedures, `sp_help`, `sp_depends`, and `sp_helptext`, will provide valuable information in determining if a trigger exists, what it references, and what its actual text or source code looks like—provided the `ENCRYPTION` option was not used during trigger creation.

Using *sp_help* `sp_help` is a generic system procedure that reports information about any object in the database. The following syntax can be used:

```
sp_help [object_name]
```

If the *object_name* is omitted, SQL Server will report information on all user objects found in the *sysobjects* system catalog table.

Sp_help is useful to determine who created a trigger and when it was created. Here is an example of the output from `sp_help` when used on the trigger created below, `Tri_Del_Authors`:

Listing 14.6   Using *sp_help* to View Information About *Tri_Del_Authors*

```
/*---------------------------
sp_help Tri_Del_Authors
---------------------------*/
Name                 Owner         Type                 When_created
-------------------- ------------  -------------------  --------------
Tri_Del_Authors      dbo           trigger              Nov 26 1995  4:37PM

Data_located_on_segment
--------------------
not applicable
```

Listing 14.7 shows a more advanced trigger that will be used in the following sections.

Listing 14.7 14_5.SQL—Advanced Trigger Demonstrating Information Returned from *sp_helptext*

```
/* create a basic trigger to stop anyone deleting an
author that still has records titleauthor table */

Create Trigger Tri_Del_Authors
On      AUTHORS
For     DELETE
As

/* First check the number of rows modified and disallow
anybody from removing more than one author at a time */
If @@RowCount > 1
Begin
        ROLLBACK TRAN
        RAISERROR ( 'You can only delete one author at a time.', 16, 10 )
End

/* declare a temp var to store the author
that is being deleted */
Declare      @nAuID id

/* now get the value of the author being deleted */
Select       @nAuID = D.AU_ID
From   AUTHORS A, DELETED D    /* DELETED is a fake table created
                                 by SQL Server to hold the values of
                                 records deleted */
Where A.AU_ID = D.AU_ID

If exists (Select       *
           From   TITLEAUTHOR
           Where AU_ID = @nAuID )
Begin
        ROLLBACK TRAN
        RAISERROR ( 'This author cannot be deleted because he/
                    she still has valid titles.', 16, 10 )
End
Go
```

Using *sp_depends*   sp_depends is a useful system-stored procedure that will return a database object's dependencies, such as tables, views, and stored procedures. The syntax is as follows:

```
sp_depends object_name
```

After adding the trigger shown in Listing 14.7, Listing 14.8 shows the output from sp_depends when run on the Authors table.

Listing 14.8 Using *sp_depends* to View Dependency Information on the Authors Table

```
/*--------------------------
sp_depends authors
--------------------------*/
In the current database the specified object is referenced by the following:
name                                    type
---------------------------------- ---------------
dbo.reptq2                              stored procedure
dbo.titleview                           view
dbo.Tri_Del_Authors                     trigger
```

Using *sp_helptext* User defined objects, such as rules, defaults, views, stored procedures, and triggers, store their text in the system catalog table, syscomments. This table is not the most easy to read, so the sp_helptext procedure is provided to enable easier access.

The syntax for sp_helptext is as follows:

```
sp_helptext object_name
```

TROUBLESHOOTING

I've tried to find out the text for a stored procedure using the sp_helptext system procedure, but the only data that is returned is garbled and unreadable. The stored procedure was stored in ENCRYPTED format. Contact the creator of the procedure to get the text for the procedure. There is no way to decrypt the data. If you have lost original text and it is critical to return the information, contact Microsoft Technical Support in your region for more information.

Dropping Triggers

There are a number of reasons why you might want to remove triggers from a table or tables. For example, you might be moving into a production environment and you want to remove any triggers that were put in place to enforce good quality assurance but that were costing performance. Or you simply might want to drop a trigger so that you can replace it with a newer version.

To drop a trigger, use the following syntax:

```
DROP TRIGGER [owner.]trigger_name[,[owner.]trigger_name…]
```

Dropping a trigger is not necessary if a new trigger is to be created that will replace the existing one. Note also that by dropping a table, all its child-related objects, such as triggers, will also be dropped.

Part

IV

Ch

14

The following example drops the trigger created above:

```
Drop Trigger Tri_Del_Authors
```

From Here...

In this chapter, you learned about the values of triggers and how they can be applied to enforce referential integrity in your application. In addition, you learned that triggers can be nested and that they can be used to provide more complex business rule validation than CONSTRAINTs that can be defined during table creation.

Look at the following chapter for more information that may be useful in helping you write effective triggers:

- Chapter 10, "Managing and Using Indexes and Keys," discusses how to enforce integrity constraints through table-based declarative referential integrity and unique indexes.
- Chapter 11, "Managing and Using Rules and Defaults," shows a different way to enforce integrity constraints on table columns through rules and bound table defaults.
- Chapter 13, "Managing Stored Procedures and Using Flow-Control Statements," provides information on how to create stored procedures that you can execute as triggers.

Creating and Using Cursors

Learn how to create and use cursors

Cursors are used to process a group of records on a one-by-one basis.

Learn the difference between front-end and back-end cursors

Where a cursor is being operated from can have a significant effect on performance.

How to optimize cursor use in an application

A cursor does not automatically yield performance gains. It must be placed and used appropriately.

In SQL Server 6.0, perhaps the biggest feature that Microsoft added to the release was *back-end*, or *server*, *cursor support*. Cursors are a way of manipulating data in a set on a row-by-row basis, instead of the typical SQL commands that operate on all the rows in the set at one time. Specifically, Microsoft added a full implementation of *back-end cursors*—cursors managed by the database and that have an easy access method from front-end application development tools such as SQLWindows and PowerBuilder or other development platforms. In referring to back-end, the distinction is made so it's understood that SQL Server always could have cursors, but these were provided by the DBLibrary layer, not the server.

Cursors provide a way of doing result-set processing inside the server without the need for a client program to manage the data sets being worked on. For example, before SQL Server 6.0, it was difficult to write a fast-performing application that had to perform multiple actions on a set of data. This was because each row in the data would need to be sent back to the front end and the client application would be responsible for initiating further activity on each row. Cursors provide a way for advanced Transact-SQL stored procedures to do all this processing without needing to return to the client. ∎

Distinguishing Between Front-End and Back-End Cursors

As just mentioned, with SQL Server, two types of cursors are available for use in an application: front-end (client) cursors and back-end (server) cursors. They are two very distinct concepts, and it's important to be able to distinguish between them.

> **N O T E**   Microsoft refers to back-end cursors, or cursors that are created and managed by the database, as *server cursors*. To avoid any confusion from this point on, unless the text specifically refers to cursors on the client or server, assume that any text referencing the term *cursor* is describing a cursor that's created in the database server. ■

When writing an application, you'll often find that you need to perform a given operation on a set of data. This set-based operation can normally be performed by using an Update statement when it's necessary to change data values, or a Delete statement when it's necessary to remove data values. These set-based operations often provide great flexibility in an application—provided that the tasks that need to be performed can appropriately be defined by a Where clause. Suppose that you wanted to change the ZIP code for all those authors in the Pubs database that lived in Menlo Park to be 94024. A simple Update could be used, as Listing 15.1 shows.

On the CD

Listing 15.1   15_1.SQL—Using *Update* to Change a ZIP Code

```
Update     AUTHORS
Set    ZIP = '94024'
Where City = 'Menlo Park'
Go
```

But what if you need to do different kinds of operations on a set of data? There are two possible solutions: you can perform multiple operations on exclusive sets, or you can get the whole set of data and, based on values in it, perform the required operations. This second solution is the concept of cursor-based processing.

Relying on the set-based updates and deletes can be inefficient. This is because your updates may end up hitting the same row more than once. It's possible to create a "view" of data in the database called a *cursor*.

One of the best advantages of cursor processing is that you can perform conditional logic on a particular row of data in a set independently of the other rows that may be in a set. Effectively, you're issuing commands or SQL on single-row data sets. This granularity of processing is often required in complex applications, and has many benefits, as follows:

- *Performance.* Set-based operations tend to use more server resources, compared with cursor operations.
- *Better transaction control.* When you're processing sets of data, you can control what happens to any given row independent of the others.

- *Special syntax.* WHERE CURRENT OF cursors allow positioned Updates and Deletes that apply to the row now being fetched and directly hit the table row without the need of an index.

- *Efficiency.* When you're performing a number of operations on a large data set, such as calling multiple stored procedures, it's more efficient for the database to process the data doing all actions per row (because data is kept in memory caches) rather than perform each task serially on the entire data set.

▶ **See** the section entitled "Updating Rows," in Chapter 7. **p. 186**

Understanding Client Cursors

Before SQL Server 6.0, Microsoft realized that its customers needed to be able to process data and to scroll backward and forward through a result set. Customers needed this scrolling functionality to support complex applications that users needed for browsing data fetched from the database.

At the time, Microsoft couldn't incorporate the server-based cursors that some of the other vendors supported, and instead chose to mimic some of their behavior in their client API to the SQL Server database—DBLibrary.

N O T E DBLibrary is a client interface that Microsoft inherited from Sybase to interact with the SQL Server database. DBLibrary is a set of commands and functions that can be executed in C to perform operations on the database. With SQL Server 6.0 and later releases, Microsoft changed its preferred interface to the database to be that of ODBC. For more discussions on interfacing with the database from client applications and programming languages, see Chapters 21 and 22. ■

To achieve this functionality, Microsoft added cursors to the data sets on the client side—client cursors.

These cursors work by having DBLibrary interact with the database as normal, fetching data from the tabular data stream (TDS) as quickly as the client requests. The TDS is the method of communication that DBLibrary uses to fetch data from the database. Typically, DBLibrary will discard any data that has been fetched from the database, and then fetched to the client application—relying on the client to perform any additional work. With cursors activated, DBLibrary will cache these records itself until the client cancels the cursor view on the data.

This caching has a number of limitations:

- SQL Server has no way of controlling or minimizing the locks held on the database, and any locks held will be held for all data pages in the cursor, not just the affected data pages. This is because SQL Server is basically unaware that anything other than a select activity is occurring on the data.

- Client-side resources can be consumed very quickly if there are large sets of data.

- The caching is inefficient when processing large amounts of data because all the data is being sent across the network unnecessarily.

Clearly, Microsoft's client cursors were just a stop-gap measure until the real work of server cursors could be completed. Server cursors provide all the same benefits of client cursors without any of the overhead or limitations. Aside from backward-compatibility issues, there are few good reasons to use client cursors in a SQL Server 6.5 application.

Server cursors generally have five states when being used, as shown in Table 15.1.

Table 15.1   The States of Existence of SQL Server Cursors

State	Explanation
DECLARE	At this point, SQL Server validates that the query that's going to be used to populate the cursor is valid. SQL Server creates a structure in shared memory that has the definition of the cursor available for compilation at the OPEN phase.
OPEN	SQL Server begins to answer the DECLARE statement by resolving the query and fetching row IDs into a temporary workspace for the use of the client, should it decide to fetch the rows that this cursor has identified.
FETCH	The data is now being returned from the cursor, and any activity that's required can be performed.
CLOSE	SQL Server closes the previously opened cursor and releases any locks that it may have held as a result of opening it.
DEALLOCATE	SQL Server releases the shared memory used by the DECLARE statement, no longer permitting another process from performing an OPEN on it.

Using SQL Server Cursors

Using a cursor in SQL Server involves following the states previously described. This section explains the steps required to use a cursor effectively in your applications.

You first must declare the cursor. Once a cursor has been declared it can be opened and fetched from. During the fetch phase or state of a cursor any number of operations may be performed on the currently active row in the cursor. When you have finished working with a cursor, you need to close and deallocate it so that SQL Server does not waste resources managing it any further.

Declaring a Cursor

Declaring a cursor is very similar to requesting data using a standard Select statement. Note that the Select statement used to declare a cursor can't include any of the Transact-SQL extensions such as COMPUTE, COMPUTE BY, or SELECT INTO.

The syntax for declaring a cursor is as follows:

```
DECLARE name_of_cursor [INSENSITIVE] [SCROLL] CURSOR
FOR Select_Statement
[FOR {READ ONLY ¦ UPDATE [OF Column_List]}]
```

N O T E Because cursors must fetch row values into variables inside the stored procedure or command batch, you can't use the asterisk (*) in your Select statement. You must use named columns in the data tables that correspond one to one with the variables used in the FETCH clause. ■

The options for the Transact-SQL command DECLARE CURSOR are as follows:

- ■ *name_of_cursor*—The name of the cursor must comply with the standard object identifier rules of the database.

- ■ INSENSITIVE—A cursor created with the INSENSITIVE keyword is completely unaffected by the actions of other users. SQL Server creates a separate temporary table of all the row data that matches the query and uses this to answer requests on the cursor. Insensitive cursors aren't modifiable using the WHERE CURRENT OF cursor syntax and therefore will impose index update hits when any updates are done.

CAUTION

Be careful when using the INSENSITIVE keyword in defining a cursor. Applications that use this keyword may run into problems of inaccurate data if the application has high transaction loads on the underlying table or tables that the cursor is being opened on. If the application being written is time driven, however (for example, "Tell me what our balance sheet position is as of right now"), INSENSITIVE cursors are a requirement.

- ■ SCROLL—The SCROLL keyword (the opposite of the INSENSITIVE keyword) allows the cursor to read from committed updates and deletes made by other server processes. The SCROLL keyword is also required if the application needs to do anything other than fetch the data sequentially until the end of the result set.

- ■ READ ONLY—As its name implies, this option stops the cursor's data from being modifiable. Internally, this makes a big difference to how SQL Server chooses to retrieve the data and generally makes it more likely to hit a clustered index if one is available. Unless you need to modify data that the cursor is declared for, it's recommended that you use the READ ONLY clause. This will provide substantial performance gains.

- ■ UPDATE—This is the default option on a single table cursor like those created when you issue a select without any join conditions. A cursor declared in this fashion will allow the WHERE CURRENT OF syntax to be used.

Listing 15.2 shows a basic cursor that's being declared to fetch the data from a single table (Employee) in the Pubs database.

On the CD

Listing 15.2   15_2.SQL—Cursor Being Declared to Retrieve Information from the Employee Table

```
Declare Cur_Empl Cursor
For    Select EMP_ID,    LNAME,
              JOB_ID,    PUB_ID
       From   EMPLOYEE
       Order By EMP_ID
Go
```

The Cur_Empl cursor, as shown in Listing 15.2, provides no greater application flexibility than a simple SELECT on the data. If, however, the application required absolute row positioning, as shown in Listing 15.3, it's possible to add the SCROLL keyword to the Declare statement that makes the cursor very different in comparison to a table SELECT.

On the CD

Listing 15.3   15_3.SQL—Scrollable Cursor Being Declared to Fetch from the Employee Table

```
Declare Cur_Empl_Scrollable SCROLL Cursor
For    Select EMP_ID,    LNAME,
              JOB_ID,    PUB_ID
       From   EMPLOYEE
       Order By EMP_ID
Go
```

Opening a Cursor

After a cursor is declared, SQL Server reserves handles for its use. To use a cursor and fetch data from it, you must open the cursor. To open a cursor, use the following syntax:

```
Open Cursor_Name
```

In the preceding examples, the code required to open the cursor would have been either

```
Open Cur_Empl
```

or

```
Open Cur_Empl_Scrollable
```

When a cursor is opened, SQL Server resolves any unknown variables with their current state. If a cursor was declared with a variable in the Where clause and then opened, for example, the value used to resolve the query would be the value that the variable held at the time the cursor was opened. For example,

```
Declare     @nHighJobID integer,
            @nLowJobID  integer

Declare Cur_Empl_Where Cursor
For    Select     LNAME, FNAME
From   EMPLOYEE
```

```
Where JOB_ID Between @nLowJobID And @nHighJobID

/* note that if the cursor were to be opened now,
probably no data would be returned because the values
of @nLowJobID and @nHighJobID are NULL */

/* now we set the values of the variables */
Select    @nLowJobID = 3,
     @nHighJobID = 10

/* open the cursor now */
Open Cur_Empl_Where


...
```

N O T E You can determine how many rows were found by the cursor by evaluating @@Cursor_Rows. If the number of rows is negative, the cursor hasn't yet determined the total number of rows, as would be the case where it may still be serially fetching the rows to satisfy the cursor definition. If the number of rows is zero, there are no open cursors, or the last cursor that was open has been closed and/or deallocated. ■

Fetching a Cursor

After a cursor is in an opened state, you can fetch data from it. Unless a cursor is declared with the SCROLL keyword, the only kind of fetching permissible is serially/sequentially through the result set.

The syntax for the FETCH statement is as follows:

```
FETCH [[NEXT ¦ PRIOR ¦ FIRST ¦ LAST ¦
     ABSOLUTE n/@nvar ¦ RELATIVE n/@nvar ]
FROM] cursor_name
[INTO @variable_name1, @variable_name2]
```

The options for the Transact-SQL command FETCH are as follows:

- NEXT—The NEXT keyword, implicit in normal fetching operations, implies that the next available row be returned.

- PRIOR—If the cursor was defined with SCROLL, this keyword will return the prior record. It's unusual for stored procedure-based applications to take advantage of this keyword unless they're responding to some kind of error condition by logically rolling back the previous row update.

- FIRST—This keyword fetches the first record of the result set found by opening the cursor.

- LAST—This keyword fetches the last record of the result set found by opening the cursor.

- ABSOLUTE n—This keyword will return the nth row in the result set. If you specify a positive number, the rows are counted from the top of the data set. If you provide a negative value for n, the number of rows will be counted from the bottom of the data set.

- RELATIVE *n*—This keyword will return the *n*th row in the result set relative to the current record that has most recently been fetched. If the number is negative, the row will be counted backward from the current row.

N O T E   In SQL Server 6.5, Microsoft has enhanced the syntax of the FETCH ABSOLUTE and FETCH RELATIVE statements by allowing @ variables to be substituted for *n*. If a variable is used, then it may only be of the types int, smallint, or tinyint. ▪

- FROM—This is an an unnecessary keyword provided to make the code slightly more readable. It indicates that the next word will be the cursor that's being fetched from.
- INTO—The INTO keyword is provided for stored procedure use so that the data returned from the cursor may be held in temporary variables for evaluation and/or other use. The data types of the variables in the INTO clause must match exactly the datatypes of the returned columns of the cursor; otherwise, errors will be generated.

Closing a Cursor

Closing a cursor releases any resources and/or locks that SQL Server may have acquired while the cursor was open. To close a cursor, use the following syntax:

```
CLOSE cursor_name
```

A closed cursor is available for fetching only after it's reopened.

Deallocating a Cursor

Deallocating a cursor completely removes any data structures that SQL Server was holding open for a given cursor. Unlike closing a cursor, after a cursor is deallocated, it no longer can be opened.

To deallocate a cursor, use the following syntax:

```
DEALLOCATE cursor_name
```

Example of Using Cursors

In the previous sections we have seen all the separate elements that are used to work with cursors in SQL Server. However, we haven't seen how all the elements are put together—that's what this section is for.

In Listing 15.4, we will examine the use of cursors and see them in action. Refer to the comments in the script (placed between /* ... */) to get a good understanding of what the cursors are doing.

On the CD

Listing 15.4   15_4.SQL—Using Cursors to Process the Stores Table in the Pubs Database

```
/* In this example we will be working with the stores table
of the pubs database.
```

To illustrate the cursors most easily, we will create a stored
procedure, that when executed:

- declares,
- opens,
- fetches, and
- processes

the data returned from a cursor. */

/* First we drop the procedure if it exists. */

```
If exists( select object_id( 'proc_Stores' ) )
    Drop Procedure proc_Stores
Go

/* Step 0: Declare the procedure. */
Create Procedure proc_Stores
As

/* Step 1: Declare some working variables. */
Declare     @nOrderCount     integer,
    @nSQLError      integer,
    @nStorCount     tinyint,
    @sState          char(2),
    @sStorId     char(4),
    @sStorName     varchar(40),
    @sCity          varchar(20)

/* Step 2: Turn off result counting.

Turns off unnecessary "0 rows affected messages" showing on the front-end */

Set NoCount On

/* Step 3: Declare the cursor that is going to find all
the data.

This step causes SQL Server to create the required
resource structures needed to manage the cursor. */

Declare Cur_Stores Cursor
For     Select      STOR_ID,      STOR_NAME,
        CITY,          STATE
    From     STORES
    Order By     STOR_ID

/* Step 4: Open the cursor.

This step causes SQL Server to create the initial result set
and prepare the data for returning to the "Fetching process. */

Open     Cur_Stores
```

continues

Listing 15.4   Continued

```
/* Step 5: Perform the first fetch.

Fetch data from the cursor into our variables for processing
and evaluation. */

Fetch      Cur_Stores
Into       @sStorId,      @sStorName,
       @sCity,           @sState

/* Step 6: Initialize counters. */

Select     @nStorCount = 0

/* Step 7: Fetch and Process Loop.

Process the data while the system variable @@Fetch_Status is = 0
(meaning that a row has been fetched from the cursor */

While @@Fetch_Status = 0
Begin
       /* Step 8: Increment counter */

       Select      @nStorCount = @nStorCount + 1

       /* Step 9: Do a quick operation to determine books on order */

       Select      @nOrderCount = Sum(QTY)
       From     SALES
       WHERE      STOR_ID = @sStorID

       /* Step 10: Return a result set to the front-end so that it knows

       what is happening */
       Select     "Store ID" = @sStorId,
            "Store Name" = @sStorName,
            "# Books on order" = @nOrderCount

       /* Step 11: Continue Fetching.

       If no rows are found then @@Fetch_Status will be set to a value other
       than zero, and the looping will end. */

       Fetch      Cur_Stores
       Into       @sStorId,      @sStorName,
            @sCity,           @sState

End

/* Step 12: Cleanup - Deallocate and close the cursors.

Note that for a stored procedure this is really unnecessary because the cursor
will no longer exist once the procedure finishes execution.
However, it is good practice to leave the procedure cleaned up */
```

```
Close     Cur_Stores
Deallocate Cur_Stores

/* Step 13: Send a totalling result.

Send total count of employees to front-end */

Select "Total # of Stores" = @nStorCount

/* Step 14: Turn on counting again */

Set NoCount On

/* Step 15: End Procedure */

Return 0
Go

/* Now we execute it to see the results. */

Execute proc_Stores
Go
```

The resulting output from running this listing is shown below so that you can see what would
have happened if you ran it:

```
Store ID Store Name                                # Books on order
-------- ---------------------------------------- ----------------
6380     Eric the Read Books                                      8
Store ID Store Name                                # Books on order
-------- ---------------------------------------- ----------------
7066     Barnum's                                               125
Store ID Store Name                                # Books on order
-------- ---------------------------------------- ----------------
7067     News & Brews                                            90
Store ID Store Name                                # Books on order
-------- ---------------------------------------- ----------------
7131     Doc-U-Mat: Quality Laundry and Books                   130
Store ID Store Name                                # Books on order
-------- ---------------------------------------- ----------------
7896     Fricative Bookshop                                      60
Store ID Store Name                                # Books on order
-------- ---------------------------------------- ----------------
8042     Bookbeat                                                80
Total # of Stores
----------------
       6
```

 TIP Sorting variables in large procedures alphabetically will make it much easier to find them. In addition,
you can sort the variables by datatype as well, so that it is even easier to find them—this will happen
automatically if you prefix variables with a datatype indicator such as: s for strings, n for numbers and
dt for date/times.

Using Nested Cursors

You can have multiple layers of cursors in a stored procedure that you can use to provide flexible result-set processing. An example of this might be when you're opening a cursor, as shown earlier in the Cur_Empl example. In addition to the cursor you've already reviewed, you can add nested cursors to impose some additional conditional logic and perhaps open a second cursor to perform additional work with the data set.

Listing 15.5 shows you what's possible with nested cursors.

On the CD

Listing 15.5   15_5.SQL—Using Cursors in a Nested Fashion

```
Create Procedure Maintain_Employees
As
/* First declare variables that are going to
be required in this procedure */

Declare      @dtPubDate    datetime,
             @nEmplCount   smallint,
             @nEmplID      empid,
             @nFirstHalf   smallint,
             @nRowCount    integer,
             @nSecondHalf  integer,
             @nSQLError    integer,
             @nYtdSales    integer,
             @sLName       varchar(30),
             @sPubID       char(4),
             @sLastType    char(12),
             @sType        char(12)

/* Now Declare the cursors to be used
Note that because variables are used in the
where clause on the second cursor, it is not
required that the second cursor be Declared inside the first.
Take advantage of this functionality so that unnecessary
declaring of cursors does not take place (this will
save resources on the server. */

Declare Cur_Empl Cursor
For    Select EMP_ID,    LNAME,
               PUB_ID
       From    EMPLOYEE
       Order By EMP_ID

Declare Cur_Titles Cursor
For    Select  TYPE,   PUBDATE, YTD_SALES
       From    TITLES
       Where   PUB_ID = @sPubID
Order By TYPE

/* open the outer cursor and fetch the first row */

Open  Cur_Empl
```

```
Fetch Cur_Empl
Into   @nEmplID,   @sLName,
       @sPubID

/* Initialize counters */
Select      @nEmplCount = 0

While @@Fetch_Status = 0              /* only fetch while there are rows left */
Begin
       /* increment counter */
       Select @nEmplCount = @nEmplCount + 1

       /* Return a result set to the front-end so that it knows
       what is happening */
       Select      @nEmplID,   @sLName

       If @sLName < 'D'  /* Skip all the D's by using a GOTO */
            Goto Fetch_Next_Empl

       /* Now open inner cursor and count the different types
       of books for this employee's publisher */

       Open Titles

       Fetch Titles
       Into  @sType, @dtPubDate, @nYtdSales

       /* Reset totals */
       Select @nFirstHalf = 0,
              @nSecondHalf = 0,
              @sLastType = NULL

       While @@Fetch_Status = 0
       Begin
              If @sType != @sLastType AND @sLastType != NULL
              Begin
                     /* send back a total record to the front-end */
                     Select @sLastType, @nFirstHalf, @nSecondHalf

                     /* reset totals */
                     Select @nFirstHalf = 0,
                            @nSecondHalf = 0
              End

              If @dtPubDate <= '6/30/95'
                     Select @nFirstHalf = @nFirstHalf + @nYtdSales,
                            @sLastType = @sType
              Else
                     Select @nSecondHalf = @nSecondHalf + @nYtdSales,
                            @sLastType = @sType

              Fetch Titles
              Into  @sType, @dtPubDate, @nYtdSales
```

continues

Listing 15.5 Continued

```
    End

    Fetch_Next_Empl:          /* label to skip inner loop */

    Fetch Cur_Empl
    Into  @nEmplID,   @sLName,
          @sPubID

End

/* Deallocate and close the cursors. Note that for a stored
procedure this is really unnecessary because the cursor
will no longer exist once the procedure finishes execution.
However, it is good practice to leave the procedure cleaned up */

Close Cur_Empl
Deallocate Cur_Empl
Deallocate Cur_Titles

/* Send total count of employees to front-end */
Select @nEmplCount

/* End proc */
Return 0
```

 TIP SQL Server treats object names case-insensitively, regardless of the sort order defined for the server. So take advantage of this and make your code easy to read by using upper- and lowercase emphasis when possible.

This was quite a complex example of the kinds of things you can do with multiple nested cursors. However, it is important to remember that using cursors is really not that difficult provided that you follow the basic steps outlined in the previous examples and throughout this chapter.

Processing Cursors from Front-End Applications

A key consideration of using cursors in an application is how they're accessible from front-end programming tools such as SQLWindows or PowerBuilder.

If the cursor returns a single set of data, which is the most common type, most front-end application languages won't be able to distinguish the data from that returned by a normal select statement. Typically, the tool will have a function for executing SELECT statements. This function is designed to work with a single set of data and, therefore, probably will work fine with stored procedures or cursors that return a single result set. Most tools provide special functions for referencing data that comes from cursors if the cursor and its associated processing returns more than one result set. A common construction might be something like this SQLWindows example snippet:

```
...
Call SqsExecuteProc( hSql, 'proc_Stores', gsResults )
While SqsGetNextResults( hSql, gsResults )
While SqlFetchNext( hSql, nReturn )
...
```

The execution of the stored procedure is followed by looping that forces the return of results to the front-end and then the fetching of the data in each result.

Most programming languages have similar functionality available and whatever programming language in which you choose to do your development should be able to support anything that SQL Server can return. For a more detailed discussion on several client/server programming tools, refer to Chapter 22, "Accessing SQL Server Databases Through Front-End Products."

From Here...

In this chapter you learned about SQL Server's new server-based cursors and how they can be used to provide much more processing power to your applications without the need to return to the client for help. After I spoke with the performance-tuning group at Sybase, whose understanding of SQL Server's cursors is very intimate, it became clear that server cursors provide greater performance than all other results-set processing mechanisms, including embedded SQL in a C application running on the server.

The reason? No networking is involved. Unless the type of work you're doing can't be modeled in stored procedures, as may be the case with arrays, then all batch operations should be moved to cursor-based procedures running on the server.

From here, I suggest that you explore the following chapters to implement what you've learned:

■ Chapter 13, "Managing Stored Procedures and Using Flow-Control Statements," explains how to start embedding cursor processing in your stored procedures.

■ Chapter 22, "Accessing SQL Server Databases Through Front-End Products," provides a full explanation of how your front-end tool of choice interacts with the database when using cursors.

Performing Administrative Operations

Understanding Server, Database, and Query Options

How to configure your server, database, and query with the available options

This chapter will show you how to configure options in SQL Server.

The purpose of each server, database, and query option

SQL Server has numerous options that can be configured. This chapter will help you understand them.

How to recover a server that won't start

Recovering SQL Server in Minimal Configuration Mode is quite difficult. This chapter will walk you through the steps involved.

SQL Server 6.5 has a number of ways of being configured. Those ways are roughly broken down into the three following areas:

- *Server Options*—These are global options that affect all operations on the currently active server. These options apply to all logins on the server and to all databases and other objects that the server owns. Server options are generally used for performance tuning and capacity or object handling management.

- *Database Options*—These are global options that affect all operations on the currently active or *used* database. Database options are generally used to limit access to the database and to enable high-speed BCP operations.

- *Query Options*—These are local options that affect only the currently executing query. Query options allow the tuning and monitoring of the activities of individual queries, and they allow the displaying of additional statistical information about the query's execution. ■

Defining Server Options

SQL Server provides a number of configuration options to enable varied and different installations of the server. These options are used to customize the way SQL Server's resources are managed. The sorts of resources that are available for management are the following:

- Memory
- User and login handling
- Sizes of objects
- Network and physical I/O handling
- Memory, disk, procedure, and read-ahead cache
- Symmetric Multi-Processing (SMP) management

N O T E *Symmetric Multi-Processing (SMP)* computers are computers that conform to a published standard for incorporating more than one CPU in the system unit. SMP computers typically offer substantial performance improvements over single CPU boxes because they can distribute the processing workload to as many CPUs as available. Windows NT has been shown to provide near-linear performance improvements on computers with as many as four CPUs. ■

SQL Server has two sets of server configuration options available. The default or *basic* server options contain the normal day-to-day sorts of things that will need to be managed. The *advanced* server options are provided to allow tuning of things in the server not generally considered necessary. Unless you have been advised by a technical support center to specifically configure one of the advanced options, it is not recommended that you change any of the advanced options. The advanced options can be enabled by turning on the configuration option, Show Advanced Option. For detailed instructions on how to set this and any option, see the section entitled "Displaying and Setting Server Options" below.

> **CAUTION**
>
> Changing server configurations can sometimes make a server unable to be restarted after the change (such as over-committed memory). To restart a server in this situation, it may be necessary to start the server in *minimal configuration mode,* which enables you to bring up the server without it attempting to apply the configurations that you set. For more information on starting the server in minimal configuration mode, see the end of this chapter.

Displaying and Setting Server Options

SQL Server provides two ways to display and set configuration options for the server. The graphical method is via SQL Server Enterprise Manager. The Transact-SQL method is by using the system-stored procedure `sp_configure`.

Using SQL Enterprise Manager SQL Enterprise Manager is a very convenient tool for the DBA to use when changing server options. The user interface makes it unnecessary to remember the syntax required for sp_configure or to know all the different options.

To use the SQL Enterprise Manager to display and set server options, perform the following steps:

1. Run SQL Enterprise Manager from the Microsoft SQL Server 6.5 group (see fig. 16.1).

Part

V

Ch

16

FIG. 16.1
After just being started, SQL Enterprise Manager shows that no server is selected.

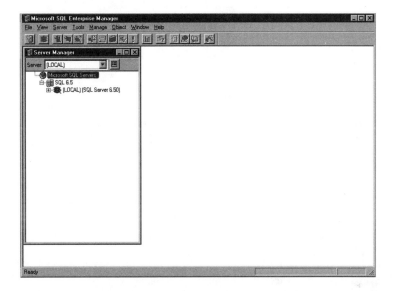

2. Select the server that you want to work on (see fig. 16.2).

FIG. 16.2
After selecting a particular server, SQL Enterprise Manager shows all of its properties and objects folders.

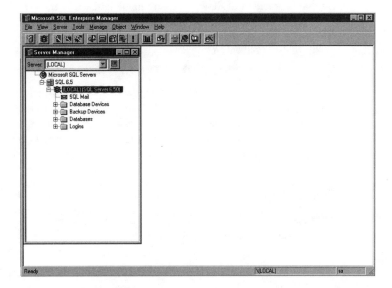

3. From the Server menu select SQL Server Configure. When the Server Configuration/ Options dialog box is displayed, click the Configuration page (see fig. 16.3).

FIG. 16.3

SQL Enterprise Manager's Server Configuration/Options dialog box shows the Configuration page.

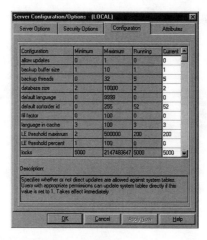

4. To change any of the settings for the server, enter the required value in the Current column and then either click Apply Now to make a change but leave the dialog box up, or click OK to apply the changes and return to the main SQL Enterprise Manager window.

 Press the F1 key on any SQL Enterprise Manager dialog box to bring up context-sensitive help that will explain the different objects/options available.

Using the System-Stored Procedure *sp_configure*

sp_configure is a system-stored procedure that is provided to allow the changing of settings on the server. sp_configure is useful for writing automated scripts that update the server without user intervention.

Sp_configure's syntax is as follows:

```
sp_configure [configuration option, [configuration value]]
```

The *configuration option* is the value that is needed to change in the server. SQL Server uses a LIKE operator on the text that is supplied so that any unique set of characters is recognized without requiring the full text value. SQL Server requires that any text with spaces or other formatting in the *configuration option* parameter be enclosed in quotation marks. Listing 16.1 shows that all of the sp_configure statements perform the same function.

Listing 16.1   *sp_configure* Requires Only That the Option Being Changed Is Uniquely Identified

```
sp_configure "nested Triggers", 0
go
```

```
sp_configure "nested", 1
go
sp_configure "triggers", 0
go
sp_configure "trig", 0
go
```

N O T E If no parameters are supplied to `sp_configure`, the resulting output is the current status of the server. Listing 16.2 shows an example of the results returned when `sp_configure` is used without a parameter.

The `sp_configure` information produced includes the advanced options. Notice that the run value for show advanced option is 1. ■

Listing 16.2 Executing *sp_configure* Without Any Options Returns the Current Server Configuration

```
/*---------------------------
sp_configure
---------------------------*/
```

name	minimum	maximum	config_value	run_value
allow updates	0	1	0	0
backup buffer size	1	10	1	1
backup threads	0	32	5	5
cursor threshold	-1	2147483647	-1	-1
database size	1	10000	2	2
default language	0	9999	0	0
default sortorder id	0	255	52	52
fill factor	0	100	0	0
free buffers	20	524288	409	409
hash buckets	4999	265003	7993	7993
language in cache	3	100	3	3
LE threshold maximum	2	500000	10	10
LE threshold minimum	2	500000	20	10
LE threshold percent	1	100	0	0
locks	5000	2147483647	5000	5000
logwrite sleep (ms)	-1	500	0	0
max async IO	1	255	8	8
max lazywrite IO	1	255	8	8
max worker threads	10	1024	255	255
media retention	0	365	0	0
memory	1000	1048576	8192	8192
nested triggers	0	1	1	1
network packet size	512	32767	4096	4096
open databases	5	32767	20	20
open objects	100	2147483647	500	500
priority boost	0	1	0	0
procedure cache	1	99	30	30
RA cache hit limit	1	255	4	4
RA cache miss limit	1	255	3	3

continues

Listing 16.2   Continued

```
RA delay                0       500         15      15
RA pre-fetches          1       1000        3       3
RA slots per thread     1       255         5       5
RA worker threads       0       255         3       3
recovery flags          0       1           0       0
recovery interval       1       32767       5       5
remote access           0       1           1       1
remote logon timeout    0       2147483647  5       5
remote query timeout    0       2147483647  0       0
resource timeout        5       2147483647  10      10
set working set size    0       1           0       0
show advanced option    0       1           1       1
SMP concurrency         -1      64          0       1
sort pages              64      511         128     128
spin counter            1       2147483647  10000   0
tempdb in ram (MB)      0       2044        0       0
user connections        5       32767       20      20

(1 row(s) affected)
```

TROUBLESHOOTING

I'm trying to change a configuration option and `sp_configure` keeps returning:

```
Msg 15125, Level 16, State 1
```

Only the System Administrator (SA) may change configuration parameters. You're not logged in to the database as SA. Only SA can change a server configuration. Log off from ISQL/w or the database tool that you are using, and reconnect to the database as the SA user.

Understanding the *RECONFIGURE* command   After executing `sp_configure`, the server may return the following:

```
Configuration option changed. Run the RECONFIGURE command to install.
```

This means that the server has changed the internal value of the configuration, but has not yet applied it. The output shown in Listing 16.3 shows that the configuration before and after is changed in the config value column, but the run value column remains unchanged.

Listing 16.3   Some *sp_configure* Options Require Reconfiguration of the Server

```
/*---------------------------
sp_configure "nested"
go
sp_configure "nested", 0
---------------------------*/
name                    minimum     maximum     config_value run_value
------------------      ----------  ----------  ------------ ----------
nested triggers         0           1           1            1
```

```
Configuration option changed. Run the RECONFIGURE command to install.
name                     minimum    maximum     config_value run_value
--------------------     ----------  ----------  ------------ ----------
nested triggers          0          1           0            1
```

Executing the RECONFIGURE command applies the change to the server (see Listing 16.4).

Listing 16.4 *RECONFIGURE* Forces SQL Server to Adjust the Run Value of a Server Option

```
/*--------------------------
reconfigure
go
sp_configure "nested"
--------------------------*/
name                     minimum    maximum     config_value run_value
--------------------     ----------  ----------  ------------ ----------
nested triggers          0          1           0            0
```

RECONFIGURE is available only to *dynamic* configuration options. These are options that can be changed without requiring the server to be shut down and restarted. The following is a list of the dynamic options that can be set with sp_configure and then applied dynamically with RECONFIGURE:

allow updates	RA cache hit limit
backup buffer size	RA cache miss limit
free buffers	RA delay
LE threshold maximum	RA pre-fetches
LE threshold minimum	recovery interval
LE threshold percent	remote logon timeout
logwrite sleep (ms)	remote query timeout
max lazywrite IO	resource timeout
max worker threads	show advanced option
nested triggers	sort pages
network packet size	spin counter

Server Options Explained

The following is a comprehensive list of all the available server options. If the word *advanced* appears in parentheses to the right of the keyword, then this option is only available if you have turned on the configuration value, Show Advanced Options. If the word *dynamic* appears in parentheses to the right of the keyword, then this option can be changed without the shutting down and restarting of the server. See the previous section on the RECONFIGURE command for more information.

In each item below, there are indications of the minimium, maximum, and default values. These values indicate the range of values that the item can have, and the default value to which SQL Server is configured when first installed.

allow updates (dynamic)

Minimum: 0

Maximum: 1

Default: 0

The `allow updates` configuration option allows the system catalog to be updated. If the value is set to 1 (one) then the system catalog is updateable. Stored procedures created while the system catalog is updateable will be able to update the system catalog even when this value is returned to 0 (zero).

> **CAUTION**
>
> Allowing updates on the system catalog is an extremely dangerous decision. It should only be done under very controlled situations and should probably be done with the server in single-user mode to prevent other users from accidentally damaging the system catalog.
>
> To start the server in single-user mode, execute `sqlservr -m` from the Win32 command prompt.

Because this option can cause so much harm, it requires an additional keyword, `WITH OVERRIDE`, when executing the `RECONFIGURE` command. So the following is the correct syntax to enable `allow updates`.

```
sp_configure "allow updates", 1
go
reconfigure with override
go
```

backup buffer size (dynamic)

Minimum: 1

Maximum: 10

Default: 1

This configuration option allows the tuning of backups by increasing or decreasing the amount of memory available to the SQL Server for holding backup data. The numeric value corresponds to 32 2K pages. So by setting the value to 4, the server will be allocating $4 \times 32 \times 2K = 256K$ for backups. A larger value will help reduce backup times but will also reduce available memory for the server.

backup threads

Minimum: 0

Maximum: 32

Default: 5

This configuration option controls how many NT service threads will be allocated to striped backup and load operations. Increase this value from the default of 5 when running on multiple CPU machines to improve backup and load times.

cursor threshold (dynamic, advanced)

Minimum: –1

Maximum: 2147483647

Default: 100

This configuration option controls how SQL Server decides to build the results to answer a request for a cursor by a client. The value corresponds to the number of rows expected in the cursor's result set. The accuracy of the cursor threshold is largely based on the currency of the INDEX statistics on the tables for which a cursor is being built. To ensure more accurate picking of the synchronous/asynchronous cursor build, make sure that the statistics are up-to-date on the base tables.

If set to –1, SQL Server will always build the cursor results synchronously, meaning that the server will attempt to build the cursor immediately upon receiving the OPEN CURSOR command. Synchronous cursor generation is usually faster for small result sets.

If set to 0, SQL Server will always build the cursor results asynchronously, meaning that the server will spawn an additional thread to answer the client and it will return control to the client while still processing other client requests. For large result sets this is the preferred option because it will stop the server from being bogged down answering a single client's request for a large cursor result.

database size

Minimum: 1

Maximum: 10000

Default: 2

This option controls the default number of megabytes to reserve for a new database being created. If the majority of the databases that are being created on a given server are greater than 2MB, it would be advisable to change this value. If the *model* database grows to be greater than 2MB, it will be required to adjust this value.

 TIP Because the minimum database size is 1MB, SQL Server databases can exist on floppy disks. See the Chapter 4 section entitled "Using Removable Media for Databases" for more information.

default language

Minimum: 0

Maximum: 9999

Default: 0

This option controls the default language ID to be used for the server. U.S. English is the default and is always 0 (zero). If other languages are added to the server, they will be assigned different language IDs.

default sortorder id (advanced)

Minimum: 0

Maximum: 255

Default: 52

This option controls the sort order that the server will be using. The sort order controls the way SQL Server sorts data and returns it to the client. The default is Dictionary, Case Insensitive.

> **CAUTION**
>
> Do not use sp_configure to change the sortorder. Use the SQL Server setup program if you wish to change this value. Changing the sortorder will require that you unload and reload the database because the data will need to be stored in a different format.

fill factor

Minimum: 0

Maximum: 100

Default: 0

This configuration option controls the default fill factor to use when creating indexes. The fill factor refers to how much space SQL Server will reserve in an index page for the potential growth of key values on the index. This option is overridden if a fill factor is specified when the CREATE INDEX command is executed.

A fill factor of 100 will force SQL Server to fill the index pages completely and should *only* be used for extremely static tables whose key values never change, grow, or are inserted into. Smaller fill factor values will allow/force SQL Server to reserve space on the index page for new values that may be added to the table/index after the initial table load.

▶ **See** the Chapter 10 section entitled "Creating an Index with *CREATE INDEX*." **p. 276**

free buffers (dynamic, advanced)

Minimum: 20

Maximum: 524288

Default: 204

This configuration option controls the amount of memory that SQL Server must maintain when lazywriting to disk. Lazywriting increases throughput because values are "written" to memory instead of disk. If this threshold is hit, then the lazywriter forces information to disk to ensure that memory pages are maintained free.

If a change is made to the memory configuration option, this option is automatically adjusted to five percent of the memory value. After the server has restarted, this value may be modified manually to any value within the range specified above.

hash buckets (advanced)

Minimum: 4999

Maximum: 265003

Default: 7993

This configuration option controls the number of buckets that SQL Server reserves for hashing (or indexing) pages of data to memory. A *bucket* is a logical storage area or counter that SQL Server uses to hold values that it needs to identify memory pages. SQL Server's hashing algorithm requires that a prime number of buckets be made available for use; therefore, if a non-prime value is specified, SQL Server will pick the closest prime number to it.

It is unlikely that this value will require modification unless the server has more than 160MB of RAM because $8000 \times 2K = 160$ MB. Note that the default of 7993 really refers to the closest prime to 8000.

language in cache

Minimum: 3

Maximum: 100

Default: 3

This configuration option controls the number of languages that SQL Server can store in the language cache simultaneously.

LE threshold maximum (dynamic)

Minimum: 2

Maximum: 500000

Default: 200

This configuration option controls the maximum number of page locks that SQL Server will permit a single query before escalating a set of page locks on a table to a full table lock. If the number of pages is exceeded, SQL Server will force a table lock—irrespective of the LE threshold percentage configured for the table. Lock escalation is performed to improve performance on the server because of unnecessary memory being allocated to manage the individual page locks.

LE threshold minimum (dynamic)

Minimum: 2

Maximum: 500000

Default: 20

This configuration option controls the minimum number of page locks that SQL Server will require a single query to acquire before escalating a set of page locks on a table to a full table lock. This configuration option is provided so that the LE threshold percentage will not hit on tables with small numbers of pages of data.

LE *threshold percent* (dynamic)

Minimum: 1

Maximum: 100

Default: 0

This configuration option controls the percentage of page locks to pages of data in the table that need to be acquired on a table before SQL Server will escalate the lock to a full table lock. A value of 0 (zero), the default, will not allow SQL Server to perform lock escalation unless the lock escalation threshold maximum is reached.

locks

Minimum: 5000

Maximum: 2147483647

Default: 5000

This configuration option controls the number of locks that SQL Server can maintain at any time. Each lock consumes 32 bytes of RAM, and so increasing this value to a large number will most likely require more RAM to be made available to the server. For example, setting this value to 20,000 will result in 20,000 * 32 bytes = 640,000 bytes or 625K of RAM consumed just by the lock manager.

logwrite sleep (ms) (dynamic, advanced)

Minimum: –1

Maximum: 500

Default: 0

This option controls the number of milliseconds that SQL Server will wait to write a log entry to disk if the buffer is not full. This can have dramatic performance gains on highly DML active databases because it will force SQL Server to write larger blocks of memory to the log at one time, rather than requiring it write less than full blocks to disk.

A value of –1 is provided to force SQL Server to always write to disk, which should only be used on systems that are extremely concerned about media failure and are not concerned with IO throughput performance. A value of 0 (zero) will force SQL Server to delay writes to disk if, and only if, there are other users on the system in the execute phase of their requests to the server.

max async IO

Minimum: 1

Maximum: 255

Default: 8

This configuration option controls the maximum number of asynchronous IO requests that SQL Server can make to the hardware devices. This value should only be changed from the default on systems that have more than eight physical disks with database devices on them or on systems that are using disk striping to improve performance.

max lazywrite IO (dynamic, advanced)

Minimum: 1

Maximum: 255

Default: 8

This configuration option is used to tune the writes from the lazywriter to the real IO subsystem. This value is dynamically configurable, but can only be configured up to the value of actual max async IO. It is not recommended that this value be modified unless someone in your primary support center tells you to.

max worker threads (dynamic)

Minimum: 10

Maximum: 1024

Default: 255

This configuration option controls the maximum number of threads that SQL Server will spawn to handle database operations. By default, SQL Server will spawn at least one thread for each listener service that is installed. In addition, there will be a thread spawned for database checkpointing, lazywriting, and for the read ahead manager. The *checkpointing process* is a process or server operation that writes dirty (or changed) pages of data that are currently cached from memory directly to disk. The *lazywriting process* manages cached writes to disk and allows transactions to be batched together for a single IO to disk containing multiple items instead of writing every transaction to disk as it occurs.

The rest of the threads that are available are allocated for user processes that are making requests. If the number of users is greater than the number of available threads allocated by the server (up to the maximum here configured), then SQL Server will use the available threads in a pooling fashion. The next request by a user process that is received at the server will be assigned to the first thread that becomes available after it has completed its assigned task.

media retention

Minimum: 0

Maximum: 365

Default: 0

This configuration option controls the number of days that a given backup is expected to be retained before it can be reused. If this value is other than 0 (zero), SQL Server will warn the user that they are performing a backup over an existing backup that has not expired its number of retention days.

This is a useful configuration for SQL Servers that are in remote areas where a full-time administrator is not available to manage the environment and where it is likely that the user may incorrectly reuse backup tapes that should be kept for a prescribed period.

TROUBLESHOOTING

My users keep overwriting their historical backup tapes with the latest backups of the database. I'm happy they're doing backups at all, but how can I stop them from using the same tape twice. It is impossible to stop a user from using the same tape twice. However, by using the media retention configuration option, you can stop them from using the tape too quickly after a backup is made. A good setting is 7, which will stop the tape from being used more than once a week.

memory

Minimum: 1000

Maximum: 1048576

Default: 4096

This configuration option controls the maximum number of 2K pages of memory that SQL Server will consume upon startup. To fully optimize your server for use as a database server, you should allocate all available memory to the server after subtracting the minimums required by Windows NT.

> **CAUTION**
>
> If you overcommit the amount of available memory, SQL Server will not start. See the section later in this chapter entitled "Starting SQL Server in Minimal Configuration Mode from the Command Line" to fix a server that is no longer starting because memory was overcommitted.

To help tune the amount of memory being consumed by SQL Server, you can use the DBCC MEMUSAGE command, which will report the way that memory has been allocated on the server and will also show the top 20 data pages and stored procedures that have been executed. Listing 16.5 shows an example of the output that is displayed without the buffer page top 20 or the stored procedure top 20.

Listing 16.5   Using *dbcc memusage* to Display Information About Memory in Use on the Server

```
/*----------------------------
dbcc memusage
---------------------------*/
Memory Usage:
```

	Meg.	2K Blks	Bytes
Configured Memory:	16.0000	8192	16777216
Code size:	1.7166	879	1800000
Static Structures:	0.2473	127	259328
Locks:	0.2480	127	260000
Open Objects:	0.1068	55	112000
Open Databases:	0.0031	2	3220
User Context Areas:	0.8248	423	864824
Page Cache:	8.8951	4555	9327184
Proc Headers:	0.2143	110	224724
Proc Cache Bufs:	3.5996	1843	3774464

nested triggers (dynamic)

Minimum: 0

Maximum: 1

Default: 1

This configuration option controls whether triggers will nest or be executed cascaded. If set to 0 (zero), SQL Server will only execute the first trigger that fires when an update or delete action occurs.

TROUBLESHOOTING

I'm concerned that we are having too many triggers firing and it seems like triggers are causing other triggers to fire and I don't know how to monitor this effectively. You can use the Nested Triggers configuration to stop SQL Server from allowing a trigger to cause another trigger to execute a procedure. Turning off this option will allow you to more closely examine the behavior of triggers in your application.

network packet size (dynamic)

Minimum: 512

Maximum: 32767

Default: 4096

This configuration option controls the server-wide maximum network packet size that is requested by a client. If the client requests a size less than the value specified in the current value, SQL Server will accept it; however, greater values than the current value will be negotiated to the maximum value specified here.

This option can improve performance on networks whose base topology supports wider or larger packets than TCP/IP's default of 4096 bytes. This is especially useful if you are running over a satellite service and wish to batch large packets of data to send through the satellite packet service.

This option should be adjusted to a higher value for reporting-only databases that are not acquiring any locks on the datasets because it will allow larger batches of data to be sent to the client at one time, improving network throughput.

> **CAUTION**
>
> Setting the packet size to be too high can cause locking problems on highly transactionally active databases. This is because SQL Server will hold locks for an unnecessarily long time in order to fill up a network packet to send to the client. Take care when adjusting this value and perform statistical analysis to prove that the values you have chosen are providing benefits to you.

open databases

Minimum: 5

Maximum: 32767

Default: 20

This configuration option controls the maximum number of databases that SQL Server can maintain in an open condition at any one time. It should not be arbitrarily set to a high value because each open database does consume some server memory.

TROUBLESHOOTING

The DBA has created a new database, but nobody can connect to it. Check to see that you haven't exceeded the number of open databases on the server. If you have, use `sp_configure` to increase the number of open databases available on the server and retry to connect.

open objects

Minimum: 100

Maximum: 2147483647

Default: 500

This configuration option controls the maximum number of objects that SQL Server can hold in memory at one time. An object can be a table page, stored procedure that is executing, or any other object in the database. Increase this value if the server ever reports that the maximum number of objects has been exceeded.

Take care when assigning values to this option because it may be necessary to allocate more memory to the server due to the consumption of memory resources by the open objects configuration option.

priority boost (advanced)

Minimum: 0

Maximum: 1

Default: 0

This configuration option controls the priority SQL Server will run at under Windows NT. The default is 0 (zero), meaning that SQL Server will run at a normally high priority, but will allow other tasks to request high threading priority too. If set to 1 (one), SQL Server will run at the highest priority under the Windows NT scheduler.

This value should be set to 1 on systems that are dedicating Windows NT to run SQL Server.

procedure cache

Minimum: 1

Maximum: 99

Default: 30

This configuration option controls the proportion of memory that SQL Server grabs and allocates to store the stored procedures that have most recently been executed. For systems that have large amounts of stored procedures, it may be necessary to set this value higher than 30 percent if the total amount of memory available to SQL Server is relatively low.

It is recommended that this value be reduced to 10 percent or less on systems with more than 512MB of RAM. It is extremely unlikely that the amount of stored procedures in memory cache will exceed 50MB.

N O T E The reason SQL Server has a stored procedure cache is because it does not store the desired query plan/execution plan of the procedure in the database until it is first executed. This explains why the first time a procedure is executed it takes more time to run. SQL Server is pulling the tokenized procedure text out of private tables and is evaluating the text and determining the correct execution path. This execution path is what is stored in the procedure cache. ■

RA cache hit limit (dynamic, advanced)

Minimum: 1

Maximum: 255

Default: 4

This configuration option is used to control the number of hits in the data page cache that the Read Ahead Manager makes before canceling itself and allowing the query to fetch data from the data page cache, instead of the Read Ahead Manager.

> **CAUTION**
> Changing this value may seriously affect performance on your server. Do not modify this value unless your primary support center has asked you to.

RA cache miss limit (dynamic, advanced)

Minimum: 1

Maximum: 255

Default: 3

Part **V**

Ch **16**

This configuration option controls the number of data page cache misses that are acceptable to the SQL Server before the Read Ahead Manager is started. Setting this value to 1 will cause the Read Ahead Manager to be fired for every access of a data page. This will cause terrible performance and a lot of unnecessary disk thrashing.

> **CAUTION**
>
> Changing this value may seriously affect performance on your server. Do not modify this value unless your primary support center has asked you to.

RA delay (dynamic, advanced)
Minimum: 0

Maximum: 500

Default: 15

This configuration option controls the number of milliseconds that the Read Ahead Manager will delay its own execution after a request has been made.

RA pre-fetches (dynamic, advanced)
Minimum: 1

Maximum: 1000

Default: 3

This configuration option controls the number of extents ($8 \times 2K$ pages) that the Read Ahead Manager will read ahead of the currently scanning execution position.

RA slots per thread (advanced)
Minimum: 1

Maximum: 255

Default: 5

This configuration option controls the number of slots per thread that SQL Server will reserve for Read Ahead processes. The number of slots multiplied by the number of allocated worker threads is the total number of concurrent read ahead activities that may be executing.

RA worker threads
Minimum: 0

Maximum: 255

Default: 3

This configuration option controls the number of Windows NT threads that SQL Server will allocate to the Read Ahead Manager. It is recommended that this value be configured to the maximum number of concurrent users expected on the system. With the option configured in this way, SQL Server will have a Read Ahead thread available to handle each user process.

recovery flags

Minimum: 0

Maximum: 1

Default: 0

This configuration option controls the information that is displayed during the SQL Server startup process. If set to 0 (zero), the default, then SQL Server will only report that the database is being recovered/restored by name. If set to 1 (one), then SQL Server will report in detail the status of every transaction that was pending at the time the server was shutdown, and what activity SQL Server took to resolve it.

 T I P To view the information captured in the error log, select Error Log from the Server menu in SQL Enterprise Manager.

recovery interval (dynamic)

Minimum: 1

Maximum: 32767

Default: 5

This configuration option controls the number of minutes that SQL Server will require to recover a database in the event that there is a system failure of some kind. This option combined with the amount of activity that is occurring on the server controls the amount of time between database CHECKPOINTS.

A database CHECKPOINT forces the writing of all the changes to dirty data pages from the transaction log information to disk instead of residing in the transaction log buffers (or lazywriter buffers). A CHECKPOINT can take considerable time if there has been a lot of activity on the server, but frequent checkpointing will reduce the amount of time required to restart the server because it will not have to ROLLFORWARD as much work from the transaction log.

remote access

Minimum: 0

Maximum: 1

Default: 1

This configuration option controls whether remote SQL Servers are allowed logon access to the server. If set to 0 (zero), SQL Server will deny access to remote SQL Servers.

remote logon timeout (dynamic, advanced)

Minimum: 0

Maximum: 2147483647

Default: 5

This configuration option controls the amount of time (in seconds) that SQL Server will wait before returning an error to the client process that was requesting the logon to a remote server. Setting this value to 0 (zero) will cause the SQL Server to wait indefinitely.

remote query timeout (dynamic, advanced)

Minimum: 0

Maximum: 2147483647

Default: 0

This configuration option controls the amount of time (in seconds) that SQL Server will wait before returning an error to the client process that was requesting the execution of a query on a remote server. Setting this value to 0 (zero) will cause the SQL Server to wait indefinitely.

resource timeout (dynamic, advanced)

Minimum: 5

Maximum: 2147483647

Default: 10

This configuration option controls the amount of time (in seconds) that SQL Server will wait before returning an error to the client process required a server resource. A server resource could be access to a memory buffer, a disk IO request, a network IO request, or a log IO request. This option should be increased if a large number of `logwait` or `bufwait` timeout warnings are in the SQL Server error log.

set working set size (advanced)

Minimum: 0

Maximum: 1

Default: 0

This configuration option controls whether SQL Server will request that Windows NT physically allocate and lock memory to the SQL Server. The amount allocated will be equal to the number of pages in the memory configuration option × 2K, plus the amount of memory requested for Tempdb, if tempdb in RAM is configured on.

show advanced option (dynamic)

Minimum: 0

Maximum: 1

Default: 1

This configuration option controls whether SQL Server will display and allow the configuration of other advanced options through `sp_configure`. If set to 0 (zero), SQL Server will respond that an option does not exist if an advanced option is attempted to be changed.

TROUBLESHOOTING

`sp_configure` is not allowing me to configure one of the advanced configuration options. Before being allowed to configure an advanced option, you must first make sure that you have enabled the show advanced option using `sp_configure`.

SMP concurrency (advanced)

Minimum: –1

Maximum: 64

Default: 0

This configuration option controls how SQL Server will operate on a Symmetric Multi-Processing server. The default configuration for a single CPU computer is 0 (zero), which means auto-configuration mode. In auto-configuration mode, SQL Server allocates N–1 CPUs to SQL Server from the Windows NT service scheduler, where N is the number of CPUs detected in the server when SQL Server starts.

If SQL Server is installed with Dedicated SMP Support chosen, SQL Server will set this value to –1, which means that all CPUs will be dedicated to SQL Server.

If the Windows NT server is not dedicated to running SQL Server and this value is configured to the maximum number of CPUs in the box, then this will result in poor performance for any other tasks (besides SQL Server) that are executing on the box.

sort pages (dynamic, advanced)

Minimum: 64

Maximum: 511

Default: 128

This configuration option controls the number of pages that SQL Server will reserve per user for sorting and resolving queries. This value should be closely tuned to the user requirements of the system that is executing on the SQL Server. A higher value will generally result in better performance for systems that do a lot of queries that require data to be sorted in memory. Setting this value high will cause each user to consume larger amounts of available memory and may necessitate that more memory be dedicated to SQL Server.

spin counter (dynamic, advanced)

Minimum: 1

Maximum: 2147483647

Default: 10000

This configuration option controls the maximum number of attempts SQL Server will make to acquire a resource from the SQL Server service manager.

This is an advanced option and should not be altered unless you are advised to do so by a Microsoft Service Center.

tempdb in RAM (MB)

Minimum: 0

Maximum: 2044

Default: 0

This configuration option controls the amount of memory that SQL Server will reserve for tempdb in RAM. If set to 0 (zero), tempdb will reside on a physical disk device (the default for which is MASTER's device). If set to any value other than 0 (zero), tempdb will be placed in a memory chunk. This memory chunk will be contiguously allocated.

If tempdb is resized through the ALTER command while it resides in memory, additional contiguous chunks of memory corresponding to the required ALTER size will be allocated to it. However, these contiguous chunks may not necessarily be next to the chunks previously allocated. It is recommended that the server be shut down and restarted if the size of tempdb is altered.

user connections

Minimum: 5

Maximum: 32767

Default: 20

This configuration option controls the maximum number of user processes that can connect to the server at one time. The logical limit is 32767; however, it is very likely that practical limits of server hardware will be exceeded before this limit is ever achieved.

There is a minimum fixed overhead for each user connection of about 40K. If this value is set to a large value it may be necessary to allocate more memory to the SQL Server.

TROUBLESHOOTING

Periodically—usually at times of heavy load on the server—users are reporting that they can't connect. It's possible that you are running out of available user connections on the server. Use sp_configure to increase the number of user connections to a higher value so that more concurrent users are permitted.

affinity mask

Minimum: 0

Maximum: 0x7fffffff

Default: 0

On SMP machines, `affinity mask` allows a thread to be associated with a processor. This is done using a bit mask. The processors on which the processes run are represented by each bit. Decimal or hexadecimal values can be used to specify values for this setting.

remote conn timeout

Minimum: –1

Maximum: 32767

Default: 60

This value represents the number of minutes that may pass without activity for a server-to-server connection. If the value is exceeded, the non-active session will be terminated. The only exception to this is when the connection is involved in a DTC-coordinated distribution transaction.

remote proc trans

Minimum: 0

Maximum: 1

Default: 0

This feature allows users to protect the actions of a server-to-server procedure through a DTC-coordinated distributed transaction. When set to true, it provides a DTC transaction that protects certain properties of transactions. After this option is set, new sessions will inherit the configuration setting as their default.

user options

Minimum: 0

Maximum: 4095

Default: 0

The user options are used to set global defaults for users logging into the system. After a change is made, all new logins will be affected but existing logins will not change. Users can override these values by using the SET statement.

SYSCONFIGURES and *SYSCURCONFIGS*: System Catalog Tables

SYSCONFIGURES and SYSCURCONFIGS are system catalog tables that SQL Server uses to store information about configuration options that are in use on the server. They are stored in the master database.

SYSCONFIGURES has information about the available options and their defaults that the server has created. Note that the sp_configure option that you see comes from the spt_values table in the master database. Rather than relying on the formatted results returned from sp_configure, it's sometimes necessary to be able to select back (and process in a result set) the configurations available and configured on the server. In Listing 16.6, the query shows you the defaults for all the configurable options in the server.

On the CD

Listing 16.6 16_01.SQL—Querying the *SYSCONFIGURES* Table to Review the Defaults

```
/*-----------------------------
Select V.NAME,   COMMENT = substring( C.COMMENT, 1, 60 ),
       "DEFAULT" = c.value
From    MASTER.DBO.SPT_VALUES V,
        MASTER.DBO.SYSCONFIGURES C
Where   V.NUMBER = C.CONFIG
And     V.NAME is not null
Order by V.NAME
---------------------------*/
```

NAME	COMMENT	DEFAULT
allow updates	Allow updates to system tables	0
backup buffer size	Backup buffer size	1
backup threads	Backup threads	5
cursor threshold	Cursor threshold	-1
database size	Default database size in megabytes	2
default language	Default language	0
default sortorder id	Default sortorder ID	52
fill factor	Default fill factor percentage	0
free buffers	Free buffers	409
hash buckets	Hash buckets	7993
language in cache	Language cache	3
LE threshold maximum	LE threshold maximum	10
LE threshold minimum	LE threshold minimum	20
LE threshold percent	LE threshold percent	0
locks	Number of locks for all users	5000
logwrite sleep (ms)	Logwrite sleep (ms)	0
max async IO	Maximum outstanding async IOs	8
max lazywrite IO	Maximum lazywrite IO	8
max worker threads	Maximum worker threads	255
media retention	Tape retention period in days	0
memory	Size of avbl phys memory in 2k pages	8192
nested triggers	Allow triggers to invoke triggers	0
network packet size	Default network packet size	4096
open databases	# of open dbs allowed for all users	20
open objects	Number of open database objects	500
priority boost	Priority boost	0
procedure cache	% of memory used for procedure cache	30
RA cache hit limit	RA cache hit limit	4
RA cache miss limit	RA cache miss limit	3
RA delay	RA delay	15
RA pre-fetches	RA pre-fetches	3
RA slots per thread	RA slots per thread	5
RA worker threads	RA worker threads	3
recovery flags	Recovery flags	0
recovery interval	Maximum recovery interval in minutes	5
remote access	Allow remote access	1
remote logon timeout	Remote logon timeout	5
remote query timeout	Remote query timeout	0
resource timeout	Resource timeout	10
set working set size	Set working set size	0
show advanced option	Show advanced options	1

```
SMP concurrency        SMP concurrency                      0
sort pages             Number of sort pages                 128
spin counter           Spin counter                         10000
tempdb in ram (MB)     TempDB in RAM option                 0
user connections       Number of user connections allowed   20

(46 row(s) affected)
```

TIP

In the above query, the reserved SQL Server keyword DEFAULT was used as a column title. To use any reserved words as text as a column title, enclose it in quotation marks.

SYSCURCONFIGS stores the currently configured values that are being used by the server. In Listing 16.7 the query shows how to get the current values for each of the configurable options in the server. Using SYSCONFIGURES and SYSCURCONFIGS together will allow you to write your own programs to dynamically set options and report options on the server.

On the CD

Listing 16.7 16_02.SQL—Querying the *SYSCURCONFIGS* Table to Review the Current Server Configurations

```
/*---------------------------
Select V.NAME,   COMMENT = substring( C.COMMENT, 1, 60 ),
       "CURRENT VALUE" = c.value
From   MASTER.DBO.SPT_VALUES V,
       MASTER.DBO.SYSCURCONFIGS C
Where  V.NUMBER = C.CONFIG
And    V.NAME is not null
Order by V.NAME
---------------------------*/
NAME                   COMMENT                                  CURRENT VALUE
------------------     -----------------------------------      -------------
allow updates          Allow updates to system tables           0
backup buffer size     Backup buffer size                       1
backup threads         Backup threads                           5
cursor threshold       Cursor threshold                         -1
database size          Default database size in megabytes       2
default language       Default language                         0
default sortorder id   Default sortorder ID                     52
fill factor            Default fill factor percentage           0
free buffers           Free buffers                             409
hash buckets           Hash buckets                             7993
language in cache      # of language information in cache       3
LE threshold maximum   Lock Escalation threshold maximum        10
LE threshold minimum   Lock Escalation threshold minimum        10
LE threshold percent   Lock Escalation threshold percent        0
locks                  Number of locks for all users            5000
logwrite sleep (ms)    Logwrite sleep (ms)                      0
max async IO           Maximum outstanding async IOs            8
max lazywrite IO       Maximum lazywrite IO                     8
max worker threads     Maximum worker threads                   255
media retention        Media retention period in days           0
```

continues

Listing 16.7 Continued

```
memory                Size of avbl phys memory in 2k pages  8192
nested triggers       Allow triggers to invoke triggers     0
network packet size   Default network packet size           4096
open databases        # of open dbs allowed for all users   20
open objects          Number of open database objects       500
priority boost        Priority boost                        0
procedure cache       % of memory used for procedure cache  30
RA cache hit limit    RA cache hit limit                    4
RA cache miss limit   RA cache miss limit                   3
RA delay              RA delay                              15
RA pre-fetches        RA pre-fetches                        3
RA slots per thread   RA slots per thread                   5
RA worker threads     RA worker threads                     3
recovery flags        Recovery flags                        0
recovery interval     Maximum recovery interval in minutes  5
remote access         Allow remote access                   1
remote logon timeout  Remote logon timeout                  5
remote query timeout  Remote query timeout                  0
resource timeout      Resource timeout                     10
set working set size  Set working set size                  0
show advanced option  Show advanced options                 1
SMP concurrency       SMP concurrency                       1
sort pages            Number of sort pages                 128
spin counter          Spin counter                          0
tempdb in ram (MB)    Size of TempDB in RAM (MB)            0
user connections      Number of user connections allowed   20

(46 row(s) affected)
```

NOTE Both queries above are joined to the SQL Server system table spt_values. This is a special table that SQL Server uses for displaying value/configuration data. ■

Defining Database Options

SQL Server has several options available at a per database level that enable the database administrator (DBA) to configure how different databases perform/act on a given server.

NOTE In versions prior to SQL Server 6.0, it was necessary to do a CHECKPOINT command in the modified database after performing a change to a database option. In SQL Server 6.0, Microsoft added the dynamic interpretation of procedural logic to stored procedures, making it possible for them to update the sp_dboption system-stored procedure to automatically do the CHECKPOINT for you. ■

Displaying and Setting Database Options

SQL Server provides two ways to display and set configuration options for the database. The graphical method is via SQL Server Enterprise Manager. The command-line method is by using the system-stored procedure, sp_dboption.

Using SQL Enterprise Manager

To configure a database using SQL Enterprise Manager, follow these steps:

1. Run SQL Enterprise Manager from the Microsoft SQL Server 6.5 group.

2. Select the Server and Database that you want to work on.

3. Either double-click the database that you want to edit or press the right-mouse button and select Edit from the menu. When the Edit Database dialog box is displayed, click the Options page (see fig. 16.4).

FIG. 16.4

SQL Enterprise Manager's Edit Database dialog box shows the Options page.

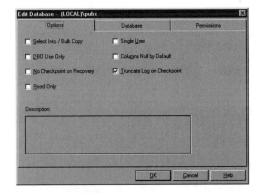

4. To change any of the settings for the database, click the required options and then click OK to apply the changes and return to the main SQL Enterprise Manager window.

Using *sp_dboption*

The system-stored procedure sp_dboption can be used instead of the SQL Enterprise Manager to set options for the database. The syntax for sp_dboption is as follows:

```
sp_dboption [database name, database option, database value]
```

database name is the name of the database that is being viewed or changed.

database option is the name of the option being viewed/changed. Place quotation marks around the option being set if it contains any embedded spaces.

database value is the new value for the option.

If no parameters are supplied to sp_dboption, it will return the available parameters that can be set for any current database. In Listing 16.8, you can see sp_dboption being executed without parameters.

Listing 16.8   Using *sp_dboption* to Report All the Configurable Database Options

```
/*---------------------------
sp_dboption
--------------------------*/
Settable database options:
--------------------------
ANSI null default
dbo use only
no chkpt on recovery
offline
published
read only
select into/bulkcopy
single user
subscribed
trunc. log on chkpt.
```

If a database is supplied as a parameter but no configuration option is supplied, sp_dboption returns the currently active configuration options for the database that was indicated (see Listing 16.9).

Listing 16.9   Seeing the *set* Option on a Database Using *sp_dboption*

```
/*---------------------------
sp_dboption pubs
--------------------------*/
The following options are set:
------------------------------
select into/bulkcopy
trunc. log on chkpt.
```

sp_dboption is similar to sp_configure in that for the option being set, it performs a wildcard-style search on the passed in option parameter (so that dbo, dbo use, and dbo use only are the same parameter).

Database Options Explained

The following is a list of all the database options that are available for configuration in user databases. In parentheses following the option name is the equivalent name that SQL Enterprise Manager uses for the option. Options without equivalent commands in SQL Enterprise Manager must be set with sp_dboption.

N O T E   The only option that is user configurable for the master database is the Truncate Log on Checkpoint option. SQL Server requires that all other configurations be left in their default setup to operate correctly. ■

***ANSI null default* (Columns Null by Default)**   This database option controls the way the CREATE TABLE statement is parsed by the SQL interpreter when defining columns. By default, if the NULL keyword is omitted in SQL Server, the SQL interpreter assumes that the column is supposed to be NOT NULL. However, the ANSI standard specifies the reverse, that if not specified a column is NULL.

If the database scripts being used to create a table or set of tables have been created for an ANSI-compatible database, it will be necessary to have this option turned on so that the tables generated/created behave the same way as they would on another ANSI-compatible database.

***DBO use only* (DBO Use Only)**   This database option controls the user access to the database. If set to True, then the only user that may access the database is the database owner (dbo). If this option is turned on while existing users have connected, they will not be killed. They will be allowed to stay on the database until they disconnect voluntarily.

***no chkpt on recovery* (No Checkpoint on Recovery)**   This database option controls the behavior on recovery of a database. The default is False, meaning that after a recovery of database or transaction log, a CHECKPOINT operation will occur.

If multiple databases are being used in a Primary and Secondary fashion and transaction logs are being rolled forward from one database to another, this option should be turned on. It will stop the database from rejecting further transaction logs being applied.

offline   This database option, if enabled, will bring a database "down" into an offline condition. This option is most often used with removable media, such as floppy disk or CD-ROM based databases, that need to be "swapped out" at any given time.

Databases that have currently connected or active users cannot be placed offline until those users disconnect. An offline database is not recovered when the server is restarted.

published   This database option controls whether a database is available for publishing and subscribing based replication. If enabled, a repl_subscriber user is added to the database and the transaction log is monitored for transactions that need to be replicated to other databases.

***read only* (Read Only)**   This database option, if enabled, places a database in read-only mode, making it impossible for any Inserts, Updates, or Deletes to occur. This is a useful option to turn on for reporting databases. For example if you are writing an application that simply does a lot of reports for your users, the read only flag will guarantee that the data does not change.

***select into/bulkcopy* (Select Into/Bulk Copy)**   This database option controls whether non-logged database operations are permitted in the current database. A non-logged operation, such as the SELECT INTO command, is highly optimized and does not write any entries to the database transaction log, making it unrecoverable.

This option must be enabled if bulkcopy (BCP) operations are to be executed against a database table without indexes. However, if a table has indexes, SQL Server will always use the slow load algorithm so that it has a chance to update the indexes.

***single user* (Single User)**   This database option limits database access to a single user. If enabled and a user connects, then that user may stay connected; however, any other user will

Part

V

Ch

16

be denied access. If single user mode is turned on, then `trunc. Log on chkpt.` will be disabled because it requires an additional user connection to the database to act as a monitor.

subscribed   This database option controls whether or not the database can be part of a subscription based replication. If set to `True`, a private account, `repl_publisher`, is given access as a DBO to the database, and the replication services are activated.

trunc. log on chkpt. (Truncate Log on Checkpoint)   This database option controls whether or not the database logs will be truncated when a checkpoint activity occurs. By default this option is off and it should always be off in production when it may be necessary to use the transaction logs for replication, backup, or recovery.

TROUBLESHOOTING

I'm checkpointing frequently, but my logs are filling up really quickly and are running out of space, stopping all activity on the server. Either perform more frequent manual dumping of the transaction logs, enlarge your logs, or use Performance Monitor to run a batch file that will dump the logs when the logs are approaching a full state. For information on Performance Monitor, see Chapter 17, "Optimizing Performance."

Understanding Query Options

SQL Server has a number of individual options that can be set while querying the database. These options control the behavior of queries when they are executed. They are also useful statistical and informational gatherers that can be helpful in diagnosing query problems, such as queries that run really slow for no apparent reason.

Displaying and Setting Database Options

SQL Server provides two ways to display and set configuration options for a query. The graphical method is via ISQL/w or through the Query Analyzer of SQL Server Enterprise Manager. The command-line method is by using the system keyword `SET`.

Using ISQL/w   To use ISQL/w to set or view query options, perform the following steps:

1. Run ISQL/w from the Microsoft SQL Server 6.5 group, and log on to the required server (see fig. 16.5).

2. From the Query menu, select Set Options to display the Query Options dialog box (see fig. 16.6).

3. To change any of the settings for the query, click the required options and then click OK to apply the changes and return to the main ISQL/w.

FIG. 16.5
The pubs database has been selected to be worked on just after starting ISQL/w.

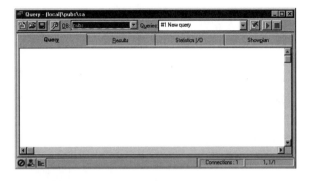

FIG. 16.6
ISQL/w's Query Options dialog box shows the Query Flags page.

SET   SQL Server provides a SQL keyword, the SET statement, that can be used to set any query option. If used in a stored procedure, the SET statement is in effect for the life of the procedure and overrides any previous settings. The syntax for the SET statement is as follows:

```
SET Option On ¦ Off
```

Option is any valid SQL Server query option.

Query Options Explained

The following is a list of all the query options that are configurable and what they do. In parentheses following the SET option is the equivalent in ISQL/w.

Arithabort (Abort on Arithmetic Error)   This option controls what SQL Server will do when an arithmetic error occurs. If set to True, SQL Server will abort any query that causes a divide by zero or numeric overflow (value is greater than the defined datatype) condition to occur. There is no opportunity to capture this error at runtime, so if this option is not set, the resulting output could be NULL results.

In Listing 16.10, Arithabort is used to stop a command batch from continuing with invalid data.

On the CD

Listing 16.10   16_03.SQL—Using the *Arithabort* Option

```
/* Declare working variables */
Declare @nDecimal Decimal( 8, 2 ),
        @nInteger Integer

/* ensure that the error does not cause an abort */
Set ArithAbort off

/* do a division that is going to cause an error
   note that the print statement doesn't
   get executed because this is a special error
   condition that SQL Server doesn't "publish"
   for handling */

Select @nDecimal = 8 / 0
If @@error != 0
    Print 'Error'

/* abort processing if the error occurs again */
Set ArithAbort on

/* This time the division will cause an error and
   the SQL command batch will be terminated, note
   that the termination stops any further activity
   and the print statement again is ignored */

Select @nDecimal = 8 / 0
If @@error != 0
    Print 'Error'
```

Here is the output:

```
Divide by zero occurred.

(1 row(s) affected)

Msg 8134, Level 16, State 1
Divide by zero error encountered
```

***Arithignore* (Ignore Arithmetic Error)**   Arithignore is the opposite of Arithabort in that it will stop the SQL Server from reporting an error condition if an arithmetic error occurs. In Listing 16.11, Arithignore is demonstrated and shows SQL Server not reporting any error conditions.

On the CD

Listing 16.11   16_04.SQL—Using *Arithignore* to Ignore Arithmetic Overflows

```
/* Declare working variables */
Declare @nDecimal Decimal( 8, 2 ),
        @nInteger Integer

/* ensure that the error does not cause an abort */
Set Arithignore on
```

```
/* do a division that is going to cause an error
   note that the print statement doesn't
   get executed because this is a special error
   condition that SQL Server doesn't "publish"
   for handling */

Select @nDecimal = 8 / 0
If @@error != 0
     Print 'Error'

/* do a print so that we know we are through the
   first part of the query */

Print 'Second Query'

/* abort processing if the error occurs again */
Set ArithIgnore off

/* This time the division will cause an error and
   the SQL command batch will be terminated, note
   that the termination stops any further activity
   and the print statement again is ignored */

Select @nDecimal = 8 / 0
If @@error != 0
     Print 'Error'
```

Here is the output:

```
(1 row(s) affected)

Second Query
Divide by zero occurred.

(1 row(s) affected)
```

NOCOUNT (No Count Display)   This option disables the display of the number of rows processed by any SQL statement. The @@ROWCOUNT global variable is still maintained even though this option is turned off. The ouput in Listing 16.12 shows the effect of NOCOUNT.

On the CD

Listing 16.12   16_05.SQL—Using *NOCOUNT* to Stop the Reporting of Rows Affected by SQL

```
/* Make sure that NoCount is Off (the default) */
Set NoCount Off

/* Do some SQL */
Select  "# Authors" = Count(*)
From    AUTHORS

/* Now turn on NoCount */
Set NoCount On
```

continues

Listing 16.12   Continued

```
/* Do the same SQL and observe the different results */
Select   "# Authors" = Count(*)
From     AUTHORS
Here is the output:
# Authors
----------
23

(1 row(s) affected)

# Authors
----------
23
```

NOEXEC **(No Execute)**   This option controls whether SQL Server will actually execute a SQL statement. If you turn this option on, SQL Server will not execute the query, but will perform only the work to determine *how* the query would have been answered. This option is most commonly used when viewing the SHOWPLAN that a query generates without fetching the data.

> **N O T E**   SQL Server processes queries in two phases: compilation and execution. In the *compilation* phase, SQL Server validates that the query is OK, checks that all the objects exist and are readable, and generates the query plan or best path to the actual data. In the *execution* phase, SQL Server starts performing the query, which could be updating the records, fetching the data, etc. ■

PARSEONLY **(Parse Query Only)**   This option is like NOEXEC except that SQL Server does not even compile the query (generate the access path to the data); all it does is check that the query is syntactically accurate.

SHOWPLAN **(Show Query Plan)**   This option shows the query plan that SQL Server generated to answer a query. The query plan can be interpreted by ISQL/w or by SQL Enterprise Manager, and a graphical representation will be shown (see fig. 16.7).

For a complete and detailed discussion on interpreting the SHOWPLAN output, refer to Chapter 23, "Understanding *SHOWPLAN* Output," in Microsoft's *SQL Server Administrator's Companion*.

STATISTICS TIME **(Show Stats Time)**   This option shows the amount of time the server spent in different areas of parsing, compilation and execution, and answering a query. This information can be very useful in helping to tune queries; however, the data can be skewed because of server caching.

STATISTICS IO **(Show Stats I/O)**   This option shows the number of logical and physical reads that the server did to answer a query. Logical reads are reads that come from cache pages; physical reads caused the database to go to disk. The number returned is the number of 2K pages read.

FIG. 16.7
ISQL/w's graphical *SHOWPLAN* output can help you understand how a query is being performed.

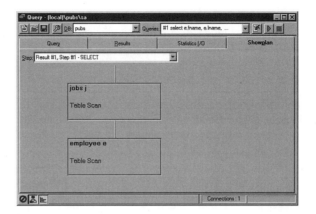

Starting the Server in Minimal Configuration Mode

Minimal configuration mode is a mode of last resort that should only be used when the server fails to start because of an invalid configuration specified with sp_configure. Minimal configuration mode starts the minimum number of services to allow the reconfiguration of the server. Minimal configuration mode is provided in SQL Server 6.0 in place of SQL Server 4.2's and Sybase's bldmaster executable. Prior to version 6.0 of SQL Server the configuration options were written to the bldmaster file and if the server was unstartable, it was necessary to edit this file manually.

> **CAUTION**
> This chapter applies *only* to SQL Server 6.x; the instructions here are not effective with prior releases. See the Microsoft SQL Server documentation on bldmaster to restart a server prior to SQL Server 6.x.

A server started in minimal configuration mode has the following limitations:

- All configuration values that affect memory, database, and server are set to their minimums as shown in sp_configure.

- The stored procedure cache is set to 50 percent of available memory as configured in the minimums of sp_configure. Therefore memory is set 1000 2K pages (or 2MB) and procedure cache is 500 pages (or 1MB).

- SQL Server is started in single-user mode at the server level (equivalent to the -m command-line option of SQL Server). Because the server is in single-user mode, the CHECKPOINT service is not started. This service is required to guarantee that transactions are written to disk.

TIP The CHECKPOINT service behaves like a user in the system and is assigned spid 3. You can check that the service is running by executing an sp_who command in ISQL.

- Remote Access is disabled because the Remote Access service (that acts as a user) is not able to connect to the server due to single-user limitations.

- Read Ahead paging is disabled because the Read Ahead service (that acts as a user) is not able to connect to the server due to single-user limitations.

- SQL Enterprise Manager will be unable to be used because it requires more than one connection to the server and consumes more resources than are available during minimal configuration mode. You must use ISQL to fix the configuration option that is causing the server to be unstartable.

- No autoexec procedures are run on server startup. Again, these procedures rely on being able to connect to the database and this connection is reserved for the user to correct the server configuration problem through ISQL.

- Tempdb is moved into RAM with 2MB of RAM designated for its use.

Starting SQL Server in Minimal Configuration Mode from the Command Line

To start the server in minimal configuration mode from the command line, perform the following steps:

1. Start a command prompt by double-clicking the Command Prompt icon in the Main group of Program Manager.

2. Type **start sqlservr -f**.

TIP The start command launches a separate process thread in which SQL Server is executed. This allows you to continue using the same command prompt to do other things. Any Windows NT task can be started.

N O T E To start SQL Server independently of the Windows NT Service Control Manager, use the –c command line switch. A server started in this fashion starts more quickly and allows more rapid fixing of the server in an emergency situation. ■

Starting SQL Server in Minimal Configuration Mode with the Services Application in Control Panel

To start the server in minimal configuration mode from using the Services application in Control Panel, perform the following steps:

1. Start Control Panel by double-clicking the Control Panel icon in the Main group of Program Manager.

2. Start the Services application by double-clicking the Services icon in the Control Panel window.

3. Type **start sqlservr -f**.

Repairing a Server Started in Minimal Configuration Mode

There may be several things that you will need to do to repair a server that has needed to be started in minimal configuration mode.

If you started your server in minimal configuration mode to reset a configuration, then this is what you should do:

1. Start the server in minimal configuration mode.
2. Run ISQL.
3. Execute `sp_configure` to change the offending configuration value.
4. Execute `reconfigure` to change the server value.
5. Execute `shutdown with nowait` to shut down the server.
6. Restart the server as you normally would, and confirm that it starts OK. If the server still does not start follow these guidelines again and adjust another configuration value.

If you started your server in minimal configuration mode because the server ran out of disk space then, this is what you should do:

1. Start the server in minimal configuration mode.
2. Run ISQL.
3. Execute `DISK RESIZE` to extend a disk device or `DISK INIT` to create another disk device.
4. Execute `ALTER DATABASE` to extend the database onto, or to add the database to, a new device.
5. Execute `shutdown with nowait` to shut down the server.
6. Restart the server as you normally would, and confirm that it starts OK. If the server still does not start, follow these guidelines again and modify the devices as appropriate.

From Here...

In this chapter you learned how to configure your server, database, and queries to get optimal performance and to maximize your use of the server. Take a look at the following chapters for more information:

- See Chapter 6, "Retrieving Data with Transact-SQL," to take advantage of some of the configuration options discussed in this chapter and improve the performance of your SELECTs.

- See Chapter 13, "Managing Stored Procedures and Using Flow-Control Statements," to take advantage of the new options to stop your stored procedures from getting error conditions and aborting.

Optimizing Performance

Performance tuning in the client/server world is somewhat of a magical art. A combination of so many factors can make an application perform well, and knowing where to focus your time is what's most important.

The most critical part of optimizing performance is to have good documentation. Document statistically how the system works or performs before even starting any performance tuning. As the performance tuning cycle begins, monitor and document the effects of all the changes so that it's easy to determine the changes that were positive and those that were negative. Never assume that all the changes made for one application automatically apply to another application. Remember you're ultimately tuning a product that a user is using, not just a database that's being accessed by some unknown client. ■

How to approximately size a database and how to estimate the amount of disk space required

Sizing a SQL Server database can make a difference to how you choose to buy hardware for your server

How to size the procedure cache for optimal performance

An optimally sized procedure cache will substantial improve performance because frequently accessed procedures will not need to be recompiled.

How to use Windows NT's Performance Monitor with SQL Server

Windows NT's Performance Monitor provides complete and up-to-date statistics to help you manage and monitor the performance of your SQL Server.

Sizing a Database

Estimating the size of a SQL Server database is relatively straightforward and can be done with a good level of accuracy. The principle of space calculation is that all the bytes of data per table should be added together along with the associated overhead per row and page of data and that this should then be used as a divisor to the page size (2K) to determine how many rows of data will fit in a page.

The actual available space of a page is 2,016 bytes because 32 bytes are reserved for fixed overhead to manage the rows on the page. In general terms, these calculations are affected by the placement of and use of FILL FACTORS on indexes and if a clustered index is on the table.

Datatype Sizes

Each SQL Server datatype consumes a certain amount of bytes based on the storage of the data. The following list defines the amount of storage that each datatype uses:

Datatype	Size
Char/Binary	The size indicated in the definition
VarChar/VarBinary	The actual data size (use an average estimate)
Int	4 bytes
SmallInt	2 bytes
TinyInt	1 byte
Float	8 bytes
Float(b)	4 bytes (numbers with precision of 1-7 digits)
Float(b)	8 bytes (numbers with precision of 8-15 digits)
Double Precision	8 bytes
Real	4 bytes
Money	8 bytes
SmallMoney	4 bytes
Datetime	8 bytes
SmallDatetime	4 bytes
Bit	1 byte
Decimal/Numeric	2-17 bytes depending on the precision
Text/Image	16 bytes per table row plus at least one 2K page for NOT NULL column
Timestamp	8 bytes

SQL Server internally defines any NULLable column as a var datatype. So a Char(12) NULL column is actually a Varchar(12) column. Therefore, for any columns that permit NULL values the average expected column size should be used.

Decimal and numeric precision affects the amount of storage required for these datatypes. The following table indicates the amount of bytes required for each range of precision:

Numeric Precision	Size
0–2	2 bytes
3–4	3 bytes
5–7	4 bytes
8–9	5 bytes
10–12	6 bytes
13–14	7 bytes
15–16	8 bytes
17–19	9 bytes
20–21	10 bytes
22–24	11 bytes
25–26	12 bytes
27–28	13 bytes
29–31	14 bytes
32–33	15 bytes
34–36	16 bytes
37–38	17 bytes

Calculating Space Requirements For Tables

The method of calculating a table's space requirements differs based on whether the table has a clustered index or not. Both calculation methods are shown here, and examples will be drawn from the pubs database to illustrate their use.

Some things to be aware of when calculating table and index sizes are that:

- Performing UPDATE STATISTICS on an index adds an extra page for that index to store the distribution statistics of the data that it contains. Performing UPDATE STATISTICS on the table will add one data distribution page per index on the table.

- For tables with variable-length columns, you should try to average the length of the row by estimating the anticipated average size of the columns on the table.

- SQL Server won't store more than 256 rows per page, even if the row is very short. So if your row is 7 bytes or less in size, the number of data pages required for N rows of data is calculated by: N / 256 = number of data pages required.

- Text and Image data will take up a minimum of 2K (one page) unless when a row is inserted, the value for the column is specified as NULL.

Tables with Clustered Indexes The Publishers table has a clustered index. This example will estimate the space required for 5,000,000 rows, and will assume that the average length of the Varchar columns is 60 percent of the defined length:

1. Calculate the row length. If the row contains only fixed-length, NOT NULL columns, the formula is

   ```
   2 + (Sum of column sizes in bytes) = Row Size
   ```

   If the row contains mixed variable-length fields and/or NULL columns, the formula is

   ```
   2 + (Sum of fixed-length column sizes in bytes) + (Sum of average
      ➥ of variable-length columns) = Subtotal
   Subtotal * (( Subtotal / 256) _+ 1) + (Number of variable-length
      ➥ columns +_ 1) + 2 = Row Size
   ```

   For the Publishers table, the second formula is required:

   ```
   2 + 4 + (60% of 92) = 55.2
   55.2 * ((55.2/256) + 1) + 5 + 2 = 75
   ```

2. Calculate the number of rows that will fit on a page. The formula is

   ```
   2016 / (Row Size) = Number of rows per page
   ```

   In this case,

   ```
   2016 / 75 = 27
   ```

 TIP For more accurate calculations, round *down* any calculations for number of rows per page.

3. Number of Rows Required/Number of rows per page = number of 2K data pages:

   In this case,

   ```
   5,000,000 / 27 = 18519
   ```

 TIP For more accurate calculations, round up any calculations for number of pages required.

4. Next calculate the space required for the clustered index. The size of the clustered index depends on whether the key columns are variable or fixed-length. For fixed-length keys, use this formula:

   ```
   5 + (Sum of column sizes in bytes) = Clustered index size
   ```

   For variable-length keys, use this formula:

   ```
   5 + (Sum of fixed-length column sizes in bytes) + (Sum of average
      ➥ of variable-length columns) = Subtotal
   Subtotal * (( Subtotal / 256) _+ 1) + (Number of variable-length
      ➥ columns +_ 1) + 2 = Clustered index size
   ```

   For Publishers, the key is a single, fixed-length column, therefore

   ```
   5 + 4 = 9
   ```

5. Now calculate the number of clustered index rows that will fit on a page. The formula is:

```
(2016 / (Clustered index size)) - 2 = Number of rows per page
```

In this case:

```
(2016 / 9) - 2 = 222
```

6. Next calculate the number of index pages by using the following formula:

```
(Number of data pages) / (Number of clustered index rows per page) = Number
of index pages at index level N
```

For this example,

```
18519 / 222 = 84
```

Index pages are at multiple levels. To compute all the levels of the index, continue to divide the resulting number of index pages by the number of clustered rows per page until the result is 1 or less. In this case:

```
84 / 222 = 1
```
, which means that one index page is at the top of the index and all the other pages are actual pointers to data pages.

7. Compute the total number of 2K pages required for the database table:

Data Pages: 18519

Index Pages (level 1): 1

Index Pages (level 0): 83

Total number of 2K pages: 19403 (or about 38MB)

Tables with Nonclustered Indexes   Tables with non-clustered indexes are calculated in size the same way as a clustered index table except for the sizing of the index itself. In this example, assume that a non-clustered index has been added to the roysched table on the `title_id` column, and that 7,000,000 rows are in the table. The following steps will help you size a non-clustered index:

1. The first step is to calculate the length of the leaf row in the index. A *leaf row* is the bottom row of an index tree and points to the data page. The leaf row's size is the size of the index's columns summed together and is affected by variable or fixed-length columns. Use this formula if you have only fixed-length columns in the index:

```
7 + (Sum of fixed-length keys) = Size of index row
```

Use this formula if you have fixed and variable-length columns in the index:

```
9 + (Sum of length of fixed-length keys) + (Sum of length of
  ➡ variable-length keys) + (Number of variable-length keys)
  ➡ + 1 = Subtotal
 (Subtotal) + ((Subtotal / 256) + 1) = (Size of leaf index row)
```

In the roysched table, the primary key is fixed-length and isn't NULL, therefore:

```
7 + 6 = 13
```

2. Next calculate the number of leaf pages that will be required by using the following formulae:

```
2016 / (Size of leaf index row) = Number of leaf rows per page
```

For example: `2016 / 13 = ` **155**

```
(Number of rows in table) / (Number of leaf rows per page) =
➥ Number of leaf pages
```

For example: `7,000,000 / 155 = ` **45,162**

3. Next calculate the size of the non-leaf row and calculate the number of non-leaf pages. The size of non-leaf row is calculated according to this formula:

```
(Size of leaf index row) + 4 = Size of nonleaf row
```

that is, `13+4=`**17**

```
(2016 / Size of nonleaf row) - 2 = Number of nonleaf index rows
➥ per page
```

In this example, `(2016/17)-2=`**116**

```
(Number of leaf pages / Number of nonleaf index rows per page)
➥ = Number of index pages at Level N
```

or `45,162/117=`**386** pages at level 1

Like the clustered index the levels of the index are determined by result division until the result is 1 or less:

`386 / 117 = ` **4** pages at level 2.

`4 / 117 = ` **1** page at level 3.

4. Finally, compute the size of the index by summing the number of pages at the various levels of the index:

Leaf Pages: 45,162

Level 1 Pages: 386

Level 2 Pages: 4

Level 3 Pages: 1

Total number of 2K pages: 45553 (or about 89MB)

Effects of *FILL FACTOR*

FILL FACTOR alters the number of rows that SQL Server will place on a page. The most likely configuration of FILL FACTOR is to assume that the table will never change its data-set and therefore you set FILL FACTOR to 100 percent to maximize the use of data pages. This affects the calculations by increasing the number of rows that can fit on a page by 2.

If you're sizing an index with a FILL FACTOR of 100 percent, don't subtract 2 from the result of the number of rows per page because SQL Server won't preallocate these rows for page growth but will instead put user data there.

Any other value of FILL FACTOR alters the size of the page itself. For example a FILL FACTOR of 70 percent reduces the amount of available space on the page to 1412 bytes.

Sizing the Procedure Cache

Sizing the Procedure Cache in SQL Server is basically a case of trial and error. Microsoft documents an approximation based on the following formula:

*Procedure Cache = (Maximum Concurrent Users) * (Size of Largest Plan) * 1.25*

To determine the size of a plan in memory, the DBCC MEMUSAGE command should be issued in ISQL. The following SQL illustrates the output from DBCC MEMUSAGE:

```
/*---------------------------
dbcc memusage
---------------------------*/
Memory Usage:
...
Buffer Cache, Top 20:
...
Procedure Cache, Top 12:
...

Procedure Name: sp_help
Database Id: 1
Object Id: 1888009757
Version: 1
Uid: 1
Type: stored procedure
Number of trees: 0
Size of trees: 0.000000 Mb, 0.000000 bytes, 0 pages
Number of plans: 1
Size of plans: 0.051249 Mb, 53738.000000 bytes, 27 pages
```

Assuming that sp_help was the largest procedure to be run on a server and that there were to be 150 concurrent users, then

150 * 27 * 2 * 1.25 = 10125K

N O T E Memory in the procedure cache is managed as a set of 2K pages; therefore, the number of pages reported by DBCC MEMUSAGE is multiplied by 2K to derive the amount of memory that the plan actually consumes. ■

Part

V

Ch

17

An alternative sizing can be estimated based on the need to stop SQL Server from recompiling procedures that fall out of the cache frequently. The procedure cache, like the data cache, works on a Least Recently Used (LRU) algorithm and procedures that are used infrequently are pushed out of the cache if there's no more room to compile a procedure that's requested by a user process.

Therefore, work out a list of the number of critical procedures or procedures that are most frequently accessed and execute each one, analyzing the memory used as reported by DBCC MEMUSAGE. Based on the total memory calculated, the size of the procedure cache can be determined.

Ultimately, the only true judge of an accurate size of procedure cache is to test, test, test an application and monitor the effects of altering the amount of cache available.

It's possible to run out of procedure cache if the number of active procedures in use (and their combined plan sizes) is greater than the cache available. In this case, you'll receive error 701, and the calling process that was trying to execute a procedure will be rolled back. If you receive this message you should resize the procedure cache to a higher percentage of available memory.

Using the Windows NT Performance Monitor

Windows NT's Performance Monitor is an advanced tool that provides statistics about the operation of the NT environment. One of the unique properties of the performance monitor is its capability to install performance heuristics and callbacks from other executables in the Windows NT system and report their statistics.

SQL Server's performance monitor is just a set of hooks for the core Windows NT Performance Monitor to call. SQL Server groups the statistics that can be displayed into what it calls *objects*. These objects group the logical similar statistics.

SQL Server gathers statistics in one of two different modes:

■ In Direct Response mode, the Performance Monitor will wait for SQL Server to gather statistics and place them in statistics tables. These tables are available at any time for browsing but refer to the last period that the server gathered information and might not necessarily accurately reflect the current server operating level.

■ In On Demand mode, the Performance Monitor will force SQL Server to gather statistics and return them whenever a period elapses in the Performance Monitor. You should take care not to saturate SQL Server with requests for statistics because this is a relatively costly operation and may in turn skew the results of the statistics themselves.

To configure either Direct Response or On Demand mode, follow these steps:

1. First run SQL Enterprise Manager from the Microsoft SQL Server 6.5 group and select the server to be configured (see fig. 17.1).

FIG. 17.1

SQL Enterprise Manager after just being started. Note that the (LOCAL) server is selected.

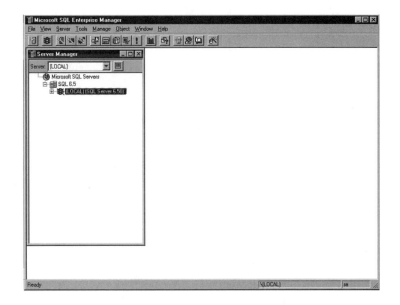

2. From the menu choose Server, SQL Server, Configure (see fig. 17.2).

FIG. 17.2

SQL Enterprise Manager's Server Configuration/Options dialog box.

3. Select Direct Response Mode or On Demand Mode and click OK.

SQL Server Statistics Objects

The following sections list the objects that SQL Server Performance Monitor can report on. Some of the counters within the objects can be applied to particular instances of activity on the server. For example, the User Object's Physical I/O counter can be applied to each user connected to the system. This process of configuring instances to the particular counter allows you to customize the statistics that you want to monitor.

SQL Server Object The SQL Server Object is the master object and provides a wide variety of statistics. The items that are monitored here are the high-level statistics that are very important to everyday management of your server. Normal monitoring of SQL Server typically watches at least the I/O and cache statistics to make sure that the physical I/O and memory subsystems aren't being flooded with requests.

They're grouped as follows:

- *Cache Statistics:* The cache options allow you to monitor the performance of both the lazywriter and the amount of free data pages available in the data cache. Also, the cache hit rate can be monitored. The cache hit rate is a useful statistic because it tells you how frequently physical I/O has to be performed to meet a user process request.

- *I/O Statistics:* These statistics report the amount of work being performed by the physical I/O subsystems of SQL Server. They can provide useful information and will allow you to monitor saturation on the I/O devices if the Outstanding Reads/Writes gets high. Careful analysis of the I/O statistics can yield an excellent set of data that will help diagnose disk problems in your environment.

- *NET Statistics:* These statistics report the number of reads and writes that SQL Server is placing out on Windows NT's network processing queues. These NET statistics are relatively unimportant and NT's statistics should be monitored instead.

- *RA Manager Statistics:* The Read Ahead Manager provides a number of system statistics that allow the monitoring of the RA's performance. Generally this information will help you tune the server using `sp_configure`.

- *User Connections:* The number of currently connected users to the server.

SQL Server Replication-Published DB Object The Replication-Published DB Object is provided to allow monitoring of the publication of transaction log information from a source or publishing database. It is highly recommended that you monitor the performance of this object if you are using replication in your environment. These statistics will help you decide how efficiently data is being published by your server.

The statistics that are available are as follows:

- *Replicated Transactions:* The number of transactions that are in the transaction log of the primary database that have yet to be placed in the distribution database but have been marked for replication.

- *Replicated Transactions/sec:* The relative performance, presented in transactions per second, of the rate of reading out of the published database's transaction log and placing the items in the distribution database for replication.

- *Replication Latency (sec):* The average number of milliseconds that elapse between the time that a transaction is placed in the transaction log and the time it's placed in the distribution database.

SQL Server Replication-Subscriber Object The Replication-Subscriber Object is provided to allow monitoring of the replication that's updating tables on the subscribing server/database. Like the Publishing Object previously described, careful monitoring of this object is essential to the management of effective replication.

The following information is provided:

- *Delivered Transactions:* The number of transactions that have been executed on the destination database.
- *Delivered Transactions/sec:* The relative performance indicated in transactions per second of delivery of data.
- *Delivered Latency (Sec):* The time, in seconds, that it takes for a transaction to be executed after it's placed in the distribution database.
- *Undelivered Transactions:* The number of transactions sitting in the distribution database that have yet to be executed on the subscribing databases.

SQL Server Locks Object The Locks Object is provided to allow central management of locks in the database. The counters provided in this object detail the totals of the different types of locks: Extent, Intent, Page, and Table. Additional counters are provided to indicate the number of blocking locks.

▶ **See** Chapter 12, "Understanding Transactions and Locking," for more information about locks. **p. 321**

SQL Server Log Object The Log Object is provided so that alerts can be placed on the size of and space free on the transaction log associated with a database. This will allow you to dump the logs at required intervals:

- *Log Size:* The size in megabytes of the transaction log.
- *Space Free:* The percentage of the log that's free and available for transactions to be placed in.

SQL Server Users Object The Users Object has the following counters available that track the statistics about user activity on the server:

- *CPU Time:* The amount of CPU consumed by a particular user.
- *Locks Held:* The current number of open locks held by a particular user.
- *Memory (in 2K pages):* The amount of memory that a particular user is consuming on the server. This memory will include any memory allocated to resolve queries.
- *Physical I/O:* The amount of physical reads and writes of data pages that have occurred as a result of the user's most recent query.

Creating and Using Chart Views

Chart views are often the most easy statistical viewing mechanism for a database administrator. With a chart you can track periodic performance in a number of criteria and see prior history in the same view.

Part
V

Ch
17

To use the SQL Performance Monitor to chart statistics for view, follow these steps:

1. First run SQL Performance Monitor from the Microsoft SQL Server 6.5 group (see fig. 17.3).

FIG. 17.3
Windows NT's Performance Monitor running the SQL Server control file (SQLCTRS.PMC) with the default objects being monitored.

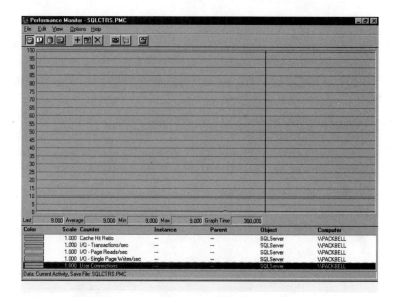

2. From the View menu, select Chart.

3. From the Edit menu, select Add To Chart. This opens the Add To Chart dialog box shown in fig. 17.4.

FIG. 17.4
The Add To Chart dialog box with the SQL Server object selected.

 T I P   Click the Explain button to get a short explanation of each counter as you select it.

4. Select the Object from which you want to monitor a counter.

5. Select one or many counters from the Counter list box and, if necessary, specify the instances that you want to apply the counters on in the Instance list box.

6. Specify the required line attributes for the item(s) being added (color, line style, and so on).

7. Click Add to add the items to the current Performance Monitor Chart (see fig. 17.5).

FIG. 17.5
The Add To Chart dialog box is ready to add SQL Server-Log counters for the master and pubs databases.

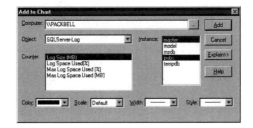

8. Add any other statistics that you want to chart and then click Done to close the dialog box. (The Cancel button changes to a Done button after you add the first item to the chart.)

Creating and Using Reports

Performance Monitor can create basic reports of data that's being gathered. These reports show the current (or most recent) values fetched from the statistics of the selected counters.

To use the SQL Performance Monitor to create a report of system statistics, follow these steps:

1. First run SQL Performance Monitor from the Microsoft SQL Server 6.5 group.
2. From the View menu, choose Report.
3. From the Edit menu, select Add To Report (see fig. 17.6).

FIG. 17.6
The Add To Report dialog box has the SQL Server Replication-Published DB object selected as well as all the counters to be added to the report.

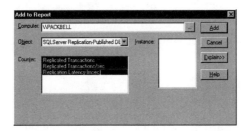

4. Select the Object that you want to report a counter from.
5. Select one or many counters from the Counter list box and, if necessary, go to Instance and specify the number of instances on which you want to apply the counters.
6. Click Add to add the items to the current Performance Monitor Report.
7. Add any other statistics that you want to report on and click Done to close the dialog box. (The Cancel button changes to a Done button after you add the first item to the chart.)

Creating and Using Alerts

Alerts are one of the most useful features of Performance Monitor. Performance Monitor not only can gather statistics from various system objects, but it can also monitor the values of those statistics. If they reach predetermined levels, Performance Monitor can execute a program that can, for example, dial a pager or alert the DBA in some other fashion.

To use the SQL Performance Monitor to create a statistical alert, follow these steps:

1. Run SQL Performance Monitor from the Microsoft SQL Server 6.5 group.
2. From the View menu, select Alert.
3. From the Edit menu, select Add To Alert (see fig. 17.7).

FIG. 17.7
The Add To Alert dialog box is
ready to add an alert that will
send a mail message to the
DBA if the used log space on
the pubs database exceeds
75 percent.

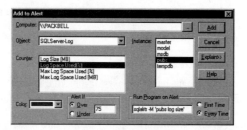

4. Select the Object that you want to add an alert counter from.
5. Select one or many counters from the Counter list box. If necessary, go to Instance and specify the instances on which you want to apply the counters.
6. Click Add to add the items to the current Performance Monitor Alert list.
7. Add any other statistics for which you want to create alerts and click Done to close the dialog box. (The Cancel button changes to a Done button after you add the first item to the chart.)

From Here...

In this chapter you learned how to identify and manage statistics that will help you determine the performance characteristics of your server. You also learned how to size a database and how to size the procedure cache.

Consider looking at the following chapters to further develop your SQL Server knowledge:

■ Chapter 16, "Understanding Server, Database, and Query Options," teaches you to further tune the server after analyzing the information provided by the SQL Performance Monitor.

■ Chapter 22, "Accessing SQL Server Databases Through Front-End Products," teaches you to examine how clients connect to the database, and perhaps tune the ODBC interface on the client.

SQL Server Administration

In this chapter you'll be presented with several issues to keep in mind as you administer your SQL Server system. There are many different concepts, routines, and ideas that you need to know for the day-in and day-out management of SQL Server.

The everyday operation of SQL Server will require some of your time to manage the database engine to its fullest potential. By staying on top of the system, you'll be able to ensure the optimum response times for users, and you'll be able to prevent some common problems with the system from happening altogether.

Some of the concepts in this chapter refer to strictly administrative tasks, and some are related more to management of performance and system tuning. Taken as a whole, these topics and the correct definition of your system will make sure you have a successful SQL Server installation. ■

Understanding and performing checkpoints

Checkpoints are used by SQL Server to maintain database integrity. You'll see how they work and how they'll impact your implementation of SQL Server.

Using the Database Consistency Checker

The Database Consistency Checker provides valuable information about the state of your database and tables.

Backing up SQL Server

Any production system must be backed up in order to remain reliable. You'll see how you can use the different tools provided by SQL Server to backup your system.

Transferring information to and from SQL Server

Whether you're bringing up a system based on information from another previously existing system, or if you're making changes to other types of existing data sources, you'll need to know how to transfer information to and from SQL Server.

Understanding and Performing Checkpoints

Checkpoints are a function incorporated by SQL Server to commit changes to a database or configuration option at a known, good point in time. As you work to configure the server or make modifications to the server that require a restart of the server, you may want to initiate the checkpoint process manually.

When a checkpoint is issued, whether by a manual intervention process or by naturally occurring server-based processes, all dirty pages are saved to disk. A *dirty page* is one containing updates that have not yet been applied to the disk image of the database. Checkpoints normally occur approximately every 60 seconds when they occur without intervention on your part. The actual time frame in which they are called will depend on server loading, recovery options you've set, and general performance tuning that SQL Server will be looking after—but should be very close to 60 seconds.

You may have noticed that if your SQL Server goes down unexpectedly, it can take longer to startup the next time. This is because SQL Server will roll back and roll forward transactions to the last checkpoint. When SQL Server does this, it is restoring the database to the last known good state, which is the one recorded when the last checkpoint was issued and successfully carried out.

N O T E You can also manually shutdown the server by issuing the SHUTDOWN command. By issuing CHECKPOINT followed by a SHUTDOWN, you can ensure that all transaction information is saved appropriately. ■

If you know that you're shutting down the server, you can avoid the longer startup times by manually issuing the CHECKPOINT command. This will accomplish the same thing as allowing the server to issue the command automatically. All information will be saved to disk, and the system will be able to simply startup and "turn on" the databases for access by your client applications. This is helpful if you're shutting down a server quickly, perhaps in a case where you've had power failure and the UPS that is sustaining the server is nearing its life cycle.

N O T E The CHECKPOINT command is issued at a database level and is applied against the current database. If you have more than one database in your system, you need to issue the command against each database. In order to issue the CHECKPOINT command, you must be the database owner. ■

Another option that will prove quite helpful is the Truncate Log on Checkpoint option. This option will automatically truncate the transaction log whenever a checkpoint is reached. To set this option, select the database in the Enterprise Manager and right-click it. Select Edit from the menu, then select the Options tab. Figure 18.1 shows the options that are available.

FIG. 18.1

You can control the interval in which the transaction log is truncated from the Enterprise Manager.

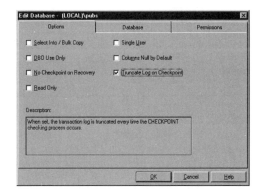

N O T E If you set Truncate Log on Checkpoint as an option, you won't be able to back up the transaction log during the course of standard backups. This may not present a problem in your installation, as you can still do database backups, but you should consider your overall backup plan prior to setting this option. See the sections later in this chapter for more information on backup and restore operations. ■

If you have Truncate Log on Checkpoint enabled for a database, the transaction log will be truncated up to the point of the last successfully committed transaction, provided replication is not in use. If replication is in use, the log is truncated up to the last successfully replicated transaction and successfully committed transaction. Because replication is transaction-log based, this prevents the log from being truncated in cases where replication has not been propagated to the subscribers for a given publication. More information on replication is presented in Chapter 20, "Setting Up and Managing Replication."

Part

V

Ch

18

Using the Database Consistency Checker

The *Database Consistency Checker* (DBCC) is a tool that you use for detailed information about the database objects that SQL Server manages. Because there are so many different facets to the SQL Server system and its handling of tables, objects, rules, triggers, stored procedures and others, it is helpful to be able to go into the server and run a "sanity check" to make sure all is well. The DBCC statement provides this functionality.

Setting Up to Ensure the Best Results: Single-User Mode

Before we get into the use and utility of DBCC, it's important to understand two different conditions that are generally in effect any time you want to use this statement. First, as a rule, you should try to make sure that as little activity as possible is impacting the SQL Server. If people are accessing the server making updates or changes, you may receive errors when DBCC runs. This is due to the nature of the calls that DBCC will perform. They are very low-level and require near-exclusive use of the database in many cases.

Second, you'll often have to ensure exclusive access to the database. In those cases, use the sp_dboption statement to set the database to single user mode. The following is the syntax of that command:

```
sp_dboption <database name>, 'single user', True
```

For example, if you want to run some checks on the PUBS database, you'll use the following command:

```
sp_dboption 'pubs', 'single user', True
```

This will prevent others from using the system while you perform your checks.

N O T E You'll need to be in the Master database prior to updating the options for the system. Be sure you issue a Use Master prior to attempting to set options using sp_dboption. ■

Once you've turned on single user mode, you can perform the checks you need to make sure the database is running in top shape. When you've completed your work with DBCC, you can set the database back to multiuser mode by changing the True noted earlier in the sp_dboption command to False. For example:

```
sp_dboption 'pubs', 'single user', False.
```

Using the DBCC Options

As mentioned earlier, DBCC supports many different options. In the next few sections, I'll describe the most often used options and what they can do to help in your administration of your SQL Server.

Using *DBCC NEWALLOC* NEWALLOC has replaced the past use of CHECKALLOC. With CHECKALLOC, the system process would stop if an error was found, sometimes obscuring other problems with the database. NEWALLOC will not stop when an error is found, but will continue on and report all errors that it finds in the database structures. It has the following syntax:

```
DBCC NEWALLOC <database name>
```

If you leave out the <database name> parameter, SQL Server will check the current database.

When NEWALLOC runs, it will return detailed information about your system and its database objects. This information can be used to point you in the direction of any problems that may be occurring on the system. Listing 18.1 shows a portion of a report, run against the standard pubs database. This sample indicates the type of information you can expect to receive from the NEWALLOC option.

Listing 18.1 Sample Output from the *NewAlloc* Statement

```
Checking pubs
***************************************************************
TABLE: sysobjects          OBJID = 1
INDID=1      FIRST=1        ROOT=8        DPAGES=4      SORT=0
     Data level: 1.  4 Data  Pages in 1 extents.
     Indid       : 1.  1 Index Pages in 1 extents.
INDID=2      FIRST=40       ROOT=41       DPAGES=1      SORT=1
     Indid       : 2.  3 Index Pages in 1 extents.
TOTAL # of extents = 3
***************************************************************
TABLE: sysindexes          OBJID = 2
INDID=1      FIRST=24       ROOT=32       DPAGES=4      SORT=0
     Data level: 1.  4 Data  Pages in 1 extents.
     Indid       : 1.  1 Index Pages in 1 extents.
TOTAL # of extents = 2
...


...
***************************************************************
TABLE: pub_info            OBJID = 864006109
INDID=1      FIRST=568      ROOT=584      DPAGES=1      SORT=0
     Data level: 1.  1 Data  Pages in 1 extents.
     Indid       : 1.  2 Index Pages in 1 extents.
INDID=255    FIRST=560      ROOT=608      DPAGES=0      SORT=0
TOTAL # of extents = 2
***************************************************************
Processed 49 entries in the Sysindexes for dbid 4.
Alloc page 0 (# of extent=32 used pages=57 ref pages=57)
Alloc page 256 (# of extent=25 used pages=34 ref pages=34)
Alloc page 512 (# of extent=15 used pages=39 ref pages=39)
Alloc page 768 (# of extent=1 used pages=1 ref pages=1)
Alloc page 1024 (# of extent=1 used pages=1 ref pages=1)
Alloc page 1280 (# of extent=1 used pages=1 ref pages=1)
...

...
Alloc page 31744 (# of extent=1 used pages=1 ref pages=1)
Alloc page 32000 (# of extent=1 used pages=1 ref pages=1)
Total (# of extent=196 used pages=261 ref pages=254) in this database
DBCC execution completed. If DBCC printed error messages, see your
     System Administrator.
```

Part

V

Ch

18

You can see that a huge amount of information is returned. The good news is that you need to look at the report that is returned and search only for the exceptions. You need to key in on problems that are reported, if any, and work with those problems. The balance of the information is provided to confirm database table structures, page allocations, etc. If you do receive an error message, you should also receive specific instructions on what needs to be done to correct the problem.

N O T E   If there are objects on removable devices, NEWALLOC might return warning message 2558. This warning can be ignored. It is caused by a necessary setting for objects residing on removable devices. ■

Using *DBCC CHECKDB*   When you run CHECKDB, each table and its associated data pages, indexes, and pointers are all validated. Each is tested to ensure that it properly links to the related information as it should. CHECKDB has the following syntax:

```
DBCC CHECKDB <database name>
```

If you leave out the <database name> parameter, SQL Server will check the current database.

The following excerpts from Listing 18.2 show what you can expect to see from the CHECKDB option:

Listing 18.2   Sample Output from the *CheckDB* Statement

```
Checking pubs
Checking 1
The total number of data pages in this table is 4.
Table has 70 data rows.
Checking 2
The total number of data pages in this table is 4.
Table has 49 data rows.
Checking 3
The total number of data pages in this table is 10.
Table has 283 data rows.
Checking 4
The total number of data pages in this table is 1.
Table has 29 data rows.
Checking 5
The total number of data pages in this table is 23.
Table has 165 data rows.
…


…
Checking 592005140
The total number of data pages in this table is 1.
Table has 14 data rows.
Checking 688005482
The total number of data pages in this table is 2.
Table has 43 data rows.
Checking 864006109
The total number of data pages in this table is 1.
The total number of TEXT/IMAGE pages in this table is 73.
Table has 8 data rows.
DBCC execution completed. If DBCC printed error messages, see your
      System Administrator.
```

You'll notice that the option will also check system tables. When you run the command, you'll be checking all tables in all aspects of the database you specify in the command.

Using *DBCC SHRINKDB* When you create a database, you often predict high on the disk volume that will be needed to support the database table. Once you've put the database into production, you are able to tell how big the database really needs to be. If you've determined that you can make the database smaller—freeing up space for other databases on your system—you can use the SHRINKDB option. Keep in mind that the SHRINKDB option works in pages. This means that you'll have to determine the size you want to make the database and divide that size by 2048 (the size of the database pages) to get the value to specify for this command. The following is the syntax for SHRINKDB:

```
DBCC SHRINKDB <database name>, <new size>
```

It's a good idea to not shrink the Master database, as this database contains all information about your system. If you find that shrinking this database is necessary for some reason, be sure to back it up first. If you consider for a moment that you'll be modifying the database that manages the different recovery mechanisms for the system, you'll quickly understand how, if a system failure occurs while shrinking the Master database, you may not be able to recover it without a backup.

 T I P If you issue the SHRINKDB statement without a <new size> parameter, SQL Server will return the size of the smallest possible database. You can use this value to determine the new size of your database.

Part

V

Ch

18

```
Current Size of Database    Size Database Can be Shrunk To
-----------------------     ------------------------------
32256                       17152

(1 row(s) affected)

Objects pvnt further shrink    Index
-------------------------      ----
syslogs                        data

(1 row(s) affected)

DBCC execution completed. If DBCC printed error messages, see your
    System Administrator.
```

N O T E A database cannot be shrunk to a size that is less than the model database.

You'll notice that, if you request the smallest possible size, SQL Server will show how far you can shrink the database. In addition, there will be an indicator about whether something additional can be done to shrink the database further. In the listing above in the current configuration, the database can be reduced to 17152 pages, or about 35M. If you are able to manipulate the other items listed as preventing further shrinking, you can make the database even smaller.

N O T E   You should rarely use the absolute minimum value when shrinking a database because any
active database is bound to grow over time and use. If you've decreased the size of the
database so severely as to limit growth for a given application, this fact will be at cross-purposes with
the design goals of your client/server SQL Server-based application.   ■

Understanding and Using *update statistics* and *recompile*

SQL Server gains much of its performance from intelligent processing of data stored in the tables. This analysis comes in different forms, but the most significant is the examination of real data in the system to determine the optimal path for retrieving the information.

As an example of this, consider the route to your house. You've likely figured out the best, fastest way to get to your house from your office. Once you've found the best route, it's a safe bet that you're more likely to take that route—even if someone were to suggest that you select a different route—because you've taken the time to consider the different roads available and selected the best one possible.

In order for you to seriously consider a new route home, there would need to be a new road offering a better route to your house, or there would have to be construction on the existing road that makes it an inefficient road home.

With SQL Server, this analogy holds true. When you implement a stored procedure, SQL Server reviews the SELECT logic of the stored procedure, along with any other data-impacting events. It figures out the best route to take in fulfilling the stored procedure's function. Once this is selected, it remembers this information so that the next time you run the stored procedure, it's optimized for the data it impacts. SQL Server's "roads" consist of the indexes on the data in the system. These are the paths that will be considered when analyzing the best way to retrieve a given value set.

If you've added a number of rows to the table, for example, more than 20 percent of the original table size, you should consider updating the statistics associated with the table. The syntax for updating a table is as follows:

```
update statistics <table name>[.index name]
```

for example,

```
update statistics authors
```

N O T E   There are no quotes around the table name you want to update.   ■

You can specify that only a given index be updated or that the information concerning the entire table be updated. If you specify the index, you must specify it as shown, indicating the table in which the index can be found.

The final step to implement these updated indexes and make the stored procedures aware of them is to indicate to the SQL Server that it should reconsider the route to take when retrieving the information from the database. To do this, you'll need to recompile the different stored procedures that are impacted by the update statistics you just ran.

In general, stored procedures are compiled the first time they're called after SQL Server is started. There are other instances that stored procedures are automatically recompiled, but simply issuing the update statistics will not cause an automatic recompile. An example of this is when an index on which a stored procedure is based is dropped. You've probably noticed that the first time you call a particular stored procedure, the execution is a bit slower. Subsequent calls to the stored procedure are often noticeably faster. This is because the optimizer is compiling the stored procedure based on the current statistics of the database tables and any relevant indexes.

You recompile a stored procedure by setting a flag on a table that will basically invalidate any copies of stored procedures that are in procedure cache. This causes SQL Server to reload and recompile the affected stored procedures the next time they are accessed if they referenced the table you flagged. To set the flag, the following command is used:

```
sp_recompile <table name>
```

where `<table_name>` is the table that will be marked for all referencing stored procedures to be recompiled. If successful, the command returns a simple acknowledgment message indicating that the stored procedures will be reloaded and recompiled.

```
sp_recompile "authors"
go
Each stored procedure and trigger that uses table authors
will be recompiled the next time it is executed.
```

TIP If you don't recompile the stored procedures impacted by update statistics, the performance gain you seek will not be realized until the server is stopped and restarted again, as this is the next time that the procedures will be reloaded and compiled.

You can't hurt anything by starting the update statistics and recompile operations, but you should run them when the fewest users are on the system. This is especially true if your database sizes are substantial. The time to update these parameters can be quite a hit on the system performance for users of your system. It's a good idea to make updating statistics a part of your regular ongoing maintenance, perhaps running the process on each of your high-use tables approximately once a month during high database throughput. When you're first bringing up a system and when you're adding information at a high rate, you may want to consider frequent calls to this procedure—perhaps as often as once per day of heavy, new data input.

Backing Up and Restoring Databases and Transaction Logs

One of the most dreaded things to hear when you call for help with your application is, "Well, when was your last backup?" It only usually happens once, but when it does, and you're caught without a backup, it can be very painful.

With SQL Server, this fact is often many times more important than on a stand-alone system. You'll often be supporting a database that is used by many, many people and having the information on the system held in good standing is very important. Data loss may incur costs across departments and may involve significant data re-entry.

SQL Server provides a couple of different ways to protect from data loss—or at least minimize it—should the worst happen. These techniques range from physical duplication of the information to backing up the databases and transaction logs at specific intervals during the course of business.

In the upcoming sections, you'll see how you back up the system and what tradeoffs to consider in determining your optimum backup scenario.

How Often to Back Up?

One of the first things that a new SQL Server customer will ask is, "How often do I need to back up?" The answer is simple, but seems sarcastic when it's first posed. Quite simply, how much data can you afford to lose?

The first answer to this is usually "none." This is fine, but then it's time to sit down and determine what the impact will be on the system plan to incur no loss of data should a catastrophic system failure occur. Typically, this involves mirroring databases, which incurs hard-dollar costs to implement. For more information on mirroring a database on your system, see "Understanding and Using Mirroring" later in this chapter.

Because the cost to mirror a system can be quite steep, the next step is to determine what amount of data can truly be at risk at any given time. To determine this, it's important to first understand that you'll be backing up two different components to the system. As you've seen throughout this book, the database contains the different tables and all other objects associated with the database. The transaction log contains an incremental log of the things that happen to a database that change it. In essence, the transaction log contains a before and after picture of the data that is changed with each block of work performed by the server.

The key thing to remember is that the database backup is a snapshot in time, and the transaction logs contain all of the changes since that snapshot was taken. At a minimum, you'll want to back up the database once a week with daily backups of the transaction log.

The best plan is to have a system of rotating backups. This is the safest and most secure way to ensure that you have the correct fault tolerance for any system failures you may experience. If you consult any computer professional, you'll find that they all agree on one thing: Your system will fail; it's only a question of when. You should have complete, concise, and accurate backups. They are the only lifeline you have in times of hardware failure.

Table 18.1 shows a suggested backup schedule. Over the course of a year, assuming you're backing up to tape, this approach will require 29 tapes. Fourteen tapes are used in the weekly backup of your system and 13 are used to maintain monthly archives. The remaining two tapes are used as 1) working transaction log backups and 2) as an initial, baseline backup of the database. Remember, this is to maintain backups, not to retain historical data on the system. You should not count on backups for retention and research on historical information. You'll need to rely on alternative backups for that purpose.

Number the tapes sequentially on a permanent label on each tape cassette.

N O T E If your database is large, you may need more than one tape per day, week, or month. In this case, consider the tape numbering scheme to be a *tape set* numbering approach. ■

Table 18.1 Suggested Backup Approach

Tape #	Used For	Comments
1	Monday backup	Backup for the first Monday of two-week cycle
2	Tuesday backup	
3	Wednesday backup	
4	Thursday backup	
5	Friday backup	
6	Saturday backup	
7	Sunday backup*	
8	Monday backup	Backup for the second Monday of cycle
9	Tuesday backup	
10	Wednesday backup	
11	Thursday backup	
12	Friday backup	
13	Saturday backup	
14	Sunday backup*	

* These tapes should be removed from the physical site and placed in a separate location.

With this backup schedule, you'll have a full two weeks of backups to fall back on should a problem arise. We recommend a two week backup cycle because you may determine that you have a problem, but it wasn't recognized immediately. Perhaps a program change or other system event caused the problem and it was undetected for a few days. By having the two weeks of backups, the odds are good that you have a clean copy of the information in those recent archives.

Backing Up and Restoring Databases

When you back up your databases and transaction logs, you do so by dumping the information in your system to a *dump device,* which is recognized by SQL Server as a repository for information and can be either a disk file or a tape device. Once SQL has dumped information to the device, the file it creates (in the case of a disk-based device) can be backed up to tape, another server, or some other location where you will be managing the backup files.

The best way to manage the backup of information is with the SQL Enterprise Manager. From the Tools menu, select Database Backup/Restore to start working with the backup subsystem. When you do, you'll be presented with the main Database Backup/Restore dialog box shown in Figure 18.2.

FIG. 18.2

The main control panel for backup and restore operations enables you to select and create devices and set scheduling options.

Setting Up Backup Devices   The first thing you'll need to do is to establish the backup devices to be used as the destination for information dumped from the working databases and tables. Devices that are already known to the system are listed in the dialog box in the Backup Devices window. You can accept one of these devices, or you can create your own device.

To create a device, click the New button below the Backup Devices window. This will call up the New Backup Device dialog box, shown in Figure 18.3, and will prompt you to name the device.

FIG. 18.3

You can create new devices that will identify a tape or disk destination for backups.

Notice that, as you type in the name for the device, the location will be updated to include the name you use.

 T I P You can specify a path that points to another physical system when you indicate the backup devices that you want to use. By doing so, you can provide good backup coverage without the need for additional storage media.

Consider creating a new device for each day in the 14-day cycle mentioned above. Then, when you create a scheduled backup, you won't necessarily have to use a tape to store the information if you point to the device on the remote system and use it as a backup destination. If you set up the system to back up to the devices without the append flag, each of the devices you create will be only as big as needed for a single copy of the database you're backing up.

Also, because the likelihood that both your core SQL Server system and the remote system will experience downtimes simultaneously is quite small, you are assured of solid backups for your system.

The downside points to remember for this approach include the following:

- The remote system must always be accessible to the backup and restore process.
- The remote system must have enough disk space to support the dump devices.
- If your building burns down and both systems are in the same building, you've lost your backup system. This is a major reason for using off-site tape or other media backups.

Keeping these rules in mind, you can see that a solution that offers the best of both worlds would be a combination of remote system backups and off-site storage for tape backups made slightly less frequently.

Part

V

Ch

18

N O T E Be sure to take note of the file name if you're backing up to a file on disk instead of tape. This file name is the name you'll need to back up to tape or elsewhere on the system when you need to copy the backup file off the system for storage. ▩

After you've indicated the name of the device you want to create, simply press Create. SQL Server will create the new device and you'll see it listed in the backup devices dialog box. You're all set and ready to start creating the backups you'll need to support your SQL Server. Figure 18.4 shows a database with 14 backup devices, one for each day of a two-week backup cycle.

The next sections will detail what's involved in setting up the backups on the system.

Running the Backup   After you've created the devices you need to support the backups, you need to do the actual backup. To that end, you have two options available. The first option is to run backups on demand. Although this will work fine, it will require manual intervention each time you want to back up the system. This approach is more prone to forgetfulness, unexpected meetings, and the like than an automated solution.

FIG. 18.4

The Master database now has a backup device for each day of a two-week backup cycle.

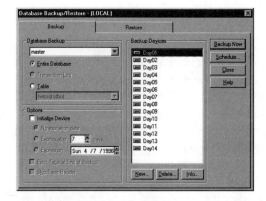

The following are some general points you need to keep in mind as you determine your backup strategy:

- Be sure you back up the transaction logs between backups of the databases. Backing up the transaction log is no different than backing up a database. It's simply an option you select during the definition of the backup.

- Be sure you back up each database that you need to protect. There is no command that backs up the entire system, so you'll need to create backup processes for all databases you are concerned with.

- Be sure you back up the Master database. Because this database includes all information about the other database objects that are in the system, it's very important to have this information in case you need to restore the entire system and rebuild from scratch.

You'll need to select the type of backup, either manual or scheduled/automatic, that will best fit the systems you are supporting.

Completing Manual Backups   Manual backups are quite straightforward and are a good way to get a feel for how the system works, the time it takes to back up, and how much impact a database backup will have on your system if other users are on the system at the time that a backup is started.

N O T E   When a backup is first run, the device must be initialized. This is done by selecting the Initialize Device checkbox in the Options section of the Backup page. If a backup is attempted without initializing the device, you will be prompted with a warning stating that the device is either offline or uninitialized. ■

To complete the backup, select the device you want to back up to and click Backup Now. The Backup Volume Labels dialog box appears (see fig. 18.5).

FIG. 18.5

If you select a device that has already had a backup completed, you'll be prompted to pick the label to which information should be appended.

Once you select the device and click <u>O</u>K, the backup will be completed. You'll be presented with a status indicator showing the progress of the backup. Finally, you'll be presented with a dialog box confirming that the backup was successful.

TROUBLESHOOTING

I've followed the steps for creating the backup, but when I run the backup, it fails. What should I be looking for to solve this problem? The first thing you'll need to examine is the free space on the dump device you've created. Make sure you have enough free space for the device to grow to accommodate the information you're saving. Remember, too, that if you have the Append option selected, the information you save will be added to the prior information each time you run a backup. This will eventually lead to some very sizable dump devices. By using the rotating tapes as noted above, you can safely back up to separate dump devices each time you back up because you'll have the prior backup's information stored safely away.

When I try to back up the Transaction Log, I get a message that indicates that I can't dump the transaction log while <u>T</u>runcate Log on Checkpoint is set. What do I do? You may recall from the previous section, "Understanding and Performing Checkpoints," that one way of helping to manage transaction log size is to turn on the <u>T</u>runcate Log on Checkpoint option. Another way to manage the size of the log is to dump the transaction log to a backup device. SQL Server will, by default, also truncate the log at that point after a successful backup. Because both operations take control over truncating the log, they are mutually exclusive. You'll need to turn back off the option to truncate the log on checkpoint before you can successfully back up the transaction log.

Part
V

Ch
18

Scheduling Automated Backups The safest bet, especially for incremental backups, is a regularly scheduled, automated backup. As shown in Figure 18.6, you have set up automated backups by clicking the <u>S</u>chedule button (refer to fig. 18.4) after you've indicated the database and the device to which you want to back up.

If you're doing append-type backups, you'll be prompted to indicate the volume you want to append to. Once you have indicated the volume, you'll see the Task Schedule dialog box, as shown in Figure 18.7, enabling you to indicate the details for the scheduled backup.

FIG. 18.6

Scheduled backups offer a way to avoid relying on human intervention for the completion of this critical job.

FIG. 18.7

You have complete flexibility in setting the times for your backups, the recurring intervals, and more. In this example, we've set up Monday, Wednesday, and Friday backups.

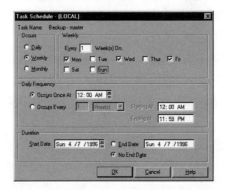

> **N O T E** For future reference, take note of the SQL Command text box (refer to fig. 18.6). It shows you what commands you can run from ISQL that will complete the backup manually. It's good practice to keep up with the commands you can enter manually, as you may want to implement them in your own application at a later date. ■

The first two options on the dialog box enable you to do a single backup at some pre-determined time. These are good first passes and we highly recommend that your first backups be scheduled *attended* backups so you can make sure all is working well, the files are created correctly, and that your backup process works in general.

Once you've determined that the backup process has gained your confidence, you can change the allotted times, create recurring backups, and more. To change the times at which the backup occurs, first select the Recurring option, then click Change (refer to fig. 18.6). You'll be presented with the dialog box shown in Figure 18.7, indicating the different options you have in determining the times for your backups to run.

The final step is to set up any options you want to enable. This is done by clicking the Options button in the Schedule Backup dialog. The most likely of these is the logging to the Windows NT Event Log. It is highly recommended that you turn on the option to log successes, as well as failures, to the log. This will give you a mechanism to check on the success or failure in a definitive sense. You'll know for sure whether it succeeded. Figure 18.8 shows this option set. The remaining options are used for e-mail notification if you're using the mail services of SQL

Server, and they enable you to establish retry parameters. If you are having failures because of network traffic to a remote server where your device is maintained, you may want to increase the number of retries.

FIG. 18.8
Be sure to check the option to log to the event log for successes as well as failures. This is a good mechanism for following up on your auto-mated processes.

> **CAUTION**
>
> If your system is in need of modification to the retry parameters, it's likely that you should investigate the cause of these before you implement retries. If you have a less reliable connection to the server containing the device you use for backup, consider moving the device. Backups are too important to leave to possible problems due to network traffic or other things that will cause you to need retries.

When you click OK to close the dialog boxes that enable you to define the backup schedule, you'll be returned to the Database Backup/Restore dialog box. You'll notice right away that there is no indication that the backup you've just created was created successfully. This is a bit disconcerting, but take heart. The information about the backup is now part of a scheduled background task. As such, you need to review it from the Task Scheduling portion of SQL Enterprise manager rather than the backup and restore utility dialog boxes. From the Server menu, select Scheduled Tasks. The Manage Scheduled Tasks dialog (see fig. 18.9) is what you'll find, and you should see your backup job listed as one of the first items in the list of things to do.

FIG. 18.9
Scheduled backups are created as background tasks that can be managed from the Tasks utility in the Enterprise Manager.

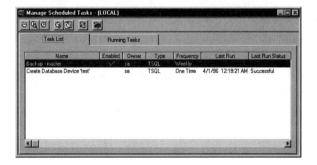

Part
V

Ch
18

> **CAUTION**
>
> If you are at all uncertain about what tasks you have created that reflect the backup job, be sure you determine which backup jobs you need before you start working with tasks. Because all background activity is managed through the Tasks listing, you can cause damage to processes that control replication, general cleanup, and many other system jobs if you remove or modify an incorrect item.

You can also use the Task listing to check the status of backups as another way of checking to see if there are any problems. You should use a combination of the Task listing and the NT Event log to determine the cause of any problems you may encounter during the backup process.

Don't forget that you need to be absolutely certain you've backed up all of the following:

- The Master database
- All databases that you would be sorry if you lost
- All transaction logs for each database you have in production or which is undergoing significant testing

Using and Understanding Information Restoration from Backups

Once you've created the backups and have faithfully been backing up your database, how do you recover the database if something does go wrong? This is where you'll be glad you put into place a formal backup plan, as it will guide you to restoring your system to full functionality in the least amount of time possible.

The following are the steps for restoring your system:

1. Install SQL Server if needed.
2. Restore the Master database if needed.
3. Re-create the devices if needed.
4. Restore the last full database backups you completed.
5. Restore the transaction logs that were backed up since the database was backed up.

At the completion of this, you'll have a fully functional system that will be up-to-date as of the last transaction log backup.

You've already learned about installing SQL Server and creating devices, so I won't cover that information here, but if you'd like more information on this, see Appendix F, "What's on the CD?" and Chapter 4, "Creating Devices, Databases, and Transaction Logs."

N O T E When you create a new database, you should create it with the Create for Load option selected. This will cause SQL Server to create the database without the initial sets of pointers in the database. Because you'll be loading this information from the backup anyway, there's no reason to have the work done twice. The time saved in creating the new database can be nearly 50 percent of the time required to create an entirely new database with the option deselected. ■

When you select the Tools, Database Backup/Restore option, and then select the Restore tab, you'll first be presented with a dialog box containing all of the valid backups available. This listing will show the date and time of the backup, the type of backup (database or transaction log), and so on. Figure 18.10 shows the options available on the Restore tab.

FIG. 18.10

The restore options enable you to designate the source and destination for restoration efforts.

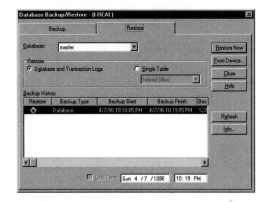

SQL Server will automatically present the list of databases for which a database backup has been completed. This enables you to select the different backups that you want to apply to the database you designate in the drop-down list box.

If you know that the information on a given backup is good until a certain time, you can indicate that in the Until Time text box. Note that any pending transactions at the time you specify will be rolled back and it will be as if they never occurred. In most cases, you'll need to restore the database and transaction logs in their entirety, so default options will be fine.

Click Restore Now and the database and transaction log(s) will be restored.

If you created the new database with the Create for Load option, you'll need to update the database options before anyone else can use the database. You'll notice that, until you do this, the database you're working with will be flagged in the Enterprise Manager's display as "(loading)." During this time, no user except the DBO can use the database. To update the options and allow other users access to the database, select Manage, Databases from the menus. You'll see a dialog box similar to the one shown in Figure 18.11.

FIG. 18.11

You must remember to update the options for any database created explicitly for loading. Otherwise users will not be able to access it.

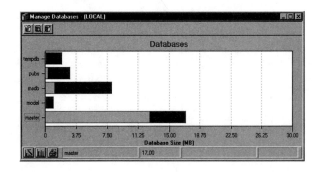

Double-click the bar representing the database you need to update. You'll be presented with the now-familiar Edit Database dialog box. Select Options, then deselect the <u>D</u>BO Use Only option (see fig. 18.12).

FIG. 18.12

The <u>D</u>BO Use Only option indicates that the database is being loaded and is not ready for production use. Deselect the option to "turn on" the database for other users.

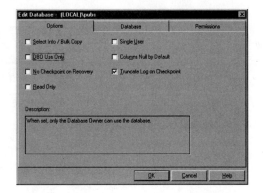

Once you've completed this step, you're restored to the point of the most recent transaction log backup and should be ready to begin some quick testing to see that everything restored correctly and boost your confidence in the process. At this point, the data is restored, all objects in the database are restored and, to the users, there should be no change in operation whatsoever.

In the cases of recovering from a system failure, practice will certainly play a key role. As a test of this process, consider using the PUBS database as a Guinea pig. Follow these steps:

1. Perform a database backup of the PUBS database.

2. Make a change to one of the authors in the Authors table. The specifics of the change don't matter: You can add a row, change a name, or whatever you will be able to easily recognize later.

3. Perform a transaction log backup of the database. You've now backed up the basic database, and you've backed up the change you made as a sort of "delta" (or difference) backup.

4. Create a new database (for example, RestoreTest). The name does not matter, only that it has sufficient size to support the PUBS database. Make the database size 33M and the transaction log size 30M. Restore the database *only* to your system. You'll have to deselect the transaction log restoration option.

5. Go into ISQL/w and select the rows from the Authors table. They should be all represented correctly, as they existed prior to your change. Your changes won't yet appear because the changes occurred after the database was backed up. In a traditional backup scenario, this was as good as it got for recovery.

6. Restore the transaction log only now. Re-query the authors table, and your changes will be there. This proves that the transaction log changes were correctly logged against the database table.

You can and should experiment with different scenarios using the test database approach. This way, when it comes time to restore your database in a real crisis, you can rest assured it will go smoothly. Think of these tests as the fire drill for database recovery!

Understanding and Using Mirroring

In addition to the backup and restore techniques covered in the previous sections, SQL Server also supports an additional fault-tolerant option: Mirroring. Because hard drives are the most likely candidate for a system failure that impacts data, you may want to consider this option to protect your databases.

N O T E   Windows NT also supports several fault-tolerant options that are enforced at the operating system level. For more information, please refer to Que's *Special Edition Using Microsoft Windows NT Server* and see the information topics regarding striped disk storage. ■

Mirroring takes place at the device level and is transparent to your applications. When you create a device and indicate that it should be mirrored, you simply tell SQL Server where you want to locate the mirror. Take care in selecting the location of the mirror. You'll be doing yourself little or no good if you place the mirror device on the same physical drive as the source device. If you do, and the drive fails, you will lose both the source device and the mirror.

Part
V

Ch
18

Overview of Mirroring

Mirroring is done when SQL Server writes changes to a device to two locations at once. The primary location is your standard device. This is the database that you are normally using and have incorporated in your system's applications. Because both devices are identical, if a switch is required from the main device to the secondary device, there is no data loss and the users of your system will not be interrupted in their use of the system.

As SQL Server uses a device, if it can no longer access the main device, it automatically switches to the mirror device, making all future changes to the mirror. When you've recovered the drives containing the problem device, you can move the information back to the original device and restart SQL Server using the corrected devices as the default once again.

Setting Up Mirroring

When you create a device—or after the fact, if you edit a device—you'll notice an option to establish mirroring. In Figure 18.13, you can see the options that enable you to work with a device.

Click on <u>M</u>irroring to indicate where the mirror file will be located. Remember, the paths you designate are relative to the server. If you're working from a workstation, be careful to keep this in mind. You can select a location that is either on the current server or on a fully qualified network path (see fig. 18.14).

FIG. 18.13
Right-click a device and select Edit to modify mirroring options.

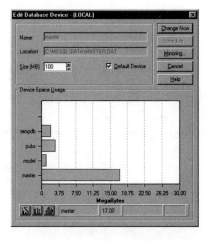

FIG. 18.14
When you select the location of the mirror file, SQL Server will mirror the requested database.

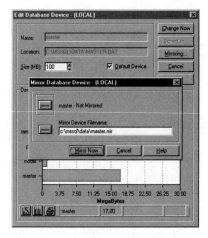

After the process has completed, the device will be mirrored and SQL Server will take care of the rest. From that point on, any informational changes to the primary device will also be reflected in the mirror device.

> **CAUTION**
>
> If you implement mirroring for a device, be sure you also mirror the Master database. This database is responsible for maintaining the system information necessary to continue processing should mirroring become necessary for any device. When you mirror the Master database, you're ensuring that you'll be able to enable SQL Server to recover to the mirrored devices that have failed.
>
> If you do not mirror the Master database, you may find that you cannot utilize the mirrors for other devices, as this information (the information about the mirrored devices managed by SQL Server) is maintained in the Master database and could be lost.

The final step is to tell SQL Server about the mirrored device in the case of the Master database. Because the Master database is used to start the server, you need to indicate to the server where the mirror can be found if it is needed. Other devices are managed automatically, so this step is only required for the Master database.

There are two parameters required at SQL Server startup that control the Master database's mirrored state: -r and -d. Figure 18.15 shows the SQL Server Configuration/Options dialog box. Choose Server, SQL Server, Configure to open this dialog box. Click the Parameters button on the Server Options page and then add the startup parameters.

FIG. 18.15

Startup options that enable mirroring the Master database can be set in the SQL Server configuration subsystem.

Part
V

Ch
18

Figure 18.16 shows the dialog box that enables you to indicate the startup options.

FIG. 18.16

Be sure to specify both -r and -d options for the Master device. If both are not found, the mirroring will not work correctly.

Add a new parameter, -r<mirror location>, that indicates the location of the mirror for the master device. Note that, even after SQL has switched to the mirror device during normal use, when you restart the system, it must still first try the primary Master device. This means that you must leave the -d specification that is showing the location of the "normal" Master device. When you add the -r option, you're specifying the fallback position that SQL should use when it has determined the master device to have become unusable.

Click the Add button to create a new parameter, and be sure to specify the entire path and file name to the mirror device file when you create the -r parameter.

What to Do When Mirroring Is in Force

When SQL Server has switched to a mirror, it automatically suspends mirroring with the original device. This frees up the device to be replaced or otherwise corrected. When the mirroring is active, the users of your system will not notice any difference in the functioning of their applications. They'll be able to continue working just as they did before the problem was found with the original device.

Once you've replaced the original device or otherwise corrected the problem that was detected, you can re-mirror the active device back to the primary device. Re-mirroring is identical to the original job of mirroring a device. You simply specify the file name that will contain the mirror, and SQL Server will take care of the rest.

If you want to switch from a current device to the mirror, as may be the case where you've just brought online a replacement for a failed device, the following are the steps you'll follow, from the creation of the original mirror through failure of the device to replacement of it and re-mirroring to return to the original state:

1. Mirror the original device.
2. The device fails; SQL Server switches to the mirror device and continues processing.
3. Replace or correct the original device.
4. Re-mirror the active device back to the original.
5. Unmirror the device, selecting the option to Switch to Mirror Device—Replace option.
6. Mirror the device—now the replacement for the original—back to the backup device.

At this point, you're back where you started with the original device being the active device and the mirror standing by as needed to back it up.

As you can see, Mirroring your devices can provide powerful backup capabilities to your key production systems. For more information about backups, be sure to review the backup and restore options presented in the first half of this chapter.

Transferring Information to and from SQL Server

The SQL Transfer Object utility provides an excellent way to move information between databases to your system. To start the Transfer utility, select the source database. Next, select the Transfer option from the Object menu (or right-click the database). Figure 18.17 shows the initial Transfer Objects dialog box.

By default, copying an entire database to a new location is as simple as selecting the source and destination database and clicking the Start Transfer button (refer to fig. 18.17). SQL Server will copy all of the different objects to the new database and set it up to match the source database.

FIG. 18.17

Select the options carefully when you use the Transfer utility. They control the objects that will be copied to the new database.

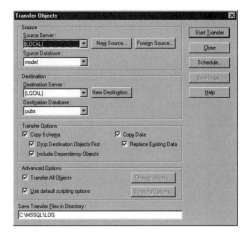

You can also initiate the copy process at a scheduled time, such as at a time when server traffic is lower and the copy process will not as adversely impact the users of the system. By selecting Schedule, you can indicate the time at which you'd like the copy to occur. As shown in Figure 18.18, the scheduling capabilities are nearly identical to those you used in setting up backups for your server.

Part
V

Ch
18

FIG. 18.18

The Transfer utility can be used to make periodic copies of key information in your system.

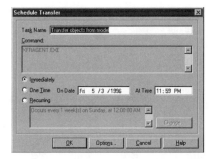

If needed, you can even use the Transfer utility to make rudimentary backups of your system by copying databases to backup devices and databases possibly located on a different server altogether. You should, however, avoid using the Transfer process as a production means of backing up your system. It's not meant to be an end-all solution to the backup needs for your system and will not support the same level of logging or critical processing checks that the backup process affords. There is, for example, no way to transfer only a transaction log for a given database.

If you deselect the Transfer All Objects option in the Transfer Objects dialog box (see fig. 18.19), you'll be able to specify exactly what objects should be included in the copy by clicking the Choose Objects button.

FIG. 18.19

You can select several options that control how objects are transferred during this process.

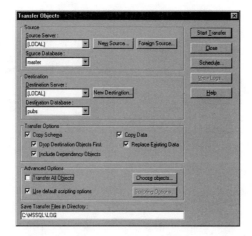

Figure 18.20 shows the different objects that you have available with a typical copy.

FIG. 18.20

You can selectively copy specific objects or attributes for your database. You can use this feature to update another system to keep it in sync.

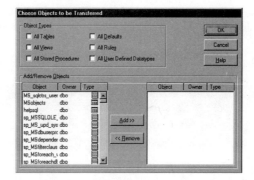

You can also indicate the different options that are transferred as part of the scripting process. As the Transfer utility puts the information from your source database into the destination system, it will script the creation of tables, logon IDs, and other such items that are not information-content based, but are structure or configuration related. You can control these items, as shown in Figure 18.21, by deselecting the Use Default Scripting Options check box in the Transfer Objects dialog box (refer to fig. 18.19) and clicking the Scripting Options button.

The Transfer Objects utility is a good companion to the backup and mirroring features you've seen earlier in this chapter. By putting these to use in your installation, you'll be able to ensure a maximum amount of up time for your user base. Use the Transfer Objects utility to make copies of critical system components, then use mirroring and backups for ongoing protection against catastrophic system failures.

FIG. 18.21

You have complete control over the objects and configurations that will be included in the transfer process. You can deselect logons if you've already set up security on the destination device, for example.

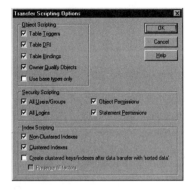

From Here...

In this chapter, we've explored some very important administrative utilities that provide the support for good, solid, fault-tolerant system design for your users. The time is now to implement these items—not later. If you wait until you need them, it will be too late. Keep in mind the old computer-support adage we mentioned earlier: Components will fail, it's only a matter of time. Plan for it; be ready for it. It will be far less painful and less difficult to recover from.

The following are some additional sources for some of the topics covered in this chapter that will help you in your administration of SQL Server:

- Chapter 4, "Creating Devices, Databases, and Transaction Logs," covers the specifics of setting up the different components for your system.

- Appendix A, "Installation and Setup of the Client and Server Software," explains the details behind the initial setup and configuration of your system. Remember to add the -r option to the startup command line if you'll be using mirroring.

- Que's *Special Edition Using Microsoft Windows NT Server* covers more specifics about disk-based recovery and fault-tolerant systems. Be sure to check into striped disk drive configurations and how you can work with backup devices.

Part
V

Ch
18

SQL Server Security

Just about everyone is concerned with the security of their data. If you're not, then you may not have considered how easy it is to get access to sensitive data on your server. One thing to remember, however, is that sometimes too much security can get in the way of productivity. Make sure that you achieve a balance between your need to manage access to data and monitor users, and the users' needs to *use* the data.

No document can categorically define every possible security option, however, this chapter's purpose is to illustrate the features that SQL Server offers and to offer suggestions on what you can do to secure your environment from unauthorized access. ■

Learn the difference between logins and users

SQL Server manages server access through Logins and database access through users.

How to protect your data from unscrupulous browsing

This chapter will introduce you to views and stored procedures as a way of hiding data from users.

Securing your environment

Get suggestions on how to secure not only SQL Server, but your physical hardware, LAN, WAN, and Internet access.

Understanding the Types of Security

Securing your data from internal and external attacks is an important job for you as a database administrator. It is important that you can control who and how data is accessed on your server. Security in SQL Server will help you manage the access that you give to your users.

Securing your data from internal attacks is probably your primary concern for most corporate environments. This security will involve the monitoring of and management of corporate databases at the direction of the managers of your company. Security is often designed to limit the sorts of data that your employees can see and when they can see it.

Securing your data from external attacks (such as over the Internet) is much more complicated, and is generally only applicable to those companies who are beginning to have an Internet presence with their SQL Server databases.

This chapter will focus more on internal security. This security will act in a layered approach, starting with logins and user permissions that secure the basic access to the server. The second layer adds views and stored procedures that limit data access. Finally, the third layer is an external security through things like physical LAN access, firewalls, and so on.

Microsoft's SQL Server security system can be implemented in three ways on any server: standard, integrated, and mixed. These security methods control how SQL Server manages user accounts on the server and how it interacts with Windows NT's own security system.

To configure a database server's security type for standard, integrated, or mixed security, follow these steps:

1. Run SQL Enterprise Manager from the Microsoft SQL Server 6.5 group (see fig. 19.1).

FIG. 19.1
After just being started, SQL Enterprise Manager shows that no server is selected.

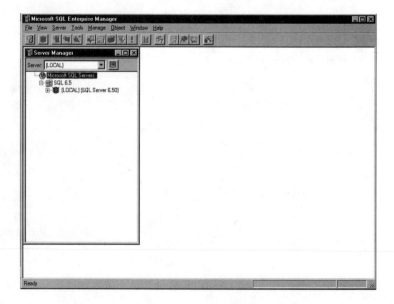

2. Select the server that is going to be managed and from the <u>S</u>erver menu, select SQL
   Server, <u>C</u>onfigure. Then activate the Security Options page (see fig. 19.2).

FIG. 19.2

To track the successful and
unsuccessful login attempts of
your users, enable (check) the
options in the Audit Level
group box.

Using Standard Security

In Standard Security mode, SQL Server is wholly responsible for managing and maintaining
accounts on the server. In this case, SQL Server is responsible for authenticating a user and for
enforcing password/login restrictions. This is the most common way of configuring SQL
Server because it behaves identically to Sybase on any hardware platform and to SQL Server
4.2 on OS/2. The majority of the rest of this chapter will discuss the features of standard security. For more information on Windows NT's integrated security system, refer to Que's *Special
Edition Using Windows NT Server*.

N O T E Standard security should be used when there are no Windows NT servers being used for file
server duties. In this case, NT's integrated security mechanisms provide no benefit to the
SQL Server. Also, standard security should be used when you expect that various different protocols
will be used to attach to the server. ∎

Using Integrated Security

Because SQL Server runs only on Windows NT, Microsoft could take advantage of, and inte-
grate into, Windows NT's excellent security system. When operating in integrated security
mode, Windows NT is responsible for managing user connections through its Access Control
List (ACL). The advantage of integrated security include single-password access to all resources on a Windows NT domain and password aging and encryption across the network.

A login to the Windows NT server is either granted or denied connection to the SQL Server
based on attributes of the user's login account to the NT server. This granting of permission or

authentication between client and server creates a *trusted* login to the server. At this point, NT only validates that the login name is valid for accessing any particular resource available on the network or server.

N O T E Trusted connections are only available via the Multi-Protocol NetLibrary (MPNL) or via Named Pipes communications protocols, so there may be networking reasons that make integrated security unfeasible in your environment. MPNL is discussed in the section in this chapter entitled "Encrypted Multi-Protocol NetLibrary." For more information on the configuration of other communications protocols for clients, see Chapter 21, "Communicating with SQL Server."

When a user establishes a trusted connection to the SQL Server, the user is either:

- Mapped to an existing SQL Server Login if a name match is found
- Connected as the default login (usually *guest*)
- Connected as SA if the user is the administrator on the NT system

All other database-based permissions, such as permissions on tables, views and other objects, are managed by SQL Server in the same way as a server running in standard security mode. These security permissions are discussed next.

Using Mixed Security

Mixed security, as its name implies, is a combination of both standard and integrated security and means that users can login to the server in either way. When a user connects to a SQL Server in mixed security mode, the server validates the login by first checking whether the login name has already established a trusted connection to the NT server. If no connection is found, SQL Server then performs its own validation of the login name and password supplied. If the requested login is not a known SQL Server login, access is denied.

Creating and Managing User Accounts

SQL Server has two levels of a user that are important to understand. The first level of a user is a *login*. A login is the ability to attach to the SQL Server itself. SQL Server manages logins on a server-wide basis. All logins are stored in the SYSLOGINS table of the master database. The second level of a user is a *user*. Users are SQL Server's way of managing who has permissions to interact with resources (such as tables and stored procedures) in a given database. A user can be in one or many databases. All users are stored in the SYSUSERS table of each database for which they have permission to access.

SQL Server uses these distinctions to allow a single user to have different levels of access based on the database that they are connecting to, and yet retain the same password. To support this, a user has a login or connection permission to the server. This login is what SQL Server associates a password to. Without a valid login to the server, a user will not have access to any of the server's databases with the possible exception of remote systems using remote stored procedures.

Once a login is created, it is then necessary to create a user of a database on that server. This process is very similar to creating a SQL Server system login and is described in the following sections.

Using SQL Enterprise Manager to Create a Login

The SQL Enterprise Manager provides a simple way of creating a login to the database. Just perform the following steps:

1. Run SQL Enterprise Manager from the Microsoft SQL Server 6.5 group.
2. Select the Server that you want to add a login to and then select Manage, Logins (see fig. 19.3).

FIG. 19.3

The Manage Logins dialog box enables you to grant access to all the databases on the server by selecting the required access level in the table at the bottom of the dialog box.

3. Enter the information for the new login and (optionally) indicate the databases that the login will be allowed to access (see fig. 19.4).

Part
V

Ch
19

FIG. 19.4

The Manage Logins dialog box shows a new login (swarner) being created with user access to the pubs and master databases.

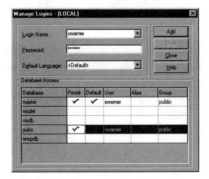

4. Click Add to verify that the information is correct and to create the login. Enter the password and verify the password assigned to the user to ensure that the information was entered correctly (see fig. 19.5).

FIG. 19.5

The Confirm Password dialog box requires verification of password information.

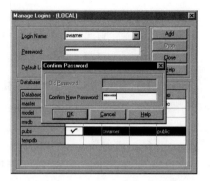

 TIP When creating a new login, set the password to be the same as the login name so that it is easy to remember.

If, at a later stage, it is necessary to add a user to a database, highlight the database in the SQL Enterprise Manager and then select Users from the Manage menu. The Manage Users dialog box will appear, as shown in Figure 19.6.

FIG. 19.6

The Manage Users dialog box shows a new user (swarner) being created for the Login swarner.

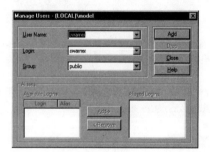

Select the user to be added to the database from the Login drop-down list box and enter the name by which it is to be identified. You should not change the name if you do not want to create an alias. Finally, click Add.

NOTE Use the Aliases group of the Manage Users dialog box to specify that other server logins can also use the currently selected database. When those logins connect to the server, if they use the currently selected database, they will not be governed by their own name, but instead will be known and managed by the system under the alias name. Note that the only logins available for selection in the Aliases group will be those logins that have not already been created as a user of the currently selected database. ■

Dropping Logins and Users with SQL Enterprise Manager

SQL Enterprise Manager's Manage Logins and Manage Users dialog boxes both provide a Drop button. Use this button to drop any user or login that you no longer want to have access to the database or server.

> **N O T E**   SQL Server Enterprise Manager is *right-click aware*—meaning that you can right-click just about anything in the tree and bring up a context-sensitive menu about the object. To quickly drop a user or login, find the user or login in the tree and right-click it. Click Delete to remove the user or login. ■

Using *sp_addlogin* to Add Logins to a Server

The `sp_addlogin` stored procedure is provided to add a login to the server using Transact-SQL statements. The syntax for `sp_addlogin` is as follows:

```
sp_addlogin login_id [, password [, defaultdb [, defaultlanguage]]]
```

- `login_id` is the name of the login being added. A login follows standard SQL Server naming conventions.
- `password` is the password to be assigned the login. Passwords are optional, but are highly recommended as the most basic of security measures.
- `defaultdb` is the default database that the SQL Server should place the login in after connecting to the database. If left NULL, SQL Server leaves the login in the master database.
- `defaultlanguage` is the default language that should be assigned to the login. If left NULL, SQL Server assigns the default language for the server.

> **T I P**   The user can change his or her password at any time using the `sp_password` stored procedure. For example, `sp_password 'Agent99', 'MaxwellSmart'` changes the currently connected user's password from Agent99 to MaxwellSmart.

The following is an example of creating a login to the server with the default database of pubs and a password of Allen.

```
sp_addlogin 'Ronald', 'Allen', pubs
```

> **N O T E**   SQL Server 6.5 has a new variation of the `sp_addlogin` stored procedure that allows a user to be added to a database while adding that user to the master.dbo.syslogins table. This new procedure takes an additional parameter that identifies the login ID. Only system administrators may use this feature. ■

Using *sp_adduser* to Add New Users to Databases

sp_adduser is similar in style to the sp_addlogin procedure. It takes an existing login and adds it to the currently active database. Note that you must issue a use database xxx and be in the required database to add a user to before running the sp_adduser stored procedure.

```
sp_adduser login_id [, username [, grpname]]
```

- login_id is the name of the login being added as a user to the database. Invalid logins will not be added to the database.

- username is provided to allow logins to be "aliased" in a database. This allows the same login to connect to different databases on the same server and have different names in each database.

- grpname allows the specification of a user group to which the user will belong. Using groups simplifies security because instead of granting permissions to individual users, the permissions can be granted to the group and then all members of the group receive them.

Below is an example of adding a user to the currently active database. Because no username is supplied, the login_id is assumed for the username.

```
sp_adduser 'Ronald'
```

sp_droplogin and *sp_dropuser*

To remove a login or user from the server or database, execute the system procedures sp_droplogin or sp_dropuser. Their syntax is very similar, especially when the username chosen for a given login to a database is the same as the *login_id*.

```
sp_droplogin login_id
```

and

```
sp_dropuser username
```

Creating and Using Groups

SQL Server provides the ability to create groups of users so that security permissions granted to all members are the same. This provides far better simplicity and is a more practical approach to security than granting individual users specific permissions on any particular set of tables.

Using SQL Enterprise Manager to Add Groups

SQL Enterprise Manager provides an easy method for adding groups to the database. Just perform the following steps:

1. Start SQL Enterprise Manager and highlight the database in the server tree for which you want to create a group (see fig. 19.7).

FIG. 19.7

The SQL Enterprise Manager shows the pubs database highlighted.

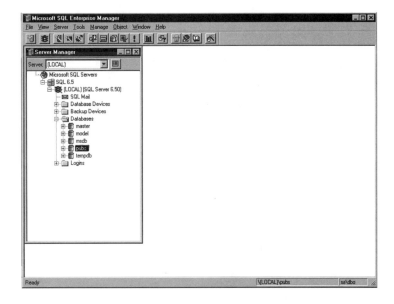

2. From the <u>M</u>anage menu, select Gr<u>o</u>ups and enter the information/name of the new group. Select any users that are required members of the group (see fig. 19.8).

FIG. 19.8

In the Manage Groups dialog box, a new group (grp_me) is created with swarner as its only member.

Part
V
Ch
19

3. Click A<u>d</u>d to add the group to the database.

Dropping Groups with SQL Enterprise Manager

Dropping security groups with SQL Enterprise Manager involves performing the same steps as creating them. You can use the Manage Groups dialog box (refer to fig. 19.8) to drop any unneeded groups from the server. Removing a group will not remove any users associated with those groups. Any permissions granted to users because they were members of the groups will be revoked.

Using Permissions and SQL Server

Permissions are the rights to access an object (such as a table) in the database. Permissions are granted to a user or group to allow that user or group to perform functions such as select data, add new rows (insert), and update data. Several permissions exist on objects in the database and descriptions follow.

Permissions are implicitly granted to the owner or creator of an object. The owner can then decide to grant permissions to other users or groups as that user sees fit.

■ The *database owner (dbo)* has full permissions on all objects in the database that he owns.

■ The *system administrator (SA)* has full permissions on all objects in all databases on the server.

SQL Server provides the GRANT and REVOKE commands to give or take away permission from a user. SQL Enterprise Manager also provides an easy way to add and remove permissions.

Object Permissions

Object permissions are the permissions to act on tables and other objects (such as stored procedures and views) in the database.

The following is a list of permissions available on tables and their descriptions:

■ SELECT enables a user to select or read data from a table or view. Note that a SELECT permission can be granted to individual columns within a table or view, not just the entire table.

■ INSERT enables a user to add new data to a table or view.

■ UPDATE enables a user to change data in a table or view. Note that an UPDATE permission can be granted to individual columns within a table or view, not just the entire table.

■ DELETE enables a user to remove data from a table or view.

■ EXECUTE enables a user to execute a stored procedure.

■ DRI/REFERENCES enables a user to add foreign key constraints on a table.

■ DDL/Data Definition Language enables a user to create, alter, or drop objects in the database. Examples are CREATE TABLE, DROP DATABASE, ALTER TABLE.

■ ALL enables the user full permissions on the object. Note that only the SA can use ALL when DDL statements are being used.

Using SQL Enterprise Manager to Manage Permissions

SQL Enterprise Manager provides an easy way of managing permissions for users and groups in a database. Perform the following steps:

1. Start SQL Enterprise Manager and highlight the database in the server tree for which you want to manage permissions (refer to fig. 19.7).

2. From the Object menu, select Permissions and choose either the By User page or the By Object page (see fig. 19.9).

3. Use the Object Permissions dialog box to specify the permissions required for the user, and then click Set to apply the changes (see fig. 19.10).

FIG. 19.9

Changing permissions by checking any of the columns does not take effect until you click the Set button.

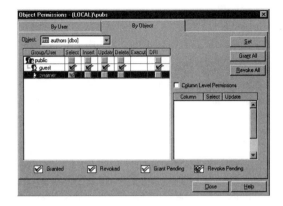

FIG. 19.10

Use the Object Filters options to limit the types of objects that are displayed in the table at the lower-left part of the dialog box.

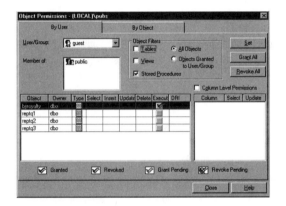

T I P Use the Grant All and Revoke All buttons to grant or revoke all the permissions on a given table or view to save time.

Using *GRANT* and *REVOKE*

SQL Server's Transact-SQL interface to permissions is through the GRANT and REVOKE statements.

The GRANT Transact-SQL command is used to give a permission or permissions to a user or group in SQL Server. Granting a permission allows the user or group to perform the granted permission.

The syntax for using GRANT is as follows:

```
GRANT permission_list
ON object_name
TO name_list
```

Use REVOKE to revoke permissions from a user. It's the opposite of GRANT and is designed to undo or remove any permissions granted from a user or group.

The syntax for REVOKE is as follows:

```
REVOKE permission_list
ON object_name
FROM name_list
```

permission_list is a list of permissions being granted or revoked. Multiple permissions should be comma separated. If ALL is specified then all permissions that the grantor has will be granted to the grantee.

object_name is a table, view, or stored procedure for which permissions are being granted or revoked.

name_list is a list of usernames or groups for which permissions are being granted or revoked. Multiple names should be separated by commas. Specifying PUBLIC will include all users.

N O T E   If WITH GRANT OPTION is appended to a grant statement it will allow the grantee to also grant his rights to other users. This is a nice option, but it should be used very sparingly—if not only by the system administrator, for security reasons. ▪

The following example grants SELECT and UPDATE permissions on the AUTHORS table:

```
Grant   SELECT, UPDATE
On      AUTHORS
To      PUBLIC
Go
```

The following example revokes DELETE permissions on the EMPLOYEE table

```
Revoke  DELETE
On      EMPLOYEE
From    PUBLIC
Go
```

Using Views to Enhance Security

Views provide a great way to enhance security because they limit the data that is available to a user. For example, you can have a group of users in grp_junior_emp that are not allowed to view any of the authors that receive more than 50 percent royalties because these are to be available only to the senior managers or other employees within the company. In Listing 19.1, the Transact-SQL shows how this can be achieved.

▶ **See** Chapter 9, "Managing and Using Views," to learn more about creating views with SQL Server.
p. 245

On the CD

Listing 19.1   19_01.SQL—Using Groups and Views to Create a Well-Secured Environment

```
/* First add the group */
sp_addgroup grp_junior_emp
go
```

```
/* now revoke select on the base tables from the public group */
Revoke Select on TitleAuthor from public
go
Revoke Select on Authors from public
go

/* now create the view that limits access */
Create View Vie_Authors
As
    Select     *
    From  AUTHORS
    Where AU_ID in (Select AU_ID
            From TITLEAUTHOR
            Where ROYALTYPER <= 50)
Go

/* grant select on the view to the members of the group */
grant select on Vie_Authors to grp_junior_emp
go
```

Using Stored Procedures to Conceal Underlying Data Objects and Business Rules

Stored procedures can be used in a very similar fashion to views to provide a level of security on the data that completely conceals the data available to a user and/or the business processes involved in manipulating the data.

In Listing 19.2, you can see the same data concealment as demonstrated in using the view in Listing 19.1 except that it is achieved through the use of a stored procedure.

Part
V

Ch
19

On the CD

Listing 19.2 19_02.SQL—Using Groups and Stored Procedures to Conceal Data Structures on the Server

```
/* First add the group */
sp_addgroup grp_junior_emp
go

/* now revoke select on the base tables from the public group */
Revoke Select on TitleAuthor from public
go
Revoke Select on Authors from public
go

/* now create the stored procedure that limits access */
Create Procedure up_SelectAuthors
As
    Select     *
    From  AUTHORS
    Where AU_ID in (Select AU_ID
```

continues

Listing 19.2 Continued

```
                     From TITLEAUTHOR
                     Where ROYALTYPER <= 50)
Go

/* grant execute on the view to the members of the group */
grant execute on up_SelectAuthors to grp_junior_emp
go
```

In Listing 19.3, the junior employees are allowed to update the contract flag on the AUTHORS table without having permission to update anything else on the table. This is the sort of procedure that enables you to hide data manipulation from the users while still giving them limited power to work on the data available to them in the server.

Listing 19.3 19_03.SQL—Stored Procedure That Allows Updating of the AUTHORS Table

```
/* First add the group */
sp_addgroup grp_junior_emp
go

/* now revoke select on the base table from the public group */
Revoke Update, Delete, Insert on Authors from public
go

/* now create the stored procedure that limits access */
Create Procedure up_SetContractForAuthor
     @nAu_Id id,
     @bContract bit
As
     Update      AUTHORS
     Set   CONTRACT = @bContract
     Where AU_ID = @nAu_Id

     Print "Author's contract flag set."
Go

/* grant execute on the view to the members of the group */
grant execute on up_SetContractForAuthor to grp_junior_emp
go
```

Using Security Beyond SQL Server

There are a number of steps that can be taken to provide a more secured environment in which SQL Server will operate. Some of the sections below may seem obvious, but are worth thinking about. We recommend that you designate a person to be responsible for system security at your workplace. This person will live, breath, and eat security and should be clearly empowered to implement any of the steps outlined below. System Security Officers (SSO) are becoming more and more common within organizations due to the highly accessible nature of public access networks, such as the Internet. Their roles are that of company custodians.

Physical Security

Often overlooked when designing the security of a system is the *physical security* of the server itself. Granted, it is unlikely that the average hacker will spend all day sitting on the system console hacking into a server trying various passwords without being noticed. However, if the server can physically be removed from its location, many unscrupulous users will be prepared to spend more time in the comfort of their homes. This would also include its mass data storage devices, such as tapes and hard drives.

Ensure that physical access to the server is limited. Provide locked doors, preferably with electronic locks, that secure the server, and optionally bolt the server to the structure on which it resides. Remember in these days of smaller and smaller hardware, the server can be a laptop or similarly small device. This makes it such that it is not so difficult to steal the box.

Because Windows NT provides excellent remote administration capabilities, you can remove monitors and keyboards from servers that must be placed in high access areas. This will stop the idle person from walking by and examining the server. As an alternative, there are plenty of hardware manufacturers that provide secure casings for server boxes that can be used to provide better security for your server.

It is assumed that the same level of physical security applied to the SQL Server will also be applied to the following:

- The network file servers
- The network hubs and routers
- Any other shared network device, such as bridges and remote WAN linkup devices

Part

V

Ch

19

Local Area Network (LAN) Access

A common mistake on LANs is to have unmonitored network nodes that allow access. Ensure that all nodes on the network that do not have computers actually attached to them have been disconnected from the hub so that no one can bring in a laptop and access the LAN at a physical level.

For highly secure environments, provide all users with SecureID cards or similar devices. These devices generate passwords that are authenticated by the Network fileserver and change constantly. This will stop users without valid identification cards from having access to the LAN, even if they have physical access to a node.

At a LAN software level, ensure that all the features of the LAN's software are being utilized. Most network operating systems provide at least government approved C2 level of security, but only if you turn it on. Unlike the B2 standard of security, C2 provides the features but does not enforce their use. Windows NT, Netware 4.1 and some versions of UNIX support C2 security.

Make sure that you are doing all the basics of good user management on your local area network, as follows:

■ Enforce password aging with a maximum life of 30 days.

■ Require unique passwords.

■ Require long (eight-character) passwords that are validated against a list of invalids. (Third party applications exist to ensure that good passwords are being used by a client.)

■ Enforce security block outs on logins that fail due to invalid passwords.

Remote or Wide Area Network Access

It's much harder to control WAN or remote access to a network than the local access provided through the LAN. However, some of the steps that you can take are as follows:

■ Assign IP addresses to all external users and do not allow them to connect with their own addresses. This will enable you to monitor closely all remote connections to your LAN.

■ Implement a software and/or hardware based firewall that physically limits external packet traffic on the server's network.

■ Enforce routine password changing per the fileserver guidelines outlined above.

■ Audit all remote transactions/IP traffic, and scan it for invalid requests.

■ Implement secure WAN protocol transport by using hardware based compression on either end of WAN bridges.

Application Security

There are a number of steps that you can take to make your applications secure independently of the security applied at the SQL Server level. Some things that you might want to consider are as follows:

■ Permission trees that allow users access to windows within your application program. You may want to break down access into three levels: view, new, and edit.

■ Application-based audit trails that track the changes of fields and the amount of time spent on any given window in the system.

■ Application-based limits on the amount of money that can be posted (for financial systems).

Remember, if the security of your database is important to you, you should always ensure that the database itself is secure with or without application programs. You must do this because sophisticated users on your network and on the Internet (if you are connected) will always be able to use a different application to work with your data if they wish. This would bypass any application-only security that was being enforced.

Encrypted Multi-Protocol NetLibrary

If security is a serious concern in the environment that SQL Server is being used, then it is possible to implement the SQL Server *Multi-Protocol NetLibrary (MPNL)*. This feature is available in version 6.0 and higher. MPNL provides a Remote Procedure Call (RPC)-based interface from clients to the SQL Server. MPNL requires that the protocol be added as a listener service to the engine—though MPNL is not actually a listener because it is RPC-based.

One key advantage of MPNL is that it can be encrypted. The encryption algorithm used can be enabled for individual clients; however, the server must be enabled for encrypted traffic. Support for clients varies. Check your SQL Server documentation for the client support available in your version.

Server enumeration via the `dbserverenum` call in NetLibrary is not supported on servers that are MPNL-enabled. Clients must know the name of servers that are operating in this mode.

From Here...

Having discovered the many facets of SQL Server security, it is most likely that you will spend the next few months trying to fill the holes that you now know exist. If you are lucky enough to be reading this book before you implement SQL Server in your environment, take advantage of what you have learned and apply as many security features as necessary to provide the appropriate control needed.

Take a look at the following chapters for more information that may be useful in creating a secure environment:

- See Chapter 13, "Managing Stored Procedures and Using Flow-Control Statements," to learn to create stored procedures to provide users with access to data without giving them access to the actual tables.
- See Chapter 9, "Managing and Using Views," to learn to hide underlying data tables with views that limit data sets available to users.

Part
V

Ch
19

Setting Up and Managing Replication

In this chapter, we'll be going over the fundamentals of replication, including how to install and use it and how it might be a good fit for your projects. Replication is an intricate feature of SQL Server. The boundaries of it have not been defined yet and there will be innovative projects that stretch these boundaries still to come.

Replication is a broad term, and to understand how to install and use it, you first need to understand what it is and what it is not. To help with this, we'll first be taking a look at some of the terms that Microsoft is using, how they implement the replication capabilities, and what it means to your system. ■

How to set up replication publications

SQL's capabilities to make information available to other servers adds new, distributed capabilities to your systems.

How to set up a SQL Server to receive information that is being replicated

Once information is available to your system, there are many different ways you can incorporate it into your database.

The different ways you can distribute information in your system to provide more meaningful data to your users

You can divide information to limit access to only certain elements of a database table.

Understanding the Basics

Replication with SQL Server provides you with the capability to duplicate information between servers. This capability brings with it the ability to synchronize information sources for multiple domains, even in cases where they are physically separated by distance and possibly poor communications links. Replication, at its most fundamental level, recognizes changes made to information in a database and sends these changes to the remote system or systems for their use.

Microsoft has employed what is called *Loose integration* in their replication model. You may have heard of the phrase, *real-enough time,* in systems implementation. Loose integration follows the real-enough time model. This means that information will flow across the system of servers not in real-time and not necessarily in batch mode, but *as quickly as it can.* The phrase, *real-enough time,* was first introduced when information was being distributed by e-mail to remote locations. It was certainly not real-time, as no live connection was maintained between sites.

Using e-mail didn't implement a batch approach, as transactions were often still addressed on a transaction-by-transaction basis. With the e-mail system, you're certain that your transactions are going to make it to the destination when a connection is completed between their system and yours.

SQL Server will synchronize the database tables—often almost immediately in many cases—but not concurrently with the transaction that made the original change that is to be replicated.

Certainly there are pros and cons to this approach. On the positive side, the user of the system will not be waiting for a remote server to respond before the application can continue. This alone can be a big time saver. Another benefit is that the system can manage some fault-tolerance in the queue of things to be done.

If you have a transaction that is going to a remote server and the remote system is down, the transaction can be queued for later processing. The server engine on the local side, the distribution engine, can retry the connection to, and update of, the remote server at regular intervals and make sure the transaction happens as soon as possible.

Another positive side-effect of this approach is a realistic approach to wide area networks that may need to be connected over slow links. Transactions can be handled as quickly as the connection allows, without bogging down applications that may be using the database tables that are to be replicated.

On the negative side, it's possible to have information in two databases that are using this schema that is out of date or different on different sides of the replication equation. With true replication as implemented in SQL Server at this time, this is a situation that you cannot control, but may have to address if this presents a problem. Remember, there are limited situations where this might occur, such as a scheduled connection was unavailable or a server went down. In either case, as soon as the connection was available, the databases would be re-synchronized at the next communication with each other.

N O T E If you have multiple databases, tables, or other entities that must be absolutely in sync, you'll need to work with the two-phase commit capabilities of SQL Server. This entails custom development on your part using the C API and working with DB-Library. Be sure to review the documentation provided with SQL Server for more information about this option. ▪

There are three different key physical layer components to the SQL replication model. They are the Subscriber, Publisher, and Distributor. Each of these components must be in place in order to have a functioning replication model.

Is It Distributed or Replicated Information?

There is a distinct implementation difference between *distributing* your information and *replicating* it. In many installations, you'll probably find that you have both scenarios. When you decide to implement a system based on multiple SQL Servers, you'll need to be very careful to define what information will reside on which SQL Servers. This sounds obvious, but you need to take it to the next step—beyond just determining functional requirements.

In many systems that are disbursed, the requirement to implement replication comes from the desire to have information available at a central location. This requirement, combined with the information to be centralized having a remote starting location, provides the foundation for a replication scenario.

This is certainly a system that can be automated using the replication capabilities of SQL Server. The primary requirement is that you put a SQL Server at each location and initiate the replication from the remote locations to the central location. Another alternative may be available if you reverse the flow of information shown in Figure 20.1.

FIG. 20.1
Basic replication model shows information flowing between different points in your system.

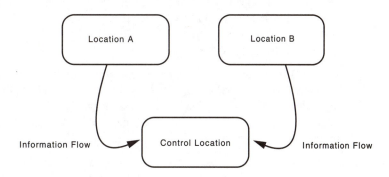

Part
V

Ch
20

Adding a distributed approach to this scenario might be helpful to enhance your application's performance. Distributed systems, or components of systems, lend themselves to situations that include some or all of the following attributes:

- The information required at each individual location is different and distinct.

- The information from one location does not need to be available, in its most up-to-date form, at other locations. Somewhat aged information, if it's needed at all, must suffice at the alternate locations.

- There is an intelligent agent running at the remote locations, and that agent must be able to respond to basic data request and manipulation requirements, such as copying working sets to a temporary database, and so forth.

A good example of a distributed system is a point-of-sale (POS) system. In a POS system, you'll often have sales information at each individual location, but other locations do not have to have that sales information until it has been posted to a central location, if at all (see fig. 20.2).

FIG. 20.2
A typical wide area network point-of-sale system lends itself to a mixed distribution- and replication-based system.

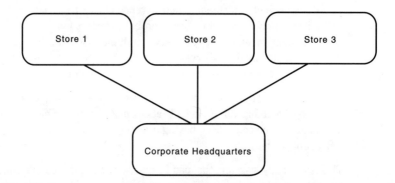

In this configuration, you can see that information flow between the store locations is minimal, and, when it does occur, it's likely to come from the corporate headquarters. Systems like this lend themselves to both a distributed information approach and a replicated scenario. First, you'll need to understand that replicated information is read-only at the recipient location. We'll cover more about how to work with this later in the chapter in the troubleshooting section, but you can use the fact that things are read-only to your advantage.

In our POS example, you can use replication to send all inventory information, including pricing, store inventory levels, and other store's sales information, to the different remote locations. Because this information is reasonably static, you can use a scheduled exchange of this information, rather than a continuous update. You'll want to keep this in mind as we walk through setting up replication in the coming sections.

Distributed information can be maintained at the stores. This information will include sales information, customer update information about purchases, credit payments, etc. You can refer to this as distributed because the stores operate on this information separately from the corporate headquarters. They can create, update, delete, and otherwise manage this information on their own.

TIP Using SQL Server to manage distributed information at the remote locations is not a requirement. You can consider using less expensive options if needed. Other databases that use ODBC are key candidates for the remote locations, as they'll be able to connect most easily to SQL Server later to update the main database systems.

In short, you should use a distributed environment to provide a fault-tolerant, independent system. The information produced under these routines, and the routines designed to create the distributed information, may or may not be required at the central location. Replicated systems are ideal for information that doesn't change very frequently at the recipients' location. Keep this in mind as you review the different replication and installation options that we'll be reviewing throughout this chapter.

SQL Server Replication Fundamentals

SQL Server's replication features follow a magazine-type analogy to relate the different roles that are parts of the equation. The model follows an *I'll Publish—You Subscribe* approach that's easy to follow and implement. In the next sections, we'll walk through setting up the different options for replication on both sides of the equation.

N O T E   SQL Server 6.5 has added the ability to replicate to ODBC subscribers, such as Access and Oracle. As stated in the SQL Server documentation, the ODBC subscriber must meet the following criteria:

- Must be ODBC Level 1-compliant.
- Must be 32-bit, thread safe, and for the processor architecture (Intel, PPC, MIPS, Alpha) that the distribution process runs on.
- Must be transaction-capable.
- Must support the Data Definition Language (DDL).
- Cannot be read-only. ▓

Publishing: Providing Information to Other Systems

When you decide you're going to be using replication to provide information to other systems, you, in effect, become a publisher. You'll be publishing your information for other systems to receive. At the highest level, the information you provide to other systems is called a *publication*. Publications consist of *articles,* which are the items that will be provided to the other systems. Articles are discrete pieces of information that range from the entire contents of a database to a single row or the result of a query. As you'll see when we review setting up a publication a little later in the chapter, there are several different ways to dissect the information you'll be providing via replication, as follows:

- Entire databases
- Entire tables
- Horizontal partitions of information
- Vertical partitions of information
- Custom views of information

Part
V

Ch
20

Each of these has its advantages and disadvantages. Which you use will depend entirely on what types of information you're replicating and how it will be used by the remote system.

N O T E Any table you want to replicate must have a unique index defined for it. If you don't have one defined, it will not show up in the list of available tables when you define the publication. ■

Entire Databases When you provide entire database articles to the remote system, you'll be asking SQL Server to monitor all activity for that database and update the users of the information with any changes that occur. This is probably the simplest form of replication to administer, as you're telling SQL Server to send everything.

Keep in mind the basic covenant of replicated tables, though; the information is read-only at the recipient. It may be that this would be too restrictive on your system to implement this type of full-blown replication.

N O T E If you're creating a *data warehousing* application—one in which you simply provide snapshot type information to other locations—this may be just the ticket. In these types of applications, you want to provide a picture of the information at a given time. You can create a database of queriable information, provide it to these remote users, and need not to worry about the information being changed. You can also be assured of the most recent and updated information at these locations, as SQL Server will be monitoring it for you and initiate updates on the schedule you designate. ■

The replication of tables and specific partitions of tables is often the way to go when you have a modifiable, production environment that you're exporting information to.

Entire Tables When you replicate entire tables, you specify a table that is monitored and sent out by the replication engine whenever changes are made. This table will be kept up to date based on the export timing and criteria you establish in setting up the publication article.

N O T E You can establish more than one article for a given table. This may be helpful if you want to provide all information to a production, administrative server, but only limited information to a reports-only server that is used by non-administrative personnel. Be aware, though, that each publication you establish will require resources on the server to process the replication event. If possible, consider publishing the table once; then create a view or other protected viewing mechanism on the receiving server as it works with the client-side software. n

Horizontal and Vertical Partitions of Information, Custom Views When you publish horizontal partitions, you're using a SELECT statement that will provide all columns of information, but is selective on the rows of information that will be considered. For example, consider the following simple SELECT statement:

```
Select * from Authors where au_lname like "W%"
```

This would select only those authors whose last names started with a *W*. These are the authors who would be included in published information.

On the other hand, it may be that you want to only publish certain columns of information to the remote system. For example, the Authors table in the Pubs database installed by default with SQL Server will include a Contract field indicating whether the author is under contract. If you're replicating a list of authors to a remote location, the users may not need to know whether you've established a contract with the author. In that case, you can select all fields except the Contract field to be included in the replication article.

You can also export a combination of a vertical and horizontal partition, or you can replicate the results of a view. The selective replication capabilities of SQL Server are the power behind the tool that really begins to broaden the appeal of replication.

Subscribing: The Recipients of Information

Once you've set up what information you'll be publishing with the articles and other information covered earlier, you'll need to move to the subscription system and let it know where to find the information that it will be the recipient of. The recipient is called the *subscriber* in the replication scenario. The subscriber sets up a connection to the distribution server and receives the information at the intervals you established when you created the article to be replicated.

Subscriptions include the ability to designate where the information will go, which will enable you to control who has access to it by using the standard NT and SQL security capabilities.

The Log Reader Process

There are two silent partners in the replication process that are always running and performing their tasks, but are much less visible when compared to the subscriber and publisher roles. These are the log reader process and the distribution database.

Replication in SQL Server is transaction log-based. As changes are made to articles that are declared for replication, they show up in the transaction log. The log reader process, an automatic background task on the server, detects these changes and logs them to the distribution server's distribution database.

Once a transaction has been processed for replication and put in the distribution database, the replication engine will publish it and make it available to the other servers that need it. You can see the log reader process if you look at the running processes in SQL Server. You'll see the process in the list of active connections.

Part

V

Ch

20

N O T E If there are any synchronization jobs pending, you'll also see those jobs listed in the pending tasks area of the running tasks list. ▪

Distribution Server: The Source of Information

The distribution server and database serve as the go-between for the publication server and the subscription server. When you set up the system—as you'll see when you go through the installation process—you'll have the option to set up a local distribution server or a remote system.

While the distribution database is separate from the other databases in your SQL Server system, it can still be on the same physical server. When you set up a local distribution database on the publication server, SQL Server will use this new database as the mechanism to keep track of the different items that need to be provided to the subscription servers on the network.

The distribution database is also the storage location for the different stored procedures that make up the replication engine. These stored procedures are automatically called when you use replication and are used to automate the different processes that happen under the covers when replication is running.

If you choose to use a remote system as your distribution database, the database is created or referenced on a different server from the publication server. This can be beneficial on a system where you may have high transaction volumes or may otherwise have a server that is bogged down just in the normal processing of transactions or network requests. In these situations, it can be beneficial to have this other system—the distribution database hosting system—manage the replication of information to the subscription servers.

CAUTION

You must have 32M of RAM on the server that will be the distribution system if you combine the distribution and publication operations on a single server. In addition, you may need to install additional memory if a given distribution server is to be used by more than one publication server. It may also be beneficial to implement a multi-processor server in cases where workload on the server is substantial.

You generally won't be working directly with the log reader processes or the distribution database, but it's important to understand their function in order to correctly set up your system.

Different Server Configurations for Replication

When you establish replication, you will save yourself time later if you take some time now to figure out exactly what the best way to lay out your system is. As with database definitions and ERDs discussed in Chapter 2, "Data Modeling and Database Design," planning early in the development process will really pay off when it comes time to move your system into production.

The configuration options for replication—at least on a physical implementation level—boil down to three different approaches, although there are certainly variations on these that may work well for some situations. The following are the basic three topologies:

- Combined single publisher/distribution, single subscribers
- Single publisher, distribution system, subscribers
- Single publisher, subscriber, publisher, subscribers (data warehousing)

Each of these is briefly described in the upcoming sections.

Combined Single Publisher/Distribution, Single Subscribers   The most basic type of installation is the combined publisher/distribution server and a single subscriber system. This enables you to configure a server where the transactions for your system take place and the information is replicated to the subscribing server. Figure 20.3 shows a simple replication configuration.

FIG. 20.3

This is a simple system using a single server as the publication and distribution system and a single subscriber.

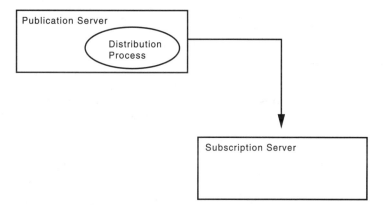

NOTE   The figures and examples we're using indicate a one-way flow of information. You can also install replication's publication features on a subscribing server and effectively replicate other information back to the original publication server. To put it another way, because a system can be both a publication and a subscription server, information can flow in both directions. In this case, you just need to establish appropriate articles for publication. ▪

It's likely that many systems that are not extremely high-volume will fall into this category, as it's the most straight-forward to set up and maintain. However, be sure to consider moving the distribution processes if your transaction volume begins to cause the server to become bogged down in processing both application and replication requests.

Single Publisher, Distribution System, Subscribers   By splitting apart the publication and distribution model, you can begin to address specific performance bottlenecks that may be apparent in your system. If you implement a model of this type, you'll be able to add processors, memory, or other resources to systems as they become over-utilized. As you can see in Figure 20.4, it may be helpful to distribute the configuration of your servers.

Part
V

Ch
20

FIG. 20.4
Moving the distribution
processes enables you to
optimize system configurations
for optimum performance.

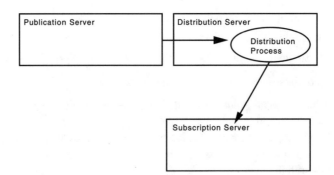

This system topology is also the first step toward a data warehousing system. By copying the information to the intermediary server, if you implement multiple subscription servers using this information, you'll be able to ensure that accurate, timely information is distributed without an overwhelming impact on the initial publication system.

In systems where you are publishing to multiple subscribers, especially in cases where the publications may be going out over a slow or remote link, a separate distribution server should be carefully considered. In each of these situations, more server attention will be required to complete the replication and is best handled by a separate system.

N O T E If you do implement this type of scenario, each system—the publication server, the distribution server, and each of the subscribers—is required to obtain separate SQL Server licenses. This cost will need to be part of the analysis when you are considering using a distribution server in this manner. ■

Single Publisher, Subscriber, Publisher, Subscribers A big topic in the database world right now is *data warehousing*. As we mentioned in the last section, replication lends itself well to data warehousing implementations, as it provides you with an automated way to provide read-only access to users of your system. You know the information will be correct and as up-to-date as you need, and because no intervention will be required, SQL Server's replication engine can be set up to update the remote systems at intervals required by your application.

In this scenario, you are publishing the information to an intermediary server that is responsible for secondary replication to subscribers. This is an excellent way to leverage your servers for their distribution to the users of your information. As you can see in Figure 20.5, one approach may be to link servers to further distribute information.

This type of installation is also a good candidate for a separate distribution server if there are other operations to be required of the initial subscription and re-publication server. It's also important to keep in mind that memory requirements may increase on the re-publication server to work with the increased number of subscribers.

FIG. 20.5
Re-publishing information leverages your resources and can be helpful in mass distribution or slow-link to multiple subscriber installations.

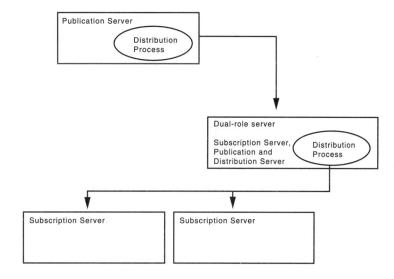

Installing the SQL Server Replication Services

The first step to installing replication is registering the remote server in the Enterprise Manager. There is nothing unique that you'll need to do to accomplish this, but you must have the server pre-defined prior to beginning the installation of the replication and subscription services.

> **N O T E** When you define servers in the Enterprise Manager, it's important that you select the correct type of security to be installed at each server. Selecting the Trusted Connection indicates that Integrated Security is in use. If you select the standard logon connection, you'll need to be sure to specify a user that is a valid user on the remote system and one that has sufficient rights to work with the database tables you are replicating. If you do not do this, you'll receive errors when the replication service tries to connect to the remote server. ▪

When you start the replication installation process, one of the first things SQL Server will do is to verify that you've declared enough memory for SQL Server processes. The minimum required memory allocated to SQL Server is 8196K or almost 8MB. You set this option in the Server Configuration dialog box, selected from the Server menu's Configurations option. An example of this is seen in Figure 20.6.

> **T I P** It's generally recommended that you allocate as much RAM as possible to SQL Server. A good guideline is that you should allocate all RAM except approximately 24M to the SQL Server process. For example, in a 64M system, you'd want to allocate approximately 40M to SQL Server. The 24M will handle the network operating system and other base operating requirements of the system.

FIG. 20.6

You must have a minimum of nearly 8M allocated to the SQL Server replication features of your system.

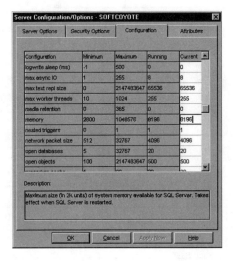

N O T E   Once you've established the memory configuration, you'll need to restart SQL Server. You can do this from the Enterprise Manager by selecting the server, and then right-clicking it. Select Stop from the menu. Once the server has been stopped, as indicated by the red traffic light, restart it. This will institute the changes to the memory configuration you just made.

The next step starts the process of installing replication as a publishing server on your system. Prior to setting up the distribution database, you'll need to have established both database and log devices. These must have sufficient disk space allocated to support the database that you'll be replicating. These are the devices that you'll be placing the distribution database and logs onto. The recommended minimum size for these items is 30M, but your size will depend significantly on several different factors, as follows:

- What is the size of the databases you'll be replicating? Remember, for each subscriber, there is an initial synchronization that must take place. This means that your distribution database should be at least as large as the combined maximum table size for each table that will be replicated. This size represents the size to support a single article. If you will be publishing multiple articles, you will want to figure out a total size based on all articles combined.

- What will be the traffic on your system be? More transactions mean more staging of information as it's passed along to the subscribing servers. This will impact the database size requirements, and, therefore, the device size requirements.

- How many different articles will you be publishing? Try to avoid using several different articles against a single information source. If you have a table that you need to provide to multiple subscribers, it's worth the effort to try to use only one publication/article combination to fulfill their needs. This is better utilization of disk resources, processing resources, and general processing bandwidth at the server.

▶ **See** Chapter 4, "Creating Devices, Databases, and Transaction Logs," for more information about setting up devices and databases in SQL Server. **p. 77**

Select Replication Configuration from the Server menu, then select Install Publishing from the submenu. This will begin the process of setting up the distribution database and other options that govern the server's operation for replication. Figure 20.7 shows the dialog box that you'll use to set up replication options.

FIG. 20.7

Set the options for the distribution database and processes for replication.

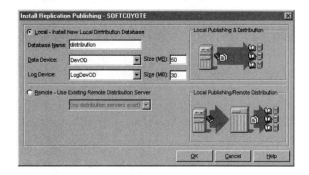

This dialog box enables you to define whether the distribution process will be local or located on a remote system. If you select local, you'll need to indicate where the distribution database will be installed. If you indicate a remote server, you'll need to know the server name and the SQL Server process must be already running on that system.

When you click OK, the new database will be added to the system and you'll be ready to start setting up specific options to enable publishing on your system. If all goes well, you'll receive a prompt, as shown in Figure 20.8, enabling you to go directly to setting up publications on your system.

FIG. 20.8

Once the distribution database is created, you can go directly to the definition of your publications and subscriptions.

N O T E If the installation of the distribution database fails for any reason, you'll need to address the problem before you can continue. A possible reason that you may experience a problem here is if you've registered a server with a user that is nonexistent or has insufficient rights on the remote system. Make sure you create an appropriate user prior to continuing if this is the problem you experience.

Once you've addressed any system problems that are presented, you may be faced with needing to completely uninstall replication before you can continue. For more information, see the "Uninstalling Replication" section at the end of this chapter. ▪

Part
V

Ch
20

Enabling Publishing

The first step to creating your own publications is to, in essence, turn on publication services, designate a frequency for the services, and indicate which databases are candidates for replication. You can get to the configuration options, shown in Figure 20.9, from the Yes/No dialog box after defining the distribution database, or you can select the Publishing option from the Server, Replication Configuration menu.

FIG. 20.9
With the configuration dialog box, you indicate frequency of updates and which databases are available for replication.

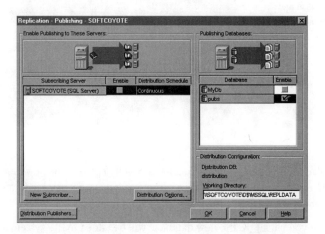

For each server you have registered to the Enterprise Manager, you can indicate whether it is allowed to subscribe to this server by selecting or deselecting the Enable option from the Enable Publishing grid. For each server you will allow to subscribe, you can indicate at what frequency you'll be replicating information to the server. The default is to replicate information continuously starting at 12:00 AM and continuing throughout the day.

If you are using a remote link or are only providing snapshot information to the subscription servers, you may want to change this value to a time when the system is generally under less load. This can help decrease the impact on network traffic that will be incurred when the replication process kicks off. Of course, this places your data into a batch-type mode and may not be acceptable at the end user's application.

Selecting or deselecting databases will control which databases you'll have to select from when you define publications. If you have a secure database that you want to control, this is the ultimate protection. By not making the database available to the replication process, you can be assured that it will not be included in publications.

You may notice the working directory option shown in the dialog box just below the designation of the distribution database. This directory is where information is kept and staged as it is sent out to the subscription servers. You can change this directory if needed. When SQL replicates a database, it is using a method somewhat like a BCP to copy the data from one system to another. This directory is where the data files are built.

N O T E It may be desirable to indicate a secured location for this directory if you have concerns about other users modifying or reviewing this information when it's staged. The information is not readily discernible, but should be protected nonetheless. ▨

If you want to create a custom distribution schedule or control how often information is sent based on transaction volume, you can click the Distribution Options button. As shown in Figure 20.10, this option also enables you to indicate how long information is maintained at the distribution server once it has been sent to the remote system.

FIG. 20.10

You can create custom distribution schedules on a server-by-server basis. This can be helpful to take into account time zone changes and other loading factors.

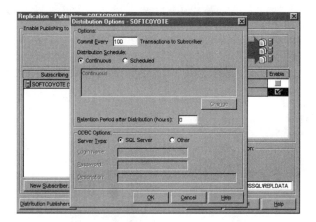

If you do opt to establish a custom distribution schedule, a separate dialog box enables you to change a number of options. As shown in Figure 20.11, you'll be able to set up how often, on a macro level, the replication will take place. This option allows values that range from daily to monthly. As you select this highest level interval, the balance of the options will change to reflect values that enable you further to define how you would like to have the replication carried out.

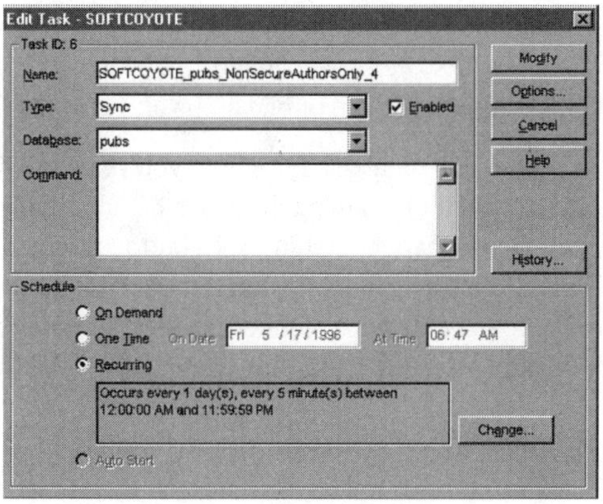

FIG. 20.11

Custom timing for replication can be defined for a number of time intervals.

Part
V

Ch
20

Congratulations—you're now ready to set up the specific publications and articles that you'll be making available to other systems. You've defined the servers that have access to the information, the frequency at which it will be provided, and you've indicated where the information will come from in your system. The next step is to create the publications that will be replicated.

Publishing Databases: How to Replicate Entire Databases

You may recall that you have two different options when it comes to replicating information on your system. You can either publish the entire database or you can select specific information in the database to replicate. In this section, we'll explain setting up replication for an entire database. In the coming sections, we'll go over setting up targeted articles. To begin, go into the replication management options (see fig. 20.12).

FIG. 20.12

Use the Manage menu to control all aspects of the replication process after you've completed the initial setup.

N O T E   Remembering which option to use from the menus or the topology dialog box can be confusing. It can help to keep in mind that you don't generally use the options on the Server menu once you've installed and set up the basic configuration for replication on your system. All aspects that deal with the specific publications and subscriptions are controlled from the Manage menu. ■

Select Manage, Replication, Publications from the menus to begin working with the different publications that are on your system (see fig. 20.13). This will take you to the dialog boxes that enable you to define and configure the publications and articles that you will be offering.

The dialog box will show each database for which you've enabled replication during the setup phase. Of course, there will not be any publications listed initially because you've not defined them yet. You use the New, Change, and Remove buttons to manage the different replications in your system. The tree display will expand under each database, showing the different publications that are available once they are defined. Under each publication, you'll be able to see the articles that have been created. From this display, you'll be able to manage all active publications.

FIG. 20.13

The initial Manage Publications dialog box shows the databases you've selected to allow for replication.

Selecting the Tables to Be Published In the first example, we'll be setting up a AllPubs publication that will replicate all eligible tables in the PUBS database. Remember, you must have a primary key defined for each table that you need to replicate. You can use the Alter Table command to institute a primary key if needed.

▶ **See** Chapter 5, "Creating Database Tables and Using Datatypes," for information about modifying table definitions. **p. 105**

When you select New, you're presented with the dialog box that enables you to set up the publication and indicate the information that should be replicated. Figure 20.14 shows the dialog box that lists the different tables that are available and enables you to set up the specifics of the article.

FIG. 20.14

Setting up the article to publish an entire database only entails selecting <all tables> for the article definition.

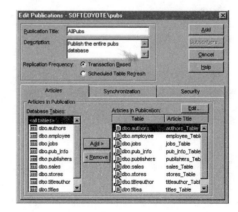

You'll need to first name the article that you're defining. When you do, make sure you do not include spaces or wildcard characters, such as an asterisk, in the name. If you do, you'll be prompted to change the name when you click Add to save the publication.

N O T E   You may want to create a naming convention for your publications to make it easier to know what information they provide. This is completely optional, but if you're publishing numerous articles, this information will help the subscription systems determine which publications they need to be working with.

Because we're first setting up an article that publishes all eligible tables from the PUBS database, simply selecting the <all tables> option will suffice for the definition. Each table is copied to the Articles in Publication pane, and you can tell that they're included by the shared icon that you're familiar with in Explorer and File Manager.

Establishing Table Synchronization   When you establish a publication, you are guaranteed that the subscribing system's tables will be initialized to contain the same information as the replicated table. To do this, there is an initial synchronization step that is completed. You can control how and when this step occurs by selecting the Synchronization tab from the Edit Publications dialog box shown in Figure 20.15.

FIG. 20.15
You can defer synchronization to a time that may suit your system requirements better, possibly saving money if remote connections are used.

If you are replicating information between SQL Servers, you'll want to make sure you leave the default copy method, using Native Format data files, selected. This will enable SQL Server to save the information in as optimized a format as possible when it creates the export file used to initialize the subscriber's database tables. The other option, Character format, will save the exported information in a format that you could use if you were importing to the receiving database using other utilities, or if you're using the information produced by the initial synchronization in a third-party system.

You can also set up the schedule of times that controls when the synchronization will occur by clicking the Change button. Establishing these times is very similar to the time frames you set up during the initial configuration of the replication services.

Controlling the Recipients of Subscriptions A key feature and concern regarding replication of databases is security. You've seen when you set up your system for replication that you can determine what subscribing systems will have overall access to your replication services. This presents a possible challenge, though, when you need to provide access to some, but not all, publications that reside on your replication server.

SQL Server enables you to indicate, on a case-by-case basis, what servers will have access to any given publication. By default, when you set up a new subscription, SQL Server will make it available to any server with overall access to the replication system of your server. To change this, as indicated in Figure 20.16, select the Security tab of the Edit Publications dialog box.

FIG. 20.16

You can easily prevent access to specific publications depending on what servers are requesting the information.

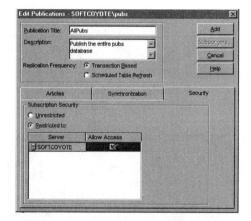

When servers look to your system to select available publications, if their system has not been authorized to use a given publication, it will not show up in the list of available items. You can change this option later to allow or disallow access to a publication by selecting Security from the initial Publications dialog box.

Making Changes to Publications Once you've set up publications, you can review them from the Manage Publications window. In Figure 20.17, you can see that each database will show its related publications and articles as they've been defined on the server.

If you want to make a change to a publication, simply highlight it and select Change. You'll be presented with the same dialog box that enabled you to define the publication in the first place. You'll be able to modify the tables that are included, how the information is synchronized, and the security aspects of the publication.

Part
V

Ch

FIG. 20.17

You can use the tree view of the replication system to select a publication or article to review or modify.

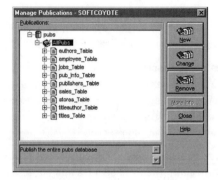

Publishing Partial Databases and/or Tables

Now that you understand how to publish entire databases, we'll review how to selectively publish information from your replication server. As you might imagine, publishing select information can be quite complicated, although it will depend a great deal on how you're trying to limit the information being replicated and how you go about defining that information.

Limiting Publications to a Single Table   The first, and most basic, selective publication is limiting the publication to a single table. You may have noticed that each table available for replication is listed when you define a given publication. In our first example, we published the entire database by selecting the <all tables> option at the top of the list of tables. The alternative to this is to select the individual tables that we want to include in the subscription from the Database Tables list. Once you've highlighted the different tables you want to include, click the Add button and they will be copied to the Articles list (see fig. 20.18).

FIG. 20.18

You can select one or more individual tables to be included in the publication.

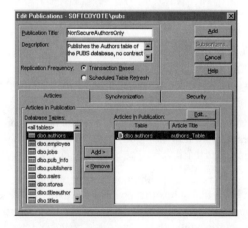

If you do nothing more for this publication, the entire table will be monitored and replicated as part of this publication. You have the same options for managing how the publication will be synchronized and what servers will have access to it as you do when setting up a full-database replication.

The alternative to publishing the entire database table is to partition it. You may recall from earlier sections in this chapter on "Publishing Partial Databases or Tables" that you can partition a table in one of two ways: either horizontally or vertically. The next section shows how you can control this functionality with your publication.

Partitioning Information to Be Included in a Publication   The two partitioning options, horizontal and vertical, correspond to looking at views of your information based on selectively retrieving rows (horizontal) or columns (vertical) from your database tables. Of course, you can combine these two techniques to provide a concise view of the information in the table if needed as well.

To establish a partition of information to be used in the article, you click the Edit button on the Edit Publications dialog box's Articles tab. This will call up the Manage Articles dialog box that shows two new tabs, Filters and Scripts (see fig. 20.19).

FIG. 20.19

You can select which columns you want to be included in the replication process.

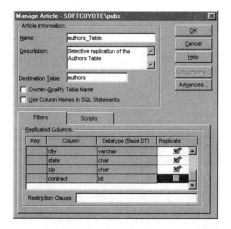

In the example, as discussed earlier in this section, we don't want to include the Contract column information in the replicated information that is provided to other sites with this publication. By scrolling down the list of columns, you can select and deselect the different columns that you want to include. When you've completed the selection, you will have vertically partitioned the database if you've deselected any columns because the publication will include only those fields that you allowed.

Normally, insert, delete, and update operations are managed by the SQL Server replication process automatically. This may be a problem if you're inserting information and need to have another process kicked off by the action of inserting a new row, for example. In these cases, you can click the Advanced button and you can specify the Insert, Update, and Delete scripts that you'd like to run when records are modified with these operations.

Part
V

Ch
20

In addition, if you need to do so, you can provide a table-creation script that you need to use in initializing tables. This script will be run instead of the standard table script generated by SQL Server based on the source table's definition. This can be helpful if you're defining tables that will receive replicated data, but perhaps not all columns that need to be in a table.

By default, when the table is created, it will be created with columns to match the article's definition. This means that, in our example of not copying the Contract column, the column would not exist at all in the recipients' databases. You can modify the creation script here and make sure all appropriate information and columns are included. Figure 20.20 shows how you can modify these values.

FIG. 20.20

You can override SQL's default methods that are used to implement changes to the underlying database tables.

▶ **See** Chapter 14, "Creating and Managing Triggers," for more information on triggers. **p. 375**

You also have the option of controlling the synchronization scripts that will be run by SQL Server. Clicking the Advanced button will let you edit what actions will be taken on synchronization of tables between the publication and subscription systems. The dialog box is shown in Figure 20.21.

FIG. 20.21

You have full control over how indexes and existing tables will be managed during the synchronization process.

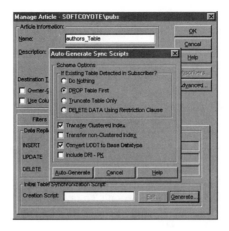

 TIP If there is a chance that the table may already exist on the user's system, be sure to check the DROP Table First option. If you don't, you may have a database table in an unknown state.

If you want to see or edit the actual script that will be created when the table is synchronized, you can click the Auto-Generate button. You'll be presented with the listing that will be used to create the table when it's initialized.

After you've completed your changes, click OK from the Manage Article dialog box, then Add from the Manage Publications dialog box. The publication will be added to the list of available publications, and you'll be ready to allow other users to start accessing the publications on your system.

You'll notice in Figure 20.22 that the AllPubs publication shows a secure publication, one with additional limits on who can see and use the information. This is indicated by the key that is showing over the book icon next to the publication name. On the NonSecureAuthorsOnly publication, there is no key, indicating that the publication is open to subscription by any subscription server with access and overall replication authority on your server.

FIG. 20.22

The new publication and articles are added to the list of active publications, ready for a subscriber to begin receiving the replicated information.

Part
V

Ch
20

In the next section, we'll go over how you set up subscriptions on the recipient side of the equation. Now that you've set up the publications, it's a straightforward process to indicate which publications any given subscription server needs to begin receiving replication updates for.

Enabling Subscribing

Once the publications have been set up on the publication server, it's a simple task to set up the subscription server to begin receiving the information. Before you can subscribe to a given article, you must follow the same installation steps outlined earlier in this chapter. These steps set up the distribution database and prepare your system to begin working with the replicated information. The only difference is that, when it comes to specifying which databases are visible to the replication process, you'll be specifying which ones can be the *recipients* of information rather than the source of the information.

▶ **See** "Installing the SQL Server Replication Services," previously in this chapter, for installation instructions. **p. 515**

When you're ready to initiate subscriptions, select Manage, Replication, Subscriptions from the menu in Enterprise Manager. As shown in Figure 20.23, this brings up a dialog box very similar to the Manage Publications dialog box used to define and create publications.

FIG. 20.23

Select the publication that you want to subscribe to from the list of available items for the server and database you are interested in.

You'll be able to drill down into any given publication to see what articles are available and whether you're already subscribed to them or not. Once you've found the publication you want to subscribe to, highlight it and select Subscribe. You'll be able to specify where you want the information to go on your local system once it begins arriving from the replication server (see fig. 20.24).

You'll notice that there are three different options available to you for synchronization of the database. The last option is to turn off the synchronization altogether. This means that you know for a fact that the database and the concerned tables are in sync with the master system by some other means.

FIG. 20.24
When you select a publication, you need to indicate where you want to store the incoming information on your server.

> **CAUTION**
>
> If you are unsure at all about the validity of the information in the database, it's best to allow the system to perform an initial synchronization on the database.

The first option enables you to let the system do the work for you and do the synchronization of information over the standard network connection between this system and the publication server. If you're on a locally attached LAN or a fast connection that is reliable, this is the best option to select and is the default.

If you're on a slower link, it may be that you've opted to bring the update to the system by another means. This includes copying the initial synchronization files from the publication server to tape or disk and then physically bringing them to the subscription system. If you have a slow link and initially populated tables, this may be a good option, as it will avoid the initial rush of information across an already slow connection between the two systems.

 Remember, you can schedule the time at which synchronization takes place. Moving it to off-hours can ease network loading significantly.

After you've set up the subscription to the publication server, you'll notice that the display of subscriptions will be updated to show the active subscription. You can see in Figure 20.25 that, although the subscription is active, it has not yet been synchronized with the publication server.

FIG. 20.25

The list of subscriptions will change to indicate that you're now subscribed to the publication. It also indicates the destination database.

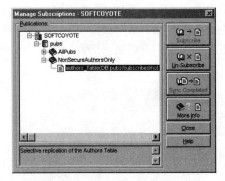

Uninstalling Replication

There may be times when you need to uninstall replication, either on a server-specific basis or on an overall basis. Examples include a server changing physical locations and no longer needing access to sensitive information, or where you've installed several test scenarios and simply want to start over!

The next two sections will show how you can cover both of these types of situations using facilities within SQL Server.

Disallowing Specific Servers

If you find that you need to remove a server from the list of servers that are eligible to receive information from your publication server, you'll need to determine whether you need to restrict only individual publications or if you need to revoke access altogether. If your intent is to remove access completely, you simply remove the server from the list of eligible candidates that can see the publications on this server.

From the Server menu, select Replication, Publishing You'll be able to indicate which servers are able to subscribe to your server. Figure 20.26 shows the server selection dialog box that will appear.

FIG. 20.26

Deselect any servers you no longer want to make publications available to.

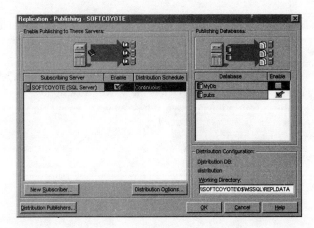

You'll be presented with a list of subscriptions that are about to be removed and asked to confirm that you want to remove the server from the list of eligible systems. Once you confirm, the server will still show up on the list, but the server will not be able to select publications on the publication server.

Uninstalling Replication Completely

Carefully consider all options before you opt to remove replication entirely from the system. This operation will shut down *all* replication to *all* subscribing servers, and it does so in a somewhat brut-force manner by removing the replication option from the server and deleting the distribution database.

There are three steps for uninstalling replication in SQL Server, as follows:

1. Discontinue all replication services—all publication and subscription services—between this system and other servers with which it is working.
2. Turn off the replication option at the server engine level.
3. Drop the distribution database.

You will need to follow these steps in order to restore your system to its state prior to installing replication. Removing connections to other servers is covered in the section immediately preceding this one. If you're removing replication from a subscription server, select Server, Replication, Subscriptions instead of Publications, but the operations of removing references to foreign servers are the same.

The next step requires issuing an interactive SQL command, so you'll need to use ISQL/w or another utility to enter the command. Enter the following stored procedure call to turn off the replication option on your system:

N O T E   You must be logged in as SA to complete this option. ■

```
sp_ServerOption "<servername>", "dist", false
```

Replace <servername> with the name of your server. In our example, because our server name is PLUTO, the command would be:

```
sp_ServerOption "pluto", "dist", false
```

N O T E   No results are returned from the call. ■

This will remove the distribution option from your system, disabling replication. The distribution database you established when you first installed replication will still remain in the system. Dropping this database is the final step in removing replication from your system.

From the Enterprise Manger, right-click the table that you specified.

Part

V

Ch

20

> **CAUTION**
>
> Be sure you're selecting the *distribution* database you specified, *not* your databases that contain active, important production information. If you have any doubt about which database to select, you can review the stored procedures for the database, and you'll be able to see the replication stored procedures there.
>
> If you select an incorrect database, you will be permanently dropping production information, and your only recourse will be to restore from a backup.

From the menu, select Drop Database and confirm that you want to drop the database. If all has gone well, you can make a quick check by selecting Server, Replication from the menus. You should have the Install Replication option available once again.

Troubleshooting

TROUBLESHOOTING

I'm trying to define publications on my server, but when I get to the point of designating the table to replicate, the table I need is not listed. Why not? Replication with SQL Server requires that you have a primary key defined for any table you need to replicate. Define a key for the table and retry the definition for the publication. The table will then appear in the list, ready for you to select it to be replicated.

TROUBLESHOOTING

I've created a publication, and I've subscribed to it. The table doesn't appear on the subscription machine. What could be wrong? A number of things can be happening that can cause the replicated table to not yet appear on the subscription system. First, keep in mind that the replication may have been established on a scheduled basis. It may be that you set up the replication to occur, at least for synchronization tasks, during the night or some other off-peak time. Check the publication setup options on the publication server to verify when you expect table synchronization tasks to be performed.

Second, it's possible that enough time hasn't passed since the publication and subscription were set up. By default, synchronization occurs every five minutes. If your table is large, it may take some time to physically transfer the information to the subscription system, or it may be that the initial five minutes has not yet passed.

Third, the connection may be down between the two servers. Check to see that you can otherwise connect to the servers and make sure that they are up, running, and allowing logons. You'll also want to check utilization on the servers. Microsoft recommends 32M of RAM on the publication system.

With less RAM, it's possible that you're running into memory constraint issues and that the server is swapping more information than it should have to while performing the operations demanded of it with replication.

TROUBLESHOOTING

I can see the replicated tables on the subscription server, but when my application runs, it generates errors indicating that I don't have sufficient rights to the information. I'm signed into SQL Server as SA, but still get these messages. What could the problem be? SQL Server's replicated tables are read-only on the subscribing system. If needed, you'll have to create either triggers on the incoming table that insert the replicated information into a working table, or you'll need to modify your system to use the tables differently, allowing for the read-only nature of the replicated tables.

From Here...

Replication is a powerful tool, especially in distributed environments. By putting replication into your systems, you can provide an excellent level of usability for applications, a great security layer for the underlying database tables, and better overall data availability.

For additional information about the topics covered in this chapter, please refer to the following chapters:

- Chapter 4, "Creating Devices, Databases, and Transaction Logs," provides additional information about creating the databases that you'll be using in the replication process. It also includes information about the management of the transaction log for your applications.

- For information on managing databases and creating databases and tables, see Chapter 5, "Creating Database Tables and Using Datatypes."

- In Chapter 10, "Managing and Using Indexes and Keys," information about defining primary keys is provided. You'll need this information to enable replication for your tables.

- Chapter 14, "Creating and Managing Triggers," includes information that may help you create subsystems for further distributing information that has been replicated—all automatically.

Part
V

Ch
20

Communicating with SQL Server

Developing applications for SQL Server can take many different forms. As you've seen throughout this book, queries executed by the server are at the heart of the system. The queries you've worked with thus far are all based in the SQL language and are generally entered or executed from the ISQL or ISQL/w utilities.

This approach won't prove very useful, however, when you're developing an application to work with SQL Server information. The client application—that portion of the program responsible for information formatting, presentation, and other user interaction—is where the power of SQL Server is presented to the average user. The way your application interfaces with the SQL Server can be just as important as all of the hard work you've done behind the scenes in defining the tables, creating the stored procedures, and optimizing the system to work at its peak.

In this chapter, we'll review a few of the top methods of working with SQL Server from an application development perspective. Each of these technologies is a comprehensive environment for working with SQL Server, and each warrants far more coverage than is afforded here. This information is provided so you'll have a starting point of knowledge for selecting the method that is right for you. ■

Different approaches for developing with SQL Server

You have several options for the specifics of how you'll communicate with SQL Server, making the versatility of the platform a good tool at your disposal.

Cross-platform development capabilities

All of the major development platforms from Microsoft and Borland are "SQL-ready."

Exposed object model for SQL administration

You can even create administrative modules for your SQL Server using new object-oriented techniques.

The most common methods of working with SQL Server are:

- DB-Library
- ODBC
- SQL OLE

The coming sections will review the basics of each of these options and explain how they may be useful in your work with SQL Server.

Understanding the DB-Library Interface

DB-Library, or *DB-LIB*, as it's often referred to, is an API for both C and VB that allows you to work directly with SQL Server. The API provides you with the different tools you need for sending queries to, and receiving information from, SQL Server. It also provides the means for working with that information by allowing you to extract information from the results sets returned from your queries.

What You Need

To use DB-LIB, you'll need to include several different supplemental files with your project. Table 21.1 shows the different files you'll need in the VB and C environments.

N O T E Some of the files listed in the following tables might not have been included with your version of SQL Server. If this is the case and the files are necessary, they can be obtained through the SQL Server SDK from Microsoft. ■

Table 21.1   Required Components for DB-LIB

C	Visual Basic
SQLDB.H	VBSQL.OCX
SQLFRONT.H	VBSQL.BAS

Table 21.2 shows the different components that you'll be working with as you develop applications with Borland's developer tools. Be sure to use the memory model that matches your application development environment.

Table 21.2   Borland DB-LIB Components

Component File	Description
BLDBLIB.LIB	Large memory model static library
BMDBLIB.LIB	Medium memory model static library

You'll use slightly different components when developing with Microsoft environments. Table 21.3 shows the required elements in this environment.

Table 21.3   Microsoft-Oriented Components

Element	Description
MSDBLIB3.LIB	Windows: Import library
NTWDBLIB.LIB	Win32: Import library
RLDBLIB.LIB	DOS: Large memory model library
RMDBLIB.LIB	DOS: Medium memory model library

Concepts and Characteristics

Working with DB-LIB typically follows a standard cycle of calls. Figure 21.1 shows the typical chain of events, starting with a logon to the SQL Server that you need to access.

FIG. 21.1
You typically log on, perform one or more calls to SQL Server, and then log off when you're using DB-LIB in your applications.

```
┌──────────────┐
│  SQL Logon   │
└──────┬───────┘
       │
       ▼
┌──────────────┐
│ Send calls to│◄───┐
│  SQL Server  │    │
└──────┬───────┘    │
       │            │
       ▼            │
┌──────────────┐    │
│ Receive and  │    │
│process results├───┘
└──────┬───────┘
       │
       ▼
┌──────────────┐
│  SQL Logoff  │
└──────────────┘
```

Two structures are used to establish your connection to the server. Both dbproc and login are used to establish and continue communications between your application and the SQL Server.

You use the DBOpen API call to initiate the connection to the server. DBOpen will initialize the DBProcess structure, giving you the information you need to continue working over the same connection to the server. Table 21.4 shows the different ways you accomplish these steps in the VB or C languages.

Part
V

Ch
21

Table 21.4 Basic Components for SQL Server Communications with DB-LIB

Description	Visual Basic	C
Initialize new loginrec structure	SqlLogin%	dblogin
Set user name for login	SqlSetLUser	DBSTLUSER
Set user password for login	SqlSetLPwd	DBSTLPWD
Set client application descriptive name	SqlSetLApp	DBSTLAPP
Open the connection to SQL Server	SqlOpen%	dbopen
Close the connection to SQL Server	SqlClose	dbclose
Close all connections	SqlExit	dbexit

Using these statements, you create a new login structure and populate the required fields. There are other properties of the login structure, but the user name and password are the only required items.

> **N O T E** If you are using integrated security, these fields are required, but they are ignored by the server when the connection is made. The server will use the user's credentials from the currently logged-on user. In this situation, if you know ahead of time that integrated security is used, you may want to pass in arbitrary information in these fields (for example, a user name and password of "blah" will suffice). Since the users will be authenticated by their network sign on, the user ID and password are not needed. The sign-on presents the user with an additional dialog box.
>
> The descriptive name is not required, but it is strongly recommended. The reason for supplying this information is simple. If you have a system administrator working with the SQL Server and reviewing the open connections, the name you provide here will be shown in the connection listing. By providing meaningful information, the administrator will know who is on the server at any given point. Because of that, you should avoid the temptation to just sign in all users on an application as the application name. If you can provide the application name and the station ID or user ID, you'll be adding some key identifying elements that the administrator can use. ■

Using the login structure and the server name, the call to open the connect is made, and the server connection is opened. When you issue the Open command, a structure is established and returned by the call. In future calls to the server, you'll be using this structure pointer whenever you issue a command to the server.

> **T I P** SQL Server login and logout operations are among the most costly transactions in terms of performance. If you log in each time you need to make a call or series of calls and then log out, you'll find that your application can be slower than you'd expect.
>
> To remedy this, consider using a separate connection for each major classification of work that is to be done. For example, if you have a point-of-sale system, at the front counter you may want to develop a

system to maintain the connection open to the Inventory table and the Accounts Receivable and Cash Drawer tables to help performance.

By doing so, you can take the time up front, during the loading of the application, to create your connections to SQL Server. Later, since the connections will already exist, the amount of time to access the separate tables will be minimized, and the user will have a much easier time using your application.

One consideration in this scenario can be the number of licensed connections you have to SQL Server. You need to make sure you end up running the number of licenses you have purchased for your SQL Server. If you use more, you may have to re-think your application, purchase additional licenses, or do both in order to have an optimal price-performance installation.

Sending Commands to SQL Server

When you send statements to SQL Server, you first build them in the SQL command buffer. Putting the commands into the buffer is done by calling `SqlCmd` with the parameters you need to place in the buffer.

> **N O T E** The examples provided here are largely VB-related. Though the actual statement varies in C, the calling conventions are similar and require many of the same approaches as apply to VB. ▨

The syntax for `SqlCmd()` in VB is:

```
Status% = SqlCmd(MyConnection%, "<statement>")
```

Each statement is appended to the previous statement, if any, that is currently in the `SqlCmd` structure. Be careful of building your statement if it requires more than one line. Remember that the string you specify is simply concatenated with any prior information in the buffer. Consider the following code sample:

```
...
Status% = SqlCmd(MyConnection%,"Select * from pubs")
Status% = SqlCmd(MyConnection%,"where author like 'A%'")
...
```

Why will this statement provide a syntax error and fail? There would not be any resulting spaces between pubs and where in the example. Be sure to provide spaces in these situations, or you'll generate syntax errors as shown.

Once you've created the buffered statement, you need to send it to SQL Server to be executed. You use the `SqlExec` statement to accomplish this.

```
Status% = SqlExec(MyConnection%)
```

Since you've queued up the commands and associated them with the particular connection, `SqlExec` will know exactly what you're executing. It sends the buffered statement to SQL Server and allows SQL to translate and run your request. In this example, the entire command that would be sent to SQL Server would be `Select * from pubs where author like 'A%'` (adding in the required spaces as indicated earlier).

N O T E If you want to call a stored procedure, you can create your command and preface it with
Execute. For example:

```
…
Status% = SqlCmd(MyConnection%,"Execute GetAuthors 'A%'")
…
```

In this case, you'd be executing a stored procedure called GetAuthors and passing a parameter,
'A%' to the stored procedure, presumably to be used as a search value. Executing the call and
processing the results occur the same as if you had issued a select statement. ■

Working With Results Sets

Once you've sent your request to SQL Server, you'll need to be able to work with the information returned from the query. To do so, you'll need to use two constants to monitor your work with the data sets. These constants are defined in the .BAS files, which are required to develop with the DB-LIB libraries.

■ SUCCEED

■ NOMOREROWS

What you're doing when you process returned results sets from SQL Server is to walk down through the rows returned until you receive NOMOREROWS, indicating that all rows which were returned have been accessed by your application. You can retrieve the current status of the record set by using the SqlResults% function. This function will return either SUCCEED or NOMOREROWS, and your application can determine what to do next based on this information.

```
Status% = SqlResults%(MyConnection%)
```

You should call SqlResults before launching into any processing loops. This will ensure that you're not working with an empty data set. If you have successfully returned information from your query, you can loop through the results by using SqlNextRow%. SqlNextRow, as the name suggests, will work down through the rows in your results, one at a time. The results are placed into the working buffer so you can work with them. When SqlNextRow hits the end of the data set, it will return NOMOREROWS, allowing your application to stop processing the data set.

N O T E Results returned from DB-LIB's functions are enumerated, rather than named, properties.
As you work with columns returned, you'll be indicating the column by number, not name.
You'll need to keep in mind the order in which you specify the columns in your select statement or
stored procedure. Otherwise, the information column you requested may not return what you expect, as
it would be returning a different column's information. ■

The final step in working with the information is to retrieve it from the buffer. SqlData and SqlDatLen are the functions that are regularly used to work with this information. The code sample below shows how a sample processing loop would be implemented, allowing you to print the author name.

```
…
Status% = SqlCmd(MyConnection%,"Select au_lname from authors")
Status% = SqlExec(MyConnection%)

While SqlNextRow%(MyConnection%) <> NOMOREROWS
      Print SqlData$(MyConnection%,1)
Wend

Print "No more information to present."
…
```

Closing the SQL Connection

After you've finished working with a given connection, you should make sure to close the connection, freeing up the memory associated with it and releasing the connection to the server. The SqlClose function will close an associated connection for just this purpose.

```
Status% = SqlClose%(MyConnection%)
```

You will need to close each connection you open for access to the server. Alternatively, you may wish to call SqlExit, which will close all currently open connections to the server. If your application has completed and is exiting, it may be easier to use the SqlExit statement to ensure that all connections are closed properly.

Client Configuration

Aside from distributing the OCX with your client application, no other modules are required with the client application. The functionality of the DB-LIB add-in is provided in the OCX and .BAS files.

In the C environment, you'll need to include the appropriate DLLs with your application and network environment. The DLLs will vary depending on the LIBs you employ, as mentioned previously. Please refer to Table 21.2 and Table 21.3 for more information.

Advantages and Disadvantages of Using DB-Library

DB-LIB is a SQL Server-specific interface layer. This means that, of the three different options presented here, this is the least "portable" between back-end database servers but also one of the faster ways to access information. This is due not only to the fact that it's an optimized interface, but also that you're developing directly in the host language. The other options, ODBC and SQL OLE, offer similar services but also impose an abstraction layer between your application and the calls to SQL Server.

One thing you may notice is that DB-LIB is very "manual" in how it is implemented. This is because you create and issue the Select statements, you create and issue the Update statements, etc. There is no concept of "bound" or automatically updating values. This can be good in that you can control the interface to the server, optimizing the connections and making sure that all data meets your criteria. In addition, you have complete control over the error trapping associated with the transactions.

Part
V

Ch
21

DB-LIB is an excellent API-level interface to SQL Server. Keep in mind that this is not the method you'll be using to work with SQL Server through more user-oriented tools like Access and Excel. These types of tools use an abstraction layer, Open Database Connectivity (ODBC), to make working with the database less developer-intensive.

Understanding Open Database Connectivity (ODBC)

If you've been working in the personal computer industry for any length of time, you know that there are a significant number of database applications which different people have installed to address different needs. Gone are the days when you could count on a specific database type at the installation site. This is especially true if you're developing a utility program, such as one that is expected to query a database, regardless of where that database came from, who designed it, etc.

ODBC attempts to rectify this, although, as you'll see, there are some costs involved with this approach. Your best-case solution will depend on a number of factors, including how diverse the database types are in the location or locations where you plan to deploy any given solution.

Concepts and Characteristics

To address the concern of connectivity to, and between, database systems, Microsoft developed the ODBC approach. ODBC is a layer of abstraction between the application and the underlying database system. This layer allows you to issue one SELECT statement and have that statement run against any supported database, including some cases where the databases do not directly support the SQL language.

Figure 21.2 shows the relationship of ODBC to the application. ODBC serves as the access layer to the operating system and database files. ODBC is responsible for taking your request for information and changing it into the language the database engine will understand and use for retrieving the information in the database.

FIG. 21.2

ODBC insulates the application developer from the specifics of the database structure and access methods.

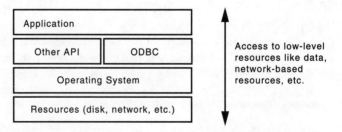

Access to low-level resources like data, network-based resources, etc.

ODBC presents a common interface to your application. This allows you to develop to a common set of calls and methodologies without having to worry about the subtleties of the underlying database. You can see an excellent example of this in Microsoft Access. In Access, you can choose to link or attach a table to a database. When you do, Access will prompt you for the type of database table you want to work with. You have the option of selecting from several formats that Access works with directly, or you can simply select ODBC. When you do, you are presented with the different ODBC configurations you've established. Thus, you are able to select any one of them, without regard to database engine.

Access will be able to attach the table to the database because it won't know about, or care about, the database, only that it can use the database table with standardized SQL statements—the key to ODBC.

Since the main purpose of ODBC is to abstract the conversation with the underlying database engine, the use of ODBC is somewhat transparent once you're connected. This is different when compared with DB-LIB reviewed earlier. DB-LIB required special syntax to buffer statements and work directly with the server. ODBC, on the other hand, requires only that you create the standardized SQL statement and then pass that statement to ODBC.

Understanding ODBC Sessions

When you work with ODBC in your application, you are working with a data source and the database engine it references. As you'll see under the Client Configuration section, when you install ODBC, you should install not only the overall ODBC subsystem but also driver-to-database combinations. These combinations are given a name and then used in your connection request when you want to access the database they refer to. These database and driver combinations are called *Data Source Names*, or *DSNs*. When you open an ODBC connection and don't otherwise specify this information, ODBC will step in and prompt you for it.

In most languages, when you specify the connect string for ODBC, you'll have a couple of options. First, you can specify only that it's an ODBC connection you want to open, in which case ODBC will step in and prompt you for the DSN to use.

```
Set db = OpenDatabase("",,"odbc;")
```

In this case, the information provided by the user will determine the database that is opened. You can also specify the connection to use by indicating the DSN, UserID and Password for the connection, as applicable.

> **CAUTION**
>
> If you allow your user to specify the ODBC connection to use, you may end up working against a database that you have not planned to interact with. In nearly all cases, your application should provide the DSN information that will allow ODBC to connect to the database, ensuring that you know the database schema for the information sources you're accessing.

```
Set db = OpenDatabase("",,"odbc;<DSN Info>")
```

Your second option is to indicate the details for the connection in the connection string itself. In this type of connection, <DSN Info> represents any of the different items you can specify as part of the DSN. Some of the more commonly used items are shown in Table 21.5.

Part
V

Ch
21

Table 21.5   Common DSN Elements

Element	Description
DSN	The DSN name you have configured in the ODBC settings
UID	The userID to use to log in to the database
PWD	The password to use for the login

For example, consider the following sample VBA statement:

```
Set db = OpenDatabase("",,"odbc;DSN=MyDSN;UID=MyUserName;PWD=MyPassword")
```

This will connect to the ODBC data source using the MyDSN configuration. It will also use the user and password indicated in the parameters. Using this command, the user will not be prompted for ODBC DSN information but will be connected automatically.

N O T E   In this example, the db variable represents a VB variable declared as a Database object type. In this example, the db variable will be the reference point for future actions against the database. ■

In this example, we're using some of the Data Access Objects, or DAO, to access the ODBC data source. Using this access method, you can work through the tables, fields and information stored in the database system by using common objects and object browsing methodologies. For a simple example, consider the following procedure:

Listing 21.1   Example of Connecting to ODBC with DAO

```
Sub DAOExample()
    'set up the variables
    Dim db As DATABASE
    Dim i As Integer

    'connect to the database
    Set db = OpenDatabase("", , "odbc;DSN=BILLING;UID=SA;PWD=;")

    'Determine how many tables there are and then print
    'the results.
    i = db.TableDefs.Count
    Debug.Print "There are " & Str$(i) & " table(s) in this database."

    'Close the connection
    db.Close
End Sub
```

The output from this routine will be a statement indicating the number of tables in the database. By using the object-oriented nature of DAO, it's easy to work quickly with the database connection once it's been established.

The final step to working with SQL is to close the connection. The specifics of how you'll close it may vary between host languages, but, in VB or VBA, you can simply use the `.Close` method. This will close the connection to the database and free up the memory structures associated with the connection.

Client Configuration

ODBC drivers are installed when you install SQL Server client utilities. They are also installed or updated when you install several Microsoft products such as Office 95 and Access 95. The drivers are installed on your system, but you still need to create the specific DSNs that you'll be referencing when you open a connection to the database.

The ODBC Administrator is located on the Control Panel (see fig. 21.3).

FIG. 21.3
The ODBC Administrator is used to manage new and existing ODBC DSNs.

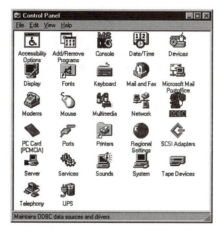

The Administrator will allow you to select from the known ODBC connections so you can make any necessary changes. You can also add new DSNs to your system. Figure 21.4 shows the initial ODBC DSN listing, and the different options you can access to manage the DSNs.

FIG. 21.4
The DSN names listed are the names you specify in the ODBC connection string.

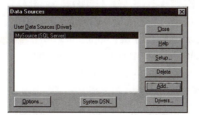

Part
V

Ch

21

In the next section, you'll see how you can work with new and existing DSNs as well as set up your system so you can take advantage of ODBC in your applications.

Working with ODBC DSNs

From the ODBC Data Sources dialog box, you have two options that relate to managing ODBC connections. The Setup and New options will let you specify the different characteristics of the DSN's you establish. Figure 21.5 shows a sample dialog of options for setting up a SQL Server connection. Note that the dialog box is the same for both setting up a new connection and making changes to an existing connection.

FIG. 21.5

When you set up ODBC connections, you should indicate as much information as possible to make connecting easier for the user of your applications.

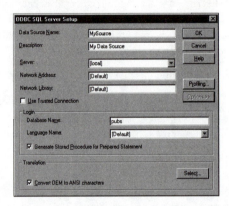

The figure shows the Options portion of the dialog extended, allowing access to the default database and other less-often used options. The key options that you should always set up are:

- Data Source Name
- Description
- Server

You should always try to establish the Database Name, as well. Doing so will help ensure that, when the connection is made, it will be to the correct database and will not rely on the default database assigned to the user that is logging in.

Advantages and Disadvantages of Using ODBC

Since ODBC provides the abstract access to just about any popular database format available, it brings a fair amount of leverage to your development effort. A key element in the ODBC framework is the capability for your DSN name to refer to any database. This allows you to develop against an Access database and implement your system in production against a SQL Server just by changing the drivers used by the DSN you've defined for the application.

The abstraction of the calls to the database engine is not without cost. The biggest downside to ODBC is that it must be able to support the capability to translate the calls. This means that additional processing overhead can slow the data access a bit. With ODBC, you can gain a significant speed advantage with a true client/server implementation. By taking the processing away from the client and into the server within SQL Server, you can eliminate much of the scrolling of information that is one of the primary slowing points for ODBC.

Consider using stored procedures as the basis for your ODBC calls when database engine processing is required. This will save processing time on both ends of the spectrum.

Understanding the SQL OLE Interface

As you may already be aware, the vast majority of development in emerging technologies is going on in object-oriented development. Microsoft, and other software tool builders, has a major push to bring out into the public object methods and classes that can be reused by third-party developers. This can be seen in the Office 95 suite of applications in their consistent use of Objects and Classes to work with their different components. Everything from sheets in Excel to TableDefs in Access is now accessible with objects and collection.

This accessibility is no different with SQL Server. In one of the newest developments for developers of SQL-based applications, the SQL OLE interface allows you to work with SQL Server by using objects, methods, and collections that relate to your database.

Concepts and Characteristics

By including Type Library (TLB) references in your application environment, you can begin using the OLE automation objects to work with SQL Server. The TLB that you'll need for Visual Basic applications is SQLOLE32.TLB. This library will expose the methods you'll be using.

In short, you'll use the .Connect method for attaching to SQL Server to begin working with the database. You'll then be able to use the different objects and collections to perform the administrative tasks associated with SQL Server. It may be easiest to review the SQL Enterprise Manager for examples of how these containers and objects relate to one another. Figure 21.6 shows the top-level hierarchy for the SQL OLE objects.

FIG. 21.6
The SQL OLE objects allow full access to the administrative objects in SQL Server. You can write the equivalent of an Enterprise Manager using these objects.

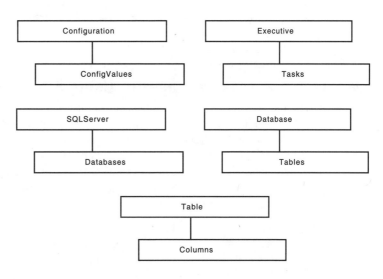

You work with the SQL OLE objects by first setting up the object variables that refer to the SQL OLE objects. The first step is to set up the reference to the TLB for SQL OLE.

Once you've established the references, you can create the routines you need to work with the objects. Listing 21.2 shows setting up a reference to the Database object, followed by printing the tables in the collection to the debug window.

Listing 21.2   Using SQL OLE in Visual Basic Code

```
Sub SQL OLEDemo()
    'declare the variables
    Dim objSQLServer As New SQL OLE.SQLServer
    Dim objDatabase As New SQL OLE.DATABASE
    Dim objTable As New SQL OLE.TABLE

    'connect to the server
    objSQLServer.Connect "pluto", "sa", ""

    'get the PUBS database
    Set objDatabase = objSQLServer("pubs")

    'iterate through the tables
    For Each objTable In objDatabase
        Debug.Print objTable
    Next

    'disconnect from the server
    Set objSQLServer = Nothing

End Sub
```

As you can see, by using the objects and collections in the SQL OLE suite, you can easily navigate the SQL Server you are administering. This gives you the added benefit of providing a concise set of capabilities to your users, possibly limiting access to certain features, while granting ready access to others.

Advantages and Disadvantages of Using SQL OLE

SQL OLE requires a good working knowledge of the architecture of SQL Server. If you haven't spent very much time in the Enterprise Manager, it may be somewhat difficult to picture the object model and work within it. This can be a hindrance for people developing their first application to manage SQL Server. It's probably not a good idea to use SQL OLE and building administrative applications as your first work with SQL Server. SQL OLE will be more meaningful and more useful to you after you've had a chance to become used to the object-oriented nature of managing SQL Server using the native tools available.

On the plus side, the SQL OLE objects provide you with easy, comprehensive, and ready access to the objects that make up the SQL Server's core functionality. By knowing these objects inside and out, you'll be able to provide more comprehensive administration of the system, simply because you'll know and understand the relationships between objects. Also, as mentioned previously, if you have people that are responsible for administering certain aspects of the system, but you need to limit their overall access to high-level tasks, a custom administrative application can be just the ticket. Also, there is no easier way to work with the SQL objects than using the SQL OLE suite of capabilities.

From Here...

You've had a whirlwind tour of the different techniques and technologies that are available to you for working with, and administering, your SQL Server system and its databases. By combining these technologies with the comprehensive coverage throughout this book on the SQL language and the capabilities of SQL Server, you'll be able to develop comprehensive applications for working with SQL Server.

From here, you may want to consider reviewing the following related materials:

- Chapter 6, "Retrieving Data with Transact-SQL" reviews the syntax for the SQL language and how you use it to work with the tables in SQL Server.

- Chapter 4, "Creating Devices, Databases, and Transaction Logs," and Chapter 5, "Creating Database Tables and Using Datatypes," detail the different objects in SQL Server and how you can create and manage them. The relationships between these objects will be helpful should you need to develop your own administrative applications using SQL OLE.

Part
V

Ch
21

Accessing SQL Server Databases Through Front-End Products

How to use some of the most popular client/server tools with SQL Server

In this chapter you will see SQLWindows, Delphi 2, and Visual Basic 4 in action.

How to configure ODBC for use with SQL Server

In the section entitled "Configuring ODBC for SQL Server 6.5" you'll learn how to install the connectivity required for accessing SQL Server through front-end tools.

Tips and tricks for client/server development

SQL Server's client interface from three popular languages is explored with sample applications that show how to develop smart applications.

With SQL Server 6, Microsoft introduced a new client-side interface through *open database connectivity* (ODBC). Rather than using the old DB-Library approach that was created by Sybase, Microsoft decided to create a new access path through ODBC.

As custodian of the ODBC specification, it was easy for Microsoft to tailor the ODBC interface, making it no longer truly "generic" and, in fact, optimizing it for SQL Server access. With this new interface, there is no longer the stigma of slow performance associated with ODBC access. Microsoft still supports the DB-Library interface for backward compatibility, but it seems that their primary focus is on making ODBC *the standard* for database access. ■

Configuring ODBC for SQL Server 6.5

ODBC is a way of connecting various different data services to different front-end applications in a consistent manner. ODBC has undergone several revisions since its inception in 1991.

ODBC is configured through a Control Panel applet: ODBC or ODBC32. In this chapter we will show you how to configure ODBC under Windows NT Workstation. In Windows 95, the only difference is the shading and etching of the dialog boxes; functionally, the methods detailed later in the chapter are identical.

To configure ODBC for use with Microsoft SQL Server 6.5, follow these steps:

1. Install the ODBC drivers that ship on the SQL Server 6.5 CD-ROM.

2. Choose Settings, Control Panel from the start menu. (See fig. 22.1.)

FIG. 22.1
Windows NT Workstation's Control Panel is really just a window with several icons in it. Each icon is an applet—a small application that manages a particular part of the operating system's behavior.

3. Double-click the ODBC icon to display the ODBC configuration dialog box (see fig. 22.2).

FIG. 22.2
ODBC's Data Sources dialog box lists available ODBC data sources that have had drivers loaded.

4. The Add Data Source dialog box (see fig. 22.3) is where you add new sources of data to be accessed via ODBC. In SQL Server's case, you add a new data source for each SQL Server that you have on the network. In this case, configure a default installation to access the pubs database.

Click the Add button in the Data Sources dialog box.

FIG. 22.3

Notice that SQL Server is listed at the bottom of the Installed ODBC Drivers list box in the Add Data Source dialog box.

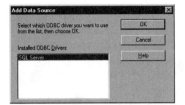

5. Select SQL Server from the list and click OK. The ODBC SQL Server Setup dialog box appears (see fig. 22.4).

FIG. 22.4

We have clicked the Options button, which displays the bottom half of the ODBC SQL Server Setup dialog box.

6. Enter a name for the data source (for example, `LocalServer`). The name can be anything meaningful to you.

7. Enter a description of the ODBC data type (for example, `MS SQL Server 6.5`) so that you can determine what source of data this ODBC service is providing without having to rely on its name.

8. Enter the name of the actual SQL Server where the data resides. If SQL Server is running locally on Windows NT, it is possible to enter (`local`) and the ODBC driver will find the server using the Named Pipes protocol.

9. Enter a network address and/or network library if your network/database administrator indicates that one is necessary. Generally, these can be left on "(Default)" and the ODBC driver will find the server when first connecting.

10. Enter a database name that the ODBC service should connect to (for example, `pubs`). Note: Some ODBC client programs lack the capability to change databases via ODBC commands, so it may be necessary to specify a data source for each database you want to connect to on the same server.

11. Unless there is a good reason to override the defaults of language and code page translation, they should be left as defaults. The completed SQL Server Setup dialog box is shown in Figure 22.5.

FIG. 22.5
The ODBC SQL Server Setup
dialog box is complete and
ready to add a new data
source for ODBC.

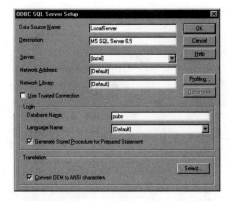

12. Click OK to add the data source. After clicking OK, the new server will be added to the list of available data sources (see fig. 22.6).

FIG. 22.6
The new entry, LocalServer, is
in the User Data Sources
(Driver) selections.

Using Gupta's SQLWindows

Gupta's SQLWindows is a classic front-end tool that has been around since the late 1980s. Since that time, it has acquired various drivers written natively to provide communications to different DBMSs. Most recently, ODBC was added with SQLWindows 5.0. However, because Microsoft revised ODBC with the release of SQL Server 6, Gupta was required to address the new functionality provided in the ODBC driver and put out a special release. Consequently, in order to connect to SQL Server 6.5 from SQLWindows, version 5.0.2 must be used.

All the source code that follows for the SQLWindows application can be found in SWINDEMO.APP on the enclosed CD-ROM.

Establishing a Connection

Connecting or preparing SQLWindows for use with SQL Server 6 involves a somewhat arcane method of using Gupta's query and report writing tool, Quest, to set up a private INI file with connection information about the ODBC data source. The INI file in question is the GUPTA.INI file and can be found in the directory that is indicated in the WIN.INI file by the keyword SqlWinDir.

Preparing SQLWindows for SQL Server 6   To use Quest to prepare the ODBC interface, follow these steps:

1. Install SQLWindows from the CD-ROM.
2. From the program group that SQLWindows installed in (usually Gupta), double-click the Quest icon (see fig. 22.7).

FIG. 22.7

Quest has just been started.

3. From the Utilities menu, select Database and then click Add. This displays the Add Database dialog box shown in Figure 22.8.

FIG. 22.8

The Add Database dialog box in Quest shows that the ODBC data source has a small ODBC icon to its immediate left.

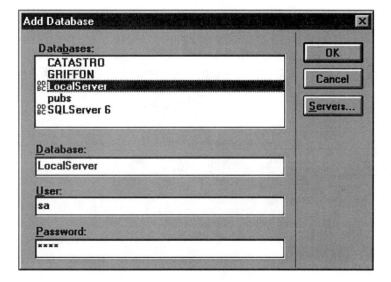

4. Select the LocalServer database, or the name that was entered previously for an ODBC data source.
5. Enter the user that is going to be used to connect to the database (for example, SA). Note that user names and passwords *are* case-sensitive.
6. Enter the password that is required for the user entered in Step 5.

CAUTION

SQLWindows and Gupta's other products, such as Quest, require that you enter a password for the database that you are connecting to. If you do not enter a password, Gupta will pass in the default password of SYSADM. You *must* have a password configured for the user that you want to access the database via ODBC with.

Remember that the default installation of SQL Server is to install SA with no password. This must be changed!

7. Click OK to test the connection and to confirm that the user and password were entered correctly. If it's successful, the LocalServer database will be added to the list in the main Quest window (see fig. 22.9).

FIG. 22.9
The LocalServer database is added to the list of available databases in Quest. Quest has connected to it, which is indicated by the lack of an asterisk next to the database name.

Connecting to SQL Server 6.5   Connecting to SQL Server using SQLWindows is relatively straightforward. SQLWindows has three reserved words that are used to specify the user ID, password, and database that are going to be connected to. Listing 22.1 shows the setting of the variables with hard-coded values. In your application you would probably have some kind of dialog box that you use to achieve the same result.

On the CD

Listing 22.1   SWINDEMO.APP—Connecting to SQL Server Using SQLWindows' *SqlConnect( )* **Function**

```
Pushbutton: pbConnect
...
      Message Actions
          On SAM_Click
                Set SqlUser = 'sa'
                Set SqlPassword = 'dell'
                Set SqlDatabase = 'LocalServer'
                If NOT SqlConnect( hSql )
                    Call SalMessageBox( 'Failed to connect to SQLServer!',
                                        'Demo - Warning', MB_IconAsterisk )
```

hSql is a local variable of type Sql Handle that is defined on the form.

Preparing and Executing SQL Statements

SQLWindows provides a simple interface for executing statements. The same interface is used to prepare and execute queries on all database server types. Listing 22.2 shows the execution of a simple SELECT to count the number of objects and place the results in the data field on the screen dfCount.

On the CD

Listing 22.2   SWINDEMO.APP—Executing SQL Statement on SQL Server Using SQLWindows' *SqlPrepareAndExecute( )* **Function**

```
On SAM_Click
      Set sSQL = '
```

```
Select     count(*)
Into       :dfCount
From       sysobjects'
If NOT SqlPrepareAndExecute( hSql, sSQL )
    Call SalMessageBox( 'Failed to execute a select from the SQLServer!',
                        'Demo - Warning', MB_IconAsterisk )
If NOT SqlFetchNext( hSql, nReturn )
    Call SalMessageBox( 'Failed to fetch on the select from the
                         SQLServer!', 'Demo - Warning', MB_IconAsterisk )
```

Notice the use of the SQL Handle hSql in all activity that involves the database. The SQL Handle is the logical entity through which all database interaction is performed.

Using Stored Procedures and Command Batches

In SQLWindows there are some extension functions for the use of executing stored procedures on the server. These functions are prefixed with the letters Odr. To add this functionality to an application, include the Gupta supplied include file: ODBSAL.APL, which should be located in the root Gupta directory.

A simple stored procedure is used to test stored procedure execution. Listing 22.3 shows the code for the stored procedure.

On the CD

Listing 22.3   SWINDEMO.APP—Simple Stored Procedure Used to Test Stored Procedure Execution in SQLWindows

```
create proc ConnectivityTest
as
Select     Count(*)
From       Sysobjects
Where      Type = 'U'
```

Listing 22.4 shows results are fetched and returned to the same dfCount data field.

On the CD

Listing 22.4   SWINDEMO.APP—Executing Stored Procedure on SQL Server Using SQLWindows' *OdrExecuteProc( )* Function

```
On SAM_Click
    Set sSQL = 'ConnectivityTest'
    If NOT OdrExecuteProc( hSql, sSQL, ':dfCount' )
        Call SalMessageBox( 'Failed to execute a select from the SQLServer!',
                            'Demo - Warning', MB_IconAsterisk )
    If NOT SqlFetchNext( hSql, nReturn )
        Call SalMessageBox( 'Failed to fetch on the select from the
                             SQLServer!', 'Demo - Warning', MB_IconAsterisk )
```

Sneak Preview of Centura

Gupta Corporation is changing its name to Centura Software Corporation in March of 1996. Along with the name change comes a whole new development tool: Centura. We had the opportunity to review a late beta release of Centura just prior to the printing of this book, and we have to say we are impressed.

As a new product, Centura was remarkably stable and feature-rich. It is fully code-compatible with SQLWindows and yet adds full 32-bit engineering to its arsenal. The new user interface embraces Windows 95's Explorer metaphor (see fig. 22.10).

FIG. 22.10
The Explorer view of Centura allows you to view the source code in style! However, for old-timers, the Outline is always available—check out the Outline tab on the lower-left corner of the right pane.

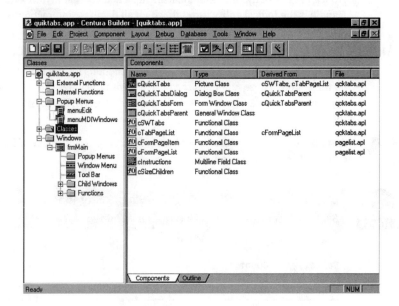

In addition to beefing up its development tool, Centura sports new class wizards that support three-tier programming through three of the most popular architectures: Novell's QuickTuxedo, Open Environment Corporation's DCE-based QuickRPC, and QuickCICS (see fig. 22.11).

FIG. 22.11
The Three-Tier Wizard supports the most popular architectures available. Centura even comes in a special edition for Tuxedo that includes all of the Tuxedo development environment.

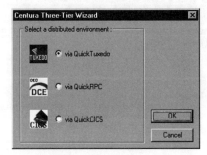

Finally, Centura adds a new tool for the developer—the Database Explorer. The Database Explorer is similar to Delphi 2's and allows easy browsing of all the key attributes. It even includes editable tables that allow you to directly manipulate the data in the database. Fig. 22.12 shows the Database Explorer editing the Authors table.

FIG. 22.12

The Database Explorer allows you to browse the data in the databases of all the different types to which Centura supports native connections: SQLBase, Oracle, Microsoft SQL Server, DB2, Sybase, Informix, and ODBC.

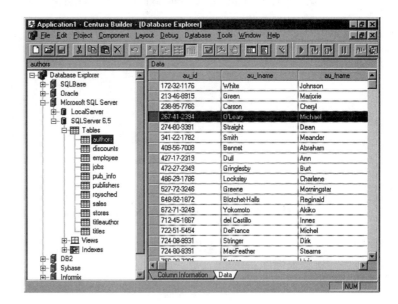

More Information and Examples

Gupta has provided two instructive sample applications—ODBSAL1.APP and ODBSAL2.APP—that can be found in the \SAMPLES directory below the Gupta directory. These examples indicate in more detail how to connect to the database and perform various operations on them.

Using Borland's Delphi 2

Borland's Delphi 2 is at the cutting edge of client/server application development. It is a new object-oriented programming language based on Pascal. Delphi 2 is the new version of Delphi that was released in 1996 to much fanfare. Delphi 2 is a fully 32-bit development environment and has received many awards.

All the source code that follows for the Delphi 2 application can be found in DPHI20.PRJ and DPHIDEMO.* on the CD-ROM.

Establishing a Connection

Delphi 2 has native drivers for SQL Server 6.5 that are shells over Microsoft's ODBC. The simplest way to prepare Delphi 2 for use with a database is to use the Database Explorer applet that ships with Delphi 2.

To use the Database Explorer to prepare the ODBC interface, perform the following steps:

1. Install Delphi 2 from the CD-ROM.

2. From the program group that Delphi 2 is installed in (usually Borland Delphi 2), select the Borland Delphi folder and double-click the Database Explorer icon (see fig. 22.13).

FIG. 22.13

Delphi 2's SQL Explorer has just been started.

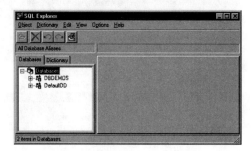

3. From the Object menu, choose New. Select MSSQL (for Microsoft SQL Server) from the New Database Alias dialog box and click OK (see fig. 22.14).

FIG. 22.14

The New Database Alias dialog box in SQL Explorer has MSSQL selected.

4. Click the editable portion of the DATABASE NAME property in the right pane and enter the name for the database to be referenced: **pubs**.

5. Enter the name of the server in the SERVER NAME property in the right pane.

6. Enter the name of the user that will by default connect to this database in the USER NAME property in the right pane: **sa**.

7. Enter any additional configurations that you want to select for this database. The completed dialog box is shown in Figure 22.15.

8. From the Object menu, select Apply to activate this database (you will notice that the arrow goes away). Figure 22.16 shows the new database is available and ready for use.

N O T E   If you want to change the alias name for this database from the default of MSSQLX (where X corresponds to the number of default databases installed so far), highlight the database in the left pane of the Explorer. From the Object menu, select Rename. Enter the new name for the database alias and press Enter. ■

9. To test that everything is configured correctly, click the plus sign to the left of the database alias name to expand the Explorer view. This will display a database logon dialog box, as shown in figure 22.17.

FIG. 22.15

A completed database definition is ready to be applied using the SQL Explorer from Delphi 2. Note that there is a highlighted arrow pointing to the database being worked on, indicating that it has not been activated yet.

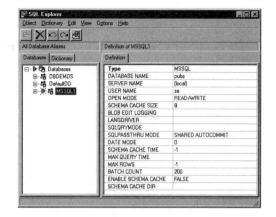

FIG. 22.16

The SQL Explorer has the new database highlighted and the name of it has been changed to LocalServer.

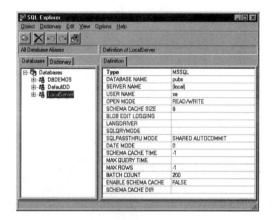

FIG. 22.17

This is the Database Login dialog box from the SQL Explorer.

10. Enter the **sa** password and the Explorer tree will expand, indicating the various components of the SQL Server that are available for manipulation via SQL Explorer.

Understanding the Delphi 2 Database Model

In its most common use, Delphi 2 has a layered approach to interfacing with databases. This layering provides several levels of abstraction from the database itself, allowing a very generic application programming interface through common objects.

Delphi 2 has a number of classes that can be used to actually manipulate the data. These classes are responsible for executing the appropriate queries to perform any DML required. The classes that can be used vary from TTable, which is used for representing a table, to TQuery, which enables a custom query to be presented to the visual objects. These physical data interface classes are typically non-visual.

These physical data sources are then mapped to a class that is responsible for interfacing with user interface objects/controls, such as data fields and lists. This interface is performed through a non-visual class, TDataSource, which transfers data from the physical data class to the visual objects that you place on an edit form.

Manipulating the data in TQuery or TTable to fetch records, update them, and so on, can be performed by invoking the methods that they have or by adding a Navigation control to the edit form. TDBNavigator is a class that interacts with TDataSource and provides the standard Next, Previous, Insert, and Update buttons to manipulate the data on the form. By placing one of these controls on an edit form and then hooking—either at design time by setting its property or at runtime by adjusting its property to the required data source on the form—you will have all the necessary components to build an edit window to a data structure (either a query or database table).

Finally, in Delphi 2 it is necessary to add controls to view/edit the actual data. Delphi 2 provides all the standard edit controls (including list boxes and combo boxes) that have properties that enable them to be hooked to a particular TDataSource. Placing the control on the form and setting its DataSource and DataField properties is all that is required.

About the Sample Application DPHIDEMO

The sample application provided here demonstrates a simple edit form to the Authors table in the pubs database. This application took less than 10 minutes to write and shows how easy it is to use Delphi 2.

The application demonstrates the use of basic TTable.Table_Authors to read from the database table directly. On top of this class is TDataSource.MyDataSource that performs the data source manipulation. There are data fields on the form that enable editing of the basic name and address information in the table; they are all of class TDBEdit.

Finally, to control the interaction with the database, TDBNavigator.MyNavigator is hooked to TDataSource.MyDataSource. To "beef up" the application and to learn a tiny part of Delphi 2, some code executes whenever the form is resized so that the Navigator control stays "docked" to the bottom of the window. The code in Listing 22.5 is so simple that it's amazing to anyone who has ever had to write this in a language such as C.

On the CD

Listing 22.5   DPHI20.PRJ—Dynamic Form Resizing with Objects That Paint Inside the Form's Boundaries

```
procedure TForm1.FormResize(Sender: TObject);
begin
```

```
MyNavigator.Top := Form1.ClientHeight - MyNavigator.Height;
MyNavigator.Width := Form1.ClientWidth;
end;

end.
```

Perhaps the nicest feature of Delphi 2 is that the data access can be tested while still at design time. The TTable class has a property of Active, which, if enabled, will connect to the database and present data to the controls if they are hooked via a TDataSource. This enables you to at least see something of what the application is going to look like at runtime.

Preparing and Executing SQL Statements

Delphi 2 represents ad hoc queries through the class TQuery. TQuery is a non-visual class that has properties that enable it to be attached to a database. The SQL property is provided to enable the setting of the required SQL statement. TQuery then interacts with a TDataSource just like TTable.

In the sample application, the Active property is set to True when the Titles button is clicked. This causes the SQL to be executed in TQuery.MyQuery and the Grid control to be populated with the results of the SELECT statement. The Grid control, TDBGrid.MyDBGrid, is hooked to the data source for presentation of the query results.

Clicking the Titles button executes the default SQL that was set in TQuery.MyQuery at design time. The Publishers... button dynamically changes the SQL and executes it. Listing 22.6 shows what is required to do this SQL changing at runtime in Delphi 2.

On the CD

Listing 22.6 DPHI20.PRJ—Setting SQL Statement in a Delphi 2 Control and Then Activating (Executing) It

```
procedure TForm1.Button2Click(Sender: TObject);
begin
    MyQuery.Active := False;
    MyQuery.SQL.Clear;
    MyQuery.SQL.Add( 'Select * from publishers');
    MyQuery.Active := True;
end;
```

Using Stored Procedures and Command Batches

Delphi 2's implementation, Stored Procedures and Command Batches, is identical to that of the general query execution principle. A StoredProcName property is provided to enable you to hook the object with a stored procedure in the server. The TStoredProc is then attached/hooked to a TDataSource and accessed as normal through other data controls.

More Information and Examples

Because the version of Delphi 2 that I was working with was an early beta, there was a limited amount of documentation and sample code supplied. However, the documentation was excellent when it was there. A neat feature of Delphi 2 is that class specific help is invoked whenever F1 is pushed during design time and when an object is highlighted. This will make it easy for you to find out about the properties and methods of the Delphi 2 classes provided by Borland.

Also, check out the Delphi forum on CompuServe where you will get a lot of help from other Delphi users.

Using Microsoft Visual Basic 4

Visual Basic 4 is Microsoft's latest incarnation of the BASIC standard. As a general tool, it has great features and has a huge install base. Microsoft has always tried to latch on to client/server connectivity, and still has some work to do to support it as cleanly as either SQLWindows or Delphi 2.

This was the first time we had ever tried to use Visual Basic for database connectivity. We were consistently frustrated by a non-intuitive environment that clearly lacked the integration of a mature database development environment.

On the CD

All the source code that follows for the Visual Basic 4 application can be found in VB4DEMO.FRM and VB4.VBP on the CD-ROM.

Understanding the Visual Basic 4 Database Model

Visual Basic and Delphi 2 have a similar approach to data access. Data access is controlled by a Data object that resides on a form. Unlike Delphi 2, VB4 does not use truly non-visual object classes or container classes. Instead, it is possible to alter the `Visible` property of the Data object to hide it if you want.

VB4's Data control is more of a combination of the `TDataSource` and `TDBNavigator` classes that are found in Delphi 2, and the visual nature of the arrow buttons explains the need to have it visible most of the time.

Once a Data control is correctly configured and bound to a particular table, it is possible to hook data fields to it as a declared data source on the form.

Connecting to SQL Server

We had expected to find some kind of configuration utility in Visual Basic 4 for database connectivity; however, VB4 is so closely integrated to ODBC that ODBC is the only interface provided.

To set up a Data control we tried to specify ODBC as the `Connect` property of the Data control that we were adding to the form; however, VB4 refused to correctly work with this. In the end, we gave up and used the Data Form Designer Wizard to create a data form and then copied the Connect string from there. This was truly an inelegant interface, which is very surprising coming from Microsoft.

For future reference, the following is a Connect string for ODBC connectivity to SQL Server:

```
ODBC;DSN=LocalServer;UID=sa;PWD=dell;
APP=Data Form Designer;WSID=DELL_NT_SERVER;DATABASE=pubs
```

The information in this string can be set at runtime by altering the Connect property of the Data control.

Preparing and Executing SQL Statements

VB4's Data control can be used to either represent tables or process queries directly. The RecordSource property can either be set to a table name or to a query. The following code snippet demonstrates a pushbutton changing the query used to populate the Data control. In turn, the Data control acts as a DataSource for a DBGrid control that is also on the form. Performing the Refresh method of the Data control causes the query to execute and in turn causes the grid to be populated:

```
Private Sub Command3_Click()
    MyDataSource2.RecordSource = "select * from titles"
    MyDataSource2.Refresh
End Sub
```

About the Sample Application VB4DEMO

The sample application that is included on the CD-ROM demonstrates a basic form that enables browsing and editing of the Authors table in the pubs database. The application has an Update button that interfaces with Data.MyDataSource and invokes its UpdateRecord method, as follows:

```
Private Sub Command1_Click()
    MyDataSource.UpdateRecord
End Sub
```

In a similar fashion, the Delete button removes a record from the table. However, for some obscure reason, there is no corresponding method in the Data control for DeleteRecord. Instead, you must resolve the reference manually by referring to the Data control's recordset, which is presumably the cache of data that the Data control is manipulating:

```
Private Sub Command2_Click()
    MyDataSource.Recordset.Delete
End Sub
```

Overall, the style of programming in Visual Basic is quite similar to Delphi 2. Here is the same logic to make the Data control appear to be docked to the base of the form window—this time as Visual Basic code:

```
Private Sub Form_Resize()
    MyDataSource.Top = Form1.ScaleHeight - MyDataSource.Height
    MyDataSource.Width = Form1.ScaleWidth
End Sub
```

From Here...

In this chapter, you learned about the basics of ODBC and how to configure it on a workstation. In addition, you were introduced to three different approaches to client/server application programming and connectivity: Gupta's SQLWindows 5.0.2, Borland's Delphi 2, and Microsoft's Visual Basic 4. In addition, there are many fine tools that were not mentioned here.

Each of the products covered in this chapter is strong in certain areas and weak in others. Choosing one of these development tools should be done after carefully evaluating a project's needs.

Appendixes

Installation and Setup of the Client and Server Software

The installation of SQL Server is relatively simple and similar to the installation of other Microsoft products. In this appendix, you'll learn about the different steps and considerations to keep in mind as you set up your server system and the clients that will access it. You'll also learn the following:

- Installing the SQL Server software at the server
- Starting and stopping the server
- Installing SQL Server client utilities
- Obtaining help for SQL Server commands ■

Understanding Server Hardware and Software Requirements

The computer system for your SQL Server installation should be on the list of supported Windows NT systems. If your system is an Intel x86-based processor, it should be 33mhz or faster, according to Microsoft documentation. In practice, it's not recommended that you implement SQL Server in a production environment on anything less than a Pentium 75mhz with 32M of RAM.

Also according to the documentation, you must have a minimum of 16M of RAM—although additional memory is recommended—for x86-based systems. A minimum of 16M is suggested for a Windows NT Server system, but 32M is more appropriate. Most RISC-based systems are usually configured with a minimum of 64M and often are configured with 128M of memory.

N O T E   These stated minimums are just that: minimums. As you bring up systems, there are a number of factors that will impact these numbers. Be sure to pay special attention to any replication tasks you may wish to run and to the number of client systems that you'll be allowing to access the server during peak periods.

One of the biggest performance boosts you can offer in the SQL Server world is the addition of memory. This simple enhancement can improve performance by twofold or more in many cases.

These recommendations aren't unreasonable for a server system. Memory has become very inexpensive in recent years. In 1977, a quarter of a megabyte of memory for at least one manufacturer's system was priced at $17,000. In recent years, you can buy 1M of memory for less than $50.

Although you might be using an Intel x86-based processor in your server system, its processing power and speed far exceeds the large minicomputer systems of 10 to 15 years ago. Physically, your server might be only as large as a client system, but don't be deceived by that. ■

You need to have at least 70M of disk space to complete the installation, and if you install the books online feature of SQL Server, you'll need to add 15M to this requirement. However, if you have only 70M, you don't have any space to create additional logical devices on which to create your databases. You should count on a minimal SQL Server installation requiring approximately 150M to start. Note that although you can create your database tables and other objects within the master database, you shouldn't. Try to keep your core objects—those installed when you first bring up SQL Server—on a common logical device. As you'll see later, when you create additional devices, databases and tables, you can designate different storage devices for those (if your primary location does not have the disk space available). You also need a floppy-disk drive for 3 1/2-inch, high-density disks or a CD-ROM drive to read the installation media.

▶ **See** Chapter 4, "Creating Devices, Databases, and Transaction Logs," for more information on creating new devices. **p.77**

Load the SQL Server software from your installation media onto a Microsoft Windows NT workstation or Windows NT Server system. You don't need any additional network software because the Windows NT system contains built-in network software. You need a network interface card (NIC) that's supported by Windows NT. If you'll access SQL Server directly only from the server system, without using a network for access, you don't need a NIC.

You can install SQL Server on a partition that uses either the FAT or NTFS file systems. You'll probably want to take advantage of the recovery and security features of an NTFS disk partition rather than the older and simpler FAT disk system, although your installation might have other considerations for other installed software that dictate this installation parameter.

▶ **See** Que's *Special Edition Using Microsoft Windows NT Server* by Roger Jennings for more information on the installation of NT Server.

Running Setup

Installing Microsoft SQL Server for Windows NT is remarkably simple. The installation is similar to the installation of nearly all Microsoft Windows products, and it'll appear familiar to you if you've installed a Windows application. You must run the setup program using an NT account that has Administrative privileges, such as the NT Administrator account.

To perform the installation, follow these steps:

1. Choose Run from the Start menu.
2. Type the drive letter of your floppy or CD drive, followed by **setup** in the run combo list box.

   The setup program displays one or more message boxes after checking whether you're working from an Administrative account and whether SQL Server already is installed. Figure A.1 shows the Welcome dialog box that appears when the SQL Server setup program is invoked.

FIG. A.1

You can change a characteristic such as the security mode only by running SQL Setup.

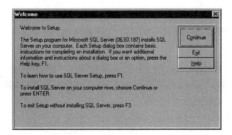

3. Click Continue.
4. Enter a Name, Company, and Product ID in the Enter Name and Organization dialog box. Then click Continue.
5. A second dialog box appears, asking you to confirm the name and company. If you want to change the name, click Change. Otherwise, click Continue.
6. The Microsoft SQL Server 6.5 – Options dialog box appears. The Install SQL Server and Utilities option is automatically selected.

When you first install SQL Server, only the Install SQL Server and Utilities, Upgrade SQL Server, and Install Utilities Only options are available. Install SQL Server and Utilities installs all the SQL Server software, including the 32-bit version of the client utilities on the server. Click Continue.

7. In the Choose Licensing Mode dialog box, you must enter the way in which you've bought licenses for the use of SQL Server, as well as the number of clients that may connect to the server. Figure A.2 shows the entry of a server-based license that will permit a maximum of 20 connections. After you click Continue, an additional dialog box appears that requires you to confirm that you've bought the number of client licenses that you've entered.

FIG. A.2

Client licensing permits you to buy the exact number of client connections that you need.

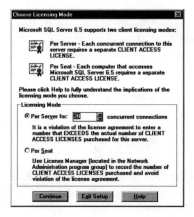

8. In the SQL Server Installation Path dialog box that appears, confirm or change the drive and directory path for SQL Server files and click Continue. Drive C is the default.

9. The MASTER Device Creation dialog box that appears allows you to confirm or change the entries for the MASTER device drive, directory, and the size of the master device.

   The default size of 25M for the MASTER Device Size may be inadequate. If you anticipate creating many devices, databases, or other objects, you can initially allocate a master device of perhaps 40M to 60M.

   The master device contains the master database and transaction log, which holds several system tables. You should avoid creating any objects in the master database, unless you want the objects to be available throughout the server system to all databases. Rows are added to the system tables by SQL Server to reference objects that you create. Click Continue.

10. The SQL Server Books Online dialog box appears, enabling you to define whether you want to install the online documentation to run from the hard disk or the CD (see fig. A.3). You should install the documentation on a hard drive of the server, unless you're short on disk space.

11. The Installation Options dialog box appears, enabling you to define the Character Set, Sort Order, and Additional Network Support (see fig. A.4). Click Sets.

FIG. A.3
You can share the online documentation from the server, saving disk space on the client systems. You can also install copies on client systems.

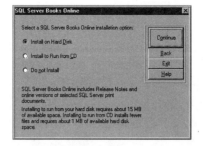

FIG. A.4
Select Auto Start SQL Server at Boot Time to automatically start SQL Server, and Auto Start SQL Executive at Boot Time to automatically start SQL Server when the Windows NT server system is booted.

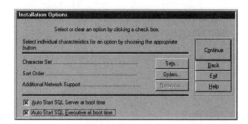

12. In the Select Character Set dialog box, select a language. If you're working only in English, you can choose 437 US English in the Select Character Set list box. If you're working in another language or storing information in multiple languages, you should select 850 Multilingual or ISO Character Set (Default). Click OK.

13. You're returned to the Installation Options dialog box. Click Orders.

14. In the Sort Order list box, confirm the default sort order or change it. If, for example, you select Binary Order, Order By clauses in Select statements are sorted by the direct binary representation of the column values. You can also select Dictionary Order, Case-Insensitive (the default) to treat corresponding upper- and lowercase letters as identical values.

> **CAUTION**
> If you later must change your character set or sort order, you'll have to rebuild the master database.

15. Click OK. You're again returned to the Installation Options dialog box. Click Networks.

16. You can install additional Net-Libraries to Named Pipes in the Select Network Protocols dialog box. For example, you can enter one or more additional Net-Libraries, such as the IPX/SPX or TCP/IP communication mechanisms. If you don't select additional Net-Libraries during installation, you can install them later.

N O T E If you have the desktop version of Microsoft SQL Server, you can't select alternate Net-Libraries; only Named Pipes may be installed. ■

17. Click <u>O</u>K to return to the Installation Options dialog box.

18. Click C<u>o</u>ntinue. Enter a Windows NT account and password to be used by SQL Executive Service in the SQL Executive Log On Account dialog box (see fig. A.5).

FIG. A.5
You should enter a password for the SQL Executive Service account that contains at least eight characters.

 TIP It's a good idea to use a separate NT account for this service rather than share the NT Administrator account. If you later change the NT Administrator account without realizing it's being used by SQL Executive Service, SQL Server might not work correctly.

19. Click C<u>o</u>ntinue. A File Copy in Progress dialog box appears, showing the progress of server files as they're copied from the distribution. As the installation proceeds, additional feedback is displayed on your monitor telling you that SQL Server is installing SQL Server.

If you successfully install SQL Server from a CD, you won't see any more dialog boxes. If you install SQL Server from floppy disks, you'll be prompted to change disks when the installation is completed successfully. Click <u>R</u>eboot if you want to begin using SQL Server.

N O T E Remember to manually start the SQL Server services after you reboot if you haven't defined automatic SQL Server startup. ■

Starting the Server

You have several options available for starting SQL Server on the system. You can configure the SQL Server services system to start automatically each time the Windows NT server system is booted. You also can use the SQL Service Manager to start the SQL Server services. Several Windows application tools can optionally start SQL Server when the applications try to connect to the server. Finally, the server can be started using a command line.

Using Automatic Service Startup

You can enable the automatic startup of SQL Server each time the Windows NT system is started. To start up SQL Server each time the server is booted, select the <u>A</u>uto Start SQL Server at Boot Time check box in the Installation Options dialog box (refer to fig. A.4). You also can define an automatic startup for SQL Server after installation.

If you don't define SQL Server processes to automatically start up, you can later change it to automatic by using the Control Panel's Services option.

1. Open the Control Panel.
2. Double-click Services.
3. In the Services dialog box, scroll down the Service list box to find MSSQLServer.
4. Select MSSQLServer. The Startup should be Manual. A manual service isn't automatically started.
5. Click Startup to open the Service dialog box (see fig. A.6).

FIG. A.6
Change the Windows NT
account that a service
uses through the Service
dialog box.

6. In the Startup Type section, select Automatic.

   You can also specify that the MSSQLServer process created by the automatic startup of the service use an account other than the Administrator system account. If you use another account, you must specify the Password Never Expires characteristic in the NT Server's User Manager utility. You don't need to specify a different account from the system account for SQL Server.

> **CAUTION**
> It's very important that you consider your future uses for SQL Server as you install it with regards to user identities for the SQL processes. If you're using, or will be using in the future, the e-mail capabilities of SQL Server and the post office resides on a Novell server, you won't be able to access the mail system unless you establish a separate account for SQL Server.

7. Click OK in the Service dialog box. The MSSQLServer Startup column should have changed from Manual to Automatic.
8. If you want to immediately start SQL Server, click Start. A message box appears, telling you that SQL Server is starting. If the SQL Server service is successfully started, Started is added in the Status column of the Services dialog box for the SQL Server service.
9. Click Close.

Starting SQL Server with SQL Service Manager

You can use the SQL Service Manager to start MSSQLServer on the Windows NT server system. To start MSSQLServer by using the SQL Service Manager, follow these steps:

1. Click the SQL Service Manager icon in the SQL Server for Windows NT group.

2. Click Start/Continue or click the green light.

   The status message at the bottom of the SQL Service Manager dialog box should change from `The service is stopped` to `The service is starting`. After SQL Server is started, the message changes to `The service is running`.

3. Either Close the SQL Service Manager or minimize it to an icon.

If you leave the SQL Server Service Manager running, you can easily Stop or Pause SQL Server as needed.

Starting SQL Server Through Windows Applications

You can optionally start up SQL Server when you connect to the server locally from the server or remotely from a client system. For example, a miniature version of the SQL Service Manager can be invoked from the toolbar of the SQL Enterprise Manager, allowing you to start and stop the server engine.

Starting SQL Server Through a Command Line

To start up SQL Server using a command line, follow these steps:

1. Open a command prompt.

2. At the command prompt, enter this command line:

   ```
   sqlservr /d drive:\directory\data\master.dat
   ```

Use `/d` to specify the name of the SQL Server master database.

The *drive* is the drive letter you entered in the Drive text box of the SQL Server Installation Path dialog box. The *directory* is the directory you entered in the Directory text box of the same dialog box. The default for the directory is SQL and the default for the drive is C.

Master.dat is the name of the data file that's the SQL Server master device. The master database is located on the master device and contains the set of system tables that defines SQL Server. Master.dat is located in the subdirectory data of the SQL directory.

NOTE The `sqlservr` command line actually starts two system processes, both of which can have multiple threads. ▪

Installing the Client Software

Many of the SQL Server utilities that you use to manage the server, issue queries against it, and develop and debug your applications are available not only as server-based applications, but also client-side applications. The utilities installed will vary depending on the client environment you are installing into. If you're using a 16-bit client (for example, Windows for Workgroups), you'll have fewer options installed than if you're using a 32-bit environment like Windows 95 or Windows NT.

For the 16-bit Windows clients, the following utilities are installed:

- *ISQL/w – the ISQL client for Windows.* This application allows you to issue SQL statement to the server just as you can from the command line. This application uses a graphical user interface to present the query, results, and any optional trace and analysis settings you may wish to establish.

- *SQL Client Configuration Utility.* This allows you to set up the different configuration options for the client software. These options include network topology and any custom DLLs required to access the server. This utility is identical in function to the Client Configuration Utility installed on the server (although dialog boxes are slightly different in presentation).

- *SQL Server Books Online.* As the name implies, this option provides you with a fully searchable online version of the SQL Server book set. This item is also the same as the version installed on the client when the SQL Server is installed.

For the 32-bit client, the following utilities are installed:

- *ISQL/w – the ISQL client for Windows.* As with the server and 16-bit versions, this application allows you to issue SQL statements to the server just as you can from the command line. This application uses a graphical user interface to present the query, results, and any optional trace and analysis settings you may wish to establish.

- *SQL Client Configuration Utility.* This allows you to set up the different configuration options for the client software. These options include network topology and any custom DLLs required to access the server. This utility is identical in function to the Client Configuration Utility installed on the server (although dialog boxes are slightly different in presentation).

- *SQL Server Books Online.* As the name implies, this option provides you with a fully searchable online version of the SQL Server book set. This item is also the same as the version installed on the client when SQL Server is installed.

- *SQL Enterprise Manager.* As you'll learn throughout this book, this application is the central command center for administering SQL Server. This includes managing the devices, databases, replication, and other features and facets of SQL Server. Chances are very good that you'll become very well-versed in the use of the Enterprise Manager as you administer your SQL Server system.

- *SQL Security Manager.* As with the server-installed version, this application allows you to manage the users and groups that access the SQL Server system.

- *MS Query.* This tool, long included with the Office applications suite as the query tool for ODBC data sources, is not only a great tool to create queries against data sources, but also one of the best hands-on tools for learning the SQL language. You can graphically create a query, then review the SQL statements that are created to carry out the request.

- *SQL Help.* This help file contains the details of the Transact-SQL dialect used by SQL Server. You can use this help file to understand the different commands you can issue against the server—above and beyond the typical standard SQL commands.

- *SQL Trace.* This facility helps you manage the flow of transactions to and from your server. You'll be using this utility with the Distributed Transaction model in SQL Server 6.5.

- *SQL Web Page Wizard.* The Web Page Wizard allows you to create interactive, single-instance or trigger-oriented Web pages to be accessed from your Web site. The wizard will create the HTML and database interface code for you, saving time when you're developing database-centric pages for your Web site.

Steps to Installing the Software for 32-Bit Clients

If you're installing the software on a 32-bit client such as Windows 95 or Windows NT, you can take advantage of the added utilities mentioned previously. To start setup, select the processor subdirectory on the CD that corresponds to your system. It's most likely that you'll be installing using the i386 subdirectory; this corresponds to the 32-bit installation of the utilities.

Here are the steps to installing the software:

N O T E   To avoid conflicts with system files, you should exit all other software applications prior to running the setup program. If you don't, you might receive an error message as the files are copied to your system. This error message will prevent you from completing the installation successfully. Pay special attention to less-obvious applications such as the Office toolbar or other applications that run in the background. When in doubt, use the Windows task manager to verify the processes that are active on your system. ■

- Start SETUP.EXE to begin.
- Click Continue at the prompt.
- If you are upgrading from a prior version of the client utilities, you'll be prompted to choose between installing the new utilities and removing the old version of the utilities on your system.

 If you're upgrading your client software, it's a good idea to remove prior versions of the utilities before you install the newer 6.5 versions on your system. If you do uninstall your old utilities, you'll need to restart the setup process to continue with the installation of the new utilities.

- You'll be prompted to specify the utilities you want to install. Your control over the installation is complete, allowing you to fine-tune your requirements based on disk space constraints or your need for a specific utility.
- The final phases of installation are automatic. The setup program will copy the routines to your system and update your system files.
- At the end of the routine, you'll be prompted to reboot the system, which will complete the process.

Once completed, you'll be able to use the client workstation to administer, inquire into, and manage the different aspects of your SQL Server system.

Installing the Software for 16-Bit Clients

As mentioned previously, the 16-bit client software offers somewhat less—although just as useful—utilities for your SQL Server installation. When you install the software on your system, you'll be following similar prompts as other Windows installations that you might have completed.

The first step is to open the Clients subdirectory on the CD containing SQL Server. Select your operating system (either DOS or Win16 for the 16-bit Windows client software). If you're running the Windows setup, select and run the SETUP program. Installation of the DOS client software simply requires copying the files to a directory of your choice.

The Windows setup program will prompt you for the destination of the files and will then ask you to confirm which utilities you want to install.

When you click Install, the utilities will be copied to your system. A program group will be created and you'll be ready to start using the utilities with your system.

SQL Server can be installed in an environment with many different chip sets and variations of the Windows operating system. All of the software needed to install and run the server, as well as to install and configure client machines, comes on the SQL Server CD. The process of installing software on the clients should be planned and consistent on clients running the same version of Windows to make maintenance and troubleshooting easier. ●

SQL Server and Web Pages

Many companies today are using SQL Server to run their businesses. It is a back-end product that is used by entire companies and possibly even the companies' customers to view data. Company employees might have an application that was developed for them to view the data or they might use a product such as Microsoft Access or Microsoft Excel to draw the data from the SQL Server database and view it. In either case, there is a cost associated with the purchase or writing of software and the training necessary to make the software useful.

Web page is one technology that is very promising because of its ease of use and ability to remain current. Web pages are viewed using Web browsers. Web browsers are very easy to use and most share standard conventions for navigating the data that is displayed on the Web pages. This common interface reduces or eliminates training costs when a Web browser is used to view data. Another advantage to using Web pages to display data is the fact that they're easy to update. Web pages are files that can simply be replaced when data is added, modified, or when data becomes obsolete. Finally, Web pages can be made widely availableby placing them on the Internet.

A company can allow customers or potential customers to view up-to-date information about its products and services.

Microsoft—recognizing the opportunity for businesses to leverage the data stored in their SQL Server databases using Web pages—has included three new system-stored procedures that aid in the creation and maintenance of such material. Microsoft also wrote a graphical interface that does the following:

- Walks a user through the thought process necessary for using the stored procedures
- Writes the stored procedures according to the information provided by a user
- Executes the stored procedures according to the information provided by a user

> **CAUTION**
> While Microsoft is committed to SQL Server running on a variety of chip architectures, the SQL Server Web Assistant and associated stored procedures can be used on Intel-based computers only. In addition, they can run on SQL Server 6.5 databases only. Running them on earlier versions will result in an error.

Following the easy-to-use example of their Office products, Microsoft has included several Wizards (or Assistants) in SQL Server 6.5. One of these Wizards is used to generate files containing HyperText Markup Language (HTML). With the appropriate server software, these HTML files or Web pages can be made accessible to a company intranet or the World Wide Web (WWW) on the Internet. ■

Using a Log In

Just as users must login to SQL Server to work in Enterprise Manager or ISQL/w, login information is required on the first page of the SQL Server Web page Wizard. The name of the SQL Server to use must be supplied along with a valid user name and password. If trusted connections are enabled on the chosen server, the user name and password can be omitted and the Use Windows NT Security... check box can be selected (see fig. B.1).

 At any time, the More Info button can be clicked to obtain more detailed descriptions of items on the page and further instructions on how to use them.

Once this page is completed, the Next button will attempt to login to the specified server (using the login settings provided) and will close this page. If the login fails, a message box will notify the user of the error and allow him to correct the information on the login page. When the correct information is given, the login is completed successfully and the Query page is shown.

Part
VI

App
B

FIG. B.1

The Web page Wizard can only be used if a valid login is provided.

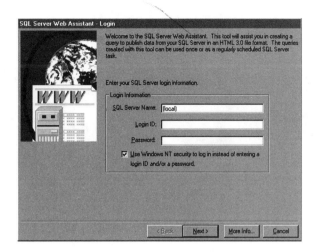

Using a Query

After successfully logging into SQL Server, a query must be provided that will be used to supply the information to be included in an HTML file. There are three ways that the query can be built:

■ Using a database hierarchy model

■ Using a free-form text query

■ Using a stored procedure

Depending upon which query type is chosen, the SQL Server Web page Wizard will prompt the user for information specific to that method. These methods are discussed in greater detail in the following three sections. Regardless of the method chosen, SQL Server will verify that the query is valid and prompt the user for modifications (if it isn't valid).

NOTE If the wrong SQL Server name was accidentally provided on the Login page, clicking the Back button will return the Wizard to that page and allow a different value to be supplied. However, when the Next button is clicked, the login settings must be verified again. ■

Using the Database Hierarchy to Build a Query

Building a query using the database hierarchy is done by simply browsing the database hierarchy in the middle of the Query page and selecting one or more tables, or individual columns within a table, to be included in the result set of the query. Figure B.2 shows this method being used to select the first and last name of authors with the last name "Warner".

Selected tables or columns are indicated by a green highlight around their representing icon. If any additional criteria are necessary to obtain a specific result set from the query, they must be entered in the text box below the database hierarchy. In Figure B.2, the authors returned by the query are limited to those with the last name "Warner".

FIG. B.2
Columns are chosen
graphically but additional
criteria must be keyed in.

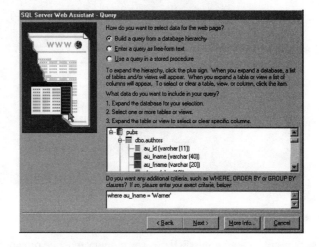

Using Free-Form Text to Build a Query

If the database hierarchy method is not flexible enough for the query needed to populate a Web page, the query can be entered free-form by selecting the Enter a Query as Free-Form Text radio button, choosing the database you want to use, and providing the actual query text. Figure B.3 shows a free-form query that will return a result set identical to that returned by the query in Figure B.2.

FIG. B.3
Column data can be formatted
and specifically labeled by a
free-form query.

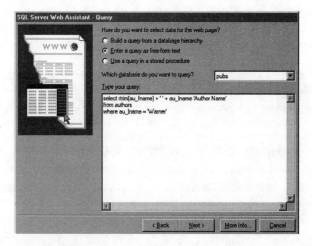

While the query in Figure B.3 returns a result set identical to the one returned by the query in Figure B.2, it formats and concatenates the data and applies a more descriptive label to the concatenated columns.

TIP Free-form queries might already exist in a system if commonly used queries are saved in text files. If a query exists that returns the necessary data in an acceptable fashion, it has already been tested and can be used as is or with formatting modification.

Using a Stored Procedure to Build a Query

Many times stored procedures exist that produce useful data that is otherwise difficult to obtain. Stored procedures that produce a result set can be used to obtain the result set for the SQL Server Web page Wizard. An example of a stored procedure that returns a result set is shown in Figure B.4.

Part

VI

App

B

FIG. B.4

Even stored procedures that require parameters can be used to obtain a result set.

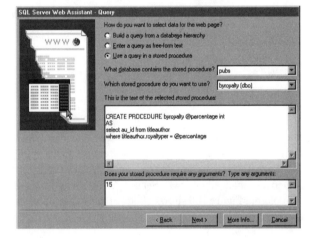

When using the stored procedure method to provide a query to the SQL Server Web page Wizard, a database must be chosen along with a stored procedure that already exists in that database. New stored procedures can't be created in the Web page Wizard.

Using Scheduling

Data can be very volatile. For data to remain valuable it must be timely. By scheduling a query to create or update a Web page at a particular time, at certain intervals, or when the data is changed in the database, SQL Server takes on the task of keeping data on Web pages up-to-date with the data in the database. When there are hundreds of pages to keep current, this becomes a very powerful and time-saving feature.

For most applications data is good for a certain period of time. The period of time might vary from hours to months. As shown in Figure B.5, the creation of a Web page can be scheduled hourly, daily, or weekly.

The creation of Web pages can also be scheduled to occur on particular days of the week at a specified time. This can be useful for information that is specific to a day of the week.

FIG. B.5
Data can be out-of-date in a matter of hours.

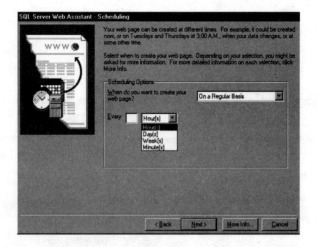

N O T E As well as recurring tasks that create Web pages over and over at scheduled times, Web pages can be created on a one-time basis. This single task can be run immediately or scheduled for a later time. ■

Some data might be so volatile—or so involatile—that Web pages displaying the data should be updated when the data changes. As with the frequency that such data might change, a Web page would have to be created quite frequently or very rarely. In either case, the update would be performed automatically by SQL Server. An entire table can be selected to trigger this event or a single column. Figure B.6 shows changes in the last names of authors, triggering SQL Server to build a new Web page.

FIG. B.6
Frequent or infrequent changes to data make it difficult to use timed updates.

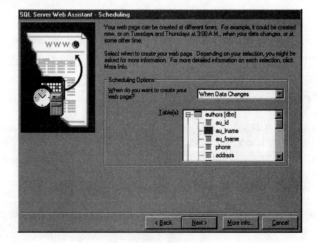

Using the File Options Page

At this point, all of the information necessary to retrieve the data to be placed on a Web page has been supplied. Now the formatting and placement of the Web page must be determined. As shown in Figure B.7, the File Options page defines where the Web page is placed, what it will look like, and what (if any) additional Web pages will be linked to it.

FIG. B.7

Web pages can be customized and even derived from templates that are built or purchased.

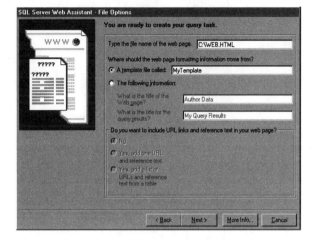

Part

VI

App

B

A template can be used for the creation of the Web pages, or SQL Server can create a generic page with a title for both the page and the query results. There is space to fill in both titles on the File Options page.

N O T E If a template isn't used, titles don't have to be provided. Titles should be used, but they aren't necessary if there is no need for them. ▣

Many Web pages contain links to other Web pages. Like titles, links aren't necessary but they do make the page more appealing for most users. A single link can be given or a list of links can be supplied. If a list of links is used, a query must be supplied that returns the address of the WWeb page and a description or reference for the page. The reference text will become the link when the page is created.

Using the Formatting Page

Finally, the Formatting page of the SQL Server Web page Wizard allows for some custom formatting of the Web page. A header style must be chosen for the title of the query results. If you didn't supply a title, just accept the default because it won't make any difference. The query results must be presented in either a fixed or proportional font and can also be formatted to be bold, italic, or both. Figure B.8 shows an example of this page.

FIG. B.8
Users may want to limit the number of rows displayed if the page is a ranking and only the top items should be shown.

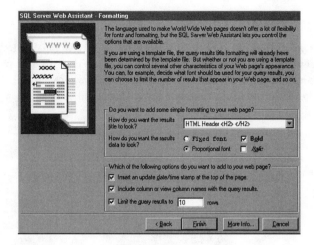

Additional information can be automatically supplied by choosing formatting options at the bottom of the Formatting page. For example, a date and time stamp can be included at the top of pages. You can include the column headings and you can limit the number of data rows placed on the page.

When you click Finish, the task you have developed is created and a final page (see fig. B.9) indicates the status of the created task.

FIG. B.9
The SQL Server Web page Wizard alerts users when the chosen tasks have been completed and scheduled if necessary.

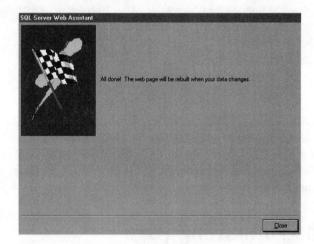

Using SQL Trace

SQL Trace is a graphical utility that is used to monitor database activity. The monitoring can be done in real time or can be done on particular users, applications, or hosts. This utility can only be used with SQL Server 6.5 servers. ■

Starting SQL Trace

The name of the SQL Trace executable file is SQLTRACE.EXE and it should be located in the SQL Server BINN directory. By default, the SQL Server 6.5 installation will place a shortcut to SQL Trace in the SQL Server program group. This (or another) shortcut can be used to start the utility or it can be started from the command line. Figure C.1 shows SQL Trace immediately after it is started.

FIG. C.1

When started, SQL Trace will prompt the user to log in to a database.

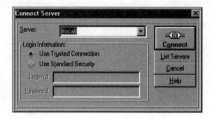

After successfully connecting to a database, the user is prompted to select which defined filters should be started (see fig. C.2). If no filters are defined, this dialog box does not appear.

FIG. C.2

Filters can begin monitoring a database as soon as the user successfully logs in to that database.

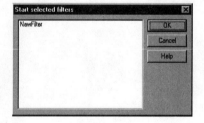

Filters can now be added, deleted, edited, started, stopped, and paused. In addition, several other utilities can be started from within SQL Trace:

- ISQL/w
- SQL Enterprise Manager
- Windows NT Performance Monitor

N O T E   When starting an ISQL/w session from within SQL Trace, ISQL/w will attempt to log in with the login information used to connect SQL Trace to a SQL Server database. ■

Using SQL Trace

The SQL Trace interface is divided into two sections:

- Active Filter Pane
- Filter Status Pane

Activities that meet a filter's criteria are displayed in the active filter pane (or window). The name of the filter being displayed is shown in the title bar. Later, in the "Setting Up a Filter" section, filters will be explained in more detail.

At the bottom of the SQL Trace window is the filter status pane. This pane is made up of several items that display information about filters defined for the current server. Figure C.3 shows a SQL Trace window with an active filter pane and filter status pane visible.

FIG. C.3

The filter status pane can be toggled between visible and invisible.

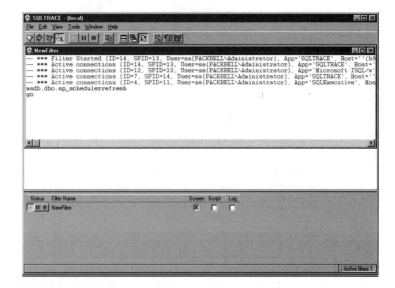

The filter status bar tracks the following information about defined filters for the current server:

- Status—Graphically represents the state (started, stopped, or paused) of a filter.
- Filter Name—Displays the name that was assigned to the filter when it was defined.
- Screen—If you check this option, an active filter pane is displayed for that filter.
- Script—Checking this option will cause the activity monitored by the filter to be saved as a SQL script.
- Log—Checking this option will cause the activity monitored by the filter to be saved in a log file.

Setting Up a Filter

To create a new filter, follow these steps:

1. Either select <u>N</u>ew Filter from the <u>F</u>ile menu or click the New Filter button (refer to fig. C.3). The New Filter dialog box appears (see fig. C.4).

Part VI
App C

FIG. C.4

Filters can be added or deleted form the New Filter dialog box.

2. Enter a Filter Name as well as any specific Login Name, Application, or Host Name to monitor. To monitor all connections, leave the default <All>.

3. Choose the Capture Options page at the bottom of the dialog box. The SQL can be captured as screen output (View on Screen), SQL script (Save to Script File), log file (Save as Log File), or any combination of the three. Each connection can be monitored separately using the Per Connection option. In addition to the commands issued, performance data can be collected by checking the Include Performance Information option.

4. Select the Events page and choose the events for which to capture data. As shown in Figure C.5, the Events page also enables you to filter SQL and RPC statements. The SQL and RPC filters are used as string values for which to search. Multiple values can be entered, separated by a semicolon, and the percent sign is used as a wildcard.

FIG. C.5

SQL and RPC statements that contain a specified string value can be filtered.

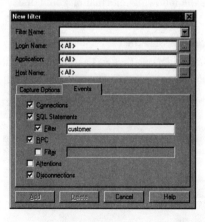

5. Click the Add button to add the filter to the defined filters for the current server.

SQL Trace is a simple but powerful tool. It can be used for many purposes. Debugging applications can be simplified by using SQL Trace to monitor SQL statements issued from an application. Performance issues can be addressed by recording a particular user's activity. And security can be enhanced by checking for dangerous activity on a server. ●

Part
VI

App
C

Redundant Arrays of Inexpensive Drives (RAID)

Redundant Arrays of Inexpensive Drives (RAID) currently has six implementations to provide a set of physical devices that will offer better data device integrity and performance. Those levels are described in this appendix. ■

Level 0

RAID Level 0 is basic data striping across multiple physical devices. The *striping* refers to the fact that multiple drives are allocated for data as a group. The data is then placed across the drives evenly so that each drive has a portion of the data. Striping provides better performance than single drives because multiple I/O threads from the operating system are allocated to servicing each drive. In addition, multiple physical reads and writes can occur simultaneously on the separate physical devices.

RAID Level 0 does not provide any fault tolerance and is purely a performance enhancement.

Level 1

RAID Level 1 is device mirroring. As discussed in Chapter 4, "Creating Devices, Databases, and Transaction Logs," mirroring provides an absolute duplication of the data on any given physical device on the mirror device. Mirroring can (depending on physical implementation) improve read performance if both drives are read in parallel and data is returned to the operating system in a single stream composed of the parallel reads. Mirroring generally imposes a slight performance cost when writing because two writes are done instead of one.

Mirroring is fault-tolerant; media failure is generally handled by an automatic and complete switch over to the mirror device.

Level 2

RAID Level 2 is an error-correcting algorithm that employs striping across multiple physical devices. It is more advanced than Level 0 because it uses error-correcting "parity" data that is striped across the devices, and copes with media failure on any particular device in the stripe set. However, the parity data consumes several disks and is quite inefficient as a storage mechanism.

RAID Level 2 is generally not used because it does not offer significant performance benefits over a straight mirroring implementation (Level 1).

Level 3

RAID Level 3 is a different implementation of the striped, parity algorithm. It differs from Level 2 by utilizing only a single device in the stripe set for storing the parity data.

RAID Level 3 offers some performance benefits to reads and writes.

Level 4

RAID Level 4 is the same as Level 3, except that it implements a larger block or segment storage size. This means that the basic unit that is being striped is large in size and generally gets better performance due to the more advanced modern physical devices that are able to read and write bigger blocks of data in a single I/O operation. RAID Level 4 stores the parity information on a separate device from the user data that is striped across multiple physical devices.

RAID Level 4 is an inefficient algorithm and is generally not used.

Level 5

RAID Level 5 is the most commonly implemented RAID level currently. It is a striped implementation that stores parity information on the same striped drives. This allows an individual device to fail and the other devices in the stripe set to contain enough information to recover and keep processing. The parity information for any particular device is always stored on another device in the stripe set, ensuring that if media failure occurs on a particular device that its parity data is not affected.

RAID Level 5 uses the same large block algorithm as Level 4, and is quite efficient. Level 5 will offer performance gains to reads and writes, until media failure occurs. When media failure occurs, reads suffer because the information on the failed device must be reconstructed from the parity data stored on the other devices. ●

Part

VI

App

D

Case Study: New York Metropolitan Museum of Art

By Jay Hoffman
Gallery Systems
New York, New York

I began developing software for the art world in 1981 with my first application, The Museum System, which is used to catalog art objects. The Museum System stores information about art, including a picture of the object that can be displayed on a PC monitor.

The Museum System is used at more than 75 art galleries in the United States and Europe. Institutions in the United States that use the Museum System include The Detroit Institute of Arts, The United States Holocaust Memorial Museum, The United States Supreme Court, The American Craft Museum (New York), and New York University's Grey Art Gallery.

I had decided to develop a similar, but more robust, system that would store information in a Microsoft SQL Server database when the Antonio Ratti Textile Center of The Metropolitan Museum of Art contacted me. The Met wanted me to develop an application that would combine the tracking of movement and preparation of textiles for storage in its new textile facility. ■

NOTE Objects in museums—even objects that are publicly displayed—are often temporarily removed by curators or art historians for research purposes. In addition, a number of objects can be removed from display to be lent to other museums. As well as the obvious information that must be kept about art objects, such as who the artist is and when the object was created, the current location of objects must also be kept. ■

The new application that I was to develop for the Met included a read-only version running on PC workstations in an area of the museum that is accessible to visitors. Visitors would be able to explore the textile database and view images and related data about the textiles.

Selecting Microsoft SQL Server for Windows NT

Many departments (including mine) within the Metropolitan Museum of Art that were already using other Microsoft products were pleased with the features and performance of the Microsoft products. The Museum staff's experience with Microsoft's word processor, spreadsheet, and PC database is the reason that I initially considered Microsoft SQL Server.

I also needed a database that could eventually store information about a nearly unlimited number of art objects, though the immediate needs only required the cataloging of less than 100,000 art objects for the textile project. Microsoft SQL Server looked as if it could meet the current needs of the textile project, as well be used to store much more data about additional art objects in the future.

Anticipating Time Required for the Project

There are several phases in the textile project, with the total time for completion specified to be one year and nine months. The first phase was completed on time, and the second phase is moving along nicely. The textile project will probably evolve into a second project with a much longer time frame.

The museum recognizes that it must eventually catalog all objects within the museum's collection so that the information about art objects can be easily and quickly retrieved. Such a project would also have to be completed in phases and would take considerably longer. It's easy to project that the museum should eventually catalog on a computer system information about its entire collection, which is far more vast than the textile information.

Choosing a Computer System

I selected a Sequent 3000 with two Pentium processors for the database server platform. The Sequent system permits me to add additional processors. I anticipated that there would only be a need to add two additional processors in the future when the museum requires additional processing capabilities.

NOTE A product such as Microsoft SQL Server is designed to leverage the power of the Windows NT operating system (see Chapter 3, "Understanding the Underlying Operating System, Windows NT"). SQL Server is written in sections that execute as separate threads under Windows NT.

The greater the number of processors within the computer system, the greater the number of threads (application code) that can execute simultaneously. Purchasing a computer system to which you can add processors as the processing demands of the system increase over time makes it less likely that you'll have to uproot your applications and move them to a larger computer. ■

Number of PC Client Workstations Supported

At this point in the project, the exact number isn't determined, but the number of PC workstations should be somewhere in the range of 12 to 60. The client workstations will be primarily used by the curatorial and conservation staff for scholarly purposes.

The PC workstations will be located on desktops in offices of the museum as well as a number that will be located in a public area. The size of the Sequent server and its expansion capability should permit the server to easily satisfy the number of clients within the range specified.

Part of the plan is to provide up to six workstations that are connected to the server in a public access area that can be used by visiting scholars or the general public. A visiting scholar or a member of the public will be able to use the PC workstation to retrieve information on textile objects in the database, using one of the public workstations. A museum visitor can make the same query that a member of the museum research staff can make to obtain information about the textiles.

For example, a query could be made based on the culture or period of an object, and all matching objects which would be displayed in a thumbnail sketch of the object found. The access to objects for the PC workstations in the public area will be limited to read-only. Information stored about the textiles cannot be changed from the PC systems that are located in the public area.

Part
VI

App
E

Structuring the Database

I allocated half a gigabyte of storage for the database. I calculated the initial allocation of space for the database knowing that I had to catalog data for 42,000 art objects, the tapestries. I didn't require half a gigabyte of space for the storage of information about the existing objects. I wanted to ensure that I had plenty of room for the addition of data for more objects that the museum would subsequently acquire. In addition, the museum hadn't completely defined the amount of information that would be cataloged for each tapestry.

The amount of space that's used for the storage of actual data is only 200 megabytes, and I expect that the final amount of space required for data about the 42,000 textiles will be 300 to 400 megabytes. I defined the storage for the database and the transaction log on different logical and physical devices, which is the usual recommendation for the best performance.

Actually, 300 to 400 megabytes is a relatively small amount of space to use for the storage of data about 42,000 art objects. The reason that a relatively small amount of space is required for the storage of the information about the tapestries is that the images of the tapestries are stored externally to the SQL Server database, as separate files.

Rather than defining the column of a database table as an image datatype (an appropriate datatype for the storage of pictures), I chose a format that permitted the greatest flexibility for subsequent access by other applications. By storing the pictures of the tapestries external to the SQL Server database, I achieved maximum flexibility in their use: their access from other applications and retrieval systems that may require use of the pictures.

The format I chose for the storage of the pictures is the Kodak Photo CD format, which actually stores multiple copies of each graphic of a tapestry, each in a different resolution. This is one of the advantages of the Photo CD format. Subsequent applications can choose one of the formats to display the graphic on the screen.

The current retrieval and display application normally displays the graphics with 4 million colors, which is required for scholarly research and proper representation and identification of the art objects. The objects also look more pleasing at a resolution that provides several million colors rather than the 256 colors that are more commonly used for graphics in computer applications.

I built a table that contains a column to link the object number to the slide or image number of the picture of the tapestry. The Photo CD format actually provides five virtual resolutions, though the application primarily uses two: one of the Photo CD formats and an additional black and white format. The application uses a black and white TIFF format that permits 256 shades of gray and the 24-bit Photo CD format that provides millions of colors.

An outside vendor scans the pictures of the tapestries and delivers the scanned images to me on compact disks (CDs). The multiple resolutions of the Photo CD format are also useful because they permit the use of client systems that support different hardware, which might vary in the resolutions that they can display because of different video cards. I'm trying to define a standard client system that permits a resolution of 1024 by 768 and displays images in at least 32,000 colors.

One of the capabilities of the retrieval system permits the display of up to twelve small so-called thumbnail representations of the tapestry pictures at a time on the screen. The thumbnail display supports only 256 colors, though the full-screen display of the tapestry permits a display of several million.

All the client systems are Intel-based PCs that are currently running Windows for Workgroups. Both the PCs and the operating system were already in place at the museum when the tapestry project was conceived, and it was decided to use them as the client system rather than replace them.

The network connectivity that is a part of the Windows for Workgroups configuration permitted a simple conversion to a server-based NT domain system. The existing Windows for Workgroups configuration was one of the reasons for implementing the storage of information for the tapestry project using Microsoft SQL Server on Windows NT.

I'm considering upgrading the client system to run Windows NT Workstation instead of Windows for Workgroups. I'll probably do this using Visual Basic 4 in order to take advantage of the more powerful client system that NT Workstation provides. Alternately, it's possible that some of the clients will be upgraded to Windows 95, which, like Windows for Workgroups or Windows NT Workstation, permits a simple connection to the database server.

Using Application Packages to Define the Database

The application that I'm creating for the tapestry collection at the Met is a direct evolution of my existing DOS-based application, The Museum System. As a result, I was also aware of the design issues involved in the type of database required. The Museum System effectively served as a prototype for the tapestry application.

Number of Tables Defined in the Database

I will need 50-75 tables in the database, though some of the tables are quite small in keeping with the type of information in the tables. Many of the small tables are authority tables in which information stored about the tapestry varies depending on the department of the museum.

Islamic art is different from Asian, twentieth century art is different from European sculpture and decorative art, and the information that is kept about each tapestry is different depending upon its origin (and hence the department that has ownership of it).

Even the same type of information that is sorted about an art object can vary. For example, the dynasties for China are different than the dynasties for Egypt, and although they are similar information, different information must be stored for each.

The differences in the information recorded for art objects also affect the entries that appear in the user interface for the tapestry application. For example, the names of dynasties on drop-down menus must be different for Chinese and Egyptian dynasties.

Formally Defining Primary and Foreign Keys for the Database Tables

I feel strongly that the database is defined correctly, and it does make sense to define primary and foreign keys. Though SQL Server will permit relational joins and triggers to be performed in the absence of key definitions, such definitions provide a descriptive structure to the database. Moreover, the formal definition of keys anticipates what may become a requirement of Microsoft SQL Server in subsequent versions for the definition of other objects dependent upon keys, such as triggers.

Defining Indexes on Tables

Both clustered and non-clustered indexes are defined for the databases tables. Generally, the smaller tables that are referenced less frequently have as few as one or two indexes defined for them. The main tables, which are referenced frequently, have several indexes defined for faster joins and retrieval.

Part
VI

App
E

Using Storage Optimization Techniques

The Sequent server that I'm using has a disk array, and I'm currently making use of volume sets to optimize data access. I'm also considering using other optimization techniques, such as striping without parity to improve performance, which I may or may not implement later in the project.

Using Fault-Tolerant Techniques

The database is backed up daily. The images are stored on CDs, so there's no need to backup this non-volatile media. The database information isn't considered critical enough to make use of additional fault-tolerant mechanisms, such as mirroring, either at the database, operating system, or hardware level. Although not a fault-tolerant mechanism, replication may be used later to make the information about the art objects available at other institutions around the world.

Allocating the Temporary Database in RAM to Optimize Performance

I initially tried doing allocating the temporary database tempdb on a logical device that was defined in memory. For the type of queries and access that I'm doing, it didn't seem to provide much of an improvement in performance. I've gone back to using the hard disk for the temporary database.

Using Triggers in the Database

I use triggers in the usual way: to maintain the referential integrity of the database tables. In addition, I use triggers to maintain an audit trail about changes that are made to data about the art objects. Some columns, of course, can't be changed by anyone, and appropriate security is provided to prevent unauthorized updates.

I also use a trigger to generate a row ID for entries in some tables to uniquely identify the rows, retrieving a value from another table. I also considered generating a unique row number using the timestamp datatype or the max function to return the largest row number in the table and then incrementing the value to use as a new row number.

The Front-End Query Application

I'm writing the application in Visual Basic using ODBC to access the database. I'm using ODBC because I want the platform independence that it provides. Visual Basic makes it easy for me to pull up the 50 to 500 objects that a user may want to browse through once he has chosen an initial object.

I'll also permit the SQL Server database to be accessible from front-end products, such as Microsoft Access. I've already permitted the access of the database using the Attach Table feature of Microsoft Access. Users have local Access tables on their clients in which they can initially store information about objects.

Through Microsoft Access, they can also attach to the SQL Server database and update the data rows. They may also need to combine the data that they've stored within the local Access tables with information from the SQL Server database.

I'm also testing the report writer, Crystal Reports, to be used to access the SQL Server database as well as Access databases. To simplify the users' access, I've set up views in SQL Server. I use the views to permit users to access multiple tables—as many as twelve tables—without having to be aware of the structure of the SQL Server database and the SQL syntax required to reference so many data sources.

Administrating the Database

The server will be located in the Textile Center, which is under construction; so for convenience, the administration of the database will be performed through the provided client administrative applications that come with the Microsoft SQL Server product.

Archiving Data

Currently, there's no plan to perform on-site or off-site storage of archives of the data. The concerns of the museum are different from those of a commercial environment. In a sense, the graphics images of the art objects are already a backup of the original art objects themselves, the tapestries.

If the CDs that contain the representations of the objects were lost, they could always be exactly re-created from the art objects. The focus to this point in time, as it should be, has been on the security and preservation of the objects themselves.

As time goes on, the museum will probably implement an archive strategy for safeguarding the information that is kept about the objects. We will be replicating the data to other institutions, which can also be used as backup copies of the data.

Existing Repositories of Information

The storage of data about art objects was started in 1988, and data was stored in dBASE III. Within the museum as a whole, each department has started committing the information that it has cataloged about art objects onto a computer system. Other PC databases were and are in use for the storage of data throughout the museum.

I've sometimes had to write custom programs for the conversion of the data from the PC databases to SQL Server. Fortunately, I often have been able to use Microsoft Access to read the data from another vendor's PC database and write it out to the SQL Server database.

Dial-Up Access to the Database

Initially, there won't be any dial-up access provided to the database, although it will be provided at a later time.

NOTE The main window of the retrieval portion of the textile project application will display a miniature view of the tapestry in a rectangle that can be seen in the upper-right portion of the window. Information that is often retrieved about a tapestry is automatically displayed in several fields of the window.

For example, the name of the tapestry is shown in a Title field, which is defined as a list box. Multiple lines of information can be stored and subsequently displayed within the Title list box field. The classification of the art object will subsequently permit other art objects to be recorded and displayed when the application is used for cataloging other objects within the museum.

A Medium Label Copy field displays information about the characteristics of the tapestry (such as its composition). Two remaining fields that display data are the Date/Period and the CreditLine (which shows the manner in which the museum acquired the tapestry).

The image of the tapestry itself can be displayed in an enlarged view in a high resolution (several million colors), permitting as detailed a view of the tapestry as permitted by current technology. The image also can be displayed in a small representation using the Make Thumbnail. In addition, the contrast and brightness of the tapestry can be adjusted to permit alternate representations of the image for research purposes.

What's on the CD?

In this appendix, you will learn about the materials included on the *Special Edition Using Microsoft SQL Server
6.5* CD-ROM that accompanies this book. It contains
applications, tools, and demonstration products. ■

In this appendix you'll learn the following:

- The CD includes several powerful applications that all work with (or around) SQL
  Server 6.5.

- Any application, sample, or code listing
  presented in the book can be found on the
  CD. That way, you can cut and paste code
  snippets without having to retype and debug
  them.

- We have provided two electonic books on
  this CD. One is in HTML format, which can
  be read using any World Wide Web browser
  on any platform. The other is in Windows
  Help file format, which can be easily
  searched and bookmarked for future
  reference.

Third-Party Products

Following is a brief description of the products and demos from third-party vendors that you'll find on the CD.

> **N O T E**   The products on the CD are demos and shareware. You may have some difficulty running them on your particular machine. If you do, feel free to contact the vendor. (They'd rather have you evaluate their product than ignore it.) ■

Using the Electronic Book

Special Edition Using Microsoft SQL Server 6.5 is available to you as an HTML document that can be read from any World Wide Web browser that you may have currently installed on your machine (such as Netscape Navigator or Mosaic). If you don't have a Web browser, we have included Microsoft's Internet Explorer for you.

The book can also be read on-screen as a Windows Help file.

Reading the Electronic Book as an HTML Document

To read the electronic book, you will need to start your Web browser and open the document file TOC.HTML located on the \HTMLVER subdirectory of the CD. Alternatively, you can browse the CD directory using File Manager and double-click TOC.HTML.

Once you have opened the TOC.HTML page, you can access all of the book's contents by clicking on the highlighted chapter number or topic name. The electronic book works like any other Web page; when you click on a hot link, a new page is opened or the browser will take you to the new location in the document. As you read through the electronic book, you will notice other highlighted words or phrases. Clicking on these cross-references will also take you to a new location within the electronic book. You can always use your browser's forward or backward buttons to return to your original location.

Installing the Internet Explorer

If you don't have a Web browser installed on your machine, you can use Microsoft's Internet Explorer 2.0 on this CD-ROM.

Microsoft Internet Explorer can be installed from the self-extracting file in the \EXPLORER directory. Double-click the MSIE20.exe or use the Control Panel's Add/Remove Programs option and follow the instructions in the install routine. Please be aware you *must* have Windows 95 installed on your machine to use this version of Internet Explorer. Other versions of this software can be downloaded from Microsoft's FTP site at **ftp://microsoft.com**.

Reading the Electronic Book as a Windows Help File Document

To read the electronic book, simply use File Manager to browse to the \HELPVER subdirectory on the CD. Double-click SQLSRVR.HLP and the file will load.

Finding Sample Code

This book contains code examples that include listing headers (for example, "see Listing 10.1") and the "On the CD" icon:

Listing 10.1 10_01.SQL—Creating the Authors2 Table and Indexes

This listing indicates that this particular *code snippet* (or example) is included electronically on the CD. To find it, browse to the \CODE subdirectory on the CD and select the filename that matches the one referenced in the listing header (in this example, 10_01.SQL).

Part
VI

App
F

Index

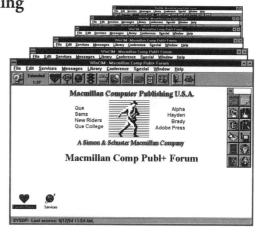

Complete and Return this Card for a *FREE* Computer Book Catalog

Thank you for purchasing this book! You have purchased a superior computer book written expressly for your needs. To continue to provide the kind of up-to-date, pertinent coverage you've come to expect from us, we need to hear from you. Please take a minute to complete and return this self-addressed, postage-paid form. In return, we'll send you a free catalog of all our computer books on topics ranging from word processing to programming and the internet.

Mr. ☐   Mrs. ☐   Ms. ☐   Dr. ☐

Name (first) ☐☐☐☐☐☐☐☐☐☐   (M.I.) ☐   (last) ☐☐☐☐☐☐☐☐☐☐☐☐☐

Address ☐☐☐☐☐☐☐☐☐☐☐☐☐☐☐☐☐☐☐☐☐☐☐☐☐
☐☐☐☐☐☐☐☐☐☐☐☐☐☐☐☐☐☐☐☐☐☐☐☐☐

City ☐☐☐☐☐☐☐☐☐☐   State ☐☐   Zip ☐☐☐☐☐ ☐☐☐☐

Phone ☐☐☐ ☐☐☐ ☐☐☐☐   Fax ☐☐☐ ☐☐☐ ☐☐☐☐

Company Name ☐☐☐☐☐☐☐☐☐☐☐☐☐☐☐☐☐☐☐☐☐☐

E-mail address ☐☐☐☐☐☐☐☐☐☐☐☐☐☐☐☐☐☐☐☐☐☐☐

1. Please check at least (3) influencing factors for purchasing this book.

Front or back cover information on book ☐
Special approach to the content ☐
Completeness of content ☐
Author's reputation ☐
Publisher's reputation ☐
Book cover design or layout ☐
Index or table of contents of book ☐
Price of book ☐
Special effects, graphics, illustrations ☐
Other (Please specify): _____ ☐

2. How did you first learn about this book?

Saw in Macmillan Computer Publishing catalog ☐
Recommended by store personnel ☐
Saw the book on bookshelf at store ☐
Recommended by a friend ☐
Received advertisement in the mail ☐
Saw an advertisement in: _____ ☐
Read book review in: _____ ☐
Other (Please specify): _____ ☐

3. How many computer books have you purchased in the last six months?

This book only ☐   3 to 5 books ☐
2 books ☐   More than 5 ☐

4. Where did you purchase this book?

Bookstore ☐
Computer Store ☐
Consumer Electronics Store ☐
Department Store ☐
Office Club ☐
Warehouse Club ☐
Mail Order ☐
Direct from Publisher ☐
Internet site ☐
Other (Please specify): _____ ☐

5. How long have you been using a computer?

☐ Less than 6 months   ☐ 6 months to a year
☐ 1 to 3 years   ☐ More than 3 years

6. What is your level of experience with personal computers and with the subject of this book?

	With PCs	With subject of book
New	☐	☐
Casual	☐	☐
Accomplished	☐	☐
Expert	☐	☐

Source Code ISBN: 0-7897-0097-2

7. Which of the following best describes your job title?

Administrative Assistant .... ☐
Coordinator .... ☐
Manager/Supervisor .... ☐
Director .... ☐
Vice President .... ☐
President/CEO/COO .... ☐
Lawyer/Doctor/Medical Professional .... ☐
Teacher/Educator/Trainer .... ☐
Engineer/Technician .... ☐
Consultant .... ☐
Not employed/Student/Retired .... ☐
Other (Please specify): _____ ☐

8. Which of the following best describes the area of the company your job title falls under?

Accounting .... ☐
Engineering .... ☐
Manufacturing .... ☐
Operations .... ☐
Marketing .... ☐
Sales .... ☐
Other (Please specify): _____ ☐

9. What is your age?

Under 20 .... ☐
21-29 .... ☐
30-39 .... ☐
40-49 .... ☐
50-59 .... ☐
60-over .... ☐

10. Are you:

Male .... ☐
Female .... ☐

11. Which computer publications do you read regularly? (Please list)

_____
_____
_____
_____
_____
_____
_____
_____
_____
_____

Comments: _____
_____
_____

Fold here and scotch-tape to m

QUE® has the right choice for every computer user

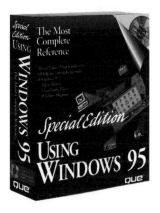

From the new computer user to the advanced programmer, we've got the right computer book for you. Our user-friendly *Using* series offers just the information you need to perform specific tasks quickly and move onto other things. And, for computer users ready to advance to new levels, QUE *Special Edition Using* books, the perfect all-in-one resource—and recognized authority on detailed reference information.

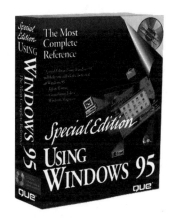

The *Using* series for casual users

Who should use this book?

Everyday users who:

- Work with computers in the office or at home
- Are familiar with computers but not in love with technology
- Just want to "get the job done"
- Don't want to read a lot of material

The user-friendly reference

- The fastest access to the one best way to get things done
- Bite-sized information for quick and easy reference
- Nontechnical approach in plain English
- Real-world analogies to explain new concepts
- Troubleshooting tips to help solve problems
- Visual elements and screen pictures that reinforce topics
- Expert authors who are experienced in training and instruction

Special Edition Using for accomplished users

Who should use this book?

Proficient computer users who:

- Have a more technical understanding of computers
- Are interested in technological trends
- Want in-depth reference information
- Prefer more detailed explanations and examples

The most complete reference

- Thorough explanations of various ways to perform tasks
- In-depth coverage of all topics
- Technical information cross-referenced for easy access
- Professional tips, tricks, and shortcuts for experienced users
- Advanced troubleshooting information with alternative approaches
- Visual elements and screen pictures that reinforce topics
- Technically qualified authors who are experts in their fields
- "Techniques form the Pros" sections with advice from well-known computer professionals

Licensing Agreement

By opening this package, you are agreeing to be bound by the following:

The software contained on this CD is in many cases copyrighted and all rights are reserved by the individual software developer and or publisher. You are bound by the individual licensing agreements associated with each piece of software contained on the CD. THIS SOFTWARE IS PROVIDED FREE OF CHARGE, AS IS, AND WITHOUT WARRANTY OF ANY KIND, EITHER EXPRESSED OR IMPLIED, INCLUDING BUT NOT LIMITED TO THE IMPLIED WARRANTIES OF MERCHANTABILITY AND FITNESS FOR A PARTICULAR PURPOSE. Neither the book publisher nor its dealers and distributors assumes any liability for any alleged or actual damages arising from the use of this software. (Some states do not allow exclusion of implied warranties, so the exclusion may not apply to you.)

CD-ROM Installation

To install the CD-ROM, run the toc.html file in the root directory.